Pawns in a Larger Game

First published 2013

Calamaish Books, Durban, South Africa, www.calamaish.co.za

ISBN 978-0-620-55629-3

PAWNS IN A LARGER GAME

Life on the Eastern Cape Frontier

by

A. D. M. WALKER

Calamaish Books

Pawns in a larger game, the 1820 Settlers came to this part of Africa at the behest of an imperial power seeking to use its own poor and unemployed in a bid to advance conquest and imperial ambitions. Though their own impulse to freedom rendered them largely unsuitable for that task, they were nevertheless caught up on the wrong side of history, unable or unwilling to acknowledge as equals those into whose homeland they had been implanted.

President Nelson Mandela, Grahamstown, 16th May 1996

Contents

Preface

History is the essence of innumerable biographies.

Thomas Carlyle, On History

The image of the British settlers in the Cape Colony has varied widely over the years. In early histories they are portrayed as standard-bearers for the colonial power bringing Christian civilisation to a barbarian country. Later their contribution was almost buried by the surge of Afrikaner nationalism – through my school years it seemed that South African history consisted only of the arrival of Jan van Riebeeck in 1652 and the events of the Great Trek. In modern times the colonist is portrayed as a villain, only concerned with exploitation of the resources of the colony.

In this book I follow the fates of a number of British settlers whose common attribute is that they are the forebears of Arthur Walker and Katie Cumming, my paternal grandparents. To understand their lives it is necessary to understand their times: to understand the times we must understand the lives of those who lived in them. I have, therefore, tried to trace their lives in parallel with the historical narrative. This is thus both a work of history and of biography: the lives of the protagonists cannot be understood without a clear comprehension of the history. Many of them were remarkable men and women and they lived in remarkable times. There are tales of murder, gunfights, war, massacre, unrequited love, and ordinary family life. They were not unique: many others whose stories are not recounted here underwent comparable experiences. They influenced and were influenced by the people they encountered and dealt with. This also a story of those people – Xhosa kings and commoners, Boer farmers and adventurers, South Africans to-be with different languages and cultures.

It is easy to be judgemental. L.P. Hartley's dictum, *The past is a foreign country: they do things differently there*, is none the less true for having become a cliché. We must judge people by the morality of their own times. These people were of all kinds – good or evil, self-interested or benevolent, brave or cowardly. They found themselves in a particular set of circumstances and dealt with them as best they could. Mostly they were concerned to survive. Some of them made significant contributions to their new country, some were involved in events that exacerbated the tensions that have always been a part of South African society.

I have tried to avoid judgement where ordinary people are concerned and let their actions and words speak for themselves with frequent quotation from contemporary or near contemporary sources. I have not hesitated to express opinions about the actions and policies of those in public office.

The lives and times of the chief characters are largely drawn from a number of primary contemporary sources, and contemporary published work, including newspapers. Edited versions of some primary sources have been published in modern times, such as the Graham's Town Series of edited works and the publications of the van Riebeeck Society. The historical framework inevitably is largely drawn from secondary sources, although in the case of events where my protagonists have been intimately involved, such as the death of the Xhosa King Hintsa, or the events surrounding the massacres of the men of the military villages in 1850, I have tried to consult as many primary sources as are available to me.

All sources are fully documented in the list of references. I have chosen to use the Harvard system of reference although I have relegated all the citations to the end-notes to avoid cluttering the text. The advantages of a consolidated list of all references in alphabetical order of author, to my mind, far outweighs the disadvantages of its relative prolixity.

The genealogy of the forebears of Arthur Walker was prepared by his nephew, G. N. "Chappie" Walker. Unfortunately I do not have a record of his sources and he is dead now. However, in every case where I have been able to check, the information he provides is correct. I know that he examined parish and press records, consulted widely among members of the family, and travelled abroad to follow up the earlier history.

The genealogy of the forebears of his wife, Katie Cumming has been constructed from a variety of sources. Their names, Cumming, Hart, Pringle, and Marillier appear frequently in contemporary and modern accounts of the history of the Eastern Cape.

The first idea for this work came from a set of reminiscences written by my father before his death. They were intended for his family, not for publication. They covered a later period than this book, the first half of the twentieth century. They were not concerned with great affairs but with providing a picture of day-to-day life of a South African family of British descent in the first half of the twentieth century. For me they gave insight into a way of life that is long gone and I was very grateful to have them.

Note on Terminology

Strictly speaking the amaXhosa[1] were the people whose chiefs were descended from Tshawe and should be distinguished from the Thembu,

Mpondo and other peoples. The common usage of 'Xhosa' as a general term to describe the people inhabiting the region roughly bounded on the east by the Mzimkulu river and on the west by a boundary (varying in response to pressures from the Cape Colony) between the Sundays and Great Fish Rivers, while using 'Zulu' for those inhabiting the region corresponding to the current province of KwaZulu-Natal is not correct. It is, however, enshrined in modern usage. In the text the word 'Xhosa' is generally used in the strict sense. When necessary, more precise designations – Gqaleka, Rharhabe, Mbalu etc – are used.

In this book there are extensive quotations from contemporary sources. In the late eighteenth and early nineteenth centuries the name given to westernmost members of the Nguni people was 'Kaffir' or 'Caffre' rather than 'Xhosa'. It was often used to distinguish them from other Nguni peoples such as the Tambookie (Thembu) or Mpondo. In this sense it was more or less synonymous with the name amaXhosa. For example, Barrow [1806, pp153 – 154] describing an expedition in 1797 writes:

> The country inhabited by the people whom the colonists distinguish by the name of Kaffers, is bounded on the south by the sea coast; on the east by a tribe of the same kind of people who call themselves Tambookies; on the south by the savage Boesjemans [San]; and on the west by the colony of the Cape.

Early black writers such as Tiyo Soga, himself a missionary to his own people, [Williams, 1983, p91], used the word quite unselfconsciously, for example, describing the opening of his new church:

> The first morning service was in Caffre and was conducted by the venerable Brownlee, the father of our Caffre missions.

The region between the Great Fish River and Natal was known as 'Caffreland' and, with variations in spelling, appears as such on contemporary maps. Later the word began to be applied to all black African people and rapidly acquired a derogatory sense.

Today the word 'kaffir' is an extremely offensive term amounting to hate speech. This provides a dilemma for writers dealing with the period who quote from original sources. I would have preferred to retain quotations exactly as written. However, I recognize that readers may find the frequent use of the word sufficiently distasteful that it disrupts the flow of the text. For this reason, I have adopted the convention (see for example Peires [1989]) of using square brackets and replacing the offensive word 'caffre', 'kaffir', and its variations by [Xhosa] in all quotations

Acknowledgements

I am grateful to many individuals who have been helpful in this work. In particular I would like to thank:

- Nellie Somers and the staff of the Killie Campbell Africana Library, University of KwaZulu-Natal, Durban.

- Cathy Dubbeld and the staff of the E. G. Malherbe Library, University of KwaZulu-Natal, Durban.

- Sally Schramm and the staff of the Cory Library, Rhodes University Grahamstown, South Africa.

- Sally Poole, formerly of the Cory Library who gave help and advice and, with her husband Graham, provided hospitality in their home while I was working in the Cory Library.

- Melanie Geustyn and the Special Collections staff of the National Library of South Africa (Cape Town Campus).

- The staff of the Cape Town Archives repository of the National Archives of South Africa.

- Prof. Jeff Peires, for his encouragement and willingness to answer all manner of questions on Xhosa history and culture. My interpretation of what he has told me, and any errors, omissions, or opinions are entirely my own responsibility.

Except where otherwise stated, all the photographs come from the author's private collection and are in the public domain. Tombi Peck generously provided press cuttings and copies of a number of public domain photographs, including those of Robert Hart Sr and James Hart, reproduced on pages 235 and 238.

The maps were prepared by the author using PlanetGIS. The topographical data originates from the South African Surveyor General and is in the public domain.

Prologue

The end is where we start from
T. S. Eliot, Little Gidding. Four Quartets

Katie's Wedding   [28th June 1899, Glen Avon, Somerset East]

Somerset East in 1899 was a small and prosperous farming centre at the foot of the Boschberg mountains in the eastern part of the Cape Colony. To the west lay the semi-desert areas of the little Karroo: to the east were the fertile mountain regions of the Amatolas. The Dutch Reformed church tower dominated the town. Clustered round the town centre, the houses of the Dutch and English colonists were attractive and solid. Few noticed the less solid and often dilapidated dwellings of the coloured people a few streets away. The town even boasted a small college offering courses leading to degrees of the University of the Cape of Good Hope[2].

A few kilometres to the east of the town lay the historic farm, Glen Avon. Seventy-five years earlier the land had been granted to Robert Hart in recognition of his services as supervisor of the government experimental farm and commissariat which, when it had been closed down, had been laid out as the village of Somerset East.

Saturday 28th June was a bright warm winter's day. Glen Avon was *en fête*. There was to be a wedding and the conveyances of the guests were pouring through the gates. The bride, Katie Cumming, was the great grand-daughter of Robert Hart. The bridegroom was Arthur Walker, a young lawyer who was beginning his independent professional life in Kokstad, East Griqualand.

The wedding was to be held in the small Presbyterian chapel on the farm. It was clearly a major social event in the small community. A local newspaper[3] devoted nearly twenty column-inches to it.

Kate had spent her childhood on Glen Avon where her father, John Pringle Cumming and his wife, Sarah Hart, had lived until their retirement the year before. Kate's paternal grandfather was the prominent Presbyterian missionary, John Forbes Cumming, now 91 years old, all dressed up, and ready to assist at the ceremony. His wife, Catherine, was the daughter of the 1820 settler John Pringle and niece of his brother, Thomas, the fighter for press freedom in the early days of the Cape Colony. Kate's maternal grandparents were Robert Hart Jr and his second wife Harriet Marillier, also of settler stock.

1

Arthur Walker   *Kate Cumming*

Arthur's parents were also from settler roots. His father, Joseph Walker Jr had been a Member of the House of Assembly. His grandparents had all been British settlers in 1820 – Joseph Walker a Grahamstown businessman, and Margaret Booth. Arthur's mother was Dorothy Driver, daughter of two other settlers, Edward Driver and Ann Thackwray.

A photograph of the wedding party shows Kate with her parents, her sister, and her bridesmaid standing under a pergola on the farm bearing large bunches of grapes. A servant stands on a ladder cutting another bunch. Somewhat surprisingly, instead of flowers, the bride is holding a bowl which is laden with fruit.

The picture is of a tranquil scene that might have taken place anywhere in the rural Britain of the time, yet the location was on the eastern border of the old Cape Colony, which had not entirely emerged from its turbulent frontier days. The Cape had been under British rule for almost a hundred years. Kate and Arthur regarded themselves as British although they had never been outside Southern Africa and thought of it as home. Soon, in the new century, would come the birth of the new Union of South Africa and they would become its citizens.

The Bridal Party

l to r. Miss Muriel McIntyre (flower girl); Unidentified farm worker; Miss Queenie Cumming (bridesmaid); Mr J. P. Cumming; the bride, Miss Katie Cumming; Mrs J.P. Cumming (b. Sarah Hart)

This is the story of how Arthur and Kate came to be South Africans. It is the saga of how a particular group of people left their homeland and built a new life in a new country. This group is defined only by the fact that they were the forebears of Arthur and Kate. Their stories are typical of the stories of their friends and neighbours. On the whole, they were neither saints nor villains. Their influences on their country were varied – good or bad depending on the point of view. Placed in a situation of great danger and great opportunity they did their best for their families and community as they saw them. Their lives must be judged in the context of their times.

Ancestry of Arthur WALKER and Kate CUMMING

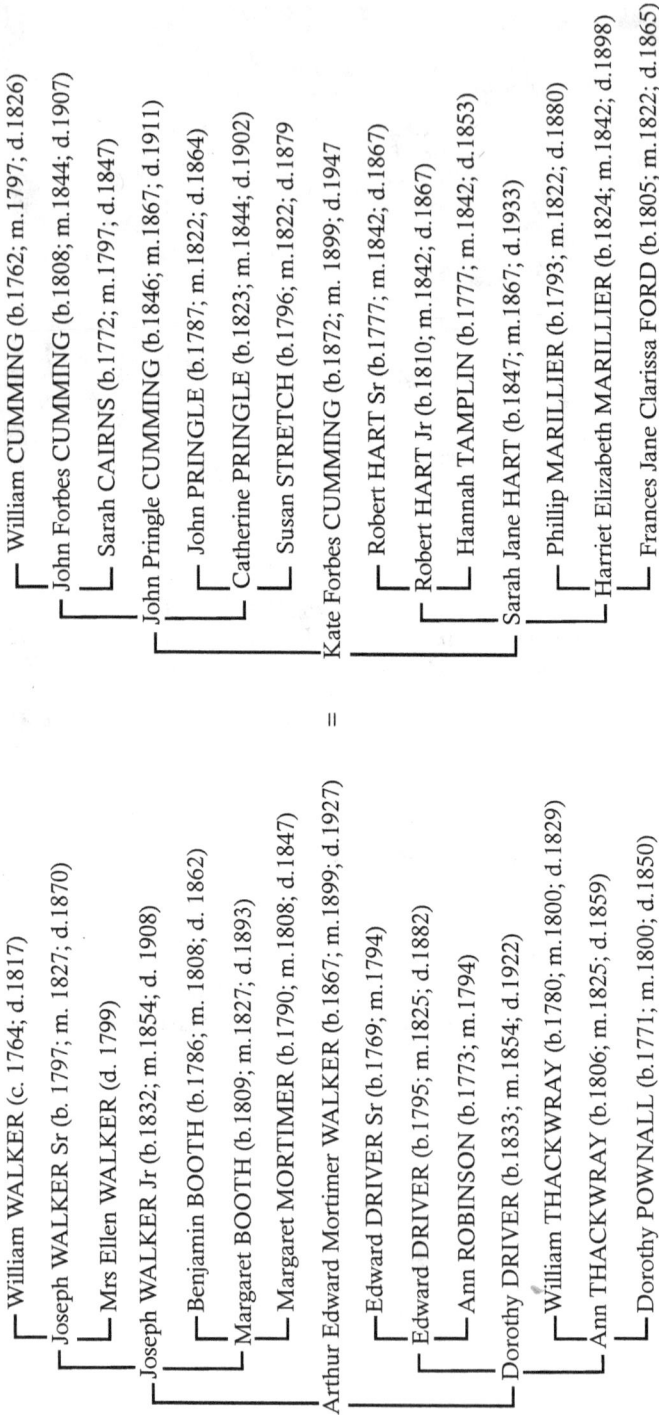

William CUMMING (b.1762; m.1797; d.1826)
John Forbes CUMMING (b.1808; m.1844; d.1907)
Sarah CAIRNS (b.1772; m.1797; d.1847)
John Pringle CUMMING (b.1846; m.1867; d.1911)
John PRINGLE (b.1787; m.1822; d.1864)
Catherine PRINGLE (b.1823; m.1844; d.1902)
Susan STRETCH (b.1796; m.1822; d.1879)
Kate Forbes CUMMING (b.1872; m. 1899; d.1947)
Robert HART Sr (b.1777; m.1842; d.1867)
Robert HART Jr (b.1810; m.1842; d.1867)
Hannah TAMPLIN (b.1777; m.1842; d.1853)
Sarah Jane HART (b.1847; m.1867; d.1933)
Phillip MARILLIER (b.1793; m.1822; d.1880)
Harriet Elizabeth MARILLIER (b.1824; m.1842; d.1898)
Frances Jane Clarissa FORD (b.1805; m.1822; d.1865)

=

William WALKER (c. 1764; d.1817)
Joseph WALKER Sr (b. 1797; m. 1827; d.1870)
Mrs Ellen WALKER (d. 1799)
Joseph WALKER Jr (b.1832; m.1854; d. 1908)
Benjamin BOOTH (b.1786; m. 1808; d. 1862)
Margaret BOOTH (b.1809; m.1827; d.1893)
Margaret MORTIMER (b.1790; m.1808; d.1847)
Arthur Edward Mortimer WALKER (b.1867; m.1899; d.1927)
Edward DRIVER Sr (b.1769; m.1794)
Edward DRIVER (b.1795; m.1825; d.1882)
Ann ROBINSON (b.1773; m.1794)
Dorothy DRIVER (b.1833; m.1854; d.1922)
William THACKWRAY (b.1780; m.1800; d.1829)
Ann THACKWRAY (b.1806; m.1825; d.1859)
Dorothy POWNALL (b.1771; m.1800; d.1850)

Family relationships between the principal characters

Chapter 1. Setting the Stage

An empire founded by war has to maintain itself by war
Montesquieu, Considérations sur les causes de la grandeur des Romains et de leur décadence

The Soldier   [1795]

It was just two years since Louis XVI and and Queen Marie Antoinette had been executed. The French Revolution was in its dying throes. The young Corsican officer, Napoleon Bonaparte, was soon to be clearing the mob from the streets of Paris with his "whiff of grapeshot." In the New World two years still remained of George Washington's term as first President of the United States.

In Britain George III – mad King George – had been King for 35 years. He had presided over the loss of the American colonies, the prolonged wars with France, the growing upheaval of the industrial revolution, and the social disruption that was accompanying it. His advisors feared for his sanity[4], and he was ultimately to be sidelined while his self-indulgent son acted as Regent. Dangerous new ideas of freedom and equality were filling the minds of ordinary people and there was a real sense that the spirit of revolution would cross the Channel and that society as then known was at risk.

The strength of Britain and its Empire was in its Navy. Control of the seas was essential to survival. The routes to India and the Far East were vital for British trade and these routes had to pass round the Cape of Good Hope, which was a Dutch colony. At the beginning of 1795 the Dutch state ruled by the Prince of Orange had been supplanted by the French-supported Batavian Republic and they held the Cape Colony with its strategic location. The British Secretary of State for War, Henry Dundas[5], (the people of the time did not see the need for euphemism; what would now be a Minister of Defence was then a Minister of War) was anxious to acquire the Cape for the British Empire.

In the Atlantic Ocean a fleet of fourteen East Indiamen was sailing towards the Cape of Good Hope, acting as troop carriers for the 98th Argyllshire Highlanders, charged with occupying the Cape on behalf of the Prince of Orange, and, of course, securing the sea route to India for Britain. They had been temporarily in Brazil while en route to provide support for a naval squadron under the command of Admiral Elphinstone that had proceeded to the Cape some time before. The regiment

5

was under the command of General Alured Clarke, and in their ranks was a young, newly-recruited Scot – Robert Hart[6].

Robert Hart was born in Strathaven[7], Lanarkshire, in 1777[8]. Strathaven was a small village in the beautiful valley of the Avon Water – Glen Avon. His parents were James Hart, a retired soldier, and Isobel Broom[9]. The main industry in Strathaven at the time was cottage weaving and this was an occupation under threat as the effects of the steam driven looms of the industrial revolution made their impact. There was widespread poverty. When Robert was 6 years old, presumably for financial reasons, the family moved from the country to Edinburgh but the memory of his earliest years in the Avon valley remained with him.

A few years later, in 1791, when he was only 14, Robert's mother died. Young Robert was an intelligent, ambitious, and adventurous lad, well educated in the Scottish tradition. He was unhappy at home where his widowed father was a strict disciplinarian. The prospects for someone of his background in late eighteenth century Scotland were poor. His father had been a soldier and that seemed to provide the opportunity for a career. Robert ran away from home to join the army. That first attempt failed; only at the second attempt did he manage to enlist in his chosen regiment and so place himself on the path to a new life of adventure and opportunity. The 98th Argyllshire was established in 1794[10] and Private Robert Hart's name appears in the list of its first recruits. He and his companions would have had little or no idea of the people, the environment, and the complexities of the land which the lumbering British fleet was approaching.

The Dutch at the Cape   [1652 – 1795]

At the end of the eighteenth century the Cape of Good Hope was a sleepy outpost of the Dutch Empire[11]. The Dutch settlement which had started in the vicinity of Cape Town had spread far into what are now the Cape Province and Eastern Cape Province. In the 145 years of occupation not much had happened to the benefit of any of the inhabitants of the Colony.

In the early days all the Dutch colonists were employees of the Dutch East India Company (The *Verenigde Oostindische Compagnie* or VOC) and the colony fell under the rule of its Council of Seventeen (The Seventeen Gentlemen or *Here XVII*). The Colony remained a fiefdom of the Company. Soon it became expedient to establish independent farms and limited rights to land were extended to a new class of free burghers[12]. The more prosperous established themselves in Cape Town and its neighbourhood. For those who had fewer resources, and needed to make a living from the land, expansion was the answer. The trekboers took their wagons, families, and herds further and further to the east, living a semi-nomadic pastoral life, differing little from that of their eastern neighbours, the Xhosa.

The Khoisan   [1652 – 1795]

When the Dutch first arrived in 1652 the indigenous people in the Cape region were the Khoikhoi[13], known at the time as "Hottentots" and, on the fringes of society the San (Bushmen). The Khoikhoi were nomadic pastoral farmers, ethnically distinct from the African people to the East and North of the settlement but closely related to the San who had a hunter-gatherer culture. In the early years of the Dutch settlement, interaction of the Khoikhoi with the settlers was largely in the form of trading livestock in exchange for desirable products such as iron, copper, and tobacco[14]. Over the years the pressures on their land led to many becoming detribalized, working mostly as servants and labourers. Others took their herds to more distant parts. By the middle of the eighteenth century there were few Khoikhoi near Cape Town, and a larger number serving as labourers on the more distant farms and in small nomadic bands. Their numbers were drastically reduced by epidemics of smallpox to which they had little immunity. There was a great deal of interbreeding with white colonists, slaves from the east, and the black community, so that the Khoikhoi within the colony began to be absorbed into what is now known as the coloured community.

The Slaves   [1652 – 1795]

There was another immigrant community in the Cape. The Dutch were a slave owning nation. Over the years there had been a steady importation of slaves[15]. Although one hears much of the "Cape Malay" slaves, the majority were, in fact, acquired from African sources, particularly Madagascar. The influence of Muslim slaves from the east, however, led to a significant level of conversion to Islam. Freed slaves and other non-Khoisan "free blacks", including those of mixed parentage from the white, black, Khoisan and slave communities, were the foundation of a growing group of people who were the forebears of many in the coloured community.

The Nguni People   [1652 – 1795]

To the East of the Colony were the black indigenous people speaking variations of the Nguni group of languages including those languages now known as Xhosa, Zulu, and Siswati[16].

The westward extent of the Nguni speaking people was the Zuurveld –
the region between the Fish and Sundays Rivers. This was also the eastward extent of the Boer farmers. It was here that competition and mutual
cultural incomprehension led to conflict. The situation was far more complicated than a simple black-white confrontation[17].

The amaXhosa[18] were the westernmost major grouping of Xhosa
speakers. To their east were other major groupings such as the ama-
Mpondo and abaThembu (labelled Tambookie[19] by most nineteenth century sources). The Xhosa chiefs all traced their descent from the great seventeenth century king Tshawe. In the eighteenth century the Xhosa had
been split by civil war arising from internecine strife between Gcaleka and
Rharhabe, the sons of Phalo[20], the followers of the former being located
to the east of the Great Kei and those of the latter to the west. A third
brother, Langa, led the amaMbalu people who were located in the
Zuurveld between the Sundays and Fish rivers. In addition other more
distantly related groups, including the amaGqunukhwebe under Tshaka[21]
and later his son Chungwa, also occupied the Zuurveld. The amaGqunukhwebe had earlier absorbed large numbers of Khoikhoi refugees from
the Cape and were extensively interbred with them. Neither the amaGqunukwhebe nor the amaMbalu recognized the paramountcy of the boy
chief Hintsa.

Conflict between the easternmost trekboers and the westernmost
Xhosa had already led to two frontier wars. The first[22] resulted in the destruction of the imiDange by the commando of Adriaan van Jaarsveld
through the treacherous murder of Jalamba, the Great Son of their Chief
Mahote. It ended in 1781 with the expulsion of the amaGqunukhwebe
and amaMbalu to the eastern side of the Fish River. Over the next few
years this expulsion was reversed as they re-occupied their traditional
grazing grounds. The second frontier war began in farce. The Boers of
Bruintjies Hoogte under the leadership of Barend Lindeque, frustrated by
what they saw as the depredations of the amaMbalu and amaGqunukhwebe, negotiated an alliance with Ndlambe, then Regent of the Rharhabe.
When Lindeque's commando first encountered Ndlambe's massed forces
in battle array, rather than accepting them as allies, they panicked and
fled. This led to a general exodus of the Boer community. The amaMbalu
and amaGqunukhwebe took advantage of the opportunity to lay the Boer
farms to waste and in May 1793 the second frontier war was in progress.

This outbreak had been precipitated by the recalcitrant Boers against
all the efforts of the new Landdrost Honoratus Maynier whose brief from
the Dutch East India Company was to promote peace on the frontier.
Maynier was eventually forced to raise a commando which drove the

Gqunukhwebe and Mbalu across the Fish River into the hands of their enemy Ndlambe where Tshaka was killed and Langa captured. Peace of a kind was negotiated with the new chiefs, Chungwa and Nqeno in November 1793.

The amaXhosa paramount succession had passed down the Gcaleka as shown in the Genealogical chart in Appendix 2. By 1785 the para-mountcy had passed to the six-year-old Hintsa and there was a regency in place. The situation of the amaRharhabe was more complicated. The amaXhosa were polygamous and the succession rules were intricate[23]. The son of the first wife of the king was not the heir. The hierarchy of the wives of the chief was carefully determined. It was only late in life that a chief took a Great Wife and the marriage was a dynastic one. The bride price or lobola was not paid by the chief himself but by his people, and the bride was inevitably the daughter of another important chief. The line of descent was followed through the Great House of each successive chief and the son of the Great Wife was the heir apparent. The next most important wife headed the so-called right-hand house, and provided a second subservient line of succession. The men of the right hand house had an advisory capacity.

In 1782 after the death of his father the four-year-old Ngqika[24] became chief in a somewhat irregular manner. His brother was heir apparent in the sovereign succession and favoured by the Rharhabe councillors. His uncle, Ndlambe, the regent, favoured Ngqika. In such circumstances the Xhosa king – at that time Khawuta – came into play, even though the amaGqaleka and amaRharhabe were essentially independent of each other. It was rather like an approach from an Australian appellant to the Privy Council in London. An appeal to Khawuta led to the proclamation of Ngqika as chief under the regency of his uncle Ndlambe. By 1795, having gone through the Xhosa circumcision ceremony, Ngqika had come of age and was ready to assume his paramountcy. Ndlambe was less eager for this to take place. Civil war among the AmaXhosa was about to erupt.

After the end of the second frontier war the frontier Boers became more and more dissatisfied with Maynier. Meanwhile Holland had been drawn into the war with France. Finally Graaff Reinet drove out the last official of the Dutch East India Company and declared their independ-ence and their sympathy to the French revolutionary cause.

Ignorant of this convoluted and tortuous situation, Admiral Elphin-stone, his Eurocentric vision firmly fixed on the resurgent threat from France, sailed his fleet round Cape Point into False Bay.

Chapter 2. The Advance Guard

Tu regere imperio populos Romane, memento
[You, O Roman, take care to rule the people with authority]

Virgil, Aeniad

The First Occupation [1795]

Admiral Elphinstone's fleet for taking over the Cape consisted of seven ships carrying a small force of marines and about 450 soldiers of the 78th Highland Regiment. They were ultimately to be supported by the troops of the 98th Argylls who were summoned from Brazil[25] when the situation became difficult.

Elphinstone had sailed into Simon's Bay and his fleet was anchored at what is now the Simonstown Naval Base on the eastern side of the Cape Peninsula. He had been confident that the Dutch would hand over the Colony to the British as instructed in the letter from from the Prince of Orange. The problem was that the Dutch authority had not yet heard of the overthrow of the House of Orange. Furthermore they were not sure whether they did not themselves favour the new Batavian Republic[26]. There was considerable division in the Colony between the royalists and those who supported the ideas of freedom that had emerged from revolutionary France. Cautiously the Governor, General Sluysken, agreed to provide supplies for the British ships, but would only allow the troops ashore if they were unarmed. At this point an American ship arrived in Table Bay and the Dutch learned more of the situation from an independent source. Newspapers reported that the new Batavian Republic was aligned with France and at war with Britain. The colonial authority decided to resist the British[27].

General Sluysken evacuated Simon's Town with the intention of burning it. The order came for the marines to disembark and prepare for action. The first step was to secure Simon's Town, which was not difficult as there was now no defence. Cape Town was to the north and the route there ran along the narrow coastal strip on the eastern side of the peninsula. The first engagement of the occupation was the Battle of Muizenberg on 7th August. Muizenberg was taken with only one casualty and the British had secured their beach-head.

Several skirmishes followed in which the Dutch were beaten off. The British forces continued to defend Muizenberg and advance slowly for the rest of August. By September they had reached Wynberg. The Dutch meanwhile had been consolidating their forces, bringing men and artillery from Cape Town. By the 3rd September they had mustered eighteen pieces of field artillery and a large body of men. At this stage the British operation had started to run into trouble but on that day the fleet of troop carriers bearing General Clarke's Highlanders at last arrived and anchored in the bay.

Robert Hart's first view of the country in which he was to spend all but five of the remaining seventy-two years of his life was of the magnificent coastline of the eastern side of the Cape Peninsula. On the shore the land rose sharply, leaving a narrow coastal strip. On the seaward side the coastline swept round False Bay. The distant Hottentots Holland mountains provided a daunting barrier between the Cape and the wild land to the east. To the north lay Cape Town – today a brief half hour away, then a hard and gruelling march.

The troops would not have been in good condition. After a long period at sea with little opportunity for exercise and a poor diet, illness and a low morale would have taken its toll. Now, at last, there was the opportunity for action. Hart was young and vigorous and it would not have taken long for him to get back into shape. Once he was on land, with fresh food available and the opportunity for physical activity, life was greatly improved.

The first task for the British forces was to establish themselves. It took ten days to complete the disembarkation of men, munitions and provisions. By 14th September they were in good spirits and ready for the advance on Cape Town.

Robert Hart and his comrades were issued with four days' supplies and began the march to Cape Town. There was no road. The Navy had the task of dragging the heavy artillery through the sand; the infantry had their own equipment to carry. They came under sporadic and irritating fire as the Dutch forces retired before them.

Meanwhile the 64-gun ship of the line *America*, the two sloops *Echo* and *Rattlesnake*, and the East Indiaman *Bombay Castle* set off round Cape Point bound for Table Bay. The arrival of the fleet in Table Bay and the threat of the advancing troops was enough for Governor Sluysken to accept that it was futile to resist further. General Clarke accepted Sluyken's surrender, the troops marched into Cape Town and entered the gates of Cape Town Castle. Bond paints a stirring picture[28]:

... the marching feet of 800 red tuniced, green-kilted men raised the dust at the Cape entrance. The Castle swallowed them up.

This was the last time for many years that the Highland uniform was worn by the regiment on a public parade. In December orders came from Britain for them to adopt the standard uniform worn by the army in India[29]. For the Cape campaigns the 98th (a Campbell regiment) did not wear Highland dress, not even tartan trews. They were outfitted as ordinary British red-jackets[30]. These orders were deeply resented by officers and men and led to much dissatisfaction during this first occupation of the Cape, which was to last until 1803.

Robert Hart's personal experiences during the years of the first occupation are partly a matter of speculation. Bond notes

> The Hart family tradition is that Hart served in all the campaigns in South Africa between 1795 and 1802.[31]

Ffoliot's account[32] also includes a number of family records in its list of sources. Such sources are not always reliable and they lead her to the statement that Hart took part in the Battle of Muizenberg, at which time he was on the high seas[33], as well as to the misidentification of Robert's mother. It is not always clear where Hart was stationed during the first British occupation. There is, however, little doubt that he was a participant in many of the activities of the regiment as it carried out the duties of the occupation.

Early Days   [1795 – 1796]

During the following year the occupation forces settled into some sort of routine. Admiral Elphinstone and General Clarke left the Cape in November 1795, shortly after the Dutch surrender, leaving Major-General J. H. Craig in charge as military governor. The 78th regiment was dispatched to India; the 98th remained in the Cape.

The dissatisfaction of the burghers of Graaff-Reinet and Swellendam with the Colonial Government was inherited by the British. Initially they refused to take the required oath of allegiance but a small threat of military force was enough to bring them temporarily into line. Dissatisfaction, however, continued, particularly in Graaff Reinet and was later to lead to further trouble.

In Cape Town the mannered tenor of life experienced by the British officers and Cape society, and later described in the letters and journals of Lady Anne Barnard[34], was not the lot of the ordinary soldiers, whose entertainments were limited to the taverns and brothels of the town. It can be assumed that it was now that Robert Hart did his growing up. From the evidence of his later life he emerged from these experiences with the stern Calvinist morality of his childhood unscathed.

The tedious routine of garrison duties was first broken almost a year after the occupation. In January 1796 news had been received in Britain that a French-Dutch assault on the Cape was being planned. Indeed, at that time, a squadron of ships was being fitted out for an expedition to the south under Rear-Admiral Engelbertus Lucas[35]. The British reaction was swift. The frigate *Carysfort* was sent to the Cape with news of developments and sailed on to India with orders recalling Elphinstone to the Cape. He returned with three ships carrying the 78th regiment. During the next few months six warships and numerous transports carrying a further 5000 soldiers were dispatched from Britain.

On 6th August 1796 Admiral Lucas, commanding eight warships and a transport vessel, anchored in Saldanha Bay almost 150km north of Cape Town on the inhospitable west coast. He had been five months at sea and was urgently in need of water and supplies. Saldanha Bay was sufficiently remote from Cape Town for him to feel that he could avoid detection and he was hopeful of French support and local sympathy for an effort to retake the Cape.

A British cavalry patrol brought the news to Craig, who immediately set off for Saldanha Bay with 2500 men, including Robert Hart[36], leaving 4000 behind for the defence of Cape Town.

It took nine days for the detachment to reach Saldanha Bay. The west coast is inhospitable. There was no road. Part of the route was through deep sand and the going was difficult. Hart's company began to get an impression of the scale and alien nature of the country. At last, on August 14th, they arrived and secured the landward side against Lucas's fleet, which was taking on stores.

Meanwhile, Admiral Elphinstone had been struggling against appalling weather to find the Dutch fleet. On 12th August he arrived in Simon's Bay and was given news of Lucas's location in Saldanha Bay. The weather prevented his sailing until the 15th.

After months of tedious garrison duty in the Castle, Robert Hart and his comrades would have both excited and apprehensive at the prospect of some action. They were frustrated when Elphinstone's fleet of 13 ships arrived on the 16th. The superior force convinced Lucas that resistance was useless and he surrendered without a shot being fired.

Ennui   [1797 – 1798]

Once the Dutch fleet had been driven off, the first event of note was the arrival of the new Governor. George Macartney, the first Earl Macartney, had had a distinguished career in the British Diplomatic and Colonial service but he was now old and ill. Reluctant to take on the responsibility of the Governorship, he accepted it out of a sense of duty, but reserved the right to retire if his illness became worse.

The party arrived on 4th May 1797. With Macartney was the new Colonial Secretary Andrew Barnard with his wife Lady Anne, and his private secretary, John Barrow. To Lady Anne Barnard and John Barrow we owe the best and most extensive accounts of life in the Cape Colony during the first British occupation[37].

During Macartney's tenure of the Governorship, while there were several disturbances, life for the troops was essentially dull. The officers had their entertainments[38]

> ... widespread deforestation had ... deprived the officers of any decent shooting. They improved their lot, however, by fetching out a pack of foxhounds and hunting jackal ...

and other ranks theirs

> ... the troops stagnated and went down in large numbers with various local diseases.

As is usually the case, military life consisted of long stretches of boredom interrupted by short bursts of sometimes terrifying activity. The latter were still to come.

During this period, at the request of the Governor and to his own delight, Barrow carried out his major expedition into the interior[39]. The immediate purpose was to provide a full report to Macartney of conditions on the frontier, particularly with regard to the simmering discontent in Graaff Reinet and to the nature of the Xhosa people. Macartney ordered[40]:

> I think, Barrow, you will have no objection to accompany one or both of these gentlemen [the expelled landdrost and minister] to the presence of these savages [the Graaff Reinet burghers], which may lead them to reflect that it must be out of tenderness to them that I have preferred to send them one of my own family rather than ... a regiment of dragoons. ... We are also shamefully ignorant even of the geography of the country ... I am further informed that the [Xhosa]s, with their cattle are in possession of the Zuur-veldt ... and that these people and the boors are perpetually fighting and carrying off each others cattle. ... my wish is that some adjustment should be made between these people.

Perhaps the most significant information that Barrow brought back was the state of the Xhosa. The civil war between Ngqika and his uncle Ndlambe, which had broken out just before the British occupation, had ended in a comprehensive victory for Ngqika, who was now undisputed Rharhabe chief. Ndlambe had been forgiven. While disempowered, he was still respected and consulted. The Gqaleka had sided with Ndlambe and shared in his defeat. The 10 year old Gqaleka chief, Hintsa, king of the Xhosa descendants of Tshawe, had been briefly captured by Ngqika, his life threatened. He had, however, been rescued and taken to a place of safety. The Rharhabe territories had been devastated by the conflict. The Rharhabe now generally occupied the area between the Fish and Kei Rivers, while the Gqaleka had retired eastward beyond the Kei. The Gqunukwhebe had over the years been much changed by the absorption of many fugitive Khoikhoi, who became completely integrated with them. Both Gqunukhwebe and Mbalu now pursued their pastoral way of life in the Zuurveld between Fish and Sundays Rivers which were regarded as part of the colony by the British. Hintsa was still recognised as *de iure* King of the Xhosa by the Rharhabe and Mbalu but *de facto* Ngqika's Rharhabe were completely independent and not under his control. The Gqunukhwebe had long been independent of any allegiance to the Xhosa royal house.

Here began the first of many misunderstandings. Barrow perceived Ngqika as the all-powerful chief of the Xhosa. He and many successive British administrators seemed, or found it convenient, not to recognize that the Xhosa were not a single integrated people, but a number of groups with varying degrees of closeness in their relationships. Barrow negotiated with Ngqika to recognize the Great Fish River as the boundary between the Colony and the Xhosa territories, with the Xhosa being confined to the region to the east of it, and the Zuurveld emptied of its Xhosa occupants. Ngqika was prepared to accept this for his own people but tried without success to explain that he had no say over the doings of the Gqunukhwebe, Mbalu or other chiefdoms in the Zuurveld. Barrow was convinced that the result of the negotiations was to remove all Xhosa beyond the Fish. This kind of misunderstanding was to bedevil relations between the Xhosa and the colony for many years.

The Graaff Reinet Rebellion and the Third Frontier War   [1799]

Macartney's tenure as Governor did not last long. In January 1799 his health had become so bad[41] that he gave up his appointment and left the Cape in the charge of an acting governor, Major-General Francis Dundas, nephew of the War Secretary. At the same time many of the British troops stationed in the Cape Colony were shipped to India, leaving the Cape military establishment dangerously undermanned.

The burghers of Graaff Reinet lost no time in taking advantage of the situation. When Adriaan van Jaarsveld, now one of their number, was arrested on a charge of forgery and was to be transported to Cape Town under escort for trial, they seized the opportunity. He was at this time one of the conspirators in a plot to resurrect the Graaff Reinet republic. His co-conspirators rescued him from his escort and began planning attacks on both Xhosa and Khoikhoi in order to increase the resources available to them.

When the news reached Cape Town Dundas wasted no time. In the latter half of February he sent Major-General Thomas Pakenham Vandeleur[42] together with a detachment of dragoons, and fifty Khoikhoi troops[43] overland to the region. At the same time infantry companies, including some from the 91st, were sent in support by sea to Algoa Bay. In addition, Dundas's instructions to Vandeleur were to take the opportunity of the presence of a strong military force to persuade the Xhosa to move to the other side of the Great Fish River.

The troops were conveyed to Algoa Bay by the frigate, *Diamond*, and the small naval sloop, *Rattlesnake* and supported by *Camel*, an armed store ship. They arrived in early March and anchored in the Bay. At that time the area was essentially unpopulated. It is a large bay, many kilometres wide, protected at the westernmost end by Cape Recife, which projects eastward into the ocean just south of the small Baakens River mouth. The landscape and vegetation were strange to Hart and his comrades, very different from the Mediterranean ambience of the Cape. There was no kind of docking facility. The ships remained at anchor, as close to shore as prudent, and the troops were rowed in ship's boats to the beach. This was a hazardous operation. The soldiers, fully equipped and mostly unable to swim, had to embark in the boats. The crews had then to negotiate the Indian Ocean breakers and beach the boats some distance from the waterline. The troops then had to wade ashore, encumbered by their equipment. A boat capsizing in the breakers would have ensured a number of drownings. The operation was completed without mishap. They set up camp and awaited the arrival of Vandeleur's overland force. The parties rendezvoused in Algoa Bay on 8th March.[44]

Dundas was concerned about Vandeleur's ability to deal with the political problems since he spoke no Dutch, Xhosa, or Khoi. John Barrow volunteered to join the troops as representative of the acting Governor and left for the frontier in early March, accompanied by Dundas's aide-de camp Lieut. Smyth and an escort from the 8th dragoons[45].

At this stage the official concern was entirely with the Boer rebellion. However, other problems had arisen when Vandeleur's party had passed the region of the Gamtoos River. Disaffected Khoi farm servants, who had long been cruelly mistreated by their Boer employers, saw this as an opportunity "to apply for redress before the English troops should leave the country."[46] Initially a small deputation was planned. Their employers forcibly dissuaded them. As a consequence there was mass desertion from the farms with an escalation of violence, Khoikhoi attacking and looting farms in the area.

Unaware of this, Vandeleur set off with his forces for Graaff Reinet, a distance of several hundred kilometres, to put down the rebellion there. Hart and his comrades were marched northwards, crossing the Sundays River at Addo Drift and labouring over the sand flats towards the Zuurberg. John Shipp, one of the soldiers on the march described it thus[47]:

> The road from Algoa Bay to Graaf-Reynett is hill and dale, and infested with lions, tigers, hyenas, wolves, and elephants; and we frequently saw eight or ten a-day, at a place called Rovee Bank, a day's march on this side of the great pass.

At the Zuurberg the land began to rise; the vegetation changed in character from the coastal strip to the terrain above the first escarpment. They continued northward on the plateau, now at an altitude of about 600 m, until they reached the Boschberg. By now they were in a region of beautiful fertile country. Hart marched over this terrain, unaware that this was to be the region where he would spend most of his long and productive life. The land rose sharply again and the expedition swung westwards over Bruintjies Hoogte towards Graaff Reinet, skirting the picturesque mountain ranges to the north of them. The vegetation began to change to the scrub of the much more arid Little Karroo. As they approached their destination they were faced with the prospect of some action to break the monotony of the days of marching, overnight camps, and uninteresting rations that could be carried with them.

There was to be no such excitement. As soon as the rebels got wind of the arrival of this force they fled, leaving an abject message of apology for their transgressions. Vandeleur refused to deal with them unless they presented themselves in person. On April 6th they did so and the rebellion was effectively over. Vandeleur arrested the ring leaders with the intention of sending them back to Cape Town aboard *Rattlesnake*. The troops, having been marched right up to the top of the hill, were now marched right back down again. They made good time to Algoa Bay where, on April 14th Barrow's party joined them.

The leaders of the rebellion were placed on board *Rattlesnake* for transport to Cape Town and trial. Vandeleur and Barrow then took their forces back into the interior with the intention of mopping up those remaining rebels who had not given themselves up, and also of trying to enforce the removal of the Xhosa beyond the Fish River. The scale of the Khoikhoi rebellion now became apparent. Many had deserted to the Xhosa, particularly to the Gqunukhwebe. Others, under various captains – Klaas Stuurman, Boesak, and Trompetter – were marauding through the Boer farmlands, looting as they went. Not far from Algoa Bay Vandeleur's force encountered a large band of Khoikhoi. Barrow described the bizarre sight[48]. The members of the group were attired in a variety of European garments, men inappropriately wearing female dress. They freely admitted to Barrow that these were the results of plundering Boer farms. Their leader, Klaas Stuurman, made a fluent speech, applying to place his party under the protection of the British forces and enumerating the many wrongs that they had suffered under the oppressive employment of the Boers.

Vandeleur disarmed them and agreed that they could accompany the party. A hundred of the young men were enlisted in the Khoi Corps. The group straggled on towards Bruintjes Hoogte along the Sundays River where they encountered a large party of Gqunukwhebe:

> ... belonging, they told us, to a powerful chief named Congo [Chungwa], who was at the head of the emigrant chiefs that had fled from [Xhosa]-land on account of some enmity subsisting between them and their King Gaika [Nqika], with whom and them I had in vain attempted two years before to bring about a reconciliation. I sent a messenger to Congo to request he would give us a meeting ...[49]

This was an opportunity to try to persuade Chungwa to move his people beyond the Fish in accordance with the British insistence that this was the colonial boundary. The Gqunukwhebe had been no part of any Dutch or British agreement to recognize this frontier. Chungwa came with an escort of thirty assegai-bearing warriors.

> He conducted himself with great firmness, said the ground on which he then stood was his own by inheritance; that, however, being desirous of remaining in friendship with the English, he would remove to the eastward in three days, but that it was impossible for him to cross the Great Fish River, as "there was blood between Gaika and himself," and that Gaika was then much too strong for him. The decided tone in which he spoke, at the head of his small party, when surrounded by British troops, his prepossessing countenance, and tall muscular figure, could not fail to excite a strong interest in his favour. Though extremely good-humoured, benevolent, and hospitable, the [Xhosa]s are neither so pliant nor so passive as the Hottentots. The consent of Congo to withdraw from the banks of the Sundays River was not given without apparent reluctance.[50]

The increasingly dishevelled British force with its rag-tag and bob-tail following continued its patrol through the region surrounding Algoa Bay and collecting the various detachments that had been assigned to different duties. On their way back to the Bay they once again encountered

Chungwa's Gqunukwhebe, who had made no attempt to move eastward. They sent a new message to Chungwa, demanding his departure but the messenger was unable to see him.

> Whatever reluctance he had shown to quit the colony, it never entered into our calculation that he would be rash enough to commence an attack upon a large body of regular troops. Such, however, was the step he chose to take; instigated, as we afterwards found out by the rebel boors. [Xhosa]s now began to appear on all the heights, with a view to attack us; numbers were observed close upon us, lurking in the bushes; our force being in a narrow defile, nearly choked with brushwood, and surrounded by [Xhosa]s, two or three rounds of grape were discharged from two field pieces to clear the thickets.

Hart and the other soldiers of the regiment had not before encountered the Xhosa. It was apparent that Chungwa and his Gqunukwhebe were no push-over and the Khoi were sent back to Algoa Bay with Barrow in charge of a small force of dragoons while Vandeleur continued with his attempt to expel the Gqunukwhebe, setting up camp on the Bushman's River, and sending out patrols to reconnoitre. The third frontier war had begun.

In Algoa Bay Barrow had a stand-off with numerous Boers who had been forced off their farms by the violence. Boers and Khoikhoi demanded British protection from each other and Barrow's party held the peace for several days with the help of a swivel gun and a naval party from *Rattlesnake*. The situation was resolved when the Khoikhoi deserted en masse and fled to the protection of Chungwa.

In Vandeleur's force, this was Hart's first introduction to the nature of war as waged by the Xhosa. The terrain included large areas of dense, thorny, and inpenetrable bush. The only paths through it were tracks beaten out by elephants. The British were burdened with inappropriate uniforms and muzzle-loading guns that required a visible enemy and that were often only useful when serving as a mount for bayonets: the Ghunukhwebe were clad in thorn-defying leather karosses, armed with assegais, and able to remain invisible in the bush.

Vandeleur's campaign was calamitous. One of his patrols under the command of Lieut. Chamney was overrun. Only four of the twenty-one members survived. Chamney himself, mortally wounded, led the Xhosa away to allow the survivors to escape. Vandeleur's main force came under attack on the Bushman's River and this convinced him that it would be better to establish fortifications. He returned to Algoa Bay. There he sent many of his troops back to Cape Town where they were needed as defence against a perceived threat from the French. A detachment, including Robert Hart[51] remained encamped at the Bay, and effectively under siege. This decision gained faint praise from Barrow[52],

> General Vandeleur, therefore, very prudently withdrew his forces, and marched them down to Algoa Bay, where part were embarked on board the "Rattlesnake," and the rest were to proceed to the Cape by easy marches.

but less complimentary opinion from military sources[53]:

> The loss of Lieut. Chumney [sic] and most of his party, cut off when detached to the coast, followed by the retreat of the general to the bay, in consequence, as I believe, Mr Barrow states, of his deeming it imprudent to wage an unequal contest with savages, the successful result of which could be only to those who had instigated them to act, – were occurrences which were certainly not calculated to inspire any of the contending parties with a high opinion of British power.

The frontier war was now complicated by a full scale rebellion of Khoikhoi against their Boer masters. The advent of the British force and the initial desertions by Khoi servants had set off an escalation of violence. Droves of Khoikhoi left the Boer farms in the Zuurveld and joined the Gqunukwhebe. In the region Agter Bruintjes Hoogte the remnants of the imiDange, now completely disaffected from the colonists, allied themselves with Chungwa and with the insurrection of the Khoikhoi. Boers fled from their farms as they came under attack right down the Langkloof. They had been without the means to defend themselves since the British authorities had cut off their supplies of gunpowder in order to put down the Graaff-Reinet rebellion.

Vandeleur sent alarmed despatches to Dundas who permitted the rearming of the Boers but the violence throughout the region continued. Dundas decided that his personal intervention was necessary. He sent *Camel* and *Rattlesnake* to the Bay carrying a prefabricated blockhouse and artisans to erect it. In early August he himself set off up the Langkloof with reinforcements.

Consider Francis Dundas's problems. He had only recently become Acting Governor as a result of Macartney's illness. His immediate superior, his uncle Henry Dundas, Secretary for War and the Colonies, was ten thousand kilometres away, and communications with the British Government, even by the fastest ships available, were subject to delays of several months. His uncle regarded the Cape as vital to British interests and had been one of the principal advocates of the British occupation. Britain, together with her partners in the Second Coalition, was at war with the French Republic under the *Directoire*. General Napoleon Bonaparte was at that very time on his way back to France from Egypt, prepared to stage his coup to take over the government. French naval vessels were a regular

threat and the probability of an invasion was high. Now came this disturbing insurrection on the most distant boundary of his Colony. If Dundas was to bring it under control he would need far greater resources than
were available to him. His concern was to stabilise the Eastern boundary.
Nothing would have pleased him more than to reach an agreement with
an all-powerful Xhosa king who had control over the people beyond the
Fish. No such king existed. The Rharhabe were in turmoil with the balance of power shifting between Ngqika and his uncle Ndlambe. Clans
that were part of the war on the Eastern Frontier – amaGqunukwhebe
and imiDange – recognized no allegiance to Ngqika or to the traditional
Xhosa Royal House under the boy king Hintsa. The trekboers were a constant nuisance with their expansionest tendencies. The Khoikhoi had his
sympathy; through Barrow's reports he was well aware of their appalling
treatment by the Boers, but they were now in revolt and in alliance with
the Xhosa. His troops in Algoa Bay did not have the resources to resolve
the situation by force of arms.

The positions of the combatants were irreconcilable. The amaGqunukwhebe were squeezed between the Rharhabe and the Boer colonists. Retreating to the other side of the Fish was not an option for them. The
imiDange had had their governing structures disrupted by the murder of
Jalamba eighteen years earlier by van Jaarsveld's men. They were split in
their allegiance between a faction that favoured submission to Hintsa and
another that desired independence. Both factions were united in their
hatred of the Boers and their distrust of any colonial authority. The
Khoikhoi were getting a heady taste of independent thought. Initially encouraged by a perception of colonial government support against the op-
pressions of their employers, they were now disillusioned and saw more
value in an alliance with the Xhosa. The Boers, deprived of the support
of their Khoikhoi servants, who had previously fought on their side and
carried the brunt of earlier hostilities, were panicked and had fled from
their farms.

Dundas's solution was to build up his defences and negotiate the best
settlement possible.

Camel arrived in the Bay in the middle of August. Hart and the other
troops were now put to work constructing more solid fortifications. The
prefabricated blockhouse was designed to house sixty men. It was sited
near the beach, commanding the landing place. On the hill behind it a
fort was constructed. An area twenty by twenty metres in size was surrounded by a massive stone wall almost three metres high. Inside was a
second blockhouse and a large powder magazine. It was armed with eight
cannon taking twelve pound shot, and commanded the Bay. In honour of

Frederick, Duke of York, Commander-in-Chief of the army, it was named Fort Frederick. Nearby was the barracks. The whole military complex could accommodate three hundred and fifty men. It must have been clear to Hart, who was no fool, that this was irrelevant to the Frontier war. It was the French that were the problem; the Boers, Khoikhoi and Xhosa could fight it out in the bush.

It soon became apparent that the French threat was not an empty one. On September 20th *Rattlesnake* and *Camel* were at anchor in Algoa Bay[54]. They were under skeleton crews, their captains being ashore with large shore parties, sampling the hospitality of the military camp. *Rattlesnake* had her yards and topmasts down. *Camel* was armed *en flute*, that is with a number of her guns removed. A brisk south easter was blowing and the surf was heavy. At 4 p.m. a ship was sighted in the east, steering parallel to the coast. At 5 p.m., having reached the anchorage, she hoisted a Danish flag and dropped anchor with her broadside trained on *Rattlesnake*, which was about 750 metres distant. *Camel's* boat, patrolling the anchorage, made towards her. Meanwhile an English schooner, the *Surprise*, had put into the Bay and sent an urgent message to *Rattlesnake* that this was no Danish ship but a French frigate, *La Preneuse*. *Camel's* boat crew, observing men with cutlasses awaiting them, retreated, while Lieut. Fothergill, in temporary command of *Rattlesnake*, signalled *Camel* that this was an enemy. Both British ships then fired warning shots towards the French frigate with no effect.

The shots woke up the forces on shore. Hart and his fellow troops watched the drama unfold. They were immediately put on alert, and the shore guns were readied for action.

By 8:30 p.m. the battle had commenced in earnest. Both British ships had to manouevre on springs. These are hawsers from bow and stern to fixed points, either on shore, or as in this case on the anchor rope. Adjustment of the lengths of these springs allowed each ship to orient herself in order to bring her guns to bear. Faced with broadsides from *Camel* and *Rattlesnake*, *la Preneuse* broke out the tricolore and opened fire.

A naval captain whose ship is under fire, in sight, and out of reach is not a happy man. All night Hart and his friends were entertained with the sight of naval officers being upset into the raging surf as they made repeated attempts to have their boats launched in order to return to their ships. The shore batteries had little effect. The main action was between the ships. Fortunately Fothergill was equal to the command and at ten o'clock the following morning *la Preneuse* limped out of the Bay under only a mainsail, to meet her fate in December when she was driven ashore in Mauritius by the British ships *Adamant* and *Tremendous* and destroyed.

Interlude   [1799 -1803]

Dundas, meanwhile, was managing negotiations with the combatants, He recalled Maynier who had credibility with the Khoikhoi and appointed him landdrost.The peace that he negotiated recognized the Gqunukwhebe rights to lands in the Zuurveld. The Khoikhoi, who were by now at odds with their Xhosa allies, were to return to the Boer farms where they would have the protection of law administered by Maynier. Relative peace was restored on the colonial side of the frontier.

Hart's regiment settled back into the boredom of garrison duty. By 1801 the situation in India required more troops. Manpower was limited and there were requests for members of the 91st Highlanders to volunteer for secondment for duty in India. It was not a popular posting:

> In September [1801] 224 men were transferred as volunteers to the 8th Light Dragoons, the 22nd, 34th, and 65th Foot which corps were proceeding to India. The Highlanders, and indeed most of the soldiers of the 91st were not very keen to volunteer into these other corps, and it was only by getting them to do so when they were drunk, or by bringing pressure to bear on them that the required numbers were obtained.[55]

Hart was a volunteer for this Indian service. Whether this was willingly or as the result of overenthusiastic pressure there is no way of telling. We know little about his time in India except that he was there in 1802. He then spent a while in Germany as a sergeant before returning to England, where his regiment was stationed.

In February 1803, under the Treaty of Amiens, the British returned the Cape to the Batavian Republic. The Dutch were to govern the Colony for just three years.

Chapter 3. Back to the Cape

*What a country calls its vital economic interests are not the things which enable its
citizens to live, but the things which enable it to make war.*

Simone Weil, The Need for Roots

England Again   [1803 – 1806]

It was while he was in England that Robert Hart met his wife-to-be. Hannah Tamplin was six months younger than him, born of poor parents in Charlwood, Surrey[56]. In September 1803 the army camp of instruction being operated on Bexhill Down was broken up and the regiment proceeded to Portsmouth in order to embark for Guernsey to form part of the garrison providing an early defence against a Napoleonic invasion. Hannah followed Robert to Guernsey and the courtship proceeded apace. Their marriage took place on 10th April 1804. It was to last for 49 years until it ended with Hannah's death in 1853.

The couple spent the first years of their marriage in England where their first child, a daughter Anna, was born early in 1805. By now Hart was a sergeant major in the army, stationed at Shornecliffe near Folkestone in Kent, under Sir John Moore, in order to be ready to repel the expected invasion from Napoleon Bonaparte. The army was, as usual, waiting for something to happen and it was a time of tedium, training recruits.

The Second British Occupation of the Cape   [1806 – 1807]

For Hart relief came in 1806. He was elevated from the ranks to become an ensign[57] and ordered to South Africa where he was to join Lieut.-Col. John Graham, commander of the Cape Regiment, as adjutant. Robert Hart's opportunity arose as a result of the occupation of the Cape by British forces for the second time in 1806. The rise of Napoleon and the renewed hostilities with France once again faced Britain with the need to protect the lucrative trade routes round the Cape of Good Hope. The second British occupation was effected in January 1806 by the 93rd Regiment, the Sutherland Highlanders[58], under the command of Lieut.-General Sir David Baird. Initially Baird acted as Military Governor.

The Cape Regiment   [1781 – 1806]

The Cape Regiment, which Hart was joining, grew out of Khoikhoi regiments that had been established in the Colony as early as 1781, when

Governor van Plettenburg established a force with the unappealing name of the Corps Bastaard Hottentotten. Later, after the disbanding of this Corps, the Pandour Corps was founded. During the first British occupation it was replaced by the Hottentot Corps, some members of whom had served with Vandeleur during the Graaff Reinet rebellion and the Third Frontier War[59].

Soon after the re-occupation of the Cape the Acting Governor, Baird, determined on re-establishing the Khoikhoi Pandours to form the Cape Regiment[60]. He appointed Major John Graham of the 93rd Regiment as its commanding officer with a consequent promotion to Lieut.-Colonel[61]. The command of a regiment has associated with it a daunting amount of military bureaucracy. Any commander can be greatly relieved by having an efficient adjutant – a junior officer with the responsibility of helping the CO with the administration of the regiment. We do not know how Graham identified Robert Hart as the man he wanted. No doubt he was looking for a young ensign, or NCO suitable for promotion to ensign, with experience not only of army management techniques but also of conditions in the Cape. Robert Hart fitted the bill admirably and in June 1806 he received orders to proceed to South Africa and his promotion to ensign.

A New Life   [1807 – 1809]

It took some time before the Hart family embarked on a transport to come to Cape Town and it was January 1807 before Robert, Hannah, and Anna – by now a toddler – saw Table Bay. Hannah was aware that she was pregnant again – not the best condition to arrive in for her husband's new posting. Officers, however, could hope to be accommodated in much better style than other ranks. The Regiment at that time was stationed at Wynberg with simple cottages for the officers and spartan barracks for the men.

Robert's work would have absorbed all his time. There were problems of recruiting. A soldier at the time received a wage of less than a shilling a day with many deductions for supplies, medical expenses, and similar personal needs. Not until later, when Lord Charles Somerset allowed wives and families to be accommodated with the rankers – a significant exception to general army regulations – could men see their families on any regular basis. With the abolition of the slave trade there was a great shortage of labour and the Dutch farmers resisted the conscription of their Khoikhoi labour. There were also the difficulties of procurement. The job was one that suited Hart's talents and he was successful in it.

Hannah had to set up her home. The cottage assigned to the Harts was primitive, not much better than a hovel. It was inadequate protection against the notorious Cape winters. Hannah's pregnancy was now confirmed and on 16th August their second daughter Harriet was born. Sadly the child was sickly and died a short time later on 30th November. The following winter was as bad. Although the Harts were able to occupy a new four-room dwelling at the end of June[62], it proved unfit for its purpose. In January 1809 Robert, supported by his commanding officer Col. Graham, petitioned Caledon to make him a grant of land[63]. He stated that his quarters were almost uninhabitable, particularly in the winter months when, in spite of attempts to repair the building, it continued to leak. His application resulted in the grant of a portion of the Government land at Wynberg that had been obtained from a local merchant, Alexander Tennant. On it he would build a dwelling house, and cultivate the undeveloped land as a garden. Graham's supporting document described him as a very meritorious officer.

The urgency of his application arose because Hannah was again pregnant. A daughter, Susannah, was born soon afterwards[64] but died in November. By the time of her death Hannah was once again pregnant. To the joy of the Harts, their first son Robert Jr was born in the middle of 1810 and was healthy. Robert's ambition for a home and a garden was not satisfied and soon afterwards he was ordered to the Eastern Frontier.

Growth of Tension   [1800 – 1812]

During the Dutch interregnum at the Cape the situation on the Eastern Frontier had not become simpler[65]. Among the amaRharhabe the balance of power had shifted between Ngqika and Ndlambe. By 1800 Ngqika's status among his people had been severely dented because of his attempted assassination of his uncle Siko, which had resulted in the flight of both Ndlambe and Siko to the Zuurveld. In 1803 Ndlambe and Chungwa of the amaGqunukwhebe had made it known to Governor Janssens that they would be interested in an alliance with the Colony against Ngqika. Other independent leaders, Galata of the amaGwali, Nqeno of the amaMbalu and Xase of the imiDange, were happy to play Ndlambe off against Ngqika as they tried to maintain their independence from the large amaRharhabe kingdom.

In 1807 one of Nqika's concubines was visiting her family in the Zuurveld and was detained by Ndlambe. Nqika retaliated by abducting Thuthula, Ndlambe's favourite wife. Ndlambe's brother, Sigcawu, fomented rebellion against Nqika. Hintsa and Ndlambe sent a Gqaleka force to support the rebellion and Ngqika was defeated. He fled to the

Amatolas. The advantage swung back and forth but ultimately the balance of power shifted sufficiently to have Ndlambe recognise Nqika as chief of the amaRharhabe. As a consequence the region west of the Fish River was occupied by Chungwa's amaGqunukhwebe and Ndlambe's supporters. In addition amaGwali, amaMbalu, imiDange and Trekboers laid claims to the area. The official British attitude was that the Fish River was the boundary of the colony and Ngqika was responsible for all the amaXhosa. Cattle rustling was rife. It was a recipe for conflict.

Clearing the Zuurveld [1806 – 1812]

Soon after the occupation, one of the appointments made by the Acting Governor, General Baird, was a second-in-command to Graham, with the rank of major in the Cape Regiment. The man chosen was Jacob Cuyler, a Dutch-speaking loyalist American from New York. He was also expected to serve as Landdrost in Uitenhage, while Anders Stockenstrom, a Swedish immigrant, had the corresponding position in Graaff Reinett. Both served with a Military and Civil Commissioner for the Eastern Cape, Major Richard Collins.

Baird's aims for the Eastern Frontier were to maintain good relations with the amaXhosa and to try to improve the relations between the Boers and the Khoikhoi. Cuyler was a poor choice to achieve them. He was ill-tempered and had negligible skills in human relations. He was equally contemptuous of Boers, amaXhosa, and Khoikhoi. His presence was to exacerbate rather than cool the tensions on the frontier. Stockenstrom, on the other hand, while identifying himself with his adopted people, the Boers, was a judicious man, ready to hear all opinions and with strong ethical standards.

Baird's short Military Governorship was ended with the appointment of Caledon in 1807. The appointment of the first civilian Governor of the second occupation was made in July 1806. Du Pré Alexander, 2nd Earl of Caledon, was a young (29) Irish Peer. He had been elected a representative peer for Ireland in 1804 and this was the extent of his administrative experience. In January 1807, before Caledon could reach the Cape, Baird was recalled, and the military commander Sir Henry George Grey[66] acted until his arrival later in the year.

Caledon's period of office was characterised by tensions between the miltary officialdom and the civil authority. The reports from the eastern frontier by Collins, Cuyler, and Stockenstrom highlighted and exaggerated the fears of the Boers, while failing to comprehend the pressures on Xhosa and Khoikhoi. Caledon was also continually at odds with Grey, the military commander-in-chief, with a lack of clarity regarding their respective responsibilities. He was less convinced of the rights of the Colonial claims to the Zuurveld region than his military officials.

His response was weak. He increased the numbers of troops on the frontier; between 1806 and 1808 the Cape Regiment grew from 500 to 800 men. Apart from those troops stationed in Cape Town, one company was stationed at Graaff Reinet and another on the frontier at the Fish River. He refused, however, the requests of the officials to permit commandos to be raised to retrieve cattle. He emphasised the rights of the Khoikhoi but required them to have fixed addresses to exercise them, effectively tying them to their oppressive employers without the opportunity to seek other employment. He failed to address the problem of the rights of the amaGqunukwhebe and other clans in the Zuurveld and confirmed the Fish River as the eastern boundary of the Colony without resolving the fundamental problem that these groups of amaXhosa had no part in any agreement with Ngqwaru and were in conflict with him. He oversaw the removal of many amaXhosa who had taken employment on Boer farms and their expulsion beyond the Fish with no means of support. Predictably this all led to an increase in the amount of cattle theft and a build-up of tension on the frontier. By the end of 1810 his feud with Grey led him to feel that he could not continue and his resignation was accepted.

Grey took charge in an acting capacity until a new Governor was appointed. Although his tenure was brief, he rapidly agreed with the proposals, over which Caledon had vacillated, that the amaXhosa should be expelled from the Colony. He ordered Major Lyster, in command of the Cape Corps on the frontier, to proceed. Lyster, in consultation with Cuyler and Stockenstrom, recommended that a commando be raised to perform the actual expulsion.

Sir John Francis Cradock, a very different man from Caledon, took up his appointment as Governor in September 1811. He was a seasoned soldier and had substantial administrative experience, having served as acting Governor of Gibraltar. He was, however, hasty in his decisions and had little patience with political subtlety. Furthermore he was not hamstrung as Caledon had been by an imprecise chain of military command; Cradock was appointed as both Civilian Governor and Commander-in-Chief of the Colonial forces.

Cradock immediately fell in with the plan for expulsion of the amaXhosa. Within a month of his arrival he had appointed Col. John Graham as Commisioner for the eastern frontier, and had dispatched him with his staff, including Robert Hart, and nearly 500 troops to Algoa Bay on board the *Upton Castle*. He also confirmed Macartney's proclamation issued thirteen years previously specifying the Great Fish River as the eastern boundary of the Colony.

Robert Hart's arrival in Algoa Bay was in very different circumstances from those of his first visit. He had left behind him his wife, his daughter and his one-year-old son. Furthermore, Hannah was again pregnant. In 1799 with Vandeleur's troops Robert had been one of the other ranks. Now he was an officer and he had been promoted to Lieutenant in 1810[67]. His accommodation on board had been relatively comfortable and he was well rested. More importantly he was far better prepared for what was to come. As adjutant he understood what the orders were; from his previous experience he had an understanding of what they implied. Furthermore he, himself, now had a crucial role to play in the forthcoming campaign.

Previously the Bay had presented a desolate appearance: now it was a bustling military camp centred on the looming presence of Fort Frederick, built twelve years earlier by his efforts and those of his comrades. The administration of the region had moved on since the last visit and Algoa Bay was not the place where Graham set up his headquarters. Uitenhage, a few kilometres inland, was the location of the Drostdy where Jacob Cuyler exercised his authority as Landdrost. It was here that the military headquarters was established.

The responsibility of an adjutant is to assist his superior officer by communicating orders, seeing that they are carried out, managing administrative detail, and taking care of the minutiae of logistics and operations. In this Hart seems to have excelled[68]. As the troops were deployed they had to be supplied and supported. The supply lines were extended. Much had to be transported from Cape Town, usually by ship. The opportunities for error and fraud among the suppliers were plentiful and needed a constant critical eye to protect the interests of the Government. Hart's rigid principles and strong work ethic were ideal for the task of oversight. He was also buoyed by news that on 21st November Hannah had safely given birth to a second son, James.

Graham's first priority was to tour the frontier to gain a knowledge of the territory on which the forthcoming campaign was to be conducted. Here Hart's previous experience was valuable and he also had time to familiarize himself further with the country that was to become his home. The Governor had instructed that the actual eviction of the amaXhosa was to be done by Boer commandos, overseen by Graham's forces. The next priority was to get these forces deployed. Graham established a line of fifty-three military posts, not for frontline attack, but to defend the Colony from possible counterattack. They stretched from the Baviaans

River westward across Bruintjes Hoogte to Riet River[69], which flows into the Sundays River. From there they extended southwards along the Sundays River, ending with Fort Frederick at Algoa Bay. These had to be kept supplied.

The Boer Commandos had to be called up. There were to be three Divisions organised under Cuyler, Stockenstrom, and George Fraser, one of Graham's officers. Their job was to bring the amaXhosa to a single collection point after which they were to be expelled beyond the Fish. By the time they had been assembled it was December. One more step in the preparations was the sending of Stockenstrom on a mission to ensure Ngqika's neutrality. This Ngqika was prepared to guarantee. The Zuurveld amaXhosa were already looking to his uncle Ndlambe as leader and no doubt Ngqika was happy to see the colonists taking on his old enemy.

On Christmas day, 1811, Graham's forces crossed the Sundays River into the Zuurveld[70]. Ndlambe left no doubt of his intention to resist. The initial days set the tone of the campaign with barbarous acts by both sides. On 26th December Anders Stockenstrom with a small party was on his way to meet Graham, and encountering a group of imiDange together with some Khoikhoi under David Stuurman, engaged in discussions with them, hoping to persude them to leave peacefully. While sharing a pipe of tobacco with some of the imiDange chiefs he was stabbed in the back by one Antonie, a follower of Stuurman, and his party was massacred. Only a few days later on the 3rd January 1812 a party from Cuyler's commando division came upon the chief of the imiDange hiding in the bush. Chungwa was old and ill; the regency had fallen on his son Kobe and he was not disposed to resist removal. Nevertheless he and those with him were shot while they lay asleep. Graham's bloody campaign had begun.

Throughout the hostilities Robert Hart kept a journal. Unfortunately this has been lost[71]. Only fragments survive in the form of quotations in other works. Thomas Pringle describes it:

> I have now lying before me a journal, kept during that campaign by my friend Mr. Hart, who was then a lieutenant in the Cape regiment. From this it appears that the [Xhosa]s were shot indiscriminately, women as well as men, and even though they offered no resistance. It is true that Mr. Hart says that the females were shot unintentionally, because the Boors could not distinguish them from men among the bushes; and so to make sure work, they shot all they could reach![72]

In the direct quotations from the journal Hart's writing is dispassionate, giving no indication of his feelings:

> Sunday Jan 12th 1812, at noon, Commandant Stolle went out with two companies to look for the chief Slambe [Ndlambe], but saw nothing of

him; they met only with a few [Xhosa]s, men and women, whom they shot. About sunset five [Xhosa]s were seen at a distance, one of whom came to the camp with a message from Slambi's son [Mdushane], requesting permission to remain until the harvest was over, and that then he, if his father would not, would go over the Fish River quietly. The messenger knew nothing about Slambi, or would say nothing of him. However, after having been put in irons, and fastened on a wheel, with a leather thong about his neck, he said that if the commando went with him before daylight, he would bring them upon two hundred [Xhosa]s asleep.[73]

The hopes of the Colonial authorities that the clearing of the Zuurveld might be achieved with minimal bloodshed had been shattered. The brutality of the Boer commandos was unrestrained by Graham. The strategy was to destroy the crops and burn the villages, a scorched earth policy to make the region uninhabitable[74]:

Friday 17th, two parties of one hundred men each were sent to destroy the gardens, and burn the villages:

Saturday 18th, three hundred men went early to destroy the gardens and huts, taking with them six hundred oxen to trample down the corn and vegetables in the gardens.

Sunday 19th, three hundred men went by daylight to destroy gardens and burn huts. About 2 o'clock P.M. a detachment returned having fallen in with a kraal of [Xhosa]s, they shot three dead on the spot, and wounded several: three women and four children they brought prisoners away.

Once the full might of the Colonial forces had been brought to bear on the amaXhosa it was all over. Ndlambe fled across the Fish with his people and cattle, successfully evading the commandos. He was soon followed by the amaGqunukwhebe, the amaMbale, and the imiDange. By the end of January all that was left was a mopping up operation and by March the region was under colonial control.

Graham's Town   [1812]

What had been a campaign now became an occupation. The region to the west of the Great Fish River must now be secured. Cradock made the decision to transfer the headquarters of the Cape regiment to the Eastern Frontier and Graham was required to set up a system of defence.

Graham ordered Lieut. Robert Hart, and Ensign Andries Stockenstrom, son of the slain landdrost, to join Capt. Donald McNiel and conduct a survey of suitable sites for a new headquarters. Stockenstrom believed he knew the perfect location. He led them to a deserted Boer farm, de Rietfonteyn, originally that of Lucas Meyer. It had a number of advantages. It was central to the Zuurveld region. From the top of a hill, a few kilometres to the east[75], the view to the east extended as far as the Keiskamma River; that to the north as far as the Tyumie valley and the Katberg. Communications with Algoa Bay, Uitenhage, and Graaff Reinet were good. There was an adequate water supply. Graham on arriving at the site was convinced and immediately gave orders to cease activities at his temporary headquarters on a nearby farm. Meyer's ruined farmstead was to be roofed as temporary officers' quarters and accommodation was to be constructed for the troops. Plots of land were alloted to the officers to construct dwelling houses.

Robert Hart as adjutant was responsible for the detailed implementation of Graham's orders. A number of lots were surveyed and allocated. They were set out around a long narrow right angled triangle surrounding the old homestead. There were seven narrow lots along the hypotenuse of the triangle on the north side and six lots along the south side. The reason for this configuration was that, at that time, two streams ran along the sides of the triangle, and these provided a convenient water supply to the officers' lots. Hart himself had a square lot at the point of the triangle. The old homestead became the officers' mess. Huts for the troops were constructed on the west side of the mess[76].

After the establishment of the headquarters a series of military posts was set up, overlooking critical areas of the region. These were not forts but wattle and daub constructions or old farm buildings. Having completed his task, Graham then departed for a long awaited leave in Britain, leaving the regiment under the command of Major Lyster. A few months later Cradock decreed that the new headquarters should be named Graham's Town in recognition of Graham's achievements on the frontier.

Robert Hart now at last had a home into which he could move his family. He was basically a city boy. Although he had been born in the country, he had been brought up from the age of six in Edinburgh. Yet some of his roots were still firmly planted in the Avon valley. In the Wynberg barracks he had tried to get a grant of land for a house with garden. In the middle of the horror and destruction of the eviction of the ama-Xhosa he had noted in his journal[77]:

> ...the gardens here are very large and numerous; and here also are the best garden pumpkins, and the largest Indian corn I have ever seen: Some of the pumpkins are 5½ feet round [1.7 metres or about 50 cm in diameter], and the corn 10 feet [about 3 metres] high.

This wistful note is followed by descriptions of the laying waste of these very same crops. Now, however, after all the destruction Robert could grow things. His plot on early plans of Grahamstown is labelled "Hart's

Garden."[78] Just a year after the establishment of the town a visitor[79] who dined with Hart wrote

> Some of the officers have already good gardens, though the town has not existed a year.

Sword into Ploughshare   [1812 – 1820]

Robert and Hannah moved their family into their new Graham's Town home as soon as construction could be completed. The expectation was that this would now be a time of peace where the regiment would perform what was basically a policing function on the frontier. Robert was immediately thrust into the duties of organizing supplies and communications for the line of military posts. Hannah, for the first time, could experience a relatively settled life. Soon she was pregnant again and their fourth surviving child, a daughter, Cecilia was born in 1813.

At the end of 1813 Cradock decided, as was common practice at the time, to allow the officers of the regiment to take ownership of their houses and land as a reward for their services. This caused a problem for Robert Hart[80]. It was felt that the location of his house obstructed further expansion of the town. Hart had already been working a large abandoned farm a short distance from the town and had 20 morgen (about 17 hectares or 43 acres) under cultivation. It was agreed that he could take ownership of this. Robert Hart was now a farmer.

Events in distant Europe were about to lead to great changes in the way of life at the Cape. Napoleon, after his disastrous Russian campaign had destroyed his apparently invincible hold over Europe, was defeated at Leipzig by the allies, forced by his Generals to abdicate on April 6th 1814, and exiled to Elba. One day earlier than the abdication, on April 5th, a ship bearing Cradock's successor as governor, dropped anchor in Table Bay. Lord Charles Henry Somerset[81], irascible and autocratic Tory aristocrat, second son of the 5th Duke of Beaufort, Privy Councillor, had arrived. Somerset for the next twelve years was to oversee momentous changes in the Colony.

With peace looming in Europe the Allied nations began meeting at the Congress of Vienna in September with a view to carving up Europe and its dependencies. In spite of Napoleon's new threat during the hundred days from March to July 1815, the meetings continued and agreements were signed just nine days before Napoleon's final defeat at Waterloo. Until now the future of the Cape Colony had been uncertain. The status of the British had been that of an occupying force. At the Congress of Vienna Dutch colonies, including the Cape, were ceded to the United Kingdom. The British were now there for the long haul. The effects of these decisions were soon to be felt by the officers of the Cape Regiment.

The policing function of the regiment kept them busy. The Cape regiment turned out to be especially efficient at patrolling the bush and evicting parties of amaXhosa who had tried to re-enter the Colony. A number of the posts that had been set up by Graham were handed over to detachments of British regiments, leaving the patrolling duties to the Cape Regiment. In 1815 Major Lyster left the Frontier, passing over command to Major Fraser. Shortly afterwards rebellion again broke out in Graaff Reinet. This time the colonial government had no mercy. The ringleaders were arrested, tried, and five were sentenced to death.

The execution on March 9 1816 was public, in the presence of the townspeople and with other rebels forced to attend. It took place at Slachter's Nek, a ridge on the Great Fish River near the Roodewal military post, the site of present day Cookhouse. Cuyler and Stockenstrom were in charge, with a troop of hundred soldiers of the Cape Regiment under Fraser. It is not recorded whether Robert Hart was in attendance but as Fraser's adjutant he may well have been[82]. The execution was botched. Four of the ropes broke leaving only one man hanged. Inexorably the process was taken forward; after a long delay more ropes were procured and the the sentence successfully carried out on the remaining four. This became an iconic event during the rise of Afrikaner Nationalism.

In early 1816 the results of events in Europe began to impinge on the regiment. After war, governments are anxious to rid themselves of the expense of large military forces. In February 1816 Lord Bathurst, the Secretary for War, consented to a substantial reduction of the establishment of the Cape Regiment. The number of officers was significantly reduced and those affected, including Hart, were placed on half pay. The prospects for the Harts did not look good. On 30th November of the previous year another daughter, Margaret, had been born. There were now five small children to be clothed, fed, and educated.

In 1817 relief came to the Harts. One of the most important military establishments on the frontier was a government farm, established by Somerset in 1815 at the foot of the Boschberg. It was named Somerset Farm, after its founder. Its main purpose was to supply the army on the frontier with produce as well as to act as an experimental farm for the development of agricure in the region. Its first director was Dr Joseph Mackrill[83] an American botanist, who was not very successful at meeting the demands of managing the farm. He resigned in 1817. Somerset agreed to the appointment of Robert Hart to the post. It was an inspired choice. Hart understood the demands of the military in complete detail having been directly concerned with procurement since arriving on the frontier eight years before. In addition he had an enthusiasm for agriculture combined with short but intense experience in Graham's Town. He grasped the opportunity with both hands.

Another half-pay officer of the Cape Regiment, Lieut. John Mears Devenish, was appointed as his assistant. Devenish needed the job even more than Hart. A member of a large Irish family, he had married his cousin Ellen Stretch in Cape Town in 1810 and they had a large growing brood of children. Ellen was the eldest of five and her siblings all had close connections with the Cape. Catherine Stretch was married to George Bennet, a Cape Town merchant. Susan Stretch was a widow who had come to South Africa to join other family members after the death of her husband, Edward Parr. Charles Lennox Stretch was an ensign in the 38th Regiment of Foot, at that time stationed in Plymouth, but soon to be ordered to the Cape. The youngest of the family, Richard Aldworth Stretch had been a member of the 60th Rifles and had returned to the Cape in 1817. All the Stretch family were eventually to live in the area where Somerset Farm was located and were to be closely associated with the Harts.

Robert and Hannah Hart packed up their possessions and with their five children, now ranging from 12 years to just 18 months old, set off by ox-wagon for the Boschberg. At last they were going to be able to set up home and live the kind of life that they had envisaged for their family and be relieved of the demands of military service.

The Battle of Graham's Town   [1817 – 1819]

Charles Lennox Stretch had arrived in South Africa with the 38th Regiment in November 1818. He could hope for a reunion with those members of his family who were already in the Cape. After several months service the Light Infantry Company of the Regiment, under the command of Col. Thomas Willshire, was ordered to the frontier. Stretch expected to be granted leave to travel to Somerset Farm to spend time with his sister Ellen and her family, the Devenishes. On arrival in Algoa Bay he found that his plans had been overtaken by events.

> But, on my arrival at Algoa Bay, we heard the [Xhosa]s headed by a chief named Lynx had entered the colony with some thousands of [Xhosa]s and actually menaced the headquarters of the commandant. I was therefore placed on duty when I landed, and continued with the troops who were sent to clear the country until October 1820.[84]

He had arrived in the middle of circumstances that had been developing for several years. Since the amaXhosa had been driven from the Zuurveldt the frontier region had never been calm. As could be expected, the expulsion of Ndlambe and his allies from their lands and the loss of large parts of their herds meant that, to survive, many amaXhosa were obliged to embark on a life of what the Colonial Government regarded as crime and what they perceived as a legitimate accumulation of assets. As a result of the expulsions, raids on the farms and cattle reaving increased rather than diminished.

In 1817, in an attempt to settle the situation, Somerset set up a conference with Ngqika on the Kat River. The years had not treated the Rharhabe ruler well. The long-running feud with his uncle Ndlambe had left his authority significantly damaged. Somerset was well aware of this, and made him an offer of active support against his enemies. The *quid pro quo* was that Ngqika would become responsible for stolen stock and ensuring that the culprits returned it. Failing this he would himself be liable[85]. While Ngqika knew full well that he had no control over Ndlambe and his allies he desperately needed the support of the British. He accepted the terms, essentially becoming a vassal of the British.

Ndlambe was eager to make peace with the Colony but Somerset, maintaining the wrong-headed insistence that Ngqika was the ruler of all the amaXhosa on the frontier, refused to negotiate with him.

Events among the amaXhosa were strengthening Ndlambe's hand. First, Hintsa the Gcaleka king had reached adulthood and taken control of the feuding amaGcaleka. He now wanted to restore the unity of the amaGcaleka and amaRharhabe under his rule. He did not trust Ngqika and gave Ndlambe moral and material support, recognizing him as ruler of the amaRharhabe. His authority as hereditary king made him a powerful patron. Second, a prophet called Nxele[86], also known as Makana or Lynx, had become extremely influential. Preaching his own blend of traditional beliefs[87] with an admixture of Christianity, he became Ndlambe's "wardoctor" – both prophet and military leader. His influence was to unite many clans against Ngqika and his British allies. In October 1818 matters came to a head when Ndlambe's forces under Nxele, with the support of amaGcaleka sent by Hintsa, comprehensively defeated Ngqika's forces, which were commanded by his son Maqoma, at the Battle of Amalinde[88].

Ngqika had appealed to the Colony for help in terms of the Kat River agreement. Somerset continued perversely to ignore the dynamics of inter-Xhosa relationships and interpreted it as a revolt against Ngqika by his subjects. The point of view taken was:

Hintza (the father of Kreli [Sarhili]) then joined with T'Slambie [Nd-
lambe] and Congo [Chungwa] in open rebellion against the authority of
Gaika and the Government, and before help could be sent to Gaika, he
was defeated in a great battle ...[89]

The thought that Hintsa, King of the Great House of the amaXhosa,
could be subject to Ngqika is ludicrous. The mere fact of the British wanting Ngqika to be Chief did not make it so. Nevertheless a large commando under Colonel Thomas Brereton was sent across the frontier on
what was supposed to be a punitive expedition. This was the start of the
5th Frontier War. Brereton's force penetrated deep into the Xhosa territory, confiscating cattle and laying the territory waste. This left the inhabitants without resources and inevitably meant that they would try to recover their means of survival. A huge Xhosa force assembled, stirred by
Nxele's messianic promises and encouraged to believe in his ability to
turn British bullets into water. This force crossed the border into the
colony, causing great destruction and havoc. By April they were approaching Graham's Town. Somerset's orders to Brereton had been to
use force only as a last resort and to try to move the amaXhosa eastwards
by persuasion. The way that Brereton's campaign was conducted alienated the amaXhosa, deprived them of the means of subsistence, and destroyed Somerset's frontier policy. Brereton was fortunate that permission
arrived for his return to Britain to settle his family affairs after the death
of his wife. This meant that he probably escaped severe censure for his vicious campaign[90]. The Graham's Town command was given to Willshire.
Charles Lennox Stretch's leave was deferred and he was despatched with
other members of his regiment to help in the defence of the town.

Years later Stretch provided a description of the events on the frontier
at that time[91]. The brutalities of Brereton's campaign caused a strong
backlash. Stretch reports that:

It was thought that this expedition would be of more benefit than any
commando that ever crossed the border and that the terror created by
it ... would effectually cause a cessation of depredations; but the result
proved the very opposite. For a short time the [Xhosa]s were tolerably
quiet, but in the beginning of the following summer, they entered the
Colony in great force, and assumed a more formidable character than
ever.

By the middle of April Nxele had mustered a force estimated by
Stretch to be 9000 strong. They secretly gathered in the Fish River Bush.
Nxele was well informed of the British strengths since he himself had
spent extended periods in the Colony and understood its ways. He had
spies to keep him informed. "Klaas" Nquka, Willshire's interpreter and
liaison with Ngqika, was one of these. On the 19th April Nquka informed
Willshire that he had information of the assembly of a large force at Kaf-

fir Drift on the lower Fish River. This was deliberate misinformation; the force was much further up-river and nearer to Graham's Town. Willshire ordered a light company of the 38th Regiment to go and investigate, reducing the garrison force by 100 men to about 350.

The first move in the Battle of Graham's Town[92] came on the 22nd April when a message arrived for Willshire from Nxele. It mockingly promised that Nxele would breakfast with him the following morning. Willshire gave the promise little credence. Next morning he was inspecting the 82 soldiers of the Cape Corps when he was approached by a new arrival in the town, Klaas Boesak, the leader of a roving band of 130 Khoikhoi who were renowned big game hunters[93]. Boesak had just received information that Nxele and his forces were approaching from the East. Willshire, with an escort of 10 men went out to reconnoitre, leaving Capt. Trappes in command[94]. The party came unexpectedly on a part of the Xhosa army resting in a ravine. These warriors lost no time in giving chase and Willshire and his small party were closely pursued towards Graham's Town.

Meanwhile Trappes, warned by a Khoi herdsman, was preparing defences. Graham's Town was essentially unfortified. The layout had not changed significantly since Robert Hart had first implemented it. There were a few dwellings. The barracks were some distance from the centre of the settlement. It lay at the bottom of a depression with a swamp in the middle of what is now High Street. A stream crossing the depression from north to south provided a slight obstacle to the advance of the amaXhosa. There were just over 300 men, with only a few cannons[95]. Sixty men were detached to defend the barracks and the remainder were formed into a hollow square. This would probably have been arranged with about 60 men on each side ranked two deep. Those in front could then fire while those behind reloaded. The cannon would have been placed to bear in the easterly direction, from which the attack was expected. Stretch and his brother officers would have been inside the square, inspecting equipment, relaying orders from Trappes, keeping up morale, and themselves preparing for a fight that would ultimately be at close quarters. The infantry weapon of the time was the Brown Bess, a flintlock muzzle loader. The rate of fire was determined by how rapidly the soldiers could reload. A well drilled force could maintain a rate of perhaps one shot in forty seconds, meaning that, at best, they could fire about 350 rounds a minute. Later estimates of the numbers of amaXhosa put Nxele's force at roughly 9000. The British cannon, however, were another matter. Charged with ball they were not very effective against large numbers. Loaded with shrapnel or grape shot – numerous small spheres about the size of a grape – they could flatten swathes of attackers and create de-moralization of an advancing force.

By midday the Xhosa forces were massing on the slopes to the east of the town. Nxele's vantage point was on a ridge near a conical hill now known as Makana's Kop.

Willshire meanwhile was galloping towards the town with his party, hotly pursued by the amaXhosa. The group had almost been surrounded before they had been aware of it and their escape was a close thing. They clattered into the town, the square opened to admit them, and their pur-suers fell away to join the main force.

The Xhosa weapons were mainly assegais. They were carried in a bundle designed for throwing and, given the skill of the users, were effect-ive at a range not much smaller than the effective musket range. At close quarters the shaft could be broken off and the blade used as a stabbing weapon. They had a few guns but relied mainly on the assegais. Nxele had divided them into three divisions on the eastern slopes overlooking the town. Two threatened the town itself; the third was positioned on the left flank to attack the barracks. Behind these 6000 men were a large num-ber of women and children with their household utensils, ready to move in to occupy the town after victory had been won.

Willshire redeployed the troops in Trappes's defensive square to meet the threat. He moved the bulk of his force into a line on the west side of the stream extending from the barracks to the square. Two cannon were placed to the north on the east side of the stream in a position to rake the open area across which the attack must come with deadly grape shot. The mounted Cape Regiment and some infantrymen were stationed to sup-port these guns. The remaining artillery were placed to cover the barracks and also the line of retreat if it became necessary.

The little force had plenty of time to anticipate what they were in for. Most must have wondered whether there was any chance of defending their position. Six thousand warriors were amassed in a position looking down on their objective. At one o'clock the attack began. First the third Xhosa division moved down the hill to attack the barracks. Next the re-maining five thousand in massed formation began jogging down the hill. As they approached the distant roar became distinguishable as Nxele's battle cry, "Tayi!", an incantation to protect themselves from harm[96].

The advancing force believed in its invincibility, both on the rational ground of a numerical superiority of thirty to one, and on ill-founded faith in Nxele's supernatural abilities. When they reached a close enough range the muskets of the troops opened fire and some assegais were hurled. Most amaXhosa broke off the shafts of their assegais ready for the hand to hand combat that would overwhelm the defenders. Then the artillery opened fire with volleys of grapeshot and shrapnel. The attackers were stopped in their tracks as great gaps were cut in their ranks. Although they had almost achieved their objective they made no further progress, taking what little cover they could find or retreating as best they could.

The attack on the barracks was a different matter. Here the cannon were ineffective as they could not fire on the attackers without destroying the defenders. It was a close thing. There was a threat that ammunition would run out. There is a well-known story of Elizabeth Salt, wife of one of the defenders, who, because the amaXhosa were always chivalrous to women and children, was able to smuggle a container of gunpowder into the barracks by wrapping it in blankets and carrying it like a baby.

The situation was desperate when Boesak and his Khoi force entered the battle. They were all skilled marksmen and Boesak knew the amaXhosa very well. They made full use of every shot and picked off the leaders, causing a leadership vacuum. Stretch gives Boesak's Khoi the credit for changing the course of the battle. The Xhosa advance was brought to a halt, changed to a retreat, and rapidly became a rout.

By the time Willshire recalled his troops from the pursuit, fearing that they would be overextended, the Xhosa dead were scattered over a wide area between Graham's Town and the Fish River. Estimates of their numbers varied widely. At two extremes Stretch estimated 2000, giving no basis for this, and Willshire 350, but this probably related only to those killed in the immediate battle and not during the pursuit. Contemporary estimates of about 1000 were supported by Cory on the basis of dubious premises[97], in which he assumed each soldier had time to get off three shots during the battle itself and that almost all these were effective; he ignored the effect of artillery and deaths during the subsequent pursuit.

This brought Nxele's career as a war leader effectively to a close. The subsequent campaign forced the amaXhosa across the Fish. Ndlambe fled, his power gone. Hintsa's amaGcaleka were forced across the Kei to the Mbashe. Nxele gave himself up and was imprisoned on Robben Island, drowning a year later while trying to escape. Somerset "negotiated" a treaty with Ngqika in which the region between the Great Fish and Keiskamma Rivers became neutral, but the amaNgqika were allowed to occupy a region between the Tyumie and the Keiskamma rivers.

A line of defence for the frontier was set up. Fort Willshire was built in the ceded territory. Strategic military posts were occupied. One of these was Roodewal, not far from Somerset farm. Charles Lennox Stretch was given command of this. This was fortunate for him in more than one way. First, his sister and brother-in-law, Ellen and John Devenish, were employed there so he had the opportunity to spend time with members of his family. Second, he met Robert and Hannah Hart, and, more importantly, their eldest daughter Anna.

Somerset Farm   [1817 – 1820]

When the Harts began work on Somerset Farm they had almost achieved what was to be their home for the rest of their lives. The nomadic life of an army officer was behind them. Although Robert was still an employee of the Colonial Government, he and Hannah now had a chance to settle down and make a life for themselves. Robert threw himself into the activity of managing a large working farm that also had the function of an experimental establishment, providing leadership and information for the agricultural community. It was also a commisariat, serving the troops on the frontier by providing an agency for buying the products of Boer farmers, and later English settler farmers, and distributing them to the army. Robert's organizational talents were a dramatic change after the indifferent management style of his predecessor and the farm was soon a busy centre of agricultural activity. The family continued to grow. Ellen Evelyn was born at the end of 1818.

Some of the activities that had considerable influence were the promotion of the merino sheep leading to the prosperous Eastern Cape wool industry, the construction of a water mill that provided a central facility for the production of flour and meal, and the importation of horses that improved the local stock.[98]

At the end of 1819 a visitor came to the farm. Once the situation on the frontier had been resolved, Charles Lennox Stretch's appointment as commander of the Roodewal Post allowed him the opportunity to visit his sister and brother-in-law, the Devenishes. Here he met the Hart family. Their eldest daughter Anna was not yet fifteen[99]. Stretch was twenty-two. Stretch was very taken with the young woman. Propinquity probably also played its part. Before long the Harts had agreed to the marriage and Charles and Anna were married in April 1820.

Life on the frontier was about to change and Somerset Farm was to play a part. The British presence at the Cape was about to change from occupation to a permanence. The frontier was on the threshold of the first substantial permanent British settlement.

Chapter 4. The Settlers

In spite of all their friends could say
On a winter's morn, on a stormy day,
In a sieve they went to sea!

Edward Lear, The Jumblies

The Land of Opportunity   [1800 – 1820]

Great Britain in the first years of the nineteenth century was a country in turmoil. The primarily agricultural country was suffering the symptoms of industrialisation as the success of British inventions began to impinge on society. New modes of travel became available. As workers began to move from country to town, consolidations of small farms into large landholdings began to transform the pattern of agricultural life. Formerly self-employed peasants were dispossessed and became wage-earning farm labourers.

The Napoleonic wars disrupted trade with France and the United States of America. At their end the discharge of large numbers of men from the Army and Navy led to a large increase in the unemployed. At the same time, notions of freedom, following on the French Revolution, led to frequent political unrest. Up and down the country there had been riots and the Luddites, opposing the introduction of machinery to replace the work of artisans, were destroying machines in their factories. Troops were stationed in the towns and the situation often became ugly. By 1819 there seemed to be a real risk that the country would become ungovernable.

At the same time in the Cape, the problems on the eastern frontier were a cause for concern. The colonial government believed that the solution was to place large numbers of settlers on the eastern frontier, where they would become a bulwark for the defence of the Colony.

The British Government saw this as an opportunity to export some of their problems of poverty and unemployment. Previous schemes to encourage emigration to the colonies on an individual basis had been relatively unsuccessful. This time the Government set up a scheme to subsidise parties of settlers to emigrate to the Cape of Good Hope.

An amount of £50 000 was voted by Parliament to support the scheme. Parties were required to consist of ten or more able-bodied men with their dependants under the leadership of a responsible person. Settlers were defined as men over the age of 18 years; their families were part of the settler unit. The leader was responsible for the payment of £10 for each such unit. Whether this was raised from his own pocket or from the individuals was a matter of choice. Each settler was to be allocated 100 acres of land which was to be subject to quit-rent[100] after the first three years of occupation.

The parties were of two main types[101]. Many, the "joint-stock" parties, were independent parties in which each family was responsible for its own deposit and each received an allocation of 100 acres of land. Others were "sole proprietor parties" where a single person financed the party. In return the members of the party waived their rights to the land in favour of the leader, and undertook to work for him for a fixed period. These leaders, who would have classed themselves as gentry, generally had visions of building up large estates in the new country with themselves playing the part of squire.

The prospect painted by the government was extremely attractive and 90 000 applications, far more than the 4 000 or so that could be supported, poured in. People were captivated by the image of a land of opportunity. Parties were organized all over the country and gaining approval to emigrate was a great prize.

The Ships   [1819 – 1820]

A fleet was assembled for the emigration. It was a collection of various vessels, many of them East Indiamen[102], assembled by the Navy Office to carry the parties of settlers. Typically they were a few hundred tons and carried about two hundred passengers. As an example the *Stentor* was described as being 382 tons sheathed in copper, and, confusingly, listed by the underwriters as having two decks and by the owners as having one. On its voyage to the Cape it carried 179 passengers. The crew's quarters were in the forecastle. Aft was the poop deck. Beneath the fore part of this was the cuddy, divided into the captain's cabin on the starboard side, and a larger area on the port side that was used as the saloon for those privileged passengers – the party leaders and gentry – who dined at the captain's table. Aft of the cuddy was the round house, divided into cabin spaces for officers and privileged passengers, and leading out to quarter galleries where the heads (latrines) were located with a drop straight into the sea. Ordinary passengers got a bit of deck that could be partitioned off with light panels. Cots could be swung from overhead deck beams but otherwise passengers had to supply their own furniture, generally a table, sofa, washstand, and bedding. Conditions were impossibly cramped. For example, another vessel, *Northampton*, was a small 19 year old ship of 574 tons. It had completed nine voyages to the Far East for the East India

Company. It travelled with about 250 passengers, 109 of them children under 18 years old.

The HMSS *Weymouth*, carrying 464 passengers, was larger. It was a naval store ship and served not only to transport a large number of settlers but also to take supplies for the settlers to the Cape.

The Walkers of Castleton [1797 – 1819]

Castleton in the Derbyshire Peak District is today an attractive village with stone houses dominated by the ruins of Peveril Castle, the Norman fortress after which the town was named. It is surrounded by fields bounded with dry-stone walls, and much frequented by hikers and climbers. In the early nineteenth century the parish of Castleton had a population of about 1300. Castleton was in a hill farming district but there was a fair amount of industry in the neighbourhood and the impact of the newly developing factories on the local home based economy was causing hardship.

Castleton churchyard contains graves of villagers going back hundreds of years. Among these are the graves of William and Ellen Walker and some of their kin.

William and Ellen had a hard life in the last quarter of the eighteenth century. Their first two children, Nancy and William, died in infancy. They then had a number of sons, William (named after his dead brother), James, John, and Richard. They then had a single daughter whom they named Nancy after her dead sister. This was followed in 1797 by their youngest son, Joseph.

Soon tragedy struck. In 1799 another child was expected. The birth was very difficult: the baby was still-born and Emily, as was then only too common, died in child-birth. Two-year-old Joseph and his five older siblings were left to grow up motherless.

In 1817, when Joseph was 20 years old, his father, William, died. The surviving family found what employment they could. Joseph and his older brother Richard found that there was not much future for them in Castleton. Both of them seem to have become shopkeepers of some kind. Whether this was as employees or whether they managed to find enough capital to operate on their own is not certain[103].

Meanwhile Lt George Smith of the 95th Regiment of Foot, which had been disbanded in 1818, had decided to try and raise a party to emigrate to the Cape Colony. Both Richard and Joseph Walker were of an enterprising character and, finding their opportunities in England limited, when the opportunity arose to emigrate they decided to try to take advantage of it. Richard at this time was recently married and had a small son, named Joseph after his younger brother, and a baby daughter. They applied to join George Smith's party which had been largely recruited from Lancashire. The two Derbyshire lads must have made a good impression. In spite of the very large number of applications they were accepted as members of the party. Lieutenant George Smith's party ultimately consisted of 63 members[104] – 20 adult men 14 of them with wives, and 29 children between them. With several other parties from the region they were assigned to *Stentor*, a tiny 382 ton ship. On 12th January 1820 they sailed from Liverpool and, after a tedious but uneventful journey, arrived at the Cape on 19th April.

The Voyage of the *Northampton*   [1819 – 1820]

In 1819 William Thackwray was approaching his fortieth birthday. His wife, Dorothy was several years older[105]. They had six surviving children, John (18), Dorothy (15), Ann (13), William (11), Joseph (6), and James (4). Thackwray described himself as an agricultural implement maker. He was obviously skilled as he later operated as a wainwright, manufacturing ox-wagons for transport over the rough or non-existent roads of the eastern Cape Colony and beyond. They came from Sheffield[106] and had joined one of the emigration societies in operation at the time. This society had been founded by one William Smith. However, Smith was refused permission to raise a large party of 100 men and their families. The Thackwrays then enlisted with Bailie's large party that was due to sail on *Chapman*. Bailie's party was a very large joint-stock party and was subject to a great deal of turmoil and disorganization. Meanwhile Smith had decided to raise a smaller party and was anxious to assemble the necessary number of members. Smith promised William the right to 100 acres of land if he joined. Since, as a late comer to Bailie's party, he would have only been entitled to 50 acres, William withdrew and, together with several other members of the emigration society, threw in his lot with Smith. They were first assigned places on board *Nautilus* but Smith requested a delay for the organization of the party and they were finally accommodated on *Northampton*[107].

William Thackwray spoke with a dialect that sounded strange to the ears of the Londoners in their party. Thomas Stubbs, a young lad in the same party, later apprenticed to Thackwray, writing his reminiscences more fifty years later, described him thus[108]:

> Old Thackwray was a strange sort of man, he was very stout, and from his talk would be taken for a Quaker, as he always said, 'yea' and 'nay' and 'thou'. But what was the strangest thing about him, he scarcely

ever spoke without farting, for instance – he would say, "George [George Wood, another apprentice] thou art a fool (Poop). George if thou doesn't alter (Poop) I shall be obliged to (Poop) get rid of thee (Poop)." Sometimes he would talk to his daughter Dolly [Dorothy] and he would say, "Dolly ist thou going (Poop) up the Town? Because if thou art thou must not (Poop) stay long (Poop)."

Five parties, numbering 253 emigrants, sailed for the Cape aboard the *Northampton*. They were led by George Pigot, Thomas Mahoney, William Clarke, William Smith[109], and Charles Dalgairn. George Pigot's fifteen year old daughter Sophia kept a diary[110] which gives a good picture of the voyage from the point of view of the privileged daughter of a party leader.

Clarke's Party included the Stubbs family, John (41), Ann (34) and their children Elizabeth (13), John (12), Thomas (10), William (6), Ellen (3) and Richard (1). It is thanks to the reminiscemces of Thomas[111] that we have such a lively picture of the voyage from the point of view of the average settler, and of the initial experiences of the Thackwrays.

The Thackwray family joined William Smith's party aboard the *Northampton* in Gravesend docks. It was the middle of December 1819. The temperatures were freezing at the beginning of the coldest winter for many years. Upstream from Gravesend the ice on the frozen Thames was six feet thick. Settler ships such as the *Aurora* and *Brilliant* had had their November sailing dates indefinitely delayed and were only able to leave in January. Further down river the *Northampton* was free of ice.

There were delays on account of the weather, but at last, on Monday 13th December 1819, *Northampton* weighed anchor. It was snowing and there was a cutting wind. It must have seemed a good time to be leaving England. It took more than a day to labour out through the Thames estuary, round the North Foreland and into the Downs in the Strait of Dover off Deal, where they anchored. They remained in the vicinity for many days waiting for suitable conditions for departure. Visitors from shore came regularly back and forth to the ship. It was only on Christmas Day that they received the signal to sail and they made their way slowly round the South Foreland into the Channel. At various times in her diary Sophia Pigot complains of how badly she and her sister Kate were suffering from seasickness. They could spend their time in the relative comfort in privileged quarters in the cuddy: the conditions of the other passengers either on the freezing deck or confined below were very different. Anyone who has spent a relatively short time below deck on a crowded cross-channel ferry in a gale can try to imagine what it would be like to spend days in a smaller and less comfortable vessel with 250 passengers on board.

Once in the channel they made fairly good progress and anchored again on the evening of Sunday 26th December at Spithead near Portsmouth. It was very cold, snowing, and the passengers could not go out on deck. On Monday 27th Sophia reported: "The ship rolled very much." That night another settler ship, *Ocean* broke from her moorings in the gale and collided with *Northampton*. Sophia laconically notes: "The *Ocean* came to pay us a visit at three o'clock in the morning – Almost all the people upon deck, I fast asleep. The ship a little injured." Thomas Stubbs, remembering the event fifty years later, describes the alarm of the passengers and the damage caused but implausibly places the event in the Bay of Biscay.

It is hard to imagine the conditions on the voyage. The journey began in December 1819 and was completed in April 1820. Presumably the children looked after each other and mostly managed to escape falling overboard. Stubbs, however, records that, while lying off Blackwell in the Thames,

> ... a heavy fall of snow occurred. Immediately the boys made a slide on the deck of the old hulk, but they had not been sliding long, when, to the astonishment of all, one of the boys went right through the porthole overboard.

Surprisingly he leaves the incident there. Did the boy survive in the freezing Thames? Was there an effective rescue attempt? There is no record.

The passengers on *Northampton* avoided the fate of those on the *Abeona* from Glasgow (lost by fire at sea with only 27 of the 132 passengers surviving) or the *Ocean* (fired on by the port batteries while at anchor in Porto Praya in the Cape Verde Islands; this by mistake as the battery was suspicious of a boat from a schooner in port that appeared similar to a previous hostile visitor). An outbreak of smallpox might have been expected to cause great alarm so it is surprising that neither Sophia Pigot nor Thomas Stubbs[112] make much of it in their accounts of the voyage. It is even more surprising that among the more than 250 people, crowded in close proximity, there were only 8 deaths from the disease – 1 adult and 7 children. It seems that the general level of immunity in the population must have been high. Vaccination by Jenner's process was becoming more and more widely used in the first years of the nineteenth century and this may have contributed to the relatively low mortality.

One of the more unpleasant aspects of the voyage was the presence of Mahoney's party. Thomas Mahoney described himself as an architect. His character was described a few years later in a document originating from the office of the Cape Governor, Lord Charles Somerset[113]:

> A very worthless character who has taken contracts from Government in buildings and not performed them.

His original large party had been split before embarkation with more than half being reorganised under William Clarke. The parties on board had all supposedly been recruited from London and its environs but Stubbs's description[114] conflicts with this

> Many of the settlers were Irish, some hailed from Yorkshire, some from Berkshire [Pigot's party] and some from London.

In fact the makeup of Mahoney's party appears to have been very different from the officially approved list. Guy Butler notes[115] that Mahoney entered fictitious names for some of his party. If one compares the lists of settlers provided by Sheffield with Morse Jones's list[116] there are many discrepancies. A number of the men enumerated on the embarkation lists never appeared and were replaced by others who were not listed[117]. Bearing in mind that Mahoney – listed as an architect – operated in the colony as a building contractor, it is not unlikely that he had filled the gaps in his party with labourers many of whom might well have been Irish.

The Mahoney party added to the discomforts of the voyage. Stubbs tends to treat their antics as comic relief but the entries in Sophia Pigot's diary paint a different picture:

> [19th Jan 1820] Mr. Mahoney very troublesome.

> [20th Jan] A meeting of the gentlemen below, sad disturbances with those Irish people.

> [11th Feb] Mr. Mahoney always very troublesome.

> [24th Feb] Disturbances with someone almost every day – very troublesome Irish people.

> [3rd Mar] Great disturbances with the Irish people, sharpening both sides of their knives. Rather frightened ... They [officers and party leaders?] were threatening to put a centinel [sic] at Mr. Mahoney's cabin door.

> [6th Mar] ... holding consultations about Mr. Mahoney ... Mr Brown and a number of people ill after drinking at Mr. M[ahoney]'s cabin the other night – Eliza Dalgairn slept in our cabin with us – they were getting in at our window.

> [8th Mar] A certain person very troublesome

Stubbs gives accounts of two disturbances. In the first a fire started near the galley. Fire on board a ship is a very serious matter as substantiated by the fate of the passengers and crew of the *Abeona*. Stubbs writes

> The sailors made a rush for the blankets to smother the fire, while some of the settlers, not knowing what the sailors wanted the blankets for, made frantic attempts to get them back. ... An Irish woman, named

Holland, made a fierce attack on a sailor, and at the same time bawled out to her son, "Dennis yer spalpeen, will ye be letting them take all our blankets to have them burned, and us and the childer starved to death with cold?"

The fire was extinguished. Something that 10 year old Thomas Stubbs found funny might have been seen as "troublesome" by an impressionable 15 year old Sophia Pigot.

The second event related by Stubbs (perhaps that on 3rd March[118]) gives a more rounded picture. The disturbance sounds less serious than perceived by Sophia but nevertheless alarming for those on board:

... the ship gave a pitch and threw the Irishman on his back, and the burgoo [porridge] on the deck. Seeing what had occurred, the second mate ... came up to our Irishman with the intention of kicking him. A stout-made settler seeing this, seized the mate by the frill of his shirt and shook him as a terrier would a rat. The mate ran aft to the Captain calling out "mutiny". The captain immediately called a muster of the sailors, armed them with cutlasses, and placed them across the quarter-deck. All the Irish rushed to the fore-castle, some armed with pieces of wood, and some with pieces of iron hoop. In the midst of them Mrs Holland could be heard calling out, "Dennis, I say Dennis, will yis be showing yourself a man this day: we're not to be bate like a lot of gilly goolies by them fellows with their big knives; so stand to it for the sake of ye's country."

The show of force seems to have been enough to calm the disturbance. Stubbs reports that the settler who shook the mate was imprisoned for a day and all was quiet thereafter.

A three-month voyage in a sailing ship could perhaps be expected to result in endless days of boredom. Instead the Thackwrays on their voyage had experienced a collision in the channel, scenes of drunken revelry, the threat of smallpox, fire on board, and a near mutiny. There were other entertainments. On 14th March the path of a total solar eclipse crossed the South Atlantic and Sophia Pigot reports having observed it. The position of the ship at the time would have been near the path of totality but her brief description gives no indication of whether they saw it as a total or partial eclipse. Crossing the line was a rough sailor's ceremony. Stubbs suggests that the morning after the revels the ship was drifting untended for some time.

At last Cape Town was sighted and *Northampton* arrived in Table Bay on 26th March.

Edward Driver and the Nottinghamshire Party   [1819 – 1820]

Nottinghamshire had for many years been a centre of the hosiery and lace making industries. These were cottage industries: businessmen in the towns would provide machines to workers and pay them piece work rates for what they produced. The income generated was barely enough for survival. Lace making had progressed (or perhaps regressed) from hand-made bobbin lace to machine-made lace using adaptations of the frame-work knitting machine. The advances made as the industrial revolution progressed led to the concentration of workers in the towns where larger machines could be operated in factories. The home industries were strug-gling. The Napoleonic wars had cut off major export markets and crop failures had led to massive inflation in food costs. The price of bread had risen to as much as a quarter of a home worker's weekly income. The number of paupers was growing; the parishes, required by the poor laws to provide relief, levied increased rates on property owners. Both rich and poor were suffering.

Near Nottingham, in the village of Kelham, lived Edward Driver Sr, an agricultural labourer, and his family. As was the case with everyone in the village, times were hard. His eldest son, also Edward, had had some employment as a ropemaker, but this was no more profitable than any of the other trades in the region.

Young Edward was intelligent, sharp, well set up, and quick with his fists. He liked to think of himself as cock of the walk and was well pleased with his nickname of Kelham Ned[119]. He was one of many young people who could see little future in Nottingham.

The disaffection and unrest all over Britain was mirrored in Notting-hamshire. In the city during 1819 there were numerous street gatherings and protests[120]. The climax came in August when 5000 people paraded through the streets of Nottingham, appealing to the Duke of Newcastle, Lord Lieutenant of the County, and the gentry for relief.

They received a sympathetic hearing. The poor laws were bearing heavily on the gentry with rates to support the workhouses ever rising. There was awareness of the government plans for encouraging emigra-tion to the colonies – particularly the Cape – and the prospect of remov-ing numbers of the unemployed from the parish was attractive. The first suggestion from the Duke was that unemployed workers should apply to join the recently announced scheme for sending workers to the Cape. The deputation could see little advantage in this. When, however, the Duke proposed setting up a fund for poor relief there was much more enthusi-asm. An appeal was launched and, in a remarkably short time the enorm-ous sum of £6 000 had been raised by local subscription. More than a hundred years before Roosevelt's "new deal" a similar scheme was set up by private charity in Nottinghamshire. The money was put towards providing employment in building roads and other public works during the winter of 1819 – 1820 and relieved some of the poverty in the region.

The temporary relief was not sustainable however. The Duke returned to his first suggestion but sought means to make it more palatable. He convened a meeting of prominent local worthies and proposed the establishment of a fund for supporting a party to emigrate to the Cape. The idea was received with enthusiasm. No doubt some of the donations were the result of altruism, but one cannot but feel that there was an element of relief at the prospect of getting rid of some of the troublemakers. Again an enormous sum – £2 000 – was pledged and a committee to administer the fund was set up including the Duke of Newcastle himself as chairman, the Duke of Portland, the Earl of Surrey, Lord Galway, Admiral Sotherton and several others, including a Mr E. S. Godfrey as Secretary.

The committee drew up a plan for selecting settlers. They circulated information widely to magistrates, parish priests, and officials concerned with poor relief. The opportunity existed for able-bodied men of good character and their families to be accepted. Paupers were acceptable, provided that five pounds was paid on their behalf from local poor relief funds. After some doubt about whether the party would be accepted, the Earl of Bathurst, in a letter to the Duke of Newcastle, ruled that, provided a list of suitable settlers was submitted to the Colonial Office, the navy would provide transport. A surgeon, Thomas Calton, was appointed as leader of the party and a Sergeant G. Dennison as administrator to help with the selection of the party and to deal with paper work.

One of the 57 successful applicants was the twenty-four year old Kelham Ned – Edward Driver. He boasted in later life that he was one who paid his own expenses and, indeed, on the page of signatures of those embarking with Calton's Party, his name is one of the very few that has been endorsed "paid £5"[121]. Edward's grandson related[122]:

> My grandfather, Edward Driver, came out with the 1820 Settlers, paying all his own expenses, a fact which he always related with pride.

Many of the party were, however, supported by the poor relief fund.

Burton's account[123] gives a fascinating picture of the preparations necessary. Godfrey, the Committee secretary, with the help of Calton and Dennison were responsible for equipping and outfitting the party. They needed to provide tools and hardware, clothing for men, women, and children, material for education of the children including paper, slates, pens, pencils and rulers, a dictionary, and spelling books. Bibles came free.

News came from the Navy Office on 5th January 1820 that the party would be accommodated on *Albury*, a 330 ton naval transport ship, and that it was bound for Liverpool from Portsmouth.

Getting from Nottingham to Liverpool was not very easy. The Pennine range, forbidding in the middle of a very cold winter, runs down the spine of the north of England. It would have been easier for the party to travel to London. One wonders why *Albury* had been sent to Liverpool. Calton's party was the only one assigned to that ship. They were 158 in number, enough to fill the small vessel. At first it was hoped that they would travel by canal boat, the quickest mode of travel at that time. They chose not to do so. Burton suggests that they were sceptical of the reliability of the service offered by the Acton canal haulage company. In any event they went by land. Sixteen and a half tons of goods were loaded on wagons and the men of the party under Sergeant Dennison accompanied them on foot across the frozen Pennine moors. It took three nights before they reached Liverpool. The women and children were shuttled by coach over a period of several days. The coaches each took about a day for the journey, following a route that avoided the mountains – westward round the southern foothills of the Pennines to Leek, then northwards on the west side of the mountains to Macclesfield, and finally westward again to Liverpool.

The party was accommodated for several day at an inn called the Saracen's Head until they could board *Albury*. This was a coaching inn that existed at the time in Dale St on the corner of Sir Thomas St. Here Bartholomew Bretherton kept 700 horses to to service his coaching business[124].

The time before sailing was occupied in trying to improve the stores. Much of the clothing that had been supplied was of poor quality and there was a shortage of pig iron for the blacksmiths. Poor weather delayed their departure. Eventually they sailed on February 20th, a month later than the departure of the other Liverpool ships, *Stentor* (with the Walkers on board) and *John*.

The voyage of the *Albury* was marred by disputes between the settlers. Dennison tried to stir up discontent against Calton. Animosities created at this time may have been the reason for violent disagreement that Edward Driver had with another member of the party, Willaim Sykes, more than a year later. Calton eventually brought Dennison before the Captain in the presence of the settler party, the matter was hammered out, and there was no more trouble for the rest of the voyage.

The Scots   [1819 – 1820]

In the twenty four years since Robert Hart had run away from Strathaven to join the army and eventually settle in the Cape, economic conditions in Scotland had not improved. Farmers, in particular, were suffering great hardship. Fifty miles to the east of Strathaven, the people in the county of Roxburghshire in the Scottish Borders were undergoing as much difficulty as anywhere. John Pringle, a thirty-two-year-old miller, but a farmer at heart, found himself trying to be a business man. He had left his father's farm, Blaiklaw, to start the milling business with his friend Kaderley and also gone into partnership with his cousin John Riddle to operate a shipping agency.

John's father, Robert had been a prosperous farmer. Now most of his capital had been lost and the family was scattered making precarious livings where they could.

Robert had been married twice. His first marriage, to Catherine Haitlie, had resulted in seven children, William, John, Thomas, Alexander, Isabella, Mary, and Jessie. The marriage had ended with Catherine's death in 1795[125]. These children were now adult and making their own way in the world. Robert's second marriage to Beatrix Scott in had resulted in a second much younger family – William Dods[126], Catherine, and Beatrice.

In 1815, as a result of the financial difficulty, Robert had left Blaiklaw in the care of his eldest son William and had moved with Beatrix and her children, as well as Mary, to a rented farm near Bishop's Auckland, in the English county of Durham. John's younger brother[127], Thomas, lame as a result of a childhood accident, was not physically or temperamentally suited to farming; he was pursuing a literary career in Edinburgh.

Alexander had left Scotland to seek his fortune. He had, in 1813, emigrated to the United States of America and was living in in a town called Wilmington[128]. John's sister Isabella was a teacher, Mary was with her father and his second family on the farm in Co. Durham, and Jessie had married William Ainslie.

Thomas was trying to make his mark in the literary world. He had had a volume of poetry published and had been the rather unsuccessful editor of the Edinburgh Monthly Magazine (which afterwards became Blackwood's Magazine). Thereafter he transferred to Constable's Edinburgh Magazine. He appeared to be respected in literary circles although for current taste his poetry is nearly unreadable. As an example take the first stanza of *Farewell to Bonny Teviotdale*, marking his party's departure from Scotland:

Our native Land – our Native Vale –
A long, a last adieu!
Farewell to bonny Lynden-dale,
And Cheviot mountains blue!

The state of his family was of great concern to Thomas; to him it seemed that it was breaking up. In addition, he was worried about his own financial situation. His literary efforts had received some critical recognition but were financially very unsuccessful. He had difficulty in supporting his wife Margaret Brown, whom he had married two years before. He must have been a difficult brother to tolerate. While criticism of him would have been inhibited because of his disability, he was only too willing to express his opinion of his siblings. As early as 1812 when he was 23 years old he was giving advice to his father about his brothers[129]:

> I have made a proposal to John [his older brother] ... to come to Edin[bu]r[gh] and study medicine ... if he himself is capable of the rigid attention and perseverance it would require. ... I have not had any answer from John. ... John has an address and accuracy of observation much better fitted for the study. Alexander [his younger brother] has a slowness and awkwardness of manner which being ingrafted in his natural disposition he will never altogether get quit of though for all this he may succeed very well in the other professions – for he is by no means deficient in good sense and reflection ...

The large ego exhibited here was probably of great use to him in his later bouts with Lord Charles Somerset during his battles for press freedom. One wonders what John's answer to this condescension was.

Thomas Pringle was attracted to the idea of emigration and proposed to his family that they apply to be included among the settlers to the Cape. There was an enormous number of applications from Scotland, but Thomas was prepared to pull strings. He went to visit his friend, Sir Walter Scott, who had been kind in his criticism of Thomas's recent work. Scott immediately wrote to the the relevant cabinet minister in London, extolling the virtues of the Pringle family and shortly afterwards the news was received that the Pringle party, with Robert nominally in charge and Thomas as *de facto* leader, had been approved to emigrate on *Brilliant*, sailing from London. The Pringle family members in the party were Thomas and his wife, his father and step-mother, brother John, and the three children of Robert and Beatrix. In addition three friends of theirs, the brothers George, John, and Peter Rennie joined them. The remainder of the party was made up of servants and farm workers.

The group made their way to London awaiting the departure of *Brilliant*. Because of the extreme weather this departure was long delayed and the ship, together with her companion *Aurora*, only sailed from

Gravesend Dock on 15th February 1820, two months after the departure of the first settler ships.

The Booth family   [1819 – 1820]

One of the strong forces driving the changes in British society at this time was the evangelical movement which had grown ever more powerful over the previous 75 years. John Wesley's Methodist movement was in the forefront of the changes. Although Wesley himself, until his death in 1791, maintained that his movement fitted within the elastic boundaries of the Anglican Church, by the early nineteenth century the Wesleyan Church was an important independent religious movement with large and enthusiastic congregations all over England. It had great influence on education, on the place in society of its members, on opening the eyes of its members to ideas of human rights, and indeed on the economic prowess of Britain. The puritan work ethic has been credited with a strong influence on the advances of the industrial revolution.

Edward Wynne was a convinced Methodist, a member of the Great Queen Street Chapel in London. He did not see much prospect of the Reform Movement making progress in improving the lot of ordinary people and so he began to investigate the prospect of participating in the Cape emigration scheme. The scheme required parties to consist of at least 10 able-bodied men and their families. However, if parties of 100 men and their families could be raised the Government was willing to pay for a minister of religion to accompany the party. This condition was crucially important to Wynne. He established the United Wesleyan Methodist Society with the object of forming a party to emigrate to the Cape. This was accomplished but shortly afterwards tragedy struck. Wynne's wife died after giving birth to a son. A new leader was briefly appointed but withdrew and finally one Ezekiah Sephton was elected leader[130]. The party was too large to fill a single ship. Most of them were to be accommodated on *Aurora* scheduled to sail in November 1819. A young Wesleyan minister, William Shaw, was approved to sail with them. The remainder of the party was to be on board *Brilliant*.

Benjamin Booth, now a Londoner, had been born in Richmond, Surrey, in 1786. He had married his wife, Margaret Mortimer, in about 1808. They lived in Lambeth where their first three children, Margaret (11), Sarah (about 6) and Jane (3) had been born. Booth and his family were staunch Methodists and were accepted by Sephton's party for emigration and were assigned to *Aurora*.

When the time came for departure the bad weather that had delayed other ships dealt a blow to the settlers plans. Departure was delayed indefinitely. The Booths, together with the rest of the party, were left to their own devices for two months. They were finally allowed on board at Deptford on the 5th February. The ship left the dock but the voyage was yet to begin. They anchored off Gravesend waiting for favourable winds. These did not occur for a week. At last *Aurora* sailed from Gravesend Dock in company with *Brilliant* on 15th February 1820.

The voyages of both *Aurora* and *Brilliant* were relatively uneventful for most of the passengers. For the Booths, however, the usual difficulties of trying to keep track of a family of young children, including a three-year-old, while coping with boredom, sea-sickness and other discomforts, were exacerbated when it became apparent that Margaret's sickness was not only the result of the ship's motion but also because she was pregnant. When the Booth family went aboard they could not have known this as she could not have been more than one month gone. The weeks waiting for departure had not been entirely unproductive. By the time the voyage was over she was well into the pregnancy and the Booth's fourth child, Benjamin Jr, was to be one of the first born to a British settler in the new country.

The Artist and his Family [1818 – 1820]

James Ford was an artist. He was also a businessman[131]. He and his wife, Frances lived in London. They had seven children, ranging in age from fourteen to three. From his house in Hackney he operated a business as a wool-stapler, buying wool from producers, sorting and grading it, and selling the wool on to manufacturers in the burgeoning textile industry. He also maintained his skills as an artist, painting miniatures. The family was not over-prosperous and took in a young couple as lodgers.

In spite of his name, Philip or Phillipe Marillier would have regarded himself as English as they come. London has always been a refuge for the exiles of Europe and his parents, being descended from minor nobility, had left Lausanne in Switzerland to make a new life in England at the time of the French Revolution. Philip had been born in Hackney and lived all his life in London where his father was a businessman. He had married Louise Droid in about 1818, and worked in the family business. The couple took lodgings with James Ford and his family.

In 1819 tragedy struck Philip when his wife and their infant daughter both died. At this time the Fords were already considering emigration to the Cape since James Ford's business had suffered heavy financial losses[132]. Philip Marillier, stricken by his own tragedy, wanted to make a new start. He wrote to his brother in Lausanne, describing his feelings at his loss[133]

My dear Brother,

Perhaps for the last time from this country I now write to you, it being my intention to take advantage of the offer held out by the government to such persons as are willing to become settlers at the British Colony of the Cape of Good Hope in South Africa.

...

I have lost those domestic comforts which repaid me for all the daily crosses and disagreements to which I was exposed in the business with which I was engaged, but which I should have been well contented to bear with, looking forward to the time when by my exertions I should have been able to retire with her, whom I loved above all others, to the country and friends she adored, ...

He goes on to describe his hopes:

... I feel that I cannot bear patiently the bustle of commerce, and the clash of interests of commercial men, and have nothing better to do than retire from the bustle of the world to the quiet and peaceable oc-cupation of husbandry ...

This quiet and peaceable pursuit he chose to undertake on the eastern frontier of the Cape Colony.

The Fords and Marillier joined Bailie's large party of about 250 members, which sailed on *Chapman*.

Bailie's party was a large joint stock party with a high proportion of professional men and artisans[134]. Members of the party who were afterwards prominent in the Eastern Cape community included John Cent-livres Chase, Robert Godlonton, and Richard "Dick" King. Many travelled with servants. Ford himself had a servant, William Gray. James Ford and his wife, Frances, had seven children. The eldest, named Frances Jane, was just fourteen years old. Philip was twenty seven years old and a widower. Nevertheless, the young girl, on the threshold of womanhood, fired his interest. Within two years they were to be married.

Chapman was one of the earliest ships to sail. She left Gravesend on 3rd December 1819 and reached Table Bay on 17th March 1820. She was the first settler ship to anchor in Algoa Bay on 10th April. The voyage was not a happy one. A number of children died of whooping cough. The crowded conditions on board and Bailie's authoritarian attitude led to a great deal of friction. Before landing relationships were so strained that the members of the party agreed to seek permission for it to be split up into five groups. When this was agreed by the authorities, James Ford became the leader of one of these.

Chapter 5. The Settlement

Have you your pistols? Have you your sharp-edged axes?

Walt Whitman, Pioneers! O Pioneers!

The Arrival at the Cape and the Journey to Algoa Bay [Mar – Jul 1820]

The settler transports straggled into Table Bay and Simon's Bay during the first half of 1820. The first arrived in March and the last in June. After three months at sea in intolerably cramped conditions the passengers must have been eager to get ashore. In most cases it was not to be. Orders were that, apart from some of the party leaders, they were to remain on board pending their onward voyage to Algoa Bay. At least conditions were improved as the ships took on fresh water and provisions. The frustration of being able to see the land, the bustling waterfront, and the town huddled at the foot of the mountain, but not being able to disembark, was intolerable. It was hard to accept that the journey was far from complete; the onward voyage to Algoa Bay involved long delays in Table Bay or Simon's Bay and then labouring eastwards along a dangerous coast. In some cases it was to be more than a month before the passengers were to reach their final destination.

Most ships docked at Table Bay or Simon's Town, sometimes both, before undertaking the voyage to Algoa Bay. There were some exceptions[135]. Nightingale's Party on board Amphitrite were landed in Cape Town and established a whaling venture there. The parties on board the East Indian and Fanny were first settled in the Western Cape but many were subsequently moved to the main area of settlement on the Eastern frontier.

Joseph and Richard Walker were irritated to find that *Stentor*, bound for India, was not able to transport them to Algoa Bay. They were required to transship to *Weymouth* for the last stage of the journey.

H.M. Stores Ship *Weymouth*, a large transport vessel, had carried 464 passengers to the Cape. Of those on board the 26 members of Captain Duncan Campbell's party were disembarked in Simon's Bay to be settled on the banks of the Zonder End River in Caledon. On board *Stentor* Griffith's, Neave's and White's parties – 84 in all – were also disembarked and dispatched to Caledon. On May 1st the remaining 95 members of George Smith's and Richardson's parties, including the Walker brothers, were crammed onto *Weymouth* for the journey to Algoa Bay. One can imagine the scene. Passengers must be assembled on deck with their personal ef-

fects. The larger items of baggage and the supplies of tools and equipment must be identified and clearly marked with their intended destinations. People and goods must be lowered into boats and transferred either
to shore or to another vessel. Numerous excited children add to the confusion. When the final exchange has been made all must be checked and
the inevitable errors corrected. Lost children must be restored to their parents and lost goods to their owners. The consequences of minor accidents
and injuries must be attended to.

Eventually *Weymouth* was able to set sail for Algoa Bay where she
anchored on 15th May. As was the case with all the parties, only the leader George Smith was allowed ashore and the remainder of the party endured a frustrating wait until the tented accommodation on shore was
available. They finally disembarked on 22nd May.

The Thackwrays had arrived in Table Bay on 26th March. After
spending a few days there *Northampton* set sail again on Easter Sunday,
April 2nd. No doubt the passengers looked forward to reaching Algoa
Bay at last. A further ordeal was to follow. Appalling weather often made
conditions on board almost insupportable. The ship beat about the ocean
making no progress against adverse winds. The settlers endured almost a
full month aboard before *Northampton* anchored in Algoa Bay at twenty
five minutes past four on Sunday April 30th.

Brilliant with the Pringles aboard, *Albury* with Edward Driver, and *Aurora* with the Booths, docked in Simon's Bay on April 30th, May 1st, and
May 2nd respectively. As was usual the passengers were frustrated by being kept on board, only the leaders being allowed ashore to consult with
the authorities in Cape Town. The delays in the Cape were much shorter
than for many of the earlier ships and the three ships set sail on May
10th, arriving in Algoa Bay on May 15th.

Algoa Bay   [1820]

In 1820 Algoa Bay, now the site of the large manufacturing city of Port
Elizabeth, was a desolate sight. To European eyes the rocks and beaches
that are now playgrounds for holiday-makers looked dangerous and forbidding. The strongly aromatic coastal vegetation, well adapted to arid
and windy conditions, was disconcertingly alien. The only permanent
structures were Fort Frederick, the military post constructed by Robert
Hart and his comrades twenty years earlier, and a few ramshackle
thatched cottages.

The Governor of the Cape, Lord Charles Somerset, was absent on extended home leave. His deputy, Acting Governor Sir Rufane Donkin, had

charged the Uitenhage Landdrost Jacob Cuyler, by now a Colonel, with the task of organizing the settlement of the immigrants. Cuyler's autocratic ways had made him very unpopular, but he was a good administrator. He organized tent villages and ox-wagon transport. When *Brilliant* docked in Algoa Bay on 15th May the organization of the settlement process was well under way. Thomas Pringle, as leader of a party, was allowed ashore. He wrote:

I then strolled along the beach to survey more closely the camp of the settlers, which had looked so picturesque from the sea. On my way I passed two or three pavilion-tents pitched apart among the evergreen bushes which were scattered between the sand-hills and the heights behind. These were the encampments of some of the higher class of settlers, and evinced the taste of the occupants by the pleasant situations in which they were placed, and by the neatness and order of everything about them. Ladies and gentlemen, elegantly dressed, were seated in some of them with books in their hands; others were rambling among the shrubbery and over the little eminences, looking down upon the bustling beach and bay. One or two handsome carriages were standing in the open air, exhibiting some tokens of aristocratic rank or pretension in the proprietors. It was obvious that several of these families had been accustomed to enjoy the luxurious accommodations of refined society in England. How far they had acted wisely in embarking their property and the happiness of their families in an enterprise like the present, and in leading their respective bands of adventurers to colonise the wilds of Southern Africa, were questions yet to be determined. Foreseeing, as I did in some degree, (although certainly by no means to the full extent), the difficulties and privations inevitable in such circumstances, I could not view this class of emigrants, with their elegant arrangements and appliances, without some melancholy misgivings as to their future fate; for they appeared utterly unfitted by former habits, especially the females, for roughing it (to use the expressive phraseology of the camp) through the first trying period of the settlement.

A little way beyond, I entered the Settlers' Camp. It consisted of several hundred tents, pitched in regular rows or streets, and occupied by the middling and lower classes of emigrants. These consisted of various descriptions of people; and the air, aspect, and array of their persons and temporary residences, were equally various. There were respectable tradesmen and jolly farmers, with every appearance of substance and snug English comfort about them. There were watermen, fishermen, and sailors, from the Thames and English sea-ports, with the reckless and weather-beaten look usual in persons of their perilous and precarious professions. There were numerous groups of pale-visaged artisans and operative manufacturers, from London and other large towns; of whom doubtless a certain proportion were persons of highly reputable character and steady habits; but a far larger portion were squalid in their aspect, slovenly in their attire and domestic arrangements, and discontented and uncourteous in their demeanour. Lastly, there were parties of pauper agricultural labourers, sent out by the aid of their respective parishes, healthier perhaps than the class just mentioned, but not apparently happier in mind, nor less generally demoralised by the untoward influence of their former social condition. On the whole, they formed a motley and unprepossessing collection of people. Guessing vaguely from my observations on this occasion and on subsequent rambles through their locations, I should say that probably about a third part were persons of real respectability of character, and possessed of some worldly substance; but that the remaining two-thirds were for the most part composed of individuals of a very unpromising description - persons who had hung loose upon society - low in morals or desperate in circumstances. Enterprise many of these doubtlessly possessed in an eminent degree; but too many appeared to be idle, insolent, and drunken, and mutinously disposed towards their masters and superiors. And with such qualities, it was not possible to augur very favourably of' their future conduct and destiny, or of the welfare of those who had collected them in England, and whose success in occupying the country depended entirely on their steady industry.[136]

In later years when the surviving settlers had achieved prosperity and status this description was embarrassing. In his account of the settlement, written more than 60 years later, Sheffield[137] wrote:

To some of the poet's [Pringle's] remarks exception will no doubt be taken. There were few, if any, parish paupers among the Settlers. The Government had insisted upon a deposit of £10 from the head of every family of man and wife and two children, and for each child and person in excess of that number £5 each had to be paid. 'Paupers' were not very likely to be able to pay such an amount as deposit money. A few there were —such as Major Pigot (after whom 'Pigot Park' was named), Mr. Scott (of 'Scott's Bottom'), Messrs. Bowker, Phillips, and Campbell, half-pay officers — who thought to build up an aristocracy of their own in the new Settlement, and who had availed themselves of the provisions of the Government regulations under which the Settlers were sent out, to bring out parties of able-bodied labourers to work on their locations or estates. These may have brought out needy but well-recommended poor people from their several parishes, but each had to produce certificates as to character from their several ministers. How, then, those who had 'hung loose upon society' could have been included among the first Settlers, we are at a loss to conceive. Taken on the whole, we believe they were above the average of intelligence and respect.

Clearly Pringle's picture was close to the truth. There were many settlers who, had they remained in Britain, would have been dependent on charity. The example of the Nottinghamshire settlers confirms that many were subsidized by the donations of wealthy gentry, anxious to be rid of numbers of unemployed who threatened to be a burden on the parish. The evidence of Thomas Stubbs and Sophia Pigot suggests that the members of Mahoney's party on board *Northampton* were in Pringle's words "individuals of a very unpromising description" while Mahoney himself was unreliable and troublesome. Stubbs also suggests that the members of Clarke's party were not of the highest calibre[138]:

> [Doctor Clarke] was the head of Clarke's Party, now called Collingham he brought out a party, mostly of young men from the penitentiary.

This may be unfair to many of Clarke's party, including Thomas's own father John, who appear to have been family men with respectable occupations. There was, however, a group of half a dozen young eighteen-year-olds listed in the party. Several have no recorded occupation. Two in Sheffield's list do not appear in Jones's list. Clarke's party originally was part of Mahoney's and was split from it[139] so it may be that there were also irregularities in its make-up.

In any event more weight can be placed on Pringle's contemporary account than on Sheffield's celebration of the settlement written for the opening of the Settler Memorial Tower in 1882. The settlers were a mixed bunch indeed. Parties such as Pigot's or Philipps's were of the sole proprietor class. Their leaders had financed the expedition and the members of the party were in their employ or contracted to them. Many of those who had come out in Bailie's party, such as James Ford and Philip Marillier, were also of this class, regarding themselves as gentlemen. In many, but not all, cases Pringle's misgivings about their future were justified. Pringle's own party had some of the characteristics of a sole proprietor party in that there were only two families – Pringles and Rennies – taking the independent role, with the remainder being agricultural workers and servants. Joseph and Richard Walker, Edward Driver, William Thackwray, and Benjamin Booth were all members of independent parties and not bound to any leader. Each looked forward to the prospect of a piece of land of his own from which he could wrest a living for his family.

Journey into the Interior   [1820]

The responsibility for the logistics of the settlement was ultimately Donkin's but delegated to Cuyler who carried them out with commendable efficiency. The allocation of sites followed Donkin's interpretation of Somerset's policy. Settlers from the same part of Britain were to be kept together. As a consequence there were two discrete regions of settlement – the Zuurveld area centred on Grahamstown that afterwards became the English district of Albany, and the inland region on the Baviaan's River that was the destination of the Scots.

Numbers of local Boers were engaged to provide transport. They were encamped round Algoa Bay with their wagons and large spans of oxen – a strange sight to British eyes used to horses as the chief beasts of burden. The nature of this transport intrigued the settlers, particularly those like

William Thackwray who was a skilled wheelwright. A span consisted of twelve oxen, sometimes more, lined up in pairs, each pair linked by a shaped wooden yoke (*juk*) resting in front of the shoulder hump that is a feature of the Afrikander breed. The yoke was secured on either side of the neck by a wooden peg (the *skei*, or *jukskei*). A long wooden shaft, (the *disselboom*[140]) hinged at its connection to the wagon, extended between the pairs of oxen, and the yokes were attached to this by leather thongs (*rieme*). A young Khoikhoi employee or a slave, the *voorloper*, would lead the oxen. In command was a driver, on the wagon or walking beside it, armed with an enormously long whip, which could be cracked with a startling noise or used with great skill to flick the haunches of any one of the beasts that might be flagging. The wagons were rugged and suited to the unforgiving terrain, simple in construction so that they could be dismantled easily for transport across otherwise impassable obstacles. They were covered by hooped canvas, providing shelter for people and goods. Here, surely, was an opportunity for William.

The parties in turn were loaded up with their goods and transported to the sites allocated to them.

When they arrived they were dumped with their possessions, rations, and agricultural supplies and left to get on with it. In an often-quoted passage one of their number[141] described their initial circumstances:

> It was a forlorn-looking plight in which we found ourselves, when the Dutch waggoners had emptied us and our luggage on to the greensward, and left us with our boxes and bundles 'under the firmament of heaven'. Our roughly-kind carriers seemed, as they wished us goodbye, to wonder what would become of us. There we were in the wilderness; and when they were gone we had no means of following, had we wished to do so. We must take root and grow, or die where we stood.

Destinations   [1820]

Stoney Vale

After the long journey the passengers on *Northampton* were finally allowed ashore. William Smith's party had been allocated land to the east of Graham's Town. It included an abandoned farm called Stoney Vale. The Stubbs family's allocation was adjacent to Smith's. Although John Stubbs had nominally been attached to Clarke's party in practice his small group operated as a separate party. It included the Stubbs family and the family of his friend John Brown as well four young men who do not appear on any list of settlers[142]. Stubbs had tried to assemble a party of his own but when this was refused managed to attach his group to Clarke's party. While these had been allocated a site at Collingham, ten miles (16 km) north west of Graham's Town on the wagon trail to Committees Drift[143], somehow Stubbs and Brown managed to be treated as an independent party and were allocated land beyond Smith's allocation, fifteen miles (24 km) east of Graham's Town on the trail passing Fraser's Camp on the way to Trompetter's Drift. The wagon train carrying the Thackwray family therefore also carried the Stubbs and Brown families.

The route followed was long and arduous. It was north of the current main road through what is now the Addo Park and then turning westwards to Graham's Town. After a break in the town the parties were reorganized – or rather disorganized - and sent off to their sites.

Thomas Stubbs[144] describes the arrival:

Arriving at Stoney Vale - we found the walls of an old house and also a tramp floor. We were given to understand the original occupiers, a Dutch family, had been murdered by [Xhosa]s. There was a laughable scene. Old Thackwray on being offloaded took possession of the ruins; but the wife of Doctor Clarke (he was the head of Clarke's Party, now called Collingham he brought out a party, mostly of young men from the penitentiary) claimed the ruins as she said the Field Cornet had told her that was on her husband's location. So as fast as Thackwray put his tross within the old walls, [she] and her men put them out. I must remark there was no roof on the ruin; At last I think Thackwray got possession and she and her men had to go back to Collingham.

In common with all the settlers, the Thackwrays were then faced with the task of building a shelter, planting crops, and constructing the way of life that they hoped would be an improvement on the grey and disadvantaged existence that they had left behind. They were more fortunate than some in having the walls of an existing house that needed only some repairs and roofing to provide them with a home.

Clumber

Albury had arrived in Algoa Bay in May 1820. The party to which Edward Driver belonged was initially disrupted by the death of Calton, their leader, shortly after they had arrived in Algoa Bay. Thomas Draper was appointed leader. The party including Edward Driver, was settled north east of Bathurst or as Dugmore[145] put it:

'... the Duke of Newcastle's protégés from Nottingham took possession of the beautiful vale of Clumber, naming it in honour of their noble patron'

Each male settler was allotted a patch of land and was left to farm it as best he could. Edward Driver became an agriculturist, faced with all the problems of finding shelter, living from hand to mouth, and cultivating virgin land.

Riet River

George Smith's party, including the Walker brothers, Richard and Joseph, was settled on a site east of the current town of Port Alfred, bounded to the east by Riet River and to the south by the coast. Today this is a remote area with magnificent beaches. Then the thick coastal forest and riverine bush made a strange impression and promised heavy labour in the clearing of land.

Neither Joseph nor Richard Walker was dedicated to the prospect of farming. Richard was a devout man much influenced by the teachings of John Wesley. His ambition was to preach but his need was to support his wife and children. Joseph, still single, more conventional in his religious observance, was not so constrained. With no special skill other than keen intelligence coupled with common sense, he was on the look out for ways to begin to build his fortune. Meanwhile, the immediate needs of the situation meant that they must set to and begin to clear the land ready for the plough and the spring planting. Soon circumstances would drive them to other occupations.

Cuyler Town

Bailie's Party from *Chapman* was the first to arrive at Algoa Bay. As a result they were not subject to the same delays as later parties. Cuyler decided to escort them to their final destination himself. The dissension in the party during the voyage, however, had left relations so strained that it was on the point of disintegration. The request to divide into smaller parties was approved and some of these did not accompany the main body of the party. Those who did included James Ford with Philip Marillier and the other members of Ford's subgroup. Their location was near the mouth of the Great Fish River. A surveyor accompanied them and as soon as they arrived, on 25th April, work began on surveying plots of land for the heads of families. They decided to call their new village Cuyler Town[146].

Salem

By the time *Aurora* dropped anchor in Algoa Bay on May 15th Margaret Booth's pregnancy was in its fifth month. Sephton's party was disembarked from both *Aurora* and *Brilliant* and housed in the camp on shore. The Booths may have wondered about their timing when they saw one of the small buildings of the camp converted to a temporary maternity hospital to accommodate two other women of the party who gave birth to new colonists within two weeks of coming ashore. The Booths' baby would be born somewhere far in the interior where their new home would be. Sephton's large party was divided into groups which set off into the interior at regular intervals.

The original plan had been for the party to be accommodated at a place that they called Reed Fountain – a literal translation from the Dutch Rietfontein – which was located east of the Kariega River. Donkin had, however, decided to accommodate Campbell's large party there, and instructed Cuyler to accommodate the Sephton party on the Assegai Bosch River, a tributary of the Kariega and the site of the future village of Salem. Somehow the instruction was not implemented and the first few groups of the Sephton party were transported to Reed Fountain and allocated land there. It is not known whether the Booths were in this group but it seems probable that, in the light of Margaret's condition, they would have been moved to their new home as soon as possible and would therefore have been part of it.

When Donkin, on his way back to Cape Town, heard about this he sent an irritated note back to Cuyler, who was forced to instruct the advance guard of the party to retrace their steps to a location on the Assegai Bosch River. In retrospect this was an unnecessary decision since the Campbell party, supposed to consist of two hundred members, eventually numbered no more than thirty initially with a futher eighteen arriving the following year.

The group was already angry. Their leader, Sephton, had asked them to pay cash for rations and they believed that he had embezzled the money provided to supply them. Sephton claimed that he had lost a draft of 2000 rixdollars he had been given for the purpose. The upshot was that Sephton was dismissed as leader of the party and Shaw, the Wesleyan minister with the party, terminated his membership of the Wesleyan Society.

In spite of these demoralizing events the party settled down with an elected committee of management in the Assegai Bosch and began to build their community, which they called Salem.

Baviaans River

Thomas Pringle's party was better prepared than many. The Pringles and the Rennies were knowledgeable farmers from the Scottish Borders. They had a balanced party which included several experienced farm hands. Further, as it turned out, the land to which they were allocated was much more suited to the type of farming that they were familiar with than in the case of most of the settlers. The reason for this was largely Somerset's policy of keeping settlers together with others from the same region. There were only two Scottish parties that arrived in the Cape in 1820.

General Charles Campbell's small advance party of 13 from Argyll was settled on the Kasouga River. Pringle's party from the Scottish Borders needed a location. A large party of 400 from Ross and Cromarty in the Highlands, led by a Captain Grant, was expected and Donkin wished to place the Scots in the same region.

Sir Rufane Donkin offered the small Pringle party a choice of two sites. They chose a distant site on the Baviaan's River far from the Zuurveld north of the current towns of Bedford and Adelaide. Ultimately the second Scottish group failed to arrive; their leader, Grant, changed his mind and the party emigrated to America instead, leaving the Scottish settlement on the Mancazana River very sparsely populated.

It was a week after they had landed before Pringle's party was ready for departure. On June 13th they set off in a train of seven wagons. Thomas Pringle gives a detailed account of their journey[147], which is well worth reading, his prose being very much better than his poetry. The party and their goods were accommodated in seven wagons. By this time it was clear that, in spite of the nominal position of Robert Pringle as leader, his son Thomas was in charge. John, though older, followed and is seldom mentioned in the lengthy writings of Thomas. This is surprising. From his later achievements it is clear that John was a strong and able personality but in the presence of his younger brother he seems to have been eclipsed and ignored. Only after Thomas had left the frontier did John begin to establish himself.

Thomas's enquiring mind ensured that the Dutch wagon master was persuaded to make side trips to investigate places of interest such as the salt pans near the Coega River, which today are still operational. Thomas's comments on the vegetation, the relationships between the Dutch, Khoikhoi, and San people accompanying them are graphic and entertaining.

Their route took them over very rugged country in a direction east of north, crossing, over a period of eight days, the Coega, Sundays, Bushmans, New Year and Little Fish Rivers. Thereafter they reached Roodewal[148], a military post on the upper reaches of the Great Fish River. Charles Lennox Stretch, now the commander, together with his junior officers, was very pleased to welcome visitors who helped to relieve the monotony of an isolated military posting. Thomas reports that:

> Here we were received by the officers of the garrison and their ladies with the utmost kindness and hospitality. ... we felt the unexpected transition to the cordial hospitalities and English comforts of our agreeable hosts altogether delightful.

Stretch's new bride, Robert Hart's eldest daughter Anna, was most probably one of those present. Since the presence of ladies is mentioned, it is possible that Stretch's sister, a young widow Susan Parr, was also there. If so, it would have been John Pringle's first meeting with his future wife.

The next day Robert Hart arrived from Somerset Farm, about fifteen miles to the west, presumably to visit his daughter and son-in-law. His surprise to find the visitors was evident. When they spoke, however, as Thomas describes, he was overcome with emotion:

> The Scottish accent, seldom entirely lost even by the most polished of the middle ranks of our countrymen, was heard from every tongue; and the broad 'Doric dialect' prevailed, spoken by female voices, fresh and unsophisticated from the banks of the Teviot and Lothian Tyne. Hart, a man of iron look and rigid nerve, was taken by surprise, and deeply affected. The accents of his native tongue, uttered by the kindly voice of women, carried him back forty years at once and irresistably, as he afterwards owned, to the scenes of his mother's fireside; and recalled freshly before him the softened remembrances of early life – those tender and sacred remembrances which, though apparently buried beneath the cares and ambitions of after years, are never, in any good heart, entirely effaced.

Hart was thereafter to be of great service to the Scottish party, providing them with farming advice, fruit trees, and other plant material.

The wagon train from Algoa Bay was now replaced by one from nearby Cradock and, after a two day stop, the party continued up to the Baviaanskloof, the gorge from which the Baviaans river emerged. Here they passed the farm of Groot Willem Prinsloo, one of the Slachters Nek rebels who had escaped execution. Their allocated territory was to be on some of the lands of the hanged rebels, but Groot Willem seemed to bear no malice, provided them with gifts of fruit and vegetables (for which in exchange he got some Dutch religious tracts), and welcomed them as neighbours. The going now became very tough; it took them five days, hacking away with pickaxe, crowbar, hatchet and sledge hammer, to negotiate the few miles up the river to their allotted site.

When they reached the hill overlooking their territory the view was worth it. Snow-capped mountains surrounded a fertile valley with distant herds of game grazing peacefully. Thomas Pringle reports the words of one of the farm labourers in the party:

> Sae that's the lot o' our inheritance then! Aweel, now that we've really got till't, I maun say that the place looks no sae mickle amiss and may suit our purpose no that ill, provided thae haughs [low lying meadows in a river valley] turn out to be guid deep land for the pleugh, and we

can but contrive to find a decent road out o' this queer hieland glen
into the lowlands – like any other Christian country.

They re-named the river the Lynden – a name that did not stick – and
the valley Glen Lynden – a name that still attaches to their farm – and
began the labour of establishing themselves in a new country.

House and Home   [1820]

The majority of the immigrants had been settled on their allotments by
the end of June 1820. It was winter on the Zuurveld. In the previous season the rains had been good. The impression that they had of the land
was of a fertile region served by adequate water supplies. For the time being they were supported by the rations issued regularly by the Government but it was imperative to get seed sown to prepare for the time when
the handouts would stop. An even greater imperative was the need for
shelter. They had tents for the interim but the region can be bitterly cold
and more substantial housing was needed. Some lucky ones like the
Thackwrays had an old structure as a basis for their houses. Otherwise,
depending on their skills, they built what houses they could. The most
substantial were wattle and daub or Devonshire cob; the least were bur-
rows excavated in the side of a slope with a canvas cover.

A wattle and daub house is built with a timber frame – posts in the
corners and wherever support is needed. The spaces between the poles
are filled in with wattle – a lattice woven of long thin branches – to form
walls. This lattice is then thickly plastered with the daub, predominantly
clay. The wattle provides the support for the daub. A pitched roof is supported by rafters made of lighter poles and thatched. The thatching material available in the frontier region was a type of light reed, used by the
Xhosa for their huts. A well made structure of this type is wind proof
and, provided that it has fairly wide eaves, reasonably weatherproof but it
has little defence against driving rain. Some kind of seal such as pitch is
desirable and this can be covered with whitewash.

Devonshire cob uses similar materials but is very different in construction. The clay or mud is mixed with straw which provides some tensile
strength and moulded into unfired bricks which provide the structural
base. The roof construction and plastering is similar.

The interiors of such dwellings were very simple. The floor was of
compressed earth surfaced with a mixture of mud and cow dung. This
somewhat surprising material is a traditional South African technique,
still used in the rural areas. It provides a smooth and reasonably water-
proof surface, but needs regular maintenance. The manure, which is very

fibrous as a result of the grass eaten by the cattle, acts as a binding agent and, contrary to expectation, does not have an unpleasant smell.

Some of the leaders of sole-proprietor parties had higher ambitions and their employees were available to construct more substantial homes. At the opposite end of the scale the less handy constructed ramshackle shacks and lived in squalor. The imperative thing was to get some land tilled and crops planted.

Chapter 6. Government

The greater the power, the more dangerous the abuse.

Edmund Burke, 1771

The Grand Plan [1818 – 1819]

In the Cape Colony the organization of the settlement was administered by a system of government that at best was labyrinthine and inefficient, and at worst was autocratic and corrupt. It was against this background that the settlers lived their lives and an account of some of the political and human background, necessary for understanding their position, is provided in this chapter.

The details of the settlement scheme had been the responsibility of the Colonial Governor, the autocratic Lord Charles Somerset, second son of the Fifth Duke of Beaufort. A patrician Plantagenet, descended from John of Gaunt, he had governed the Cape since 1814 with an hauteur characteristic of the aristocratic class of the time.

Somerset had been given *carte blanche* to plan the details of the arrival and settlement. The official boundary to the east of the Colony was the Great Fish River. Between the Fish and Keiskamma Rivers was the neutral territory declared after the war of 1819. Somerset's intention was that the settlers would occupy the Zuurveld region between the Fish and Sundays Rivers so that the westernmost Xhosa would not be tempted to infiltrate the region. To this end he envisaged a densely populated region with the inhabitants conducting agriculture similar to that practiced in Britain. The plan was lamentable. The Zuurveld had previously been occupied by pastoral farmers, both Dutch and Xhosa. It supported cattle only on a seasonal basis. In summer the grazing was good: in winter the herds were driven elsewhere. Neither the climate nor the soil was suitable for intensive cultivation of European crops. Rainfall was erratic. The hundred acres of land per man allotted to the settlers was woefully inadequate for successful cultivation. The settlers had supposedly been selected on the basis of their ability and desire to farm the land but many of them had no agricultural experience and little interest in farming.

The plan was also based on the assumption that the agreement with Ngqika would ensure that the Xhosa would remain on the far side of the Keiskamma River, with the territory that had been ceded after the war of 1819, remaining unoccupied except by a British military presence, centred on Fort Willshire on the west bank of the river. This depended on

Somerset's perception that Ngqika had the status of paramount chief who would be obeyed by all Xhosas. It failed to recognize that Ngqika had little or no control over the westernmost Xhosa and held him responsible where he had no power. It also overlooked the fact that, since these people had been expelled from the region, their crops destroyed, their cattle confiscated, they had no resources other than those they could win from their surroundings. Trapped between the Xhosa heartlands and the ceded territory, they would be forced into what the Colony called cattle theft and they regarded as recovering the spoils of war.

The Somersets   [1814 - 1819]

When Lord Charles Somerset had first come to the Cape in 1814 he had generally been popular and respected. There were signs, however, that it was his own interest that was highest on his list of priorities. The Colonial Secretary, Colonel Christopher Bird, soon encountered a problem[149]. The Governor's salary took effect from the date of his assumption of duty, when that of his predecessor ceased. Bird discovered that Somerset, on arrival, had drawn pay for the period of his journey to the Cape. Assuming this was an error, Bird drew the matter to the attention of the Governor, who promised to write to Bathurst, the Secretary of State, to explain and rectify the matter. He failed to do so, however, until the creation of the new Audit Office in June 1816 threatened to expose the matter. He then applied to Bathurst to allow the money to be kept: the request was refused. Only in 1821 was the money at last repaid, and then he chose to do so in rixdollars which had substantially depreciated since the loan.

Things became worse when Lord Charles's eldest son, Henry Somerset arrived in the Cape in 1817. He was recently married, a veteran of the Peninsular War and of Waterloo, where he had served with the 18th Hussars and achieved the rank of captain. His father was anxious to secure him a position suitable for a gentleman of his standing. Initially he was assigned to the Cape Regiment under Colonel Graham as was his younger brother, Charles.

Patronage was a fact of life in matters of Government at the time. In the Colony it was taken as a matter of course that no advancement was possible without the support of the Governor. For many British officers of the time having the sons of the Governor as members of their mess was an opportunity. At least one such officer, Captain Andries Stockenstrom, was not impressed[150]:

> From my profound respect for, and attachment to, his father, there are
> few sacrifices that I would not have made to serve the son and gain his

good will; but with an infatuated parent who could not believe it possible for his son to be in the wrong, who possessed despotic sway in
the Colony, and all powerful influence at head-quarters, civil and military, it was but natural that the young aspirant Captain should become
the focus of a set of hangers-on and flatterers ...

Patronage had become nepotism. Both young Somersets obtained advancement in the Cape regiment at the cost of other longer serving officers.

Soon the twenty year old Henry Somerset had become Assistant
Landdrost of Uitenhage. Stockenstrom was, of course, Landdrost of
Graaff Reinet at the time. When the first settlement was being planned he
was consulted by the Governor on allocation of land and found himself
at odds with him over the location of settlers on existing Boer farms in
the district. Shortly afterwards, in a discussion with Bird, he brought up
some difficulties over a decision made by Henry Somerset in his capacity
as Assistant Landdrost. Bird, with his permission, discussed the matter
with the Governor, and Stockenstrom found himself on the wrong side of
a diatribe from the Governor.[151]

... and let me tell you, sir, that no one has ever embroiled himself with
any one of my family without repenting it.

This was the start of a feud between Henry Somerset and Andries
Stockenstrom that was to have a long-lasting effect on the eastern frontier.

The Stand-In   [1820 – 1821]

Lord Charles, somewhat against the wishes of Lord Bathurst, the Secretary of State for the Colonies, went on leave shortly before the arrival of
the settlers. The Colony needed to be placed under the control of an Acting Governor. The man chosen by the high command was Sir Rufane
Donkin. He had been in India but was temporarily on leave in the Cape.

Donkin had been deeply affected by the death of his young wife, who
had died in India as the result of a fever. He himself was in poor health.
When he found himself ordered to take over the Acting Governorship he
dutifully, but somewhat unwillingly, accepted the responsibility.

Lord Charles first tried to manipulate the appointment of his replacement while on leave in England. He hoped to appoint his next in command for a small salary while he continued to be paid the balance. Government policy was that an effective Governor must at least be of the
rank of Major General. Donkin was on leave and unless he took up the
post before his period of leave was completed he would have to return to
India. Somerset tried to delay the whole process so that this would happen, until Donkin threatened to provide a complete report to the Com-

mander in Chief. Somerset, fearing that his own leave would be lost, sailed for England[152]. This was the beginning of a serious enmity between Somerset and Donkin.

Before his departure for England, Somerset, a rigid Tory, had a meeting with Donkin, a flexible Whig. Both would have agreed after the meeting that Somerset's policy was to be implemented by Donkin. Somerset expected exact adherence to the policy. On Donkin, therefore, fell the responsibility of dealing with the consequences of some of its inadequacies. He expected to make sensible pragmatic adjustments if they became necessary.

As it turned out, his pragmatic adjustments were far from minor and nor, so far as his relationship with Lord Charles was concerned, were they sensible.

Lord Charles had tended to regard Government property as his own. His official residence was Government House in Cape Town, but he also maintained a seaside villa at Camps Bay on the west side of the peninsula, a shooting estate, and his summer residence, Newlands, on the south-east side of Table Mountain. These were operated at Government expense and serviced by military personnel. Donkin slashed expenditure on these and returned the soldiers to their normal duties. The historic company gardens had been closed and used for growing feedstock for Lord Charles's own stables. Donkin reopened them to the public. Lord Charles had relied on a system of spies and informers, spread through the military and civil service. Donkin dismantled the network. Donkin envisaged changes in allowing trade with the Xhosa and closing down the government supported Somerset farm, because it competed unfairly with private farmers. These changes did not come to fruition during Donkin's tenure.

Donkin's character, however, was by no means flawless. His letters[153] suggest insecurity, defensiveness, and indecision, with the consequence of ill-considered decisions.

One such was his reversal of Somerset's policy on missionaries. Lord Charles wished to prevent missionaries from operating outside the Colony. Donkin reversed this, not as a result of rational consideration, but because he had wilted under a fiery verbal onslaught by Dr John Philip of the London Missionary Society. This may or may not have been a good thing but it was not done by deliberate analysis and argument. His granting of land to individuals seems to have been somewhat capricious and provided a weapon for Lord Charles Somerset to try to bring sanctions against him after his term of office. His letters tend to carry unnecessarily extensive arguments explaining and justifying his decisions to subordinates when a simple order might better have achieved his purpose.

Hooray Henry [1820 – 1821]

Lord Charles Somerset's constant concern after his departure was obtaining a position for his son Henry. He believed that he had made his wishes clear to Donkin that Henry should be appointed to the position of Commander at Simon's Town, the Naval Harbour.

Henry Somerset was at the time stationed on the frontier and a divisive influence there. His toadies began spreading rumours about Andries Stockenstrom and his younger brother Charles, who was also an officer in the Cape Regiment. One of the most assiduous of these was the medical officer of the 72nd Regiment, Dr Robert Knox, a Scot. Stockenstrom's brother was accused of theft. Andries Stockenstrom himself found himself under attack for not having resigned his post in favour of Henry Somerset[154]. He also was apparently accused of cowardice, if that is the correct interpretation of what he wrote:

> I accidently found that it was rumoured and believed that I had sworn the peace against a man whom I ought to have fought.

This last accusation decided him. He approached a former associate who had been sidelined from the regiment to a half pay position as Assistant Magistrate of Cradock to act as his second, and challenged Knox to a duel[155]. There was a hasty withdrawal. The events led to a Court of Inquiry and an apology from Henry Somerset, leading to further enmity. Knox had a promotion reversed as a result of this.

The case occasioned some outcry. A recently arrived settler, Mr Bishop Burnett, of whom we shall hear more, was so outraged that he accosted Knox in the street in Graham's Town and horse-whipped him[156]. These incidents set the pattern for the relationship between Andries Stockenstrom and Henry Somerset for the next forty years.

Back in England, Lord Charles's anxiety to get preferment for his son continued. He had discussed the matter with Donkin before leaving and now began pressing him. Donkin was dismayed by the overt nepotism and was unconvinced of Henry's suitability for the post. He expressed his opinion to Bird in a letter dated April 19th 1821:

> I have quite made up my mind not to sacrifice the public interests here for any plans Ld. C. Somerset may have had for his son Henry – I have never made him the most distant promise that I would realize those plans; altho' you well know that I was on the point of doing so when I thought I could thereby benefit the public service.

He also made his feelings known in a letter to Lord Charles dated May 1st 1821[157]:

> ... but to put so young a Capt. as Capt. H. Somerset into such a situation when I had under my command so many old and deserving Field Officers with claims on me & on the service, would have been, (unless I could have put him in on some evident public Ground,) to draw on myself the just remonstrances & the odiums of the army here. The case however is very different in regard to your Lordship – what would in me be an act of offensive partiality, in you will be only the natural act of a Father providing for his son – and – if your Lordship places Capt. H. Somerset at Simonstown, as no doubt you will do, however others may be disappointed, they cannot reasonably blame you.

Would Somerset have understood the last sentence as the blistering sarcasm that seems to be intended or would he have taken it at face value? In any event he appears to have brought out his big guns.

Both Donkin and Bird had begun to hope that, in fact, Somerset would not return as Governor. Their hopes were dashed when the mails arrived from England in early June. Some threat, it is not clear what, was brought to bear on Donkin. His frustration is evident in a letter to Bird, dated June 4th 1821, reporting the arrival of the mails:

> ... one communication is of such a nature that on public and unavoidable grounds I must place Capt. H. Somerset at Simons Town.

So Henry Somerset took up his new position at Simon's Town.

He was soon in direct conflict with Donkin.

In common with his father, Henry Somerset did not distinguish clearly between the property of the King – that is to say Government property – and the property of his father. He was outraged by the changes in his father's policies that in his mind interfered with the smooth running of what he had seen as his father's possessions. A herd of mules, considered by Henry to be family property, was grazing on the Newlands Estate and he made arrangements for them to be taken elsewhere. Donkin refused to allow them to be removed from the estate. Henry was further infuriated. When, therefore, he encountered Donkin and Bird on the road between Cape Town and Rondebosch, he accosted the Acting Governor and addressed him in terms that could not be ignored. He accused him of insulting the Governor and Commander of the Forces by his actions, and required to know how he could act against the interests of his superior. The encounter almost came to blows. It ended with Donkin placing Henry under arrest and confining him to his post at Simon's Town.

Henry appealed to Bird and got short shrift. Bird wrote him a letter[158] carefully spelling out why he was in the wrong, that Donkin was the representative of the king and not of his father, that the quarrel could not be regarded as personal, and that his arrest was on account of the insubordination to his superior and through him to the monarch. Relief was, however, on the way.

On 30th November, 1821, the ship carrying Lord Charles Somerset back to resume his duties dropped anchor in Table Bay.

Among the first to board was Henry Somerset. He spent an extended time in private discussions with his father. Also among those to come aboard was a staff officer acting as Donkin's emissary. He brought an invitation informing Somerset that dinner had been arranged at Government House and offering Lord Charles a carriage to take him there.

Lord Charles emerged from his discussions with his son in a fury. He was reported as having exclaimed that he would undo everything that had been done by Sir Rufane Donkin[159] and he soon set out to do just that. Donkin's emissary was unable to bring any reply to Donkin save that Lord Charles would remain on board that night.

Next morning, as Donkin left to meet Somerset, Lord Charles entered Government House by another door and took possession. He sent a curt note to Donkin:

> Lord Charles Somerset presents his compliments to Sir Rufane Shaw Donkin, and if Sir R. S. Donkin has any official communication to make to Lord Charles, he will meet Sir Rufane at the Colonial Office at any time Sir R. D. will appoint. Saturday December 1st, 1821.

A few days later Donkin left Cape Town without having met Somerset. Lord Charles set out to make good on his promise to undo everything that he had done.

Officialdom [1820 – 1821]

Local government was in the hands of the Landdrost of a District, assisted by Heemraden. The Dutch position of Landdrost was roughly equivalent to magistrate. The Heemraden were appointed from prominent citizens of the community.

The only established village in the Zuurveld settlement was Graham's Town. At the time that Donkin assumed duty as governor, the landdrost was Colonel Fraser of the 72nd regiment, but he was in England and his duties were effectively in the hands of his assistant, Henry Somerset. The nearest neighbouring centre of consequence was Uitenhage, close to Algoa Bay. Their landdrost there was Cuyler, but after he had dealt with the location of the settlers they largely fell outside the region of his juridiction.

Graham's Town was awkwardly placed as it was located on the edge of the region where settlers had been located. This led to some difficulties in administering the settlement from there.

As early as May 1820 Donkin, in the interests of more efficient administration, decided to establish a new township that was more central. It was called Bathurst after the Secretary of State for the Colonies. Captain Trappes of the 72nd Regiment was dispatched from Algoa Bay to take charge of the administration there and in September was appointed as Acting Landdrost. Donkin's intention was that Bathurst was to become the centre of administration.

Trappes had been in the Colony for some time. It was he who had been in temporary command at the battle of Graham's Town until Willshire had galloped into town a short distance ahead of the pursuing Xhosa. Those in the know were not optimistic about the appointment and he rapidly lost popularity as he began to apply the policies of the Government:

> I soon discovered him to be the horrid character he was universally thought to be. He is a Bachelor between 50 and 60, a sensualist, a Scoffer of Religion, and the greatest Misanthrope I was ever acquainted with. I never heard him speak well of any body, added to this he was Col Bird's spy[160]

Trappes was, in fact, a relative of the Colonial Secretary, Colonel Bird. The policies that made him unpopular initially were those of Somerset, applied by Donkin. Somerset had at first been determined not to allow the Xhosa to move from their territory. To this end he required that the settlers remain on their lands. The law of the Colony was still the Dutch system, far more restrictive than the settlers had known in Britain. Initially, under Donkin's regime, each settler was confined to his own area with a pass system rivalling that of modern apartheid years. Contact with the Xhosa in the form of trade was forbidden.

When protests began, the leading settlers discovered to their dismay that freedoms they had enjoyed in Britain did not exist in the Cape. Meetings with a political intent were forbidden. The solution of some of the leading settlers was to form a cultural society[161]. This met once only in January 1821. A petition was circulated complaining of ill-judged decisions by the landdrost and stating the position that a landdrost should be a "man of character, penetration and general knowledge" as well as a citizen rather than a military man. Trappes appears to have fitted none of these criteria in their minds.

The chairman of the society was Thomas Philipps, one of Trappes's Heemraden. Trappes demanded and failed to get a withdrawal from him.

The matter was referred to Donkin, who upheld the law by removing Philipps as Heemraad[162] but recognized that Trappes was a problem and must ultimately be removed.

A feature of Donkin's personality was a desire not to cause offence to those responsible to him. This was perhaps characteristic of the time; many individuals were in their positions by patronage; offence to the individual might mean offence to a more powerful patron. Removal of Trappes from his position was not simply a matter of transferring him. He was a relative of Colonel Bird and Donkin did not wish to offend the Colonial Secretary. There were other individuals with claims to positions that he must satisfy.

Donkin had two problems that were not directly related to individuals. The first was that the removal of the centre of administration from Graham's Town to Bathurst had created a divided civil authority. There was little case for two landdrosts in Albany. The second was the division of responsibilities between the military commander of the frontier forces, Colonel Willshire, and the civil authority.

Donkin's first attempt to rationalise matters was to appoint Colonel Graham, the founder of Graham's Town, as District Landdrost for Albany. Trappes, whose position was only provisional, received the news by letter. Philipps, his Heemraad, described his disappointment[163]. A letter from Bird followed, telling his relative that it had all been an action of the Governor while Bird had been absent. Some of Donkin's correspondence suggests that Bird might not have been a strong supporter of Trappes. Graham's appointment, however, came to nothing as he was already seriously ill, never took up the post, and died in April 1821.

Graham's death triggered Donkin's next move to try to integrate the command structure of the frontier region by combining the position of Landdrost and Military Commander. Donkin did not want Willshire in the post and had a plan for him. At this point Henry Somerset was still in Graham's Town and Donkin had no intention of placing him at Simonstown. This was the position intended for Willshire. The position of landdrost at Tulbagh was vacant and he intended to move Trappes sideways to this post thus avoiding any overt criticism of him. He wrote a careful letter to Willshire explaining his plans for him on April 19 1821. Next he tried to make sure that Bird was on his side. He wrote to him from Uitenhage where he was just beginning a second tour of the frontier[164]:

> When you some time ago suggested to me to send up Colonel Monc[k]ton in both capacities, you did not hesitate a moment in putting out of your view Capt. Trappes, a relative of your own. ... I will not

touch on all the complaints I have had against Capt. Trappes – it is unnecessary to do so, if he be removed by the arrangement I have in view
[placing Willshire at Simonstown and Trappes at Tulbagh].

The plans to keep everyone satisfied were blocked by Lord Charles's
force majeure in getting Henry the Simonstown position. Donkin was
forced to write to Willshire on June 5th stating that Simonstown was no
longer available and offering him a token post as *Aide-de-Camp*; although
this post was only likely to last as long as Donkin's tenure, it would show
that Willshire's removal was not as a result of dissatisfaction with his performance. Needless to say, the attempts to please everyone pleased no-
one.

Shortly afterwards Trappes was removed from Bathurst and Major
James Jones was appointed to the post.[165] This appointment did not survive Lord Charles Somerset's return. Lord Bathurst refused consent for
the appointment ostensibly because of his short period of service in the
Cape and consequent lack of experience

Somerset's choice for landdrost was one Harry Rivers and Rivers was
the man with whom the settlers had most dealings in the early years[166]:

I [Thomas Philipps] got a letter from a person who has always been very
careful in what he says –

"I fear you will have to regret the appointment of Mr Rivers, you may
feast him to your advantage, but promises renewed and broken are the
usual currency he deals in, he is much too lazy ever to be of use."

Rivers arrived in Graham's Town and organized matters for his own con-
venience.

A Most Litigious Man   [1820 – 1821]

When Robert Hart had been given charge of Somerset Farm in 1817 he
and his family had left behind their first small farm on the outskirts of
Graham's Town. It was called Doorn Valley and was much too far from
Somerset Farm to get enough attention from Robert. When in 1820 a settler with private means approached him with a view to leasing the property, he was only too pleased to let the farm to him.

His new tenant was Bishop Burnett[167], the same who was shortly to
distinguish himself by publicly horsewhipping Dr Knox. Burnett had
failed in his application to bring a party of settlers so had travelled
privately to the colony at his own expense. When he first arrived in Graham's Town he learned from Henry Somerset that there was a very good
market for fodder for the numerous horses belonging to the military on
the frontier. He applied to Donkin for a large tract of land adjacent to

Doorn Valley and invested a large amount of capital in setting himself up as an unofficial commissariat to the army. All his own funds were sunk in the project so to bridge the time before his lands became productive he bought cattle on credit from Robert Hart and food supplies for his labour force and himself from a Cape Town firm, Ebden & Eaton.

Burnett's character was to have a large impact not only on his creditors but also on the Colony as a whole. He was a man of strong opinions reinforced by a complete absence of good judgement and common sense.

His first illustration of this was the Knox affair. A more perspicacious man, knowing that his whole future depended on the good will of the army, might have considered whether it made good sense to antagonize Henry Somerset by taking the part of Andries Stockenstrom so dramatically as to assault Henry's friend Knox.

By the beginning of 1821 he was in financial trouble. Hart was threatening to sue for the recovery of what was owed to him and he could only hold off Ebden & Eaton by mortgaging all his assets to them. His real problem, though, was one of cash flow. He had supplied the army with substantial amounts of fodder but had not been paid because, in spite of numerous applications, the responsible officer, Henry Somerset, failed to certify delivery.

He received several summonses from the Cape High Court on behalf of Robert Hart. The law was administered in Dutch. He felt he should be addressed in English and ignored them, resulting in a judgement by default. His debts could have been setted if the army had settled his bill. Henry Somerset's successor after he left for Simonstown would only certify deliveries that he himself had received, stating that the earlier debts were Somerset's business.

Burnett was then declared bankrupt which meant that he could neither carry on his business nor sell his property to settle his debts. The matter came to the Graham's Town Circuit Court. The whole case escalated, eventually resulting in six different actions with Hart suing Burnett for recovery of monies owed and Burnett suing Hart for defamation and conspiracy. All the actions ended in Hart's favour, but one thing that had been exposed was the inadequacy of the colonial system of law. Hart never actually recovered the full amount of the debt.

Burnett petitioned the Governor in terms that led to the Fiscal[168] suing him for libel. The matter now escalated into a full scale dispute with the Governor and the Colonial Government ending in Burnett's sentence for imprisonment and banishment. The first of these sentences was not implemented in the interest of getting rid of him as soon as possible. The

matter ended in debates in the House of Commons in Britain and played
no small part in the downfall of Lord Charles Somerset.

The Rise of Henry Somerset   [1821 – 1824]

Once his father had returned to his position as Governor Henry Somerset
could begin his rise in the hierarchy. His position at Simonstown was a
useful stepping stone but what he needed for the future was military rank
in the Cape command. Major Fraser, seriously ill by the beginning of
1823, sold his commission to Henry who became Major Somerset, commanding the Cape Corps on the eastern frontier but still serving in Simon's Town[169]. The Governor had been making a strong case for increasing the strength of the frontier forces. Balfour approved, but insisted that
the commanding officer be stationed on the frontier. In October 1823 Major Henry Somerset and his wife settled in Graham's Town. He became
Lieut. Colonel, again by purchase, in July 1824. His progress was not impeded by the fact that his uncle, Lord FitzRoy Somerset[170] was now secretary to Wellington, the commander-in-chief of the army.

The nature of Henry's rise to his position was not unusual for the
time. He was a naturally affable man and became well-accepted and liked
by Graham's Town society. He was to remain in positions of command
on the Eastern frontier for the next thirty years. His estate in Graham's
Town, Oatlands, was a centre of social activity.

The Fall of Lord Charles   [1821 – 1827]

Henry's father, on the other hand, became less and less popular. His character permitted no opposition to his ideas. Some of the more perceptive
or more obstinate of the settlers, who had seen the dawn of the age of
liberty in Europe, were in the forefront of opposition to him.

Donkin had been regarded as a friend of the settlers. Many of Lord
Charles's actions to reverse his decisions were deeply resented. He reversed the decision to make Bathurst the capital of Albany, placing it
once more in Graham's Town. A number of settlers suffered losses from
this decision. He instituted an inquiry into grants of land made by
Donkin, maintaining that they had not complied with the rules for such
grants. Many of these grants do appear to have been arbitrary, but his
case would have been stronger if he had not excluded a grant of land to
Henry Somerset in Graham's Town from the list supplied to him by Bird.
He was the sole arbiter of appeals against judgements of the Cape Court
and his decisions on such matters were made in private without assessors
to advise him, unsupported by reasons. One of his most resented meas-

ures was the prohibition on public meetings expressed in a proclamation on 1st May 1822. The penalties were draconian and from this time a constant stream of complaints against actions by the Governor were received by influential contacts in Britain. The feeling of isolation of the residents of the eastern Cape, and their indignation, was increased because Somerset failed to visit the frontier after his return in 1821; not until 1825 did he pay them a visit.

Furious correspondence flowed from Somerset and Donkin to Bathurst, each accusing the other of a variety of offences. Through men like John Philip, British parliamentarians began to get a picture of an administration in trouble. What troubled them most, however, were not the grievances of the people, but growing evidence of severe financial problems. The purpose of a colony was to make money not absorb it; if in addition it appeared that the finances were mismanaged there was compelling need to take action.

There were already plans to investigate the governance procedures in several colonies. On 26th July 1822 the British Parliament appointed two commissioners to make recommendations on improving the system of government in the Cape and, nearly a year later, on 12th July 1823, William Colebrooke and John Biggs arrived in Cape Town to carry out this task.

The presence of the commissioners was only one of the pressures felt by Lord Charles. Others from within the Colony made themselves felt.

For Thomas Pringle farming on the frontier was only an intermediate step in his career plans. His physical disability prevented him from participating fully in the work of the farm. His half-brother, William Dods Pringle, was as a fourteen-year-old able to be useful to his father on the farm. His brother John was making his own way. Thomas's ambitions were literary, so, in September 1822, he made his way to Cape Town.

At first he was optimistic about his prospects there[171]. He obtained an appointment to take charge of the new public library[172] and took on some pupils from prosperous Cape Town households for tuition. After discussion with officials there seemed to be good prospects of taking charge of the Government Gazette, at that time the only publication in the Cape, and turning it into a useful news medium. He wrote enthusiastically to his friend John Fairbairn in Scotland. Fairbairn replied[173]:

> I will join you (D.V.) after you receive this epistle. My resolution was finally taken upon reading your last letter, and all my friends here approve of it.

Before Fairbairn ever arrived Pringle was disillusioned. He had collaborated with a Dutch reformed minister, the Rev. Mr Faure, to make plans to publish an independent journal. They discussed them widely and were surprised to get a visit from an associate of Lord Charles who tried strongly to dissuade them from publishing. When they persisted he informed them that Lord Charles was strongly opposed to such an enterprise and suggested that persisting might cause them personal harm. Pringle had been befriended by Col. Bird and through him petitioned the Governor for permission to publish. Five weeks later Bird came to him with a verbal refusal from the Governor. When Pringle suggested asking for an interview Bird strongly advised them to take the matter no further because of Somerset's extreme prejudice against any free press. For the time being they desisted. The arrival of the commissioners of inquiry gave an opportunity for Pringle to give evidence to them. He took full advantage of it. The evidence he gave to them was full and critical. Shortly afterwards he published a document in London[174] outlining the difficulties that the British settlers were having; doubtless this was similar to his evidence given to the commission.

Fairbairn arrived soon after. Precluded from continuing with plans for a journal, he and Pringle opened an academy, expanding the few pupils into a formal organization. This was initially a great success. Then, on 2nd December 1823, Pringle was summoned by Lord Charles. To his surprise he was informed by Somerset with ill grace that Bathurst had given permission for his publication. Publication of the *South African Journal* edited by Pringle and *De Zuid-Afrikaansch Tijdsscrift* edited by Faure began soon afterwards. Fairbairn joined Pringle to assist him. At the same time a newspaper, The *South African Commercial Advertiser* was started by a printer named Greig. Soon he found the need for editorial assistance and Fairbairn and Pringle were drawn in.

For a few months the publications appeared. It is hard to imagine the level of paranoia that found them objectionable. A poem by Pringle, on the suppression of constitutional government in Spain, ended:

> Yes! Congresses and Courts must yield
> To nations bursting from their chain;
> While, under Britain's guardian shield,
> Law, Freedom, Truth, begin their reign.[175]

To Lord Charles this probably echoed the Paris mob bellowing "*Liberté, égalité, justice*".[176] The crisis came, however, with reports of a legal case.

Two Cape Town residents, William Edwards, a man as contumacious as Bishop Burnett, and Launcelot Cooke, submitted a petition to the Governor for onward transmission to the Secretary of State. In it a favourite of Lord Charles was accused of corruption. Somerset's reaction was to instruct Mr Daniel Denysson, the Fiscal, to prosecute them for libel. They were acquitted but Edwards was imprisoned for contempt of court in that he abused the Fiscal. The following month he was charged with writing an abusive letter to the Governor. On 4th May 1824 the Fiscal visited Greig, placed restrictions on the paper and censored the article. Pringle, Fairbairn and Greig agreed that they could not continue to publish in the circumstances and the next day the *Advertiser* carried an article reporting the censorship and stating that it was ceasing publication. Greig's refusal to comply with Denysson's demand led to his expulsion from the Colony and he returned to England. The press was seized and transferred to a printer who published a Somerset-supporting paper for the next few years.

Fairbairn and Pringle were next in line. The *South African Journal* raised Lord Charles's ire. Pringle was summoned to a meeting with the Governor and the Chief Justice where Somerset tore into him.

> I [Pringle] would not submit to be rated in the style he had assumed by any man, whatever were his station or his rank. I repelled his charges of having acted unworthy of my character as a government servant and a loyal subject; – I defended my conduct in regard to the press, and the character of our magazine which he said was full of "calumny and falsehood;" – I asserted my right to petition the king for the extension of the freedom of the press to the colony; and I denied altogether the "personal obligations" with which he upbraided me, having never asked nor received from him the slightest personal favour, unless the lands alloted to my party, and my own appointment to the Government Library, were considered such, – though the latter was, in fact a public duty assigned to me, in compliance with the recommendations of the Home Government.[177]

Pringle then resigned his position in the library.

Somerset backtracked but Pringle was adamant. He and Fairbairn continued to try to run the academy but were so strongly opposed by the Governor that prospective parents of scholars were intimidated. Pringle, financially ruined, ultimately decided to return to Britain. He left Cape Town in October 1824 to return to Albany for a visit. Fairbairn remained in Cape Town in charge of the Academy. A year later Thomas Pringle left South Africa for good.

Lord Charles was now under siege. He had achieved a situation where some of his most strident critics were in London making use of every opportunity to lobby influential acquaintances. Donkin was strenuously defending his record as Governor. Philip was attacking the treatment of the Khoikhoi and other coloured inhabitants of the Colony. Greig was campaigning for the overthrow of press censorship and the resumption of publication of the *Commercial Advertiser*. Less measured criticism was flowing from those who felt they had been wronged by the Governor, such as Burnett and Edwards. Petitions and reports were arriving from complainants in the Colony. Reports were flowing in from the Commissioners, recommending substantial changes in the system of government of the Cape (but not containing personal criticism of Somerset himself).

Colonel Bird had been dismissed as Colonial Secretary in March 1824, ostensibly on the grounds of his Catholicism but possibly because he was suspected by the Governor of supplying Donkin with information[178]. He was succeeded by Sir Richard Plaskett who arrived in the Colony in November and was horrified by the state of incompetence in government and particularly in the courts of law.

Bathurst was a supporter of Somerset by inclination but he could not ignore the furore. Greig was given permission to return to the Cape and publish the *Commercial Advertiser*; he appointed Fairbairn as editor and publication was resumed in August 1825. Fairbairn was to become proprietor and editor for many years. Some check was placed on Lord Charles by the appointment of a Council of Advice in February 1825, consisting of three officials and three members appointed by Bathurst. On the recommendation of the commissioners a Lieutenant Governor, Major-General Richard Bourke, was appointed. He did not immediately take up office. Lord Charles had requested leave to refute allegations against him, but had delayed coming for almost a year. Finally Bathurst summoned him and Bourke took up the post of Acting Governor. Lord Charles only resigned his post when Lord Liverpool's Tory government was replaced by the Canning administration – still Tory but more forward looking – in April 1827. Lord Charles died in 1831.

Donkin spent the rest of his life largely in literary work and was elected to Parliament. His personal demons continued to trouble him and he committed suicide in 1841.

Chapter 7. Fear, Famine, and Flood

They rather hoped, man, child and wife
To find a somewhat easier life,
But found instead, through weary years,
A life of blood and sweat and tears

Harold Goodwin, May I throw a spanner?, Grocott's Mail

Flight from the Land   [1820 – 1822]

From the first arrival of the settlers on their allotments the grand plan for a densely populated agricultural region at the frontier began to crumble. The leaders of the sole proprietor parties, had envisaged the establishment of large estates. They had paid for the costs of bringing their parties to the Cape and in exchange had acquired the rights to the land. The members of their parties had contracted to work for them for a fixed period. An immediate problem was that of labour. Their neighbours, the Boers, were still served by slaves and by cheap Khoikhoi labour. Wages for the settlers were by comparison unaffordable. At the same time the needs of the military and of the new population meant that there was an explosion of building activity in Graham's Town. Many of the settlers were skilled tradesmen rather than farmers and used every means to get released from their indentures and earn good wages in the town. This was often to the advantage of their masters who were having difficulty finding their wages.

The members of the joint stock parties each had a hundred acres (about 40 hectares). Initially they began to till them by hand but soon found that without draught animals they were powerless. Some gave up and managed to get official permission to move to the towns, others persisted, acquiring oxen by barter, and learning to use them for ploughing. The shrewder among them began to enlarge their holdings by acquiring land from their neighbours as they left for the town.

It was not long before it became apparent that the land was ill-suited to agriculture. To live off the Zuurveld they needed to farm cattle and sheep. This could not be done on 100 acres. The Boers used vast tracts for their pastoral life. Such sparsely populated farms were the exact opposite of the densely populated buffer area envisaged by the colonial authorities.

As early as the end of 1820 the nature of the changes to the plan was apparent and the original parties were substantially broken up. Those who elected to remain on the farm were faced with the prospect of learning how to make things work in a new country that was very different from Britain.

The Rust [1820 – 1823]

The settlers came from Britain where the staple food was bread. A wheat crop was important to them. Had they looked to their neighbours, the Xhosa or the Boers, the grains they would have seen growing would have been mealies (maize) or mabela (sorghum). While interior high-altitude regions of South Africa have proved to be ideal for wheat, the regions nearer the coast are climatically unsuitable. The more industrious of the settlers laboured to get the land ploughed and the seed sown. With spring the wheat crop grew and flourished and the novice farmers contemplated the prospect of a good harvest. Then just before they came to maturity the stalks of the wheat began to develop elongated blisters on the stems and leaves parallel to the axes. After some days these burst open revealing a rust-red powdery interior. These later turned black and the crops withered and died. The more knowledgeable of the settlers recognized the fungal disease that they called rust[179].

This was the first of several plagues visited on the settlers. The reddish powder consisted of the spores of the fungus. Wheat is particularly susceptible to the disease which develops easily in warm, moist conditions. The spores can be borne great distances in the wind, infecting crops over a whole region. It can be treated with appropriate fungicides but the best defence is the use of resistant strains of wheat. These remedies were not available to the tyro farmers and they faced starvation.

The disease was not confined to the Zuurveld. It also affected the Somerset district. Thomas Pringle described the tribulations of the farmers[180]:

> The year 1821 began rather gloomily at Glen Lynden. In the first place the whole of our wheat crops were destroyed by the rust or mildew. Then a severe drought, which had commenced in December, lasted more than three months: so that the pastures were parched up; the river ceased to flow, except near its sources; the irrigation of our gardens and orchards was interrupted, and many of the young trees and other plants destroyed.

The Pringle party was far better off than the bulk of the settlers in the Zuurveld for several reasons. They were practical farmers who understood what they were about, they had a congenial and experienced neighbour in Robert Hart[181], Thomas Pringle was an eloquent and committed advocate for their interests, and circumstances were to lead to an improvement in their land holdings.

Sir Rufane Donkin was keenly aware of the difficulties of the new colonists. In June 1821 he set out on his second tour of the frontier region. First he journeyed through the Zuurveld hearing complaints and making arrangements to improve the situation. Next he travelled to the Scottish settlement for the same purpose. The most immediate effect of his visit was approval of an extension of the scheme of issuing rations. He extended the scheme until the next harvest. This removed the immediate threat of starvation. He also made a number of other reforms which, for his supporters, proved his ability to react humanely and pragmatically to circumstances, and, to his detractors, illustrated his *ad hoc* approach to decision making and his failure to apply consistent standards.

The whole area of the Zuurveld together with the neutral territory between the Fish and Keiskamma Rivers was proclaimed as a new district called Albany, moving the frontier of the colony to the Keiskamma River. This was in contravention of Somerset's concept of a neutral zone. He established military posts.

He also relaxed the restrictions on movement. Many settlers moved to the towns of Graham's Town and Bathurst.

Deluge   **[October 1823]**

As early as October 1820, when Robert Hart made a visit to the Zuurveld, he was alarmed to see the sites that the settlers had chosen for their dwellings. John Ayliff[182] noted remarks that Hart made when he visited Willson's party on the way to Bathurst:

> We heard that the principle [*sic*] man of this party was Mr Hart of Somerset, who was going through the settlement, as we heard, to see how the settlers were getting on, that he might report to the Government. He looked a terrible stern man, tho' he talked kindly. One thing he said, but that we paid no attention to, as it was the most unreasonable thing in the world, it was most absurd, he said, "I shall expect to hear that half the settlers houses are washed into the sea, building as they are so low in the valleys, all of which are sometimes covered with water. You should always build up on the side of the hills with the front of your house and your cattle kraals looking to the rising sun ..."

Doubtless Hart's report to the Government included this advice. The Government paid no attention and nor did the settlers.

Three years after Hart's visit his advice had been forgotten. The land was in the grip of of a prolonged drought. The wheat crop had been destroyed by rust for the third successive year. Many had left the land and migrated to the towns. The proprietors of large parties had long since released many of their farm workers; a number had been ruined. Those re-maining on their allotments continued fighting the elements.

At last, in October 1823, the drought was broken. First there were some violent thunderstorms. Then, next day, relieved farmers woke to the sound of steady set-in rain. The spring rains had come and they could look forward to relief from the long months of aridity. What they had, however, was a cut-off low pressure system that was to remain in place for a week, with water being efficiently transferred through the atmo-spheric system from the Indian Ocean to the whole frontier region.

The pressures and vicissitudes of the last three years had not provided time for buildings more substantial than the early wattle and daub or Devonshire cob houses to be built. As time passed the soaked thatch began to fail and the water ran in. The walls began to disintegrate. The Devonshire cob walls had no framework to support them: they disinteg-rated and collapsed. The wattle and daub fared not much better.

Worse than this was what happened to the lower lying houses. Water courses that had been completely dry through the long drought-stricken winter began to run as vigorous streams, rose to become large rivers, and overflowed onto the flood plains as irresistible torrents. Houses, crops, and livestock were swept away. Miraculously, in the whole of Albany, there was only one man drowned. The floods described in Robert Hart's unheeded warning had come to pass.

When the skies cleared a devastated land was revealed. Many were ruined. After several years of struggle this was the final blow for many who abandoned their lands and went to seek employment in the towns. Those who struggled on met with further setbacks when, early the follow-ing year, the surviving wheat crops were, for the fourth time, destroyed by rust.

In Salem, Benjamin and Margaret Booth had begun to establish a fam-ily home. Since the birth of Benjamin Jr. they had had another daughter so that their children now numbered five. Margaret the eldest was four-teen: Elizabeth the youngest was an infant. Their allotment was one of those strung along the banks of the Assegai Bosch River on the inside of a long horseshoe bend. There is no record of the damage that they suffered, but Salem was badly hit by the flood and the location of their al-lotment was such that it was likely that they suffered badly. Over a period of a week Salem had changed from a well ordered, although poor, com-munity to muddy wasteland.

The land drained. The people faced the drudgery of clearing up and starting again.

The *Mfecane*   [1822 – 1827]

While the settlers were beginning the arduous process of establishing themselves, other developments that would have a profound effect on the dynamics of frontier relationships were taking place outside the borders of the Colony. In Natal, on the distant eastern coast of South Africa, a new power had arisen, changing the loose clan structure of the Nguni people of the region. The Zulu nation had been born.

The rise of Shaka, the first Zulu king, is the stuff of legend[183]. The early accounts of his rise and tyrannical reign[184] also credit him with almost single-handedly having built the Zulu nation and turned it into an invincible military force. Modern studies are more nuanced[185] and present a complex picture. Nevertheless, by 1822, a few years after his seizure of control, the Zulus were a military force feared by and providing great pressure on their neighbours.

The colonists on the eastern frontier soon became aware of great disturbances on the other side of the border with reports of marauders provoking battle and bloodshed to the east and north of the Colony. These were understood to be either Zulu invaders or their victims fleeing from Shaka's hordes and seeking territory of their own. The invaders were often labelled Fitcane or variations of the word. The whole process of displacement of peoples such as the Ndebele, Sotho, or Ngwane, attributed to Zulu conquest, began to be called the *mfecane*[186] in the late 19th century, and became the received wisdom of the first half of the twentieth century[187].

More recently Cobbing has introduced a revisionist picture in which it was not Shaka's expansionism but essentially pressures of the European slave trade, centred on Delagoa Bay to the north of the Zulu kingdom[188] that was the cause of the *mfecane*. In its most extreme form this picture has the group of Natal settlers such as H. F. Fynn, F. Farewell and J. King, Cape officials, sundry missionaries and later "liberal historians" colluding to conceal this motive, and placing the blame on Shaka. The debate about the exact nature of the *mfecane*[189] that resulted was sometimes intemperate and Cobbing's extreme position was comprehensively attacked. Nevertheless his work was influential in provoking a substantial rethink of the paradigm of the *mfecane*. Wright[190] gives a more balanced view suggesting that the history of African societies across South Africa must be understood in terms of the forces on them as a result of the expension of the European frontiers.

What is clear is that the causes of the *mfecane* are more complex than simple Zulu expansionism and also that the image of Shaka as both military genius and bloodthirsty tyrant may have been influenced by early writers such as Fynn and Isaacs whose descriptions were calculated to serve their own interests and are not always reliable.

Whatever the precise causes of the *mfecane*, for our purposes it is enough to know that between about 1817 and 1828 turmoil existed in the regions to the north and east of the Colony, leading to significant population disturbances and migration. We shall not attempt to disentangle the conflicting accounts of these events.

The increased population pressure resulting from the Colonial forces on the one hand, and the ravages of the *mfecane* on the other, affected the frontier Xhosa severely. The livestock of the settlers became a more and more desirable target for the impoverished people to the east and cattle theft, sometimes accompanied by violence, was soon a problem to the farmers. Enthusiastic retaliation meant equivalent insecurity for the western Xhosa.

Chapter 8. Taking Root

How 'Ya Gonna Keep 'Em Down on the Farm (After They've Seen Paree)
Joe Young and Sam M. Lewis, Title of popular song

Starting up   [1820 – 1823]

Different individuals responded differently to the challenges of the first years of settlement. Some held fast to the land and continued grimly dealing with the demands of the environment until they either made a success of their farms or, in a number of cases, died in the attempt. Some grasped the opportunity to use their special skills – in the new settlement artisans of all types were soon in demand. Other able people without these skills began to exercise entrepreneurial abilities in various forms of trade. Many of the least able drifted away from the frontier to wherever in the Colony they could find some form of manual labour to support themselves. The names of many of those who were recorded on the original lists have simply disappeared from the record.

Religion   [1820 – 1830]

Inevitably religious faith had a strong influence in maintaining the spirits of some, but certainly not all, the settlers during these early years. At the time of the British occupation the established religious denomination in the Colony was the Dutch Reformed Church. Calvinist and conservative, it served the needs of the Dutch colonists. Missionary activity among the Khoikhoi in the colony and the Griquas to the north had been largely through the efforts of the Moravians, a German organization with links to the Lutheran church, and the London Missionary Society, a non-denominational Protestant organization supporting missionary activity in many parts of the world.

When the British settlement was planned it had been envisaged that ministers of religion would be part of the settlement. One of the conditions in the plan was that parties larger than 100 members would be able to appoint a minister whose fare and stipend would be the reponsibility of the Government. Few parties were large enough to take up this offer and only three such appointments were made. Two of these had little influence on the religious life of the settlement. The third was a different kettle of fish.

William Shaw was a Wesleyan Methodist. Twenty-two years old, newly ordained, he was appointed to Sephton's party and sailed with them in *Aurora*. Sephton's party had, as we have seen, been established as a group of devout Wesleyans from the Great Queen Street Chapel in London. It was a large party, highly motivated, and fortunate to have Shaw's enthusiasm to inspire them. Shaw saw his responsibilities as extending to the whole settlement. Shaw's preaching was soon attracting substantial congregations and soon services were being held all over Albany. Many of the settlers had been lay preachers in England and they too rallied to the cause. A number of them were from Sephton's party.

Richard Walker in later life

Three prominent ones were not. They were John Ayliff, William Shepstone, and Richard Walker.

Richard and Joseph Walker were both religious men. Joseph's religion formed a background to his life: Richard's was central to his. Over the next few years Richard was a mainstay of the Methodist roster in Albany. He, Shepstone, and Ayliff were "received into full connexion" as lay preachers. Later all three were to spend years in missionary service among the Xhosa. Shepstone and Ayliff became ordained Wesleyan ministers. Walker was never ordained. He remained a lay preacher while serving the missions in other ways.

Further north the Scots followed a different course. The non-arrival of Grant's party and the loss of the *Abeona* meant that the Harts, Pringles, and Rennies were a small minority in a largely Dutch-speaking environment. These Scots were devout Presbyterians. The region in which they lived was dominated by Dutch farmers – Calvinists whose religious observances differed from the Scots only in language. For the Pringles and Rennies, however, the establishment of the missions of Tyumie and Lovedale in the early eighteen twenties provided a source of visiting Presbyterian ministers. Robert Hart at Glen Avon was further from this but a number of Presbyterian ministers, the most notable being Andrew Murray, had come from Scotland at the call of the Dutch Reformed Church. Murray was based in Graaff Reinet. Robert Hart was naturally drawn to the Dutch Reformed Church in Somerset, became one of its elders in Somerset East and remained one until his death.

Before the second British occupation most missionary activity had been among the Khoikhoi in the Colony and Griquas to the north, with the London Missionary Society and the Moravians playing a prominent part. Once churches had been established in Albany the minds of evangelical Christans began to turn towards the Xhosa. At the time missionary activities tended to be carried out under the auspices of the various missionary societies, many interdenominational. The London Missionary Society (LMS) already had a strong foot in the door. Now the Glasgow Missionary Society (GMS) also became active. William Shaw began enthusiastically to promote the interests of the newly established Wesleyan Methodist Missionary Society (WMMS). Shaw himself set up the first Wesleyan mission to the Gqunukwhebe at Wesleyville and he left Salem to serve there in 1823. During the eighteen-twenties the missions of the various societies spread steadily eastwards[191].

Farmers   [1820 – 1827]

Some farmers did stay down on the farm. There were two kinds. Some, the sole owners of parties, had large holdings, derived from the allocation of 100 acres per adult male in the party. The members of their parties were contracted to them for labour but, in many cases, after a short time there were no resources to pay them and they were released. The members of joint stock parties had only their 100 acre plots: on the Zuurveld this was an uneconomic smallholding. Many of these left their allotments and their neighbours began to take steps to acquire their land to build up viable holdings. In this process the patronage of the Governor was crucial. Land grants could be made as a reward for services, or simply to take in hand abandoned holdings. Donkin during his acting governorship made many such grants.

There were several things that favoured the farmers of the Scottish settlement. Firstly, the Pringles and Rennies were experienced farmers, although they had much to learn about their new environment. Secondly, because Grant's party had changed their plans and emigrated to America, there was considerably more vacant land available if they could get access to it. Thirdly, they had a neighbour of vast experience in Robert Hart at Somerset Farm.

By 1820 the Harts had made a great success of the Government farm. Its function was both to serve as a commisariat for the military and to conduct research into farming in the region. Hart was among the first to introduce merino sheep to the region, imported horses, placed hundreds of acres under cultivation, planted varieties of fruit trees, and set the farm up as an agency for supplying the produce of Boer farmers to the military. Now, with the arrival of the settlers, he was also responsible for sourcing and supplying the rations with which they were provided for a some years until they were established on the land. He was very helpful to the Pringles[192]:

> Some young fruit trees, sent by our friend Mr Hart of Somerset, as a present to my father were planted at Clifton on the 15th of August [1820]; being the first commencement of an orchard on the location.

The Pringles made rapid progress in settling in. Initially they built a central camp. Within a few days of their arrival they were alarmed by an encounter with a large lion. Only two of the party were armed and their muzzle-loaders were not charged. By the time they were ready to defend themselves the animal had retreated. Lions and hyenas were a threat to their livestock and it was necessary to mount a guard at night. The burden of night-time guard duties and long hours of heavy labour during the day was debilitating. The Pringle party was, however, in different circumstances from the settlers in Albany. Because they were so few they were able to get a great deal of help from their neighbours. Thomas wrote to Charles Stretch at the Roodewal post and asked him to find horses for them to buy; shortly afterwards one was procured. Andries Stockenstrom, the landdrost of Graaff Reinet and Captain Harding, the Deputy at Cradock provided a squad of 10 Khoikhoi guards to help with their security.

In spite of some snowfalls – Glen Lynden is at high altitude – they got their Scots plough into operation. This was a new technology for the region. The Dutch plough used in the region was a simple device with a ploughshare to cut the bottom of the furrow and a mouldboard to turn over the soil. It was clumsy and inefficient and required a full span of oxen to pull it, with at least three men – a driver, a voorloper, and a ploughman. The older European ploughs were more complex, with the addition of a coulter, a vertical blade in front of the ploughshare. As it was drawn through the soil the coulter made a vertical cut. The ploughshare then cut horizontally at the bottom of the furrow between the previous furrow and the current position. It was fixed to the front of the mouldboard, which was shaped to turn over the sod. The Scots plough, invented some years before by James Small, was a technological advance. The ploughshare and mouldboard were replaced by a carefully calculated cast iron shape designed to turn over the sod efficiently. Unlike an English plough it had no wheels and could be operated by one ploughman and a pair of horses. In the absence of draught horses it was necessary to use a pair of oxen. The notable efficiency of this new machine impressed those that saw it:

> [We] ploughed and sowed with wheat the first cultured land on the location on the first of September. It was tilled with a Scotch iron plough, without wheels, guided by one man and drawn by two oxen, – to the great admiration of our Hottentot guard, who had never before seen any other plough than the enormous and unwieldy Dutch colonial implement of tillage, which has only one handle and no coulter, and is usually drawn by eight, ten, or twelve oxen, and managed by three or four men and boys.

One of the men they had brought with them, James Ekron, was a skilled ploughman. Soon a team, consisting of Robert Pringle, his sons John and William Dods, and James Ekron had the first fields ploughed and planted. Thomas with his disability could not help in this but made furniture and concerned himself with construction and carpentry. Ditches had to be built for irrigation. They constructed irrigation channels and planted vegetables.

Initially they were dependent on the Government rations but by the end of the year they were beginning to profit from their industry. Thomas's journal entry for 19th December 1820 records that

> My brother John finds stones fit for millstones, and, with the aid of one of the Hottentots, begins to construct a small mill on the pattern of Wentzel Coetzer's[193]

The hope of flour from their own crops was dashed when, in common with farmers all over the country, their wheat crop was destroyed by the rust. At Glen Lynden they were not quite as badly affected by this plague over the next few years and their planting of diverse crops meant that, relative to many of the settlers in Albany, they prospered.

In June, 1821, Sir Rufane Donkin visited the region on a tour of inspection to assess the progress of the settlers. Thomas Pringle, on hearing that, after visiting Albany, he was going to be at Somerset Farm, lost no time in hurrying there to meet him and tell him of their troubles. Donkin accepted that the non-arrival of Grant's party and the loss of the *Abeona* with the Highland party on board was a blow to the Scottish settlement, which was now sparsely filled – the Pringle party was the only settler party in the region, although they had a number of Boer neighbours. He offered to resettle them in Albany. This was not at all what Thomas had in mind. They were well satisfied with their site. What they wanted, and what Donkin was persuaded to give them, was more land. Glen Lynden was extended down through the Baviaans River valley, substantially increasing their holding.

Nevertheless, the failure of the wheat crop in two successive years was a severe blow. When, at the end of 1822, the rust had destroyed the crop for the second time in succession John Pringle decided to leave the party. In his own words[194]

> [I] was induced by the failure of two successive crops to accept the situation of second assistant on the colonial Government establishment at Somerset

It was not an abandonment. He went to work as an assistant to Robert Hart, leaving some employees to look after his land. The reason he gives for the move may not be the only one. Of course the additional income would have been important. Another possibility, however, is that he felt the need to learn from Robert Hart, who had such a wealth of experience. Also, one cannot but feel that Thomas must have been a difficult younger brother to live with. In the whole of Thomas's account of the settlement[195] John is only mentioned in passing two or three times. It is also clear Thomas enjoyed laying down the law – in the eyes of an older brother he must have appeared impossibly bossy. One does not get the impression that they were close.

There was one other reason why John might have thought the move a good one. Susan Parr, née Stretch, had been widowed when her husband Edward Parr had died in 1818. Her brother, Hart's son-in-law Charles Lennox Stretch, who had previously commanded the Roodewal post, had been granted a neighbouring farm. Her cousin, John Mears Devenish, was Robert Hart's assistant on Somerset farm and was married to her older sister Ellen. After her husband's death, Susan, with her daughter, also Susan, lived at Somerset with her relatives. If John Pringle did not meet her at Roodewal on his first journey to the Baviaans River he must surely have met her as a neighbour during the first years of the settlement. Thomas Pringle describes a number of journeys round the region to make the acquaintance of his neighbours, including the Harts. While he says nothing of his brother it can be assumed that John would not have remained on his farm for two years without ever making similar journeys. At some point John Pringle and Susan Parr became acquainted. Whether or not this contributed to John's decision to move to Somerset Farm at the end of 1821, they were soon betrothed and were married on March 26th 1822.

John Pringle's arrival at Somerset Farm was of mutual benefit. Hart gained a hard-working and knowledgeable assistant and Pringle gained the opportunity to get the best available experience of local farming conditions and an additional income as well.

Charles Lennox Stretch's brief flirtation with independent farming had not lasted long. In 1822 he, too, had moved to Somerset Farm and was employed in keeping the accounts. Yet another appointment was John Ayliff in 1822. He took a post as manager and was also appointed to take charge of the post for what was becoming a large settlement. The traveller, George Thompson visited the farm in May 1823 and described a flourishing undertaking[196]:

> Somerset Farm, at the time I visited it, was an extensive Government establishment, under the superintendance of Mr. Hart, formerly adjutant of the old Cape Corps, assisted by Lieut. Devenish of the same corps, and Mr. J. Pringle, a practical farmer, from the Scotch party of settlers. ... The greatest activity and bustle appeared to pervade every part of the establishment; and even the languid Hottentots seemed here to emulate the ardour of Englishmen [*sic*], as if they had caught a portion of the activity and enterprize for which the indefatigable Mr. Hart has been long distinguished.

In spite of its success, even in 1823 the status of the farm was becoming precarious. The reason was that the need for it was no longer so great now that there were many farmers ready and willing to supply the military. Furthermore they were resentful of the effective monopoly that the Government establishment had for this purpose. John Pringle wrote a "memorial" to the Governor[197]

> ... The memorialist being now married with the prospect of an increasing family and in the uncertainty of the continuance of that establishment [Somerset Farm], is anxious as to his future subsistance for which his location is incapable of affording adequate means. Memorialist therefore humbly requests your excellency will be pleased to grant him such a portion of land as your excellency may deem proper, at or near the place called 'Jalouses Kraal' on the Mankanzana River, a short way above its junction with the Koonap, and situated North-East of the request place called 'Thorn Kloof,' or if that spot be already disposed of, an allotment near the head of the river adjacent to Memorialists location. That Memorialist can produce the highest recommendation from Mr Hart of his conduct and service since his connection with the Somerset Farm. ...

The Government process ground slowly on, and, a year later, in May 1824 John was awarded a large tract of land on the Mankazana River.

The axe fell on Somerset Farm in January 1825. Hart received a letter informing him that funding would cease, the employees were to be given one month's notice, and the farm would be closed, "it being the intention of his Excellency the Governor to establish a Drosdty on the farm site and to found a new district." In March the farm was divided into 94 erven (plots) to be sold by auction. The town was known as Somerset –

later to become Somerset East to distinguish it from Somerset West near Cape Town.

Robert Hart, as a reward for his service, was granted a farm a few kilometres from the new town on the Naude's River immediately below the Boschberg. As a salute to his roots and his memories of childhood he called it Glen Avon. The farm is still in the possession of fifth and sixth generation descendants and a small house that he built is still there. Charles Stretch obtained a position as Government surveyor, for which he was well suited. His father had been a surveyor in Britain and Charles had had a good deal of experience of surveying in the army. John Ayliff was appointed by Shaw as Assistant Superintendent of Mission Schools in Graham's Town.

For some reason John Pringle did not yet feel ready to strike out on his own. He took a position on a farm near Graaff Reinet. Only in 1827 did he move his wife and growing family of three daughters to the Mankazana River. By this time his brother Thomas was long gone – first to Cape Town for his struggles with the Governor for the freedom of the press, and then back to Britain. Thomas's farm, Eildon, had been passed on to their older brother William, who had arrived in the Cape in 1822. Their young half-brother William Dods had another large farm on the Baviaans River. John called his farm Glenthorn. By 1827 members of the Pringle party were working a total of 20 000 acres (about 8000 hectares) – 18 times the 1100 acres to which the original size of the party had entitled them.

Merchants and Businessmen   [1820 – 1834]

In adversity some of the settlers saw opportunity. Faced with the same difficulties as many of his fellows, Joseph Walker set out to take advantage of what skills he had. It was clear to him that his immediate hope was in overcoming the disadvantages posed by the inadequate land allocations that had been thought suitable for the settlers. In the longer term, however, he needed to accumulate some capital. His instincts were those of a businessman; his experience in England, such as it was, was of retail trade; his ambition was to set himself up as a shopkeeper.

The acquisition of land was an important part of his activities during the first years of the settlement. When he had arrived he had been a member of George Smith's joint stock party and had received his allotment of 100 acres at George Vale, the original location of the party to the west of Riet River near the coast. Like many of the other parties, Smith's had disintegrated relatively soon after arrival. Smith was replaced as leader and many members of the party left the land at an early stage and migrated to the towns. Joseph took this as an opportunity. In addition to his own 100 acres he acquired a further 300 acres at George Vale, the allotments of Henry Warner, William Elliott, and John Kirkman, who had abandoned them. Other opportunities arose:

> Decision of His Excellency the Governor on the Claims of the under named Persons
>
> Mr. J. WALKER (of Geo. SMITH's Party)
>
> His Excellency the Governor has no objection to granting to Mr. WALKER an extension of land as prayed for by him, provided it will not interfere with the farm of Bester, whose claims must not be prejudiced. The District Surveyor will decide on this.
>
> Graham's Town, February 23rd 1825
>
> By Command of His Excellency the Governor
>
> Signed Richard PLASKET, Secretary to Government[198]

In 1826 he applied for, and was granted, a separate farm, on the western side of the Kowie River, downstream of the confluence of the Blaauwkrantz River. This, for a while, became his home; he called it Wesley Wood.[199] At some stage he also acquired a farm near the Kowie River mouth on the land originally allotted to William Cock's party[200].

He now decided that he was well enough set up to marry. Benjamin Booth's eldest daughter, Margaret, was seventeen years old. He courted her and they were married on May 10th 1827. Margaret, of course, was a staunch Methodist. Her father was one of the Sephton party that had come out complete with its own minister,

Joseph Walker in later life

the Rev. William Shaw. Joseph's brother Richard was a convert and pillar of the Wesleyans, a lay preacher. It is therefore a little surprising that the wedding was carried out in the military chapel in Graham's Town by the Rev. Thomas Ireland – an Anglican ceremony in an Anglican chapel, with an Anglican celebrant. This may just be that the boundaries between Anglican and Methodist churches on the frontier were still blurred – after all, John Wesley had regarded himself as a member of the Anglican church until his death. It might also have been the because of the availability of a suitable marriage officer. There was a short period when the legality of marriages carried out by the Wesleyans was questioned by an Anglican clergyman[201], but doubts were removed when all such marriages that had taken place were legalized by proclamation. Could it have been that a marriage in the Established Church of Joseph's childhood was felt to have a little more social status? In any event the Walkers were to become pillars of the Graham's Town Wesleyan congregation.

Farming was, however, not Joseph's first interest. By early 1828 the Walkers were living in Graham's Town and Joseph had opened his small store in Bathurst Street selling the necessities of life to the townspeople. From some later evidence he appears to have placed managers on his farms. Their first daughter was born on 11th February 1828, and afterwards children came at at well managed two year intervals, Ellen in March 1830, the first son Joseph in June 1832, and Sarah in April 1834. The precision was to continue. Ultimately Margaret gave birth to eleven children, neatly scheduled in the first half of even numbered years until 1848.

In 1834 Joseph bought another hundred acres at George Vale from one John Holt who had just acquired it from Daniel Flinn. Joseph now held 500 acres there as well as Wesley Wood.

This kind of accumulation of wealth was typical of a small group of men with entrepeneurial flair. Their means of accumulating capital varied. Some took part in the illegal trade or later legal trade with the Xhosa, some took up ivory hunting, some used their skills as artisans. Not all of them were successful in assembling the capital that allowed them to invest in businesses. Those that were successful were to become some of the leading citizens of Graham's Town. By the eighteen thirties the town was a prosperous community of 7000 people surrounded by successful farms.

The Illegal Trade   [1817 – 1824]

Even before the British occupation of the Cape, there was regular trade between the frontier colonists and peoples outside the colony. By the time the British settlers arrived it had long been regulated in one way or another by the Colonial authorities[202]. As part of the Kat River deal with Ngqika in 1817, Lord Charles Somerset had given Ngqika exclusive rights to trade with the Colony. Only those Xhosa who carried Ngqika's token were allowed to cross the border and trade.

After the Nxele war and the Battle of Graham's Town, Somerset's agreement with Ngqika, granting him the control of the Xhosa side of trade with the Colony, fell away. Trade across the border was forbidden by law. Once the settlers had arrived, Sir Rufane Donkin saw the advantages of establishing trade again. He planned the establishment of a fair to be held near Fort Willshire, on the bank of the Keiskamma River. The first was cancelled because of the murder of a settler herder. Before the second could take place Somerset returned to the Governorship. In a fit of autocratic pique he cancelled the fair along with all the other Donkin policies that he had reversed. Trade with the Xhosa once again became illegal.

While many settlers were looking for any chance to turn a penny – honest or not – this would not have been much of a problem if the separation between Xhosa and Colonists, envisaged by Somerset when he decreed the neutral territory, had been effective. His solution to the problem of cattle theft was total separation. Inevitably there were, however, points of contact, where the opportunity for trade to mutual benefit arose.

One of the earliest of these points of contact was near the road between Graham's Town and Trompetter's Drift. In the Coombs Valley there were a number of deposits of fine red clay and it was at these that for years the Xhosa had gathered clay for decorative and ceremonial use.

The farms closest to the clay pits were those of settlers who had arrived on the *Northampton*. William Thackwray's farm was a few kilometres up the road towards Graham's Town. The Stubbs family farm included clay deposits as did the farm of John Brown, Stubbs's partner until they agreed to divide up their allocations. The troublesome Thomas Mahoney also had a farm that included clay deposits.

On 7th January 1821 this community was startled and alarmed by the appearance of a large company of Xhosa at the clay pits. These were Mbalu and Mdange people, led by their chiefs Nqeno and Bhothomane, who had been granted permission by the frontier commander Lt. Col. Willshire to gather clay. The Stubbs boys drove their cattle home early and were forbidden by John to go out again; the cattle were allowed to roam free without herders during the period of the Xhosa visit. Thomas Stubbs records that none were lost, which was significant given later problems with cattle theft.

A threat is also an opportunity. Thomas Stubbs writes[203]:

> The [Xhosa]s brought a great quantity of ivory. They had a camp about three miles from us on the Coombs River. We bought a large quantity for beads and buttons.

He also bought an ox and this was the beginning of a thriving illegal trade. Most of the settlers in the neighbourhood – Stubbs, Mahoney, Brown, Shaw, and Thackwray – rapidly became involved.

There were regular visits by the Xhosa for clay for the next eight months. At the instigation of Harry Rivers, the landdrost, the rules were then changed. The Xhosa were thereafter required by the Government to trade for the clay, not with the Colonists but directly with the Government agent. Participation by the settlers in trade was still strictly illegal. Stubbs was not complimentary to Rivers "alias pumpkin guts, alias humbug." He firmly believed that Rivers was himself heavily involved in trade through the medium of Boesak, the leader of the same group of Khoikhoi hunters that had been the heroes of the battle of Graham's Town. They were based at the mission station Theopolis, and Rivers had licensed them to hunt for ivory in the trans-frontier region.

A regular series of clay pits markets was established for which the Xhosa were encouraged to bring ivory, hides, and other useful trade goods. The Xhosa were not pleased by this requirement to pay for what had previously been a free resource. Nevertheless they soon found that there was a far more profitable way of trading the goods that they brought to the clay pits fair. They could meet with settlers surreptitiously and obtain more desirable goods such as buttons, beads, and ironware. The goods they made available at the clay pits fairs were relatively scanty.

Gunfight at Governor's Kop   [1821]

The Clumber valley, where the Nottinghamshire party was settled, is a beautiful rural setting. The environment was not entirely congenial to someone of Edward Driver's temperament. He was looking for other opportunities. By the middle of 1821 by barter, or quite probably by illegal trade with the Xhosa, he had managed to acquire a number of beasts of his own. He kept them, along with those of other settlers, in a kraal[204] at Governor's Kop, about seventeen kilometres from Graham's Town, close to the Thackwray farm at Stoney Vale[205]. Clumber, where Driver had originally been located, was nowhere near. The location at Governor's Kop was suspiciously convenient for trade with those Xhosa who came to the clay pits.

Driver was tempestuous, intelligent, stubborn, and cocky. His grandson remembered him as an old man[206]:

> ... even in later life when I remember him, he was a most domineering and independent old gentleman. And that was his reputation in the family.

On 5th August 1821 he was occupied in letting a herd of cattle belonging to himself and Jeremiah Honey[207] out of the kraal in which they had been confined for the night[208]. He was accosted by a neighbour, appropriately named William Sykes. Sykes, an older man, had been aboard *Albury* and was also a member of Calton's party. Like several others of the party he was illiterate. On the list of signatures at embarkation his name appears with "X His mark" beside it. Bill Sykes and Kelham Ned would have had ample opportunity to get acquainted during the five month voyage from Liverpool.

Sykes disliked Driver and was drunk. He was carrying a charged shotgun – in the words of later court proceedings *"een met hagel geladen Schietgeweer."* What his motivation was is not clear but he seems to have thought that Driver was acting without authority and demanded to know what he was doing. Driver, not a man for diplomacy, told him it was none of his business. The drunken Sykes was incensed and threatened to shoot him. Driver ignored him, infuriating the other man who twice repeated the threat.

"If you do I'll break your gun all to pieces," Driver replied – this is the court record of his response, which may in reality have been expressed a little more forcefully.

Edward Driver in later life

For Sykes this was the last straw. "Then I will!" he yelled, and fired. The range was only about eight or ten paces. Driver fell wounded and Sykes expressed his satisfaction: "I have closed your gob!"[209] he shouted and ran off.

The muzzle loaders of the time were notoriously inaccurate. The distribution of Edward's wounds suggest that the main force of the blast missed him. One piece of shot hit him in the throat, one penetrated his abdomen, and fourteen pieces peppered his breast. Fortunately the gun was charged with birdshot[210]; a blast of buck shot at that range would certainly have killed him. In 1820 even a small gun shot wound was dangerous with the ever present threat of infection. Edward was young and fit. He was taken into Graham's Town where his wounds were treated by Robert Currie, a young surgeon who was a member of Phillips's party on *Kennersley Castle* and who had set up practice in Graham's Town. The pellets were removed from stomach and neck and picked from his chest without antiseptics and with no anaesthetic other than the probable use of brandy or other spirits. He survived surgery and recovered rapidly.

Sykes was soon arrested and brought to trial before the Commission for Administering Justice in the Country Districts at the Drostdy of Bathurst on the 19th October 1821. The Colony was still administered under the Roman-Dutch law of the previous colonial power and the proceedings are recorded in Dutch, with an English translation attached. Sykes offered no defence, other than that he was drunk. The Court was unimpressed with this:

> And as it therefore appears that the Prisoner in this case has been guilty of intentionally wounding of Edward Driver, without being able to allege anything in his Defence, than that he had done so in a State of Intoxication, & as such a claim cannot be tolerated in a Country where Justice prevails, but on the contrary should be vigorously punished, according to the Laws, as an Example to deter others from doing the like ...

William Sykes was sentenced to be imprisoned on Robben Island to await the arrival of the next convict ship and thereafter to be transported for fourteen years to New South Wales.

Murder at Fraser's Camp   [June 1823]

Now that Edward Driver was located at Governor's Kop, he and John Stubbs were near neighbours, strategically located along the road to Trompetter's Drift. In June 1823 the two agreed to cooperate in a trading venture. On a winter Wednesday Stubbs, his 16 year old son John Jr, his nephew Thomas Hood, and Edward Driver secretly crossed the Great Fish River at Trompetter's Drift[211] and rode off across Xhosaland. They were accompanied by three Khoikhoi cattle drovers. They led pack horses loaded with trade goods. On the banks of the Keiskamma River, by arrangement, they met a Gqunukwhebe Chief, identified as Congo. Chungwa, the prominent Gqunukwhebe Paramount, was often called Congo in contemporary sources but he had long been dead. This Congo was Kobe kaChungwa, a minor son of Chungwa, known in the Colony as Kobus Congo. By this time he had constructed a special hut for traders, and there was a steady stream of illicit travellers visiting him. The Landdrost, Harry Rivers, wrote:

They had met the [Xhosa] Chief Congo and a party of his people at the Drift of the Keiskamma nearest the Coast and had there purchased eighty five head of Cattle for Beads Copper wire &c.[212]

John Stubbs Jr's deposition attached to this, also mentions eight elephant tusks. The currency for the trade had been bought a week in advance at about 2 Rixdollars per lb[213] of beads. The negotiated price of a cow was 1lb of beads and that of a tusk 2 lb. At the time there were about 12 Rixdollars to the pound. After their successful negotiations the party set off home. John Jr and Tom Hood rode ahead while John Sr and Edward Driver supervised the cattle drovers. Once back in the Colony, as they approached the top of the long rise from the river gorge, near Fraser's camp, Driver and Stubbs saw John Jr and Thomas coming back towards them. They had disquieting news. A large group of Khoikhoi was bivouacked ahead of them at Fraser's Camp. They had no wish to encounter anyone else when encumbered with the proceeds of illegal trade, including a large herd of cattle.

Stubbs Sr rode ahead to reconnoitre. He was surrounded by Khoikhoi. It was Boesak and his band of hunters. Boesak told him he was under arrest[214]. In his own report Rivers states that some weeks before he had asked Boesak to keep an eye open for illicit traders and Boesak was aware that there could be substantial rewards for apprehending them. Thomas Stubbs maintained that Boesak's hunting activities were a cover for illegal ivory trade with Landdrost Harry Rivers as a partner and that Boesak was simply protecting his own interests.

Stubbs's reaction was that of someone encountering a gang of rivals rather than a patrol with any legal power of arrest. He levelled his gun, threatened to shoot any one who laid hands on him, and retreated to find the others. He found Driver, but John Jr and Thomas had disappeared; they had by now been arrested by Boesak, who had confiscated the cattle and ivory. Driver and Stubbs retreated into the bush. There they separated. Driver's own account, reported by Cowper Rose[215] states:

... we fled different ways, — and I wandered on foot, unarmed and alone; night was coming on, when, on suddenly turning a rock, I saw three armed [Xhosa]s within three yards of me; they had seized some of the cattle, and the bleeding body of my companion lay by them. I turned without a hope of escape, and almost felt, in thought, the assegai whizzing into my back.

Edward Driver made good his escape. John Stubbs was not so fortunate.

At 11pm Mrs Stubbs and her younger son Thomas were woken by a loud knocking at their door. It was Edward Driver. Thomas's account is that he gave them the news, saying that the cattle and ivory had been confiscated and that he expected that the other members of the party would be home soon. This is at variance with Driver's own story, as it implies that he was still unaware of John Stubbs's death. Both accounts of the events, by Thomas Stubbs and Cowper Rose, are second-hand. Driver might have been embroidering the story for Rose: Stubbs was recalling events fifty years later.

According to Thomas, Driver then asked him to take his horse and ride to Hobson's farm, about 13 km away, to deliver a letter. If he met anyone he should destroy the letter rather than let it be taken from him. The Hobsons[216] were also heavily involved in illegal trade and may have been partners in the trading enterprise, needing to be informed. Why did Driver not deliver the message in person? Perhaps he believed that he had been recognized and needed to go in to hiding. In any event Thomas Stubbs set off at midnight and delivered the letter.

On his way back from Hobson's, Thomas Stubbs met Boesak's hunters with young John Stubbs and Thomas Hood. They were able to whisper a quick account of what they knew of the night's happenings to Thomas Stubbs before they were hustled away.

The next morning a group of soldiers from the 6th Regiment brought in the body of John Stubbs. He had several assegai wounds and had apparently fought his assailants to the death with the butt of his gun when it had misfired. Thomas Stubbs believed from the evidence of some tracks that he had tried to retrieve some stolen cattle from some marauding Xhosas and had died in the attempt. The suggestion[217] that when the boys, the cattle, and the ivory were seized by Boesak "the [Xhosa]s considered that this was a trick of Stubbs to get the cattle before they had completed their bargains and murdered him" assumes that the trade had taken place nearby. It is absurd when it is known that they had traded with Kobe on the Keiskamma deep in Gqunukwhebe territory some days earlier.

Driver is reported as stating:

> ... we were seized, taken to Graham's Town, brought to trial, — the court was divided in opinion and we got off.

Neither the Court Report nor Thomas Stubbs makes any mention of Driver's arrest although Rivers's report states

> ... Stubbs and another man, whom I have not been able to detect but strongly suspect to be Edward Driver of the Nottingham Party, had gone with the two boys into [Xhosa]land to traffic with Congo.

Driver may well have been embroidering his account when talking to Cowper Rose.

According to Stubbs, next day John Stubbs Jr and Thomas Hood were sentenced to six months imprisonment each in the Court of the Land-drost, Harry Rivers. They were released next day as part of a cover-up when Hood laid information against Rivers that he had been engaged heavily in the ivory trade with Boesak as his agent. The Report of Prisoners for the Graham's Town District for the period 31st May to 30th June 1823[218], lists John Stubbs and Thomas Hood as having been confined on 21st June for the crime of "Trafficing with the [Xhosa]s" and released on the same day with the comment "Released by the Landdrost." Because of Rivers's unpopularity with the settlers Stubbs's account may be prejudiced. Rivers's letter, however, does state

> I shall proceed against Hood and the young Stubbs for the penalties under the proclamation of September last, and for the Confiscation of the Cattle and Ivory, to a third of the proceeds of which the Informer Boesak and the R O Prosecutor will be each entitled, and I request the directions of His Excellency as to the disposal of the remaining third.

Many questions remain, not least that of what happened to Edward Driver in the immediate aftermath of these events. It appears that he successfully managed to keep his participation out of the record. The suspicions of Harry Rivers came to nothing.

Artisans and Apprentices   [1820 - 1823]

A large proportion of the settlers did not have the grounding in agriculture that the architects of the settlement plan had envisaged. They were townsmen, often skilled in various trades, without the desire to take on the problems of starting from scratch in difficult circumstances. Within months many of them had resolved to try to make use of their skills in the towns. They had contractual problems; they had to obtain release from their undertakings either to the government or to their masters in the case of sole proprietor party leaders. They flocked to Graham's Town, whose new status as capital of the region provoked a boom in building and related trades.

William Thackwray was one of the settlers who did have a trade. He was a skilled wheelwright and agricultural toolmaker. He lost little time in setting himself up in trade, being established in Graham's Town before the end of 1820. There was a demand for his skills and he was soon able to take on an apprentice, George Wood, a lumbering lad who gave no indication of his future destiny of becoming one of the richest men in the Colony. William's son John was also expected to help in the business, although his temperament was not suited to steady work. Along with making wagons, William also began to use them for transport and John was of help with the oxen.

George Wood was not a conscientious lad. Some interesting social history is contained in two official letters[219]:

Letter from Lord Charles Somerset [Governor of the Cape Colony] to Earl Bathurst [Secretary of State]

Government House

Cape of Good Hope, 24th September 1822

My Lord, – I have had the honour to receive your Lordship's note dated 8th May 1822, requesting that enquiry be made relative to George Wood Smith, who is represented to have emigrated from England to this place, and in reply I beg to transmit to your Lordship a copy of a report from the Magistrate of Albany District, which will put your Lordship in possession of the information required. I have &c

(Signed) Charles Henry Somerset

[Enclosure]

Graham's Town 3rd September 1822

Sir, – I have the honour to acknowledge the receipt of your letter of the 17th ulto. transmitting a copy of a note from the Secretary of State requesting information relative to George Wood Smith, and in reply to the representation of his mother I have the honour to inform His Excellency the Governor that George Wood came out as an apprentice to Richard Smith a carpenter of Mr. Sephton's party under articles for seven years. The indentures are dated 5th November 1819, and were formally transferred or assigned on 8th December 1820 by the mutual consent of the Master and apprentice, and in the presence of a Magistrate, to W. Thackwray a Wheelright [sic] and Carpenter residing in Grahamstown, with whom the boy now lives.

I informed the lad that his mother had made inquiries respecting him, and he has assured me that he would write to her, which he stated that he had not done since his arrival in the Colony. He is in good health and learning a trade under a respectable Master.

I have &c.

(signed) Harry Rivers

Lieut.-Col. Bird, Colonial Secretary

What else would a mother who had not heard from her son do but take the matter up with the Secretary of State who in turn would instruct the Colonial Governor to look into matters? This correspondence shows that William had set himself up as a wheelwright before the end of 1820, less than nine months after his arrival in the district, and certainly before he would have had time to assimilate the difficulties of farming in Albany.

It was not long after this that Lord Charles Somerset caused consternation among the growing business community in Graham's Town. On 4th October 1822 he issued a proclamation[220] "... for the purpose of securing the Country against [Xhosa] depredations." It listed regulations for conscripting settlers to Commando[221] forces. The portion of the proclamation that caused concern was one reading:

> ... all Persons serving therein shall be subject to all the Provisions contained in the Act of Parliament then in force, for the prevention of Mutiny and Desertion, and of the Articles of War, made in pursuance thereof.

The autocratic removal of their limited civil rights was anathema. A group of prominent settlers responded with a "memorial" to the Governor. Matters moved slowly – the document was dated 8th April 1823[222]:

> ... In consequence of a recent Proclamation your Memorialists are called upon to take an Oath to which they cannot acquiesce.

> Your Memorialists trust your Excellency will not from this circumstance consider them as disloyal Subjects; they have carefully considered it, and are anxious to testify their loyalty in any way which does not interfere with their personal liberty, but they cannot divest themselves of the idea that after taking that Oath they are bound under the Martial Law equally with any Private in His Majesty's regiments. ...

The document was signed by 56 "memorialists", the eighth on the list being Wm Thackwray. It was an early indication of the friction building up between the settlers and the colonial Government.

The necessity for such a home guard force was brought home just two months later. The death of John Stubbs was a great shock to the community, more especially to the Thackwrays. Stubbs and Thackwrays had been near neighbours. Furthermore, the loss was too much for Ann Stubbs. She was dead within a few months, leaving her children destitute. It fell first to the Thackwrays to help out. Dorothy was sent to the Stubbs home to help with the children. The authorities soon stepped in and made arrangements for the family, which was split up. One of the babies was sent to Glen Avon to be fostered there. Thomas Stubbs, now in his teens, was expected to take up a trade. Agreement was reached that he should be apprenticed to William Thackwray.

Young Stubbs was a lively addition to the Thackwray business. He did not get on well with some other members of the group. His description of his fellow apprentice is caustic:

> OLD GEORGE WOULD[223]: First knew him when apprentice to Old Thackwray. He was a great bulk of a fellow and was so confoundedly stupid, that it was thought he was not able to learn the trade. He was so filthy

in his habits, that old Thackwray would not allow him into the house but made him get his food in the kitchen.

The description must be taken with a pinch of salt. It was written many years later in a satirical work, and Thomas Stubbs in his old age was resentful of the success of Wood in the light of his own lack of financial success.

The Beginning of Legal Trade   [1824 – 1827]

By 1824 it was apparent, even to Lord Charles Somerset, that the farming experiment had failed. The rust, drought, flood, and the inadequacies of the land allocations, made European style agriculture impossible in the Zuurveld. Only those few who had the knowledge, nous, and resources to assemble viable tracts of land and embark on stock farming were likely to make a success of living off the land. The rest had fled to Graham's Town or Graaff Reinet, or had left the frontier area. Some had the option to use their skills as artisans. The remainder had to scratch a living in one way or another. Many entered the black economy, turning to illegal trade or smuggling. The Government was powerless to stop it. Edward Driver was one of these.

It had long been apparent to him that farming of itself was not sufficient to keep body and soul together. He became more and more involved in commercial ventures in the form of trading and smuggling. The risks of trading were substantial, both personal and financial. Patrols of the Cape Corps consisting of Khoikhoi soldiers were sparse, but, if encountered, would arrest the traders. Because of the illegal nature of the trade settlers were vulnerable to exploitation by Xhosa chiefs. On one occasion he was trading across the border with the amaRharhabe and Ngqika confiscated all his trade goods. Cowper Rose[224] describes a conversation with Driver:

> When pursuing his first dangerous trade, his stock of beads, he [Driver] said, had been frequently seized by the [Xhosa]s, and his life threatened, — for they knew well that the life of the smuggler was not protected — that Gaika [Ngqika] had once taken every thing from him, and was about to give him up to the English troops; — "When, you know," observed the [Xhosa] calmly, "you will be hanged;" and that he was only saved by the intervention of another chief, Duchany [Mdushane, son of Ndlambe and Ngqika's cousin], who prevailed on Gaika to let him escape.

His initial ventures were enough to show him that illegal trade held considerable dangers and in later life he gained the reputation of a courageous but prudent man.

Many other settlers exploited the presence of the Xhosa people on the other side of the Fish River. Apart from livestock, the most important commodities to be obtained were ivory, ostrich feathers, other game products, hides and skins and similar goods. The commodities with which to trade included innocuous merchandise such as beads, ironware, and other hardware. Illegal, less innocuous commodities were guns, ammunition, and liquor.

Young John Thackwray quickly got into the business:

Another of the illicit traders was John Thackwray, a slight, good-tempered young man who seems to have been attracted by danger.[225]

Wagon making did not agree with any of William Thackwray's apprentices. Thomas Stubbs soon left his service and, by agreement, became apprenticed to a saddlemaker. George Wood also ended his apprenticeship. May Bell continues:

George Wood's apprenticeship to the elder Thackwray had not lasted long. Young Wood may have downed tools and walked out – he was that kind of lad. But why should his master, to whom the indentures gave a cheap servant for six years, allow him to go? ... According to later gossip, Wood was seen leading oxen, barefoot, in Grahamstown streets ... Since it was about this time that young Thackwray took to trading, the chances are that young Wood led John Thackwray's oxen, and that an anxious father had released a difficult apprentice so that his son might have a companion to help him on his dangerous trips.

It is possible, however, that this refers to a time after trade at Fort Willshire had become legal and William Thackwray was one of the traders. Wood may have simply still been serving his apprentice master. Another contemporary account[226] states that

... the Honourable George Wood was a leader to old Thackeray's [sic] wagon...

so it might be that he was merely performing a menial task expected of an apprentice.

In 1824, bowing to circumstance, Somerset at last reversed his trade policy. He decided to revive the idea of a market at Fort Willshire. Here the idea was to licence Colonists to take part in the fair, bringing trade goods from the Colony to exchange for desirable products such as ivory, hides, and skins. This would mean that the commerce was taking place deep in the Ceded Territory – Fort Willshire was on the banks of the Keiskamma River – and that there would be no need for the Xhosa to enter the Colony as had been the case for the Clay Pits Fairs. On 23rd July 1824 the Governor issued a proclamation establishing the fairs. Anyone of good character could obtain a licence from the Landdrost and, armed with this and a list of his approved trade goods, could attend the fair and take part in the trade.

The first licence[227] was issued on 5th Aug 1824 to one John Testard who was a storeman at Fort Willshire. Among the first licencees were young John Thackwray and his father William (licences number 16 and 18 issued on the 20th and 21st August) and their neighbour John Brown (number 13). Edward Driver followed soon afterwards with licence number 26. Young William Thackwray, only 15 years old, was issued with licence number 51 on 9th October.

The Fort Willshire fairs soon took off. They were held weekly. Initially each fair lasted for three days, from Wednesday to Friday. Fort Willshire was seventy kilometres from Graham's Town. The wagon trail ran from the town to Committees Drift on the Fish River, upstream from Trompetter's Drift. Across the river was the Ceded Territory. After passing through the steep and difficult terrain of the Fish River valley, it turned north for a while along the high ground between the Fish and the Keiskamma. Fort Willshire overlooked a drift on a bend of the Keiskamma where it made its closest approach to the course of the Fish. Trading at the fair was a full-time job. Assuming that the traders kept the Sabbath, Monday was devoted to disposing of goods obtained at the previous week's fair and obtaining goods suitable for trade. On Tuesday the long trek to the fair took place. It was wise to travel in convoy as there was always the risk of encountering bandits bent on acquiring the trade goods without cost to themselves. Some traders, such as William Thackwray had their own wagons and supplied a service to other traders who preferred to entrust their goods to the wagoners and ride independently. Pack oxen were also in use. It was a day-long journey. In the evening the traders camped on a site outside the Fort.

From contemporary accounts Beck[228] has constructed a lively description of the proceedings. The Xhosa camp was confined to the other side of the Keiskamma River. Fixed times were set for the market. The start and finish were signalled by a cannon shot. At the beginning of the day this was the signal for the Xhosa to stream across the drift, carrying their goods with them. In the early days few of the settlers could speak Xhosa and few Xhosa could speak English or Dutch. Communication was by gesture and demonstration. The military kept order. At the signal for the end of the day both sides returned to their camps. Saturday was taken up with the return journey.

The Government was concerned that the trade should be in goods that were "useful" to the Xhosa.

The Articles most desirable to induce the [Xhosa]s to purchase, would be Cloths of every description; Woollen and Cotton Articles of any kind that they could be tempted to receive, particularly Blankets; also, the Leather Trowsers of the Colony, Knives, Tinder-boxes, Agricultural and Horticultural Implements, red Clay, Tea, Coffee, Sugar, Hatchets, Cast Iron Cooking Pots and Kettles, &c. &c. &c.[229]

The Government knew what they wanted themselves

The Articles to be received from the [Xhosa]s are Ivory, Ox Hides, Skins of Animals, Natural Curiosities, Corn, and small Manufactures, such as Baskets, Mats, Sambocs [sjamboks], &c. Barter in Cattle is for the present prohibited.

Wealth for the Xhosa was measured in cattle. Only those few who lived on mission stations were interested in clothes. What they wanted was something which, while ornamental, was also useful as currency that they could use in the interior to trade for cattle. They wanted beads and buttons. The Government wanted them to learn the value of the goods of British civilisation.

Buttons, Beads, and Trinkets are to be limited, though not entirely prohibited; that is, no staple commodity, such as Ivory, Hides, &c. is to be purchased solely by Beads, Buttons, and Trinkets; but Beads, Buttons, and Trinkets are allowed in Barter, combined with any of the above named Articles.

The other things that were, of course, highly desirable, were precisely those things that were strictly forbidden:

It is most strictly forbidden to take to the Market, for Sale or Barter, or to exchange or give away there, any Firearms or Ammunition, or any kind of Spirits, Wines, Beers, or other Liquors.

These were a constant temptation to indulge in clandestine trade.

Into the Interior   [1823 – 1830]

The Fort Willshire fairs continued for a number of years. Initially there were scores of traders. As time went on those who were less committed to the weekly toil found other occupations. The successful ones had to be tenacious, steadfast, and enduring. Probably most of those who were successful also indulged in illegal trading away from the restrictions of the fair.

Edward Driver was one of those who was unlikely to be constrained by the exact letter of the law. He clearly had entrepreneurial skills and maintained a trading activity for many years, while also finding other means of making a living. His grandson W. I. S. Driver[230] wrote of him:

He was known from one end of the Transkeian Territories to the other, and everywhere on the Frontier, to the Chiefs and natives by the name of "Sonyakatya", and it was only a few days ago that here, in Quthing, Basutoland, where a number of Tembu natives live, that one of them asked me if I was a descendent of "Sonyakatya" Driver about whom his own ancestors and others had told him much.

He and many other licencees were keen on the opportunity to be legally on the other side of the border in order to continue with clandestine trade using the contacts already set up, never mind the more controlled environment of the fair.

The military establishment had a jaundiced view of the traders. Officers and gentlemen regarded those who indulged in trade as socially inferior; those who engaged in it, whether legally or illegally, were beneath contempt. The need to keep body and soul together was no excuse. Charles Lennox Stretch expressed his view forcefully[231]:

Many of that class of the settlers of 1820 got into Caffraria as "traders", where Fort Willshire was the scene of barter, and were equally mischievous among the [Xhosa]s in robbing and cheating the natives ... A trader named Driver – I believe that was the name – knowing the propensity of the heathen to steal, was journeying with his waggon, and having a companion equally dishonest with him, made a plan as follows to rob the [Xhosa]s. It was midday in the summer month of January, and taking a roll of brass wire such as the women wear on their arms, they laid it at the end of their waggon on the grass; and throwing themselves down at the other end pretended to sleep. It was not long before a [Xhosa] who was passing beheld the wire and sleepers, and thinking he was unobserved, seized the bait. He was allowed to go a short distance, and was then taken to his chief as a thief and had to pay 4 head of cattle of £20 value for the wire which cost a shilling in Graham's Town. The same parties, taking advantage of the native ignorance, sold the seed of the stremonium or stinkblaar for coarse gunpowder. When there I saw "settler traders" were beginning to introduce guns among the [Xhosa]s, which became a very profitable trade between Graham's Town and Caffraria for many years until the war of 1835 and long after.

Sharp practice was common among those who began to take advantage of opportunities for trade. From Driver's point of view he probably felt that he was only taking advantage of the fact that he knew that Xhosa passers-by were liable to help themselves to his stock. Driver's grandson wrote:

He did well at trading as well as hunting and, although the story is told of another 1820 Settler as well, we have always understood that "Sonyakatya" sold bullets at a great profit to natives as "pot seed", from which iron pots would grow if properly planted.

This seems much more reprehensible than the entrapment of the wire thief. The other settler referred to may well be George Wood; his descendant May Bell[232] relates a similar story about him, but is at pains to point out that he afterwards returned to make good his promise to deliver bullets.

Driver's father-in-law, William Thackwray, was more inclined to legal trade. He remained prominent among the Fort Willshire traders. When this trade declined he was, however, also prepared to go outside the bounds of what was permitted, being more adventurous than many of his fellows. He became known to the Xhosa, according to contemporary spelling, as Calamaish[233].

William became a pioneer in opening up the territory beyond the eastern frontier to trade when, in 1825, he made a major journey into Pondoland, to the banks of the Umzimvubu River, where the Mpondo king Faku had his homestead[234]. This was well before the legalization of trade with the Xhosa. The expedition traveled through what is now known as the Ciskei and the Transkei and must have been extremely arduous as well as dangerous. New trails were being opened. There were many deep river gorges to be crossed. This sometimes entailed dismantling the wagon and carrying it and its cargo piece by piece down one side of a gorge and up the other. A very good contemporary description of such a journey is provided by Andrew Geddes Bain[235] who in 1829, after such expeditions became legal, following what was by then a better developed trail, made a similar journey, covering what was much the same route as Thackwray four years earlier. William's travels convinced him that there was the prospect of better profit in such ventures than in trade at the highly competitive Fort Willshire fairs.

In 1826 there was a new opportunity. After the departure of Lord Charles Somerset, an acting Governor, Major-General Richard Bourke was appointed[236] and served between 1826 and 1828. This coincided with a major change in the system of government of the Colony as a result of the recommendations of the Commission of Inquiry. The Dutch colonial system of administration of government was replaced by a British one, leading to the abolishing of posts such as Landdrost. In the criminal courts English law replaced Dutch, although, to this day, Roman-Dutch law is the basis of civil law in South Africa.

As part of the reorganization, Bourke was concerned to clean up the law covering all trade. Ordinance 23 of 11th Sep. 1826 consolidated the laws governing trade, made provision for border fairs to be set up, and, importantly,

> ... it shall and may be lawful for the Governor for the time being of this Colony, to authorise the Landdrosts, and Deputy Landdrosts, of the Frontier Districts, to Grant Licences, under Hand and Seal, to such Col-

onists of good character as may desire to trade privately with the nations beyond the boundaries of such District; such Licences to be perfected on a Stamp of Six Pounds value, or of such other amount as may hereafter legally be required, and to be in force for one Year only ...[237]

At last trading beyond the borders of the Colony might become a legal way to make a living. William Thackwray lost no time in consulting Major Dundas, the Landdrost in Graham's Town. He was assured that he would be regarded as a suitable holder of a licence and on the strength of this he set about the expensive business of stocking up for a journey into the interior.

To his dismay when he went back to Dundas for his licence he was told that instructions had arrived from the Governor that no licences were to be granted under this ordinance. This placed him in great financial difficulty[238]. He composed a strong memorial to the Governor pointing out his problems[239] and requesting an exception. To his relief he was successful. Just two licences were issued, number 1 to one George Joseph and number 2 to William Thackwray.

This was the beginning of a new increase in prosperity. In the first six months of 1827 Thackwray brought back 460 cattle and 170 lb of ivory from successful trade in Thembuland[240].

In the period that followed William apparently travelled up as far as the Northern Cape and deep into what is now the Transkei. By the late eighteen twenties he had a profound knowledge of the region and the opportunities for trade and hunting.

Another form of trade into the interior arose from the activities of the missionaries. Those who went beyond the borders of the Colony had always found it necessary to trade simply for the everyday necessities of life. In the early eighteen twenties, however, this trade became more formalised with the establishment of stores on many mission stations. John Philip had set up stores first at Bethelsdorp and then at Theopolis, serving the Khoikhoi people at the missions. These were run by storekeepers and were intended on one hand to free the missionaries from concerns with store keeping and on the other to supply the converts with clothes and suitable missionary goods that were intended to provide a "civilising influence." These LMS mission stations were in the colony. When the Wesleyans started setting up mission stations they served the Xhosa beyond the borders of the Colony.

By 1826 at Wesleyville William Shaw could see the need for a store. He enlisted help from William Ritchie Thomson, the missionary and Government Agent at Balfour to get permission from Bourke. The Acting Governor reacted by inviting a plan[241].

Shaw's response proposed a number of principles. A missionary could not, himself, be involved in trade. The shopkeeper would be employed and under the control of the resident missionary, and subject to dismissal for failing to abide by the regulations set up for the store. He would not trade on his own behalf. Only residents of the mission could make use of the store; others must use the Fort Willshire fair for trade. The store would only provide useful goods such as ironware, clothing, or tools in exchange for the staples of trade such as ivory, hides, or cattle; if the customers wanted beads or trinkets for these goods they would have to go to the Fort Willshire fair. This was to avoid competition. Up to one quarter of the value could be paid in colonial currency. Only small items of handy work such as woven baskets or mats could be paid for by beads and trinkets. Customers having colonial cash could purchase whatever they desired. There was an absolute ban on trade in guns, ammunition, or spirits. Ultimately, as the plan worked, the mission would pay employees in cash rather than kind – this was to encourage an acceptance of money as a useful exchange for goods.

Bourke immediately accepted these conditions and Shaw's first task was to employ a suitable shopkeeper. His choice was Richard Walker. It was a very successful one from Shaw's point of view. The commercial activities were placed at arms length from the missionary society. Stock was obtained from William Cock's store in Graham's Town and a commission on sales paid by Cock to the mission store[242]. The Walker family arrived at Wesleyville on 28th July 1827. The first few days that the store operated were chaotic[243]:

> The store has been commenced, but the Natives either did not or would not understand our plan, which restricts the traffic to useful articles, whereas the majority of them are still more anxious to receive beads etc. For several days, hundreds of Natives came with hides , ivory, corn etc. etc. intendg. to Barter for [Xhosa] ornaments, but when they found nothing could induce me to sanction Mr. Walker in departing from the above general regulation for his traffic, they ceased to trouble us by coming in such crowds, and the comparatively small number who are desirous of obtaining cloathing, Hatchets, Iron cooking pots etc., traffic with Mr. W. in as quiet and orderly a manner as can be expected from such rude people. Those who still seek Beads & Trinkets, and which at present are the great mass of the people, traffic with the regular dealers at the Fairs established by Government, ...

Initially all went well. Richard's salary was paid from the profits of the store. Not only the Xhosa were served. Other missionaries, both at Wesleyville and at neighbouring stations could obtain supplies from the store, saving them long and difficult trips to the Colony. In addition Richard served as a preacher working over the whole region.

It was not to last. By the end of the year the Fort Willshire traders were complaining about the impact of both the mission trade and the licenced inland traders on their business. These traders were strictly forbidden to engage in any commercial activities other than those at the fair. The licences of the inland traders precluded them from trading near Fort Willshire. The mission shop operated with no licence but the permission of the Governor. By the late eighteen twenties the Fort Willshire operation was losing ground. At the beginning of 1829, in a memorandum to the Governor, a number of traders at the fair complained[244]

> The Fair at Fort Willshire has been severely injured by exclusive Licences granted to Mr. Walker at the Missionary Station, and Messrs Collet, Wood, and Trollip, this private Trade has been carried out within 12 miles of Fort Wiltshire [sic], whereas formerly the Fair was protected by your obliging all holders of Private Licences to take such route as might prevent any injury to it.

The complaint does not seem to have been against the trade itself, but against its taking place too near the location of the fair. Shortly afterwards the complaints were of the existence of the mission store. The ordinance that permitted trade beyond the borders on issue of a licence was used to try to persuade the Public Prosecutor to bring a case against Richard Walker for trading without a licence. When the prosecutor declined to prosecute, a licensed trader, Edward Hanger, brought a private case against him. Richard was summoned to appear in the Magistrates Court in Graham's Town[245]. Shaw, much to his dismay, appeared for the defence. The outcome was a finding that the mission store was in technical violation of the Ordinance, but in view of the circumstances a suspended fine of £20 was imposed, pending an appeal to the Governor. To cover himself for the future Richard Walker applied for and was granted a licence. There the matter rested until near the end of 1829 when the Fort Willshire traders again appealed. It was decided to revoke all the licences but when Walker came to hand his in he was permitted to keep it. Shaw tried to get clarification from the Governor without success. In 1830 the Fort Willshire traders again registered a complaint, but before the matter had been resolved the border was opened to trade and thereafter Richard Walker was able to continue operating in common with many others who began to expand the commercial activities of the colony into Xhosa territory.

The Beginnings of Prosperity   [1830 – 1834]

The decade from 1820 to 1830 had produced a transformation of conditions on the eastern frontier. Those settlers who could not cope had, one way or another, disappeared from the scene. The farmers had found what worked in the climatic conditions and had consolidated their lands to provide viable farms. The businessmen were doing well in the towns. There was work for tradesmen and artisans. The system of government and legal system had been improved (but was far from perfect). In 1834 Thomas Pringle – now in London, but receiving information from his many family and friends in the Colony – was able to write[246]

> ... the commercial affairs of the district have progressed beyond expectation; and the internal trade with the [Xhosa] and other native tribes, which has been created almost entirely since the arrival of the British settlers, is becoming every day more extensive and important. Graham's Town, the capital of the district, which in 1820 was a mere military post, is now a thriving and bustling country town, with about 3500 inhabitants, chiefly English. Besides the established church (English), it boasts three chapels for protestant dissenters (Independent, Wesleyan, and Baptist), a free school for youth of both sexes, and an infant school, supported by voluntary subscription. It also now possesses two subscription libraries, agricultural, missionary, and temperance societies, a savings bank, and a weekly newspaper.

There was soon to be a rude awakening.

Chapter 9. The Elephant Hunters

Nature's great masterpiece, an elephant
The only harmless great thing

John Donne, The Progress of the soul

Opportunity   [1820 - 1931]

When the settlers arrived the land was teeming with game. Vast herds of antelope roamed the Zuurveld. Lions and leopards (referred to as tigers by the settlers) preyed on this bounty and now man took advantage of the supply for his own purposes. Hippopotami – sea cows – were common in the rivers. Rhinoceros roamed through the bush. The largest animals were the elephants that trod paths through the dense thorny riverine forests, making them penetrable by other animals and man.

The elephants had long been hunted by the amaXhosa[247] but a successful hunt was a rare event. The first stage was to locate an animal that was separated from the herd; without guns a troop of elephants is impregnable. Fires were set to surround the animal and it was then attacked with volleys of assegais. Many of these did not penetrate the skin and the elephant would be able to withstand the assault for long periods of time. After nightfall it might penetrate the ring of fire and move long distances. Next day the process would be repeated until, sometimes after several days, the animal succumbed. Tusks, ears and tail were the privilege of the chief, the ears and tail as trophies and the tusks for the making of arm rings and as gifts and items of trade.

Some of the young and more courageous settlers saw their opportunity. With guns of enormous calibre they were able to stalk and kill elephants and rapidly build up wealth. The leading hunters each killed hundreds in a year[248].

Availing themselves of the recently granted freedom to move beyond the Colonial boundary several settlers devoted themselves to big game hunting (chiefly the elephant, buffalo, lion, hippopotamus and rhinoceros), a pursuit in which they soon made a name for themselves. The famous lion hunter, George Rennie, and such men as J. Stubbs, [William] Carey Hobson, Edward Driver, Henry Stirraker, Thomas and Henry Hartley, William Gradwell, John Thackwray, [Richard?] Hayhurst, James Jennings and the four Cawoods (Samuel, James, Joshua and David) all acquired a great reputation as intrepid big-game hunters; unfortunately their exploits in the field have not been formally recorded, their fame being now a matter of family tradition only.[249]

The combined effect of this steady slaughter and the loss of habitat as man began to dominate the land led to a catastrophic collapse in the elephant population. By the eighteen forties the plentiful herds were no more.

As late as 1920 the Union Government was employing a hunter to eliminate the last vestiges of the herds that still remained in the Addo Bush[250]. Interestingly, at that time it was noted that many of the elephants were tuskless. There is no doubt that in the early nineteenth century most were favoured with large and valuable tusks, the reason for their attraction to the hunters. There were a few tuskless ones. Driver told Cowper Rose that the tusks could not be for defence, as he had thought, because "the most fierce and dangerous among them is a breed that the Dutch call Koeskops, and they have no tusks." It would be tempting to speculate that the selective pressure arising from the hunters' choice of specimens caused animals with smaller tusks to survive best – a case of Darwinian unnatural selection. Recent research, however, while recognising a rapid increase in the incidence of tusklessness, suggests that the changes are due to non-selective genetic drift in a small isolated population[251]. At last, in 1931, public outcry led to the establishment of the Addo National Park, dedicated to the preservation of the elephants.

In order to judge the elephant hunters we must discard twenty-first century prejudice. Today selling ivory that is not certified as antique is criminal in most countries and forbidden by a treaty to which 173 countries adhere[252]. This is not just the result of bunny-hugging sentimentality but of a hard-nosed understanding of the importance of preserving the ecology for the benefit of the earth and of further generations. In the eighteen twenties such understanding did not exist. The sentiment was almost precisely opposite. The great naturalist, William J. Burchell, who spent five years on scientific exploration of the length and breadth of South Africa between 1810 and 1815[253], clearly understood that species could be eliminated by the impact of man. He expressed an establishment view when he wrote:

> The great and powerful cause which will long operate to check the extension of the cultivation of grain, is the abundance of wild animals to be met with in all parts of the country; and until these shall be reduced in number or driven out of the land, it is hardly to be expected that the natives will turn to settled agricultural pursuits. The introduction of fire-arms among them would ultimately operate to the promotion of tillage, notwithstanding that their first effects might occasion the neglect of it. By hunting, this people would obtain food in a manner so much more agreeable than by agriculture, that grain would probably become but a secondary resource; but the evil would remedy itself, and the more eagerly they pursued the chase, and the more numerous were

the guns and the hunters, the sooner would the game be destroyed or driven out of the country.

Read that statement again! It is a significant example of the dangers of making judgements in hindsight. From a twenty-first century point of view the shooting of elephants almost to the point of extinction might be judged as cynical exploitation and destruction of the eco-system for personal profit. From Burchell's perspective it was not only harmless but positively beneficial. The benefit of mankind through the promotion of agriculture was to be pursued at all costs. Furthermore, giving the amaXhosa and Khoikhoi guns would encourage them to increase the rate of slaughter, eliminate the game, and take up peaceful agricultural pursuits that would tie them to the land and reduce their propensity for war and cattle theft. The wild life was a hindrance to be removed. The hunting of elephant and other big game was a valuable pursuit and the hunters were respected as courageous and valuable members of society. Judgement of individuals operating in this environment should be made in the light of the ethics and norms of their time and not in the context of twenty-first century sensitivities.

How to hunt an elephant

The African elephant is the largest living land animal. A full-grown male stands between three and four metres at the shoulder and has a mass between four and seven tonnes. The tusks may be as long as two metres with a mass of forty kilograms and both male and female have tusks. Although the female Addo elephants are now tuskless, this was not the case in the eighteen twenties when these elephants were part of the larger population of African elephants spread over the whole country. They have a close-knit social structure with strong family loyalties and are fiercely protective of their young. When provoked they can be very aggressive. Notwithstanding John Donne's words at the head of this chapter, they are truly formidable animals. At the beginning of the nineteenth century they ranged widely over the whole country, dangers to be avoided by prudent men. Despite the dangers, the rewards of elephant hunting in the eighteen twenties persuaded several courageous men to go after them.

What was needed? The first and most vital piece of equipment was a suitable gun. There was no real choice of weapon. The only options were variations of the smooth-bore, flintlock muzzleloader such as the Brown Bess used by the British forces. These were either imported complete or manufactured by skilled gunsmiths in the colony, using imported barrels and other parts. Such guns came in various calibres: for elephant one obviously wanted the largest calibre possible. The monsters known as elephant guns were typically four-bore[254] weapons with fearsome barrels of length one and a half metres, bore greater than 1 inch (about 2.6 cm), and weighing about twenty pounds (9 kg). The ball used in them was a quarter of a pound (about 113 grams) in mass. Stubbs records that John Thackwray had such a weapon[255]

He [John Thackwray] had a gun that carried a quarter pound ball ...

The other equipment needed included (i) a container for gunpowder, invariably a powder horn, (ii) a ramrod, slightly longer than the gun barrel, (iii) a supply of balls of the right calibre, large enough to fill the barrel but able to move freely within it, (iv) spare flints and scraps of leather for clamping them on the hammer, (v) a supply of wads – pieces of cotton fabric (pillow ticking) big enough to wrap the ball, (vi) a measure for the powder required for a single discharge (if you had any sense you measured out small parcels of the right quantity before the hunt), and (vii) oil of some sort to keep the gun lubricated. The gunpowder was black powder, the classic mixture of charcoal, sulphur, and saltpetre (potassium nitrate), quite different from later smokeless powders. It was coarsely ground except for a small quantity that was ground finely for use as primer.

To load the gun one first ensured that it was empty (Feel with the ramrod. Do not look down the barrel!) and clean (Now you may look down the barrel). The butt was then placed on the ground and a measure of powder poured into the mouth. The elephant gun was long enough for this to be done while mounted on a horse (although hunting while mounted, as the boers did, was scorned by hunters such as Driver and Thackwray). A man on foot had to hold the gun at a slant when loading. A ball was then placed on a wad, rested on the mouth of the gun and forced gently down the barrel with the ramrod.

Next the flintlock, which was the heart of the gun, came into operation. It had a priming pan to contain fine black powder. The pan had a hinged lid to which was attached a contoured steel which controlled the opening of the lid. A sprung hammer was fitted with a clamp to hold a shaped piece of flint. The hammer was arranged so that when released by the trigger, the flint struck the steel and was dragged across it, so opening the lid of the pan and generating a spark to ignite the primer. This, in turn, ignited the powder in the barrel through a small hole. When the hammer was pulled back to the half cock position, a safety catch prevented the trigger from releasing it. In this position the lid of the pan could be opened for priming and snapped shut. To fire the gun the hammer was pulled back to the full cock position, releasing the safety catch. A release of the hammer by pulling the trigger initiated the firing process.

> When the musket was fired, the ball bounced down the sides of the bar-
> rel and out in the general direction in which it had been aimed; the
> smooth bore was an inaccurate weapon[256].

Even the most skilled hunter needed 20 to 30 seconds to reload. The kick
of the gun was enormous. The famous hunter, Selous, much later in the
century used such guns:

> I have never used or seen used a rifle which drove better than these
> common-made old muzzle loaders. ... they kicked most frightfully, and
> in my case the punishment I received from these guns has affected my
> nerves to such an extent as to have materially influenced my shooting
> ever since, and I am heartily sorry that I ever had anything to do with
> them.[257]

Imagine, then, the practical problems of stalking a herd of elephants, selecting those animals making the best targets, and organizing the firing
and reloading needed to bring down the quarry. At any time one might be
faced with a charge by an enraged and wounded animal. One needed a
trusted gunbearer standing by with a second weapon, a good horse, and
an oxwagon to bring home the spoils. Stubbs reports of Thackwray

> He had been known to shoot seven elephants out of one troop before
> they got away.

This is a nearly incredible feat given the tools available.

A Dangerous Occupation   [1823 – 1825]

What, then, would cause a man to choose hunting of elephant or other
big game as a career? First, obviously, would be the need for an income
and the availability of the quarry. After that comes the quality that some
would call *machismo* and others foolhardiness linked with undoubted
courage. These traits are characteristic of men who are still young enough
to believe in their own invulnerability. The hunters listed above in the passage quoted from Hockley's book[258] were all young men with the exception of Henry Stirraker, who was 40 on arrival at the Cape and possibly
the Hayhurst mentioned who may have been the father Richard (40 on arrival) but might have been the son, John, when he grew to adulthood. The
J. Stubbs listed would have been Thomas's brother not his father – John
Stubbs Senior was dead before there had been for him time to gain a
reputation as a hunter. Our two protagonists, Edward Driver and John
Thackwray, both fell squarely into the youthful category.

John Thackwray's trading activities had not been very successful. His
partner George Wood soon went his own way and eventually achieved
great financial success. John was not a good businessman. The early traveller Andrew Steedman recorded a conversation with him[259]:

He [John Thackwray] was an English settler, and made no secret of having been concerned in an illicit trade with the [Xhosa]s, previously to
the removal of restrictions, and the establishment of the fair at Fort
Wiltshire (sic). He recounted several instances of good faith observed
by the [Xhosa] Chiefs with whom he had dealt in transactions of this
nature. Having laid in a large stock of beads in order to carry on this
species of traffic, he became at last, in consequence of great depreci-
ation in their value, and through a combination of other unfortunate
circumstances, much involved in pecuniary difficulties; and was under
the necessity of having recourse to the dangerous pursuit of elephant
shooting, as the readiest means of extrication.

Edward Driver, on the other hand, after his experiences at the time of
the murder of John Stubbs, probably found elephant hunting no more
dangerous than trading and he pursued both activities, spending more
and more time in the bush in pursuit of ivory. He, too, was initially forced
into hunting by trading failures, although later in life he was a successful
trader. He and Thackwray were natural allies. Edward found John Thackwray a man after his own heart. He admired his courage:

I have heard Driver say that he [Thackwray] was the coolest man he
ever saw. On one occasion those two were returning home, and were
riding up the old road from Committees, passed [sic] the Spitz Kop:
Thackwray was in front, when they heard a noise in front - and after
Driver called directly out, "Look out for the Rhinoceros" and got out of
the road. But before Thackwray could turn his horse the beast caught
him and completely took the horse from under him leaving Thackwray
on his stern on the foot path. He said, "By the mortal man - I will have a
shot at him for that" and fired. He was obliged to walk home, as the
horse was so much injured[260].

Edward Driver was as courageous but not as reckless. It is perhaps
from his experience at the hands of Bill Sykes in the gunfight at Governor's Kop that Edward learnt to be "cautious like an astronaut"[261]. Being shot is likely to concentrate the mind. Throughout his life he frequently found himself in situations of great danger, yet from this time on
he seldom seems to have put himself needlessly in hazard or behaved
recklessly. Kelham Ned was transformed into Canny Edward. In this he
was quite different from John Thackwray whose temperament was better
illustrated by the imaginative description by Dugmore[262]:

... little John Thackwray, who engaged to write his own initials on the
haunches of an elephant and shoot it afterwards, and who died the victim of his own daring.

One thing seems consistent in descriptions of John Thackwray. Dugmore
speaks of "little John Thackwray." May Bell describes him as "slight and
good-tempered." Steedman remarks that he was "of low stature, a spare,
bony young man." Could it be that his small stature led to overcompensa-
tion by exaggerated feats of daring?

Brothers-in-Law   [1825]

John Thackwray was a member of a large and lively family: Edward
Driver was solitary with no family members nearer than Nottingham-
shire. They must have met quite soon after arriving in the Cape. Although
Driver was initially based at Clumber, he was soon farming at Governor's
Kop, and was a neighbour of the Thackwrays. John Thackwray would
have been a congenial acquaintance. However, soon it was not John that
Edward came to visit.

The Thackwray family included two young women. Dorothy, the elder, was twenty-one, maturing, destined for the career of a missionary's
wife in distant and inhospitable parts of Southern Africa. Ann, the
younger, was eighteen when she met Edward. She was the very good
reason for him to find excuses to visit the Thackwrays. By the beginning
of 1825 they were very close. By the second half of the year they were
faced with the need to tell Ann's parents that she was pregnant. They
were married on 6th Oct 1825 and their first daughter Anne was born five
months later. Edward seems to have been a welcome addition to the family. His transformation from young tearaway to family man was complete.
He appears to have joined the clan at Stoney Vale rather than remaining
at Clumber. He and his brother-in-law, John now became associates in
the endeavour to wrest a living from the unforgiving frontier territory.

Escapades and Adventures   [1825 – 1828]

Two early nineteenth century tourists, Andrew Steedman and Cowper
Rose, have each provided insight into the nature of elephant hunting on
the eastern Cape Frontier. Each spent an extended period in the eighteen
twenties touring the Cape Colony and its environs, each wrote a book on
his experiences[263], and most importantly each went on an elephant hunt.
Steedman engaged John Thackwray as guide and Rose engaged "Mr
D–." We have already noted and substantiated the identification[264] of Mr
D– as Edward Driver. Each author describes his own elephant hunt in de-
tail and in addition provides accounts of conversations with Driver or
Thackwray, as well as descriptions of their appearances and personalities.
The incidents described here are largely based on their descriptions.

Cowper Rose's impressions of Edward Driver on their first meeting
give a very good physical picture of the man and his equipment:

> ... a thin, spare, bony man, formed for activity, whose sun-scorched
> countenance and eye of habitual watchfulness bore that expression so
> frequently to be traced among poachers. His manner was bold and
> open, as one who felt that in such situations the petty distinctions of
> society ceased. His quick grey eye glanced from beneath the broad

brim of the boor's hat; his powder-horn hung from a black leathern
buckled shoulder-belt, to which his pouch was attached: he was mounted on an active, well-formed, small horse, and followed by nine dogs
of every variety of the cur and lurcher ...

On this occasion he was accompanied by "a little boy whom he was
training to his dangerous trade," and two Khoikhoi "shooters", one of
whom was called Skipper. One can speculate on the identity of the boy.
Edward's young brother-in-law Joseph Thackwray would have been about
thirteen years old at the time, older brother William (18) was too old to be
a "little boy" and James (10) was probably too young to carry an elephant
gun. The Thackwray boys were bold youngsters who had grown up on
the frontier and Edward had just become a member of the family. He
might well have taken a young brother-in-law with him.

Skipper was one of the many nearly undocumented characters that
gave colour to the society of the time. He was an independent, courageous, and feckless hunter of indeterminate age, colourfully dressed and
living in the present. Cowper Rose's description of him was so vivid that
it was quoted verbatim by Steedman when he, too, encountered him:

> Skipper was one of the boldest and most successful shooters in the
> country; but his gains, while they lasted, went only to keep the canteen
> in a roar, for he never could be persuaded to purchase cattle or acquire
> property. Methinks I see the extraordinary old man now before me,
> coolly shaking the ashes from the large pipe, while the elephants are
> feeding within a dozen yards of him: [265]

Such experienced mentors were invaluable to the young settlers who embarked on the life of an ivory hunter.

Andrew Steedman gives an equally vivid picture of John Thackwray:

> ... he evinced so much kindness of disposition, that the natives, to
> many of whom he had been previously known, welcomed him with a
> degree of cordiality and esteem highly creditable to each party. His un-
> assuming manners, his coolness in the moment of danger, far removed
> from all foolhardiness, created a favourable impression on his behalf.
> He was of low stature, a spare, bony young man, whose sun-burnt fea-
> tures gave him the expression that belongs to a wanderer over the
> mountains, whose life is a succession of perils.

An example of the hazards met by the hunters is a story told to Steedman by Thackwray[266]. Thackwray was on a hunting expedition with a
companion – probably his bearer. They came upon a herd of elephants.
Thackwray's practice was to stalk the herd from the downwind side and
get as close as possible to his quarry, thus minimizing the risk of missing
his target with the clumsy elephant gun. On this occasion the herd detec-
ted the pair of hunters and charged. Elephants give some warning of an
imminent charge: the ears are spread, the head is tossed, the trunk is ab-

ruptly unrolled and is used to toss grass and dust about. The animal trumpets. There may be a mock advance. It is as well to have such a warning as an elephant in full charge moves much faster than a man can run. On this occasion Thackwray and his companion decided to make themselves scarce but, to their alarm, found themselves on the edge of a steep krantz[267] with no escape route and an elephant threatening them at short range. Their only option was to go over the edge. Fortunately there was a ledge a few metres below them and they scrambled down to it. The elephant knelt down at the edge of the precipice and tried to reach them with its trunk. It was a perfect target but right above them so that shooting it would have placed them directly beneath a toppling elephant. Shooting birds from below is one thing – elephants quite another. They were forced to cower there until eventually the herd made off so that they could make their escape.

Rose also provides insight into the motivations of the hunters. Driver told him:

> I have a wife now, and shall have children, and have been driven to this [ivory hunting] by debt and necessity. I have nearly got over my difficulties, for in twenty months, I and my hottentots have killed eight hundred elephants; four hundred have fallen by this good gun; and when I am free, I quit it.[268]

This would place the account as being at the end of 1825 or beginning of 1826 – Edward married Ann Thackwray in October 1825 and his first child Anne was born in March 1826.

The description by Cowper Rose of his hunt in Driver's company gives a good idea of the dangers. Much of the time was spent in strenuous walking, trying to track down the prey. When a herd was located, Rose and young Joseph were provided with lighted brands and told to fire the grass and escape if there should be the danger of a charge. By the end of a long day Rose was exhausted. The remainder of the party was anxious to continue so Edward Driver detailed Joseph Thackwray aged thirteen (if the young boy was indeed he) to remain with him and protect him. They endured the night, and survived, despite a close encounter with a rhinoceros. Next day Joseph guided Rose back to the party. Driver had been concerned:

> "... your meeting with the rhinoceros might have been a very serious one; for it is the most savage beast in the country and fears nothing bu the elephant." He [Driver] asked us whether it had come towards us grunting, and rooting up the turf with his horn; and on my replying that, as far as I could tell, from the slight glimpse I caught of him, it was not so, and, that I only heard his heavy tramp, he said, "Then it could not have been seeing you, but had probably been frightened by the elephants crossing the ravine."

Compared to present day attitudes, the settlers were not over protective of their children.

The hunters' skill led them to great success in harvesting ivory, laid the basis of the fortunes of Edward Driver and his family, and contributed to the improving finances of the Thackwrays. For the next two years the pair continued to hunt ivory. The Thackwrays older daughter Dorothy was wooed by James Allison Jr, who had arrived with the settlers as an 18 year old and had now set himself up as a hatter in Grahamstown. Edward and Ann had their second child, a daughter Mary, in September 1827. William Thackwray's trading expeditions continued successfully. The family was beginning to prosper and life was improving.

Captains, Kings, and Unicorns   [1827]

In the middle of 1827 John Thackwray, filled with curiosity, confident in his bush expertise, and at home in his dealings with the Xhosa, undertook a pioneering expedition into Thembuland which, had it been described with the eloquence of a Cowper Rose or a John Barrow, would have excited the same interest as was shown in the works of those authors at the time. That we know anything of it is thanks to a correspondent of the journal *The Colonist* with the nom-de-plume "A Traveller." There is little doubt that this correspondent was, in fact, Andrew Steedman[269].

Thackwray's letter is dated "Graham's Town, Oct. 11, 1827," and begins, "I returned two months ago from an excursion in to the interior." It continues with a delightful account of this journey. Thackwray was the son of an artisan father and is unlikely to have had more than an elementary school education. Nevertheless, his prose, in its clarity, fluidity, and style, would put many modern school leavers to shame.

The composition of the party is not stated. He speaks of "we" in the letter but does not mention the name of any companions. In the later part of his letter he speaks of remote people "most of whom had never seen a white man before" seeming to suggest that he was the only such person in the party. It seems likely, therefore, that his only companions were one or two of the Khoi bearers, who usually accompanied him on hunting expeditions. They were mounted, since he writes of their horses, and would certainly have had an ox-wagon containing their baggage and supplies.

Apart from a spirit of inquiry, his objectives were threefold: hunting ivory, trade, and a quest to find a unicorn. This was by no means as quixotic as it sounds to a twenty-first century ear. Much of Africa was still *terra incognita*. Explorers returned from their travels with tales of strange creatures. There were rumours of anthropoid apes in the central African forest. The first specimens of gorillas only became available to western science twenty years later, in 1847. As late as 1860 David Livingstone was convinced of the likelihood of unicorns in the African interior. John Barrow, a naturalist of good credentials, had devoted several pages in his widely read and serious account of his travels to attempts to find such an animal[270]. He described witness's accounts of sightings, some from trekboers, others from San. He was shown a San rock painting from which he produced a drawing that he called a facsimile. It is far from such, being closer to the unicorn in a mediæval tapestry than any San rock art ever seen. He wrote:

> The unicorn, as it is represented in Europe, is unquestionably a work of fancy; but it does not follow from thence that a quadruped with one horn, growing out of the middle of the forehead, should not exist. The arguments, indeed, that might be offered are much stronger for its existence than are against it.

The hunting fraternity was captivated by the unicorn. Two years earlier George Rennie of Pringle's party applied for a licence to search for the unicorn[271].

> ... As I am informed that a number of curious animals are to be found beyond the Orange River (amongst which the unicorn is said to be) will you have the goodness to permit Diedrich Muller, Christian Muller and myself to travel for a few months in that quarter.

Many other authors of the time were convinced of the likelihood of the existence of unicorns. A hunter of ivory, intending to make a journey into the unknown interior, could dream of the enormous profits to be made by the hunter who brought home the first specimen.

John Thackwray started his adventure by travelling north, only turning eastwards when he could travel directly from the Cape into what he thought of as Tambookieland – the country of the abaThembu. He crossed the Black Kei River near the site of present-day Queenstown. He was all set to visit the kings, and the clan chiefs and headmen, or captains as he called them. At the beginning of his letter, with the bizarre spelling typical of the time before Xhosa was a written language, he lists the great kings:

> I visited the principal chiefs in Tembooka land, who are very numerous; but the most powerful are Vosany, the King of the Mahaala tribe; Foubow King of the Macquaties, and Galeyka, King of the Machadula tribe.

These can be identified as follows[272]:–

The royal clan of the abaThembu were the amaHala and this is essentially synomomous with the abaThembu. Their king at the time was

Ngubencuka Vusani[273], usually known as Ngubencuka. Fubu was king of the amaQwathi.

Galeyka is more difficult to identify[274]. There is no tribe that can be identified with the Machadula. It is likely, however that this was Galeka, also known as Magadule, a son of the right hand house of Gambushe's son Ntchunga. Gambushe was chief of the amaBomvana. His daughter was Hintsa's Great Wife and the amaBomvana, while vassals of Hintsa, were a powerful unit in the region. Gambushe died in about 1826[275]. The king at the time would have been Ntchunga, Gambushe's Great Son, who might well have been a minor at the time. Galeka's position would normally have been that of an influential councillor but we can speculate that it would have been normal for him to be serving as regent if the king was a minor. This would be consistent with Thackwray's identification of him as on a par with Ngubencuka and Fubu.

As John Thackwray moved into Thembuland the ravages of the *mfecane* became apparent. The first people that he encountered were the amaTshatshu, a dispossessed Thembu subgroup, under the leadership of a surly and demoralised headman called Bawana. They had fled from an onslaught by a roving band of marauders, identified by Thackwray as "Feycanie" – in fact they were amaBhaca – under a chief "Matekan" (Madikane). Madikane had driven them westward from their homelands to an area near present-day Whittlesea south of Queenstown[276]. There they had sought refuge and Maqoma had allowed them to settle. Bhurhu, brother of the Xhosa king Hintsa, had seized the opportunity to occupy the vacated territory. This visit, the start of Thackwray's encounter with the Thembu, was not a success. He found Bawana to be "a cowardly wretch and a sad thief besides." This opinion was occasioned by the fact that a number of buttons, valuable trade goods, had been stolen from him during his stay. He also claimed to have been swindled out of five cattle. He left Bawana's kraal without regret.

The next stop that he planned was at a place that had excited his interest. He had heard of the existence of a female Thembu chief called Nojungo. This was sufficiently unusual to deserve a special visit. When the party arrived, however, the site was abandoned and destroyed. Thackwray attributes this to a disastrous flood. This seems unlikely. Unlike the settlers all the Nguni people of southern Africa were well aware of the dangers of building in apparently dry areas that were subject to the occasional but enormous flash floods that occur on the flood plains after heavy rains. Traditionally dwellings are built at the top of hills, even though this means long walks for women and children carrying water containers balanced on their heads from the small streams in the valleys

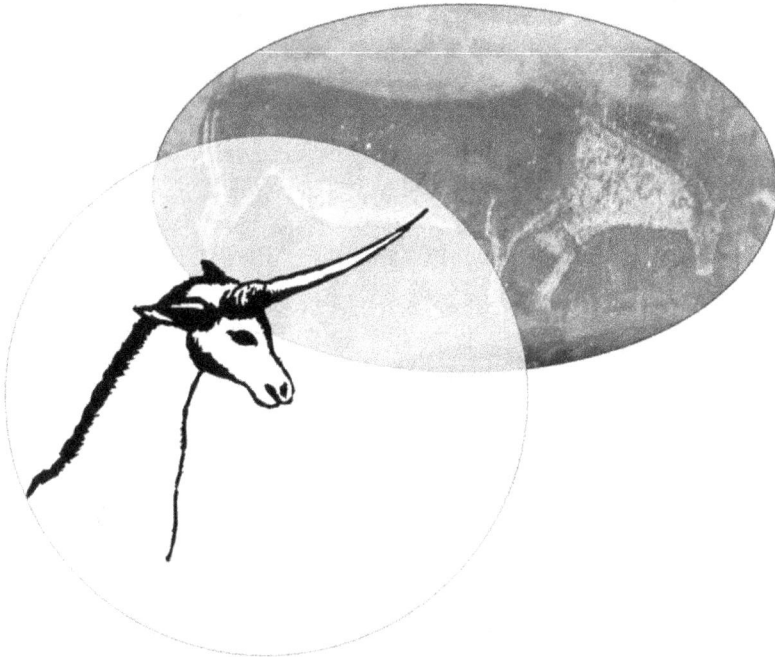

Barrow's drawing of a unicorn compared with a photograph of an actual San rock painting of an eland.
[Drawing from Barrow [1806] in the public domain. Photograph by the author]

to the homesteads at the summits of the hills. This practice is reinforced by fear of the tikoloshe or tokoloshe – evil water sprites of Nguni folklore that lurk in the night, causing havoc, and hoping to rape the women with their enormously long penises. It is hard to believe in habitations destroyed by flood. It is more likely that Nojungo's people had also been driven out as a consequence of the *mfecane*.

From these scenes of desolation the little party trekked on towards the abandoned lands of the amaTshatshu. There they arrived at the Great Place of Bhurhu who had extended the range of the amaGcaleka by occupying the Bawana's territory on the "N'Eber" or Kei River[277]. Here they found an illustrious visitor. Hintsa, King of the Xhosa nation, was visiting his brother. At that time he was thirty-nine years old and at the height of his powers. Thackwray found him impressive. Both Hintsa and John Thackwray would have been anxious to take advantage of the meeting to gain information and intelligence. Unfortunately Thackwray does not record the details of their conversation. He merely reports

> He seems a very superior man for a savage – very inquisitive, and seems partial to the English.

After this encounter with Xhosa royalty Thackwray set off towards the Mbashe River where the great place of Ngubencuka, king of the aba-Thembu, was located. He was "reckoned the most powerful chief in Tembookaland." On the way he stopped at the kraal of one of his vassals,

> ... Quainqway [unidentified], a Tembooka captain under Vosany; though he resides perhaps more than 50 miles from Vosany's Kraal, which is on the river Bashee [Mbashe].

Here he received a warm welcome that greatly impressed him:

> The kindness, which was shown to me by this old captain, could not have been exceeded by any civilized person whatever. He told me his cattle had been stolen by the Feycanies. I left his place much gratified by his behaviour...

He showed his gratitude with a gift a fifteen buttons, a generous amount in the trade currency of the time.

He was now approaching the heart of the Thembu kingdom. Ngubengcuka's Great Place was near Clarkebury on the Mbashe river. He was in the direct line of descent from Hala. His Great Wife was the daughter of Faku, the Mpondo king. He was still youthful, about 30, although he was to die only two years later. When they met, Thackwray was impressed:

> He is quite a hero among the Tembookas and I think he is the greatest warrior I have met with. He is a man of few words but his conduct seems regulated in a great measure by honourable principles. His appearance is rather forbidding at first; but that impression soon wears off. He told me he was at war with the Macquaties [amaQwathi], and his great men seemed to expatiate largely on the injuries they had received.

The next port of call was the great place of Tyopo, chief of the amaGcina. Tyopo's father Phato (not Phatho, the Gqunukwhebe chief) had taken as his great wife the daughter of a San chief. Their son Tyopo showed this by the fact that he spoke the San language fluently[278]. Thackwray described him as "a very amiable mild young man." The exact route followed by the expedition is uncertain. Twenty years later Tyopo's lands were near the present site of Queenstown, not far from where Thackwray had crossed the Black Kei to enter Thembuland. At this stage of the journey Thackwray had left this region far behind. He was somewhere between the Mbashe and Mthatha (Umtata) Rivers, and this must have been where Tyopo was located in 1827. Wars were raging and there was great mobility as the fortunes of the participants fluctuated.

> He was once able to fight with Vosany; but his power is much reduced by his wars, and he is now under Vosany.

By now he was deep enough into unknown territory to begin his enquiries into the existence of unicorns. He began to question people he saw about whether they had ever seen an animal about the size of a springbok but with a single horn in the middle of its forehead. There was a woman at Tyopo's Place who came from a different part of the country. She told him that she had often heard of such animals in her home country.

He continued to explore Tyopo's country, finding that the deeper he penetrated the more populous it became. Standing on top of a hill he was able to count more than forty settlements, each associated with large extended families. But the country was badly ravaged by the *mfecane*. He visited many of Tyopo's captains or headmen all of whom had suffered heavy losses. It would have been easy to yield to the temptation to use his firepower to become a mercenary:

> One captain of the name of Umpolwain [Unidentified: the name may be Mpolweni], wished me to persuade ten or twelve Englishmen to come with guns to assist him to go to war with another captain, and if we were successful we should divide the cattle we took.

This was not Thackwray's ambition. Other traders of the time, however, particularly members of the group of English adventurers in Natal, were already enthusiastically contributing to the havoc in the more distant lands of the Mpondo and Mpondomise people.

In Tyopo's country he also met the Rain-maker. This was a man who was believed to be able to make rain by magic in time of drought:

> This man was of great service to me. I found that he had great influence over the minds of the people, not one of whom could have sold a single head of cattle without his permission. I gave way to his advice in every thing, and made him several presents: in return he persuaded the people to exchange their cattle with me for beads, buttons &c. to a good amount.

By now Thackwray's entourage was enlarged to include the herd of cattle that he had been building up by trade. He took this caravan with him on to the territory of the amaQwathi:

> I next went among the Macquaty tribe to Mongongo [unidentified], Foubow [Fubu], Maposa [Maphasa, son of Bawana] and many other captains, most of whom had never seen a white man before. But I found, that the further I went the greater was their awe of the English, which secured me always civil treatment.

He did not forget to maintain his pursuit of the fabled unicorn:

> I often made enquiries respecting the Unicorn. At Mongongo's, in the Macquaty country, I found two men who said that they had seen many of them, and gave a very feasible account of the animal. They said the

country where they were found was about two months journey from the place where I then was.

On then to the Mthatha River, to the land of Galeka Magadule:

He was much surprized to see a white man on horseback, as he had never before seen a white man, or a horse. He seemed a good sort of man, and brought me plenty of brandy to drink, which they make from corn at this place.

This is not likely to be any sort of distilled drink but *tywala*, the mildly alcoholic beer made from sorghum millet, served ritually at celebrations. It was here than Thackwray heard news of Henry Francis Fynn who had been on an expedition from Natal into nearby Pondoland. Two abaMbo men told him that they had seen Fynn at "Mampondo's kraal," in other words at Faku's Great Place[279]. Here Faku, the king of the amaMpondo, had given him five tusks of ivory. This was the second time that a Thackwray had just missed linking up with Fynn. In 1825 Fynn had been in Pondoland and had just failed to encounter John's father, William, who was in the region. Fynn wrote in his journal[280]:

... whilst on one of the excursions I made from there to the Umzimvubu River, I heard of a European who passed among the natives under the name of Calamaish ... He afterwards proved to be a Mr Thackwray, a [Xhosa] trader.

After months of wandering through unknown parts of the country John Thackwray began his return journey. He first cut down to the coast and then made inland for Vusani's Great Place "through a country they call Hentooly[281]". He then more or less retraced his path home, his caravan much augmented by cattle and the other products of successful trade, but without a unicorn. John Thackwray was now not only a notable elephant hunter, but also an explorer, and, at last, had begun to be successful in trade. The leaders he had met were all to meet their own fates. We shall encounter Hintsa, Bhurhu, and Tyopo again. Galeka Magadule was to meet ultimate defeat at the hands of Faku and Mweli, his head hacked off and his skull used by the amaMpondomise as a container to mix charms[282].

John Thackwray returned to the welcome of his family with the right to feel that he had begun to make a success of his life. He too had no idea of what was to come.

Death in the Ecca Forest   [1828]

Thursday the 28th of February 1828 was a quiet, late-summer's day at a Mission north east of Graham's Town on the road from Herman's Kraal[283]. The Rev. John Ayliff, newly elevated from the laity, was visiting the station and was about his mid-week business. Ayliff was one of the several Wesleyans who had risen from being lay preachers. His journal[284] gives a clear picture of the opinions and prejudices of the missionaries of the day, particularly those who came from the ranks of the settlers themselves.

In the distance, from the direction of the Great Fish River, a small procession appeared. Two ox-wagons with attendant voorlopers and drivers were making their way slowly up the long slope towards Graham's Town. Ayliff made his way down to meet them. The driver in charge of the wagon train was distressed. He told Ayliff that in one wagon was the body of his employer, John Thackwray, who had been killed the previous day by an elephant while hunting[285].

On Wednesday 27th John Thackwray had visited the house of his friend George Wood. George was recently married; he and his young wife, Susan, had set up house at Herman's Kraal, where their increasing prosperity had allowed them to establish a trading station[286]. George was not at home but Susan entertained him to a meal while his Khoikhoi bearer was scouting for elephants. Eventually the bearer arrived with a report of a large herd of elephants in the nearby Ecca Forest. John could wait no longer and set off on the hunt leaving George a cheerful message.

John's massive four-bore elephant gun was out of order so he had left it in Graham's Town for repair[287] and was using a borrowed and unfamiliar weapon. The two men had encountered a herd of elephants and John had picked out a large bull elephant as his target. His shot felled, and apparently killed it. They were watching the remainder of the herd when the elephant that they had thought dead rose and charged. The Khoikhoi bearer was knocked over but escaped by ducking under the elephant's body. John scrambled frantically to reload but the unfamiliar gun misfired and the elephant seized him with his trunk and carried him off. The Khoikhoi gun-bearer remembered nothing more and had been found at the side of the Fort Beaufort Road in a semiconscious state. When John's body had been tracked down it was almost naked and terribly injured. His leg and shoulder were broken and his thigh had been pierced by a tusk. He was terribly bruised round the waist where he had been crushed by the elephant's trunk[288]. The body was brought back to the Woods' house and lay there for the night until it could be transported to Graham's Town the next day.

The news was a dreadful blow to the family. Ayliff visited them and reported:

I feel very much for the parents for they have had to contend with great difficulty since they came into this country and it was only on Monday

that the father was saying to me that his trials had been greatly multiplied and his case was something like Job's. Little did he then think of
this great trial, that it was so near him.

I visited the family this afternoon and found them in the greatest possible
distress. The poor old gentleman seemed quite borne down with the
greatness of the trial. For my own part I do not know that I have ever
[seen] such distress in a family. He being the eldest son, & much beloved
by all the family, [his death] was deeply deplored. It was literally a house
of weeping.

Later Andrew Steedman wrote[289]:

Few will read his brief and mournful history without regretting that experience so valuable, courage so undaunted, and fortitude so enduring,
had not been made subservient to higher aims than merely seeking a
scanty provision for the supply of his daily wants, and that his end
should have been so untimely and distressing.

Forty years later Stubbs remembered:

Thus ended one of the bravest elephant hunters in those days.

The Rev. John Ayliff's comment at the time was a pusillanimous:

This will, perhaps, prove a warning to these elephant hunters not to be
too venturesome. ... May the Lord sanctify this affliction to the eternal
good of those that are left behind.

The epigram by Dugmore quoted earlier, suggesting that John Thackwray had wagered that he could write his initials on an elephant's
haunches before shooting it and was thus killed, while perhaps in accord
with the temperament and spirit of John Thackwray, is neither plausible
nor consistent with the contemporary account. He might at some time
have made bets similar to Dugmore's story but it is very unlikely that,
with only his bearer for witness, he would have tried to meet with the
terms of such a bet on this occasion.

John's death was the first of the tragedies that were to strike the Thackwray family. There was worse to come.

Chapter 10. Sorrows of a Settler Family

The nameless men who nameless rivers travel,
And in strange valleys greet strange deaths alone,
The grim intrepid ones ...

Robert W. Service, To the Man of the High North

Carrying On   [1828 - 1829]

Life went on. John's death must have been a significant blow to the Thackwray family finances with the loss of income from his ivory hunting. William and Dorothy may have found some comfort from the birth of another grandchild – Hannah Driver was born on 10 Jun 1829.

William Thackwray and Edward Driver continued with their extensive trading and hunting activities. By this time they had acquired a large fund of local knowledge. A contemporary newspaper correspondent states[290]:

> ... he [William] had latterly been familiar to misfortune; and it was to re-pair his shattered circumstances that he thus became the object of chance – to forgo the comforts of home for a novel and adventurous uncertainty – and thus after repeated journeys during which he had travelled almost every country between Lattakoo [Dithakong in what is now North West Province] and the Indian Ocean, ...

Many of the expeditions were across the Fish and Kei Rivers and up as far as Faku's Mpondo kingdom on the Umzimvubu, which he had first visited in 1825. Early in 1829 he set off on another such journey.

The Outlaw   [1795 – 1829]

Jan Nicholaas (Klaas) Lochenberg was a large swaggering Boer renegade – one of those who had left the colony with Coenrad de Buys at the time of the Graaff Reinet rebellion in the seventeen nineties. These rebel Boers, with bands of followers, at first ranged through what are now the Free State and North West Provinces, living as bandits, looting and pilla-ging to build their fortunes[291]. These regions were the badlands of the time, subject to no law, occupied by shifting bands of refugees such as the so-called Bastards, the issue of fugitive Khoi, runaway slaves, and reneg-ade Boers.

By 1799 Lochenberg was living on the Wild Coast of the Transkei, married to his second wife Sarah, a Khoi woman, and to several other Khoi wives. He traded in ivory and supplemented his income by gun-run-ning. Over the years his family and followers grew in number, sometimes serving as a mercenaries to various chiefs in the frequent warfare of the region. By the eighteen twenties he was established at Mazeppa Bay, an idyllic spot on the Wild Coast.

Lochenberg had acted as a translator for Shrewsbury, the Wesleyan missionary who set up the Butterworth Mission, and as an advocate for Mdepa[292], chief of the Tshomane clan, in persuading the Wesleyans to establish a mission in his territory which he hoped would provide some protection against the ravages of Shaka's Zulu invaders of Pondoland. Passing traders and hunters would obviously make contact with him to keep informed of the latest news and make use of his extensive local knowledge. Indirectly Lochenberg was to be one of the triggers that set off the events of Thackwray's last journey. In the meantime they encountered each other whenever Thackwray was in the neighbourhood.

The Wreck of the *Éole*   [1829]

By April 1829 William Thackwray, still devastated by the death of his son John, was trading in the neighbourhood of Lochenberg's Place[293].

Off the coast, a three hundred ton French ship *L'Éole* was in serious trouble. Bound for Bordeaux from Calcutta she had encountered some of the foul weather for which the region is notorious. The ship was struggling in heavy seas with no visibility. For three days the crew had no idea of where they were until, on April 12th, they ran aground on the rocky coast near the mouth of the Mbashe River.

The Wild Coast is aptly named. Forbidding cliffs flank seemingly peaceful beaches. Rivers emerge from deep gorges into wide river mouths. In times of drought these may form closed lagoons but in times of flood they open into raging torrents that carry the topsoil washed from the interior miles out to sea in muddy stains. The rocky outcrops that stretch into the sea on either side of the beaches are razor-sharp and covered with abrasive barnacles. Strong cross currents can drag swimmers away from beaches. The Indian Ocean breakers roll in and crash on the rocks with huge force and then rush back over the rocks dragging objects in their path into the ocean.

Of the fifteen crew members and five passengers on board *L'Éole*, only eight struggled ashore, battered and abraded. The only other survivor of the wreck was a small dog called Zizi. Three bodies were washed ashore. The remaining nine passengers and crew were lost. The first people that the exhausted survivors encountered were a group of Xhosa. This was a terrifying encounter for them. Precipitated onto the shores of Africa, unable to defend themselves, entirely ignorant of the nature of the land in which they found themselves, these Europeans were faced by a near naked group of people that they perceived as savages. They spoke only French: the Xhosas spoke only their own language. Normal Xhosa conversation is frequently carried on in a loud voice. It is impolite for a conversation to be inaudible to others present. This might well have sounded threatening to traumatized shipwreck victims who were not in good physical condition and their interpretation of it was recorded by Shrewsbury[294]:

> Here they found themselves amongst a race of savages but knew not who they were. Some of the [Xhosa]s were for putting them to death, but others, supposing them to be Englishmen, and that the colonists would revenge their death, opposed it; merciful counsels prevailed, and they were saved alive and withal treated with a degree of kindness.

The exact sequence of events is confused. On the one hand this description of the attitude of the Xhosa to the castaways is attributed to Thackwray, on the other Thackwray is only supposed to have seen them the next day after they had been found by Lochenberg[295]:

> The shipwreck survivors were first discovered by Nicholas Lochenberg, who asked the trader William Thackwray to convey them to Lochenerg's abode.

Only Thackwray or Lochenberg could have translated the tenor of the Xhosa conversation and, if either or both of them had been present they would surely have been participants in the discussion. The castaways could not have followed and understood any argument about their fate and this makes Shrewsbury's account implausible. One might speculate that, given Xhosa traditions of hospitality, the conversation was more likely to be along the lines of: "What on Earth are we to do about these people? Well! Old Lochenberg's in the neighbourhood. Let's pass them on to him." In any event the survivors reported that Thackwray "treated them with great kindness"

> ... to his [Thackwray's] active benevolence the survivors from the wreck of the French ship Eoli, owed, under Providence, their delivery from the cruel death ...[296]

He helped bury the bodies of the three victims who had been washed ashore, and guided them to the mission station at Butterworth about 65 km away. where Shrewsbury welcomed them. Shrewsbury sent them off with a guide to take them to Graham's Town. On the way, near Mount Coke Mission, they met with a wagon train that included Henry Francis Fynn, Andrew Geddes Bain and John Burnett Biddulph who were on an expedition making for Pondoland[297]. The traders fed them and gave them further directions. The survivors of the wreck, in gratitude for what Bain described as common hospitality, presented Zizi to Biddulph and the final image of the resilient little dog is of it trotting off beside the wagons of the Bain expedition towards Pondoland.

Having delivered his charges to the Butterworth Mission, William Thackwray completed his business in the region and returned to Graham's Town.

The Traders of Natal   [1824 – 1829]

Lt Francis Farewell, RN (rtd)[298] was a prominent figure in early Natal history. After a distinguished spell in the Navy he was retired on half pay and after some time in India as a ship owner set out to make his fortune in Africa. He set up a consortium of maritime merchants to support him in opening up trade on the east coast of South Africa in what is now the province of KwaZulu-Natal and persuaded Lord Charles Somerset to grant permission for his trading activities[299]. He rapidly established a reputation as a swashbuckling adventurer. His associates included Henry Francis Fynn, Nathaniel Isaacs, and John Cane, all daring adventurers with dubious ethical standards. By the middle eighteen twenties Farewell had set up relations with Shaka, the Zulu King, and had notionally had a large grant of land from him. He built and occupied Fort Farewell at Port Natal, near the centre of the future city of Durban. Farewell Square in front of the City Hall is named after him.

Farewell was energetic, ambitious, and had an eye for the main chance. A major objective was to bring Natal under the control of the British crown and to this end he was unscrupulous in his reports to the Colonial authorities of conditions in the region. Another ambition was to open a trade route between the distant Cape Colony and Port Natal. His associate Henry Francis Fynn was a regular trader with Zulu and Xhosa.

Trade was not the only occupation of Fynn and his associates. It is quite likely that they also on occasion acted as mercenaries for Shaka in the Zulu raids carried out against the Mpondo and other peoples to the south east. Fynn was by now established in a stronghold on the Umzimkulu River where he maintained his private army.

The Flight of the amaQwabe   [1828 – 1829]

The reign of Shaka came to an end in September 1828 with his assassination by his half-brothers Dingane and Mhlangane and the assumption of power by Dingane. Shaka's capital, Buluwayo, was in the territory of the amaQwabe and Nqeto, Chief of this Clan, was Shaka's close ally. Nqeto was not prepared to accept the authority of the new King and he and his clan were driven out of their territory, retreating south west into Pondoland. They made their way as far as the Umzimvubu River. By the second half of 1829 they had reached the edge of Faku's territory, not very far from his Great Place. There they asked Faku for permission to settle.

To Faku their presence was not just an irritant but a very real threat. Endless Zulu raids over the previous five years had tested his patience to the limit. Not only did he refuse Nqeto's request: he was determined to drive him out of the region. He decided to get a little help from his friends. Klaas Lochenberg was available with a small private army. Lochenberg took on the job, no doubt encouraged by the prospect of rich pickings of cattle.

Lochenberg's son[300], years later, maintained that his father had had premonitions of his death for several days before the battle. Whether one believes this or not, the battle was a disaster. Nqeto allowed Lochenberg and his Khoi mercenaries, supported by an Mpondo force, to approach ever closer. Nqeto was injured in the leg by a shot from the attackers. The amaQwabe warriors waited until Lochenberg's men were close enough for hand-to-hand combat and, when they dismounted to reload, overwhelmed them with the short Zulu stabbing assegais. Lochenberg was killed, the attacking forces routed and the amaQwabe launched on a bloody campaign of plunder and pillage through Pondoland.

The Last Expedition   [Aug – Oct 1829]

At this time Francis Farewell was pursuing his ambition to open a trade route from Graham's Town to Port Natal. In August 1829 he sailed from Port Natal to Algoa Bay and set about making a splash in Graham's Town society while he organized an expedition. Thomas Philipps had his measure. He wrote in a letter dated 25th August 1829:

> I have lately seen a good deal of the celebrated Lt. Farewell, the Sir Gregor McGregor of Port Natal as I have named him. He is an enterpris-ing man, but so fond of society as he is, it is surprising he should like to lead the life he has hitherto done ...

"Sir" Gregor McGregor[301] (the knighthood was his own invention) was an adventurer and confidence trickster of the time who had left the British army and joined Simon Bolivar in South America. Among other adventures he annexed part of Spanish Florida with his private army in order to gain it for the United States and almost succeeded. Later he declared himself ruler of a fictitious territory in South America and returned to Britain inviting investment in his new country and duping many investors. His exploits had been the talk of the Empire at the beginning of the eighteen twenties and Philipps clearly recognized similar characteristics in Farewell.

Farewell's purpose in visiting Graham's Town was to employ a team to take his wagon train on an expedition to open up the route to Port Natal. William Thackwray was clearly his man:

> When Lieut. Farewell, of Natal fame in its very early history, went from Durban to Port Elizabeth by sea, and then took a train of wagons overland through the Transkei to Natal, he asked William Thackwray, father-in-law of Edward Driver, to accompany him owing to the great knowledge of the then unknown territories which William Thackwray possessed[302].

Farewell planned to send the wagon train ahead while he spent time with his wife and family in Uitenhage and then follow on horseback. He had set up a relationship with the authorities and on the journey provided several reports to Duncan Campbell, the Graham's Town Civil Commissioner[303].

Thomas Philipps's description of Farewell's visit to Graham's Town continues:

> He [Farewell] has just dispatched a person with about 20 hottentots with a waggon, pack bullocks etc overland. He intends to follow in a few weeks, leaving his wife and family for the present in Uitenhage.'

The 'person' was William. Edward Driver was with the party. According to a later statement he made[304], he had "left the colony in August with Mr Farewell's property." Other members of the expedition were William Walker, a young English naturalist who had accompanied Andrew Steedman to the Cape[305], Henry Foulds, a settler who had been in the same party on the *Albury* as Driver, and three companions called Whittle, Howard and Painter. Walker's objective on the expedition was not trade but exploration and scientific study of the flora and fauna found on the way. He had expressed a desire to his mentor, Andrew Steedman, to follow in the footsteps of Mungo Park. Foulds and Driver were cooperating in elephant hunting and ivory trading.

Some of the others may have been independent traders with their own wagons. Farewell's wagon was loaded with goods of several kinds. Cane[306] mentions '5000lb of beads.' He significantly fails to mention explicitly muskets and a large supply of ammunition[307]. This was either intended for trade with Dingane or possibly to supply Henry Fynn.

By 1829 the route was quite well established. It is likely to have been similar to that followed earlier in the year by the well-documented expedition of Andrew Geddes Bain and John Burnet Biddulph[308]. It started off along the road from Graham's Town, past Stoney Vale and the Clay Pits to Trompetter's Drift on the Great Fish River. From there it wound from mission station to drift[309] to mission station. The route across the major rivers – the Keiskamma, the Buffalo (Qonce), the Kei, and the Mbashe – all involved dangerous paths down the sides of the great gorges through the drifts, and up the other sides. Near the Colony the missions, Wesleyville and Mount Coke provided resting places. The advance of Wesleyan missions into the interior was proceeding apace, bringing not only the word of God but also the gospel of the British Empire, and acting as a source of intelligence for the colonial government. Butterworth near Hintsa's Great Place had been in existence for some years. Morley on the far side of the Mthatha (Umtata) River had only recently been established.

Farewell set off on horseback after his party early in September. On the 17th near the Mbashe River he was surprised to encounter his associate John Cane, on a mission from Zululand. Cane brought the news that Dingane had been confirmed as the Zulu king and had appointed Cane as an emissary to the Governor or even, perhaps, to King George. He had sent a gift of ivory to accompany his good wishes. Cane also warned Farewell that Fynn was taking advantage of his absence to damage his interests. He did not see much advantage to himself in continuing with Dingane's errand and decided that it would be better to forget his responsibilities to Dingane and join Farewell's expedition. The next day the two arrived at Butterworth where they discharged Dingane's commission by persuading Shrewsbury, the resident missionary, to take charge of the tusk and to send it and Dingane's greetings to Campbell in Graham's Town with covering letters.

After resting at Butterworth the two began the journey to Pondoland. They reached Morley on the 24th September. The missionary, J. William Shepstone welcomed them with the news of Lochenberg's death and the subsequent ravages of Nqeto's amaQwabe warriors. Farewell knew Nqeto well from his time at Shaka's court and trusted him. He wrote a report on the situation to Campbell and undertook to negotiate with Nqeto to persuade him "to live peaceably." Those in the Mission tried to dissuade him from this dangerous path but without success.

They rested their horses for a few days and then left for Faku's Great Place on the Mzimvubu. By the time they reached it they were reunited with William Thackwray and the wagon train. They all made camp at Faku's place. Apart from their engagement in trade Farewell was probably after intelligence which he could have used both to make his case as a responsible citizen to the Colonial government and to increase his credit in future negotiations with Dingane.

Farewell sent word to Nqeto that he would like to meet him. In due course a messenger arrived inviting Farewell to visit him. Faku was suspicious of Nqeto's motives and strongly advised against the visit[310]. Family tradition[311] suggests that Edward Driver also advised against it. Farewell was dismissive of the warnings. He was confident that his old acquaintance, Nqeto, would not cause him harm. He asked Thackwray to accompany him and William Walker, eager for new experiences also agreed to join the group. The party, accompanied by a Xhosa (or possibly Khoikhoi) interpreter called Lynx, and several servants, set off on 10th October[312] for Nqeto's place. The other members remained with the wagons, camped a few kilometres from Nqeto's place. Edward Driver, after delivering his warning, set off elephant hunting. His intention was to rejoin the expedition somewhere along the route between the Mzimkulu and Mzimvubu Rivers.

Nqeto greeted Farewell and his party with ceremony. A cow was slaughtered and a feast took place. Lynx and the servants were very uneasy. There is a possibility that one of them was indeed a spy for Dingane, and that he was fearful of being recognized. Soga notes[313]

> Nqeto was a fugitive, and a desperado determined to preserve his life. Now what was Farewell's object in going there, for one of Dingane's spies accompamied him and was furnished on his way to Nqeto with a greatcoat to conceal his identity? But Nqeto was not deceived and recognized him. It was natural, therefore, for Nqeto to think that this conduct of Farewell's proclaimed him to be a spy of Dingane's, and equally to be anxious to secure his destruction.

Thackwray and Walker also began to feel the tension as the tone of the evening changed. Nqeto showed the wound he had sustained in the battle with Lochenberg and began to mock his guests, parading the horses that he had won from Lochenberg while boasting of his victory. Farewell throughout remained determinedly sanguine while the other members of the party became more and more alarmed.

At last the festivities ended and Farewell, Thackwray, and Walker retired to their tent. Lynx and the servants were assigned to a nearby hut. What followed depends on Lynx's account[314].

At midnight, when all was quiet, a group of armed Qwabe warriors emerged from the shadows. The moon was almost full[315] and the scene was well illuminated. At a signal the guy ropes of the tent were slashed. The first and last things that the occupants knew was the collapse of the canvas onto them and the multiple thrusts of short Zulu stabbing assegais. Lynx and the servants were woken by cries for help and anguished calls of "Oh my God!" They fearfully looked out and saw Thackwray and Walker lying dead on the ground and the body of Farewell surrounded by the assailants. It was not clear whether he was already dead or whether they were trying to rob him and for some time afterwards there was fruitless speculation about whether he might have survived. The warriors then turned on the hut. Lynx tried to rouse the servants to defend themselves but most were frozen with terror and unable to respond. He took up his gun, shot his way to freedom and, with two other fugitives brought the news to Cane's wagon camp.

The situation was alarming. Cane and his companions fled and hid. When they returned the wagons had been looted. On October 12th Cane wrote from the place where he was hiding to Shepstone at Morley:

'... three natives escaped and gave us the intelligence. I intended to stand and protect what property we could take in the wagon, but was basely deserted by all the people. I returned in the evening to the wagon, such a destruction, I suppose was never seen in [Xhosa]land; they had taken about 5000lb of beads, every article of clothing, and what else could be of service to them. ... Messrs Whittle, Howard, Fowles [Foulds], Painter and self, remained to the last moment, and escaped in the night to the Onsomvoobo [Mzimvubu] where we now remain in a very critical situation. Some doubts remain as to the safety of Mr. Driver's party, who have not been heard of since this day week. ...'

The amaQwabe continued to rage through Pondoland. Edward Driver was still missing and there were serious fears that he, too, had been killed. Cane managed to make his way to Morley and word was sent to Uitenhage and Graham's Town. The mission station, threatened with attack, was abandoned and the refugees set off towards Butterworth.

Misfortunes Come in Threes   [Oct 1829 – May 1830]

The news of William's death came as a terrible shock to the settler community. To Dorothy Thackwray and her family, little more than a year after John's death, it was devastating. Young Dorothy and her husband James Allison lived in Graham's Town where James had his hatter's shop. In the absence of Edward, Ann Driver and her children were with her mother, as were young William, Joseph and James. Ann faced not only the loss of her father but also the fears for her husband of whom there was no news. Worse was to come.

Young William was just twenty-one years old, feeling his oats, and already gaining a reputation as a philanderer. Just two days after the news had arrived, on about the 27th or 28th of October, he was at the home of his elder sister, Dorothy. Her husband James Allison does not appear to have been at home. According to some accounts they heard a disturbance outside the house, originating with a group of Khoikhoi. William went outside to remonstrate with them. There was an altercation, a flurry, and the group scattered and fled, leaving William writhing on the ground. He had been stabbed in the abdomen.

In 1829 such a wound was inevitably fatal. Perforation of the intestine and leakage of the contents into the abdominal cavity meant peritonitis and an agonizing death. William survived until the next day when he died of his wounds.

The circumstances of his death were variously described at the time as follows:

– in two press reports[316]:

> ... we were informed that the eldest surviving son, a youth of about 18 years of age, had been stabbed, last night, as is supposed by a Hottentot, a number of whom were drinking and dancing on the premises of Mr Allison, his brother in law. An investigation is going on but the circumstances are yet involved in mystery.

> ...a number of Hottentots had congregated on the premises of Aitcheson the hatter and were making a noise. Mr. A. not being at home, Mrs A. sent young Thackery [sic] to disperse them: on his going to the door a rush was made to it by several, with bottles of brandy, and who as he passed plunged a knife in the bowels of the unfortunate youth.

– in gossip[317]:

> killed by a Hottentot girl, instigated by jealousy...

– in a later newspaper[318]:

> ...killed by some person at present unknown

– and by family tradition[319]:

> stabbed by a Hottentot woman.

Some sources are confused. Morse Jones[320] identifies William the son as the victim of Nqeto's assault. The confusion over the multiple deaths is compounded by Hockly who at various points in his text has John Thackwray killed by an elephant (correct), listed as one of the dead in the frontier wars (perhaps confused with James who was wounded in the war) and elected to the Cape House of Assembly in the eighteen fifties (this was James).

There were in fact good reasons for the confusion, which only came to light at the trial of the perpetrator.

The press reports variously place the event at the premises either of a Mr Aitcheson or a Mr Allison. This disagreement is easily resolved. William's sister, Dorothy, was married to James Allison and it was indeed at his sister's house that the events had occurred. James Allison was a hatmaker, trained by a Boer farmer[321]. and practised as a hatter before entering missionary work. Thus "Aitcheson the hatter" is a slip on the part of the writer, which should read "Allison the hatter." The two accounts in the *Commercial Advertiser* on Oct 30th, which agree except for the name of the property owner, say no more than that the perpetrator was a Khoikhoi. Is Philipps's letter then just malicious gossip? It was written two weeks after the events when more would have been known. One of the two letters written in the *Commercial Advertiser* refers to the suspect being a "boy of N—'s." A later letter of Feb 3rd 1830 refers only to "some person at present unknown." This letter was an appeal for donations for the support of Dorothy, William Jr's mother, and appears to be drawing something of a veil over the circumstances.

William was buried on the 30th October 1829. The funeral was held at the Anglican St George's Church. The register erroneously gave his age as twenty and described him as a "[Xhosa] Trader."

The murderess, for it was a woman, was captured and brought to trial some months later. The Graham's Town Circuit Court sat in April 1830. Its proceedings, dealing with rape, assault, and robbery, were reported in great detail over a number of successive issues by a correspondent of the *South African Commercial Advertiser*, which, appearing every Wednesday and Saturday, was the only regular newspaper published in the Colony at the time. Only at the end of the third report is there a single paragraph stating[322]:

> The girl for the murder of poor Thackwray is found guilty and sentenced to be hanged; there appears to be no chance of escape.

Readers had to wait another ten days for an account of the trial[323]. On April 15th 1830, Flora Kiewiet, a young Khoi woman, had appeared in the Graham's Town Circuit Court before Judge Menzies, charged with the murder of William Thackwray. She pleaded not guilty. The witnesses included the District Surgeon Dr John Atherstone[324], and the sister of the accused, Elsje Valminck. The story that emerged during the trial, largely as a result of the evidence of these two witnesses, is as follows[325].

According to Flora[326], who seems to have been in some sort of employment with the Allisons, she and William had been lovers for some time. Their affair was a compendium of all the agonies of young love. He had told her, perhaps truthfully perhaps not, that he wanted to marry her. She had at first refused him because she believed that he was involved with other women. After much argument he had sworn to be faithful and they made a mutual pact that if he was ever unfaithful she could kill him. He did not take this seriously but it appears that she did.

On the evening of the murder Flora and her sister Elsje were walking from Allison's hatter's shop to the associated dwelling house when they surprised William and Catharine Piet, a household servant in a corner of the grounds. Catharine retreated from Flora's outrage, which was compounded when, far from expressing regret, William told her that he was tired of her. When she asked whether he intended to desert her for Catharine he replied, "Yes, I cannot do otherwise." Flora demanded that Elsje call Catharine back. Elsje wisely refused:

> I refused to go and shortly afterwards I saw the prisoner stab Thackwray with a knife in his belly and heard her say "I am guilty of one death" or [perhaps] "I can only die once." Thackwray said "Oh God!" I said "What is that?" when Thackwray said "Flora has stabbed me."

Afterwards Flora told Atherstone that she had not meant to do William a serious injury but, seeing the blow coming, he had turned round to avoid the knife and as a result had received the thrust in the belly. This seems implausible; it is more likely to be a rationalisation of her actions.

Elsje pulled out the knife, probably exacerbating the injury. William begged them both not to say anything as he did not want his sister to know the reason for his wound. It became apparent that William was gravely injured and they called for help. John Atherstone, the District Surgeon, was called in to attend to the wound. Flora was taken into custody.

Atherstone was horrified at the extent of William's injuries. About 45 cm of his intestines were protruding and they were perforated in four places. Infection was already setting in. He asked William what had happened:

> He had stated that the Hottentots in the shop had got hold of a quantity of brandy, and had been making a great noise; that he had gone out to see what was the matter; his sister was frightened at the noise; and that just before he met with the accident he heard a greater noise in the shop, when he ran from the dwelling house with a knife in his hand and was not certain whether he received a stab from someone or fell upon his knife.

Atherstone did not believe him – it was an implausible account and he had already got the impression from other witnesses that there had been a murderous attack. He did his best with the wound, enlarging the aperture in the abdominal wall so that he could replace the intestine and suturing the perforations, but he knew perfectly well that there was no hope. He was concerned to get to the bottom of the matter and, as District Surgeon, well aware of the law. For a hearsay deathbed statement it was necessary that the patient should clearly understand that he was dying:

> I told Thackwray when I first saw him that there was no chance of his living and begged him to inform me how the accident occurred. He seemed alarmed and agitated and said that he hoped not for his sis-

ter's sake. Thackwray insisted on his story right up to the time just before he died.

There was more corroborative evidence from other witnesses that Flora had stabbed William and, at last, the jury was asked for its verdict. They found no need for any delay in pronouncing her guilty. The correspondent described the macabre ceremony that followed with relish:

> His Lordship then placed the black cap upon his head, and addressed the prisoner shortly, but with great solemnity and sentence of death was passed upon her. This impressive scene had little effect upon the prisoner who watched with a fixed and inquisitive eye every look and motion of his Lordship during this awful ceremony: and she heard the irrevocable sentence, which is to cut short her mortal career, without a muscle being disturbed, or the slightest indication of a nerve being affected.

Flora was more likely to have been in shock and denial. Modern day proponents of the death penalty might wish to consider not only the victim but the brutalising effect on those responsible for its execution, by which is meant society as a whole.

In a document written on behalf of William's mother more than five years later there is confirmation that Flora was indeed hanged[327]:

> ... another son was murdered by a Hottentot and who suffered the extreme penalty of the law ...

Where was Edward Driver? [Oct. 1829 – Jan. 1830]

When the news of the elder Thackwray's death reached Graham's Town it also brought fears that Edward Driver had been a victim of the mayhem unleashed by Nqeto after the encounter with Lochenberg. The family's mourning was intensified by their concerns for his life. Ann by now had three small daughters. Hannah had been born just six months earlier.

Their fears were eased in January 1830 when Edward arrived back in Graham's Town. He had been unaware of the disasters that had fallen on his family until he had started his journey back. He must, however, have stopped at rest places such as mission stations on the way and heard the news of the massacre of Farewell's party although, it appears from his statement, that his information might have been uncertain. The reunion was naturally a blessing for the Thackwray family, but his arrival also caused a sensation in the town because not only had he been feared dead, there were also fears for Henry Foulds who had initially been his companion. Donald Moodie, the Acting Civil Commissioner in Graham's

Town during an absence of Campbell, took a statement from him and reported his evidence[328]:

> Mr E. Driver left the colony in August with Mr Farewell's property which he conveyed to near the Umbzimfuba [Mzimvubu], from which time he remained between that river and the Umzimcola [Mzimkulu] until 1st January when he left and returned to Graham's Town. H. Foulds, 3 hottentots and 3 [Xhosa]s remained behind in charge of a quantity of ivory (800lbs) [this would have been in the company of Farewell's party before the massacre] which they were to convey on 7 horses to the wagon of Ralph Manley at the Umtata. From that date I [Driver] heard nothing certain until today.

Moodie's document also reports evidence from Manley that led him to conclude that Foulds had been killed. This news was a dreadful financial blow to Edward and led him to compose a memorial to the Governor[329]:

> To his Excellency
>
> The Governor
>
> The humble Memorial of Edward Driver
>
> of Stony Vale Albany
>
> Sheweth
>
> That Memorialist accepted an offer of the late Mr Farewell to convey for him two Wagon loads of Goods under the expectation of being remunerated by shooting Elephants. At the time of Mr Farewell's Murder Memorialist lost twenty two head of Oxen, and Beads and Buttons to a very considerable amount. -
>
> Memorialists expectations of obtaining Ivory were fully realised, and he commenced his journey home, at arriving at the Omsoomphobu, the River being too high for the Wagons to cross. Memorialist having been long absent from his Family proceeded home on Foot leaving his property in charge of one Englishman, three Hottentots and three [Xhosa]s –
>
> Memorialist has now ascertained that a tribe of Tambookies, the same whose cattle were restored by Major Dundas have attacked and murdered his Party, taken the whole of his property, consisting of
>
> 5 Elephant Guns
>
> Abt 800 lb of large Ivory
>
> 7 Horses
>
> 6 Saddles
>
> and thereby reduced him to absolute ruin.
>
> Memorialist prays the protection of Your Excellency, and interference to obtain the return of his property , or an adequate compensation
>
> And Memorialist will ever pray
>
> Edward Driver

Happily Foulds and his party had survived and Edward's fortune was intact. A subsequent memorial on his behalf by his neighbour John Brown[330] withdraws the application, and states that Foulds's party had returned safely and had been well-treated by all the Xhosa they had met on the way. Also with them was another servant of Farewell's who had been presumed dead.

Aftermath   [1829 – 1844]

The third death of a man in her family left Dorothy Thackwray destitute. Joseph was nineteen years old and James only fourteen. She was effectively dependent on her sons-in-law. Edward Driver was by now reasonably well established; James Allison was making only a marginal living as a hatter.

It seems that Edward must now have taken on the responsibility for the farm at Stoney Vale. It is possible that he purchased it from his mother-in-law, which would have provided her with some capital support[331]. For many years Driver's farm was a landmark and a stop for travellers on the road from Graham's Town to Trompetter's Drift. On various documents Edward gave his address as Stoney Vale, Governor's Kop or Driver's Hill.

The townspeople took up a collection. Between them they raised £11[332]. It was felt that other residents of the Colony in Cape Town might be prepared to contribute and a letter, signed by a number of Graham's Town residents was sent to the Commercial Advertiser[333]:

Mrs Thackwray's Case

The attention of the charitable is earnestly requested to the distressing situation of Mrs Thackwray, who has been within the space of a few months deprived of all means of support, by the melancholy death of her husband and two grown up sons.

Mr Thackwray senior had for some years been engaged in trading with the tribes beyond the Boundary; and in an appeal in favour of his widow, it must not be improper to state, that to his active benevolence the survivors from the wreck of the French ship Eoli, owed, under providence, their delivery from the cruel death that soon after befel [sic] their preserver, Mr Thackwray being treacherously murdered by a predatory tribe on 8th October last.

His eldest son was a few months before killed by an elephant and a few days after the arrival of the intelligence of the death of the father, a second son, the only remaining support of the widow & two young children was killed by some person at present unknown.

This statement is submitted to the Public, with the view of obtaining for the unfortunate widow such a sum of money as will enable her to set

up a small business, at Graham's Town, as a confectioner, for which
she is qualified.

Subscriptions for this purpose will be thankfully received at the office
of this Paper, and by the Rev. Mr Monroe at Graham's Town.

The confectionery business never amounted to much. After the frontier war of 1834 – 1835 there seemed to be a case for her getting some sort
of pension. Two widows whose husbands had died in the war had received support. She submitted a memorial to the Governor, Sir Benjamin
D'Urban, dated Graham's Town, July 30th 1835, requesting financial
aid[334]:

... That she is near sixty-three years of age and has no means of subsistence save her own individual efforts by knitting children's socks,
and she laments to state that her sight greatly fails and she is therefore
compelled to anticipate a period with sorrow when even this slender resource fails her ...

Governors can afford to be sympathetic. D'Urban referred it to the
Civil Commissioner as "a case deserving sympathetic attention." Campbell was, however, a bean counter. He reported:

Although I sincerely comiserate [sic] the case of this poor woman I fear
it will be impossible to relieve her to the extent she prays for or to assimilate her circumstances with those of the widows of Armstrong and
Purcell. Her husband was not killed in Caffraria but in the Zoola country
by a rebellious chief of the nation. Her two sons were killed in this
colony and they came by their deaths by means unconnected with
[Xhosa]s or [Xhosa] warfare. I do not see, therefore, that her case can
be assimilated to that of Purcel [sic] and Armstrong.

William Thackwray Sr was one of the first cross border traders. At the
twenty fifth anniversary celebrations of the settlement, held on 10 April
1844 in Port Elizabeth, the chief speaker, J Centlivres Chase, had this to
say[335]:

Numbered also amongst their victims is to be named, the bold, the intelligent, the enterprizing THACKWRAY, the elder – one of the pioneers
of the Settlement, who cleared the way for British commerce into the interior, and who, with his companion WALKER, was treacherously massacred at midnight by the natives of the Amaponda country, on whose
protection he at a fatal moment had unfortunately confided.

An account of William's temperament, more respectful than that of
his apprentice, Thomas Stubbs, occurs in a letter written immediately
after his death[336]:

Poor Thackwray was well known here [Graham's Town]. He was an amiable and intelligent man; and few, very few, possessed, like him the
qualifications requisite for the casual life he had adopted ...

Finally one has to wonder about William Thackwray's appearance. Stubbs's description of a stout, farting, old man with a strange accent is satirical – the description of a master by his apprentice. What did he mean by "stout"? Anyone who had endured the vicissitudes of life in the first few years of settlement is unlikely to have been corpulent. The older meaning of "thickset" or "sturdy" is more likely intended. Certainly by the time of his death he had travelled by ox wagon as far as any trader, through inhospitable country. Travel by ox wagon demands a lot of walking. At river gorges and mountains it was often necessary to dismantle the wagon and carry it piece by piece to the other side. Anyone living that kind of life would have ended spare and muscular. A number of different writers describe him as "old Thackwray". When he died he was less than 50 years old and when he first reached the Cape he was 40. Does the adjective imply a level of gravitas making him seem older than his years or was he merely worn down by circumstance? There is no way of knowing.

Chapter 11. War

The conquest of the earth, which mostly means the taking it away from those who have a different complexion or slightly flatter noses than ourselves, is not a pretty thing when you look into it.

Joseph Conrad, Heart of Darkness

The Empire Strikes Back [1819 – 1833]

The decade between 1820 and 1830 not only represented a turning point in the history of the Colony but also a watershed in that of the western Xhosa. Before that time Colony and Xhosa had coexisted. The lifestyles of the Boers on one side of the frontier and the Xhosa on the other were pastoral and well understood by both sides. The frictions were frictions between two different peoples competing for the same territory for similar reasons. After the eighteen twenties the relationship was between an aggressive colonial power and a people threatened both militarily and culturally.

For the Xhosa of the eastern frontier the Battle of Graham's Town and the defeats that followed it initiated a new level of pressure on their way of life[337]. The period of uninhibited expansionism was gone: contraction of their territory was now the norm. Their culture was deeply rooted in their pastoral way of life with land the foundation. Their system of succession assumed that the junior sons of their chiefs could find lands of their own for their people. Space for the welfare of their herds, the basis of their riches, was essential. Without it their whole way of life was threatened.

We recall that Ndlambe, the loser in the war, had retreated to the inaccessible upper Kei. Ngqika and his allies Bhothomane of the imiDange and Nqeno of the amaMbalu had been pleased to have the British support against him and thought of themselves as allies of the Colony. They were now to find out the cost of this support. They, together with Kobe of the amaGqunukwhebe and Habana of the imiDange[338], were summoned to a meeting with the Governor at which they were informed of his new dispensation for the frontier. The treaty – in reality an ultimatum – that Lord Charles Somerset now forced on Ngqika created a no-man's land between the Colony and the Xhosa. They were to be expelled from this region between the Fish and the Keiskamma rivers – called the ceded territory – and it was to be patrolled by colonial troops, based in Fort Willshire and the line of forts protecting the frontier. These forts were well within the so-called no-man's land. The Rharhabe were now irretrievably split between the amaNgqika and the amaNdlambe. Ngqika's people were pushed into a small region between the Tyumie and Keiskamma Rivers.

Next in the succession of provocations was the arrival of the settlers who began to occupy what many Xhosa had seen as their land. Worse, the squeeze from the east was intensified by the *mfecane*. Over Southern Africa populations were decimated. Bands of refugees competing for territory caused havoc. There was wholesale resettlement of peoples. In the frontier region, dispossesed groups struggled for resources.

Naturally, in the circumstances, the incidence of cattle theft increased alarmingly. Ngqika found himself in the position of being expected to control this. Since some of the most enthusiastic cattle reavers were the Mbalu and the imiDange over whom he had no authority, he was placed in a difficult situation. He was not a strong character and often took refuge in alcohol. He lost influence and his sons Tyhali, Maqoma, and Anta took more and more control.

Maqoma in particular went his own way. A few years after the establishment of the ceded territory he and his people had occupied the region in the Kat River valley. This was tolerated for a number of years, causing Andries Stockenström great disquiet, as he strongly favoured an exclusion zone as the solution to the Colony's problems. Maqoma, nevertheless, for a number of years, acted as a moderating influence, cooperating with the military authorities in returning stolen cattle and making himself popular with the officers of the colonial army.

Another provocative influence was the presence of the Christian missionaries. There was great lack of understanding between the missionaries and the Xhosa. The missionaries of the evangelical movement were locked in their own paradigm, with no understanding or empathy for Xhosa beliefs and customs. They were horrified by nudity, sexual customs, polygamy, and the pagan beliefs of the Xhosa. They were confident in their own faith, with each man in his place in the world, hellfire and eternal damnation awaiting the sinners, and eternal bliss for those who accepted the word and repented of their sins. Most Xhosa, equally confident in their own culture, listened politely and found the message irrelevant. There were a few notable exceptions, such as Dyanie Tshatshu of the Ntinde and Khama of the Gqunukwhebe, who became converts, but on the whole there was initially little success in converting the Xhosa. On the other hand, the missionaries were not unwelcome, and permission was given for them to establish mission stations. They provided a useful conduit for communication with the colonial government; in some senses their missions were as much diplomatic as religious. They brought knowledge of agricultural techniques and education, but provoked justified suspicions of spying for the Colony.

Among the Xhosa the old guard was changing. Ndlambe died on the 10th February 1828. His son Mdushane succeeded but only survived him for a year. When he died the amaNdlambe disintegrated into smaller groups led by Ndlambe's brothers, Mhala and Mqhayi, and Mdushane's son Qasana[339]. Ngqika was becoming more and more erratic, coughing from tuberculosis, often drunk, suspicious of others, greedy for the gifts from the Colony that he regarded as his due. He died on the 14th December 1829.

Ngqika's heir apparent was a child, Sandile, born in 1820, handicapped by a withered leg, and fiercely protected by Ngqika's Great Wife Suthu. Maqoma was the obvious regent and his influence grew, both with the Ngqikas and with his neighbours.

Events leading to war   [1829 – 1834]

By the late 1820s the pressures from the colonial side were intolerable. Lord Charles Somerset's reprisal policy, imposed on Nqqika in 1818 was a great source of friction. Stolen cattle were tracked into the Xhosa territory by commandos raised for the purpose. When the followers reached the first kraal, they commandeered replacements for the stolen beasts, whether or not the owners had had anything to do with the theft. It was then expected that these owners, through the authority of Ngqika, would seek compensation from those responsible for the theft. There was an obvious opportunity for abuse, often seized with alacrity. With justification, many Xhosa saw this as simply tit-for-tat theft.

The man in charge of overseeing this policy was Lord Charles's son Henry and he pursued it enthusiastically. By the middle eighteen twenties he was an established figure in Graham's Town society, generally popular among the town gentry, but even an adulatory biographer[340] labelled him "a military man with little intellectual pretension." His style was epitomized by a commando he led in December 1825. In spite of standing orders that commandos were not permitted to cross the frontier without the permission of the civil authority, he decided that it was necessary to conduct a secret raid to retrieve horses and cattle, allegedly stolen by a vassal of Ngqika. Without informing Major Dundas[341], the newly appointed Graham's Town Landdrost, he assembled a force consisting of Khoikhoi troops, Boers from the north, and some artillery men, and set off across the frontier, leaving both Landdrost and townspeople uninformed and apprehensive.

When Somerset's forces reached the village of the suspected thieves they attacked it at dawn and seized what they regarded as the appropriate number of cattle. This was not, however, an amaNgqika village, but an imiDange settlement. After they had been convinced of this they returned their booty, but this had the effect of enraging Bhothomane, normally well-disposed towards the British. The commando then proceeded to another settlement, which they attacked and made off with 500 cattle. This, too, was the wrong village; it was an amaMbalu group. They too were infuriated and Nqeno was alienated. A number of Xhosa were killed and two soldiers of the commando fell victim to pursuing Xhosa. All in all, it was an inept and irresponsible military disaster.

The uproar that followed was headed by Dundas who threatened to resign. Even Lord Charles Somerset, now under severe pressure from the ongoing commission of inquiry, upheld Dundas. Nevertheless, no court martial, inquiry, or other sanction followed. It seemed to be regarded as a personal difference between Dundas and Henry Somerset. Six weeks later reconciliation was achieved at a ball given by the officers of the Cape Corps:

> ... my [Mrs Thomas Philipps's] good husband with the Assistance of some other Friends, accomplished his long-wished for object of reuniting the Powers here. ... an unfortunate difference had occurred between the Landdrost and Col. Somerset so that they would not meet each other and it was only by Tom's [Philipps's] interference between them and a little soothing with each party, that the Colonel was induced to commence the ball with Mrs. Dundas, lead her into supper, etc. The next day he was persuaded to acknowledge that he was in error through misinformation, which Major Dundas has said he should consider sufficient. Each party was anxious to have it made up, particularly the Ladies. It was agreed that the gentlemen should meet together on the Race Ground ... They met and were Friends, and the next day called reciprocally at each others' houses.[342]

The effect of this and other raids across the border by commandos was to alienate more and more of the Xhosa and led to ever increasing cattle reaving.

Notwithstanding these military adventures, Henry Somerset failed to guarantee the integrity of his father's ceded territory. He was openly supportive of Maqoma's occupation of the Kat River valley.

The recall of Lord Charles Somerset to face an inquiry into his erratic stewardship and the appointment of Bourke as acting Governor, led to major changes in Government. As well as changes to the law under which the Colony was governed, the abolition of slavery took final effect and, in addition, the legal disabilities suffered by the Khoikhoi and other coloured inhabitants of the Colony, were removed, leaving them as free citizens on paper, although not in practice. Part of the reorganization of Government meant that the post of Lieutenant-Governor for the Eastern Cape, to which Bourke had been appointed before becoming acting governor, was abolished and the affairs of the frontier were put in the hands of a Commissioner General. For Andries Stockenstrom this meant a major change of circumstances. As Landdrost of Graaff Reinet he found himself out of a job. While still pondering his future he was appointed to the new post of Commissioner General for the eastern frontier, which he accepted. Now the chief civil authority on the frontier was Stockenstrom and the chief military authority Henry Somerset, two men whose dislike for each other was so acute as to make reasonable cooperation nearly impossible. Stockenstrom was touchy and always ready to see a slur: Somerset was insensitive, imperceptive, and resentful as a result of his earlier brushes with Stockenstrom. Furthermore, the relationship between the two offices was not properly defined: it was not clear to what extent Somerset was responsible to Stockenstrom.

They were at odds over policy. Stockenstrom was totally against the presence of Maqoma in the ceded territory: Somerset, with the support of his father, tolerated it and made the case that he was a stabilising influence. Stockenstrom believed that the reprisal policy was counterproductive and ineffective: Somerset pursued it with enthusiasm.

In the ceded territory, in the region of the Kat River, Maqoma was about to embark on actions that would impinge on these disagreements and have heavy consequences for both Colony and Xhosa. When John Thackwray had visited the region on his way into Thembuland in 1827 he had met an unhappy clan, dispossesed of their territory, and settled on land by permission of Maqoma. Their chief, Bawana, who had not impressed John Thackwray, now had even less to satisfy him. Galela, a minor Gcina chief, was at odds with him and attacked him. Maqoma chose to enter the dispute and fiercely attacked Galela. The missionary, John Ross was told by Maqoma that he was supporting Bawana as legitimate clan chief against a rebel Galela, while an oral source suggested that he wanted to gain the amaGcina as vassals[343]. The opinion of the Moravians at Shiloh was that Bawana had incited Maqoma to attack his old enemy[344]. Whatever the reason, the consequences for both Bawana and Maqoma were serious. Many of the amaGcina fled into the Colony creating a refugee problem. Bawana, shortly afterwards was killed by his enemies.

Bourke's interregnum had been ended by the appointment of a new Governor, Sir Galbraith Lowry Cole[345], who arrived in 1828. When the news of the incursion of the Thembu refugees reached Cape Town it was discussed by the Legislative Council. Stockenstrom, a member of the Council was asked by the new Governor for his opinion. Stockenstrom stated that he strongly believed that it was important that a consistent rule of law be applied in dealings with the Xhosa. Maqoma was in the ceded territory by special permission of the former Governor, provided that he kept the peace. Stockenstrom was of the opinion that Maqoma had not met his side of the bargain and therefore should be expelled from the Kat River region, thus achieving what Stockenstrom had always thought should be the case. Cole was happy to take the advice.

The Kat River Settlement   [1828 - 1834]

With a force of three hundred soldiers Stockenstrom carried the message to Maqoma that he was to be expelled from the Amatolas. His people were driven from their homes and the old cycle of hut burning and crop destruction began. The resentment of Maqoma and his people was to influence relationships on the frontier for many years.

Stockenstrom now had the opportunity to achieve a cherished goal. The Governor agreed to the establishment of a settlement of Khoikhoi and coloured people in the region. Soon the new settlers were flooding in with the organizational ability of Stockenstrom ensuring its initial success.

Stockenstrom invited James Read, a missionary from the London Missionary Society, to lead the first party to the Kat river. Read had a controversial background[346]. He had first come to the Cape in 1800 and had assisted Johannes van der Kemp with the setting up of Bethelsdorp. After van der Kemp's death he continued to run the mission station. He and his Khoikhoi wife, Sarah, had eight surviving children. This marriage and Read's strong advocacy of the Khoikhoi cause, accusing Boer farmers of criminal mistreatment of their Khoikhoi servants, had, as early as 1816, made him greatly unpopular with the colonists and a hero to humanitarian societies in Britain. While the spirit of his criticisms of the colonists was probably justified, he was intemperate in making many accusations without sufficient evidence. When he confessed to adultery with the Khoikhoi daughter of a church elder and moved with both his wife and mistress to Lattakoo there was a scandal within the London Missionary Society. An investigation by Dr John Philip highlighted many inadequacies in the management and operation of Bethelsdorp. The result was that Read spent many years in the missionary wilderness, first at Lattakoo and then at Theopolis.

To Stockenstrom's dismay, Read set himself up as a permanent missionary at the settlement. This had not been the intention. He was likely to be a cause for criticism from the neighbouring colonists. In addition, the LMS was viewed with suspicion by the colonial government. William Thomson, from the Glasgow Missionary Society was quickly appointed as official government missionary and occupied Balfour, a mission station abandoned by John Ross when Maqoma had been expelled. The Khoikhoi tended to associate themselves with Read; the "Bastards" (those of mixed race) with Thomson.

The settlement remained a focus of suspicion for the neighbours. There was a constant fear that the settlers would ally themselves with the Xhosa. It is probably true that Maqoma hoped to gain their support but there was never at this period any serious danger of this.

Robert Hart found himself in the position of having to damp down suspicions. News reached him that a party of Boer colonists were advancing on the settlement to forestall a rumoured and entirely fictitious attack:

> ...the Boers, being imposed upon from some of those whose only hope was in war, were made to believe that the Kat River Hottentots were going to attack the Colony. They assembled armed, and were advancing against their supposed enemies, when my old friend Robert Hart Senior, and Mr Onkruid rushed forward to prevent the bloody conflict, but found the Boers already convinced that they were fools and dupes, whilst the credit of this gallantry was allotted to those, who could by no possibility have acted in the matter before the bubble burst.[347]

Certainly there were some Khoikhoi who took the part of the Xhosa, but, on the whole, the settlement for many years provided an important source of recruits for the army and was crucial to the defence of the Colony.

Trouble in Gcalekaland [1833 – 1834]

Hintsa's Gcaleka people lived far from the Colony. The people of the royal house of the Xhosa occupied the land to the east of the Great Kei River, bounded to the north by the Thembu and to the east by the Mpondo and Mpondomise kingdoms. Hintsa had come to manhood. While the rift between the amaGcaleka and amaRharhabe still existed, and the amaRharhabe themselves were divided between the amaNgqika and the amaNdlambe, all these groupings recognized Hintsa as their king. His political power base was with the Gcaleka: his status with the Rharhabe, however, was titular only.

The eighteen twenties had also been a turbulent time for the Gcaleka people[348]. There had long been tension with their Thembu neighbours. The fragmented abaThembu had been unified under their great king Ngubencuka and clans such as the amaGcina subordinated. John Thackwray in 1827 had noted how the formerly strong Tyopo of the amaGcina was now "under Vosany [Ngubencuka]". After this strengthening of the abaThembu there had been strong tensions between the Thembu and Gcaleka peoples over competing territorial claims in the upper Kei region. To the east, in the early part of the century, conflict between the amaMpondo and the amaBomvana had led to the Bomvana chief Gambushe and his people fleeing to Hintsa and becoming subject to him. Hintsa had taken Gambushe's daughter Nomsa as his Great Wife. This alliance led to tensions between the Gcaleka and the Mpondo peoples.

The mix came to the boil in the first half of the twenties with the troubles that have been labelled the *mfecane*. The first impact came when the fugitive Bhaca, an aggressive, fast-moving group headed by their feared leader Madikane, entered Thembuland in about 1823. They attacked and defeated the Tshatshu and Gcina – John Thackwray had seen some of the effects of this when he visited Bawana of the Tshatshu. The invasion could not be tolerated. Madikane's army was defeated by an alliance of Xhosa, Thembu, and Mpondomise forces and Madikane himself was killed in the battle. The Bhaca, hungry for land of their own, allied themselves with the Mpondo to attack the Bomvana. This was the equivalent of an attack on Hintsa himself. His Gcaleka army combined with the Bomvana and drove the Bhaca out of the region.

The next major pressure came from across the Orange River. The Ngwane people, also fugitives from Zululand, under the leadership of Matiwane, crossed the Orange River in 1827, searching for a place of refuge. At the same time, threats from the Zulu king Shaka alarmed both Hintsa and Ngubencuka. They appealed to the Colony for help. The Albany Landdrost, W. B. Dundas, was sent with a small force to investigate and try to settle matters. He found a great deal of devastation resulting from the earlier conflict between the Xhosa and Bomvana on one hand and the Bhaca and Mpondo on the other. He then encountered a group of Ngwane whom Ngubencuka had led him to believe were Zulus. He drove them off, confiscating their cattle, and returned to the Colony with a defeat of the "Zulu hordes" under his belt.

The Ngwane then took steps to recover their cattle from Ngubencuka's Thembu. Ngubencuka sent a message to Henry Somerset warning that the "Zulu" had returned and Somerset set off with a much larger force.

Matiwane's people were by then in very difficult circumstances. Short of food, with no place of their own, they were suddenly faced with a threat that they did not understand. Somerset had brought Hintsa and Ngubencuka into a fragile alliance. Their motive was the prospect of booty: his was the repulse of the "Zulu." The Ngwane had never before encountered gunfire in warfare. They were destroyed by the British troops, while the Gcaleka and Thembu at their rear plundered their cattle, murdered their wounded, and abducted their women. This Battle of Mbholompo was the death of the Ngwane as a force. Matiwane, with a few of his followers struggled back to Zululand where Matiwane was to be killed by Dingane. A number were brought back to the Colony by Somerset where they added to the labour pool. Many were allowed by Hintsa to settle in Gcalekaland as new subjects.

The refugee Ngwane became part of the displaced people known as the Mfengu[349]. These included Bhele and Hlubi people who had themselves been displaced by the Ngwane as well as survivors of the Bhaca invasion. Soon afterwards Ngubencuka and Hintsa quarreled and the Thembu moved northwards, leaving Hintsa in command of the large tract of land east of the Kei.

By 1830 Gcalekaland was no longer isolated from the influences of the Colony. The removal of restrictions on trade introduced trade goods and traders to the region. Previously the Gcaleka would either have traded with their western neighbours who had direct contact with the colony through the Fort Willshire fairs or with occasional adventurers such as William Thackwray: now they were frequently exposed, first to itinerant traders and then to men who came and asked permission to set up trading stations in the territory.

Edward Driver was one of these. His farm near Governor's Kop was prospering and included Driver's Hill and the old Thackwray farm at Stoney Vale. The ivory trade was doing well. In 1831 he spent five months elephant hunting in the region between the Umzimvubu and Umzimkulu. He returned just in time for the birth of his first son Edward Bailey. He was by now well known in the Xhosa territories by the name Sonyakatya. Growing prosperity allowed him to establish a trading station on the Mbashe River, well placed for trade with the Gcaleka and the Bomvana. He installed a manager, Ephraim Dicks, who had arrived in 1820 on board the *Weymouth* as a 16 year old orphan, his father having died on the voyage.

Not only traders had settled in the territory. Other new alien influences were the settling of Boer farmers in the region and the activities of evangelical Christian missionaries.

The farmers were a group of some thirty families under Louis Tregardt, who had previously been a farmer near Somerset East and a neighbour of Robert Hart. Tregardt had found it expedient to remove himself from the Colony under suspicion of receiving stolen cattle and had been allowed by Hintsa to settle in his territory[350]. Tregardt was later to be one of the earliest leaders of the Great Trek, but he had already left the Colony by 1834. For Hintsa, he was a source of information about the nature of the Colony.

The relentless spread of the missionaries, especially the Wesleyans meant that a number of mission stations had been established in the region. Near Hintsa's Great Place, at Butterworth, William Shaw had set up a station. Initially under the guidance of William Shrewsbury, by 1830 John Ayliff was in charge.

Ayliff had risen from the ranks of the lay preachers. He came from a relatively humble background and, while he appears to have been an observant man, he did not have much breadth of mind. His ideas were locked into the teachings of evangelical Christianity. Like most of his fellows he initially had little success in converting any of the Gcaleka. They were happy to hear what he had to say but it had no effect on them. Their customs and beliefs were deeply shocking to him[351]. He was delighted, therefore, when he began to gain numerous converts among the Mfengu who began to settle at the mission.

Just as many Khoikhoi had been absorbed into the Gqunukwhebe, or as white shipwreck survivors had been absorbed, the Mfengu were accepted by Hintsa to become so-called *busa* clients[352]. Under this system a destitute individual was attached to a member of the tribe and worked for him. As part of that work, as a result of an occasional gift such as a calf, he could build up wealth in the only form recognized, as a small herd of cattle, and thus achieve ultimate independence. Ultimately he and his family would be absorbed entirely.

Many Mfengu were willing converts to Christianity which seemed to promise what they had been unable to achieve. Ayliff was immensely proud of his congregation. He was achieving what had previously been unobtainable, a significant following of Xhosa converts. The converts were alienated from the Xhosa traditions. They wore a version of European clothing; they gave up Xhosa customs; their allegiance was to their congregation rather than to Hintsa. Ayliff totally misunderstood the relationship of the refugees with their hosts. He wrongheadedly saw them as slaves and thought of Christianity as releasing them from bondage[353].

In addition, many Mfengu began to surreptitiously build up herds that they had acquired illicitly, hiding them in the bush. With their own tribal affiliations damaged, they were still not always prepared to be absorbed into those of the Gcaleka. The mission station became something of a thorn in the flesh for Hintsa.

The traders also became a focus for dissatisfaction. Initially they had been a welcome source of trade goods, now they became less popular.

The reasons for this are not entirely clear. It is possible that they acquired a reputation for sharp dealing. Ayliff did not think so[354]:

> Some have attributed the change of feeling to the improper conduct of the traders themselves. That there might have been some unprincipled men among the traders, I admit; but as far as the tribe of Hintza is concerned, of the traders lately residing therein, I can bear testimony to the fact that their general conduct to the [Xhosa]s has not been bad. Indeed, for a trader to injure a [Xhosa] in his person or property with impunity was almost impossible, the trader being so completely at the mercy of the [Xhosa] chief, and living so far from any other trader.

One of the earliest incidents was at the beginning of 1833. On 16th March, Edward Driver's Trading Store at Butterworth was attacked and burnt out[355]. The manager, Ephraim Dicks, escaped but the store and its stock were lost. This was a considerable financial blow. Driver held Hintsa responsible:

> He [Hintsa] had robbed him [Driver] "to a very great amount, repeatedly himself, personally", and had threatened the lives of his servants, and perpetrated many acts of injustice, which it would take too long to enumerate.[356]

There is no way of determining to what extent this opinion was justified. Driver's feelings about his treatment were the culmination of a long history of trading across the border. His early experiences with Ngqika had not been happy. It is also possible that sharp dealing on his part or on the part of Dicks could have led to resentment. Whether or not Hintsa was in any way personally to blame for Driver's losses the fact remains that Driver's perception was that he was directly responsible and he was resentful.

Matters became more serious in the middle of 1834. There were a number of incidents in which traders were robbed or terrorized. The manager of one trading station, John Rowles, was terrorized with his wife and family for a whole month[357]. Their goods were plundered and, their house occupied. Gallows were erected outside and they were threatened with hanging. They had no transport to provide a means of escape. They were rescued when Richard Walker arrived with his wagon. Richard was still the storeman at Wesleyville. He also traded throughout the region providing a mail service and trading opportunities to other mission stations. He took the family to Driver's trading store at Butterworth, which had been reopened. At about the same time another trader, William Purcell was murdered.

Both missionaries and traders began to consider the possibility of evacuating the region.

The Invasion of the Colony   [Dec 1834]

Although Edward Driver had suffered a substantial loss by the destruction of his trading station in Gcalekaland, he was still a prosperous hunter and farmer:

> [He] possessed at that time as large a stock of Cattle as was to be found the property of one individual on the Frontier, the greatest part of which were Trek Oxen[358]

Shortly before Christmas in 1834 he took a party of military officers under Major Gregory out on a buffalo hunt. Returning home a day or two before Christmas the party found Driver's farm under attack. Over a wide front the invasion of Albany by the Xhosa had begun.

The final trigger that had set off the war had been yet another reprisal raid to recover stolen cattle. A military patrol set out from Fort Beaufort to seek missing horses in the Mancazana valley. They came across some cattle and seized them. This was a big mistake. The cattle belonged to Tyhali and the taking of a chief's cattle was an attack on the chief himself. They were pursued by a group of warriors led by Xhoxho, brother of Maqoma, Anta, and Tyhali. Hard pressed, the patrol opened fire, killing two of the pursuers. Another shot that produced a far less serious physical wound had far more serious consequences. One of the musket balls grazed Xhoxho's head. The wounding of a chief was an attack on the nation. The outrage arising from this event precipitated the invasion that had already been planned by Maqoma and his allies.

All over the Colony farms were burnt and pillaged and the occupants driven out. A major objective of the attacks was to acquire some of his cattle and the group at Driver's farm had this in mind. He and his companions, however, were literally loaded for buffalo. They fought off the raiders, killing three in the process. It was clear to them that the engagement was part of a much larger incursion.

The officers had to return to their posts urgently. Edward's first priority was to get his family and stock into safety. They moved into Graham's Town where the scale of the invasion became apparent. The cattle were placed with what was termed the "general herd" under the care of the army, as it turned out not the most secure place for them. Lodgings of some sort were found for his family. Refugees were streaming into the town. The townspeople had been woken to the seriousness of the situation. On Christmas morning it became official:

> ... the town was disturbed at dawn by the firing of a cannon from the Fort, and the ringing of the heavy bells of St George's Church. All hurried thither and heard the fearful news.[359]

For several days the town had been buzzing with rumours of raids and pillage by the Xhosa. Now the extent of the problem became apparent to the townspeople. Fort Willshire had been attacked by a strong force under Maqoma at daybreak on Monday 22nd December. The attack had been plotted together with some mutinous Cape Corps troops in the garrison, who failed to meet their side of the bargain during the night. The dawn attack was driven off and Maqoma's force crossed the Fish River at Trompetter's Drift, spreading out to attack the farms and homesteads of the Colony. These attacks began in earnest on Tuesday. The farm nearest to the drift, belonging to James Howse, was laid waste and attacks began on other farms along the road to Graham's Town. Meanwhile along the whole length of the frontier thousands of the warriors of Maqoma and his allies streamed into the Colony. It was a party of these that Edward Driver and his friends had driven off from their farm.

Col. Henry Somerset, commander of the military forces on the eastern frontier, was at the Kat River settlement when hostilities broke out. There were only about 750 troops in the region. Half formed the garrison in Graham's Town under Col. England. The remainder were spread out manning the thin line of forts in the ceded territory. Both Somerset and England were out of their depth. Neither had a reputation for daring or intelligence. Somerset gathered a troop of Khoikhoi and tried to plug the holes in the frontier without success. England conceived his duty to be the defence of Graham's Town and remained with his troops in the barracks. He was not encouraged by a panicky dispatch from Somerset estimating that the attack involved many thousand Xhosa.

It soon became apparent that all the settlements of Albany had been under attack. Only Salem had been spared as a result of the courage of Richard Gush, a Quaker who had ridden out unarmed to face down the attacking force, berated them, promised them food and supplies, and persuaded them to depart.

In Graham's Town itself there was a leadership vacuum. A group of young men rode out to see what they could do along the road to Trompetter's Drift. They found pitiful sights. Mrs Mahoney, the wife of the same Mahoney who had been so troublesome during the voyage of the *Northampton* was found wandering in a shocked state. Her husband, who was now a prosperous farmer and neighbour of Driver, had been slaughtered before her eyes and she had been told to run by the attackers who were not ready to harm women and children. Other refugees and corpses were found along the way.

The responsible authorities in the town were the Civil Commissioner, Duncan Campbell, and the ranking military officer Lieut.-Col. Richard

England. They were joined on the 29th December by Somerset, who had now ordered the evacuation of the main forward defensive post, Fort Willshire, and the satellite forts, and had left only Fort Beaufort manned and in a state of siege. He now gloomily contemplated a possible evacuation of Graham's Town.

In the absence of effective military leadership the citizens of the town did their own thing. Some prominent citizens formed themselves in to a "Committee of Safety." The more active inhabitants began to organize themselves into various voluntary militia units.

Edward Driver claimed that he "raised a force of volunteers"[360]. Certainly a number of like-minded people in the town got together and organized themselves into groups. Those like him, who had experience of the bush, were good horsemen, and had an easy familiarity with firearms, were to play an important part in the volunteer forces that later supported the army.

By the time of the invasion both Joseph Walker and George Wood were the owners of shops in Bathurst St. Each had managed to build up enough capital to be optimistic about the future. Now all was threatened. They each had a spirit of entrepreneurship. Neither was particularly fitted to military activity. Nevertheless, something had to be done. The two cooperated in organizing all the Khoikhoi and coloured population of the town into a force that they called the "Sharpshooters." This was a confusing name, as the settler Volunteer Corps called themselves the "Albany Sharpshooters." Wood and Walker set their force to assist in guarding and patrolling the town.

Harry Smith Takes Charge   [1834 – 1835]

In Cape Town the first news of the invasion arrived on 28th December in the form of a dispatch from Somerset which pre-dated the worst of the irruption. D'Urban decided he needed a presence on the frontier. He ordered the Chief of Staff of the army in Cape Town, Lieut.-Col. Henry George Wakelyn "Harry" Smith[361] to proceed to the frontier, giving him full power to impose military law as required. Smith was a veteran of the Peninsula campaign in Spain, the American war of 1812, and Waterloo. Flamboyant and gallant he had managed to get a posting to the Cape a few years before as Deputy Quartermaster-General. Sir Lowry Cole merged the post of Deputy Adjutant General with this shortly afterwards. He and his beautiful Spanish wife Juana, whom he had rescued from British atrocities in Badajoz and married when she was just fourteen, cut a dash in Cape Town, but what Smith wanted was action (and promotion), and now he had the opportunity. Further dispatches described the worsening situation and his mission gained even greater urgency.

The logical mode of transport was by ship, which, if winds were favourable would take about 10 days to reach Algoa Bay, but could be delayed for substantially longer than this. Impatiently Smith chose to undertake his epic journey on horseback. The ride, along the route followed by military dispatch riders and taking advantage of the changes of horse available, took just six days, well over 100 kilometres a day.

After a frenetic few days organizing the despatch of reinforcements and supplies by ship, he left Cape Town before dawn on New Year's day 1835 and rode into Graham's Town on 6th January. What he found horrified him.

The defence of the panicked town could be described as a tragi-comedy. Without effective leadership the defences in the town were ill-placed and ineffective. The small forces of the army garrison were supplemented by various volunteer groups, armed with whatever weapons they could find, assembled by individuals showing a level of leadership qualities. In the absence of an adequate command structure these tended to act at cross purposes. A few settlers had military experience. William Gilfillan hd served as a lieutenant in the 60th Regiment between 1812 and 1819, had returned to Britain, and had then joined Thornhill's party of 1820 settlers. Robert Bagot of William Smith's party had been a captain in the 47th regiment before emigrating to South Africa. Others, without such experience, such as Edward Driver, George Wood, and Joseph Walker, by organizing militia groups, also achieved positions of command.

Smith made his way through the ragtag and bobtail army towards Oatlands, Somerset's estate in Graham's Town, preparing to meet the local commander.

Smith was never moderate in his opinions. In addition, his vocabulary was extensively influenced by that of the lower ranks of Wellington's army. In masculine company his ordinary conversation was embellished with profanity, scatology, and blasphemy. It would have been entertaining to eavesdrop on his debriefing of Campbell and Henry Somerset.

He made it absolutely clear that he was not satisfied with the supine air of defeatism. The way to win the war was to take the fight to the enemy. Within days he had made sweeping changes to the forces available[362]. He formed the Albany Sharpshooters, Bathurst Volunteers and other militia groups into a Corps, consisting of four companies of infantry and one of cavalry. Edward Driver had the command of the 1st Troop of the Albany Sharpshooters. The Khoikhoi Sharpshooters became part of this Corps with George Wood and Joseph Walker rapidly advancing to Major and Captain respectively.

Smith had two objects in view. The first was to provide an immediate response to the invasion by attacks on the invaders in their own territory. The second was to build up a force of invasion as quickly as possible to defeat the Xhosa and impose a state of peace on the frontier region.

Four hundred volunteers were organized under Major Cox of the regular army and, on January 10th, less than three weeks after the first hostilities, crossed the Fish River with orders to attack and destroy Nqeno's Mbalu village and the village of Ngqika's son Tyhali. This mission had been completed by the 13th January. The Cape Corps, under Henry Somerset, was dispatched to secure the route to Algoa Bay. Detachments of the regular army were sent to reoccupy Fort Willshire and the chain of military posts in the ceded territory. By the time Sir Benjamin D'Urban arrived in Algoa Bay, on the 20th January, the Xhosa had retreated from the Colony.

When the news of the war came, Charles Lennox Stretch was living at Glen Avon, the estate of his father-in-law Robert Hart. He felt he had a unique perspective to provide, having served during the Battle of Graham's Town. He wrote offering his services to his friend, and recent boss as Surveyor-General, Major Charles Michell, who had joined the staff of the Governor and was based in Graham's Town. The letter was dealt with by Smith who summoned him to Graham's Town in order that he might be placed in an appropriate position. He arrived there of February 6th and his first task was to write a report for D'Urban on the operations of the army during the war of 1819[363]. He was soon appointed as Captain in the Provisional Corps on 22nd February, having prodded Smith the previous day with a letter reminding him of his availability.

The Corps of Guides   [1834 – 1835]

After the punitive thrusts against Nqeno and Bhothomane, D'Urban and Smith began preparations for their major campaign into the ceded territory and beyond. Smith was convinced that the Fish River was untenable as a boundary because of the harsh terrain and the dense bush into which the Xhosa could disappear. He made the case for the Buffalo (Qonce) River, a much more open and defensible barrier. This was deep in the territory of Hintsa's Gcalekas. First it would be necessary to clear all the Xhosa from the ceded territory. Both D'Urban and Smith held the delusion not only that Hintsa, as Xhosa king, was responsible for the war, but also that he would have the power to compensate the colony for the loss of livestock and war damages and would be able to control the Xhosa people if he were coerced to do so. The territory was unknown to them. They had a need for tough young guides who were intimately familiar with the region and the people in it. The enormous pool of refugees in Graham's Town included many such, most already enrolled in the variety of voluntary militias. The man he chose to lead this new Corps of Guides was the twenty-four year old Richard Southey. He took charge of what was to be the Corps of Guides for the headquarters column and and had the responsibility of selecting the guides for the other columns.

Richard Southey[364] was the son of George Southey Sr, the leader of a settler party that came out to the Cape on board the *Kennersley Castle*. George and his wife Jane had had seven children who had grown to adulthood in the first years of the settlement. A year or two after the initial settlement, Jane's brother John Shaw, with his wife and nine children had also emigrated to the Colony. By the end of 1834 George Sr was dead and the younger members of the family were taking advantage of the increasing prosperity in the Colony and striking out on their own. Three Southey brothers, William, Richard, and George Jr, had purchased a farm on the Kap River, about halfway between Graham's Town and the Fish River mouth. They were erecting the buildings on what they envisaged would become a large estate. Their cousin John Shaw Jr had joined them on the farm to help them with the construction. His brothers William[365] and Robert may also have been involved.

> They had nearly completed the erection of commodious and extensive farm premises when the war of 1835 broke out. The [Xhosa]s drove off 800 head of their cattle and waylaid and murdered a young man named John Shaw, a near relative who had quitted Graham's Town to their assistance.[366]

The Southey brothers, and William and Robert Shaw retreated to Bathurst, faced not only with a family tragedy but also with the loss of their property and an uncertain future. They enrolled in the militia units that were being hastily put together to support the troops in Harry Smith's conduct of the war. Two and a half months later, in March 1835, Robert Shaw was killed in an engagement at Trompetter's Drift.

Richard Southey, Captain of Guides, assembled a group from the Albany sharpshooters.

> Fifty two volunteered and were accepted, among whom I [H. E. Halse] was one. When we elected Richard Southey our Captain and George Southey Lieut., fifty others, young Albany farmers, also volunteered, under the command of Mitford Bowker, calling themselves the 'Bathurst Volunteers'. These were mostly friends and relations of our fellows. Thus the Grahams Town [I.e. Albany] Sharp Shooters were disbanded and returned to town ...[367]

The Corps included Southey's brothers, William and George, his cousin, William Shaw, the brothers Bertram and William Bowker, a young man John Bisset and Edward Driver[368].

The Southeys were very experienced. They had served on Somerset's bumbling campaign against Matiwane in 1828, and had been involved in a number of skirmishes since the beginning of the war. Richard was to end up as the distinguished colonial administrator, Sir Richard Southey KCMG. The Bowkers were two of a large settler family. Miles Bowker, their father had been the leader of his own sole proprietor party and the boys had been brought up on the frontier. The Bowker farm had been overrun in the first assault of the colony. All the male members of the family had been prominent among the volunteers. John Bisset was the baby of the group, while Edward Driver was the old man. The others were in their twenties apart from Bisset the teenager who was 17. Bisset, too, was to end up in later years with a distinguished military and administrative career, ending as Sir John Bisset KCMG, Acting Governor of Natal. Driver's 39 years and vast experience separated him from his companions and gave him a mentorship role.

The new Corps began its duties on 17th March 1835. Richard Southey's squad of eight was assigned to Harry Smith. Uniforms were scarcely different from their regular bush attire, the only point of distinction being a swaggering ostrich feather in each hatband of their broad-brimmed wideawake hats. The squad assigned to D'Urban were distinguished by a leopard-skin hatband[369].

Horse Trading   [1835]

After Smith's arrival, as the military force was built up in Graham's Town, what had been a sleepy village woke up to find itself the military centre of a campaign involving 4000 troops and their activities. The army needed horses, oxen, wagons, equipment, clothing, and rations. For the merchants and entrepreneurs of Graham's Town this was a bonanza.

One of the first to see the opportunities was George Wood. Wood had come a long way since his days as an apprentice to William Thackwray and a barefoot voorloper to John Thackwray's wagon. His trading station at Hermanus's Kraal had been successful, he had a modest shop in town, and his prosperity was growing. His and Joseph Walker's efforts to organize the Khoikhoi inhabitants of the town into the Sharpshooters meant that he had a point of contact with Harry Smith and, within days, he had secured the contract to supply horses to the army. Item 3 of the military orders signed by Smith on 17th January 1835 states

Dr Campbell and Captain Wood, of the Graham's Town Volunteers, are appointed to purchase horses, according to a schedule of rates (Marginal Note: Minimum £6 Maximum £11 5s) which will be given them.

By section 4 of the same orders Captain Wood has become Major Wood and is placed in charge of the depot for keeping the horses. Wood needed help so he brought in the services of another crony:

He [Wood], and Joseph Walker, and Dr A G Campbell were to buy horses.[370]

Whether in times of war or in times of peace, arms contracts, and anything else to do with military procurement, offer opportunities for very satisfactory profit. If, as is sometimes the case even up to the present day, these dealings are not according to the highest ethical standards, the profits can be even better. The chief source for an account of the dealings of Wood, Walker, and Campbell is Thomas Stubbs[371] and his story should be taken with a pinch of salt because Wood was Stubbs's *bête noire*. When Thomas Stubbs wrote his reminiscences nearly forty years after these events he could not forgive the fact that while he, Stubbs, had lived a hard dangerous and relatively unrewarded life, Wood, whom he regarded as stupid, had become the "richest man in the Colony." Wood became a leading citizen, Member of the Legislative Assembly, and public benefactor in Grahamstown as a result of astute financial dealings: Stubbs spent the last years of his life, nearly destitute, on his brother's farm writing his reminiscences.

There is little reason to doubt that the three entrepreneurs could acquire horses at as little as two pounds ten shillings each and sell them again for between five and ten pounds. That is the way of arms contracts and can almost be regarded as an honest profit. Another settler[372] recorded:

I employed myself in purchasing and selling horses to the Govt agents and from a very small beginning – £10 the proceeds of my only Horse – I made in a week about £150 profit. With this I was enabled to fit myself out comfortably for taking the field for some months.

Horses were not the only source of profit. George Wood also sold cheap brown fabric to equip the Khoikhoi volunteers[373]

It looked well when new, but a march into the Fish River Bush which soon followed, made the bush brown and the [men][374] scarecrows. A fresh contract to clothe the naked being inevitable, a little foresight dictated to the previous contractor that something more substantial would be required, all the available moleskin was therefore purchased. When the second contract was called for the first contractor got it, but with the understanding that he must abandon the military rank of major in the Hottentot Battalion, which he held. Of course the military rank was readily parted with and the contract retained.

Wood cleared £7000 from these sales[375]:

> The most notorious [of the incidents of profiteering] was the clothing of the Provisional Colonial Infantry by a person named "Wood" who reaped the sum of £7000 for this job.

Stubbs's account of more murky activities[376] than simply making outrageous profits is less certain. Wood apparently used Walker and Campbell as suppliers while Wood handled sales. Stubbs then describes how, after a horse was sold, it was led around a block, up an alley, and back to the place where the sale was taking place. It was then sold again, and possibly more than twice.

> He [Wood] not only made his store, but I believe he humbugged both Old Dr Campbell and Walker.

If this fraud was successful then either the army had no checks on delivery of purchases (quite possible) or someone on the procurement side was in on the act. Whatever the truth of the situation, by the end of the war not only had Wood had made his pile, but so had Joseph Walker. In spite of Stubbs's suggestion that Walker and Campbell had been cheated by Wood, Joseph Walker does not seem afterwards to have been at odds with Wood. They appear to have maintained a cordial relationship after the war.

These were not the only irregularities. Stubbs records that the cattle placed with the Government for safekeeping at a depot called Coldstream were plundered:

> A party of civilians were posted there on cattle guard but, the greatest enemy they had was the Contractor. The Government allowed him to look out fat cattle there (no matter who owned them) and bring them into town for slaughter. I know several who saw their favourite cows slaughtered, and never got a farthing for them: horses were taken in the same way - and no compensation was ever made.[377]

During the war the leading meat contractors for the government had been William Cock and George Lee[378]:

> I [Thomas Stubbs] then began with the manner the settlers were humbugged by the government from the time we arrived in the Colony and as to the protection they got for their cattle in the war - I would describe it - ... I told them that the cattle was sent to a depot about six miles from town and that the contractors, Cock and Lee, had the pick of the cattle to slaughter for the troops, and that I knew several settlers who had seen their favourite cows at the slaughter house and claimed them, but were not allowed to have them.[379]

William Cock was the leader of a party that had arrived in the Colony on board *Weymouth*. By the start of the war he was already a substantial businessman in Graham's Town.

Edward Driver was one of those that suffered:[380]

> ... although his large herd of cattle were saved from capture by the
> [Xhosa]s yet that by being placed in charge of the Government the
> greater part of them perhaps all with the brand mark upon them were
> sold to Transport Contractors others were slaughtered for rations for
> the Troops or others receiving Government supplies.

He complained afterwards that, while on campaign with the army, large
numbers of cattle had been sent up for the use of the troops, many of
which were his property:

> His Excellency accompanied by Col. Smith and Staff and also many Col-
> onists among whom were the Messrs Southeys, Bowkers, Thackwrays
> and Shaw with many others rode out and saw them. His Excellency in
> presence of a good number of persons said that both he [Driver] and all
> the Colonists should get compensation for their cattle so consumed.

No such compensation was ever forthcoming.

The Press   [1831 – 1835]

Robert Godlonton and Thomas Stringfellow were printers by trade and,
when they came to the Cape with the settlers in 1820, they brought with
them a printing press. The authorities at the Cape could not allow such
an instrument of sedition at the frontier, so when *Chapman* put in at Cape
Town, the press was confiscated and sent to Graaff Reinet, where for
many years it was used to print government notices. The two printers,
after an initially unsuccessful period on the land, found themselves,
dressed in livery, employed as assistants to the messenger of the Court[381],
with no opportunity of pursuing their chosen trade.

In 1831, while on a shooting trip passing through Graaff Reinet, a
young printer, Louis Meurant, had his attention drawn to a wooden press
that was for sale. It was the one that had been confiscated. He bought it at
an auction and used it to start the first newspaper on the eastern frontier[382], which he called *The Graham's Town Journal*. He employed Godlonton as printer, reporter, and editor, and soon the responsibility for the paper was largely in Godlonton's hands. He was later to become its owner.

In the eighteen thirties, after press censorship was ended, the standards
required of journalists were not what is hoped for today. Separation of
news and comment was not a familiar concept. Writers happily expressed
their opinions in terms that would now be regarded as libellous. Editors
found their news where they could. Unsubstantiated reports, rumour, and
even invention were seized upon to fill their pages. Godlonton was no exception. Much of the newspaper was filled with tedious reports of the

minutiae of small town life but when more substantial events took place he made the most of them.

Robert Godlonton was conservative, narrow-minded and self-right-eous, not broadly educated, a pillar of the Wesleyan congregation in Graham's Town, and entirely one-sided in his identification with the interests of his own community. This was not unusual, but his position in control of the only newspaper in the region put him in a unique position to promote these values.

From the beginning the *Journal* had been strong in attacking the neglect of the frontier region by the Cape government. The settlers had been placed on the frontier and over the years had suffered drought, flood, crop failure, stock theft, and pestilence, with little control over their own destiny. The government was in Cape Town: even by fast ship it was more than a week away. They were largely dependent on their own community and inevitably became isolationist. Outsiders were the enemy. The *Journal* reflected and intensified these views. In an uninhibited stream of vituperation, Godlonton attacked the Governor, the Xhosa, the Colonial authorities and any other targets on which he could bring his sights to bear.

The attack by the Xhosa on the settlement exacerbated this. Graham's Town was filled with refugees, many of whom had lost family and property in the invasion. Rumours stoked the fears of the people and *The Graham's Town Journal* propagated them with enthusiasm. Godlonton's style can be judged from the polemic that he wrote after the war, *A narrative of the irruption of the Kaffir hordes into the Eastern Province of the Cape of Good Hope, 1834-1835.* It was not, however, a unique style at the time. Ambrose Campbell, the horse trader of the previous section, wrote an equally vituperative work, *The Wrongs of the Caffre Nation: a Narrative,* strongly attacking the treatment of the Xhosa by the Government and the nature of the military campaign. This lost its force because, while it made significant points, many of its allegations could not be substantiated[383].

The sniping of the Journal spared no-one. An exasperated Harry Smith wrote to his wife:

> I have desired you have a Graham's Town Journal sent you, and I beg you not to believe more than one-half of the alarming lies that will be published in it. This place ought to be called "Necessity" for it is the mother of invention.[384]

The war, just as it made the fortunes of many on the frontier, also shaped the future editorial stance of *The Graham's Town Journal,* and the views of the community it served. Over the subsequent years the *Journal* continued to propagate an isolationist view, vehemently anti-Xhosa, strongly advocating a separatist Eastern Province, a view that mirrored and shaped the opinions of many, but not all, of its readers.

A Convenient Scapegoat   [1835]

The objectives of D'Urban and Smith in responding to the invasion were threefold. First was the task of securing the Colony and expelling the invaders. Second was the intention of exacting retribution by recovering the losses of the Colonists, especially in stock, from the invaders. Third was the determination to ensure that the future of the Eastern frontier region would be safe from the prospect of another such incursion.

The first objective was obtained relatively easily. Once an effective command structure had been achieved, the frontier colonists had been organized into a semblance of a military force, and commando reinforcements from other parts of the Colony had arrived, the invaders rapidly retired to the bush across the Fish River, driving their newly acquired herds as far from the risk of reclamation as possible. The line of military forts was repossessed and the first activity would be a mopping up operation in the Amatolas.

The second objective was less straightforward. From whom would the missing cattle be retrieved? The herds were dissipated throughout the Xhosa territory, in the possession of a variety of groups of men with many allegiances, melting into the bush. The solution to that problem was also uncomplicated in the minds of D'Urban and Smith. Retrieve cattle wherever you can find them and never mind the niceties of their actual origin.

Smith believed he had the solution to meeting the third objective. The ceded territory had been a problem from the start. His solution was straightforward: annex the territory between the Fish and the Kei and occupy it. In his mind the Kei could be defended: the Fish could not. D'Urban would take some convincing.

As a background to all this they had a nagging problem. Who were they fighting? Military minds, honed in the Napoleonic Wars, were comfortable with a European command structure, with the ultimate responsibility in the hands of the Emperor. Any such structure was absent in the Xhosa. The one figure that could be identified as being at the head of things was Hintsa, the Gcaleka king, by virtue of his descent from Phalo through the Great House succession, recognized by the Rharhabe as king, but only in a titular sense. The *Graham's Town Journal* had been stridently pushing the point of view that Hintsa was responsible for the war.

While Smith was a man who always allowed action to be a substitute for thought, D'Urban was of a different calibre. He was quite prepared to make decisions but he wanted them based on hard intelligence.

> Master [D'Urban] is always floundering in the midst of information, whilst I like to take a look at the ground, march, and take possession[385]

It is hard for a twenty first century mind to appreciate the level of isolation of those who bore ultimate responsibility at that time.

Before D'Urban had ever left Cape Town, the stream of reports bringing intelligence from Gcalekaland predisposed him to be suspicious of Hintsa's motives. John Ayliff at Butterworth was a focus for the gathering of this intelligence. While there is no reason to doubt the reports of incidents of murder and pillage, Ayliff's interpretation of the motives of Hintsa were strongly coloured by his own prejudices.

As we have noted, Hintsa's position with respect to the easternmost Xhosa was a titular one, and he could not be regarded as responsible for the war. On the other hand, there is little doubt that he was consulted before the war broke out and gave his approval[386]. He also did not prevent a number of his subject chiefs from participating. Furthermore, after the invaders had been pushed back from the Colony and had begun to retreat, Gcalekaland provided a refuge for them and their plunder. Evidence for this continued to accumulate while D'Urban and Smith planned their campaign. Richard Walker, for example, who was in a good position to observe as he took his wagon through the territory, initially for trading purposes and thereafter to bring isolated traders and missionaries to safety, provided a report, dated 9th February 1835[387]:

> ... I have seen five droves of colonial cattle pass here in one day, besides horses, all brought by Hintza's people; added to this, it appears Hintza sent men to order the plunder of the last two trading stations belonging to Fowler & Co., on the other side of the Kye, occupied by Eccles and Horton, which was immediately put into execution and the men turned adrift; and were I to tell you of their sufferings it would make your heart ache; suffice it to say, they stripped them naked all to their shirts, and left them in this state for half a month both night and day, not even so much as allowing them a kaross to cover themselves at night, and then drove into a small outhouse without a bit of fire, and almost starved them to death, besides many other indignities too numerous and disgusting to mention, and this all done by Hintza's people. ...

Other reports giving similar information arrived from D'Urban's own officers in the field.

The losses of the colonists in buildings, crops and live stock were enormous. The Governor was certain that not only should the enemy be defeated, but also retribution should be exacted. Convinced of the complicity of Hintsa – D'Urban by weighing the evidence, and Smith by emotion – the Governor agreed to the invasion of Gcalekaland.

An invasion to retrieve cattle would have been acceptable. What was actually planned was taking on an enormous responsibility and politically extremely hazardous. No British Government wanted to take on responsibility for additional colonial possessions that were a drain on the exchequer rather than a source of wealth. What D'Urban was unaware of was that, while these events were taking place, Robert Peel's Tory government had fallen, to be replaced by a Whig Government under Lord Melbourne. The new Secretary of State for War and the Colonies was Charles Grant, 1st Baron Glenelg, a man far less likely to approve of the action than his predecessor Lord Aberdeen.

D'Urban, persuaded by the mercurial Smith, resolved to annex the territory from the Fish to the Kei, drive on into Gcalekaland, obtain retribution from Hintsa and force him to take responsibility for all the Xhosa. Smith began to plan the invasion.

Chapter 12. Invasion

And tell sad stories of the death of kings:
How some have been deposed, some slain in war
William Shakespeare, Richard II, Act III Scene 2

Preliminaries [1835]

The troops and volunteers available to Smith were divided into two parts. One, under Col. England, consisting of about 500 regulars and 1500 volunteers, remained in Graham's Town for the defence of the Colony. The force that Smith built up for the invasion was also made up of about 2000 men. They were a medley of regular troops, Boer commandos, settler volunteers, and Khoikhoi "volunteers" such as those that Wood and Walker had assembled – in Smith's words[388]:

> [I] organized two corps of Hottentots consisting of every loose vagabond I could lay my hands on, called the 1st and 2nd Battallion Hottentot Infantry.

The troops were organized in Four Divisions, under the overall command of D'Urban, with Smith as Chief of Staff. The 1st Division mustered at Fort Willshire commanded by Col. Peddie of the 72nd Regiment. Somerset's 2nd Division assembled in the Southern part of the ceded territory. Major Cox commanded the 3rd Division at Fort Beaufort, and the 4th Division, consisting of the Boer force, was placed in the north under Field Commandant van Wyk. Among the settlers were some with previous military experience who were put in command of various units. One such was William Gilfillan, a former officer of the 65th Regiment, who had served in the Cape from 1813 to 1818, and then returned as a settler in Thornhill's party. He was put in command of a unit of Harry Smith's "loose vagabonds". Equipping them had been a nightmare, with the first flimsy uniforms, supplied by George Wood, destroyed in the bush, and they were still outfitted in what clothing could be found. Gilfillan's diary shows his exasperation with Smith's style of command, painting a different picture from the hero of Graham's Town[389].

> 16th and 17th [March 1835] ... He [Smith] rides up to the camp in the evening and in a most ridiculous speech where he calls the Hottentots his children and promises fifty things which he never intends to give. By way of clenching [*sic*] the matter and ingratiating himself with the men, he tells them that he throws all the blame of their not being clothed to the Officers ... and a deal of trash of the same sort leading to vilify and render the Officers unpopular with their men (meaning perhaps thereby to promote unanimity and the good of the service).

...

> 18th ... The balance [of the parade] move off towards the Fish River
> most thoroughly disgusted with the Chief of Staff and praying that
> some lucky accident would place them under the command of Col
> Somerset or some equally rational company.

This undermining of the authority of his officers is yet another aspect of
Smith's flawed character as a commander.

The start of the push was into the Xhosa territory of the Amatola
mountains. D'Urban had joined the 1st Division at Fort Willshire on 28th
March together with the last of the troops. On the 30th and 31st the push
began. The initial objective was the removal of the Xhosa in the region of
the Amatola mountains. There were a number of skirmishes. In most of
these there was little direct engagement. Generally the Xhosa melted into
the bush and cattle were "repossessed." These were not necessarily the
cattle that had been stolen but whatever beasts had been captured, no
matter what their previous history.

The headquarters were temporarily set up in a camp in the Amatolas
where the 1st Division awaited the arrival of the other Divisions. Unlike
the Xhosa, who could move through the bush, living off the land unen-
cumbered by equipment other than a bundle of assegais, the Colonial
forces were constrained by the need for maintaining adequate lines of
supply. The only available way of moving equipment was by means of
ox-wagon trains which moved through the rugged country at a slow walking pace. Smith, with the Governor now on the spot, was heavily occupied with his duties as Chief of Staff. He could only bear the tasks of administration for a finite time. His mercurial character required action. On
April 7th D'Urban gave him permission to take a detachment into the
bush:

> I took with me a detachment of the 72nd Highlanders, under Captain
> Murray, my faithful attendant always; one of the Hottentot Battalions;
> and my Corps of Mounted Guides, gentlemen of the country and mer-
> chants who had traded all over [Xhosa]land and knew the country per-
> fectly. Never was there a more useful body[390].

The guides in this detachment included Edward Driver, a
"merchant", Bertram and William Bowker, Henry Halse, and John Bisset, the "gentlemen of the country".

The target was a large group of Xhosa, with large numbers of cattle, in
a mountain stronghold. They consisted of groups of amaMbalu and
amaNdlambe supported by some Khoikhoi led by Louis Arnoldus, "a
noted rebel Hottentot."[391] With better weapons their position would have
been nearly impregnable. At the eastern end of the Amatola mountains

two deep ravines or poorts disgorge watercourses that converge to form the Buffalo River, which flows roughly southward. Between two branches of the river a ridge runs down from the mountain top with steep cliffs on either side.

> On coming in sight we saw in the bush an isolated hill, not very high, for the ascent was gradual from all sides until you came to a precipice about 30 or 40 feet high rising abruptly, smooth and perpendicular, on the top forming a flat level piece of tableland of about 150 yards across, with one or two good fountains which trickled over the rocks in many places. At the bottom of the krantz the dropping water had made a sort of cavern all round, or rather, by the washing away of the ground, the rock was over hanging and formed a sort of ledge. There were only two paths by which this krantz could be ascended – one immediately in front and one behind which we did not then know of.[392]

The main Xhosa position was at the top of the krantz. Smith had sent the Khoikhoi battalion round to the north to outflank the Xhosa while he proposed to occupy the ridge with the 72nd, under Murray. From the top of the krantz the narrow access path was bombarded with rocks and boulders. The Xhosa were ready with assegais to defend the gap through which only one man could proceed at a time.

Bertram and William Bowker with Edward Driver had taken cover. Captain Murray, in charge of the group of 72nd Highlanders, gave the command to his troops to advance up the hill towards the krantz. The soldiers set off:

> Old Driver was with us; about as fine an old chap as ever I knew. William began to climb the rocks, the [Xhosa]s firing and shouting, when Driver shouted to William "Come back you fool and let them go up that's paid for it'. I thought this very good advice.[393]

As usual Edward Driver did not see the need to place himself needlessly in danger. Nevertheless, when it became necessary to try and force a path through the narrow gap he was one of the first to try and as a result was slightly wounded by an assegai in the face. The assault on the fortress continued leading to several casualties. Captain Murray himself was quite seriously wounded. Eventually the Khoikhoi Battalion was in position to make an assault from the rear and the battle to take what became known as Murray's Krantz was over. The Xhosa fled, Louis Arnoldus was captured, and many thousands of cattle were repossessed.

The skirmishes throughout the Amatolas continued. Smith relied more and more on his scouts to get intelligence about the movements of the Xhosa. He began to get the measure of Driver's usefulness and also of his character[394]:

... [Driver] on one occasion was late in returning from a scouting expedition and the hot tempered Sir Harry Smith was fuming and swearing at the delay. One of his officers ventured to suggest to Sir Harry, as
the river had come down in flood and Edward Driver was on the other
side, that Driver might have got drowned and they had better go down
the river to look for his body. Sir Harry replied, with his usual accom-
paniment of oaths, that they all ought to know Driver's body would not
float downstream, if he were drowned, but would float upstream.

Eventually D'Urban and Smith were ready to make their major incursion
into Hintsa's territory. D'Urban was the commanding officer, but he depended heavily for advice on Smith, who was the driving force.

Across the Kei   [April – May 1835]

The British force invaded Gcalekaland, Hintsa's territory, on 15th April
1835[395]. D'Urban's doubts were overcome by Smith's forceful arguments
and, starting from their camp near the present position of Komgha, they
wound their way down into the Kei Gorge. As they crossed the river, relatively low compared with its flow during times of flood, they were
watched by a group of Gcaleka. With them was an emissary from
Bhurhu, Hintsa's brother, who had been sent to gauge their intentions.
Smith's reply was unencouraging. It amounted to stating that the army
came in peace provided that Hintsa would restore all cattle stolen from
the Colony and would provide a sufficiently large force to support the Colonial Government against the Rharhabe. The force would continue to
advance until Hintsa made himself available for discussions with D'Urban. In the absence of any resistance they did so, arriving at John Ayliff's
ruined mission station of Butterworth, adjacent to Hintsa's Great Place,
Gcwa, on 17th April. They were joined by Somerset's exhausted and be-
draggled Division on the 20th. They had encountered rough country, bad
weather, and more opposition and were badly in need of rest and recuper-
ation.

Sorties in the Amatolas   [April 1835]

While D'Urban and Smith were advancing on Hintsa, the harrying of
Maqoma and Tyhali continued. This was the task of the third division
under Major Cox. Their tactics were exactly same as the those that
Robert Hart had experienced when he had been involved with Col. Graham in clearing the Zuurveld more than twenty years before. Now Hart's
son-in-law, Charles Lennox Stretch found himself involved in a similar
war of attrition as a captain in Cox's division.

The Xhosa had invented the guerilla war for themselves. They were
able to live off the land, waiting their opportunity to attack any isolated

army groups, liberate some cattle, or pick off stragglers. The British army was equipped and trained as a force that would obey orders unthinkingly so that they could maintain a steady disciplined action while under fire during pitched battles on European soil. It was difficult for them to come to terms with an enemy who struck without warning and then melted away into the bush. The Colonist volunteers, both Dutch and English, while untrained, were better suited to this kind of warfare.

The need to maintain supply lines was a significant burden on the army: the Xhosa lived off the land. The strategy adopted by the army was, therefore, one of making the land uninhabitable. Just as Graham had done, they set out to burn the huts and destroy the crops, leaving a wasteland that provided no sustenance to the enemy. Among the Xhosa it was the women who tended the crops and looked after the homes. On attack they fled into the bush. While the army orders were to protect the women and children, a figure moving in dense bush was a potential danger, whether male or female.

On 27th April intelligence had been received that Tyhali was in the bush near Burnshill. Stretch was leading a small detachment in search of him. From the bush they heard the cries of someone in agony. With their guns at the ready the party advanced cautiously. What they found appalled Stretch. A young woman with a severe abdominal gunshot wound was lying on the ground. Her child was crying beside her. She was attended by other women who could do nothing for her but try to soothe her. They told Stretch that she was one of Maqoma's younger wives. She was clearly dying. Stretch in his journal that evening admitted that he could not stand the sight. Unable to do anything to help, the soldiers left them, after briefly trying unsuccessfully to persuade the women to move to open ground where they could not be mistaken for hidden warriors.

Later they found other women in the bush:

> Many women were met soon after. We explained to them the folly of remaining in the bush and advised them to go out to the open country where they would be safe. But (as it was stated) those who had fled to the Governor's camp at the Buffalo had been prostituted, [so] the [Xhosa]s would not allow the women to leave the bush, preferring the risk of being shot to the licentious conduct of the Christians; and unfortunately for the respectability of the army, there is too much cause of regret that such things do occur even by the officers.[396]

Stretch was in his home territory. His farm was not very far off, and in his years as a Government Surveyor he had trudged round the region meeting the farmers on the Colonial side of the boundary and many Xhosa in the Ceded Territory. It was no surprise to him when, one evening, while camped on the ridge between the Tyumie and Keiskamma

Rivers, three visitors came into camp. They were Stretch's brother-in-law, John Pringle, his neighbour, George Rennie, and Thomas Scott, who had married Beatrice Pringle, John's half-sister. This was a chance to catch up with family news. John had recently had a letter from England and it carried sad news. He showed it to Stretch:

> Read a letter informing John of his brother's death and his happy end from his minister, John MacDonald.[397]

The death of Thomas Pringle had occurred in London on 5th December 1834, where he had returned some years before. After his battles with Lord Charles Somerset over the freedom of the press he had been left without an income and had returned to England in 1826. There he became secretary to the Anti-Slavery Society and worked for them until his death seeing the successful passing of the anti-slavery act in 1834. He had maintained his contacts with the Colony, remaining in touch with his former partner, Fairbairn, and with Dr Philip of the London Missionary Society. Had Thomas survived until the period after the war he would have been a strong voice for the philanthropist cause, but it was not to be.

The Murder of Hintsa   [April – May 1835]

As Smith's force advanced into Hintsa's territory the first delegation that they met had nothing to do with the Gcaleka. A large group of men approached them waving white rags and asked to speak to the Governor. They were Mfengu – Fingos as the Colonists called them – Ayliff's converts. By this time Ayliff himself had been forced to abandon the mission. He had left his congregation with assurances that they would receive the protection of the British Government. D'Urban took them under his protection. He saw them as a future source of men for the defence of the frontier and for the time being they were allowed to remain with the army.

By 24th April Hintsa had not appeared. D'Urban lost patience and declared war. He and Smith left Somerset's Division to protect the communications lines while they recuperated, and advanced deep into Gcalekaland, setting up a base of operations near the junction of the Tsomo and Isolo rivers. From there he launched operations to capture cattle, acquiring several thousand and making it clear to Hintsa that his problem was not simply going to go away. Hintsa had good reason to stay clear of the army but he could not leave them to ravage his people and confiscate his cattle. He decided to parley.

On the 29th April Smith returned to camp from one of his raids to be informed that

... a deputation had arrived from Hintsa consisting of four [Xhosa]s mounted on capital horses which were detained and themselves made prisoners. They stated that Hintza was near and wished to visit the Governor for the purpose of coming to terms[398]

This treatment of the deputation could not have impressed Hintsa who was waiting in the neighbourhood. He was, with good reason, apprehensive of the motives of D'Urban and Smith. A little while later:

Thirty nine other messengers arrive whose first question was why must Hintza die what had he done? And concluded enquiring what had become of Hintza's first messengers, and informed us Hintza was on his way and would be in the camp that afternoon.

Indeed, later that afternoon Hintsa arrived with a large mounted escort. The Corps of Guides was detailed to stand guard over the escort while the king was greeted with ceremony by D'Urban and began what he had expected to be a process of negotiation.

Hintsa was rather out of his depth. He was not comfortable with a process in which long series of conditions were taken from extensive documents that he could not read. He had long recognised that he was between a rock and a hard place with pressure coming from the Mpondo and Thembu in the east and the Rharhabe being forced back by the British in the west. He had been coerced unwillingly to the negotiating table by the British invasion and now he found that he had no room to manoeuvre. Instead of a negotiation he was now faced with an ultimatum in circumstances where he had good cause to fear for his personal safety.

D'Urban laid out his terms. Hintsa was required to return 50 000 cattle and 1000 horses which had allegedly been stolen during the time leading up to the war. The fact that they were largely not the responsibility of the Gqaleka was not taken into account. He was expected to return all firearms and to order and police a cessation of hostilities. Hintsa and his son, Sarhili, far from being regarded as protected under a flag of truce, were to be held as hostages pending the fulfilment of the British demands. In vain he made the case that his position as Xhosa king was a ceremonial one and that he had no effective authority over the Rharhabe, let alone the Mbalu or Gqunukwhebe. He was given twenty four hours to make a decision.

A process of softening him up then began. He was invited to dine with Smith that evening. By the end of the dinner Hintsa had agreed to cooperate. There are some suggestions that he might not have fully understood what D'Urban's terms implied; they were set out at length in a complex document. If he did understand them there is no doubt that he would have clearly understood that he was not in a position to deliver. He had come to negotiate and now found himself subject to force majeure. One could legitimately argue that any agreement was made under duress. Nevertheless D'Urban and Smith professed to be delighted at his acceptance of "peace."

> The whole force was paraded at day light and the officers ordered to the front to be present at the ratification of the peace. The terms were read to Hinza and upon his stating that he perfectly understood and agreed to the terms the Governor shook hands with him and three guns were fired. We were then dismissed and a present was made to Hinza – several articles valued at £100 sterling –[399]

Orders were then given to return to the base camp at the Kei River. In D'Urban's and Smith's minds the war was won. At the same time an exodus of the Mfengu began. Offered a place in the Colony by D'Urban, seen as a future source of labour and of troops for the defence of the frontier, many thousand refugees began to desert their temporary home in Gcalekaland and make their way across the Kei, most eventually settling in the ceded territory near the present town of Peddie.

The expedition slowly made its way back towards the Kei. On 2nd May Hintsa's brother Bhurhu, with a large number of supporters, rode into the British camp to join the king. He brought with him a token number of cattle, about twenty, which he stated was all that he had. It is difficult to disentangle precisely what the attitude of the British commanders was at the time but there was probably some suspicion of Bhurhu's motives. During the day a party under Col. Peddie brought intelligence that Mfengu refugees were being attacked by Gcaleka warriors. Smith was enraged and threatened Hintsa that he would hang two Gcaleka for each Mfengu killed.

During the day they were joined by several other parties of Gcaleka but these were prevented from following the march. There were now several hundred armed warriors in the camp. This clearly presented D'Urban and Smith with a problem. There was a strong presumption that they planned some effort to release Hintsa. Smith demanded that the Gcaleka surrender their weapons and when they refused he brought up a squad of the 72nd Regiment to face them. In a journal entry dated that day Gilfillan described the scene[400]:

> ... the Colonel desired the piquet to prime and load which they immediately did. He then ordered a reinforcement and called to the corps of guides to stand to their arms, which they immediately did. When the bugle sounded a flourish the 72nd fixed their Bayonetes [sic] and the Col calling for Hinza, desired him peremptorily [sic] to order his men to give up their arms instantly. All this so intimidated the [Xhosa]s that they very unwillingly gave up their assegais and Hinza, trembling like a leaf, seized Col Smith by the hand, as claiming his protection.

This contemporary description is the only one that suggests Hintsa's alarm at the time. Gilfillan on the day thought that

> Hinza having informed his inferior chiefs that he was forcibly detained, it is not improbable that these [Xhosa]s came either to attempt his release, or act as his guard.

Notwithstanding the fact that Hintsa had originally come to negotiate with the Governor, that his safety had been guaranteed, and that there was a strong case for understanding that his presence was effectively under a flag of truce, the opinion among the officers and men was that he was a prisoner. At this early stage, after a peace treaty of sorts had been agreed, there was a perception that he might try to escape. A case could, however, be made that his confinement was part of the peace treaty to which Hintsa had agreed.

By the 5th May it was clear that no cattle were forthcoming. The suggestion arose that it would be much better for Hintsa to be taken back into Gcalekaland so that he could persuade his people to bring in the cattle[401].

Either through crass insensitivity, or as a deliberate tactic, Smith had assigned members of the Corps of Guides to guard Hintsa. They included George Southey, William Shaw, and Edward Driver, all of whom had suffered severe personal losses in the war, and held Hintsa personally responsible. The situation was not improved by the fact that Hintsa's entourage included Mqhayi[402], who had led the group that had killed John Shaw. When William Shaw heard of this and was told that Mqhayi was carrying his brother's gun, he

> ... looked for his gun. [Richard] Southey told Col. Smith, who sent and had Shaw brought before him – "Well Sir," he said "what are you thinking about? I understand you want to shoot Umkye [Mqhayi]. Do you not know that as he has come into the camp as a friendly chief I should have to try you – and you would be hanged?" Shaw said, "Only let me get a chance at him, and when I have shot him, you can hang me as soon as you like."[403]

But Mqhayi had left the camp so the threat was not carried out.

The process of softening Hintsa up, probably deliberate on Smith's part, continued. Part of the time he was treated like an honoured guest; he dined with Smith in the evening and was given presents. At other times Smith berated him for failing to meet the obligations of the peace treaty. Worse, his guards were constantly provoking him. Holden Bowker noted in his journal[404]:

> 7 May, Thursday. ... Yesterday Driver told Hintsa if he would give him a good horse he would speak a good word for him. Hintsa sent him a handsome mare and Driver sent him word that he would ask the Governor to hang him.

The general tone of this entry is approving. In the light of the Smith's be-haviour, and the threats of his guards, it is not surprising that Hintsa feared for his life. Nor is it surprising that he might have planned to es-cape.

The army reached the drift on the Kei on the 9th May. Few cattle had been forthcoming. D'Urban agreed that a detachment under Smith's command would escort Hintsa on an expedition back into his territory, leaving his son Sarhili and brother Bhurhu as hostages. This would then give Hintsa the opportunity to see his people and tell them to give up the cattle. Smith's detachment left on 10th May, but not before D'Urban had taken dramatic action. He formally annexed all the territory to the east of the Colony, as far as the Great Kei River. This was a very bold step and contributed greatly to his future downfall. D'Urban then moved west-wards to set up headquarters on the Mpotshane River. Smith's force, con-sisting of about a hundred men from the 72nd regiment, volunteers, and members of the Corps of Guides, escorted Hintsa back towards the Mbashe.

By the 12th May there had still been no success in retrieving signific-ant numbers of cattle[405]. The party had reached the region near Hintsa's Great Place. George Southey noted[406] that that they were on the road to Edward Driver's Trading Station, the one that had been looted and burnt two years earlier. Hintsa, after some days walking, had been mounted on what was described as a good horse. The Guides responsible for his safe-keeping were nearby, including Driver, George and William Southey, Bis-set, Halse, and Shaw. Further behind was Gilfillan with his Cape Corps men.

The column was stretched out over a great distance. They had crossed the Nqabara river, which ran along the bottom of a deep valley. The wa-ter course ran for the most part between steep rocky krantzes, heavily wooded. Beyond the crossing point the path ran up a steep hill. The party of officers surrounding Smith included his aide de camp, Balfour, and formed the vanguard. They had reached the brow of the hill, about 1.5 km from the drift while Hintsa, who was leading his horse, and the Guides laboured up the slope. Many of the party were still to cross the river. Caesar Andrews was with the guides when Hintsa caught his eye:

> Southey still guarded him but about half way up the mountain Hintza made a sign for me to hold his assegais while he mounted, which I did, but kept my gun in rest. He immediately pressed forward, passed most of the troops and at the top of the mountain got alongside of Col. Smith[407].

With hindsight, Andrews saw this as indicating an intention to escape. Precisely what happened next is impossible to tell. Hintsa's horse broke away from the party. It was later advantageous for Smith and those supporting him to claim that Hintsa was trying to escape. Others have claimed that his horse bolted. It really does not matter which. He had every reason to want to escape and, whatever his original intention, he very shortly found himself in a race for his life.

Smith was mounted on an excellent horse, while the mounts of many others were exhausted; most were leading their horses. He set off in pursuit of Hintsa, trailing a stream of curses, with Balfour and other officers well behind. The Guides, who were close to the top of the climb, struggled to mount. Hintsa followed the line of the ridge with Smith in hot pursuit. From the river at the bottom of the slope Gilfillan could see the chase along the skyline. The Guides, now mounted, struggled to catch up.

> Southey, William Southey, myself [Bisset], William Shaw, old Driver, Balfour, A.D.C. Oliver and many others were all in this race, but behind.[408]

After covering about fifteen hundred metres Smith caught up with Hintsa. He yelled at him to stop. He had a pair of pistols but they had been loaded and primed some time before and, with the damp weather of the previous few days, when he tried to shoot at the fugitive both misfired. The enraged Smith struck at Hintsa's head with one of the pistols, losing it in the process. The second he flung at Hintsa with as little success. He then seized Hintsa's kaross and forcibly dragged him off his horse, causing him to fall heavily. At this point Smith's horse had had enough and bolted, carrying him a further five hundred metres along the ridge before he could bring it under control.

Several accounts state that Hintsa then threw an assegai at Smith:

> Hintsa, having gathered himself up [after the fall], let go an assegai at Col. Smith.[409]

> ... he unhorsed him, Hintza falling heavily among the legs of the Colonel's horse, which fortunately bolted with the Colonel, for Hintza nimbly gathered himself and drawing an assegai hurled it after Colonel Smith, but luckily it fell short.[410]

> As he fell, Hintza drew an assegai and hurled it at Col. Smith. It was a narrow escape, for the point narrowly missed his throat, the wood handle striking him on the cheek, leaving a trail like the blow from a sjambok.[411]

It is quite difficult to picture how Hintsa managed to do this after recovering from a heavy fall with Smith disappearing into the distance on a bolting horse. The accounts are, however, from partisan sources. Bisset, another partisan source, claims implausibly that before Smith had fired

> ... the chief (who had always been allowed to carry his arms, consisting of the usual bundle of seven assegais) made a stab at the General [sic]. It was well that it was a bundle and not a single assegai, for although parried with his right arm the points of the seven assegais penetrated his coat over the right breast and slightly entered the skin.[412]

No other witness suggests that Smith was not the first aggressor.

Hintsa's horse, too, bolted and Hintsa ran, slid, and stumbled his way down the steep slope towards the river. Some of the officers, including Balfour, and the Guides, led by George Southey, now reached the point where Hintsa had started down the slope. It was too steep and rugged for a chase on horseback so a number started down the slope on foot.

> We were many of us good runners, George Southey one of the best I had seen. He was in advance, I and a lot of the others not far behind.[413]

Others picked their way down on horseback. Smith, having brought his horse under control let slip the dogs of war by bellowing after the runners "Shoot George! And be damned to you!"[414]. Hintsa was by now a good distance ahead. Smith retrieved one of his pistols and swore, "Damn his hard iron skull, for I have bent my pistol on it."[415] George Southey, now within range and an excellent shot, stopped, took aim, and fired. Hintsa was brought down and the winded pursuers eased their pace, thinking that the chase was over[416]. Hintsa, however, only had a flesh wound. The ball had passed through his calf. Driven by adrenalin, he rose and continued his headlong flight. The pursuit was resumed and once again Southey fired. This time he caused more damage. The ball struck him on the right side, entering below the rib cage, a potentially fatal wound. The river was about eight hundred metres from where Hintsa had been dragged from his horse. By this time Hintsa had almost reached the refuge of the riverine bush. Once again he got to his feet. Others were now firing. William Shaw got off a shot that missed. Hintsa disappeared into the bush.

> As he was jumping into it [the bush round the river] I [Henry Halse] fired and the bullet struck where I last saw his head and I thought I had given him a quietus[417].

But Halse was wrong; he had missed.

Caesar Andrews was watching from a vantage point. There was some concern on the part of the pursuers that there might be an ambush.

> George Southey, however, reloaded and went into the bush on the river bank. While these movements were taking place several of our mounted men arrived near the river. Lieut. Balfour and Oliver, Bisset, Driver, Sergt. Jupp, Cape Rifles etc.[418]

The first to enter the bush were George Southey and Balfour. They were followed by other pursuers and a hue and cry began up and down the river bank. Those who were closest to the position where the quarry was found included George Southey, Balfour, Edward Driver, Bisset, Robert Daniels, and two Cape Corps soldiers, Windfogel Julie and Nicholaas Africa, the latter a member of Smith's escort.

The river ran in a small ravine, bounded by near vertical rock faces about three or four metres high. These were a sufficiently severe obstacle to cause Southey and Balfour to hesitate before clambering down. The watercourse itself, well below the maximum flood level, was between low banks in the middle of the ravine. The bush growing on either side of the water was dense. Hintsa, already mortally wounded by Southey's second shot, must have tumbled down the drop and could not have gone far before seeking cover. He hid himself in the water below a rock that provided some concealment.

Several of the searchers came upon Hintsa almost simultaneously[419]. Walking downstream, Nicholaas Africa saw a man in the water. It was Hintsa. He raised his gun. Across the river Julie also saw the fugitive and began to wade across. Hintsa raised his head. "Taru, amapakati [Mercy, gentlemen]" he called. Africa lowered his gun and signalled to Julie to do the same. From the downstream side George Southey also saw the fugitive and heard his call[420], as did Edward Driver, who was close behind him. He brought up his gun and fired. The ball struck Hintsa on the side of the head and killed him instantly.

Andrews, watching from the hill above, was joined by Smith, still swearing and believing that Hintsa might escape. They heard the report and saw the smoke from the shot rising above the bush. Shortly afterwards, George Southey appeared, waving a handkerchief[421]. Andrews estimated that the whole incident had taken about an hour to play itself out.

In the bush the hunters approached the body.

> I [Bisset] took his assegais and the charm from around his neck, and left immediately to carry the news to Sir Harry Smith ...[422]

Edward Driver, having been an immediate witness to the killing, went to find and calm his horse[423].

The news spread through the ranks. More than just news, some were shown the gruesome evidence of something much more sinister:

> Before leaving, William Southey cut off Hintza's ears and Dr Ford of the 72nd the upper lip and flesh of the cheeks and chin, which they carried away as souvenirs.[424]

The body was carried up to one of the Xhosa huts in the neighbourhood and left there. While many were unconcerned a few had reservations: even though they held no brief for Hintsa

> Thus miserably ended the life of the mighty Hinza , who had so long
> held a despotic sway over the lives of Thousands. I regret to add the
> body was much mutilated by some individuals who allowed their insati-
> able thirst of possessing a relic of so great a man to get the better of
> their humanity and better feeling, which teaches us not to trample on a
> fallen foe[425].

By late in the day Smith gave orders to march. With Hintsa's death,
the steam went out of his campaign. The drive to recover 50 000 cattle
disintegrated into some sorties that recovered small numbers of cattle,
and the invasion force was back in D'Urban's camp five days later on 17th
May.

The great invasion was over. The campaign to bring back the cattle
petered out. In D'Urban's eyes peace had been signed, the recalcitrant
Hintsa was dead, and his son Sarhili had succeeded and would prove
more malleable.

Chapter 13. Consequences

Auferre, trucidare, rapere, falsis nominibus imperium; atque, ubi solitudinem
faciunt, pacem appellant.
[Robbery, slaughter, and pillage, they falsely style government; and where they
make a desert they call it peace.]
Calgacus, a British chieftain, on the Romans. Quoted by Tacitus in Agricola.

Settlers vs Philanthropists

The climate of opinion that formed a background to the frontier conflict arose from the dramatic changes that took place in Europe during the end of the eighteenth and the beginning of the nineteenth centuries. The pressure for social justice in Britain had grown steadily since the French revolution. The appalling social conditions flowing from the pressures of the industrial revolution were one focus of reform. The vicious slave trade provoked strong abolitionist fervour. A strong influence for change was the evangelical Christian movement, which was itself a consequence of the pressure for reform.

The evangelical movement was not confined to the non-established churches. Within the Established Church groups of reformers arose. One such group was in Cambridge. Another in London, named the Clapham sect by its detractors, consisted of a group of prominent wealthy evangelical Christians including William Wilberforce, Charles Grant Sr, and Fowler Buxton.

By 1834, under the influence of men such as Wilberforce, the abolition of slavery within the British sphere of influence had been achieved. Many other reforms had yet to come.

In the Cape most of the colonists were conservative. Not surprisingly, on the frontier, both Boers and settlers were inward looking, their own interests being paramount. The majority of the settlers had their origins in the working class. The leading citizens of Graham's Town had mostly risen from this group by what they saw as their own efforts – the large advantage to those who had managed to attract Government patronage was overlooked. Fourteen years after the settlement they were sceptical of the Colonial Government's motives, convinced that their concerns and grievances were ignored by the authorities in Cape Town, let alone in England. Their losses and setbacks were attributed to outside influence, not least to the depredations of the Xhosa. The more extreme opinions were articulated by Godlonton's *Graham's Town Journal*.

These opinions were by no means universally held on the eastern Frontier or in the Cape as a whole. There was a small, but vociferous, body of reformists, with influence in England, propagating a different point of view. These men provoked outrage amongst the Graham's Town opinion makers who saw them as prejudiced in favour of the Xhosa and who were unable to look beyond their own concerns and fears.

Chief among these bogymen was Dr John Philip. Philip, a Scottish Congregationalist minister, came to the Cape in 1818 as the second of a two-man commission to investigate troubles in the missions of the London Missionary Society – not least the sexual peccadillos of James Read and other missionaries. He remained as Superintendent of the Society's stations in the Colony. Soon came into conflict with the authoritarian Lord Charles Somerset and campaigned for the rights of the coloured people within the boundaries of the Colony. In 1823 he returned to England to press his cause with influential members of the reform movement. There he became familiar with influential reformers such as Fowler Buxton and Charles Grant Jr, afterwards to become Lord Glenelg. They became convinced of the need for giving Khoikhoi and other coloured inhabitants of the Cape the same political rights as the colonists; the emancipation of slaves was futile if all it did was to release them into the same conditions as the Khoikhoi. The pressure was successful in principle, but the change in status of the Khoikhoi during the tenure of Governor Bourke were not really effective because of the inability of the beneficiaries to establish the residential status that they needed to exercise their rights. Philip's criticisms of the conditions in the Colony were set down in detail in a voluminous report[426], which was published in 1828. This work shows the nature of his advocacy. It is a fierce polemic. Much of what it says can be recognized today as true; much of this, however, is unsupported by credible evidence. Philip tended to take the allegations of his correspondents as truth and was sometimes embarrassed when required to justify what he wrote. As a result it was all too easy for his embattled opponents on the frontier to persuade themselves that the position he held was based entirely on prejudice and to demonize him and those who held his point of view.

The cause of reform had an influential mouthpiece at the other end of the Colony in Cape Town, where the *Commercial Advertiser* took a diametrically opposite point of view to that of the *Graham's Town Journal*. The editor was Thomas Pringle's old friend, John Fairbairn. He had, in 1831, married Elizabeth, the daughter of Dr Philip. Fairbairn provoked outrage among the frontier colonists as, fed by sympathetic correspondents such as his father-in-law, Charles Lennox Stretch, and Ambrose Campbell, he regularly published articles critical of their beliefs and actions.

Andries Stockenstrom did not really belong to this group. He was his own man so far as his ideas about government of the frontier region. Disillusioned by his service as Commissioner General for the Eastern Frontier[427], he had been allowed to take leave of absence from his post at the beginning of 1833. He had travelled to England, intent on putting the case for his frontier policy, which he had been unable to advance, to the Government. He was there at the time of the war and in 1835 was an important provider of evidence to the Committee on Aborigines. His views, those of someone from the Dutch community who had been born and brought up in the Colony, were influential. While by no means coincident with those of many reformers, they led him to be regarded by the settlers as one of the reformers, vilified by the eastern press.

The opinions of the group consisting of Philip, missionaries such as the Reads, Fairbairn, Stockenstrom, Stretch, Campbell, and others, were anathema to many on the frontier. They were labelled philanthropists and much of what they alleged was dismissed as propaganda.

It is easy to present this as a conflict between the two extremes articulated by Philip and Godlonton. It is also easy to revile the Graham's Town settler community and praise the reformists for views that are so much closer to modern ideas. At the time it was just as easy to revile the Xhosa as pagan barbarians. Men deal with the situations in which they find themselves. The situation on the frontier was a recipe for conflict. The interests of colonists and Xhosa were irreconcilable. Both Xhosa and colonists perceived their actions as reasonable self-interest. The reformist drive came largely from outside the settler community and it is not surprising that it was regarded as a threat.

Spin Doctors   [1835]

Smith's written report to D'Urban, describing the events surrounding the death of Hintsa, was dated 18th May 1835, the day after he had arrived in camp. Of course he had made a verbal report as soon as he arrived. The Governor was not pleased to receive the news:

> Major Maclean was dining with His Excellency Sir Benjamin when the news was announced of his [Hintza's] death, which was anything but pleasing. And when Major Dutton mentioned at table having some of his 'curiosities' Sir Benjamin was very angry[428].

The implications of the killing of the Xhosa king were just beginning to sink in. Among the troops the details of the incident were freely discussed and letters from the camp bore the news. At the time the younger troops did not grasp the seriousness of the events. Many years later Henry Halse reflected:

This was a very wrong and barbarous thing to do, but we did not think so at the time, and it might have been the cause of doing the Colony a serious injury. [429]

Those who had been most closely involved freely discussed what had happened with others who had been with D'Urban on the other side of the Kei at the time. Charles Lennox Stretch was no admirer of Smith. As early as May 2nd he had written in his journal:

It appears the general sentiment that Colonel Somerset would have conducted the command with less expense and more ability than Colonel Smith.

When the news of Hintsa's death arrived in the camp he was outraged and expressed his opinions very forcefully, so much so that Balfour visited him to try to put a clamp on the gossip and propound a more acceptable version:

Directly I [Stretch] heard of the manner [in which] Hintza had been used, I did not conceal my sentiments at such brutal conduct, and Dr Murray and Balfour came to my tent to apprise me my expressions relative to this event had reached the Governor's ears and he was very angry. Balfour appeared to desire it might be a personal subject, but I referred him to 6 officers of his own regiment, Colonel Peddie, Leslie, Fisher, Lacy, and I put this question to them: 'Gentlemen, do you not [remember?] that Mr Driver Southey and Shaw stated repeatedly that the late Hintza called out for mercy several times?' Colonel Peddie put this question to the officers, and they all answered, 'Yes, yes, yes - perfectly well.' I then told Balfour he should hold his tongue in future about contradicting the report[430].

D'Urban had reason to be concerned. As soon as he received Smith's report he would have seen the implications. Apart from the wisdom of the invasion in the first place, there were three aspects of Hintsa's death that caused great concern. The first was his status under the equivalent of a flag of truce, the second was the fact that he was shot out of hand while begging for mercy, and the third was the mutilation of his body. Stretch's outrage was typical of the rumours, some exaggerated, going round the camp:

Mr Simmons informed me [Stretch] when the former chief fell, having in vain called for mercy, Mr Nourse cut out the emblems of his manhood, Mr Shaw the ears and skin of his chin, while a certain doctor with a bayonet endeavoured to extract some of his teeth[431].

D'Urban's despatch[432] to the Secretary of State, describing the outcome of the campaign, was dated 19th June 1835 and only states the fact of Hintsa's death and D'Urban's regret, referring the recipient to Smith's report to D'Urban, which was attached as part of the document. Between them the two reports contain the basis of the response to the critical issues. First, D'Urban made the case that Hintsa had been a voluntary hostage, but that his status changed when the attacks were made on the Mfengu refugees; he did not go so far as to state unequivocally that he had made him a prisoner:

> I therefore signified to Hintsa that this proceeding [the attacks on the Mfengu], by which he had broken the treaty, had altered his position, that I held him, and all who accompanied him, responsible.
>
> ...
>
> Hintza with his son and followers remained as before, without any alteration in their treatment, but avowedly now held under a stricter and more ample obligation of pledge than before.

Second, Smith, in his report, turned the shooting into self defence on Southey's part:

> ... he [Hintsa] precipitated himself down a kloof into the Kebaka, and posting himself in a narrow niche of the rock, defied any attempts to secure him; when still refusing to surrender, and raising an assegai, Mr George Southey fired and shot him through the head[433].

Third, the issue of the mutilation was simply ignored; later the protagonists denied any knowledge of it.

This was the beginning of the construction of the official version of events. Compare Caesar Andrews's entry in his campaign diary[434]

> Hintza sought the cover of the thick wood bordering the River but Geo. Southey fortunately coming upon the exact spot where he was concealed put his gun to his head and he paid the just forfeit of his life for his treacherous attempt to escape the fulfilment of his treaty.

with the official version that he wrote in his reminiscences[435]

> Southey on entering the bush saw Hintsa standing up to his knees in the river with assegai poised to throw at him. He had only time to bring his gun round and fire. The ball penetrated Hintsa's head and instant death took place.

The shooting became self-defence and the mutilation was denied. The public perception in the settler community at the time was still the received wisdom of the frontier community in 1884:

> The operations closed, after a most spirited and successful campaign, with the death of Hintza, who was shot by Mr G. Southey while attempting to escape after having surrendered himself as a prisoner of war.[436]

Whistle Blowers   [1835]

The news of Hintsa's death rapidly spread beyond the headquarters camp as volunteers and soldiers wrote home.

As it was, I [Henry Halse] was the cause, unintentionally, of much excitement on the subject. I had written to my father from the camp and
among other things had given him a full account of the affair. As news
from the camp was greedily sought after, he shewed the letter to several persons, among others Dr Ambrose Campbell who was always at war
with the authorities, and was the editor of a paper. [He] got hold of it
and made so much of it in England that a commission of enquiry was
ordered two years after to enquire into particulars.[437]

Ambrose Campbell was, indeed, a major player in bringing the whole affair into the public eye. He was soon in touch with Dr Philip who through
the London Missionary Society began a campaign to bring the matter before the British Government and public. He also provided a great deal of
ammunition to Fairbairn, who kept the matter firmly before the citizens
of the Colony in the pages of the *Commercial Advertiser.* Meanwhile Godlonton in the *Graham's Town Journal* fiercely painted Hintsa as the villain-
ous architect of all the woes of the settlers and Southey as a hero.

Those who had been present in Smith's detachment at the time of the
shooting knew very well what had happened. Different participants reacted in different ways. One was Frederick I'Ons, the artist who left a
great legacy of lively paintings of the frontier[438]. Having heard all the accounts of the participants he painted a picture. This picture is still in the
possession of a descendant and the family tradition is that I'Ons left instructions that it should never be allowed to leave the family. While it is
painted from imagination, the key feature of the painting is that it shows
Southey in the act of shooting a defenceless Hintsa in the back.

Seeking Peace   [May – Sep 1835]

The various volunteer groups, both Boer and Briton, were discharged during June. This was essential as the demands of their farms made it essential for them to return to the land. Edward Driver returned to his farm to
start the rebuilding process. Harry Smith provided him with a fulsome
testimonial:

HEADQUARTERS

KING WILLIAM'S TOWN

9th June 1835

The Bearer Mr Edward Driver has served with me in the capacity of
Guide since 1st of February, he has been of the greatest use upon every
important occasion, he is a man of undaunted courage and persever-
ance and has performed his Duty upon all occasions as becomes a
brave man and I hold him to be an honor to his Country – it would afford me the greatest satisfaction to be able to render him any service in
my power upon any future occasion.

H. G. SMITH – Col.

Chief of the Corps[439]

The problem was that the war was not over. A peace agreed by the dead Hintsa under duress had no influence with Maqoma and his allies. Harry Smith found himself fighting an enemy that melted away into the bush, emerging when least expected, to ambush, retreat, and live to fight another day[440].

As early as May, even before the death of Hintsa, the Xhosa were feeling the strain. A long war of attrition had no place in their thoughts. There were some early overtures for peace. On May 11th Suthu, Ngqika's Great widow, mother of the boy chief Sandile, made the first approach. She sent a message to Cox asking for a meeting. Too heavy to walk any distance, she asked for a conveyance to be sent, and Cox had her brought into his camp in a wagon. Her message was that Maqoma and Tyhali wished to talk. At this stage of the war Cox was not prepared to make many concessions. He agreed to a cease fire for twenty four hours but threatened an immediate return to full hostilities if the meeting failed to take place. The news of Hintsa's captivity had spread throughout the region. Maqoma and Tyhali were understandably suspicious. If Hintsa had been made a prisoner when he came to parley, was this not just a ploy to place them in captivity?

Cox sent one of his Lieutenants ahead to persuade Maqoma and Tyhali to meet with him. As part of the persuasion a bottle of brandy was produced. By the time Cox arrived, Maqoma, showing the same weakness as his father, was in no state to conduct any business and the process collapsed.

Brownlee's destroyed mission on the Buffalo River was selected as the site of the capital of the new Province of Queen Adelaide. It was named King William's Town on 24th May. Smith was placed in charge, and D'Urban returned to Graham's Town on 12th June.

While Smith, in King William's Town, began to set up the mechanisms for the government of the new province, the guerilla war continued. The Xhosa continued their refusal to fit in with his preconceived idea that they had been defeated. The army suffered increasing losses. The worst was the loss of a skirmishing party of thirty under Charles Baillie. All were killed. Maintenance of the supply lines remained difficult. The Boer and English volunteers were released to return to their farms. The Khoikhoi troops bitterly resented that they were not similarly treated. By August even Smith was forced to abandon his determinedly sanguine view of the ongoing hostilities. He cast about for a scapegoat. To him it was unthinkable that the Xhosa could hold his forces at bay. James Read, who had been seriously ill in Graham's Town since the beginning of the war was accused of masterminding the proceedings as well as supplying arms and ammunition.

Throughout Major Cox's bush campaign Charles Stretch kept up his journal. By early August the appetite for war on both sides was low. Stretch's journal entry for August 15th provides an extended and some-what confused account of the next stages towards negotiating a peace.[441]

The previous day a Xhosa warrior had been encountered by two members of the regiment, Sergeant Jephta and Corporal Dirks. What he told them caused them to take him to Major Cox at his camp on the site of what was to be called Fort Cox. The man agreed to take a message from the eponymous commander to Maqoma and Tyhali. The response from the chiefs was to send one of their counsellors with a proposal for a meeting with Cox. The condition was that the delegation should include one Captain Warden, who was well known to and trusted by Tyhali. Warden was summoned by Cox, and the two of them, supported by Stretch and other officers, with the Kat River Legion and some recently drafted Mfengu troops, set out for the meeting. Near the Xhosa camp on the Gxulu River, Warden was sent ahead to say that Cox was willing to parley. Shortly afterwards he returned with a message from Maqoma to say that Cox and Warden should enter the Xhosa camp. Since the Xhosa force was over 1000 men, Cox's officers advised him against this. Maqoma was asked to meet him at a halfway point between the two forces but he said:

> "No! My people must hear what the major has to say. But I will as-semble my principal men, and he must come to that tree (pointing out a certain bush)." As soon as this was communicated to the major he moved towards this spot, and Macomo and Tyali with their principal fol-lowers forming a crescent, met him just at the tree. It was a formidable party to meet, but Warden observed we [i.e. Cox and Warden] had bet-ter show them we placed confidence in them, and they both went up and saluted the chiefs.

There were about 120 men in the party supporting Maqoma and Tyhali, with more than 1000 warriors a few hundred metres away. Cox and Warden were alone, with Stretch, the other officers, and the relatively small number of troops, watching from a small distance. The two chiefs contrasted strongly in behaviour and appearance. Maqoma was dressed in European clothes, and maintained a stern formal demeanour: Tyhali wore the leopard skin regalia of a chief, and, while he generally remained solemn, was not above greeting his acquaintance Warden jovially. After exchanging compliments, the participants got down to business. Cox was not empowered to negotiate; he could state D'Urban's terms but could provide no response to the Xhosa overtures.

> The major informed them that he had not come to discuss past griev-amces on either side (with which they all seemed much pleased), but to inform them the Governor was still anxious to entertain any tenders they might make of submission, and would extend his clemency as not to insist on their passing the Key [Kei], but would assign them land on this side of it where they might live in peace.

Cox did not (and could not) specify where this land would be, but the concession that the Xhosa would not be expelled to the other side of the Kei was a recognition by D'Urban that Smith's grandiose plan was impracticable and unenforceable.

Maqoma and Tyhali agreed to submit. Stretch reported their words as, "We have now no father since Gaika is dead, and therefore we will that the Governor is our father." Aside from some friction because of the presence of the Mfengu, of whom the chiefs "desired their servants might be restored to them," the discussions went well and a cease fire was agreed until Captain Warden had taken the news to D'Urban and returned with his response.

Several days passed before the Governor's reply was received. There was frequent contact between Xhosa and British during this period and, in anticipation of peace, the mood was upbeat.

D'Urban's terms were brought to the camp on Sunday August 22nd by his aide-de-camp, Captain Alexander. When they saw them, Cox, Warden, and Stretch were both downcast and sceptical of any success. The Governor, influenced by Smith and the bellicose citizens of Graham's Town, was still under the impression that he held all the cards and that the Xhosa would accept his terms unconditionally. There were a number of quite unacceptable conditions:

- Sandile, the boy king of the Ngqika, and his mother Suthu must be handed over to Warden and taken to the Governor, after which they would remain under his control.

- All guns and ammunition must be surrendered.

- Khoikhoi deserters who had been fighting on the side of the Xhosa must be handed over.

- All Xhosa must evacuate their ancentral country of the Tyumie valley, the Amatolas, the Keiskamma valley, the Ntabakandoda, and the Buffalo Mountains, and travel to King William's Town where they would be well treated and shown the new territories that had been assigned to them between the Kei and Gonubie rivers.

The amaXhosa were to submit within twenty four hours, failing which hostilities would be resumed.

A meeting at Cox's camp was arranged with the chiefs who attended with a large well-disciplined body of men. Their bearing, organization, and discipline made a strong impression of the British officers. The amaXhosa listened to the terms and, when Warden had finished reading them, Maqoma expressed their opinion. Stretch's account purports to represent Maqoma's speech directly. Clearly it would have been written afterwards in his journal from memory and was his English interpretation of the Xhosa oratory and its translation. It appears, however, to be an attempt to represent fairly both the content and the passion:

> "That is not peace; it would be purchasing peace, and what better would we be? Is that the way of making peace between nations that have been at war? ... you said it was the wish of your Governor to forget the past, and in that paper [i.e. the terms that Warden had been reading] things gone past are referred to. Besides, what guns do you want, and what do you want to do with them if there is peace? The Hottentots were born in our country. Sandilla is our chief and we cannot be separated. Besides our graves are here (pointing to Gaika's) [The discussions were held within sight of Ngqika's grave]; many of our fathers were buried at the Bavians River. That country you now possess. However, with that we are satisfied. But you must allow us to remain where we are. ... We will fight for the [Colonial] government, for we are the children of government. Therefore don't send us to a country where we cannot live. This [indicating the accompanying mass of Xhosa] is only half my people, and how can so many exist in so small a country as you speak of?"

Maqoma went on to ask why they should give up the Khoikhoi who were in their territory and also whether the British would give up the Mfengu "who are our Hottentots and who in the day of public calamity rose up against us and carried off all my cattle." Cox unwisely replied that "he had no doubt when peace was restored they would be put in possession of the Fingoes." Finally Maqoma asked the unanswerable question:

> We see Gaika and Hintza no more with our eyes, and our cattle are all taken. And when you treated Hintza the way you did, how could you expect me to entrust my person in your hands?

He finished by expressing his trust in Cox and his companions and asked them to intercede with the Governor on their behalf. Notwithstanding D'Urban's twenty four hour ultimatum, he stated that they would not resume hostilities.

The British negotiators were impressed with Maqoma. Messages were sent to D'Urban the following day. Cox confided in his officers that his records showed numerous examples of wrongs done to the Xhosa in Somerset's raids on cattle under the policy of restitution. He wrote a private letter to the Governor strongly recommending that Maqoma should be allowed to remain in his territory in the Amatolas. Stretch observed:

> A most favourable opportunity is offered for a conference with the chiefs and re-establishing peace which is the object of Major Cox and the design of all who are in any way acquainted with the true state of affairs to accomplish. *Terms have however been offered that we knew would not be accepted* [Stretch's emphasis]. And, had Sir B. D'Urban descended from his pinnacle of military etiquette and held this interview himself with Macomo, if he did not succeed in his requests he would likely in his heart have felt the justice of them. And I feel certain he would have come if he had not been influenced and surrounded by advisors whose object is to gain by the misfortunes of others...

The advisors to whom Stretch was referring were the Graham's Town merchants who, now that the immediate threat to their safety had been removed, were finding the war very profitable.

Maqoma's response was sent to Harry Smith at Fort Willshire for onward transmission to D'Urban. It reached him on 28th August. Smith's reaction was outrage at the weakness of the British negotiators. He hoped that D'Urban would reject it; he sent three hundred men and an artillery piece to Cox's camp in order to be ready to restart the war. At the same time, it appears that Maqoma was striving to show his good faith by restoring some cattle and trying to get the message to all his people that they should refrain from doing anything to provoke a hostile reaction. As always the control of the chiefs was not complete. Individual bands of Xhosa continued sporadic raids. The British preparation for the peace was also continued. Construction was begun on the buildings for Fort Cox, making use of the large supply of manpower that Smith had made available.

D'Urban, too, was infuriated at Cox's private letter. It had, however, become clear to him that the army was in no state to continue the war indefinitely and while he was angered by the arrogance of Maqoma's demonstration of the Xhosa strength, he could not fail to recognize that he must reach agreement with them. To be sure that his new terms would be forcefully presented he decided to send Smith himself to meet with Maqoma and his allies.

D'Urban abandoned his most unacceptable demands. He no longer required the surrender of Sandile and Suthu, or the Khoikhoi rebels. He conceded the right of Maqoma to remain in the Amatola region.

Smith arrived at Fort Cox with D'Urban's conditions. They were not entirely to his liking. He expressed his intention of adding his own twist to the ceremony at which they were announced to the chiefs, quite at odds with D'Urban's intentions. Cox, Stretch, and Warden were alarmed:

> From his (Colonel Smith's) disposition and manner various were the opinions and doubts entertained as to the success of the embassy, and we began to fear that His Excellency's kind intentions would be frustrated by some additional demands which Colonel Smith had committed to writing, to be made from the chiefs contrary to the rules of the commission with which Captain Warden and he were charged – such as demanding the Hottentots and arms, and making them say, 'We cry Mercy! Mercy! Mercy!', a fabrication of his own fertile genius in military despotism.

Stretch's response to this was as contemptuous of Smith as Smith's intentions were of D'Urban. He took matters into his own hands, and confident of knowing the "feelings of all friends of Peace", privately sent a message to Maqoma, advising him to remain silent while Smith spoke, not to be concerned with what Smith said, and to listen only to the Governor's terms when Smith read them. It appears that the message was sent with the connivance of Captain Warden and Lieutenant Sutton, another of Cox's officers. Had it not been sent, it was not unlikely that Maqoma and his allies would have been so angered by Smith's posturing that the war would have continued much longer.

What drove Stretch and the other officers to this action? Stretch, himself, came from a background in the regular army and had been recalled for the war; the other two were part of the standing army in the Colony. As an act of disloyalty to a superior officer it was remarkable, and an indication of the lack of respect that Smith had elicited in many officers in the army. Stretch was a complex man. He came from an upper middle class family with strong military connections. After sowing his wild oats in Wellington's army, he had become a committed Christian and often found himself at odds with the opinions of his brother officers. When he had settled at Glen Avon both he and his father-in-law, Robert Hart, had been greatly influenced by the preaching of the Reverend Andrew Murray, a Scottish Presbyterian minister who had been called to the sister Dutch Reformed Church in Graaff Reinet. Both he and Hart had joined the Dutch Reformed congregation in Somerset East, and Hart was for many years an elder of that church before establishing his own Presbyterian Church on his farm. Stretch found more in common with the Dutch colonists than he did with the English settlers. His opinions of his fellow countrymen seem to have been influenced by the pressures of English class distinctions; he regarded the majority of the settlers, particularly the traders and shopkeepers, as of an inferior class. The Dutch and the Xhosa fell outside the framework of such class distinctions and he was able to relate to them far more easily. He had been truly appalled by the death of Hintsa and found himself very much in the same camp as Dr Philip, Fairbairn of the *Commercial Advertiser,* and Andries Stockenstrom, providing ammunition for the philanthropist movement that brought the attention of the British public to the events of the war and, *inter alia,* to the circumstances of Hintsa's death.

Cox was unaware of the action of his subordinates although later, on 15th September:

> Sutton informed Major Cox, we (Sutton, Warden and Stretch) had sent a private message to Macomo that he was not to lose his temper with Colonel Smith on the 6th, for the which he was much obliged.

Smith, on arrival at Fort Cox on September 5th, sent a peremptory message to Maqoma, demanding a meeting within the next two hours. Maqoma, unwilling to dance to Smith's tune, let him wait. Cox, Warden and Stretch spent two hours at the meeting place before returning to camp with the news that there had been no response from Maqoma. In the evening a message arrived to say that the chiefs would be at the meeting place the following day.

September 6th was a Sunday. The Xhosa deputation let the British wait for an hour before they appeared. When they arrived they were broadly representative. Maqoma was accompanied by his brothers Tyhali and Anta and the Rharhabe Great House was represented by Suthu. Nqeno of the amaMbalu was attended by his sons Stokwe and Sonto. The imiDange were represented by Fandala, the son of their chief, Bhothomane. All the chiefs were attended by their senior councillors.

The chiefs were not at ease with Smith. They clearly did not trust him. Smith tried to put them at ease, taking the arms of Maqoma and Tyhali.

> ... the colonel thoiught to pay them an honour by taking them on each arm, they were much embarrassed to find themselves linked so closely to with the 'King Killer' (alluding to Hintsa's death). Macomo disengaged himself and fell back among his followers, but Tyali remained arm-in-arm till we got to the bush, where we all sat down.

Smith made his bombastic speech. The matter of giving up arms was an issue but they agreed to do so only if the governor desired it. Peace was announced and celebrated with a seven gun salute. The land that would be allocated to them was pointed out but they wished to know exactly where each tribe would be located. They agreed to send emissaries to D'Urban at Fort Willshire, but were reluctant to meet him personally.

Warden and Stretch remained in the camp at Fort Cox while Smith set off for Fort Willshire with the emissaries of the chiefs. While waiting for news of D'Urban's arrival, meetings continued between Maqoma, Tyhali, Warden and Stretch. On Wednesday 9th September Stretch entertained Maqoma and Tyhali to dinner in his tent where discussions about the necessity for them to meet D'Urban took place.

That evening a message arrived from Smith to say that the Governor had arrived at Fort Willshire and would see them the following day. There were a few delays and it was not until Friday that they were introduced to the Governor and dined with him in the evening. There were a number of delays in the days that followed. Reports were received of continuing cattle thefts and D'Urban refused to have any further discussion until they ceased. Maqoma and Tyhali went off to bring matters under control.

On Wednesday 16th Cox sent Stretch to locate Maqoma and find out his intentions. He found him in command of a significant force of warriors and in a state of indecision. Mistrust of the British motives had again arisen. Phatho, chief of the amaGqunukwhebe had sent him a message that the intention was to take the chiefs prisoner and incarcerate them on Robben Island. Stretch brought them to meet Cox for reassurance.

> The major [Cox] told him he knew that Pato would be sorry to see them reconciled with the Governor, and therefore they were by these means endeavouring to thwart the reconciliation. Besides there were many shopkeepers in Graham's Town whose interest it was also to prevent it.[442]

After various negotiations, eventually D'Urban met with Maqoma, Tyhali, Nqeno, and Mhala at Fort Willshire. On the 17th agreement was reached and peace was declared.

Under the terms of the peace the Ngqika were permitted to remain in the Amatolas. In so doing, however, they became subjects of the King. They were allotted lands in what was now firmly British territory and became subject to English law.

For those farming near the frontier, the end of the war meant a return to ravaged farms and the effort to rebuild. What had been acts of war were now transformed into simple theft. Just three days after peace was declared, on 16th September, a number of cattle belonging to Driver and Thomas Manley were stolen from where they were grazing on Manley's Flats near Grahamstown. A patrol led by the owners set off in hot pursuit and overtook some of the rustlers and recovered 75 head of cattle. The farmers who had suffered most in the past were, however, were to become much better protected as the country on the other side of the Fish River became settled by colonists. Edward Driver probably felt that his losses to the Xhosa were trivial compared to those he suffered from the army commissariat.

Repercussions   [1835 – 1836]

D'Urban's first despatch reporting the war to the British Government was tardy, being only written in June, 1835. While addressed to Aberdeen it was read by the new Secretary of State, Lord Glenelg. Charles Grant, first Baron Glenelg, had gained the title on becoming Secretary of State a few months before. He was a devout evangelical Anglican, the son of Charles Grant Senior.

D'Urban's despatch was taken to London by one of his aides-de-camp, Captain G. de la Poer Beresford, who was charged with the duty of making the case for D'Urban's actions, particularly the annexation of the new province of Queen Adelaide. On the same ship a package arrived for the Secretary of the London Missionary Society, William Ellis, from Dr John Philip. Philip's report contained an extensive exposure of what had been going on, including letters from Charles Lennox Stretch, Ambrose Campbell, and various missionary sources, as well as press reports from Fairbairn's Commercial Advertiser and accounts of the statements of individuals such as the soldiers of the Cape Corps who had been witnesses to Hintsa's death.

Ellis enlisted the help of Fowler Buxton M.P., a noted abolitionist and reformer in Parliament, and they began the process of lobbying Glenelg. Buxton had already been well appraised of events on the Eastern Cape frontier by Philip, and as early as May had persuaded parliament to appoint a select committee, the Select Committee on Aborigines, and appoint him chairman. By the time it came to sit in August, news of the war and the death of Hintsa had arrived in England, and lent urgency to its proceedings. The evidence of men such as Stockenstrom and soldiers who had served on the frontier provided more information to Glenelg, who was clearly appalled by events.

The Secretary of State was a scrupulously fair man with legal training and he set about preparing the response of the Government to events in the Cape with thoroughness and careful attention to the evidence from both sides. This resulted in a document that was despatched to D'Urban on the 26th December 1835 and which reached him on 21st March 1836.

In prose that was cool and measured, courteous and devastating, Glenelg spelt out the long sequence of events that led to war. He carefully approved the necessity for ending the Xhosa incursion and then demolished the case for annexation of the Province of Queen Adelaide, for the devastation of homes and crops of the Xhosa, and for the level of retaliation. He then turned to the death of Hintsa, enumerating all the concerns about the nature of Hintsa's imprisonment, his treatment and the details of his death, and expressed his intention of setting up an inquiry into the circumstances of his death.

The despatch ended with a series of instructions. The sovereignty over the region between Kei and Keiskamma Rivers, while it could not be justified morally or on principles of international law, was accepted for practical reasons. Occupation of the Province of Queen Adelaide must cease by the end of 1836 and the annexation must be reversed. This requirement was couched somewhat ambiguous terms as the original draft had aroused the ire of King William IV; as a result there was an opportunity for D'Urban to argue the case for its retention. The Mfengu were to be settled on lands west of the Keiskamma under British protection. The Xhosa who had been expelled from the conquered territories should have their ancient possessions restored, subject to each tribe being assigned clearly defined territory. A Lieutenant Governor would be appointed to administer the functions of government on the eastern Frontier. He would be supported by a Commissioner whose function would be to investigate and adjudicate on incursions across the border by both colonists and Xhosa. A Government agent would be appointed to be stationed in the independent Xhosa territory whose function would be to protect the interests both of the British traders and of the Xhosa.

The despatch resulted in great dissatisfaction among the British and Dutch colonists[443]. For D'Urban and Smith it was a huge blow. The actions following from it were to lead to D'Urban's recall and Smith's transfer from the Colony.

Inquiry   [1835 – 1837]

Glenelg's request for an inquiry into the death of Hintsa was made to the Commander-in-Chief of the Army, Lord Hill. Hill's instructions resulted in the consitution of a Court of Enquiry which was to open its proceedings at Fort Willshire on August 29th, 1836. Smith was alarmed at the threat to his career and indignant at what he regarded as a slur on his honour. He enthusiastically set about doing what he could to influence the proceedings. D'Urban was not prepared to accept his suggestions for membership of the Committee of Inquiry, but allowed Smith a privileged position in that he was given the opportunity to read the documentation in advance and to interact with the witnesses. Since many of these witnesses were soldiers under his command, he was able to instruct them in the manufactured story. Some of the eyewitnesses were settlers who had already been discharged and they reacted to summons to give evidence in various ways:

> I heard of it [the inquiry], a summons for me as witness was prepared, but as I was at the time preparing for a journey into the interior, I hurried my movements and started on horseback, leaving my wagon to follow. Thus the summons was not served. All the other witnesses being well primed, denied any knowledge of the mutilation, ...[444]

Edward Driver was one of those summonsed and made no difficulty about attending.

After the initial formalities the first witness called by the Court of Inquiry was Ambrose Campbell[445]. He made an unimpressive witness, not least because all he had to offer was hearsay evidence. He was unable to back up many of the allegations that he had made during the period leading up to the Inquiry. Two critical questions were whether Southey had shot Hintsa when he was begging for mercy, whether Hintsa's body had been mutilated after death, and, if so, who had been responsible. All Campbell had to offer was the statement that had been made by Klaas, an interpreter of mixed Khoikhoi and Xhosa descent, and other hearsay evidence.

Klaas's evidence when he was called was thus crucial. He essentially confirmed everything that had been in his statement. He, however, had not personally witnessed the critical events. He had been with the column that had been climbing the hill well behind the vanguard who had been in pursuit of Hintsa, Fortuitously, however, he had been at the level where the hunt for Hintsa had occurred. He had heard the shots and shortly afterwards seen Windvogel Julie and Nicholaas Africa emerging from the bush where Hintsa had been killed. They had been carrying arm rings and tobacco from Hintsa's body. Klaas made his way to the site of the killing, by which time many onlookers had arrived at the scene. That evening Julie and Africa had asked Klaas what "Taru" meant and he had told them it was a request for mercy. They then told him that Hintsa had repeatedly asked for mercy before Southey shot him. Klaas's evidence regarding the mutilation was equivocal. He denied knowledge of any mutilation whereas he had previously in a statement declared that William Southey had cut off Hintsa's ears.

Julie and Africa were still serving soldiers. When their turn came to give evidence they described the pursuit of Hintsa from his first dash to his death as eye-witnesses. Both denied hearing him call for mercy but said that they had lowered their guns because others were in the line of fire. They denied having discussed matters with Klaas afterwards. Both, however, unequivocally stated that George Southey had cut off Hintsa's ears.

Pretorius in his analysis of the evidence writes that[446]:

This meant that Klaas's word was the only foundation on which the humanitarians based their claim that Hintsa had cried for mercy.

This is true so far as the evidence presented to the inquiry was concerned. Pretorius, however, was not aware of the journals of Charles Lennox Stretch and the reminiscences of Henry Halse. Stretch, in particular, reported later that Driver, George Southey, and Shaw all had stated that Hintza had called for mercy several times. The humanitarians who had so strongly lobbied Glenelg had been very much aware of the reports of these conversations. Halse's letter to his father was brought to the attention of the Court but Halse, himself, had taken good care to make himself unavailable. Godlonton in the *Graham's Town Journal* was providing regular and vituperative comment on the proceedings of the Court, much of it manifestly untrue; he asserted that Halse was a hundred miles away from the site of Hintsa's death when it occurred. With no support in Court, Halse's observations had no influence on the inquiry.

After the Court had shown a strong interest in pursuing these allegations with other witnesses, Smith decided it was time to get his carefully prepared story on record. He demanded to be allowed to submit a statement to the Court. With some reluctance this was agreed. Smith's account had evolved since his original report to D'Urban. His story now had a strong suggestion that Hintsa's escape had been planned. The break for freedom was described as before but now there was a large force of Xhosa waiting in the neighbourhood for the escape of their king. When Southey had gone into the riverine bush it was swarming with Xhosa. He had seen an enemy figure threatening him with an assegai and had immediately fired to defend himself. Only afterwards had the dead man been discovered to be Hintsa. There had been no calls for mercy; the shot had been an instantaneous reaction to defend himself. The mutilation was not mentioned.

Captain Balfour's evidence was a valiant attempt to support Smith. He was not a fluent liar and number of contradictions in his evidence were exposed by the Court.

Other witnesses supported Smith's story. Young Bisset was Smith's creature. As a result of the events at the time Smith had offered him a commission and given him a horse. He parroted the official line that Southey had fired in self defence, a line quite at variance with what he had written in a letter at the time:

> Hintza sprang up and leaped into the Water, keeping only his head out under a projecting stone. Geo. Southey and several others came up by this time while I [Bisset] was engaged reloading. ... Lt Balfour made three attempts to fire, but his percussion gun missed fire. Geo. Southey who was first, then took deliberate aim at his head, and blew his brains out[447].

William Shaw stuck obstinately to the official story and got himself confused in the process.

Now it was Driver's turn.

Edward Driver was his own man, stubborn and secure in his own opinions. If Smith had tried to influence him it was without success. His instinct was to be straightforward and outspoken. At the same time several comrades with whom he had served – the Southey brothers and William Shaw in particular – were threatened by the proceedings of the Court. He also had little sympathy with the abstract principles of the humanitarians. To him Hintsa was a principal instigator of the war and a personal enemy. Driver was not, however, prepared to lie on oath. The Court was one of Inquiry not one of Justice and, under the rules of procedure, there was no obligation on him to answer their questions. The course that he appears to have adopted was to speak the truth and nothing but the truth. The whole truth, however, was another matter: when truthful answers would have incriminated the Southeys or Shaw he straightforwardly stated that he refused to answer the question, as he was entitled to do[448].

One of the first questions he was asked was if he knew why Southey had shot Hintsa. His presence near the scene of the shooting had been mentioned by other witnesses and we can assume that something was known by the Court of the circumstances surrounding the detaining of Hintsa. Driver and the Southeys were reported to have threatened Hintsa in various ways at the time. His answer to the Court's question was unequivocal. He could not speak for Southey but, had he had the opportunity, he would himself have shot the king, and he regretted not having done so. He denied that this was for private revenge although he had many personal grievances against Hintsa; his reason was because of what he saw as the injuries to the colonists caused by the war.

He described the events at the river. To the surprise of the members of the Court he stated that he had been present when Southey fired the shot. He had seen Hintsa hide himself behind the rock and had seen him shot. He saw no assegais near the body, but the tail end of one protruded from beneath the rock. This demolished the argument that Hintsa had threatened Southey with an assegai. He had not noticed whether Julie and Africa and been in sight, but they could have been there, unobserved by him. They were certainly there shortly afterwards. He had been distracted by the need to see to his horse and had left shortly afterwards. The body had not been mutilated at the time.

Asked whether he had he seen the body mutilated he answered, "I saw the body at the top of the hill where it had been dragged. I decline answering the question. I did not mutilate it myself." Had he seen Hintsa's ears in the possession of anyone? He again declined to answer. Had he heard Hintsa cry for mercy? "That is a question I decline to answer." Frustratingly, while it would have been clear to anyone present what the answers were to the questions to which he refused to respond, the Court could make no use of such inference.

It must be concluded that, had Driver provided replies to the questions that he had refused to answer, the findings of the Court would in all probability have been very different. In this sense his evidence was central to the whole proceeding.

The remaining witnesses added nothing much that was new. The Southey brothers trotted out the official story. Dr Ford described the condition of the body, including the fact that an ear had been cut off. He refuted the suggestion that the ear could have been lost as a result of the bullet wound.

After the witnesses had been heard the Court moved to Graham's Town to prepare its report. In many ways it was damning. It found that Hintsa may have premeditated his escape, but there was no conclusive evidence showing whether his status was that of "a friendly guide, a hostage, or a prisoner." Up to the point where Hintsa entered the riverine bush it followed Smith's account. In particular it found that Smith had ordered Southey to fire at Hintsa. Thereafter it differed sharply with the stories of Smith and Southey. They found that Hintsa was hiding, and in extremity. They discounted any idea that there were large numbers of Xhosa waiting in ambush and that Hintsa might have been leading his pursuers into a trap. The evidence did not allow them to determine whether he had cried for mercy – an important point it attributing culpability. They found that the mutilation had occurred and condemned it forcefully, but were unable to assign responsibility.

Nothing had been found that could criminally implicate Smith or any other individual, although his reputation had received a blow.

The report was eventually submitted to Glenelg by D'Urban along with a further justification of D'Urban's own decisions. The reply dated 1st May 1837 accepted the findings and provided faint praise for both D'Urban and Smith. It concluded, however, by relieving D'Urban of his position as Governor of the Colony.

Chapter 14. Interbellum

Rights are often entangled with wrongs, and wrongs wear the air of good.

St Thomas Aquinas, Summa Theologiae: Prudence

Winners and Losers [1835]

The peace was a turning point for many[449]. For the settlers of Albany it heralded a time of increasing prosperity and relative security. For the amaRharhabe, the amaMbalu, the amaGqunukwhebe, the amaNtinde and the imiDange it was the beginning of a new existence, with different relationships between them and the Colonial Government. For the Mfengu it was the end of their wanderings; they surrendered their former existence for a life within the Colony, providing a new source of labour and becoming key to the defence of the frontier with many being recruited into the new Fingo units. For many frontier Boers the new political dispensations that followed the end of the war were too much to take and many were soon to leave the Colony in the Great Trek, providing a new source of strife and instability in the South African interior to the North of the Colony. For the Colonial Government there was the new problem of how to assimilate the Mfengu now living as British subjects within the Colonial boundaries; unlike the Khoikhoi and coloured communities whose culture had been stifled by long years in contact with western ideas, there was no prospect of their immediately embracing western political systems and customs. For the British Government there was the problem of what to do to prevent this turbulent Colony from becoming a drain on the Exchequer. And for D'Urban and Smith there was the problem of dealing with the consequences of their ill-judged actions during the war.

Uneasy Interlude [1835 – 1837]

The pace of developments in the first years after the war was controlled by the three months or so that it took for a ship to make the voyage between Britain and the Cape. As soon as Glenelg had received D'Urban's reports and the submissions of the reformists and the Select Committee on Aborigines had made its report, D'Urban's new dispensation, as well as his Governorship, was doomed. It was not until January 1838, however, that his successor, Lieut.-Gen. Sir George Napier arrived to succeed him. In the mean time many pressures made him a lame duck governor.

Initially D'Urban and Smith were hailed as heroes by the colonists. They had defeated the enemy. They had extended the boundaries of the Colony providing opportunities for expansion. Soon their star was to fade. Smith, after the inquiry into Hintsa's death, found himself marking time in his old position in Cape Town. Only when Glenelg had gone and Melbourne's Whig government was in its last stages was he posted to India in 1840. His career once again began to flourish there.

The Lieutenant Governor [1836]

Those who supported a separate seat of government for the Eastern Cape were delighted when the decision was made to fill the position of Lieutenant Governor. The post had been created at the end of Somerset's term of office. General Bourke had arrived to fill it but had had to step in as Acting Governor. The delight turned to anger when the name of the appointee became known. Andries Stockenstrom arrived in 1836 to take up the position. He became solely responsible for the Government of the eastern region unless the Governor was actually present. On Glenelg's instructions he set out to implement a frontier policy that was very different from what D'Urban and Smith had conceived.

There were now numerous Xhosa resettled in the ceded territory. The treaty policy that Stockenstrom set up was based on agreements with the chiefs. No longer could colonists pursue those who stole their cattle beyond the border. The chiefs were responsible for restitution.

Before Glenelg's final instructions had arrived D'Urban had seen the inevitable and reversed the annexation of Queen Adelaide Province. Stockenstrom was now faced with the responsibility not only of governing the eastern part of the Colony, but also of managing relationships with the Xhosa in the ceded territory and also in the abandoned Queen Adelaide Province. He took over responsibility for managing the reversal of the annexation on 14th September 1836 shortly after the end of the Commission of Enquiry into Hintsa's death. Smith organised a large gathering of Xhosa who were to be harangued on his departure. Smith believed that the Xhosa were desolated by his departure: Stockenstrom thought that it was only the knowledge that there were to be changes in frontier administration that prevented further violence. Many of the Xhosa apparently thought that Smith had been dismissed after having been found guilty of murdering Hintsa. Smith returned to Cape Town to resume his military position. He was rewarded with the consolation prize of promotion to full Colonel and waited for better times. In 1840, once Glenelg had gone, he was appointed as Adjutant-General to the British

Army in India. There he resumed his swashbuckling career and advanced to further military glory.

Stockenstrom was a complex man. He had grown up among the eastern Boers, son of a Swedish immigrant, but part of the Dutch community. As a young man his father had been killed treacherously at the beginning of the fourth frontier war. He had joined the Cape Corps as a young ensign and had been befriended by the adjutant, Robert Hart. They remained lifelong friends. He was in many ways a misfit. His keen sense of justice and respect for the rule of law had led him to positions that meant that he was identified with the philanthropists by the Colonists, and thus lumped together with missionaries, British humanitarian politicians, and other groups that they regarded as favouring the Xhosa at the expense of the Colonists. He had all the qualifications for being an excellent Lieutenant Governor except that he was unacceptable to those he was expected to govern. He was totally at odds with his superior, Sir Benjamin D'Urban, yet his appointment made it clear that he was himself responsible for interpretation of policy and for governing the region; only if the Governor was actually present in the region could he be overruled.

Throughout his time on the frontier Stockenstrom had been totally opposed to the reprisal system and had advocated a system where the Xhosa were kept strictly on their side of the frontier and their chiefs would regulate their own affairs including being responsible for controlling cattle theft. He now had the opportunity to put his ideas into practice. During December 1836 he set about negotiating treaties with the various Xhosa chiefs.

The treaty system that he developed had several aspects. Before he could even start he had to ensure that those Xhosa who had been on opposite sides during the war reached some accommodation. The amaGqunukwhebe under Phatho had supported the British and first the various chiefs had to negotiate a settlement. This took some days. The position of the Mfengu needed to be secured. The ongoing problem of cross-border cattle-reaving had to be addressed. The tangled political legacy of D'Urban's and Smith's invasion had to be unwound.

Stockenstrom's principle was the clear separation of Xhosa and Colony with the boundary being at the Great Fish River. The annexation of Queen Adelaide Province between Keiskamma and Kei was cancelled by D'Urban's proclamation on 2nd February 1837. On Stockenstrom's orders the troops withdrew. In the ceded territory between the Fish and the Keiskamma the protection of both the Mfengu and the Kat River Settlement meant that this could not be abandoned. It formally remained British but within it the Xhosa chiefs ruled subject to their own law. Colonists could not cross the Fish without the permission of the chiefs: the Xhosa could not enter the Colony without permission. White settlement was excluded from the ceded territory. Some of the forts remained occupied but there were to be no military patrols. Only in the event of threats to the Mfengu or the Kat River Settlement would these troops be ordered into action. Two agents were appointed as representatives of the Colony – one to the amaNgqika, the other to the amaGqunukwhebe, the remnants of the amaNdlambe, and the other smaller clans. Xhosa equivalents using the title pakati – the name for tribal councillors – were appointed to the frontier region. Cross-border cattle theft was to be handled by complaints to the military authorities who would refer them to the chiefs. They in turn would be responsible for following up the complaints. In no circumstances could pursuit of stolen cattle take place across the border.

In many ways it was a perverted form of this policy that was the philosophical basis of Hendrik Verwoerd's "Separate Development" more than a hundred and twenty years later. The difference was that the Stockenstrom's system recognized an existing independent and culturally strong Xhosa people located in a well defined region: Verwoerd's system tried to impose quasi-independence forcibly on a people whose cultural values had been subject to a century of abuse and when the geographical and economic integration of the South African people was irreversible.

D'Urban was totally opposed to Stockenstrom's policies and there is suspicion that he was involved in plots to undermine his Deputy[450]. The sniping went on until their relations had completely broken down. Eventually D'Urban was relieved of his position by Glenelg. He thereafter resumed his military position in Cape Town, only leaving in 1846 when he was appointed Commander of the British forces in North America, located in Montreal. He was succeeded as governor by Sir George Napier in January 1838.

At first relations between the new Governor Napier and Stockenstrom were cordial. Napier was Glenelg's man and anxious for the treaty system to work. His main concern, however, was to maintain the frontier at peace with the least possible expense. The dissatisfaction on the frontier because of Stockenstrom's unpopularity impeded him and led to strained relations.

The opposition to Stockenstrom from the settlers became more overt. Not long after his appointment accusations of murder were brought against him relating to an incident more than twenty years earlier in 1812 when, as a young ensign on campaign with Col. Graham, he had shot an unarmed Xhosa youth. The matter was pursued by Duncan Campbell, the Graham's Town Civil Commissioner, who collected affidavits regarding the matter. D'Urban gave Stockenstrom no opportunity to defend himself but sent the allegations straight to London. Stockenstrom failed to get an enquiry instituted and unwisely brought a libel case against Campbell. The Court was a local one and unsympathetic to Stockenstrom. They decided against him and awarded a judgement with substantial costs. It was the beginning of the end for the Lieutenant-Governor. The official enquiry into the alleged murder was held in the Cape and he was fully exonerated. He travelled to London to clear his name there, but, while Glenelg was sympathetic, he was in no position to support him as he was about to be dropped from the Melbourne cabinet and replaced by Lord Normanby who oversaw Stockenstrom's resignation as Lieutenant-Governor. Stockenstrom returned to the Cape to retire to his farm. Later he was rewarded for his services by a baronetcy. He was succeeded as Lieutenant Governor by Colonel John Hare who satisfied Napier's feelings that a military man should occupy the position, but who was in all other respects unsuitable for the post.

The Great Trek   [1835 – 1836]

The Great Trek is a catch-all description of the migration of Dutch frontier farmers who, in large numbers left the Colony and travelled northwards in search of what they hoped would be a better life. It was the Dutch of the frontier region who trekked; the more prosperous farmers and merchants of the west had no reason to go. The story of the trekkers forms the basis of the tradition of the Afrikaans community in South Africa with large emotional impact for them. It is full of the idealization that one would expect in such circumstances.

While the aftermath of the war, particularly the reversal of the D'Urban postwar frontier policy, was in the past cited as the major reason for the departure of the trekkers, the motivations of those who trekked were varied. General dissatisfaction among the Dutch community arose from a multiplicity of causes – the change from the Dutch to the English legal system, the imposition of English as the language of government, the abolition of slavery, the odium cast on them by the activities of the humanitarian movement, the insecurity of life on the frontier, the upsetting of the relationship between farmers and labourers, the distance of a Colonial government perceived as unsympathetic to and ignorant of their concerns. Where the British settlers remained and agitated for separate representative government, the Boers tore up their roots and trekked north looking for a better life. Piet Retief laid out their rationalization of their motives in a manifesto[451], concluding:

> We are now quitting the fruitful land of our birth, in which we have suffered enormous losses and continual vexation, and are entering a

wild and dangerous territory; but we go with a firm reliance on an all-seeing, just, merciful Being, whom it will be our endeavour to fear and humbly to obey.

The motives of the trekkers were were not always in line with the lofty ideals expressed in the manifesto. Piet Retief, himself, had recently been suspended from his position as a field commandant by Stockenstrom, both because of his opposition to Stockenstrom and also because of unacceptable actions taken against the Xhosa[452]. Another well-known trekker, Louis Tregardt, had already left the Colony well before the war, possibly to escape allegations of cattle stealing[453]. He had been granted land by Hintsa close to Butterworth. He was suspected by the British of encouraging the war against the Colony. When Harry Smith invaded Hintsa's territory, Tregardt, hearing that Smith had issued a warrant for his arrest, trekked north and settled beyond the Orange River for about a year before setting off on his ill-fated trek to Delagoa Bay.

From the point of view of the British settlers the trek vacated large numbers of farms in the region giving the entrepreneurs the opportunity of picking them up at bargain prices, which they did with enthusiasm.

The Merchants   [1836 – 1842]

Forty years after the end of the war one of the Wesleyan ministers who had been a vociferous supporter of the war against Hintsa, the Rev. William Boyce, remembered the group of people who were prominent among his friends in Graham's Town.[454]

> I am obliged, however, to confess that we Methodists were on the whole a plebeian set. Except an editor and printer, and a few wholesale shopkeepers, who by general consent were termed "merchants" as importing their goods direct from Europe, and a few persons connected with the army or commissariat, the rest of us were retail storekeepers and artizans. [Xhosa] traders, and wagon proprietors engaged in the carriage of goods within the Colony, were, next to the merchants our enterprising class, commanding no small degree of respect. In the country we were small farmers and graziers. In those days we made no pretensions to the gentility which is supposed to be connected with freedom from labour, for we all had to work for our living. None of us were ashamed of this, or of our useful occupations, however lowly they might be. Our successors and descendants need not to blush for us, - for we made the Colony what it is! ... But as I recall the names of these fathers of the Colony, small and great, I feel that their memory is blessed. I dare but mention the names of William Cock, of the Kowi River; Robert Godlonton, for many years the Editor of the Graham's Town Journal; Captain M'Donald, George Wood, Richard and Joseph Walker, Carey Hobson, James Powell, Charles Penney, William Wright, J. C. Wright, Robert Lee, B. Booth, Daniel Roberts sen. and jun., James Howse, J. Kidd, C. White, J. Jubber, J. Weeks, Charles Slater, Thomas

Cockroft, W. A. Fletcher, with the Cawoods, Cyruses, Webbs, Lucases, Prices, Hartleys, Daniels, Oateses, Trollopes, Bonnins, Temletts, Ushers and Hooles. Other names, not identified with Methodism, deserve to be respected by all Methodists for their work's sake: - old Dr Campbell[455] and Dr. Atherstone[456], Mr. Driver (the elephant hunter), Mr Hart of Somerset, and Mr Gilfillan of Cradock, and J. O. Smith of Algoa Bay, though mentioned last, not least in the loving respect of the writer of these reminiscences.

These Wesleyans, mostly business men, included most of those who dominated the commercial growth of Graham's Town for the next thirty years. Graham's Town businessmen had had a significant injection of capital into their businesses from the military. While the end of the war had meant a reduction in these returns, the army associated with the administration of the expanded territory of the Colony still required supplies, and the new capital allowed their businesses to expand and to meet the demands of an increasingly prosperous frontier region. The small shopkeepers of Graham's Town were evolving into prosperous merchants.

Of these men, at the end of the war in 1835, Joseph Walker was not the most prosperous – that was George Wood. He was not the most politically outspoken – that was Robert Godlonton. He was not the most visionary so far as the future of Albany was concerned – that might have been William Cock with his grand plans for a port on the Kowie River. He was not the most fervent Methodist in the Wesleyan congregation – his brother Richard might have competed for that status had he not been far away on a lonely mission station. Nevertheless, Joseph had reason to be well satisfied with his position. He was a prominent member of the town's business community. He was happily married and had four children. He had a clear idea of where he was going. He was a leading member of the Wesleyan congregation, important for his position in the town. His shop in Bathurst Street was a success, and his dealings during the war had provided him with capital to improve his position. In fifteen years he had come a long way from penniless immigrant.

After the war Joseph and George Wood found room to cooperate in looking for further profit. In a memorial[457] addressed to Sir Benjamin D'Urban, Governor, dated 16th Oct 1835, signed "George Wood, Major, Sharpshooters, and Joseph Walker, Captain, Sharpshooters," the memorialists note that

> ...Memorialists jointly used their utmost ... exertions to collect all the Hottentots and Natives which they possibly could, and by the exertions of memorialists only was that useful body of men kept in hard active service by night and day until your Excellency was pleased to form the first and second battalions from them and send them into the field ...

and go on to ask the Governor to

> ... grant them each a farm of the usual size on the Keiskamma R.

The request is endorsed by an official:

> I am afraid neither of these gentlemen would go to live upon his location ...

This was probably an administrative kiss of death for this particular grant. A major reason for the granting of a farm was to place farmers in the ceded territory to provide a further line of defence. After the war, with the occupation of the ceded territory, farms were granted throughout the region, leading to an increase of prosperity among the settlers that was mirrored by the loss of power, land and territory by the Xhosa. Land speculation became extremely profitable. Apart from land in the new territories, farms were available at knock-down prices from departing trekkers.

Over the next few years Joseph Walker maintained an interest in dealings in land. In 1839 the five portions of land at George Vale were sold to Miles Bowker, and Wesley Wood to William Cock and George Hodgkins. Like other town businessmen Joseph was often litigious in protecting his rights. An ongoing grievance was the fact that his party leader, George Smith had acquired title to a large portion of the land allocated to his party. Smith's party was a joint stock party and the land should initially have been allotted to the individuals who had all paid their share of the costs. Joseph wrote a memorial to the Governor, Sir George Napier, in 1842 seeking to prevent the land, which now belonged to Smith's widow, being transferred on grounds that while deed had been made out in name of Smith it was on behalf of the party, quoting an earlier judgement against Smith which had stated that "Your Title Deed is worth no more than so much brown paper." The Registrar of Deeds replied that the land had already been transferred to M Norden.[458] The next step was for Joseph to join with Christopher Wedderburn, also of Smith's party, to apply for an interdict to prevent the land being transferred to another buyer, Frederick Carlisle[459].

Such disputes were common as the more prosperous settlers consolidated their holdings. They were complicated by the rather chaotic state of the records of the holdings of Trekkers who had left their farms and the need to survey those lands which were granted in the new territory. Joseph Walker, however, after divesting himself of many of his land holdings concentrated on business in town, keeping only one farm under management near the Kowie mouth.

His shop in Bathurst Street had started as a small store selling the necessities of life. After the war it was well capitalised by his profits from supplying the military and he grew the business, beginning to import goods himself and stocking the shop with luxuries. By 1842 he could advertise in the *Graham's Town Journal* that:

JOSEPH WALKER

Bathurst Street

Begs to inform his friends and the public that he has just received a Great Variety of GOODS suited for the season, amongst which are to be found the following, viz:- a large assortment of Chali, Saxony Muslin de Laine and other Dresses, also superior Muslin de Laines and Chalis in the piece. Also Gros de Naples, plain and figured and plain Satins. Satinette, Watered Silks, China Silks and Silk Velvet. Also narrow Velvet for the hair. A handsome assortment of fringes, Blond and Blond Edgings, fancy washing Blonds, Thread, Brussels and other Lace and Lace Edgings, Muslin work of all sorts. A large and fresh assortment of Ladies Work Boxes, Superior Metal Tea Pots etc. etc. Bathurst Street, 4th August 1842

The atmosphere of the frontier is maintained by the juxtaposition of fashionable fripperies and utilitarian utensils, but it is clear that he catered to a clientele that had money to spend and were no longer living in want.

Other opportunities were seized as they became available. Associated with the growing economy other services were established. Joseph invested in these. He became a shareholder in the new Eastern Province Bank[460]. Like other good Wesleyans he became involved in public service and charitable activities.

Family connections began to be established as the younger generation grew up and married. In 1838 Joseph Walker's sister-in-law, Jane Booth married James Thackwray, younger surviving son of William, and in 1842 his brother-in-law, Benjamin Booth Jr – the same who had been conceived in London and born in the Cape – married Robert Godlonton's daughter, Matilda. Joseph and Margaret Walker's family grew. In March 1846 they had nine children with another due when, sadly their youngest child James died at the age of 18 months. One month later Mortimer Booth Walker was born. It is perhaps significant that of all their eleven children only James did not survive until adulthood. In England, both in town and country, child mortality was very high. The healthy outdoor life on the frontier was an extra advantage to the emigrant settlers.

The flourishing of Graham's Town went hand in hand with the establishment of more representative municipal government. Its beginnings were in 1836 with the promulgation of the municipal ordinance of that year[461]. Under this ordinance any resident magistrate or justice of the peace could call a meeting of the inhabitants of a community to decide whether to set up a Municipal Board; if twenty five residents demanded it, such a meeting had to be called. If the majority of those present supported the concept then a committee was elected to draw up regulations, which were submitted to the government for approval. The regulations determined the extent of the municipal area, the number of wards into which it was to be divided, the number of municipal commissioners constituting the board, whether or not there would be ward masters. They also defined the responsibilities of the municipality – these were typical of local government: roads, services, local police, operation of the market and so forth. The commissioners formed the executive of the Board and were elected for three year terms by a public meeting. In sufficiently large towns, each ward elected its ward master to administer municipal affairs within the ward.

In April and May 1837 the regulations for the small frontier towns were promulgated – Beaufort[462], Somerset[463], Graham's Town, and Cradock. The largest was Graham's Town with eight wards and seven municipal commissioners. The *Graham's Town Journal* announced the results of the election of commissioners on May 25th 1837. Among them was Benjamin Booth[464].

Unsafe Harbour   [1835 – 1889]

When the settlers had arrived in the Cape, the only route to Graham's Town had been the rugged wagon road from Algoa Bay. Algoa Bay itself had no harbour. Ships anchored in the bay and small craft transferred the cargo to shore. By the end of the war in 1835 nothing much had changed. The road had been improved slightly but the mode of transport was the same. The needs, however, had changed. Initially the traffic had been largely one way: goods and people were needed to support the settlement. As the economy of the eastern region improved, export became a priority. The inadequate facilities for transporting goods not only to Cape Town and its environs, but also to the outside world, handicapped the growth of markets for the products of the region.

From the beginning the potential of the estuary of the Kowie River as a port seemed obvious to many businessmen in the region[465]. Early attempts to set up a shipping service between Algoa Bay and the Kowie mouth had been encouraged first by Donkin and then by Lord Charles Somerset. The growing town at Algoa Bay had been named Port Elizabeth after Donkin's dead wife. Those proposing the establishment of a port at the Kowie had asked Lord Charles to allow it to be named Port Frances after Henry Somerset's wife. For a while there had been a harbour master and a magistrate, (the latter was Donald Moodie who had married Sophia Pigot, the diarist of the *Northampton*). The project failed as a result of shipwrecks, lack of commitment from Government, and some incompetence. By 1835 its use as a harbour was only remembered in the name of Port Frances, a name that was not to survive.

The estuary was a broad tidal wetland with many sandbanks exposed at low tide with the main outflow on eastern side and a smaller branch on the western. The whole was contained between two high hills, called the West bank and the East Bank. The early use of the estuary as a harbour had been on the East Bank. Now, in June 1835, a letter from Samuel Bennet[466] was published in the *Graham's Town Journal*. In it he proposed that the western channel should be opened and the eastern filled, providing a way into the river that would serve as a well protected harbour. The idea was a spark that fired some local entrepreneurs.

In 1835, William Cock, his fortune made as a result of his dealings during the war, returned for a while to England, intending to settle there. Like many emigrants he found that, while the call of home was insistent in a distant place, once he had returned the grass was not as green as he remembered it. It was not long before he was back in the Cape, now to settle there for good. He built himself an elaborate home on the West Bank of the Kowie. He called it Richmond House but its crenellated design immediately meant that it was ever afterwards called Cock's Castle. The modern Richmond House retains traces of the original building.

Bennet's idea set him off. He became obsessed with the project of developing the harbour. Over the next few years, with the support of a private members bill in the Cape Legislative Council, he and various partners met numerous obstacles to the construction of a protected western harbour entrance. The project was hampered by lack of expertise among the principals, inadequate resources – a large number of labourers with pick axes and spades – and the dangers of the site. By 1841 there was a channel of sorts, even although there had been considerable damage of the embankment by high spring tides the previous year. The ebb tide cleared it out but the flood tide tended to silt it up with sand from the adjacent beach. A surveyor's report concluded that on completion of the western pier the port would be viable. Shortly afterwards a schooner, the *Africaine*, commissioned by Cock for the Kowie trade, managed to tie up in the port after having run aground on the beach and having been refloated. After spending some time there she set sail loaded with cargo but, on leaving the port, she was driven ashore and wrecked, fortunately without loss of life. Notwithstanding this setback, the Albany public was fired with enthusiasm for the prospects of the new harbour and clamoured to invest their money in various companies associated with shipping and the port. Steam power was now a viable option. The Albany Steamship Company – Cock a director, of course – was set up in 1842 and two ships, *Sophia* and *The British Settler* built. A paddle steamer, the *Sir John St Aubyn*, was purchased for Cock and docked in June 1842. She serviced the port for a short while and then, on February 2nd 1843, while acting as a tug for the *Sophia*, both she and her tow were wrecked on the beach.

These setbacks seem to have done little to quell the enthusiasm of the entrepreneurs of Albany. Just three weeks later Joseph Walker read the prospectus of the Graham's Town, Bathurst, and Kowie Shipping Company. Two days later on 23rd February he committed himself to investment and, as a shareholder, attended a meeting to establish the Company[467]. All the usual businessmen were there. Thomas Philipps was in the chair. Cock proposed the establishment of the company. Godlonton proposed the adoption of the propectus. Joseph Walker was elected to a committee that, among others, included Cock and George Wood, with the responsibility of preparing a deed of constitution. The next month, on March 17th 1843, the first annual general meeting of the company elected its board of directors – William Cock and Joseph Walker prominent among them – appointed auditors, and received a highly favourable report from Major Wortham of the Royal Engineers on the suitability of the port for receiving military supplies.

Of all the schemes, good and bad, in the Colony at the time, the port at the mouth of the Kowie River probably caused more grief to those investing in it than any other. Its promise for the future was regularly interrupted by misfortune and disaster. The competition from the growing city of Port Elizabeth was intense; the opening of the Zuurberg pass provided Port Elizabeth with a better route to Graaff Reinet and neighbouring towns. Wrecks of ships associated with the Kowie were frequent, although in the early years this must be understood in the context of the loss of one thirtieth of the British merchant fleet in each year. Eventually the Colonial Government assumed responsibility for the port works in 1857. The harbour, renamed Port Alfred regularly silted up and could not take the larger steam ships as the century progressed. At last, with the wreck of the tug *Buffalo* in 1889, the harbour's useful life ended.

The original investors in the port, Joseph Walker among them, would have been astonished by the final twist in the tail. During most of the twentieth century Port Alfred, was a sleepy village with one hotel, a number of holiday homes, and one run down café serving the magnificent beach. The latest development in the history of the port came in the nine-teen nineties. Port Alfred became fashionable. A new marina was excav-ated with a system of canals onto which opulent waterfront properties were faced. Sail, in the form of pleasure craft, once more is a feature of the town. It is a sought after retirement town and holiday destination with an opulent yachting marina, luxurious waterfront homes, and numerous hotels and restaurants.

Government Servants   [1820 – 1836]

The growth in prosperity of the frontier businessmen was balanced by the dashed hopes of many who had hoped to build up prosperous country es-tates. Thomas Pringle's reservations about the capacity of many of the would-be gentry to cope with conditions on the frontier had in many cases been justified. On the whole, it was not the leaders of sole propriet-or parties that became the leading citizens of the frontier region. From the beginning, far from being able to establish themselves as a squire-archy, these men found themselves unable to afford the labour necessary to establish their estates and unable to survive the misfortunes of the early years of settlement[468]. Their parties splintered. These were not men with an entrepreneurial spirit. Many ended up as salarymen in government posts.

James Ford and Philip Marillier were cases in point. Philip's dreams of retreat "from the bustle of the world to the quiet and peaceable occu-pation of husbandry" had been dashed. His father-in-law, James Ford, after a brief and unsuccessful spell as the leader of a subgroup of Bailie's fragmented and unhappy party[469], had eked out a living as a painter of miniatures in Graham's Town:

> He clung to his 300 or 400 acres until he saw that he was ruined, when he resolved to put into practice, what in his youth he had followed as an Amusement.[470]

At this time, in late 1822, he is recorded as having visited Ngqika and made drawings for a portrait of him, which unfortunately does not ap-pear to have survived. He and his wife eventually left the frontier and went to live in Cape Town. There he continued as a miniature painter while Frances opened a seminary for young women.

Philip was forced into a succession of menial government jobs. Before the war he had briefly been a clerk to the Graham's Town Landdrost and then had been transferred to the same position in the new town of Somer-set when the Albany and Somerset magisterial districts were combined in 1827. By this time he and Frances had four children. One of their grandchildren remembered her mother's description of the town as it was then[471]:

> My mother (Harriet, daughter of Richard and Frances Marillier) told me there were only seven large houses (brick, I think she meant) when they came to live here; and also that it was only when they came to Somerset East that she and four or five other children of the family were baptised. She remembered it well. Whether Grandmother did not care to have it done before I don't know, but a brother-in-law, an Anglican minister, baptised them. There was no church built then.

This was shortly after it had been laid out. The leading citizen of the town was, of course, Robert Hart, with whose family the Marilliers were to become connected.

After his service in the war Philip resumed his occupation as clerk to the magistrate. It was seven years before he had worked his way up to an appointment as magistrate of the district in 1842. Philip's spell as magistrate did lasted only two years. He resigned to go into business with his son; it was not successful and ended in bankruptcy.

Frances Marillier's father, James Ford, had died in Cape Town in 1835. His wife returned to Graham's Town where she ran a school with the help of one of her daughters. She converted to the Roman Catholic Church and after her death her school became the nucleus of the Catholic convent school.

The end of the war had a significant effect on the fortunes of Charles Lennox Stretch. He was selected by Stockenstrom as the government representative to the amaNgqika – the so-called "Gaika agent." The missionary William Chalmers had been considered as one possibility for this post but was ultimately not considered; one significant reason was that his activities during the war had not increased the trust of Maqoma in him. The other agent for the southern Xhosa was one of the numerous Bowker brothers, John Mitford Bowker. Stretch was appointed to this post and he and Anna left Graaff Reinet to set up home at Fort Cox on the Keiskamma River. Since the death of their first-born son in infancy, there was no prospect of further children and Anna's new life was lonely compared with the society of the people of Graaff Reinet.

Wool [1749 – 1842]

The Dutch had never regarded the Cape Colony as having any significant contribution to make to world trade. It was a staging post for their trade with the east. With the coming of the British, during the second occupation, the point of view changed. At first the only significant product was wine from the Western Cape vineyards. By the time the settlers arrived in

1820, wine constituted more than 70% of Cape exports. It continued to dominate until the advent and growth of a new product – wool. The Eastern Cape turned out to be ideal for farming the Spanish bred merino sheep. At the beginning of the eighteen thirties this trade began to take off.

Merino sheep[472] had first come to the Cape in 1789 as a small flock of six – part of a gift from King Charles III of Spain to the Government of the Netherlands. Later Lord Charles Somerset had imported some from France. Some of these he sent to Robert Hart on Somerset Farm where there was an opportunity to evaluate their merits[473]. During the early years of British rule they remained a curiosity. Some of the more affluent British settlers experimented with them in the early years. The wool boom was precipitated by the needs of the industrial cities of the north of England, as steam power increased the capacity of the mills. Although the textile industry came to be dominated by cotton, wool was still important enough to demand increasing imports from the colonies.

Robert Hart in later life

Robert Hart at Glen Avon and John Pringle at Glenthorn both recognized the advantages of the merino sheep whose fleeces were to be a key to the growth of Eastern Cape prosperity. Hart's interest had first been aroused when he had evaluated Somerset's flock at Somerset Farm. Pringle was given a small flock in 1824 by Andries Stockenstrom when he was first granted after Somerset farm was closed[474]. On the whole, the Dutch farmers of the region had only been interested in sheep as a source of meat. Their flocks consisted of the Dutch fat-tailed sheep, good eating but not a good source of wool. Before the arrival of the settlers the trekboer economy had been largely a self-sufficient, subsistence one. Now, as the economy grew, the advantages of trade became apparent. Those Boers who remained in the region eagerly followed the example of the forward-looking settlers who took up wool farming. Before the war wool exports from the Eastern Cape grew from 4500lb, worth £222, in 1830, to about 80 000lb, worth £4261, in 1835.

While Albany was not as well suited to sheep farming, in Graham's Town itself the local merchants invested strongly in the wool trade. Much of the land speculation that followed the opening of the ceded territory was related to wool farming. The trade in importing sheep and exporting wool flourished:

Graham's Town Journal, 7th April 1842

The attention of flock masters is most particularly called to a public sale which will be held on account of Mr. W. R. Thompson, on Thursday next, 25 ewes and 5 rams selected in France from a pure merino flock, formerly the property of the Empress Josephine. ... Rams from the same flock imported last year by Mr Thompson, clipped 7¼ lb wool each.

Hart and Pringle had farms located in the heartland of what was to become South Africa's premier wool farming region. Glenthorn celebrated the 150th anniversary of the establishment of its merino flock in 1970 when the farm was still in the hands of descendants of John Pringle[475]. Glen Avon today is still owned by direct descendants of Robert Hart.

Ups and Downs   [1838 – 1846]

Robert Hart and John Pringle were devout Calvinists. Although Hart had become an elder of the Dutch Reformed Church and Pringle had regular access to Presbyterian ministers at relatively close mission stations like Tyumie and Lovedale, each felt the need for a Presbyterian ministry closer to home. The new wealth that came from wool led each to resolve to build a Scottish church.

John Pringle was the first to do so. With the help of a detachment of the 91st Regiment under Captain Ward a solid stone structure was built on his farm at and completed at the beginning of 1840. It remained to find a minister. His ambition was to have it operate not just as a family church but ministering to the entire community including the local Khoikhoi. He approached the Glasgow Missionary Society for a minister and was promised a candidate as soon as one became available.

Robert Hart built his chapel later. He was well served by the local Dutch Reformed Church so there was less urgency. There were, however, other reasons that delayed him.

Robert Hart's *Annus Horribilis*   [1838 – 1844]

To modern eyes the fortunes of the Hart family at Glen Avon during the first part of the eighteen-forties have all the elements of a soap opera. To the sternly moral Robert and Hannah Hart they must have been hard to bear. Their family was growing up. In 1838 Ellen had married William Dods Pringle, John Pringle's half-brother, and Sarah had married Robert Mitford Bowker. Anna, Robert and James had long been married – Anna to Charles Lennox Stretch, Robert to a neighbour's daughter, Johanna Meintjies, and James to Maria van Aarde.

The first troubles came as a series of misfortunes, not unusual at the time. James's wife Maria died on 21st December 1839. Ellen Pringle died on 29th June 1840. On 18th July 1841, Johanna, Robert Jr's wife, died, leaving him with six motherless children. He lost no time in remarrying. Just seven months after Johanna's death, on 11th February 1842, Robert Jr. married the Marillier's daughter Harriet. The relationship with the Marilliers was to be further complicated when, in 1857, Harriet's brother Frederick married her stepdaughter, Ann Margaret Hart. James married a second wife, Martha Louisa Klopper on 10th April 1842.

The year 1844 was a really bad one. Late in the year Robert wrote to his great friend R J Eaton[476]. The letter is filled with information about his family. But, on page 2, after providing news about Ann and Robert Jr, he wrote sadly:

> My second [son] James the prodigal I am sorry to say has a second wife and 7 children but is in Somerset gaol for Murder or Manslaughter he has been a great Trouble to us what the result may be God only knows but his conduct has been and is a great affliction. ... All [my family] are doing well but James and I hope it has pleased God to allow this Visita-tion for his good and others however painful it may be for the present.

The events leading up to this happened on 18th September 1844[477]. That morning Cornelis van Rooyen and his kinsman Jacobus Smit set out with a wagon, driven by Jan Platje, to visit James Hart, with whom van Rooy-en had had previous dealings. Their objective, apparently, was to retrieve a saddle that belonged to van Rooyen. They arrived at Roodewal and were received cordially by Hart who invited van Rooyen and Smit into the house. At first the conversation was friendly, but then the matter of the saddle was raised. When asked where it was, Hart said that it was in the house but that he would not return it until van Rooyen had fulfilled a contract with Hart. Some time before he had been engaged to work for Hart for a year and had not completed his time. Both Hart and van Rooy-en appear to have been on a short fuse. Cornelis van Rooyen stood up and threatened to take the saddle. Hart grabbed him by the shoulder and told him to leave. They walked out of the house, followed by Smit. The first real threat came from Hart: "I will not give you the saddle and if you assault me I will shoot you!" The argument became acrimonious and after a short while Hart and van Rooyen went back into the house while Smit remained outside.

When they next appeared the quarrel had escalated. Hart was carrying a gun. It was loaded and primed but not cocked. His right hand, however, was on the hammer and the situation was tense. He advanced on van Rooyen with the gun levelled. Van Rooyen grabbed the barrel and pushed it aside while they both grappled for the gun. Both were young, fit farmers. They were closely matched in strength and neither was able to gain the upper hand. As they strained for advantage, Hart made a move. Keeping hold of the gun with his left hand, he reached into his pocket with his right and pulled out a clasp knife, managed to open it one-handed and made a thrust at van Rooyen.

James Hart

This was more than van Rooyen could take. He let go the gun and ran for the wagon, closely pursued by Hart. When they reached the wagon he turned at bay, grabbed the barrel of the gun, and pushed it aside. "Don't shoot, James!" shouted Smit. Hart made a back-handed thrust at van Rooyen with the knife and he fell. This was more than enough for Smit; he leapt on his horse and rode off, followed as closely as possible by Platje with the wagon. When they looked back, van Rooyen was lying on the ground, Hart was walking slowly towards the house, Martha, James's wife, watched in shock from the front door, and a young apprentice, Henry Mould, stood horrified at the corner of the house.

James Hart walked into the house, sat down, and wrote a note to the field cornet:

Mr. O'Reilly

I have stabbed a man. Come and investigate the case

(signed) James Hart

He then wrote a note to his father and settled down to await events.

Eventually O'Reilly, together with the local magistrate and a police escort arrived[478]. Hart calmly provided evidence and statements were taken from the witnesses. Hart was arrested and arrangements were put in hand to transport him to the gaol in Somerset. While he was waiting he was allowed to console himself with a bottle of brandy. This was a bad mistake. As they walked out of the house to start the journey to Somerset Hart saw his horse, which was saddled and ready for him. The brandy meant that he saw this as an opportunity. He broke away from his escort, leapt onto the horse and galloped off into the distance.

It was a foolish move. The pursuit was immediate and the constable following him was armed with a gun charged with buckshot. He ignored calls to stop and the policeman fired. Hart was brought down with quite serious injuries. A doctor was called and treated nine wounds in his back, wrist, and leg. He was judged fit to be moved to Somerset and was taken there to await the consequences.

The autopsy showed that van Rooyen had been killed by a single thrust of the knife into the right ventricle of the heart. James Hart was brought before the magistrate, charged with murder, and referred to the Supreme Court for trial.

The case was heard several months later on 14th April 1845 in the Graham's Town Circuit Court before Judge Menzies. It lasted three days. Had James been found guilty on the murder charge he would have been hanged without delay. He was lucky that the jury, all men of the district who knew him well, decided that there was enough doubt about the degree of intent to reduce the charge to culpable homicide. He was known to be very erratic and a local press report attributed his actions to insanity, believed to have arisen from the bite of a rabid dog when he was fifteen years old. On the 16th April 1845 James was found guilty of that charge and sentenced to ten years imprisonment with hard labour. Attempts by his father to have him transferred to the gaol in Somerset or Graham's Town were unsuccessful[479]. Robert's later attempts in 1847, using all his influence, to appeal to the Governor to have the sentence reduced also failed[480].

Meanwhile the marriage of Robert Hart Jr and Harriet Marillier was coming under strain. Harriet's first child, named after her mother, had been born on 13th April 1844. In 1846, her second child, Richard, was born in May, and about the same time Harriet's unmarried elder sister, Frances, gave birth to a son, Wilfred, who was acknowledged as having been fathered by Robert[481]. On the positive side, Wilfred seems to have been comfortably absorbed into the extended Hart family at Glen Avon.

Robert Hart Jr (Comparison with the photograph of his father, Robert Hart Sr, shows that both pictures were taken in the same studio – probably at the same time)

Harriet Marillier (Mrs Robert Hart Jr)

It was now, in 1846, that Robert Sr felt it was time to build a chapel on his farm. This was to serve the Presbyterian community of Somerset for many years.

The Silver Jubilee   [1844 – 1845]

One would assume that the British settlers, or at least the leaders among them, were able to count. The new mathematics from Arabia introduced the concept of zero to the western world in the middle ages. This has not yet been completely internalised by the public, as illustrated by the heated press correspondence over whether the new millenium began on 1st January 2000 or 1st January 2001[482]. In any event, for the settlers, the celebration of the twenty fifth anniversary of their arrival in Algoa Bay was held in April 1844, twenty four years after the landing. To be fair, one of those responsible for initiating the celebrations was clear about the matter in his own mind when he wrote[483]:

The Tenth of next April [1824], I beg to remind you, will be the anniversary of the debarkation on the sands of Algoa Bay of the first parties of Settlers which came to this country, and it is moreover the Half-Jubilee year – that of our entrance upon the twenty-fifth year of our sojourn in this fine Colony.

This way of looking at things also had the potential advantage of allowing a second celebration at the end of the jubilee year.

The first suggestion of a celebration came from John Ayliff and was taken up enthusiastically by John Centlivres Chase in Port Elizabeth. An inaugural meeting was held in Graham's Town in February and all the usual suspects were rounded up to form an organizing committee, including Joseph Walker, Benjamin Booth, Robert Godlonton, George Wood, and several others. Thomas Stringfellow, Godlonton's former associate, was elected chairman. They planned a gala day in Graham's Town on April 10th 1844. A parallel celebration was held in Port Elizabeth on the same day. Bathurst scheduled their celebration for 10th May[484] and Salem for 23rd July, the day of arrival of Sephton's party.

The Graham's Town celebration started off well[485]. Henry Somerset, playing the part of country squire, had lent the grounds of his estate, Oatlands, for a function that mimicked a church fête. The adults and children of the town gathered, bought food from stalls, picnicked under the trees, and listened to the bands of three different regiments. Before that, in the morning, those with enough stamina had listened to a long address by the Rev. William Shaw, delivered in St George's Church. This had been followed by a procession through the streets from St George's to the picnic grounds.

It was in the evening that things went wrong. A grand banquet was planned. Initially it was intended to restrict it only to settlers who had arrived in 1820. In the face of protests the organising committee threw it open to the public and in spite of the large expense – nine shillings per head[486] – it was over-subscribed. A newly completed shop provided space for 250 diners. More than this arrived and there was a great deal of confusion. It is probable that many were gatecrashers. The tables were set out in an E-shape with dignitaries at the head. The committee, however – among them George Wood, Joseph Walker, Thomas Stringfellow, and Benjamin Booth – were distributed among the other diners. An amateur band provided background music. Many of the leading citizens of the town were Wesleyans who supported the growing temperance movement, but plenty of alcohol was available, mostly in the form of the local brandy. The meal proceeded convivially. Afterwards the tables were cleared and the after-dinner speeches began. Thomas Philipps was in the chair. After the traditional toast to the Queen a number of toasts were proposed, with the key-note address being the toast to the settlers of Albany by Col. Henry Somerset.

At the other end of the room was Thomas Stubbs, sitting with some of his cronies. Near them were George Wood, William Smith, and Thomas Stringfellow. Stubbs had been doubtful about coming to the dinner at all. He did not believe that there was much cause for celebration. His family had been destroyed as a result of their move to the Cape. His father had been murdered, his mother had died, the family had been split up, and he had had a difficult life, during which, in spite of courageous service in the volunteer forces, he had failed to prosper as many others had done. Near him was sitting his fellow apprentice George Wood, who was now rich and a leading citizen of the town. By this time all in the neighbourhood had drunk freely.

Somerset, who, according to Stubbs, was a very poor public speaker, was bumbling on about the good deeds of the Government in protecting the settlers and looking after their interests. This was too much for Stubbs. When Somerset praised the Government for protecting the settlers' cattle during the war he spoke out. "That's a lie," he announced to his companions[487]. Stringfellow, sitting nearby, was incensed. He threatened to have Stubbs ejected. "I am a Justice of the Peace and I will have you turned out!"

A police officer would have been more use than a J.P. to stop things. Stubbs, in full voice, repeated, "That is a damned lie!" The man next to Stringfellow found the idea of sitting next to a Justice of the Peace distasteful and threw his brandy into his face. The company quickly divided into those supporting Stubbs and those wanting to expel him. When someone tried to hustle him out Stubbs's brother-in-law, John Miller, seized the man and threw him "completely over the heads of some others." The battle was on. Diners began to break up chairs in order to use the legs as weapons.

Inside the sober merchant George Wood there was still a riotous apprentice trying to break out. Wood could not restrain himself and nor could William Smith. They lifted Stubbs onto a table and pressed him to make his case[488]. Stubbs began to attack the record of the Government in looking after the interests of the settlers. He gave full value, naming William Cock and George Lee as corrupt contractors who misappropriated the cattle in their care, cheered on by Wood, Smith, and the neighbouring crowd.

Somerset bumbled on, persevering to the end of his speech, and William Shaw rose to propose the toast to those settlers who had died. In Godlonton's words

> The next toast was ... introduced by the Rev. W. Shaw with some seri-
> ous and appropriate observations, but which unhappily were but par-
> tially heard from the confusion which then prevailed in several parts of
> the room.

Stringfellow and William Smith both struggled to the platform to try to
propose their scheduled toasts:

> Several other toasts were proposed and drunk in the course of the
> evening; but as a large proportion of the company had departed, and
> as very little order was preserved, it falls not within our province to re-
> cord them.

The scandalised good and faithful of the community melted away leaving
the field to Stubbs who noted that

> When I concluded, those that remained gave me three hearty cheers.
> We then, all that remained, drew up to one table and spent the evening.

By contrast, a month later, the celebrations at Bathurst were a model of
propriety. This time George Wood, possibly mending fences, was the
speaker charged with the responsibility of proposing a toast to William
Cock.

The citizens of Bathurst, a year later, celebrated the 25th anniversary
of the arrival on a more appropriate date, Wednesday the 14th May
1845[489]. It was something to please the sober citizens of the village with
no room for frivolity. In the preceding year Benjamin Booth had retired
and moved to Bathurst, so he was roped in as secretary of the organizing
committee, bringing his experience of the rumpus in Graham's Town.

To those with a twenty-first century attention span it would have been
a day of mind-numbing boredom. The village was thronged with 400
people, many of whom had ridden in from as far away as Graham's
Town. The Graham's Town Amateur Band had been roped in to provide
music. The Wesleyan Chapel was decorated as if for a harvest festival and
at 11 a.m. a service of thanksgiving was addressed at length by the Rev.
John Ayliff. At 2 p.m. the pupils of the Sunday School were gathered together by their teachers and, led by the band "playing some of the best
and most lively national airs," processed round the village. There was a
merciful break for tea and then at 4 p.m. they gathered for a meeting in
the chapel. This was addressed by no fewer than thirteen speakers. Benjamin Booth, himself, was one of them, and both his sons-in-law, Joseph
Walker and James Thackwray had come from Graham's Town to give
speeches. James had married Benjamin's daughter Jane a few years before. Joseph was now a Graham's Town wardmaster; James was beginning to make his mark in Graham's Town, running a business in Somer-

set street identified as a "bazar". The procedings continued until 9 p.m. –
five full hours. If the official account is to be believed we learn that:

> ... although the proceedings occupied five hours, not terminating until
> about 9 o'clock, the only regret was that time had sped so quickly, and
> that prudence required the meeting should be brought to a close. ...
> there was no indulgence in strong drink, no artificial stimulants, no al-
> tercation of any kind; – all was harmony, good order and cheerful en-
> joyment.

Ethos

To understand the mind-sets of the settlers it is necessary to put aside our
prejudices and try to immerse ourselves in their times. It is much easier to
understand the nature of technological and material changes than to understand the faith, ethos, ideas, and social attitudes of those who lived
through them. What were the feelings of those who lived on the frontier,
experiencing the autocracy of Governors like Lord Charles Somerset, un-
controllable natural disasters, conflict with the amaXhosa, and the constant insecurity of making a new life in a strange land?

In Georgian Britain, in the first third of the nineteenth century, the
changes wrought by the industrial revolution had brought hundreds of
thousands of economic refugees from the country to the large industrial
conglomerations of London, the north of England, and Scotland, where
they lived in squalor, labouring in the new factories, on the construction
sites, and in the ship building yards. Among the working classes in some
of these places, only 25% survived to adulthood. In Manchester and Liverpool the average life expectancy among the working class was less than
twenty years. Ignorance of the relationship between disease and hygiene
meant that mortality across all classes of society was high. In their
struggle to survive, the only recourse most people had was to their own
community or to patronage.

Among country people the next county, or even the next village, was
foreign territory. In the melting pots of the cities, people from this background formed new communities, inward looking and interdependent. At
the same time these attitudes were leavened by those who had had contact with the world – in the army, the navy, or, for the more privileged
classes, in Colonial government. Foreigners were either enemies like the
French, subservient like the Indians or the Khoikhoi, or remote and in-
comprehensibly alien like the Chinese. Class distinctions were large.

Unsurprisingly, crime was at a high level. Penalties were draconian.
Public executions were carried out for a wide range of crimes. The last
public hanging in England was in 1868. When the settler ships sailed

down the Thames at the end of 1819, they passed Graves Point, where the tarred corpses of executed pirates hung in chains on gibbets as a warning to all. Lesser crimes provoked severe punishment. Edward Driver's assailant in 1821 was transported to Australia for fourteen years for a murderous assault. In 1833 Edward's brother Charles was charged in Nottingham with stealing fifteen fowls. Their father, Edward Sr, was charged with receiving them. Edward Sr was discharged but Charles was found guilty and sentenced to transportation to Australia for seven years[490]. Life was cheap and property highly valued. The ostentatious, and often hypocritical, morality of the later Victorian age, with its emphasis on keeping up appearances, was yet to come.

And in parallel with all this was the pressure to reform. The French and American revolutions had swept away the assumptions of the past. Belief in the divine right of kings, in the necessity of government by a hereditary ruling class could no longer be held without challenge. Nevertheless, the property owning classes, in general, would confidently have asserted that the poor could not be trusted with the responsibility of government. Man was inherently sinful and corrupt and needed to be strictly controlled. Before 1832 fewer than 3% of the population of England and Wales had the financial qualifications to vote; an even smaller proportion of Scots, fewer than 2% were enfranchised[491]. George Washington and Thomas Jefferson found no contradiction between the American Declaration of Independence and the maintenance of their estates by large numbers of slaves. Religion preached equality in the after life but not in this one:

> The rich man in his castle,
> The poor man at his gate,
> God made them high and lowly,
> And ordered their estate[492].

Whatever denomination anyone chose, or whether they were religious at all, there was no questioning of the fundamentals. Genesis was a literal description of the creation. The threat of eternal hellfire troubled both good and wicked. God's hand was seen every day in natural occurences, in matters of life and death, and in determining one's station in life. Heathens needed to be converted for their own sake; if they perversely refused to accept the word of God it was through inherent wickedness.

Most men are not revolutionaries. Their aims are not to change the system, but to find success within the system in which they find themselves. Men like Robert Godlonton, Joseph Walker, George Wood, Benjamin Booth, and their fellows had taken huge risks in emigrating to the Cape to escape from their working class backgrounds. They had achieved positions in the Colony that were not open to them in England. Having achieved these positions they were intent on preserving them. On the whole the reformists did not come from their ranks. Charles Lennox Stretch came from a family of landed gentry. Thomas Pringle and John Fairbairn were from a more liberal Scottish background. The reformist missionaries were well educated men sent from Britain. It is notable that many of the more conservative missionary workers like Shaw, Ayliff, Shrewsbury, and Richard Walker, had themselves come from the ranks of the working class settlers.

These then were the circumstances that shaped the attitudes of the settlers. To understand their words and actions we must understand their environment.

Chapter 15. The Young Missionary

Did you want to be a missionary in your youth? I did. I think most kids do some
time or another, which is odd, seein' how unsatisfactory most of us turn out.
Dorothy Sayers, Clouds of Witness

The Young Dominie   [1836 – 1839]

On a winter's day, in the Royal Burgh of Arbroath on the east coast of
Scotland, a young Scottish dominie sat down at his desk, opened an expensive new octavo notebook that he thought suitable for his purpose,
dipped his pen into the inkwell and, in a tiny copperplate hand suitable
for making the maximum use of his investment, began to write:

Arbroath Dec 17 1836

No School. Went to Friockheim[493] – In walking along the road it struck
me what a beautiful analogy might be drawn between commencing a
journey in the early part of the day and a person beginning the Christian life.

John Forbes Cumming had begun a task which would occupy him on
a near daily basis for more than fifty years. His diary occupies fifteen
volumes which, together with notebooks, correspondence, various writings and miscellaneous items, form the collection of his papers in the
South African National Library, Cape Town[494].

Cumming was born on 14th July 1808, the son of William Cumming
of Inverness and his wife, Sarah Cairns. He was one of several children[495]. He was well educated with a knowledge of mathematics, medicine, law, and theology, and was thus a suitable appointment as a teacher
in a town such as Arbroath. In his late twenties he he had now acquired
the ambition to become a minister and ultimately a missionary in the
Presbyterian Church.

Over the next few years he built up his experience and reputation by
preaching frequently at many different churches in Scotland.

News from the eastern frontier of the Cape Colony often arrived in
Scotland. The 6th Frontier War had ended in 1835 but unrest continued
sporadically on the frontier. The desire to bring Christianity to the Xhosa
nation was very strong, particularly in the Methodist and Presbyterian
churches. John Cumming determined on trying to obtain an appointment
that would take him to the Cape. He put himself forward as a candidate
to become an agent of the Caffrarian Mission in Africa.

John Forbes Cumming in later life

On 16th July 1839 he was called for an interview in Edinburgh. It had been arranged by the secretary of the Edinburgh Missionary Society, Mr Gavin Struthers, who, together with the Directors of the Mission, formed an interviewing board. It was a new experience for Cumming. He was surprised to be asked what kind of income he expected and had little idea of what would be necessary. He managed to give an answer that would have pleased the Directors – he was sure that the income provided to other missionaries was adequate and he would be quite satisfied with the same. Another question related to the divisions in the church at the time. Would he have any objection to working with ministers of the established church[496]? He replied that he would have none. At the end of the interview a last ordeal remained. He was expected to show off his abilities that evening by preaching in Greyfriars church.

His efforts were successful. He was accepted by the Society and began to plan the daunting journey to the Cape.

Travail and Tribulation   [January – February 1840]

By the beginning of 1840 John Cumming's preparations were nearly completed. He spent the last days before the planned journey travelling to meet his friends and colleagues to say farewell and preaching at any opportunity. At last it was time for the departure. At 5 p.m. on 27th January 1840 he left Glasgow docks in one of the new sea-going steamers bound for Liverpool, which was reached the following day. From there he took another new form of transport, the railway train via Birmingham to London. There accommodation had been arranged at a respectable lodging house, Providence House in Falcon St, much used by clerics.

London was *en fête*. Preparations were in hand for the wedding of the young Queen Victoria to Prince Albert of Saxe-Coburg Gotha. Several weeks were to pass before passage could be arranged to the Cape. John Cumming made full use of the opportunity to see the sights of the city.

He visited Regents Park and the fashionable Madame Tussauds. He did not forget to take the opportunity to attend the sermons of various prominent preachers. Then on 10th February:

Went out with Mrs S— to see Queen and Prince Albert [on] their wedding day – Saw both.

Having stood among the excited crowds, next day Cumming visited the location of the wedding. Clearly the splendour impressed the austere Calvinist:

Went to Westminster Abbey. Oh this was the noblest of all the scenes I have witnessed in London.

It was now time to embark on the voyage. Passage had been arranged on a brig, the *Henry*. On 13th February, an all too appropriate date, he began his travels. He left Providence House with his luggage and was driven to the dock where he had expected to embark. The *Henry* had already sailed. His alarmed enquiry elicited the information that the ship had moved to Gravesend Docks further down the river. He spent the rest of the day arranging transportation of his luggage to Gravesend where he found the ship and had his luggage stowed on board. He was told that they were expected to sail four days later on the 17th so, rather than remaining uncomfortably on board, he returned to Providence House.

After his first experience he was taking no chances. He left Providence House again the day before the date of sailing, took a steamer down the river to Gravesend, and joined the ship.

The captain of the *Henry* was either extraordinarily unfortunate or remarkably incompetent. The ship finally sailed as planned on 17th February. It did not proceed far. Cumming notes laconically:

Weighed anchor at 4 o'clock afternoon. Ran foul of a Brig – much damage

The ship had to put into harbour for substantial repairs which took several days. At last, on the 20th she sailed once more, but had not made much progress when once again disaster struck. Cumming wrote:

Weighed anchor again. Schooner ran foul of us – drove us upon a large ship – did much damage.

This time the repairs did not take quite as long. The next day the Captain was taking no chances, employing a steamer to tug them downstream towards the Estuary until they had enough sea-room to set sail. They then made slow progress until they were preparing to round the North Foreland and pass through the Straits of Dover into the Channel. It was too much to expect that things would go smoothly. Cumming's diary on the 24th February has a short but eloquent entry:

> Wrecked on Margate Sands. Got passengers out to Whitstable - re-
> turned to vessel - stayed all night.

During occurrences of great importance to them, diarists have little
time to write and, at best, make brief notes of the events: when nothing
much is happening they indulge in pages of tedious introspection. Cumming is no exception. Very little detail is given of the wreck. It appears
that they must have beached under the influence of an unfavourable wind
without doing too much damage and in a position where it was possible
to get everyone off the ship without casualties. The ship was later
salvaged and several months later was to be seen moored in London.
Why did Cumming return to the ship after the passengers had gone to
Whitstable? Possibly it was to secure his ill-fated luggage. He tells us
nothing of this.

Finally on the 27th he records that he walked to Canterbury. This was
the end of the journey. He returned to Scotland with his tail between his
legs.

Interlude   [April – May 1840]

The whole tedious process began again. It would not have been surprising if John Cumming had decided that the Almighty was unconvinced of
the necessity of his mission. He himself had begun to have misgivings.
Nevertheless he went about the business of arranging another voyage. He
occupied the time with preaching, visiting friends and colleagues, and agonizing over his own perceived inadequacies. His doubts were not reduced by news received by the Society:

> April 10 1840. "Heard that Williams, missionary, is Murdered[497] – Pos-
> sibly this may be my fate too, but should not like it till I had done some
> great thing promoting the cause of Christ. I hope I [live] to an old age
> for the longest time in earth is too short to do good."

One of the colleagues with whom he had contact was a Dr King, the
father of two daughters, Margaret and Eliza who lived at Bridge of Allan
near Stirling. It is clear that during this period Margaret in particular had
aroused John's interest. Towards the end of April he was doing his last
round of farewells. On 25th he bade goodbye to Dr King in Glasgow and
set off by canal boat to Stirling. A series of diary entries at the end of
April gives an impression of the progress of an acquaintanceship that had
already proceeded quite far:

> 25. Went out [from Stirling] to Bridge of Allan. Saw Margaret and Eliza
> King - walked to Stirling again [about 5 miles or 8 km each way].

26. ... again walked to B[ridge] of A[llan] for tea with M— and E—. Expressed my mind to M— did not receive a satisfactory answer – slept at inn B[ridge] of A[llan].

27. Breakfasted with M and E – went to Stirling for my bag to stay in Knockhill Farm along with M and E

28. Residing at Knockhill Farm – Oh what a delightful society – Got donkey and went with M and E to Dunblane ...

How firmly was his mind fixed on Margaret? The entry continues:

... E has a noble interesting spirit. I do admire her – she is a lovely intelligent bold spirited creature. Happy the man who gets her.

Nevertheless his sights were still set on Margaret:

29. We are becoming more [intimately?] acquainted and appreciate each others company more.

30. Feel more and more delighted with their society.

Unfortunately the time had now come to continue his journey. It seemed that Margaret would not say yes or no:

M won't give me a satisfactory answer yet. But I shall hope against hope.

The two sisters accompanied John to the canal stop for Edinburgh. He boarded the boat with his hopes unfulfilled. He then describes a scene that was very much at odds with his expressed desires. It was to Eliza that he said, "Give me something to keep as a memorial to you." It was Eliza who asked him to lend her his new knife. It was Eliza who publicly "in the presence of all the people" cut off one of her ringlets and handed the hair and his knife to him over the rail. To his diary he soliloquized:

I shall keep it [the ringlet] most sacredly. M wants the energy of character that E posseses. She is a pure gentle intelligent creature however. Adieu ye fair ones for the present – the hope of return takes away the sting from adieu.

One wonders what Margaret thought of all this. She could scarcely be blamed if she felt his commitment was less than complete.

Misfortune and Misadventure   [1840]

The next day he embarked on a coaster at Leith bound for London. The voyage was far from comfortable. He found to his alarm that the experiences on board the Henry had affected him so that he lay in his bunk dreading another disaster. He could not bring himself to announce to the Captain or the passengers that he was a minister and to offer to conduct a service on Sunday. He wrestled with his conscience about this and felt doubts about his vocation. The voyage was not an easy one and there was a considerable amount of fog which delayed the ship.

He arrived in London in the early afternoon of the 5th May. He called in at Providence House and went on to see the shipping agent who had arranged his voyage on the *Meg Merrilees*. She had sailed the previous day.

"Thus the fog on the passage from Leith to London has caused me to miss my passage to the Cape.

After spending the night at Providence House the following day he went back to see the agent who had a suggestion. Why not proceed to Deal and hope to pick up the *Meg Merrilees* there? He took a coach to Canterbury and arrived the following day in the small hours of the morning. At the first opportunity he took another coach to Deal to find that the *Meg* had passed the previous afternoon. This trip was turning out to be almost as disastrous as his previous one. He lamented his misfortune in his diary, donning a metaphorical hair shirt and attributing his troubles to a punishment from God for his loss of faith while on the voyage from Leith.

The next day he returned to London, having been without sleep for 48 hours, and frantically suggested to the agent that he should try to catch the ship at Portsmouth. The agent dissuaded him from a course that might have led to his staring after the ship as it disappeared over the horizon at Lands End. Instead he was persuaded to seek passage on another suitable vessel. This led to his spending another month in London.

This time the stay was much less enjoyable than previously. He was laid low by serious influenza and confined to bed for a considerable time. His chief entertainment seems to have been attending various churches and religious meetings around London and fiercely criticising the intellect, erudition, articulation, and style of the preachers.

By late May he had arranged alternative transport. On the 27th he visited the ship in which he was to make his voyage.

Called down at the London Docks and saw the captain of the "Mary Nixon" who told me he did not think he would sail till about the 10th or 15th of next month.

After his experiences on Henry one might have expected his judgement of the captain to be made on the basis of professional competence rather than piety:

He is a smart intelligent man – I do not think a religious one however. I hope I shall have prudence and firmness to conduct myself properly while sailing with him.

John had long been waiting for a letter from Bridge of Allan and it failed to arrive. On the same day as he was arranging matters with the captain he noted:

Wrote a letter to Eliza King God bless her.

but nothing was sent to Margaret and nothing came from her.

A day or two later he notes that he is still waiting for a letter from Dr King but has little hope that it will arrive. Then in the diary two long closely written paragraphs have been deleted. They are not just scored out but each letter is separately obliterated with heavy vertical strokes of black ink so that the passage is impossible to read. This is followed by:

Let Christian love burn purely between them and myself .... I know it [the relationship with Margaret and Eliza] has taken up my attention most absorbingly – perhaps to the hurt of His cause and therefore He has done this.

With these Calvinistic thoughts of a vengeful God, John Cumming made a break with his past life and set off on his journey to Africa to start a new one. On the 25th June the *Mary Nixon* was towed down the river by a steamer. It was bitterly cold for a summer day:

"This is a strange beginning to our voyage says me. Why the weather is as cold as a December evening."

The vessel made her way into the Channel and set off on the long voyage to the Cape.

Cape Town   [September – December 1840]

Exactly three months later, on 24th September 1840, John Cumming recorded that he spied Table Mountain and made a tiny marginal sketch of it in his diary. The next day the ship docked in Table Bay[498].

Cape Town by now was a well populated town, the centre of government and an important trading port. John Cumming's first impressions were of an attractive place but he was astonished at the number of people idling on the streets. This did not accord with his idea of fit behaviour and he commented on it, comparing it unfavourably with industrious Calvinist Scotland. Even today Cape Town has a reputation of being very laid back.

He quickly called on Dr John Philip, who was now no longer Superintendant of the London Missionary Society's stations in the Cape, but an unofficial advisor to the British government on the interests of the indigenous people. The unpopularity of Philip's efforts on behalf of the coloured and African people had not changed in the years since 1835. Philip welcomed Cumming to the Cape and was at pains to introduce him to the local society. There was some time to wait before he took passage to Algoa Bay so it was expected that he would make himself known and also make himself useful by preaching and assisting with pastoral duties.

In spite of these distractions his mind was troubled. No doubt he was homesick. He could not forget the immediate past. Now that his new life was close upon him he began to have second thoughts:

> [Oct 5th 1840:] Have written letter to [heavy erasure] in which I tell plainly that I do think I shall yet return to Scotland and work in the vineyard there. Have had much struggling to send this .... Have prayed much for direction sending it. Would willingly not do so but I feel as confident as I live that to Scotland I shall return. How I know not. The Lord will bring it to pass in his own time.

It seems unlikely that he was referring to an official letter – why erase the name of the addressee? Surely he would discuss doubts about his vocation with his local superior in the form of Dr Philip. It seems more likely that the letter was personal and very probably directed to Margaret King, or possibly even to Eliza. In any event his confidence in a return to Scotland was misplaced. In his long life he was only to return once on furlough, and his future was in the Cape Colony.

The arrival of a personable and presentable young man in the small Cape Town society was always welcome and John was rapidly absorbed into local activities, dining out, meeting a wide variety of people, and also participating in the religious life of the community, preaching and meeting the local congregations. Although his mind was not on the young ladies of Cape Town his arrival did not go unnoticed by them. He noted that

> I have always suspected that Miss— has entertained the idea that I was wishing her to go with me to Caffraria. I have as much as possible endeavoured to destroy this impression.

In spite of this suspicion he was unwise enough to accept an invitation to join a walking party that was planning a hike round the kloof at Lion's Head[499]. The party consisted of himself, the unidentified Miss— referred to above, a pair of young ladies, a pair of young gentlemen, and two servants carrying provisions for the day. They set off at 9 a.m. on October 12th – just three weeks after John's arrival in Cape Town. He wrote

> I was like a sheep led to the slaughter. I went unresistingly thinking it was to pass off as a mere party of pleasure ...

As time went on the objective of the expedition became apparent:

> They all appear to have [arranged the expedition] with the view of giving me the opportunity of putting the question to Miss— thinking I sup-

pose that I was too bashful to do anything else. The unfortunate girl seems to have inflamed their minds with this idea and the plan was conceived accordingly.

He was acutely embarrassed but at the same time flattered:

... there appears to be something in my manner that induces many to suppose I love them. No doubt I have to gain the good opinion of any lady – but my keen sensibility apparently awakens other feelings in their minds and makes them imagine an object I have not in view.

In spite of his embarrassment he could see the absurdity of the situation:

I grieve exceedingly at the result of this day's scene altho' it certainly is a distressing ridiculous one.

He describes the continuation of the walk. They all began to feel tired and he began to get the feeling that they were willing him to take Miss— aside and propose to her. As he describes the scene his embarrassment grows and his handwriting gets smaller and smaller as if he is trying to shrink into a small hole. Eventually he took the bull by the horns and decided to make it clear to her that he was not interested. His technique was to expand at length on his future plans and the dangers of a missionary's life "without at the same time acknowledging that [he] was aware of her intention or theirs." Miss— was disappointed:

She perceived my drift but was loathe to receive it. ... It was confusion thrice confounded. [The members of the party] will doubtless blacken me for what they will term my duplicity unless the ridiculous situation in which they have placed themselves seals their lips.

Covered with mutual embarrassment the group made its way back into town. Fortunately for John's equanimity he was due to leave Cape Town just a week later. His embarrassment was further eased when he paid a visit to the school in the "Scotch Church" and was approached by his companions on the walk. He gained the impression from them that they were sorry for the misunderstanding and that Miss — had misled them.

Journey to Glenthorn   [October – November 1840]

John Cumming's first assignment was to the church on John Pringle's farm, Glenthorn. Pringle, a deeply religious man had built it to fulfil what he saw as an urgent need both of his family and of the community. It was just complete and Cumming was to be its first resident minister, filling the position until the designated incumbent arrived from Scotland, when Cumming would be able to fulfil his ambition to take his ministry to the Xhosa.

He embarked in Cape Town on a 100 ton ship called the *Cench*[500] with "6 passengers in cabin and about 35 in steerage." A fellow passenger was the newly ordained and married Mr Solomon who was to take up a position at the mission station at Griquatown. His wife was a niece of Dr Philip who came aboard to see them off. They sailed at 3 p.m. on the 27th October and had an easy passage, arriving in Algoa Bay on the afternoon of November 1st.

John Pringle had come down to Algoa Bay to meet his new minister but was conducting business in Uitenhage on Cumming's day of arrival. Summoned by a message sent by the shipping agent, he arrived the next day, anxious to set off on the journey home as soon as possible. True to form, Cumming's luggage was not yet out of the hold, and there appeared little prospect of its emerging for several days. In any event Pringle had only brought with him one spare horse for Cumming and one for light baggage only. They left instructions for Mr Kemp, the shipping agent, to dispatch it later by wagon.

They were faced with a journey of about 250 km. Cumming eyed the horses with some trepidation:

> I felt rather uncertain as to the success of my horsemanship on account of my never having been on a horse's back with the exception of twice all my previous life ...

The Cape boerperd (farmer's horse) is descended from a number of breeds, some having been brought to the country at the time of van Riebeeck. It is small, rugged, and undistinguished in appearance, but has great endurance and is relatively immune to African horse sickness. Many are five-gaited[501], the fifth gait being the trippel or rack. The forelegs are thrown out in a kind of equine goose-step while the hindquarters shimmy from side to side. As late as the middle of the twentieth century, in the towns of the Transkei, one of the more stirring regular sights was the progress of a Xhosa man come to town on business, in full red-blanket regalia, astride a trippeling horse. From the side the rider appears to glide smoothly forward as though seated in a limousine. Nevertheless, as an alternative to the trot, the trippel is not a comfortable ride. In the trot the horse's back moves up and down and the rider must either either rattle in the saddle or learn to post – move up and down in the stirrups in synchronisation with the horse's gait. In the trippel there is little or no vertical movement but the rapid side-to-side movement of the saddle is disconcerting. The trot or the trippel are the only gaits, other than a walk, that the horse can maintain for significant distances. A novice, faced with a long ride, is more or less condemned to do most of it at a walk.

In terms of the skill required, Cumming surprised himself:

> [I] was agreeably disappointed to find that I could manage so well.

The party set off in the late afternoon of the 5th November[502] to cover the short distance to their first stop, the mission station Bethelsdorp. Cumming called on an Edinburgh teacher there and noted with innocent cupidity that he had a salary of £230 per annum. Next day they reached Graham's Town where Cumming stayed with the Rev. Mr Locke. They remained there several days, Pringle with business to transact and Cumming hopefully waiting for his luggage which failed to arrive. Cumming was entertained by members of the local clergy such as William Shaw. By 13th it was time to proceed, still with no news of the luggage. Accompanied by two missionaries, Henry Calderwood and Richard Birt, for part of the way, they set off after dinner, taken as was the custom of the time in the middle of the day. Calderwood and Birt had arrived in the country the previous year, sponsored by the London Missionary Society.

In the evening Cumming's lack of equestrian skill became apparent. The party upped the pace and disappeared into the darkness, leaving him to find his way as best he could in the darkness of the African night. He was equal to the task, slackening the reins and allowing the horse to make its own pace in order to rejoin its companions. They rode until midnight, stayed at a farm and went on to the next day:

> In riding up by the Mankazana River, the beauty of the scenery was overwhelming and on nearing the valley in which the homestead of Glenthorn was situated the view was simply grand. We stood still to gaze upon it. At a few miles distant rose a hill with the appearance of a lion couchant on its top, as if on a natural pedestal; and with uplifted head it seemed to look down on the valley below, with the hills on each side covered with the most beautiful mimosa trees, and in front of the hill, in the midst of the vale, there stood a Building, rising above the verdure. Pringle with heaving voice exclaimed "O bonny Glenthorn! There is the Church!"[503]

The household had been waiting anxiously for their arrival. The Pringles had six children. Catherine, Isabella, and Mary Ann were teenagers, Catherine at 17 just entering adulthood. The first son, Robert Pears, was 11. Then there were two *laat-lammetjies* (late lambs), Ellen Stretch (4), and James Lennox Stretch (2):

> The children had been out on the hill looking for our approach for two days.

As always, John Cumming enjoyed the attention of the young women:

> Alas! For the young minister, he was the object of much sympathy and more especially by the gentler sex, who all protested at the cruelty exercised at causing him to ride such a journey in such a short time. This was balm to his battered body, as well as grateful to his gladsome heart.[504]

John Cumming remained at Glenthorn for several months. There was no manse so he was accommodated in the Pringle home and came to know the family well. They were very pleased with the new young minister, who became a family friend. He was introduced to his duties by the Rev. Mr William Chalmers of the Glasgow Missionary Society who was in charge of the Tyumie Mission and was a regular visitor to Glenthorn. Chalmers was a plump, jovial man, later nicknamed "the Fat Parson" by Harry Smith, and he, too, became a good friend to Cumming. Another mentor who became a friend and colleague was Robert Niven of Iqibira.

Journey to Tambookieland   [1841]

By March of 1841 John Cumming had settled in and it was time to begin the next stage of his career. A new team of Presbyterian clergy was due in Algoa Bay and he undertook to travel there to meet them. By now his horsemanship was up to the task. Apart from Hepburn and Withers, who were respectively to take on the church and school at Glenthorn, there was also a so-called Missionary-Catechist and Artisan, Mr Thomas Campbell and his wife[505]. John Cumming was ear-marked to spend some time at Iqibira with Niven before setting up a Mission Station of his own.

In September he began serious preparation for his Mission. He and Niven set off, each with a pair of horses. They had with them Jonas[506], a young Mfengu man, as interpreter and assistant. On setting out they seemed to have little idea of where they wanted to go. Their first need was advice and they journeyed to Philipton in the Kat River settlement to consult with James Read Sr, who was still ensconced at Philipton as missionary, while his eldest son James Jr ran the school. His second son Joseph ran two nearby mission stations, one – then known as "Bushman's School" – to the San people headed by a headman Madoor[507], and one at a small village called Qumbu about thirty kilometres south west of what is now Queenstown[508].

After discussions with Read "about the state of Tembuland, as he had Mission schools in that part of the country", they continued to the Wesleyan mission at Mvane, run by Joseph Warner. Warner was well-placed to advise on a location. His mission was in the territory of Mthirara, the Thembu king, who had succeeded his father Ngubencuka Vusani[509]. Warner advised that there was no mission in the amaGcina territory where Tyopo reigned. Warner agreed to accompany them on a visit to Tyopo to ask his permission to set up a mission.

The amaGcina were now established on either side of the White Kei River. Tyopo, the "amiable mild young man" that John Thackwray had visited twenty four years earlier, was now secure in his status as part of the Thembu kingdom, and was just as amiable. The three missionaries had no difficulties in getting his permission to set up a new mission station wherever they pleased in his territory.

Pleased with the success of their application, they began the journey home. Cumming and Niven left Warner at Mvane and continued towards Iqibira for another two days. The first night they spent in the open. The next they were accommodated at the mission station recently established by Jacob Döhne of the Berlin Society. At the end of the following day things began to go wrong. Night fell and in a steady drizzle they found themselves in heavy bush without shelter. In the distance a dog barked, giving some hope of shelter for the night. They led their horses down a steep slope to a stream. Cumming jumped it easily; one of his horses followed him, but the other blundered into the water and found itself in deep mud. Niven and Jonas found a better crossing place, and the three tried to extricate the horse from its predicament. All efforts failed. They could still hear the dog barking and Jonas was sent for help. He soon returned in great alarm[510]:

> "The [Xhosa]s are coming to kill us" he said "I came to a hut and asked the people to give me a brand to kindle a fire to see and get the horse out of the mud. A [Xhosa] said who are these Abelungu [sic][511], where are these men that are come?" He replied "They are Abafundisi" (the teachers) "The teachers" exclaimed the [Xhosa] in a terrified tone, "these are the people going about killing the people with the small pox" and stretching out his hand to lay hold of his assegai, I [Jonas – the punctuation and syntax is muddled] rushed out of the hut.

The missionaries were alarmed to say the least. They had nowhere to go so they hunkered down for the night. They managed to make a fire – perhaps not the best strategy if they were hoping to avoid an attack – and sat beside it, singing the twenty-third psalm for the curious comfort of realising "what it was to be in the valley of the Shadow of Death." Meanwhile the horse – his name was Hector – sank deeper in the mud.

No attack came. In the morning they found Hector still alive but there was no hope of releasing him. Guiltily and reluctantly they abandoned him. As they set off they saw some of the men who had threatened them. Niven reproved them for their behaviour and threatened to report them to Sandile, the Ngqika king[512]. In the light of day fear and distrust evaporated and the missionaries promised that, if the men would extricate Hector, they would send a man to fetch the horse with a blanket as a reward. They continued to the Pirie mission where they were welcomed by John Ross, the missionary. He was upset by the condition of their clothes. John Cumming accepted the loan of a jacket but drew the line at buckskin trousers. After a brief rest they continued to Iqibira, and were home by nightfall.

An elder, Ungunana[513], was sent with the promised blanket, but he found Hector dead on the bank of the stream.

Chapter 16. The Mission to the AmaGcina

I have been a stranger in a strange land.

Exodus, 2:22

Getting Started [1842]

The decision to set up a mission to Tyopo's people was not implemented rapidly. For a year John Cumming continued his work as assistant to Niven at Iqibira. The mission served the amaMbala, the Xhosa clan under Nqeno. Cumming was learning his trade, and making his first attempts to learn the Xhosa language.

His time at Iqibira was punctuated with the opportunity of frequent visits to Glenthorn. Hepburn, his successor there, had not been a success. He had provoked a schism in the congregation and taken half of it elsewhere. He was afterwards to join the Wesleyan Church. Cumming seems to have been fairly unperturbed by this, unlike the Glasgow Missionary Society, from whom several agitated letters were received. The Glenthorn Church was served for several years by visits from neighbouring ministers, giving John Cumming plenty of opportunity for maintaining his friendship with the Pringles and their daughter Catherine.

After a year of preparation the time for establishing Cumming's own mission came[514]. The organization and cost required was extensive. Crucial to the establishment was the acquisition of a wagon and oxen. Funds had to be obtained from the Missionary Society. The cost of the wagon was enormous – £200, twice the annual salary of the young missionary. Supplies of staple foods sufficient for long periods had to be found.

Shortly before the time of departure a delegation arrived at Iqibira. It consisted of Nqeno, Chief of the amaMbalu who were served by the mission, together with his sons Stokwe and Sonto. Nqeno was the son of Langa, the brother of Gcaleka and Rharhabe. He, too, had previously agreed that Cumming could have a place for a mission in his territory, and he was now demanding to know why the mission was to go to Tyopo. The establishment of missions was fraught with diplomatic problems that the missionaries were not always equipped to handle. It is surprising that, if there had been previous discussions with him, he had not been kept informed. Niven explained to him that the Directors of the mission in Scotland had decided that, since there was already a mission in his territory, Cumming's station should go to a place where there was not one. Nqeno and his sons went away, having heard this explanation, but

unsatisfied. This competition between various clans to get a teacher was
to lead to further difficulty.

In September 1842 John Cumming and his Xhosa interpreter, chosen
from the Mbalu congregation at Iqibira, set off for Tyopo's country in the
new wagon. On the way they paid their respects to Joseph Warner at
Mvane before continuing to the White Kei River where they camped for
the night. Next day they continued to Tyopo's Great Place.

Tyopo received them formally, dressed in a leopard-skin kaross, and
surrounded by his counsellors. John Cumming made his best effort in a
formal address to Tyopo, translated by his interpreter. He told him of the
preparations and delays and that he was now coming to take up his abode
in accordance with the kind invitation. He was expecting a gracious welcome, but

> ... what was my astonishment when the interpreter turned round to me
> and says, "The Chief he has heard my words but does not wish me to
> come among his people." Confounded at this unexpected turn of af-
> fairs, I told him that while my heart was deeply grieved to hear the
> words coming from the lips of the Chief I would not press myself upon
> him, but would immediately remove my waggon from his land, and go
> away.

This new obstacle in the path towards establishing his own mission left
Cumming disconsolate. He packed up his wagon and made his way to
Joseph Read's nearby mission, which was about twelve kilometres away,
poured out his troubles, and spent the night there.

Next day he rode across to Mvane to consult Joseph Warner, who had
already been so helpful with advice. Warner was indignant at his treatment and told him, "I will go with you to Tyopo and I shall give him my
mind on the matter."

The next morning they set out to the Great Place and were received
by Tyopo. Warner was a fluent Xhosa linguist and his indignation led
him to speak forcefully:

> ... he said, "Well Tyopo, what is this I hear respecting you? You invited
> this young man to become your teacher who with great trouble and
> much expense has come a long journey, and now that he has come you
> tell him plainly that you don't want him." In this strain Mr Warner went
> on ...

Tyopo was astonished. He:

> ... declared that the charge was without foundation. He had never said
> that he did not want him on the contrary he had welcomed him gladly
> in the presence of these his Pakati and was quite confounded when he
> said that he would go and remove his waggon from his ground.

Now the situation became apparent. The interpreter had been pursuing his own agenda. Knowing Nqeno's wishes, and being a loyal member of the amaMbalu, he had been putting his own spin on the translation.

Ruffled feathers were smoothed. Apologies and regrets were expressed. The interpreter was sent off in disgrace and

> As to Tyopo, when Mr Warner had expressed our regret at what had taken place, he brightened up, and expressed his gratification, declaring that his whole country was before me, and that I might select whatever place I pleased to erect my house in the midst of his people.

Kirkwood   [1842 – 1843]

At last John Cumming had achieved his ambition. He found a site on the banks of the White Kei (Xonxa) River not far from Tyopo's Great Place and outspanned his wagon. Having dismissed the unreliable interpreter, he allowed the driver and voorloper of the wagon to return to Iqibira. He was left with two horses and a span of oxen, alone in the wilderness.

His first action was to engage a man as servant and interpreter. His own Xhosa, as was evident from the debacle of his arrival, was still rudimentary and an interpreter was essential. Together they constructed a hut in the pattern of the time – a circle of flexible branches planted vertically, drawn together in the middle, and thatched with reeds. The floor was finished with the ubiquitous cow manure screed. This was his own mission and he named the place Kirkwood, after his first mentor in Glasgow, a man to whom he thought Tyopo bore an astonishing likeness.

In his reminiscences Cumming lists his nearest missionary neighbours who fell under the auspices of either the Glasgow, or the London Missionary Society. Those under the Glasgow Society were Chalmers at Tyumie who served Sandile the Ngqika king, Govan, Bennie, and Weir at Lovedale, Laing at Burnshill, and Ross at Pirie, all serving various Ngqika people under Sandile. In addition Niven was at Iqibira serving the amaMbalu under Nqeno. Those under the London Society were Calderwood at Blinkwater serving Maqoma, Birt near Fort Beaufort serving Bhothomane's imiDange, Kayser at Knapp's Hope serving another group of Sandile's amaNgqika, and Brownlee on the Buffalo (Qonce) River, supporting the Christian chief Dyani Tshatshu of the amaNtinde.

These were not his only missionary neighbours. Warner's Wesleyan station, Lesseyton, was nearby and, of course, there was the controversial Read family.

An important objective was to improve his Xhosa. There were almost no printed aids. It was a spoken language with only a small beginning towards developing its orthography. Boyce's Xhosa Grammar had been published by the Wesleyans[515] but, if it was available to Cumming, he felt he needed to amplify his vocabulary. One of the items in his papers is a notebook, set up as a dictionary. Entries are set out alphabetically, with extensive gaps for new entries. This was started for him by Niven. The work does not progress very far; as his skill increased there was less and less need for its assistance. With total immersion his language skills grew and later he became a fluent Xhosa linguist.

Slowly he began to make the acquaintance of his neighbours, and began the business of building a relationship of trust with them. The two most important objectives were the setting up of regular church services and establishing elementary school classes. This could only be done by going out and meeting the people, trying to raise their interest in what he had to offer. Unlike the Khoikhoi who – with their culture essentially destroyed by nearly two hundred years contact with Europeans – were susceptible to the attractions of evangelical Christianity, all the Xhosa were much more secure in their culture.

Why then did leaders such as Tyopo and Nqeno compete to have missionaries in their territories? There were some advantages but a belief in Christianity was seldom a motive, except in the case of one or two converts such as Dyani Tshatshu of the amaNtinde. An important motive was the belief that supporting the establishment of a mission station provided some guarantee of support from the Colonial authorities when under threat as a result of the frequent outbreaks of unrest between different peoples. The missionaries were a point of contact with the Colonial Government, and able to act as intermediaries. The establishment of a school was also sometimes regarded as an advantage, but could also give rise to the suspicion that the people were being alienated from their traditions.

On the whole Cumming was well received by the amaGcina. There was mutual respect but he was prepared to stand up for what he believed was right. On one occasion he had a potentially dangerous encounter. One day he was alone in his cottage when it was approached by a group that appeared threatening

> ... Anta, Gaika's great warlike son, was on a visit to Tyopo. He called on me with a number of his followers. I was alone in my humble cottage. Entering, and after mutual salutations, he looked around, and then in a kind of imperious tone he said "Give me tobacco"

It might have been wise to accede to this request but Cumming was provoked by the demand and refused.

With flashing eyes, and pressing his assegai in his uplifted hand within a yard of my breast, he with a thundering voice repeated the same demand. I quietly looked at him and said "No! I will not." He loosened his hand, and turning went out to the outside of the door. On his part I now saw that all this action was dramatic, but it was very trying to me ; seeing that I was but a stripling he no doubt thought to frighten me into compliance ...

Having made his point Cumming then presented Anta with a handful of tobacco which he accepted with satisfaction.

Cumming's solitary state was not regarded as ideal by the authorities of the Missionary Society. The ideal situation was for a missionary to marry and have a wife as a companion. Dr Philip visited the area during this period, mainly to inspect the two London Mission stations in the charge of James Read. Cumming rode to meet him where he was camped near the Qumbu station:

Speaking concerning my own solitary situation in the midst of the people, so far away from all Christian society, where I was exposed to so many temptations before which many missionaries in like circumstances had fallen he [Philip] said that if he had been asked his advice, he certainly would not have encouraged me to come here. But my only safety was to keep close with God, He alone would be my Refuge and my Protector. I acknowledged his [Philip's] kindness in suitable terms, I had preached in his pulpit while in Cape Town, and now we parted never to see each other in the flesh.

Cumming's solitude was soon to be relieved. Thomas Campbell, the artisan missionary who had arrived in the country in the party with Hepburn, had been assigned to Iqibira. His arrival had been marked by tragedy. His young wife, shortly after she had given birth to their first child, became ill with one of the many infections that were simply labelled as "a fever", and had died, leaving Campbell with an infant daughter. As soon as the baby was old enough she was sent back to her grandparents in Scotland, and Campbell was assigned to assist Cumming at Kirkwood. Together they were able to build a more substantial wattle and daub house.

The day to day life of the two missionaries was still arduous. Cumming relates the story of an journey that illustrates the kind of self reliance that they needed. He and Campbell had visited the school operated by Joseph Read for the people of the San chief Madoor. They were riding back from the station which was some 20 km from Kirkwood. Cumming was cantering some 50 m behind Campbell when an armed warrior appeared suddenly from the bush on his right, and immediately attcked him with an assegai. Cumming jerked the reins, the horse reared, and the thrust just missed.

> Seeing that he had missed his mark, he lifted up his eyes, and seeing
> my white face under my broad brimmer he exclaimed "Ngumlungu, un-
> gubani wena?" "It is a white man, who art thou" "I am Tyopo's teacher"
> said I. In a moment he turned, and with a sping into the bush was out
> of sight.

Cumming realised that he was one of Tyopo's people who had mistaken him for a Gcaleka cattle raider and was horrified that he had almost killed someone under the protection of his chief.

On another occasion the two had been out on an expedition hoping to
buy meat from some trekboers in the area. During the night their horses
were cut loose and disappeared. They suspected their hosts and after
complaints two horses were "found" and they left with their needs unsatisfied. The third horse and the promised sheep never appeared. On the
way home they were caught in a torrential storm in an exposed ravine on
the White Kei River. The water was rising dangerously and they were
threathened with drowning so they pushed on until they came to a place
where a flooded tributary must be crossed. Cumming thought it was too
dangerous but Campbell decided to make the attempt. He borrowed
Cumming's sjambok gave the horse a sharp cut and was immediately
swept away by the flood. Cumming realised that, if he was swept as far as
the main river there would be no hope. He leapt off his horse and ran to a
promontory where he was able to make a grab at Campbell's hair and get
him out. The horse also managed to scramble out. Campbell's arm appeared to be broken but on examination he decided the shoulder was dis-
located. With Cumming supporting Campbell, they found some boulders
that allowed them to cross the stream and made their way painfully to
where there was a small settlement. The headman made them as comfortable as he could, given that the water was streaming through the hut that
was to accommodate them. Cumming was now faced with the responsibility of treating the injury. The nearest doctor was about 80km away.

> I knew that the longer the dislocation was unattended to the more diffi-
> cult it would be to restore it to its place. In these circumstances I saw
> that much depended on myself.

An attempt to relocate the arm in its socket with the help of two of his
Thembu hosts, Cumming holding the patient while the two men heaved
on his arm, failed. Cumming did what any missionary would do. He
prayed:

> Suddenly my thoughts were wafted to a scene which I had seen in Edin-
> burgh many years ago. There lay a person with a dislocated arm. The
> doctor enters. He examines and then removing his shoe from his foot
> he places [his foot] under the armpit, and gently pressing it gave at the
> same time a smart pull at the wrist, and in a moment the arm was in its

place. Mentally I said I will do the same and immediately a voice came from Campbell "O it is in."

Next day they thanked the headman and promised a gift if he would send to the mission for it. They made their way to Read's other school which was nearby and rested for several hours.

In the afternoon we reached home after a tedious walk of some 8 miles wearied and disappointed at our fruitless journey in search of meat to fill our empty cupboard.

Such experiences together with the daily labour of maintaining the mission station weighed hard on the missionaries. The lack of irrigation at Kirkwood was a great disadvantage. In addition Campbell was anxious to have a station of his own. They had blanket permission from Tyopo to settle where they pleased and identified a site on the Bonkolo stream. It had the advantage of a plentiful water supply; today it is the site of the large Bonkolo reservoir that serves Queenstown. The problem was that, while Kirkwood was located near the centre of the Gcina territory, Bonkolo was at its edge. They called in advice. John Pringle came from Glenthorn and Robert Niven from Iqibira. Cumming had little experience as a host. He depended on a mission cook who was navigating without a map. After an attempt to bite on rock-hard lumps of unleavened "bread" Niven asked for mealie-meal and made porridge on the fire himself. The pudding at dinner consisted of a doughy casing with a handful of un-cooked spices and condiments in the middle.

In spite of their culinary adventures, in giving advice Pringle was principally concerned with the nourishment of the land and Niven with the nourishment of souls. Pringle saw no prospects of irrigation at Kirkwood; Niven said of his own choice of Iqibira "When I chose the site of the station, it was to seek people and not to seek water." The final decision was to build another rough dwelling at Bonkolo and serve both sites. For a while they took turns to occupy each changing places from time to time.

A Clash of Cultures [about 1843]

All missionaries found great difficulty in coming to terms with the culture and customs of the Xhosa. Many were appalled by polygamy, the lobola bride-price system, the casual attitude to nudity. Their minds were seldom open to a morality different from their own.

John Cumming was more tolerant than most but he was profoundly shocked when, one day, a young woman arrived at the mission, distraught and begging protection. She told him that Tyopo had sent men to summon various young women to his Great Place to "to carry out one of their customs – 'upondlo'," as Cumming coyly described it[516]. *Upundlo* was a variety of *droit de seigneur* exercised by a chief. Cumming was so incensed that, telling her to remain behind at the mission and assuring her that she would be safe there as Tyopo had declared that the mission was under his protection, he set off for the Great Place. The journey from the mission was quite arduous and he reached his destination in the late afternoon. There he found Tyopo and his councillors presiding over a large gathering of his people. Tyopo was in full regalia with leopard skin kaross and his councillors in "holiday dress." The missionary's state of mind was such that he spoke without discretion or diplomacy:

> Although by no means an expert in speaking the language but roused by the peculiar circumstances in which I was engaged, I had no fear. After saluting the Chief, I told him the object of my visit, and expatiating on the wickedness of the custom in which they were engaged, I poured to my own astonishment the threatenings of God's law against such conduct.

This effrontery might have been expected to have led to trouble but, while Cumming was talking, nature took a hand. Late afternoon thunderstorms are a common feature of summer in the Eastern Cape. The clouds build up rapidly, the frequency and intensity of the lightning and thunder is frightening, and the violence of wind and rain is dramatic.

> ... a fearful clap of thunder burst forth echoing and re-echoing amongst the rocks around. The lightning flashes were awful, and every one seemed struck with terror. Tyopo cowering and covering his head with his tiger kaross put forth his hand and said "That is enough, I have heard what you have said, go home, and I will send and recall the men now waiting at your place."

Cumming, awed at the success of his advocacy, shook hands with Tyopo and set off home through a developing flood. He had to lead his horse through the night, often ankle deep in water, and reached Kirkwood at about midnight. Next morning he made sure that the waiting men had indeed been withdrawn and told the young woman that she was safe to go home.

It is easy to regard these events as a cynical exploitation of a natural phenomenon for Cumming's own ends. One must, however, understand things in context. Cumming's fundamentalist beliefs were as strong a superstition as Tyopo's dread of the storm:

> I myself felt awed and like Moses of Old feared and trembled at this manifestation of Power.
>
> ...
>
> His daughter was never molested again, and attended hopefully on the services. A kind of sacredness seemed to be thrown round her, as she was the first person who had given such a blow to that vile custom of

the tribe. It was no longer in the estimation of the people, a law like that of the Medes and Persians which changed not.

The Fate of a Rain-maker   [about 1843]

When John Thackwray had travelled through Thembuland seventeen years earlier he had been very impressed with Tyopo's rain-maker. Rain-makers were a feature of Xhosa life. Often Mfengu or Khoi refugees, they claimed to be able to bring rain to a parched land and their supposed skills brought them great respect. Tyopo's rain-maker, when Thackwray met him, was successful, prosperous, and influential.

One Sunday, when Cumming and Campbell were both still at Kirkwood, they were surprised by a remarkable visitor. He announced to them that he was Tyopo's rain doctor and that he had come to pay his respects to the teachers. Was this the same rain-maker that had received Thackwray? Each was described as Tyopo's rain-maker and it seems plausible that they were one and the same but there is no way of being certain[517].

For Cumming and Campbell a visit by a notable practitioner of pagan rituals was an opportunity not to be missed, and they engaged in a long dialogue on the nature of Christian religion, emphasizing that only God could make rain. Surprisingly, their visitor appeared to be convinced and they were delighted when he finally agreed that indeed his powers were spurious and only God could make rain.

Some time after this, when Cumming had moved to Iqibira, and Campbell was in charge of the mission to the amaGcina, Cumming received a letter from him telling the story of the fate of the rain-maker.

There had been a long and crippling drought and Tyopo had sent messengers to the rain-maker asking that he should take steps to bring the drought to an end. The reply he received showed that the exhortations of the missionaries had deeply affected the rain-maker. Whether he had simply lost faith in his own powers or had indeed been convinced of the power of a Christian God is impossible to say, but, for whatever reason he is reported as having sent the reply that "Only God can make rain." Tyopo was infuriated and summoned the man to appear before him.

> In great indignation the Chief called him before him and said "The country is burned up, and you say the God only can give rain, where then did you get the cattle that you have? Was it not from your promising rain? If you cannot give rain now then you must be a deceiver, you have been telling big lies. See! I will give you three days to make rain, and if you do not give it in that time you shall die." "It is no use my try-

ing," he said, "God only can give rain" and he persisted in saying this in spite of all the Chief promised to give.[518]

Even in the face of this threat the man persisted in his refusal to exercise his rainmaking ability and was sentenced to be beaten to death:

> ... they sprang and dragged him away and fell upon him with their ker-
> ries in a most savage manner. The wretched man cried in his agony "O
> put a reim [sic] about my neck and cast me into the river." This they did
> and he perished amidst the infuriated shouts of the people he had de-
> ceived so long.[519]

Finally Cumming provides an epitaph

> He was a Fingo and one of the wealthiest in the tribe. How striking was
> his testimony to the power of God.

The tragedy is a morality tale rather than an accurate description of events. Cumming would not simply have invented the story and presented it as truth, so we can assume as basic facts that (i) Tyopo's rain-maker existed and engaged in debate with the missionaries about his craft, (ii) there was a severe drought (iii) when called on to make rain, he failed to do so, and (iv) he was put to death as a result. The natural course for most nineteenth century minds was to attribute natural or unusual or momentous events to God. Whether the rain-maker had indeed been convinced by the missionaries is doubtful. More likely, having failed in his rainmaking activity, and threatened with the consequences he attempted to excuse his failure by recalling his conversation with the missionaries. If so, the explanation failed to impress Tyopo. Cumming's account is fitted into his own paradigm and turns the story into a parable, illustrating the power of the Christian God. Nowhere does he seem to have any sense that he might bear some responsibility for the rain-maker's death.

Love and Marriage   [1843]

The lonely days at Kirkwood were relieved by memories of, and occasional visits to, Glenthorn. John's memories of what he had left behind in Scotland became less intense as time went on and his diary of the time is no longer focused on the past but is devoted to the day to day concerns of his mission. By the middle of 1843 he was approaching his thirty-fifth birthday. He no longer dreamt so much of returning to Scotland. His sense of mission was far more secure and he began to contemplate a permanent future.

When he had first arrived at Glenthorn, John Pringle's eldest daughter Catherine had been just seventeen years old. Now she was all but twenty. Proximity is the strongest ally of romance. As always, John Cumming's own subconscious wish was rationalized into God's will. A few days before his birthday he wrote in his diary:

> Sabbath 9th July [1843]. While engaged in prayer and meditation on the subject of C[atherine] P[ringle] felt a strong conviction that the Lord willed me to go forward and make her the wife.

Once he had made the decision he was quick to act on it. As soon as he could arrange it he set off once more for Glenthorn. It was a five day journey and he arrived on a Sunday ready to complete his campaign for Catherine's hand. He knew where the domestic power in the Pringle household rested and his first approach was not to Catherine's father as might have been expected from Victorian convention:

> Tuesday [22nd Aug 1843]. Open my mind to Mrs Pringle after breakfast imparting my intention to marry Catherine – quite agreeable.

There was a last chance for second thoughts but he was commited:

> Wednesday [3rd Aug 1843]. Sleepless night – rose early went out wrestled with God – spoke to Catherine – asked if agreeable to share her lot with mine in Mission field – ... agreeable.

Finally, now that the important part of the process was complete, permission was sought from the head of the family:

> Friday [5th Aug 1843] Speak to John Pringle regarding Catherine agreeable if she is.

With everyone agreeable and agreed, John returned to Kirkwood. There he continued with his strenuous labours. Only occasionally did he see visitors. His human contacts were almost entirely with his parishioners.

One distant neighbour was Henry Fynn, now removed from Natal and with a position of respectability as Government Agent to the abaThembu. His post was some 60km away but on his rounds he occasionally visited the missionary. On one of his visits he found Cumming gravely ill with dysentry. The nature of the water supplies made such illnesses common at the time. Fynn returned to his station to get medicine:

> On reaching home he found the Colonel Napier who was travelling had just reached the Residency. He told him of my case, and in the most generous manner he said "And I have a case of the best brandy, send him a bottle from me and it will do him good" When it arrived I took a little once or twice, but it seemed to burn up my inside and make it worse. I laid it aside.

The treatment was typical of the time. Not surprisingly, when Fynn made a second visit, he found Cumming in a state of collapse. He insisted that he be taken to somewhere where he could be cared for and, with Campbell's help loaded him into the wagon and sent him to Iqibira. There he was gradually nursed back to health until he was fit for work. He continued assisting at Iqibira and never returned to Kirkwood.

By now he was well-established in the eyes of the Glasgow Missionary Society and ready to take more responsibility. When Robert Niven was temporarily summoned back to Scotland, the responsibility for Iqibira fell on him. One thing was left to be done. Before leaving for Scotland, Niven accompanied him to Glenthorn, and on the 20th April 1844 officiated at the wedding of John and Catherine. The marriage was to last for fifty-eight years.

Chapter 17. The War of the Axe

Thou art my battle axe and weapons of war: for with thee will I break in pieces the nations, and with thee will I destroy kingdoms

Jeremiah 51:10

Pressures [1837 – 1846]

The Governor who replaced D'Urban, Major-General Sir George Thomas Napier, was a distinguished veteran of Wellington's army. He had been severely wounded in the Peninsula campaign, having lost an arm. By the time he took up office he was 54 years old. After the differences between D'Urban and Stockenstrom he took great pains to clarify the working relationship between governor and Lieutenant-Governor. He began his term of office intent on making the frontier system work. That meant ensuring the success of the treaty system, maintaining peace on the frontier, reducing the incidence of cattle theft by the strict application of the agreements with the Xhosa, and above all preventing the Colony becoming too great a drain on the Exchequer.

He was soon to become aware of the impossible strains between those with a responsibility for the administration of the frontier. Stockenstrom, responsible for the civil administration and Somerset, the military commander were longstanding enemies, barely on speaking terms, and with radically different attitudes to the problem of frontier control. The two agents to the frontier Xhosa, Charles Lennox Stretch and John Mitford Bowker were at opposite poles of opinion. Stretch was associated with humanist opinion and believed by the colonists to be prejudiced against them in favour of the Xhosa: Bowker was a close associate of the Graham's Town establishment, a friend of Godlonton, and suspected (rightly) of fomenting opposition to the treaty system. The first casualty was Bowker who was forced to resign and replaced by Theophilus Shepstone[520]. The next to go was Stockenstrom. Napier, while supporting him in his fight to clear his name after his legal woes, was relieved to accept his resignation. His relationship with many of the leading citizens of the frontier made his position untenable, whatever its rights.

Stockenstrom's successor as Lieutenant-Governor, Colonel John Hare, was a totally different character. First he was a military man, which pleased the Governor. He was, however, old, tired, and out of his depth.

Charles Lennox Stretch carried out his duties as Ngqika Agent watching the situation deteriorate. His official home was at Block Drift on the

Tyumie River near the present town of Alice. There was a military post
there and further up the river William Chalmers still ran the Tyumie Mission Station. Stretch believed firmly that Stockenstrom's treaty system
had worked well. He was indignant at Napier's easy acceptance that it
had failed and kept statistics on the incidence of cattle theft to prove it.
His account book of all the claims for theft is prefaced with some notes
expressing his opinion of the Governor:

> During the period Capt Stockenstrom was in England Sir George Napier
> requested Col. Hare to state officially the quantity of Cattle taken from
> the Colony from the period when Stockenstrom Government com-
> menced & contrary to the Treaties both the Reclaimable and irreclaim-
> able Lists were [Exercised?] and the number of cattle in both were ad-
> ded together and a claim of £13,000 made against the Gaikas. It was
> very disgraceful of Sir George Napier by this making it falsely appear
> the system was bad. The procedure was ruinous to the [Xhosa]s. It was
> as bad as the reprisal system.[521]

Tyumie 1844   C.   L.
Stretch

For the early years of his tenure Stretch had been very satisfied with
Maqoma's efforts to fulfil the terms of the treaty. He was impressed with
his intellect and qualities of leadership. His counterparts further south,
first Bowker and then Shepstone provided contrary opinions.

Maqoma was Regent of the amaNgqika acting for Sandile, the heir
until he should come of age, this being defined by when he underwent the
circumcision ceremony. Sandile was a weakly child. He was crippled by a
withered leg, perhaps the result of poliomyelitis. His mother, Ngqika's
Great Wife Suthu, was fiercely protective of him. Maqoma, his brothers,
Tyhali, Anta, and Xhoxho, and their councillors felt considerable concern
about his capacity to rule.

Sandile underwent the circumcision ceremony in 1840. It took place at
the Great Place of his mother Suthu. Maqoma and Tyhali attended in order to preside over the proceedings.

Circumcision among the Xhosa[522] is a crucial rite of passage in which
a boy becomes a man. It has cultural and religious significance. Before
the ritual the preparations included the gathering of materials for the ceremonial costume – a palm leaf kilt and mask – and the construction of a
lodge for the accommodation of the initiates during a period of seclusion,
during which they would receive instruction. The initiates had some
choice as to when circumcision would take place and it was very desirable to undergo the ordeal at the same time as a chief. To be part of the
same group as the king of the amaNgqika was even more desirable.

The actual ceremony took place on 22nd February 1840. After the ceremony the initiates, the abakwetha, went into seclusion in the lodge where they underwent instruction for several months. At the end of this period they emerged to a ceremony of celebration of their manhood. Sandile could now assume his position as king of the amaNgqika.

This was a bitter time for Maqoma. He knew himself to be the ablest leader among the amaNgqika. He was deeply sceptical of Sandile's ability. The new missionary to his clan, the same Henry Calderwood that had accompanied John Cumming for part of the way on his first journey to Glenthorn, had been impressed with the depth of the discussions he had held with him. Maqoma's critical mind, however, was not going to be easily swayed by the blandishments of Christianity and, when it became apparent that he was not a candidate for conversion, the impetuous young missionary became as deeply disillusioned as he had previously been impressed with him.

There are many reports at this time that Maqoma was often to be seen drunk in the canteens of Fort Beaufort. While the treaty system was still working he was often at the Fort for discussions about the administration of the border, and there is no doubt that he sometimes drank to excess. Many sources at the time describe him as a hopeless alcoholic. If he was, then he was an extremely hardy one. He lived until 1873 and later photographs show an apparently vigorous old man. In fact contemporary sources were often intent on vilifying the man who was held responsible for the 1834 invasion of the colony. Calderwood was increasingly critical of him, and Godlonton, in The *Graham's Town Journal* frequently published personal attacks on him. The much more likely picture is of someone who, on occasion, drank to excess, but was not uncontrollably addicted[523]. Nevertheless, at this time there seems little doubt that he was often incapacitated[524]

In 1842 matters came to a head when an opportunity arose for Maqoma to gain political advantage. Tyhali was seriously ill with a lung disease, most probably tuberculosis. Maqoma, through Andries Botha, a Khoikhoi headman at the Kat River Settlement, knew of a Mfengu diviner whom he summoned to treat Tyhali. In the circumstances – Tyhali was clearly dying – the treatment was bound to be ineffective. The reason for an illness of this sort was always understood to be the result of witchcraft, and, in order to counteract this, the sorcerer responsible for the malicious spell had to be identified and executed. This was done by a diviner who conducted a "smelling out" in which the people gathered together and the diviner, by interacting with them, identified and pointed out the supposed sorcerer[525].

The smelling out justifiably invoked horror in all who came in contact with it. It was not unusual for it to be used as a political weapon. The power behind Sandile's throne was his mother Suthu. For Maqoma to gain control over Sandile it was necessary to eliminate Suthu. Maqoma, supported by other chiefs such as Mhala, Ndlambe's successor, plotted to ensure that Suthu was identified as the sorcerer responsible for Tyhali's death; if she were eliminated the young and inexperienced Sandile would be vulnerable to a coup.

Stretch's job meant that he needed to know what was going on. On April 14th 1842 he had received a deathbed statement[526] from Tyhali spelling out what the dying man believed was Maqoma's plan.

I am a dying man, and I speak to my Father before my Spirit breaks and he will see Tyali no more.

Maqomo has told his House lies regarding my illness not having been reported to him, and the reason is he wishes when I am dead to Eat up my people and destroy Gaika's house. When my messengers went to him he was always drunk and knew not what they said. The Governor must not believe him – I hope my people will follow my advice to them to live in Peace with the Government and themselves.

Tyali X his mark

The language is, of course, Stretch's attempt to render the meaning and rhythm of the Xhosa.

On May 1st Tyhali died[527]. When news reached Stretch that Suthu had been summoned to Tyhali's Great Place and on arrival had been arrested he took action.

The smelling out process was delayed; for such an important occasion other chiefs had been summoned and Bhothomane and Nqeno had not yet arrived. Charles Stretch, together with William Chalmers and his wife, Mary, descended on Tyhali's Great Place. Stretch took the official line. He informed the diviner that, as he was resident at the Kat River Settlement he was a British subject. Should he choose to continue with the procedure he should be in no doubt that he would be arrested and tried for murder. Andries Botha was also present and Stretch threatened him with legal action as an accessory. William Chalmers harangued Maqoma on the iniquity of witch doctors and their charlatanism. Mary Chalmers took Suthu under her wing and with Victorian vigour told her captives what she thought of them.

The game was up. Botha and the diviner made a hasty retreat to the Kat River Settlement. Maqoma abandoned the arrangements for the *mhlahlo*. Suthu was escorted back to her Great Place where she sought temporary refuge with James Laing, the missionary at neighbouring Burnshill.

No matter how appalling the smelling out, and how important it was to prevent it, the effect of the actions was to bring home to Sandile, Maqoma and the other Xhosa chiefs the extent to which their independence had disappeared. Their relationships with Stretch and Chalmers were soured and the tensions driving the two sides to conflict were increased.

Hare had initially been determined to maintain the treaty system. As time went on, however, cattle theft continued and the Graham's Town lobby for stronger action against the Xhosa became more strident. Soon he became disillusioned. He had no time for the the Xhosa, for the citizens of Graham's Town, or for his own officials such as Stretch. He was just serving time in his post with little vision for what it entailed.

Matters changed in 1844 when Sir Peregrine Maitland replaced Napier. Maitland was from an old military family, yet another veteran of the Peninsular war. He had previous experience as Lieutenant Governor of Upper Canada and and then of Nova Scotia where he had established a reputation for piety and inaction. As a young man he had played first class cricket as a batsman for Surrey, Hampshire, and the MCC, finishing after 32 innings with an average of 6.8[528]. Many people in Canada, angered by his identification with conservative political causes, would have rated his period in office as comparable with his cricket average.

Maitland had no insight into the complexities of frontier relationships. By September he had decided that the treaty system must be changed. He arrived on the frontier and unilaterally informed Nqeno and Stokwe of the amaMbalu, Phatho of the amaGqunukwhebe, and Mhala of the amaNdlambe that Stockenstrom's treaties were no more. Sandile and Maqoma heard this by messenger. Some days later, again with no consultation they were informed of the new conditions to be imposed. Among other things, these reimposed the patrol system and removed Christian converts from the authority of the Chiefs. The insult was no less hurtful in that it was delivered as a result of abysmal lack of understanding.

The settler community, while rejoicing at the end of the hated treaty system, was disappointed that they were not allowed to acquire land in the former Xhosa territory. The situation continued to deteriorate through 1845. With the abrogation of the treaties, the chiefs no longer put emphasis on preventing cattle theft. The youthful Sandile failed to balance the desire of his people for confrontation and the demands of the Colonial Government. Even Calderwood tried to warn the Government that their lack of understanding of the Xhosa was leading to disaster. A severe drought placed even more strains on the region. By the beginning of 1846 an explosion was imminent.

Iqibira   [1844 – 1846]

After their marriage John and Catherine Cumming settled down at Iqibira acting for Robert Niven during his absence in Britain. Thomas Campbell continued to manage Kirkwood and Bonkolo. Campbell, after the loss of his first wife, had remarried. His new bride was Elizabeth, niece of Charles Lennox Stretch and daughter of John and Ellen Devenish who had worked with Robert Hart in the days of Somerset Farm. Elizabeth was just 18 years old when she took on the task of accompanying her new husband to his remote and isolated station. The two of them started and ended their married lives in the primitive conditions at Bonkolo.

In the latter part of 1845 Cumming got word that Campbell was ill and he decided that he had better visit him. The Cummings had wasted no time since their marriage and Catherine was pregnant. She could not be left alone at Iqibira so they first set off in their ox wagon to Glenthorn, where John left her in the care of her parents and set off to ride to Bonkolo:

> In ascending the height from which the Ubonkolo stream emerges from the valley above, I spied on the distant side a waggon travelling on, and a white man slowly following after. What! I said to myself. Is that Campbell? I crossed over and found that it was so. He was thin emaciated, and what struck me was his long neck rising from what formerly was his broad shoulders and sturdy frame. Alas! I said can this be he? Mrs Campbell was in the waggon, and it may easily be understood how gladly surprised they both were at meeting them so unexpectedly.

Campbell had severe dysentry and was clearly unable to struggle on. Cumming took over. Elizabeth could not be left alone with a gravely ill husband. He escorted the waggon back to Glenthorn, a three day journey of jolting discomfort, during which Campbell lay in agony in the back of the wagon.

There was no medical help in the region and it was decided that the patient should be sent to Graham's Town. Withers, the teacher who had arrived in South Africa at the same time as Campbell escorted the wagon there. Cumming remained with his wife for a day or two, sending a letter to William Chalmers at Tyumie to tell him of the situation, and then travelled to Graham's Town.

He and Chalmers arrived in the town at the same time and found Campbell on his death bed. He died that evening and his Elizabeth was left a widow after six months.[529]

Cumming and Chalmers had had the realities of their own situations brought home to them. Like good Scots they took practical precautions for the future:

> ... with a sigh he [Chalmers] said Well! Which of us will be next? He had already insured his life in the Mutual[530], and going with him to the Agent of that Company, I also insured my life at the same time for £600.

Catherine stayed with her family at Glenthorn until the birth of her first child. On the 3rd January 1846 John made an entry in his diary:

> Birth – Mrs Cumming of a son at 6 o'clock evening – at Glenthorn – Mrs Albert attending.

The birth was a cause for rejoicing, a son for John Cumming, a grandson for John and Susan Pringle. The celebration came three weeks later. James Read was invited to come from Philipton and Cumming noted in his diary:

> Jan 25. [I] Preach in English – My boy baptised and named John Pringle by Mr Read.

John and Catherine brought the infant John Pringle Cumming to Iqibira immediately after the baptism, just three weeks after the baby's birth. They broke the journey at Block Drift to visit Catherine's uncle, Charles Lennox Stretch. By this time Stretch's disillusionment meant he was despairing of a peaceful solution to the frontier situation. Distrusted by his superiors on account of his defence of the Xhosa position, and distrusted by the Xhosa as the agent of the British, he was now isolated. His position in the public service would not survive long.

A few days earlier the tension had been increased when, unannounced, a party of soldiers crossed the Keiskamma into Xhosa territory and set up camp near Stretch's Residency. They had orders to survey the site with a view to erecting a military post there. At the same time Stretch had happened to send a message to Sandile about a complaint from a trader that Sandile had taken goods from his store and assaulted him in doing so. Sandile sent an intemperate message back to him, the tone of which was very threatening. He demanded that the troops should leave Block Drift immediately. Stretch had sent a communication to Fort Beaufort that resulted in the arrival of a strong contingent of troops. Sandile, alarmed by this, back-tracked and apologized, Hare, nevertheless, insisted on a conference at Block Drift. When he reached there with about 100 soldiers he found himself facing several thousand Xhosa in a tense stand-off. While Sandile and Suthu were intent on defusing the situation, their supporters were more belligerent. The conference lasted all day and ended in a temporary agreement. The Xhosa dispersed, derisively firing shots over the heads of the British troops.

No doubt Cumming and Stretch discussed all this, although Cumming does not mention it. The two had much in common and their relationship was that of friends rather than of connection by marriage. When it was time to continue with their journey, the Cummings left Block Drift with no illusions about the future.

Outbreak of War   [March – April 1846]

One of the more troublesome clans on the border was that of Tola, a minor branch of the imiDange. Deeply involved in stock theft, their attitude towards the British was aggressive. In the middle of March, 1846 Tsili, one of Tola's men was visiting Fort Beaufort. The fort itself was surrounded by a small village, and one of its amenities was a trading store. The trader observed Tsili concealing an axe stolen from the large stock of implements. He apprehended the thief who was placed under arrest. Tola, who refused to recognize any authority by the British over his people, unsuccessfully tried to get him released. On 16th March Tsili and three other prisoners, handcuffed in pairs, were dispatched for trial to Graham's Town. Some way along the route the party was attacked. The Khoikhoi man attached to Tsili was stabbed to death. In order to release their clansman the attackers hacked off his hand. One of the rescue party was killed during the engagement.

Hare was outraged and demanded the return of the prisoner. Tola refused and was backed up by the senior Dange chief, Bhothomane. All the Xhosa in the region agreed with the decision: so far as they were concerned the matter was subject to their authority, not Hare's and, since one of their people had been killed during the rescue the matter should be regarded as closed. Hare was not prepared to accept this. On 21st March he announced that he would attack the Xhosa.

Maitland in Cape Town approved the decision and sent some reinforcements by sea. He followed soon after.

Alone at Iqibira   [January – May 1846]

The Cummings had very little time to settle in at Iqibira. Maitland's and Hare's declaration of war against the Xhosa was in March and soon alarming reports of threatening hostilities began arriving at the mission station.

The Mission at Iqibira served the amaMbalu. Their chief Nqeno had died early in 1846 and had been succeeded by his son Stokwe[531]. Before his death he had been anxious to avoid conflict with the British and had extracted a promise from Stokwe and Sonto to remain neutral. He was buried in the presence of a British detachment that accorded him semi-military honours. Cumming, therefore, had hopes that Iqibira might avoid the consequences of the war. When, however, reports of the evacuation of other mission stations began arriving, he decided that his wife and child could not remain at the mission; he sent them to Glenthorn. He himself was determined to remain at his post. The ox wagon was loaded with valuables and supplies and mother and child set off accompanied by a number of Christian Xhosa who wished to avoid the war. The most prominent of these was Nomaza, the Great Wife of Langa, Stokwe's grandfather, the founder of the amaMbalu and younger brother of Gcaleka and Rharhabe. Nomaza had been baptised many years before by van der Kemp and now lived near the mission. She was old, blind, and infirm. The Cumming's installed her in their wagon

> Dali, a nephew of the chief [Nqeno] seeing Nomaza in the waggon, asked where we were going to take her to. I [Cumming] said, to Glenthorn on the Mankazana. "Oh, that is well," he said. I believe it was indeed well, as her presence there, it is said, prevented the [Xhosa]s from attacking that place during the War. I accompanied the refugees as far as the Karoma, and then returned to the lonely Iqibigha.[532]

There he remained under the protection of Stokwe for the next two months while matters developed.

The Governor, Sir Peregrine Maitland arrived in Port Elizabeth at the beginning of April and reached Graham's Town on the 10th. Hare's leisurely preparations for the invasion were almost complete. Maitland was in overall command but left the planning to Hare, who was wholly ignorant of the nature of war on the frontier. Nevertheless, with experienced subordinates such as Somerset to advise him one might have expected some level of competence in the planning. There was not.

The country was in the grip of a severe drought. Even in the best of times the problems of supply lines for an army in the rough country was considerable. There were no storage depots for ammunition or food. Everything needed had to be carried over the rough terrain by ox wagon with an enemy that could melt away into the bush, reappearing to harrass the British when they were most vulnerable.

The day after Maitland's arrival the army set off towards the Amatolas, under the command of Somerset. Apart from the troops and their equipment there were 125 wagons carrying supplies, each with a full span of oxen.

Maitland stopped at Block Drift to ask Stretch about the situation.

> Mr Stretch afterwards told me that when Governor Maitland came to Chumie Vale, he anxiously enquired if all the Missionaries had been able to leave their stations, and get to places of safety. He replied "I believe all are safe, but Mr Cumming the Missionary of Stock [Stokwe] Chief of the Amambalu, still keeps to his station. "What![''] exclaimed the Governor "Can nothing be done to rescue him? I give you authority to employ men at any expense and try and bring him out from that place" Mr Stretch said "I will do what I can, but I doubt very much if I can accomplish it."[533]

Cumming, on the other hand, was under different pressures. His decision to remain arose from Stokwe's neutrality:

> One thing that tended to my remaining at my post, though surrounded with war, was that Stock the present Chief of the tribe, was the only one in [Xhosa]land not proscribed by Government in the Proclamation against [Xhosa]s in general. The Chief, who lived some 15 miles away from the station, sent a messenger to me saying "I hope you will not leave me, for if you leave me I will soon be treated as if I were at war with the Government, and you know that I am sitting still, and I have the Governor's word that I will not be molested." I returned my word to the Chief that as long as he continued to protect the Station, I would remain. I carried on as usual my work among the people Sabbath after Sabbath[534].

By the 17th April, Saturday, Somerset's force had established a camp at Burnshill and he had taken a major part of his troops into the Amatola valley in search of the Xhosa, leaving the wagons under a light guard.

Cumming in his lonely house at Iqibira heard the ominous sounds of battle:

> In the meantime Colonel Somerset crossed the Keiskamma with a large body of troops, and passed near the station on his way to Burnshill. On the following day [18th April] – Sabbath – while we were at worship in the Church, we heard the booming of the great guns at Burnshill. It was a solemnising time. We waited anxiously to hear the result.

The result was a disaster for the British[535]. The wagon train had been given orders to rejoin Somerset, who should have known better, on the other side of the Keiskamma. They had already been under attack and suffered casualties. No longer were the Xhosa fighting with assegais and shields. They were well-armed, thanks to the commercial enterprise of the Graham's Town merchants. The wagon train, 5 kilometres long, set off. Thousands of Xhosa waited. The route to the drift on the Keiskamma led through a narrow pass. When the wagons were strung out through this cleft the attack came. It was overwhelming. The troops fell back to defend the ammunition wagons and fought their way back to Burnshill, abandoning 65 wagons. The spoils for the Xhosa included the regimental silver, lost for ever, almost as bad as the loss of an standard by a Roman legion. Also gone were guns, food, wine, medical supplies, clothing, and all the impedimenta of a nineteenth century military campaign. Somerset was compelled to retreat with his entire force, under heavy attack, all the way back to Block Drift.

The jubilant Xhosa flooded across the border into the Colony.

The Threat to the Colony   [April – May 1846]

For those in Graham's Town who had been advocating the cause of war and supplying the needs of the Xhosa for weapons, the chickens had come home to roost. It was 1834 all over again but with no Harry Smith to ride to the rescue. Refugees streamed from the farms in Albany. Once again the defence of the streets of Graham's Town was in the hands of its citizens.

Joseph Walker, in common with many of his friends and colleagues once again found himself manning the barricades:

Graham's Town Journal, Saturday May 30th 1846:

The following gentlemen are requested to give their best aid in maintaining the Barricades in good repair, viz: Messrs. KIFT, STUBBS, THOMPSON, SMITH at those near the Drostdy Barracks. Messrs. NELSON and LEVEY at those adjoining their own houses; Messrs. SHAW and RUTHERFORD at those on the east of Hill Street; Mr. CAWOOD at those near the Wesleyan Chapel; Messrs. WALKER and LEE at those across Bathurst Street; Mr. DAVIS and M. MEURANT at those near their respective houses.

This time, however, the town was not directly threatened. It was the farms that suffered immediate loss. While Graham's Town was on the agenda of the Xhosa, there were obstacles in the ceded territory to be overcome first.

Cumming's Ride   [May 1846]

For Stokwe the capture of the British wagons at Burnshill was a turning point. He was under considerable pressure to join the conflict. He sent a message to John Cumming at Iqibira:

... Stock sent word to me [Cumming] "Go out to your friends in the Colony, the country is filled with strange [Xhosa]s, and as I am far away, they may come upon you before I can help you." I said to myself, the door is now opened for me to leave my post. I will arise and depart for this is not my rest.[536]

During his lonely spell at Iqibira he had been served by a young convert, Pepe Gongwana[537]. They had spent their spare time during the previous months on maintenance tasks at the mission. Now the two of them saddled up and set off to visit Stokwe at his Great Place. There they told him of their plans for getting back to Glenthorn. Stokwe himself had probably by now resolved to join the war – his warriors may well have already been part of it. He was, however, concerned for the safety of Cumming. A major problem was how to secure the mission property. The buildings would inevitably be destroyed in the conflict: it might be possible to save the contents. They needed wagons. Cumming's own wagon had gone to Glenthorn with his family months before.

The direct route to Glenthorn was to the North West but was long and dangerous. Cumming had a better idea. South of Iqibira, in the ceded territory on the Colonial side of the Keiskamma was Fort Peddie, occupied by a significant British force. It was about 40km from Iqibira and Stokwe's Great Place lay between. He and Pepe rode south.

When they reached the fort it was bustling with troops and refugees – both missionaries and traders. John Brownlee, whose mission station on the Buffalo River had been commandeered by Harry Smith in the previous war to form the capital of the short lived Province of Queen Adelaide, had arrived with his family. After the previous war he had re-established his mission: now he was again forced out. Traders from throughout the Xhosa regions were camped in their wagons. John Cumming had his own priorities.

The local Government agent, Captain John Maclean, introduced him to the local Commander, Lieutenant-Colonel Martin Lindsay of the 91st Argyllshire. The fort itself was manned by the 91st and large numbers of Mfengu troops were encamped outside. The latter were later to bear the brunt of the defence of the fort.

Lindsay was expecting an imminent attack. Since the beginning of the hostilities he had been receiving regular intelligence from Mqhayi[538]. This had made it clear that the major objective of the Xhosa was first to destroy Fort Peddie and then advance on Graham's Town, sixty kilometres to the west. He was now faced with an importunate, travel-stained missionary who was demanding the loan of some wagons in order to bring the property of his mission station to safety.

> "What! said he "How can you take waggons for such a purpose, and at such a time? The [Xhosa]s will seize them" I said if he could favour me, our mission would be responsible for the value of the waggons. "Well," he said If you will get Stock to give you men to accompany you, I will spare you two waggons" This I did.

The following morning the refugees in the camp were astonished to see the little wagon train, manned by Cumming, Gongwana, two drivers, and two voorlopers, setting off northwards. There was a certain amount of jeering:

> ... one of the Refugee Traders said "I bet you £500, that you will not bring these wagons back again.

They made their way safely as far as the Great Place where Stokwe gave them an escort that was armed only with sticks. It had, however, considerable authority, consisting of Stokwe's brother[539] and two other relatives. They travelled on to Iqibira.

The mission station was still untouched. The most valuable contents were Niven's books. They loaded his whole library and as much of the furniture as fitted on the wagons and set off on the return journey. Niven's favourite horse, which had been left in Cumming's care, was placed on a leading rein. Near the Keiskamma, Cumming sent the wagons ahead to set up camp while he and Pepe made a diversion to bid a final farewell to Stokwe.

They reached the Great Place in the evening and were welcomed by Stokwe. Just like Fort Peddie, Stokwe's Great Place was awash with rumour and alarm:

> ... at night we all lay down in the hut on the ground with our feet to the fire in the centre like so many spokes of a wheel. About midnight we were all aroused by a [Xhosa] putting his head in by the door and loudly saying the Fingoe's [sic] of Fort Peddie have seized on the cattle, and the [British] soldiers are coming up in the morning to attack the Great Place. Stock looked to me and said "Do you hear that? "Yes" I replied "I hear but I do not believe it all ..."

Cumming, showing a faith in the integrity of the British command that was perhaps unjustified, explained that while it was quite possible that some errant Mfengu had stolen the cattle, Stokwe was not on the proscribed list of those who were at war with the Colony and the British would not attack without provocation. He offered to to take a message to Fort Peddie provided that Stokwe supplied him with an escort. The escort soon absconded, being terrified of falling into the hands of the British, but Cumming. after a brush with a frightened sentry, was able to see Maclean, who immediately provided a message of reassurance. Cumming was able to return to Stokwe to tell him that, if he sent two representatives the following morning, Maclean would compensate him for the stolen cattle.

Cumming's departure the next day was the occasion of a remarkable scene:

> In the morning before leaving I said to Stock "We are about to part, and may never see one another again. I would like that you would call your

people here, and we shall worship God before leaving. ... in a short time a large number of [Xhosa] warriors with their arms gathered into a half circle on the hill slope, while I took my station above them and gave an address, and engaged in prayer. ...In the far distance were the Amatolas where a few days ago the battle of Burnshill had taken place, where the [Xhosa]s had burnt the commissariat waggons, and taken a great spoil of oxen and other spoil from the troops and thus forced them to retire. The intervening country was now lying at the mercy of the victorious [Xhosa]s, and what the end of all this might be who could know.

John Cumming and Pepe Gongwana then said their farewells and rode to rejoin their wagons. The situation was very tense, so when a burly Xhosa warrior suddenly appeared out of the bush and seized Cumming's bridle they were alarmed. He interrogated them about who they were and asked if they knew the whereabouts of a large body of British troops in the neighbourhood. During the conversation he let go the bridle for an instant, Cumming immediately spurred his horse, and the two of them made their escape.

Their arrival at the wagon encampment was just in time. The drivers were preparing to leave. The tense situation and the delay in Cumming's return had made them increasingly nervous and they had decided to flee. Cumming reassured them and the situation was resolved when a column of troops appeared at the end of the road. It was a large detachment of reinforcements from Fort Hare. An imminent attack on Fort Peddie was expected and they had been sent to strengthen the garrison. The Cumming wagon train followed them and in due course reached the fort. Cumming wryly observed that:

... in due time we all entered safely. The betting trader was astonished when he saw the two waggons coming in preceeded by such a welcome force. However he failed to hand me the £500 which he had betted.

John Cumming had now achieved his first objective of saving Niven's and the mission's property. Lindsay allowed him to store the goods in the Commissariat where they remained for more than a year; Niven was able to retrieve them after the war. Cumming was now free to pursue his second objective – to reunite himself with his family at Glenthorn.

It was the 30th April. The source of the threat to Fort Peddie showed how matters had deteriorated during the last few years. The attacking force consisted of amaGqunukwhebe under Phatho; in the 1935 war he had been loyal to the British. Now completely alienated from them he had thrown in his lot with Xhosa threatening the Colony. In the camp there was near panic among the civilians and many of them abandoned their shelters for the night to take refuge within its walls. Cumming did not join them and was not above gently mocking them in his account:

I felt ashamed to join them, and so I determined to remain in the unfin-
ished Commissariat rooms which had been given me. No attack took
place. Next morning they all returned to their houses apparently feeling
very small at the thought of having left them so unnecessarily.

On this occasion the British had sent out a column to attack . When
the large force of Gqunukwhebe warriors advanced on them they had
simply retreated to the fort. Phatho had satisfied himself with looting a
nearby Mfengu village and had then departed. It was not until some
weeks later, on 28th May that the main attack on Peddie was mounted.
By that time not only Phatho, but also Dyani Tshatshu, the Christian
chief of the amaNtinde, and Mhala of the amaNdlambe had turned their
backs on the colony. Stokwe, too, had joined the Xhosa cause and Cumming was far away at Glenthorn.

Getting there had not been easy. The morning after his night in the
Commissariat he found out from Maclean that a party of 17 dragoons
was going to Graham's Town and he and Pepe were welcome to accompany them. The Sergeant in charge of the party looked at their small and
scruffy mounts doubtfully and, rather than placing them in the safer position at the front of the column, said that they would have to bring up the
rear and keep up as best they could.

The first stage of the journey took them as far as the Post at Trompetter's Drift. The country was still in the grip of a disastrous drought and
there was no grazing for the horses. Next day they continued along the
perilous route, watching for ambush from the dense scrub in Driver's
Bush. At this point the horses of two of the dragoons began to fall back
and others began to flag. The mission *boerperde* continued without difficulty.

I said to the Sergeant "There is no use for us to wait, we will just ride
on to Grahamstown (which perhaps 10 miles more or less distant from
where we were)" He seemed a little touched at the idea of our now taking the van and reaching Town before him.

Two of the grain-fed well-bred military horses died on the journey and
another on arrival in Graham's Town. The little mission horses showed
no ill effects.

The following day they joined a Burgher force bound for Fort
Beaufort. The journey took two days. The first night was spent at a way-
side halt on the Koonap river, called Tomlinson's Hotel. Cumming had
hopes of a bed for the night, but they found the accommodation entirely
occupied by Governor Maitland and his party so had to sleep outdoors.
Fort Beaufort was reached the next day but there was no prospect of a

party travelling towards Mankazana Post near Glenthorn so they set off alone.

> On coming out of the Drift we met 8 well armed Burghers, who seeing us unarmed going into the mouth of danger said "Where are you going?" "To Mankazana" I said. "Are you mad? Where is your gun?" Before I could answer Pepe exclaimed "God is our gun" They went their way and we went ours. As we rode along the Karooma the sky was obscured with clouds of smoke arising on all sides from Farm houses burning …

They then encountered troops from Mankazana Post who said that they had the previous day been heavily attacked by a force under Maqoma and advised them against continuing. On hearing that they were determined to proceed they were asked to take a message to the Post commander giving him directions to Stuart's Road where there was the possibility of retrieving a large number of cattle. This was successful and the next day the commander, Lieutenant Tom, agreed to escort them while another foray was made.

The last stage of the journey had to be taken alone as the army horses needed to be returned to their stables.

> We mounted the Black Hill and keeping to the side of the river along the ridge so as to see our way on every side, we went on till we saw a great smoke arising from what we knew as McMaster Kraal, where we knew the [Xhosa]s were at work.

> However, we kept out of sight and went on till we reached Glenthorn in safety in the afternoon.

> I cannot describe the congratulations of all my beloved ones there at our wonderful journey from Igquiligha [Iqibira] through the country in a state of barbarous strife and war, and that without our having met an enemy all the way.

Wearisome War and Phony Peace   [May – Dec 1846]

The Xhosa had learned a lot about warfare since Nxele's army had been destroyed at the Battle of Graham's Town[540]. They were now better armed, with substantial fire power in the form of muskets supplied by the illegal arms trade. While these were usually inferior to the British equipment, in their large numbers they could produce a daunting counter to the British operations. The Xhosa had always been masters of guerilla techniques. They could now apply these with to very good effect in a strategic plan that concentrated on the British supply lines. The Colonial army relied on constant replenishment of supplies and these could only be delivered by slow moving extended ox wagon trains. The Xhosa success at Burnshill showed the way.

On May 22nd a relief supply train of 43 wagons set off from Graham's Town to Fort Peddie. Impossibly extended over a distance of several kilometres, there was no sure protection. As the wagons climbed out of the Fish Gorge on the other side of Trompetter's Drift the Xhosa attacked. It is easy to stop an ox wagon. All that is needed is to shoot a few oxen. The small escort, hopelessly outnumbered by 1500 Xhosa abandoned the wagons and retired to the Trompetter's Drift post. The wagons and their contents were destroyed. This disaster was the final trigger that created euphoria among the Xhosa and brought the uncommitted Xhosa into the war. Even Stokwe was forced by the pressure to abandon his neutrality. The commander of the escort, Captain Campbell, was later court martialled for failing to protect the supply train although he had had no possible alternative.

On 28th May another attack on Fort Peddie was carried out by an estimated 8000 warriors drawn from the united Xhosa forces – amaNgqika, amaNdlambe, amaMbalu, imiDange, amaGqunukwhebe, and amaNtinde.

The defences held. Eventually the Xhosa withdrew, taking with them the prize of about 4000 cattle. The battle was temporarily won by the British but Fort Peddie was left stripped of food and ammunition, deep in Xhosa territory. The next relief wagon train needed an escort of more than 1000 troops and succeeded in reaching the fort only after an eleven hour engagement ranging along the length of the track out of the Fish river gorge.

This was the high point of the war for the Xhosa. Not long afterwards forces under Henry Somerset, planning to attack Stokwe's Great Place, encountered substantial amaNdlambe forces under Mhala and Siyolo. In an open area, in the Mgwangqa ("Gwanga") valley, the Xhosa warriors were vulnerable to cavalry, being unable to use their normal tactics of melting into the bush. In a bloody conflict, in which more than 300 Xhosa died, they suffered their first major reverse of the war.

This led to a withdrawal from the Colony and a period of stalemate. While Maitland was able to claim that the Colony was unthreatened and that he would shortly attack the Xhosa armies, he was, in fact, stymied by the inability to supply an invading army because of the Xhosa threat to the wagon trains.

Skirmishing continued for the next few months. The Colonial forces were augmented by a large burgher force. Maitland was more or less forced to give Andries Stockenstrom the command as the volunteers were unwilling to serve under Hare. At the end of August Maitland relieved the ailing Hare of his position and took over command. Hare was now able to embark for home, for a retirement for which he had yearned. It was not to be. He died not long after the ship had left Cape Town. Later Maitland named the new fort at Block Drift after him[541].

Eventually Stockenstrom persuaded the Governor to allow him to pursue the Gqunukwhebe into Sarhili's territory. Once again unenforceable demands were made of the Xhosa King. Sarhili denied responsibility for the war but undertook responsibility for the future behaviour of the Xhosa, an undertaking which he was not in a position to honour.

Then in September the rains came. Maitland and Hare, in their ineptitude, had failed to beat the Xhosa. It was the demands of the seasons that led to their defeat. It was imperative that the lands be ploughed and the crops sown or starvation would be the consequence. Maqoma had for some months been anxious to negotiate an independent peace for his own amaJingqi, but Maitland refused to treat with him, determined eventually to invade and annexe the Xhosa territory. This reversal of Glenelg's policy had been approved by the Secretary of State, Earl Grey[542]. Eventually a delegation including Sandile, Maqoma, Bhothomane and Tola, met with Colonel Campbell, the commander of Fort Cox to negotiate peace. Maitland's terms required that they give up their guns, return all cattle and other spoils of war, and forfeit all the lands west of the Kei. This they were not prepared to do. Instead they left the meeting and went to plant their crops, simply refusing to fight. Maqoma, sick and disillusioned, formally surrendered. Sandile, while not surrendering, made overtures by handing over Tsili, the axe thief, to the Colony.

Maitland, in his own mind, was satisfied that this was the end of the hostilities with the Ngqika and he reported as much to Grey. It remained to bring the whole of the region west of the Great Kei under British control. This involved subjugating Phatho, who was still fully engaged in the war, and, more significantly, Sarhili. It was while he was leading a futile expedition that was commandering cattle in Sarhili's territory that he received a dispatch from Grey informing him that he was being recalled and that he was to be replaced.

The new Governor, Sir Henry Pottinger, was distinguished by having negotiatied the treaty of Nanking which ended the first opium war with China. In so doing, exceeding his instructions, he had annexed Hong Kong and had served as its first Governor from 1841 to 1843. Now, accompanied by Sir George Berkeley who was to command the army, he arrived in Cape Town on 27th January 1847 and immediately assumed office.

For the Cummings this was a time for recovery – Catherine from the months of worry while John had been isolated at Iqibira, John from the rigours of his journey of escape. They remained at Glenthorn with Catherine's parents for the rest of the year while the skirmishing dragged on in the south and the phony peace in the north continued.

When John had arrived back at Glenthorn he had caught up with the news. To his dismay, he discovered that Tyumie had been plundered and burnt and his old mentor and friend, William Chalmers, had fled with his family to the Kat River Settlement. At the end of the year he went to visit him there and found him ill with dysentery and greatly depressed at the loss of his home. He persuaded the Chalmers family, his wife Mary, and eight children[543] to come back with him to Glenthorn for rest and recovery.

With the situation in the Colony under control and the low level of hostilities removed far to the east, the Cummings and the Pringles could contemplate a holiday. They did what generations of Eastern Cape residents have done since, they travelled to the mouth of the Kowie at Port Alfred where they had hired a cottage facing the magnificent beach.

> About this time Mrs. Pringle and a number of the family had gone with the waggon and were at the Kowie sea bathing. Before leaving Glenthorn in order to join them I stepped into Mr Chalmer's [sic] room, and found him very low.

John Cumming then set off to join his family on their seaside holiday. In Victorian times sea bathing was undertaken more for health than pleasure. At British holiday resorts bathing machines concealed those changing into suitable dress until they could reach the water. Men and women were segregated and costumes were designed to completely cover the body. The Kowie beach would have been less formal but it is still probable that men and women would have bathed separately and unlikely that the costumes would have been less complete. Walking, relaxing, and visiting neighbours would have been the main entertainments.

In spite of the phony peace the holiday was not completed. A message arrived from the local militia commander to get to Graham's Town as soon as possible as a new invasion was expected. This was a false alarm as there was no major incursion into Albany at the time. Nevertheless they loaded their wagons and set off. It was a two day journey to Graham's Town and it was eventful. Although there was no invasion, cattle theft was still frequent and the party was alarmed to encounter what appeared to be a battle in which many shots were audible. This turned out to be a party of Mfengu troops who were firing guns randomly into the bush in the hope of frightening the enemy so as to clear it before they entered. Eventually on the second day they reached Graham's Town and engaged rooms at Harding's Hotel on the Market Square. There they were joined by John Pringle who had come to meet them.

The bad news was brought by messenger. Chalmers had died on 8th Feb 1847. John Cumming immediately left for Glenthorn. When he arrived on the 10th February he was too late. The funeral had already taken place.

Chalmers's death was a new beginning for John Cumming. The Tyumie Mission was an important one and he had no immediate commitment. This was to be his next post. Within a few weeks he recorded in his diary:

> Feb 19, 1847 Start early morning with Mrs Chalmers for Chumie. Stopped at Balfour for night. Feb 20 travelled from Balfour to Philipton and later to Tyumie
>
> Reached Chumie in a drizzling rain. The kitchen is the only place left by the incendiary with a roof. Mr Chalmers suffered much for living in such a place. Neither door nor window, black as smoke can make it, filled with vermin etc.[544]

The war was by no means over, but Tyumie was within the Colony and not under immediate threat. Surprisingly Mary Chalmers was determined to remain in her home and a house on the mission grounds was set aside for her. The work of restoring the station began.

The New Governor   [1847]

Is there such a thing as a good bureaucracy? It can be imagined. The line of command is unambiguous. Officials have distinct areas of responsibility. They have the authority to make decisions and take initiatives within these areas according to well-defined rules of procedure. They are accountable for their actions which are subject to audit and review. Real bureaucracies, however, lie between two extremes. At one extreme is the tightly controlled, centralized organization, where every action has a laid down procedure with no room for discretion, no one can take a decision without referring it to a superior, there is no reward for initiative, and the main objective is to produce the right paper work. At the other extreme the lines of command are a tangled network, the rules are not clear, the bureaucrats find themselves accountable to more than one master, and communication between the centre and the operating parts is poor. The only way to get things done is, for the first kind to break the rules, and for the second to make them up as you go along.

The new Governor, Sir Henry Pottinger, hoped to find in the Colonial Government a bureaucracy of the first kind. What he found was one of the second. There were many problems. The Government was in London, the Colonial Administration in Cape Town, and the problem on the frontier. Communications were slow. Until the advent of steam the voyage from London lasted months. The military post riders, providing a relay between Cape Town and the frontier, took more than a week, as did the shortest voyage under sail. Cape Governors were usually, but not always, military men. This meant that some Governors were in overall command of the army and some were not. Civilian posts, such as magistrate, were often filled by military officers. Conversely, because the regular army was much too small to defend the frontier adequately, during time of war a variety of civilian militias was called into play, with varying command structures. The relationship between these and the regular army was often difficult. The army served both as combat troops and as a police force. In this environment patronage, nepotism, and corruption flourished.

The exploitation of the system for personal gain was common. The example was set from the top. From the time of Lord Charles Somerset's appointment of his son Henry to a sinecure at Simon's Town, and Donkin's arbitrary grants of land[545], the system invited the solicitation of patronage if any advance in circumstances was to be achieved. If your cattle were stolen you sought compensation from the government. If you thought you had served the Colony well you sent a memorial to the Governor requesting a grant of land as a reward. This led to a culture of entitlement.

There were obvious examples of fraud. A more insidious problem was the need to get things done in the face of a system that was unresponsive. Relatively junior officers often were isolated in remote locations and had to make executive decisions without the guidance of clear rule and precedent. As a result different parts of the defence and civil structure on the frontier received different treatment, leading to resentment. Regular army officers milked the system by drawing allowances for wagons that were never used. Militia commanders inflated the numbers of their men, pocketing their extra pay. On the other hand, the difficulty of operations often meant that isolated commanders had to meet expenses out of their own pockets, hoping – often in vain – that they might later be reimbursed. The fact that there was no money available for the business of government meant that suppliers to the commissariat were no longer willing to give credit. Many went unpaid.

As an example, the Civil Commissioner for Somerset East was unable to pay for supplies and, on behalf of the Government, borrowed £750 from Robert Hart[546]. Hart was forced to accept repayment in a Treasury Bill that could only be redeemed in England by an agent with the loss of six months interest while the process took place. He had to go through

the same process to obtain payment for meal supplied to the Fort
Beaufort Commissariat.

Thomas Stubbs, was, on the whole, an honest man and strongly critical of the system. In spite of his criticism of entrepreneurs such as George
Woods, he had come out of the 1835 war with some capital:

> In the war [of 1835] I made some money besides doing lots of duty. I
> then moved into a larger shop [for his business as a saddle maker] in
> Church Square ...[547]

In spite of some errors of judgement he was doing quite well by 1846;
his brother was running the saddler's shop and he had set up a transport
business, which had the mail contract between Graham's Town and Port
Elizabeth. In 1843, he had established a club – The Sporting Club – with
an interest in gunnery and hunting, but with strong overtones of a private
mounted militia. On the outbreak of the 1846 war their services were
offered and accepted for the defence of the Colony. Other such militias
included the Yeomanry Corps under John Norden, the Tirailleurs under
William Surmon, and a foot corps called the Guffies, commanded by
Samuel Dell. After Norden became one of the first casualties of the war
Stubbs was put in overall command of these by Major O'Reilly, the military commander in Graham's Town. In addition, some time later the
Burgher forces from the western part of the Colony arrived. All these
private armies had their own arrangements for allowances

> The Yeomanry being all big [i.e. prosperous] fellows, would not receive
> pay, but had half-ration of forage for the horses. Not so the Sporting
> Club: they found their own horse, saddle, bridles and guns and we re-
> ceived full rations for horse, man and family. Commandant pay fifteen
> shillings per diem, Captain ten shillings and sixpence, privates six
> pence.[548]

Stubbs was very critical of the level of corruption in the army and
among the town businessmen, but he was not above manipulating the system for the benefit of his own men:

> But then, the men's pay was made up – horses shod, suit of clothes,
> cloak, blanket, and long boots each: and besides, most of them were
> tradesmen and any of them that got a job of work, I put them down on
> leave until they had done, they drawing rations all the time.

Pottinger arrived and was appalled. Although he held the military rank
of major-general, it was honorary. Most of his experience had been civilian. He was a former Governor of Hong Kong and steeped in the ways of
colonial government in the Far East. His instincts were those of a bureau-
crat, not a soldier. He was impulsive, often leaping to conclusions on the
basis of untested advice. He was greeted by letters from the Government
agents to the Xhosa, petitions from the people of Albany, and military re-

ports that made it clear that, notwithstanding Maitland's assurances, the war was far from over. He decided to travel immediately to the frontier[549].

Of all the problems that he found, the one that seemed to exercise him most was that of bringing order to the organization of the military structures. There were three kinds of units: the regular army, the commandos, and the levies. The commandos were supposedly burgher reservists, subject to call-up but not paid. The levies included voluntary groupings such as Stubbs's Sporting Club, as well as Mfengu and Khoikhoi units; they received varying emoluments[550]. This mish-mash of organizational units, an obvious invitation to corruption, offended Pottinger's bureaucratic soul.

One of his early impulsive actions was, without consultation, to terminate Thomas Stubbs's position as leader of the Rangers, only to have to reinstate him when he found he was without the services of the Sporting Club which was at the time performing important service[551]. He fell out with the people of the Kat River Settlement by assuming that they held their land on military tenure and demanding that they provide 400 men; the entire male population of the settlement was only 1000, of whom 900 were already serving[552].

But, of all those that fell foul of him, the one that most raised his ire was Charles Lennox Stretch.

Stretch on the Rack   [1846 – 1847]

Charles Lennox Stretch was of Anglo-Irish descent, his father from a Protestant, and his mother from a Catholic family. As a young officer, stationed in Paris after the Napoleonic Wars he sowed his wild oats, but not without agonizing over his actions:

> On leaving college and finding myself uncontrolled, the depravity of my heart soon appeared by giving way to the invitations to sin; and the example of the officers only seemed to blind me in Satan's service to everything that was good, and they often laughed at me for refusing to allow the bad women who came about our camp in the Bois de Belogne to enter my tent. My resolutions were as the morning cloud, and until I was married in 1820 I continued being in rebellion against the Lord, a stranger to my heart, and without hope in the world. During a storm in the British Channel, the ship I was in being in imminent danger induced me to call to Him who stilleth the mind and the storm, and while I addressed a short prayer to the throne of grace, I was filled with confusion for my disobedience and neglect of performing my vows.[553]

During his courtship and marriage to Anna, the eldest daughter of Robert Hart, he became greatly attracted by the Calvinist preaching of the Presbyterian and Dutch Reformed Churches, and although an Anglican by upbringing, like his father-in-law, became a member of the Dutch

Reformed Church in Somerset East[554]. His later strong moral stands were heavily influenced by his religious convictions.

His term as Ngqika Government Agent became a burden to him as he saw the whole basis of Stockenstrom's treaty system undermined and the climate of opinion both among his superiors and on the frontier move towards the bellicose attitudes that had led to the war. When he was informed in August of 1846 that he was to be relieved of his position it probably came as a relief. The manner of his dismissal, however, was brutal.

During the progress of the war Maitland had become more and more influenced by the advice of the more belligerent of the colonists. The supporters of Stockenstrom's policies had lost all influence. Before he finally gave up office, Maitland was concerned to make the point that the Xhosa were now subjugated and recognized British rule. In such circumstances the presence of a Diplomatic Agent to the Xhosa was anomalous. There was no more need for Stretch's post. This was a reasonable decision. The manner of the termination of the office of Charles Stretch, however, was the beginning of series of mean actions and allegations against him that show the malign influence of advisors who had been opposed to his views. The Governor's private secretary, his son Brownlow Maitland, wrote to Stretch on 5th December 1846 informing him that

> His Excellency has therefore decided on its [Stretch's office as Ngqika Agent] immediate abolition and your salary as Resident Agent will not be drawn after today.[555]

There is no acknowledgement of his service, no suggestion that he might be entitled to a pension, and a mean-spirited quality pervades the letter.

Stretch had believed that there were faults on both sides; he despaired of the policies that had led to the inevitable clash of interest and to the war. It was clear that the opinions of the more extreme anti-Xhosa colonists had now become Government policy. His disillusion was complete when Henry Calderwood was appointed by Maitland as Ngqika Commissioner, essentially replacing Stretch although his post was as the Government agent over a subject people where Stretch's had been that of a representative to an independent people.

Since Calderwood had accompanied John Cumming on his first ride to Glenthorn he had changed radically from the idealistic young missionary who had come to the Colony filled with optimism. His mission to Maqoma's people at Blinkwater had been a failure. His intolerant and judgemental temperament led to clashes with Maqoma. He also became involved in a vicious campaign within the London Missionary Society to discredit John Philip and the Reads[556]. He became identified with the anti-Xhosa, anti-reformist frontier opinion. Even although many of the missionary community had come to hold similar views he did not have their support. What he did have, however, was the ear of the Governor – first Maitland and then Pottinger. When Pottinger first arrived at the frontier in February 1847 the first people that he summoned for advice were Calderwood and his counterpart at Fort Peddie, Captain John Maclean.

Stretch, an ex-military man, with experience in several wars, was committed to the defence of the Colony. He had been an obvious choice for the position of Commander of the Mfengu levies at Block Drift. At the time he was still Ngqika Agent but aware that his position was precarious. The dual appointment was not unusual. Many civilian posts were routinely assigned to military officers and, in time of war, men served in the various defence units while maintaining contact with their civilian occupations. On 10th August 1846 he was officially appointed with the rank of Captain. The levies were woefully ill-clad and he applied to Hare for uniforms. Hare approved the supply of a shirt and a pair of moleskin trousers for each man.

After his removal as Ngqika Agent in December, Stretch's only position was his military one.

At the beginning of the war, a number of refugees from Richard Birt's mission station at Mxelo were accommodated at Glen Avon. Birt had recently married Margaret Fleischer, the widowed daughter of Robert Hart, so his father-in-law's farm was the natural refuge. It is very probable that his brother-in-law, Charles Lennox Stretch, also had a hand in the arrangements. At the beginning of 1847 Stretch recruited the men from this party into his Fingo levy. This meant more uniforms and he indented for 400 more shirts and pairs of trousers. The request was approved by Henry Somerset.

Stretch's was not the only such unit in the region. Another was the so-called Tarka Levy. This had been raised in June of 1846 by a Captain T. L. Minter of Cradock. This consisted of adherents of Hermanus Matroos and Kama. Hermanus was leader of a group at the Kat River Settlement. Kama was the brother of Phatho, the Gqunukwhebe chief who, after being an ally of the British in the 1835 war, was now one of the most active of the belligerents. Kama, on the other hand, was a committed Christian, and he and his followers had moved into the Colony to escape the Xhosa. Minter had drawn about £560 from the military chest for the expenses of his unit. Of this he had spent approximately £260 in settling his personal debts in Cradock and the balance had been used to purchase goods to trade on his own behalf[557]. Despite the ease with which the military funds were generally being milked, this was too obvious. Minter was tried and sentenced to prison. His leaderless levies were assigned to Stretch, who now had a very substantial command. He applied for a further 188 uniforms.

And that is where the trouble started.

Stretch found himself the focus of a vituperative campaign by Pottinger that seemed to have its origins in the Governor's hatred of bureaucratic untidiness and his reliance on Calderwood's advice. Indeed, the disorganization of the Government and military machines concealed a good deal of dishonesty but Pottinger focused on this problem to the detriment of the conduct of the war.

One opinion was that[558]:

> Apparently, the principle which actuated him was to regard every man as utterly dishonest until proof of the reverse was forthcoming. But, as in the case of Captain Stretch, no one had an opportunity of defending himself, pleading honourable motives or showing that the circumstances of 1846 precluded that detailed reverence for red tape which was quite proper in those who could at a distance regard danger with equanimity.

It is difficult to understand why Pottinger concentrated his attention so much on Stretch unless one takes into account the fact that he was advised by Calderwood. Calderwood had been in the forefront of the campaign against Philip and the Reads and harboured a similar attitude towards Stretch, who was closely associated with them. No doubt he made these opinions clear to the Governor. Nevertheless, even if he was convinced by Calderwood of Stretch's culpability, the near hysterical tone of Pottinger's correspondence, written in emotive language, sprinkled with underlined phrases, and rich in condemnatory adjectives and adverbs, suggests someone out of his depth in facing his problems and displacing his frustration by identifying suitable scapegoats.

On 25th March Pottinger wrote to Earl Grey from Fort Peddie:

> A Mr Stretch, who was diplomatic agent at Block Drift (where he claims a large quantity of ground ceded to him by the [Xhosa] chiefs!) was appointed – I think most unwisely – to the command of the Fingoe levies in that part of the country, and I am told he has taken a number of [Xhosa]s into his pay at double the rate sanctioned for the [Xhosa] police. His being left there at all – or at least with any authority – was objectionable, and he has availed himself of that error to thwart all Mr Calderwood's plans. It is very generally believed that he deceived Sir P. Maitland as to Sandilli's having consented to an outpost at Block Drift ... and that his object was to secure protection, by that outpost, to his alleged property. I am only waiting to obtain proofs of these acts to dismiss him from all employment ...[559]

The property concerned is now the famous Lovedale Mission Institute. During his tenure as Ngqika Agent Stretch had been granted the land for his house by Sandile. He had given up part of it for the use of the Mission and at his own expense constructed a conduit to provide a water supply for it. The suggestion that he deceived Maitland about Sandile's consent to a fort at Block Drift seems to occur only here.

Pottinger was swift to act. On 3rd April he wrote to Berkeley:

I have therefore resolved to remove Mr Stretch from Her Majesty's service, but as I am not quite certain under whose immediate orders he is considered to be at this moment I think it advisable, to prevent any appearance of clashing with authority, to consult you in the first instance and await your answer. I can see no possible extenuation of Mr Stretch's misconduct. Situated as he is, and has been, with the commissioner residing on the spot, it was doubly his duty to refrain from the most trifling interference with the [Xhosa]s, and I can only ascribe his proceedings to a desire to thwart the important matters entrusted to Mr Calderwood's superintendence when he was appointed to supersede Mr Stretch in political charge of the Gaikas.[560]

Stretch was by no means the only target. In the same letter he writes:

I learn ... that a Mr Chalmers has 300 [Xhosa]s attached to him at the Tyumie station, of whom 150 are rationed 'by the late governor's orders' – for which I have called – and that an equal number who are called Mr Calderwood's have 'neither rations, pay or clothing, and are well placed for their own support ...'

At this time the mission had been destroyed, all its crops lost, Chalmers had been dead for some time, and Cumming had already returned with Chalmers's widow to try and bring it back to life. Who had authorized the rations for the devastated people is not clear, but the comparison with those at Calderwood's mission, who were settled within the Colony with viable crops, is scarcely reasonable.

Pottinger's wishes were put into effect by a general order dated 6th May 1847[561]. This order 154 included the following clauses:

6. The services of the following four individuals, lately or at present in the public employ, are dispensed with from the dates opposite their respective names :-

Mr. (Captain Commandant) Stretch of the Fingo Levy attached to the 1st Division, 30th April, 1847.

Mr. (Captain) Alcock, commanding the post at Commando Kraal, 30th April, 1847.

Mr. (Captain) Smith, of the Graaf-Reinet Levy, from the 15th May, 1847.

Mr. (Lieutenant) Knight of the Graaf-Reinet Levy, from the 15th May, 1847.

...

14. It appears from the returns submitted that the Fingo Levy attached to the late 1st Division at Fort Hare, consists of one Commandant, two Captains, two Subalterns, one Lieutenant and Adjutant, one Lieutenant and Quarter-master, nine sergeants, eight corporals and 206 privates.

Mr. Stretch, the Commandant, has been already removed by a preceding part of this Order (6), and the services of Adjutant McGlashan and Quartermaster Hamilton are likewise no longer required for these duties. His Excellency the Governor &c. is however, pleased to direct that the above officers and men shall be embodied into two companies,

...

Cory in his history comments that

By May the 6th, he [Pottinger] tells us, that by dint of withholding his sanction to the issue of all pay and rations, he obtained sufficient data to enter upon his task of bringing forth his famous despatch, No. 154. It is testimony to the comparatively good and quiet behaviour of the [Xhosa]s during 1847 that the Governor was permitted to devote so much time to this work.

Charles and Anna Stretch found themselves without employment, and expelled from their house. Their first hope was when Pottinger had a Court of Inquiry set up. His motives were set out in a memorandum issued on 10th May[562]:

It is needless for me to comment on the extravagance, impropriety and absurdity of a person in Mr Stretch's situation having had the power to squander the public money in this manner. ... there are certain circumstances connected with Mr Stretch's unaccountable (and as I understand unauthorized) absence just after the clothing is supposed to have been issued and at a moment when it was already his duty to be at his post at the head of his men, that have excited my strongest suspicions and lead me to hope that sufficient proof of his delinquency will yet be obtained to enable me to have legal measures instituted against him for breach of trust and defrauding his employers.

The hope expressed was not to be realised. The Court of Inquiry, consisting of three senior officers Lieut.-Col. Johnstone, Lieut.-Col. Montressor, and Major Hind, met on the 12th May at Fort Hare and found that the 223 members of Stretch's levy were all wearing their issued uniform and that the remaining 177 uniforms were accounted for and in store awaiting issue. All the requisitions from stores had been approved by superior officers. Stretch was exonerated. Pottinger was incensed:

What pretension had a man of Stretch's station and authority to have such a quantity of property belonging to Her Majesty in his possession. The affair bears fraud and absurdity on the face of it and should have been condemned by the Courts as it deserved.[563]

Not unreasonably, Stretch asked for a review of his dismissal and that he be given a chance to defend himself against the unwarranted charges. Pottinger's response was[564]:

> The idea of ordering a Court of Enquiry on a person like Stretch, amidst such gross neglect, confusion and irregularity [he meant in the army not in his own mind], would have been involving myself in useless diffi-culties and worry.

Charles and Anne Stretch were now without a home and without em-ployment. They moved to Glen Avon where Robert Hart, Ann's father, provided temporary employment in the administration of the farm.

Peculiar Malignity [1847]

The influence of Henry Calderwood was to be seen throughout the re-mainder of the war. Calderwood, as Macaulay wrote of Thomas Wentworth,

> ... felt towards those whom he had deserted that peculiar malignity which has, in all ages, been characteristic of apostates[565].

His ideals as a missionary abandoned, he blamed the Xhosa people and those who sympathised with them for his failure to convert the heathen. He was regarded by Pottinger as one who knew the ways and customs of the Xhosa, and his advice and recommendations were accepted and acted upon.

The focus of his disfavour was Sandile. While all the other Ngqika chiefs had made token surrenders of arms and cattle and negotiated peace, Sandile had refused to do so. The only other chief to hold out was Phatho of the amaGqunukwhebe, who was being harried by Henry Somerset's force, melting into the bush and leaving the army with scant reward in the form of cattle. Calderwood used the theft of 14 goats from Mfengu living in the Kat River valley as a *casus belli*. Sandile was blamed by Calderwood who refused his offer of restitution of the goats and a search for the thief. Calderwood recommended to Pottinger that Sandile be seized. Pottinger agreed and approved a secret force of 150 regular sol-diers to carry out the raid.

It was nearly another disaster. Sandile escaped and the British had to fight their way out of the area under heavy fire, bringing with them a few cattle.

This was the signal for Pottinger to declare war which he did on 27th August, in a proclamation declaring Sandile a rebel[566]. Calderwood had recommended that planting and harvesting of crops by the amaNgqika should be forbidden except to those who broke away from Sandile and accepted British rule. Pottinger's orders to Berkeley included the following[567]:

> Sandilli having refused, as shown in my proclamation, to make any reparation or in fact to listen to any terms, he and his people must be reduced to submission or expelled from the country they inhabit, their cattle taken or killed, their fields destroyed and kraals burned.

The campaign against Sandile was ruthless. By October he was ready to discuss terms. By this time Pottinger had heard that he had been appointed Governor of Madras. On October 19th John Bisset, now a captain in the army as a result of his services to Harry Smith in the 1835 war, reported that Sandile had surrendered to him.

The circumstances of the "surrender" were controversial at the time. There was strong evidence that Sandile had come to discuss terms, not to surrender, and was outraged when he found himself a prisoner[568]. All that remained for Pottinger were mopping up operations against Phatho. By the time he was relieved in order to take up his new position in Madras the war was over. The situation, however, had not been resolved.

Chapter 18. Brief Peace

My argument is that war makes rattling good history; but peace is poor reading

Thomas Hardy, Dynasts

The Governor [1847]

Sir Henry George Wakelyn Smith, 1st Baronet of Aliwal, Knight Grand Cross in the Order of the Bath, the same Harry Smith who had left the Colony smarting at Glenelg's revocation of D'Urban's frontier policy, returned triumphantly to the Cape on 1st December 1847 to replace Pottinger as Governor. His service in India had culminated in a famous victory at the Battle of Aliwal, leading to a baronetcy, the plaudits of both the House of Commons and the House of Lords, fulsome praise by the Duke of Wellington, his GCB, the Freedom of the Cities of London and of Glasgow, and the degree of Doctor of Laws (*honoris causa*) from the University of Cambridge. He was still, however, the same excitable, hotheaded, foul-mouthed, vainglorious character that he had always been.

He set out to stamp his authority on the region.

Initially most of the colonists on the frontier regarded him as a saviour. The reputation that he had acquired during his previous service at the Cape coupled with his later deeds in other parts of the Empire seemed to fit him uniquely for the task of pacifying the Xhosa and advancing the interests of the colonists. The missionaries saw the opportunity of being able to return to their missions under his protection. No-one was more convinced of his fitness for the position than Smith himself. He believed that he had a unique insight into the minds and customs of the Xhosa and proceeded to demonstrate it by projecting himself as the *nkosi nkulu*, dominating and insulting their kings and chiefs.

Ten days after his arrival, in Cape Town, he boarded *Rosamond* and sailed for Port Elizabeth, arriving on 14th December. He immediately provided a foretaste of his intentions. At his hotel he was acknowledging the cheers of the welcoming crowd when he saw his old adversary Maqoma among them and began the process of thoroughly alienating the Xhosa. Summoning Maqoma[569] he berated and insulted him and finally forced him to kneel and place his head on the ground. He then placed his foot on Maqoma's neck and told him that this was the way that he treated the enemies of the Queen. It was spiteful, humiliating, and counterproductive.

Next he proceeded to the frontier and, on 17th Dec 1847 in Graham's Town, issued a proclamation, abrogating all treaties with the Ngqika, Ndlambe, Gqunukwhebe, and Thembu, annexing the former ceded territory in the name of the British Crown and defining the new boundary of the Colony on the east as the Keiskamma River, and to the north as the line of the Tyumie River to its source, then along the crest of the Katberg and from there to the Orange River. That day he also met and addressed the Ngqika chiefs and people while the citizens of Graham's Town and the military forces looked on.

First he introduced some symbolism. He produced what he described as a stick of peace. In his despatch to Earl Grey dated 23rd Dec[570] he stated that it was customary to use a stick called *umsila* as a sign of the authenticity of a message. In fact the word "*umsila*" means "tail." The tail of a leopard or elephant – never a stick – was, in pre-colonial times given as a token of authority to a messenger in the same way as a European king might have used a ring or a seal as a token[571]. By extension the name *imisila* became applied to the messengers themselves. Smith however now turned his stick into a symbol which he required the chiefs to touch in order to pledge their commitment to peace. This idea of a "stick of peace" was Smith's own, an example of the mumbo-jumbo that he considered appropriate in his interactions with the Xhosa. In his despatch to Earl Grey, describing the occasion, he continues:

> I then in a very impressive manner read and explained the proclamations, with various comments, threats, and promises, as the tenor of the documents turned; which being concluded, each Chief came forward and kissed my foot; a custom of their own in doing homage; exclaiming "Inkosi Inkulu" (great chief).

As an act of hubris this takes some beating. Nowhere else except in Smith's despatch do we find this "custom of their own." Harriet Ward described the ceremony approvingly

> The Chiefs, having declared their perfect understanding of everything that had been said, were then told to step forward separately, each being required to place his hand upon "the staff of peace" or upon that of war, should he prefer it, and to kiss his foot, in token of absolute submission, and deep humility for their past aggressions upon the Colony, and hostility to the British Government.

> ... their chiefs, one after another, approached the Governor, who sat proudly on horseback, and as, with their hand on the staff of peace, they bent their heads in lowly submission, and kissed the foot of him whom they had agreed to acknowledge as their future great chief.

Smith believed that he understood the Xhosa and that this performance was calculated to impress them. The later consequences demonstrated his folly.

The same despatch from Smith to Earl Grey has a number of enclosures. The first proclaims the new territory of British Kaffraria. Those Xhosa living between the Keiskamma River and the Kei and up into the Amatola mountains now, like it or not, found themselves subjects of the Queen. While the ceded territory between the Fish and Keiskamma was incorporated into the colony, British Kaffraria was created as an administratively separate entity from the Colony, and the Governor acquired an alter ego as High Commissioner. He proclaimed King William's Town as the capital of the new territory. Day to day administration was to be in the hands of a Chief Commissioner, Colonel George Mackinnon, who was also the military commander. He was to be supported by Charles Brownlee, son of the missionary John Brownlee, who replaced Calderwood as Assistant Commissioner to the amaNgqika, and Captain John Maclean, from Fort Peddie, who served the same function for the ama-Ndlambe. The smaller houses, the amaGqunukwhebe, amaMbale and others, were lumped in these two groupings. In addition, across the Kei, Henry Fynn was appointed to represent British interests at the Great Place of Sarhili, the successor of Hintsa. A further proclamation enabled the founding of new villages in British Kaffraria in which land would be available for long serving soldiers who had been honourably discharged. They would also provide a military reserve in case of need.

Next he had a message sent out summoning all the kings and chiefs of the frontier Xhosa to a great meeting. This was held in the new capital of British Kaffraria, King William's Town, and was attended by all the major Xhosa leaders. The list of those attending[572] included Sandile, king of the amaNgqika, Mtirara son of Ngubencuka and king of the abaThembu, with Tyopo of the amaGcina, Siyolo of the amaNdlambe, with his brother Siwane and uncle Mhala, Stokwe of the amaMbalu with his brother Sonto, Phatho of the amaGqunukwhebe with brother Kobe, Dyani Tshatshu of the amaNtinde, Bhothomane of the imiDange and his cousin Tola, and the minor Rharhabe descendant Toyise. Maqoma was not present. He was still in detention in Port Elizabeth.

The assembled chiefs and their followers gathered on one side. Smith stood in front of lines of troops in full uniform. With his usual emotionalism, he addressed the assembly informing them of the terms of the proclamation. He made it clear that the proclamation meant that Sarhili was no longer to be regarded as king of the amaXhosa. He, Harry Smith, was now the only authority. The Ceded Territory was now lost to the amaXhosa. They would be confined to the region beyond the Keiskamma, each clan in a prescribed area. As far as the Kei they would be in the territory of British Kaffraria. The Gcaleka beyond the Kei remained independent but were required to provide free access to the mission stations. Sandile remonstrated; the remaining chiefs saw no value in arguing with Smith in full flow. In a histrionic climax Smith had a wagon, previously charged with explosives, blown up to provide a spectacle that he believed would terrorize his audience. The pastoral existence of the amaXhosa, dependent on extensive lands, was now in irreversible decline.

After the War   [1845 – 1850]

While the Xhosa chiefs lamented over their lost territory and watched their authority dwindle, the British community on the frontier prospered. No longer were they living from hand to mouth as they struggled to survive on a dangerous frontier. The lands vacated by the Boer trekkers had provided many opportunity for profitable investment and now there were many opportunities in the former ceded territory. The wool trade had brought many to prosperity. The towns and villages were settled communities rather than collections of haphazard shelters. Graham's Town had grown to a bustling centre of business.

When the British immigrants had arrived the only colonial settlements of any consequence were Graaff Reinet, Graham's Town, and Uitenhage. Now municipal government was well established. Joseph Walker, George Wood, and James Thackwray, William's youngest son, were elected as municipal commissioners. Joseph's shop was now a landmark. Robert Godlonton, not to be outdone by the Cape Town businessmen, published an Eastern Province Directory and Almanac in which Joseph was proudly able to advertise his general store as having been established for twenty years, using every fancy font in Godlonton's tray to do so.

Stretch's Quest for Justice   [1847 – 1854]

With the arrival of Harry Smith, Charles Lennox Stretch hoped for some compensation for his dismissal:

> Memorialist humbly appeals to your Excellency's known justice, that he may be informed of any accusation, or suspicion of criminality, or the least possible dereliction of duty, has been alleged against him during the period he held office - and if any such thing exist as a reason why memorialist be excluded from office - that Memorialist be allowed the means of the most scrutinizing investigation, in order to clear himself ...[573]

Stretch had little reason to expect Smith to be sympathetic to him and, indeed, received a reply from Richard Southey, now a colonial aide, stating that the matter was a dispute with Maitland and complaints should be addressed to him. This seems to have been a regular tactic of the period. Holders of office took no responsibility for the actions of their predecessors in the same office, making the pursuit of a grievance an impossible task. Surprisingly, however, Southey's letter went on to refer favourably to Stretch's performance during Smith's previous service in the colony

... he [Smith] not only was perfectly satisfied with your services, but placed that confidence in you which he is not aware was ever abused.

Stretch was not prepared to give up his case. Within a week he had written a long description of events for the Secretary of State and sent it to Montagu, the Colonial Secretary, for onward transmission.

Stretch had three major grievances, his mode of dismissal by Maitland as Ngqika Agent, the accusation of dishonesty that arose when Pottinger removed him from his military position, and the loss of what he considered his property at Block Drift.

Block Drift had become his home when, in the eighteen thirties, Stockenstrom, then Lieutenant-Governor, had agreed that Fort Cox was not central enough for the residence of the Ngqika Agent[574]. It was located on the Keiskamma River, close to Sandile's Great Place but at the time Sandile was not of age and Maqoma was regent in his place. Stockenstrom arranged a meeting with Maqoma and Tyali and they settled on Block Drift on the Tyumie River, about 20 km to the west, as a suitable site.

Stretch had already invested a significant amount in the Fort Cox residence which was lost to him. He also had to buy a cottage at Block Drift as temporary accommodation. He was unwilling to invest further in a more adequate house without some security of tenure so he consulted with Maqoma and Tyali who agreed that "Block Drift should be mine [Stretch's] forever."[575] This was later ratified by Sandile when he came of age, with the concurrence of his councillors. Stretch built a house on the land at his own expense. The Lovedale Mission was adjacent to his land. He admired the work of the missionaries in setting up a school there[576] and he presented the mission with a parcel of land and, at his own expense, had a watercourse constructed to bring a water supply to the school. At the beginning of the 1846 war the house was commandeered by the army, ruined, and Stretch was not allowed to claim it after the war.

His efforts to obtain recompense for his losses gained little sympathy from Pottinger. His strenuous appeals to Montagu did have some effect. He began to garner support from public opinion. The *Herald* in Port Elizabeth on 6th February 1847 thundered that Stretch deserved compensation. A two man commission of enquiry into his title to Block Drift was set up. He was not, however, satisfied when Henry Calderwood was appointed as one of the commissioners. He wrote to Montagu objecting to Calderwood's nomination[577]:

> The selection of the latter individual for this duty compels me most re-
> pectfully to observe I have been painfully called on to refute, and repu-
> diate as libellous, a letter of the Rev. H. Calderwood ... on the subject
> of the Native Levies ...

Public sympathy was expressed in the press (but not in the *Graham's Town Journal*). The *Cape Frontier Times* of 4th July 1848 wrote:

> We need scarcely add that if Mr Calderwood values public opinion he
> will decline to act as a member of this board ... His appointment to
> such office shows an evident want of just, proper, and generous feel-
> ing. Who recommended His Excellency to appoint Mr Calderwood to de-
> cide a case in which Mr Stretch's interest was concerned? Has the
> bungling frontier policy pursued prior to the [Xhosa] war of 1846, os-
> tensibly by Sir P. Maitland, any connection with the scandalous manner
> of Mr Stretch's dismissal from office?

The final outcome of the Block Drift affair was that Stretch's right to the house and a small fraction of the land was recognized and he was granted some compensation.

The reply to his submission to Earl Grey, seven months after it had been sent, was not encouraging. Montagu wrote to inform him that the Secretary of State saw no reason for interference. The question of re-employment or a pension was a matter for the Governor. Stretch's response was, on those grounds, to make an immediate application to Smith for a job or a pension. The curt reply from Montagu on 24th May 1849 was that Smith had no position available and Stretch's position as Ngqika Agent – held for more than ten years – was temporary and there would be no pension.

His last effort, a few days later, was an attempt to get an impartial inquiry into his dismissal. He wrote an letter to Earl Grey that was an impassioned condemnation of the general acceptance of the patronage and privilege that pervaded the Colonial Service at the time[578]

> ... Sir H. Pottinger may be a most fortunate and most powerful man,
> perhaps one of great ability – he may believe himself vested with cer-
> tain prerogatives, which place him beyond the reach of ordinary means
> of redress; he may hope to be shielded by that species of patronage
> which have in earlier times too often insured impunity to such tyrannic-
> al outrages, but I believe I may presume to claim the right to maintain,
> that although I may have made mistakes, I have principles of truth,
> justice and morality quite equal to his. I am by birth and conduct quite
> as much the gentleman as he is – but above all, I am a British subject
> like himself, and as such as much entitled to your Lordship's protec-
> tion, not in the shape of office, pecuniary compensation, or other favor,
> but by the mere urgent repetition of my request for the investigation

already solicited ... whilst I hereby pledge myself to prove the said in-
sinuations and accusations to be false and slanderous.

This too was refused.

For the time being he had shot his bolt. Some closure was only
achieved a number of years later when, in 1854, he was elected to the
newly established House of Assembly. As a result of a petition by Stretch,
a Select Committee of the Parliament was set up consisting of four members of the Legislative Council, chaired by Andries Stockenstrom. It put
aside the land claim, pending additional information, but found in
Stretch's favour on all other points. It found that his position as Ngqika
Agent had been a permanent one, found that he had performed his duties
conscientiously, quoting favorable testimonials from D'Urban, Smith,
Stockenstrom, and Napier, and most importantly, referring to the accusations of fraud

> ... there is not the slightest ground for the said charge of fraud, which
> appears to them groundless and caluminous, and that there has noth-
> ing transpired throughout the investigation injurious to the character
> and conduct of the Petitioner, either as a man of honour, or as a public
> officer[579].

Scandal and Outrage   [1850]

After the end of the War of the Axe, as soon as Smith's actions as Governor had made it possible, the missionaries had began to re-occupy their
missions. Some were abandoned, some new ones were set up. For John
Cumming there was a new authority.

The fractious Presbyterian Church now underwent another reorganization. Several denominations had broken from the established Scottish
Church in 1733. Now two of these, the United Secession and the Relief
churches, united to form the United Presbyterian Church. The activities
of the Glasgow Missionary Society in the Cape were handed over in 1847
to a new Mission Board of this Church. Initially the only two ministers
under the control of the new Board were John Cumming and Robert
Niven. The missions were Tyumie and Iqibira. Since Campbell's death
the small outposts of Kirkwood and Bonkolo had been served by visits
from the main missions.

As a result of the death of William Chalmers, John Cumming was assigned to take charge of the Tyumie mission. Chalmers's widow had lived
for many years at Tyumie and preferred to remain there with her children
– an adult daughter Janet and younger sons William Jr. and John. She
was assigned some land on the mission property and a house built for her.
Robert Niven, now back in the Colony, was assigned to a new mission,

Uniondale, on the upper Keiskamma River above the Boma Pass. From Scotland a new young missionary, George Brown, arrived and was placed in charge of Iqibira.

John Cumming at first welcomed Brown, who was pleased that a new incumbent could serve the Iqibira community that had been his responsibility before the war. He and Catherine entertained him in their home and John was ready with advice. After some time, however, disquieting rumours reached him about Brown's conduct. Brown was a young and virile man and, it appeared, not as resistant to sexual temptation as Cumming had been during his isolation at Kirkwood. Stories of his relationships with women of his congregation shocked the missionary community and appalled Cumming[580]. In addition Cumming became concerned at Brown's influence on his own congregation.

Matters began to come to a head towards the end of 1849. Cumming recorded[581], in the minute handwriting that he used when his emotions were deeply engaged, the contents of a letter he had written:

Rev. G. Brown   Chumie 9 Nov. 1849

Sir

I regret that I should ever have cause to express an unfavourable opinion of you. I deem it right to acquaint you however that on account of what has already taken place after your reception into the confidence of my family I have written to the Secretary of Mr Nupen [of the Glasgow Missionary Society] and declared that my confidence in you is shaken to the very foundation. I trust that you will also see the propriety of abstaining from interfering in any work of whatever kind that is considered as placed under my superintendance in connection with the Chumie station.

Yours

John F. Cumming

Quite apart from any sexual misconduct on Brown's part it seems there was a disagreement between Cumming and Brown over the conduct of their missions. It is not clear precisely what this was. A few days later, however, a Presbytery meeting was held to discuss these disagreements. Writing in the third person Cumming records parts of it:

20 Nov - Mr Niven arrives - Presbytery meets at 4 o'clock p.m. ... Mr Brown proposes 3 questions to be answered by Mr Cumming - agreed that the answers be given at meeting on 3 Dec.

Niven was anxious to settle the matter

31 Nov - Met in church Mr Niven, Cumming and Brown - Mr N. proposes it's taken [I.e. accepted that the] case being [i.e. should be] settled by mutual explanations. Mr C. agreed but Mr Brown would not.

...

> 4 Dec – Morning Presbytery meeting of complaints against Mr Brown to
> be put to Presbytery – complaint respecting Mr C put and Mr B required
> to retract ..

The affair simmered on.

> 17 March 1850 – Mr Brown went in morning and held worship with the
> disaffected members at the Gwalana without asking my permission.

When the allegations against Brown reached Glasgow the directors of the Missionary Board were bound to take action. It had been their intention that a commisioner, the Rev. Henry Renton, should be appointed to carry out an inspection of their missionary activities in South Africa, and he was charged with investigating the affair.

Back at Tyumie matters were reaching a climax. Brown had now been pressing his attentions on Janet Chalmers. Janet was 21 years old and had lived on the mission all her life. Her widowed mother became aware that she was pregnant. The news added a new breath of scandal, which could only be dispelled by marriage. A scandalised Cumming wrote;

> Aug 6 [1850] – Mr Brown married to Miss J. Chalmers who is leaving for
> Igqibigha after the ceremony. She has shamed herself in H[eaven].

By November Renton had arrived and was lodged with Mrs Chalmers at Tyumie. Cumming, with a mixture of shock and *schadenfreude* recorded:

> Nov 30 [1850] – Received note from Mr Renton intimating that he had
> received a note from Mr Brown saying his wife (Mrs B) had been prema-
> turely delivered of a male child this morning. Married 6 Aug 1850!! Tiyo
> [Soga][582] who had previously told me of the matter ... smote upon his
> thigh exclaiming I cannot contain myself for joy. He meant joy at the
> deliverance which the cause of truth and righteousness had received ...

The investigation of Brown's conduct was instituted. Over the next weeks meetings were set where Renton could begin his inquiry.

The Military Villages   [1847 – 1850]

Smith's proclamation enabling the establishment of military villages was put into effect in May 1848. Four such villages were created on the western side of the Tyumie. They were named Auckland, Woburn, Ely and Juanasburg. Juanasburg was named for Smith's wife and Ely for his birthplace. They were occupied by discharged soldiers, supposedly of good character. Each had a commander. Their location was a provocation to the Xhosa people who had previously regarded the area as home.

The provocation was increased by the behaviour of some of the residents of Woburn. When Maqoma's brother, Tyhali, had died he had been buried according to custom near the site of Woburn. The burial had included grave goods in the form of his weapons and regalia. The site of the grave was now outside the area occupied by his people, a cause in itself for resentment. For some of the rougher veterans at Woburn the grave was something to be looted. They dug up the relics in the grave and scattered the contents. This sacrilege was witnessed by Tebe, the great widow of Tyhali, who was regent until her son came of age.

Tebe visited the Tyumie mission and vented her frustration on the missionaries. Renton was the senior man there at the time and afterwards reported her comments on the behaviour of the veterans as well as generally on British policy towards the Xhosa. She expressed the frustration of all the chiefs with Smith's actions when she said[583]:

> You [the British Government] have taken away all my power; you take away the power of the chiefs; and then you find fault with us for not keeping the people in order.

The general resentment by the Xhosa was reaching crisis level.

Chapter 19. Massacre, Siege, and Ambush

I and the public know
What all schoolchildren learn,
Those to whom evil is done
Do evil in return

W. H. Auden, Another Time

The Wizard Mlanjeni   [1850]

In hard times prophets and soothsayers prosper. Relationships between the western amaXhosa and the British had reached their nadir. The Xhosa people longed for promises of better times and their chiefs could not provide them. The rise of Mlanjeni, as a prophet in the mould of Nxele, coincided with Harry Smith's assumption of direct British rule over the amaXhosa[584].

Mlanjeni was one of Mqhayi's people. Although he was youthful, slight, and emaciated, the Xhosa found him charismatic and compelling. He first came to their attention in early 1850 as a diviner, performing his own rituals for the exorcism of witches. His method was very different from the smelling-out ceremonies of the time. Those who were suspected of witchcraft found that, through autosuggestion, they could not pass between his pair of witch's poles until they had been cured; there was no torture and execution. He taught that witchcraft was an affliction that could be cured, and encouraged the people to discard all the tools of the practice.

It was, however, his prophecies that had the greatest impact. His reputation soon spread to Pondoland and even to parts of Zululand. He could eradicate witchcraft, and since sickness and death were the result of witchcraft he had the secret of immortality.

The Assistant Commissioner for the Ndlambe, John Maclean, determined to stamp out the practice of witchcraft, first summoned Mlanjeni's chief Mqhayi to explain what was going on. Although Mqhayi defended Mlanjeni, Maclean demanded that he move to Mqhayi's Great Place where his activities could be monitored. Mlanjeni responded by going into hiding. From that time, the middle of 1850, reports began to reach the colony of his activities. He told the Xhosa to kill all dun-coloured cattle to prepare themselves for war. Like Nxele thirty years earlier, he made promises about the invulnerability of warriors if they followed his commands. He issued medicines that would turn the white man's bullets to water and make the Xhosa armies invulnerable. Alarming reports began to filter back to the Colony about Xhosa preparations for war.

Smith was at first reluctant to give any weight to Mlanjeni. He failed to recognize the ominous signs of trouble to come. Still less did he recognize that it was his own policies that were a prime cause of the unrest. Eventually even Mackinnon was convinced that vigorous measures were necessary and wrote to Smith telling him so. Smith reluctantly decided to come to the frontier and deal with the situation. On arrival he summoned Sandile to meet him on 26th October 1850. Sandile, deeply mistrustful after his experiences at the end of the previous war, made excuses and failed to attend. Smith was furious. On 30th October he issued a proclamation:

> ... I hereby depose the said Sandilli from his rank as chief, and that I appoint Charles Brownlee Esq., Commissioner for the Gaika tribes, to assume direct control of Sandilli's tribe, whose loyalty I have no reason to doubt, under the instructions of the Chief Commissioner of British Kaffraria [Mackinnon][585].

This was almost the last straw for the Ngqika people. It resulted in Sandile's instructions to his people to begin killing light coloured cattle according to the instructions of Mlanjeni. Smith, well-satisfied with himself, returned to Cape Town.

Disillusion in the Kat River Settlement   [1847 – 1850]

It was not only the Xhosa who were dissatisfied and preparing for trouble. The people of the Kat River Settlement had been deeply scarred by the events of the previous few years.

The settlement had grown substantially since its establishment by Andries Stockenstrom thirty years earlier. It consisted of a number of groupings. These included the missions Philipton and Balfour and other villages. Many of the residents had been there for many years with full rights to their homes. Others were squatters, some of long standing and others recent arrivals. The two most significant groups of incomers were settled at Blinkwater, where Henry Calderwood had first had his mission. The areas where they lived were controlled by local chieftains Andries Botha and Hermanus Matroos[586].

The white colonists at this time would still have referred to the inhabitants of the settlement as "Hottentots". Up to this point we have used "Khoikhoi" as a neutral synonym for this unacceptable term. This becomes less and less appropriate as our narrative progresses and the heterogeneity of the people lumped under this label increases. "Khoikhoi" can only reasonably be applied to the ethnic descendants of the original indigenous inhabitants of the Western Cape region. The assimilation of the Cape Khoikhoi into the much larger "coloured" population was by now far advanced. The assignment of racial labels by the modern democratic South African Government is as all-pervasive as it was in the days of apartheid, although the purpose of the labelling is different. Today it is still the practice of people in South Africa to distinguish those who call themselves "coloured" from those who call themselves "white", although the cultural, linguistic, and genetic pool from which these groups are descended is a continuum. A more appropriate label for the people of the Kat River Settlement at this time would be "coloured" and that is what we shall call them collectively.

Andries Botha was a Gonaqua, a grouping that was largely of mixed Khoikhoi and Xhosa descent, although his name suggests some Dutch ancestry. Ethnically the Gonaqua were similar to the Gqunukwhebe but they would not have recognized any connection: the Gonaqua were culturally closer to the white colonists and the Gqunukwhebe were Xhosa. Hermanus Matroos was the son of an escaped slave and a Xhosa woman. Both had served the British for many years. Matroos had been an interpreter in 1819 after the Battle of Graham's Town, when he replaced Nxele's spy Ngquka. Later he had interpreted for Harry Smith during the 1835 war. Botha had led his adherents with distinction in the 1835 and 1846 wars. He had been rewarded with his property in the Kat River Settlement and an appointment as Field Cornet.

The men of the Kat River Settlement had borne the brunt of the fighting in the 1846 war. Their reward had been Pottinger's demands for yet more men when 90% of them were already in the field. Their crops had suffered. The women and children had had a hard time while the men were away. They resented the different way in which they had been treated from the volunteers of the English and Dutch communities. Their genuine grievances included one that throws a clear light on the fiction that the reason for confiscating Xhosa cattle was to retrieve what had been stolen.

> The men returned very much dissatisfied with the treatment they had received in the performance of this service, inasmuch as they were promised that all the cattle they would take from the [Xhosa]s should be given them; and on complaining that they were naked and without blankets, they were promised that these also would be provided for them. But the cattle which the people captured on this expedition were given to the boers.
>
> ...

On the cattle being divided, however, the seventy Kat River men, instead of sharing equally with the levies and the soldiers, only got a hundred head of cattle, while many thousand had been captured.[587]

The winter of 1850 was extreme. The land suffered the twin inflictions of bitter cold and harsh drought. When men are desperate for food they will look to any source to find it. Cattle theft increased markedly. The white farmers in the neighbourhood blamed the squatters of the Kat River Settlement and they might well have been right. The complaints reached the Governor and through Montagu, the Colonial Secretary, his instructions to remove the squatters were sent to the local magistrate, Holden Bowker.

Bowker leapt at the opportunity. With a detachment of the newly formed "[Xhosa] Police", a force of Xhosa recruited since the war, he went through the settlement evicting those he suspected of being squatters and destroying their homes. The new police force consisted of Xhosa from the annexed region who had been recruited. It was not long since they had faced the coloured people of the Kat River Settlement in battle. They relished the opportunity to be on the dominant side. Men, women and children were turned out into the freezing weather on Bowker's say-so, without any appeal except by travelling 30 km to Fort Hare. Their homes were burned and their possessions destroyed.

Andries Stockenstrom and the Reads tried to intercede on their behalf but got no sympathy from Harry Smith or anyone else in authority until Charles Brownlee, the Assistant-Commissioner to the Ngqika, became aware of the events and was sufficiently disturbed to set up an enquiry. Bowker was forced to resign his post and Botha was reinstated but the damage was done. Dissatisfaction among the community of Kat River had now been replaced by hostility; a mood of open rebellion prevailed.

Portents of War   [Dec 1850]

The farmers of Somerset had every reason to fear what was in store. Recurrent rumours of Mlanjeni's activities kept filtering through from Xhosa sources. The widespread slaughtering of cattle was disturbing. Their confidence in the British authority had been severely shaken over the past few years. Their experiences during the War of the Axe, in which all had suffered severe losses, and many had lost family or friends, weighed on their minds. When Xhosa servants began deserting the farms at the call of Mlanjeni, often before they had received their pay, the farmers began to feel the pressure. Many abandoned their farms and drove their stock to safer regions. On 14th December 1850 a large group of them met at the farm of L. Tregardt[588]. They elected Robert Hart as

Chairman and, after a long meeting, crafted a resolution for the chairman to transmit to the Governor[589]. After summarizing their concerns it expressed

> ... their general determination of for ever abandoning their farms and thereby desolating the frontier.

It was signed by most of the leading farmers of the district including Robert Hart Jr representing his father's farm Glen Avon. As chairman, Robert Hart Sr wrote a covering letter and sent the resolution to Smith. They duly received a somewhat anodyne reply, by which time the situation had been overtaken by events.

Smith returned to the frontier in early December. First he tried to reassure the colonists that the military were well prepared. Next, at King William's Town, he called a meeting of the Ndlambe and Gqunukwhebe chiefs, Mhala and Phatho, to ensure their support. Neither had any wish to become involved in an Ngqika quarrel with the Colony and both promised neutrality. Phatho also undertook to protect the road between the port of East London and King William's Town. Mackinnon was sent with a force of almost 600 to Fort Cox. Somerset took a further 460 to defend Fort Hare. A new arrival in the Colony, Lieut.-Col. William Eyre, was put in command of a column of nearly 400 and sent to Kabousie Nek in order to guard possible escape routes for Sandile to the east. Having made his dispositions, Smith then prepared, as he thought, to bring the Ngqika firmly back under control. He instructed Brownlee to call a great meeting of all the Ngqika chiefs to be held at Fort Cox on December 19th. It was to be another of his showpieces. The missionaries in the region were also summoned to this "meeting of peace."

The Presbyterian missionaries from the neighbouring stations gathered at Tyumie the previous day[590]. The Church Commisioner, Henry Renton, Robert Niven from Uniondale, and Ritchie Thomson[591] from the Kat River Settlement all spent the night at Tyumie with John Cumming. On the 19th, shortly after sunrise before 6 o'clock, the four missionaries mounted their horses and set off for Fort Cox, 24 km to the south-east. The summer day, which had started mild and cloudy grew in oppressiveness as the sun rose higher. By midday it was blazing down with full force, baking through the sober clothing suitable for a meeting with the Governor.

Fort Cox, Brownlee's residence, the mission station Burnshill, and Sandile's Great Place were located close to each other on the Keiskamma River at the position of modern day Burnshill. The sight that met the eyes of the missionaries as they approached was striking:

... the Fort perched upon a rock at the termination of a kind of peninsula ... the scene was bustling with the tents of the troops recently arrived ... men women & young & old coming ... All indicating that they
were going to the meeting of peace.

They were welcomed by Brownlee who told them that half of his
house was occupied by the Governor and his staff. He went to inform
Smith that the missionaries had arrived and they were invited to meet
him. The resulting conversation was more than disappointing and John
Cumming was not impressed:

His rude manner left no favourable impression upon our minds. There
is no doubt of his being a brave and skilful soldier but if any expect to
see the courtesy of a gentleman he would be sorely disappointed – and
far less the dignity and intelligence of a statesman. His remarks for he
had no conversation are an amusing jumble of [illegible word – possibly depravity], war, politics, philosophy, coarse jests, and abuse of all
it included.

Shortly after noon the Xhosa assembled. Cumming records

... the Chiefs in soldiers dress came up on horseback followed by a
multitude of [Xhosa]s carrying sticks over their shoulders. [They] arranged themselves in front of the veranda of Mr Brownlee's house.

Maqoma and Xhoxho were present with their councillors. Of course,
Sandile and Anta were not there. With a price on their heads, and with
Smith having deposed Sandile, it was unlikely that they would have been.
Nevertheless, Smith made much of their absence. The printed record of
Smith's speech[592] suggests a harsh but sober address. The reports of witnesses do not agree. Of the clergymen present, Renton's impression was
that at first this was the case but his later remarks were insulting and ill-
judged. Cumming noted that "... Sir Harry addressed them in a bombastic style." Brown was more approving.

The Governor addressed the assembly saying his intention was not
war but the punishment of Sandile and Anta. He promised that he would
not send soldiers in pursuit of them. If it were so that he did not want to
make war and would not pursue Sandile, asked one of the chiefs, then
what were all the soldiers for? In his address Smith made much of his
"stick of peace." Renton described this as[593]

... what might have passed for a long broomstick, seven or eight feet in
height perhaps, with a brass round handle of a door stuck at the top of
it, which the Governor held during his interview with the [Xhosa]s, and
which he called the stick of peace, and flourished, and he required all
those of the chiefs that were pacific to touch the stick, and those who
would not do so he regarded were not in favour of peace.

Smith, in his official report maintained that his stick was according to
custom[594].

> I shall continue to govern you by the stick (the baton of authority called in [Xhosa] 'Umsila')

Renton's opinion was that

> I think such exhibitions do harm and not good before a grave, subtle, and discriminating race like the Gaika [Xhosa]s

Smith's speech then descended into vituperation. He insulted Maqoma, who was present, accusing him of drunkenness and lying, and expressing a desire to see him expelled from the Colony. Maqoma had little reason to respect Smith from his previous contacts with him and the comments found little favour with the audience. At the end of the speech Cumming records that the Governor

> ... called to choose a chief instead of Sandilla who was now thrown away. At an after meeting Sutu was named by the [Xhosa] chiefs and offered for Sir Harry.

George Brown, entirely in sympathy with Smith, noted[595]

> He [Smith] proposed that the assembled chiefs should elect one in the place of Sandilli who, by his obstinate refusal to make his appearance when called, and taking to his hiding place, had confirmed the worst suspicions entertained regarding him. Sutu, the mother of Sandilli, was elected by the chiefs according to this proposal, and one half of her councillors was nominated by the chiefs, and the other half by the Governor.

Smith's own account stated:

> After the meeting the chiefs retired, according to my desire, for the purpose of consulting and reporting to me their feeling as to the person whom it was expedient to appoint as Regent of the Amambombos. They returned in about an hour, expressing their hope that Sutu, the great widow of Gaika, might, for the present fill that station which she had done with so much discretion on a former occasion.[596]

Smith's proclamation seven weeks earlier, deposing Sandile, has been interpreted as replacing him by Brownlee as Chief[597], with the insult that that implied. This does not appear to have been Smith's intention. The wording of the proclamation is that Brownlee was "to assume direct control of Sandilli's tribe". The mechanism that Smith envisaged seems to be that a regent would be appointed who would be directly responsible to Brownlee. Brownlee in his Residency at Fort Cox and Suthu at the Great Place lived within two kilometres of each other allowing close oversight. Smith seems to have overlooked the fact that Suthu was Sandile's mother and supported him strongly. Whatever exact relationship was intended is irrelevant, as the whole matter was shortly afterwards overtaken by events.

After the great meeting Smith again met with the missionaries. What he told them shows just how out of touch he was with the real feelings of the Xhosa[598]

> He said "Gentlemen, you are no doubt aware that there is a scare in the Colony that the [Xhosa]s are about to break out. I do not believe it. I therefore request that you remain at your stations, for if you leave that will confirm the truth of the rumour. But rest assured that if I hear of danger I will cause you all to be duly warned" In deference to this request I [Cumming] gave up my purpose of removing the school people.

The consequences of the meeting at Fort Cox were that the amaNgqika departed to prepare for war.

Folly   [Dec 1850]

Delighted with his own performance at Fort Cox, Smith now decided that what was needed to ram his message home was a demonstration of British military might. Sandile and Anta were believed to be hiding in the mountains near Niven's mission, Uniondale. This overlooked the large oxbow on the Keiskamma River some 18 km north-east of Fort Cox, where present day Keiskammahoek is located.

The display of strength took place on Christmas Eve 1850. At the Fort Cox meeting Smith, in response to an indignant question, had denied any intention of sending soldiers to capture Sandile and Anta: the meeting had been one of peace, he said. Nevertheless, most of the army had the impression that this was an expedition against the fugitive chiefs. Smith's orders reinforced this. A large force was to proceed from Fort Cox to Uniondale under the command of Mackinnon, approaching from the west. It was to be an exhibition of the strength of the British army. At the same time Colonel Eyre was to take a smaller force round to the east, ready to mop up Xhosa warriors escaping from the British, with the hope that they would include Sandile and Anta.

In the small hours of the morning of Christmas eve, the column set out for Uniondale. Five hundred strong, they were led by a squad of the newly formed Xhosa Police. These had been recruited from the defeated Ngqika after the previous war, and their loyalty was to prove fragile. They were followed by Mackinnon, the commander, accompanied by Jack Bisset, in command of a detachment of CMR[599] coloured troops. The bulk of the force, in the form of detachments of the 6th and 73rd Regiments of Foot and the Rifle brigade, followed next. At the rear came the support forces and baggage train, the latter formed by pack horses rather than wagons on account of the nature of the country and the necessity for rapid movement. As they left, they passed Brownlee's Residency and the

Burnshill mission. Close by was Sandile's Great Place, occupied by his mother Suthu. Ngqika's grave was on the hillside. The column marched north-eastward, following the route along the broad Keiskamma valley[600].

Only the CMR had experience of fighting in these conditions. The British troops were newly arrived, magnificently trained for a pitched battle, unbeatable when lined up in a double rank firing volley after volley to well-drilled command. The British commanders, however, had learned nothing from the experience of the previous war, fought only three years earlier. The vulnerability of a long strung out column, with no means of communication, and the troops left to make their own decisions, had not yet been absorbed into their military paradigm. Only Bisset, with his long experience, tried to persuade Mackinnon of the danger. He failed to do so. Mackinnon ordered that guns should not be loaded as no trouble was expected.

The river followed a winding course, carved out by æons of erosion. Several times it had to be forded. They made good time and by breakfast had travelled about thirteen or fourteen kilometres. After eating, it was not long before they reached the foot of the Boma Pass, leading up into the Amatolas to Uniondale. The pass was on the south-east face of the mountain, a slowly rising path with the river down a steep slope on the right and the mountain face rising sharply on the left. There was dense bush on either side. The track provided a steady climb to the summit and then continued for a short distance on the level to Uniondale. For almost 2 km it was only possible to progress in single file. The leading units emerged from the top before the rear guard had entered the pass. The narrow single file meant that no messengers could ride to or from Mackinnon. The only means of communication was by imprecise bugle call.

When the CMR were clear of the top of the pass, the attack fell upon the extended British forces. Xhosa warriors, hidden in the bush, attacked along the whole extended line. With no effective communication, confusion reigned. At first Mackinnon refused to believe in the reality of the attack. Bisset and his orderly, showing great courage, fought their way back into the pass where Bisset was seriously wounded. Ultimately the troops, severely mauled after suffering the loss of twelve killed and many wounded, fought their way out of the pass at the top.

Robert Niven had returned to his family after the great meeting at Fort Cox. He too had been reassured by Smith and, not expecting trouble, was preparing for Christmas with his family. Instead he was faced with the arrival of a large body of defeated troops. On Mackinnon's advice he decided to take his family to safety at Tyumie the following morning and then return to Uniondale.

At 5 a.m. on Christmas Day Mackinnon's demoralised column set off to make their way to Fort White, taking the eastern track down to a wagon road that led to their destination. Robert and Rebecca Niven, their four children, Rebecca's niece, a mission carpenter named Ball, and Tause Soga, Tiyo's sister, set off early on Christmas morning in the opposite direction, making for Tyumie. One of Sandile's councillors, Vika, who lived nearby provided them with a three man escort.

Black Christmas [1850]

Until recent times, overshadowed by Hogmanay, Christmas was not a particularly important festival for the Scots. No unusual celebration was planned by the missionaries at Tyumie. On Christmas Eve[601] George Brown said goodbye to his wife Janet and their baby and left Iqibira for Tyumie to resume what he called "the business then occupying our attention," which was actually the investigation of the charges of immorality against him. This investigation was scheduled to continue through the Christmas season. He arrived at Tyumie at about midday where Renton and Cumming awaited him. Brown was accommodated in his mother-in-law's house at the mission. Mr and Mrs Renton, too, were allotted a room there, making a strained and uncomfortable household[602].

The Tyumie mission was quite spread out. John and Catherine Cumming and their family occupied the main mission house, which had been rebuilt after it had been destroyed in the previous war. Another house had been provided some distance away for Mary Chalmers. There was a small church and accommodation for individual assistants and a number of converts who worked on the mission, as well as large mission gardens; the mission had to be as self-sufficient as possible.

In the small hours of Christmas morning, before the midsummer sun had risen, John Cumming was woken by an urgent knocking at his door. For doctors and men of the cloth such summonses always indicated someone in trouble. It was Festiri, brother of Tiyo Soga, one of the elders of the mission church[603]. He was very agitated. Cumming invited him in and asked him to sit down. Festiri reported that he had received a messenger who had told him of the engagement in the Boma Pass. He gave a figure of 10 soldiers killed – not far off the actual number. But the major news was that there was a force of Xhosa in the region and that they were going to attack the military villages that day. As always on the frontier, communications were the problem. It was just 6 a.m. when Cumming scrawled a letter to Calderwood with this information and sent it by messenger. Then, conscientiously, he "Had worship as usual in the church."

It is not clear whether that message ever got through to Calderwood. Even if it had, it would have been too late.

Cumming told the Rentons, Mrs Chalmers, and Brown of what had happened when they woke. While they were talking three men in the uniform of the CMR rode up. They carried a letter to Renton from Calderwood, written at two o'clock that morning. In it he warned them that he had had a message from Smith, giving the first news of the Boma Pass battle. It also asked if the mission could defend itself and whether they needed weapons. Renton scrawled a request for twenty-four guns and ammunition. Brown afterwards expressed the view that this was only likely to provoke an attack on them[604].

As the CMR men were leaving a large Xhosa force appeared on a distant ridge and then disappeared over the top in two parties bound for unknown destinations. It was clear that there was considerable danger and the missionaries advised the soldiers to charge their muskets before they left. There was great concern for Niven and the people at Uniondale who had been right at the centre of the events at the Boma Pass. Brown was agitated about his wife Janet and the baby and wanted to return immediately to Iqibira. He saddled up his horse but, as he was about to mount, the group saw smoke rising on the horizon from the direction of Woburn, which lay between Iqibira and Tyumie. It was Janet's mother, supported by Renton, who dissuaded him from leaving.

Alarms now came thick and fast. In a cloud of dust, a rider came down the track at a gallop, pursued by two Xhosa warriors[605]. The disturbance brought Cumming to the door of his house. The man arrived at the gate, with his mount in a lather, shouting for help, "Oh, Mr Cumming! Save me, save me! The [Xhosa]s are after me." Cumming beckoned him in and he flung himself from his horse, leaving the reins trailing, and not caring whether the valuable mount was taken as booty. His pursuers stopped at the hedge round the mission house. Renton and Brown, hearing the commotion hurried down from the Chalmers house to see what was happening.

Dukwane, son of Ntsikane[606], who lived at the mission, grabbed the reins of the frightened horse and faced up to the pursuers. They demanded that their quarry be surrendered to them.

Dukwana's reply was:– "This station was pronounced by Gaika, at its establishment, as a sanctuary, a city of refuge; the white man is within the ramparts; therefore no man may give him up or molest him." They then said "deliver up his horse to us." Dukwana replied "You have no business here; the horse will not be given up; and you know as well as I do that according to the laws of our Chiefs you are now doing a thing that will bring you into trouble." As the blood-thirsty [Xhosa]s walked

> away they said to Dukwana, "then know that you have this day joined
> league with our enemy, and you will suffer for it."

These details of the confrontation were written forty-six years later by
William Chalmers Jr[607]. The actual exchange in Xhosa may have been
very different and the reporter's English rendition is clearly written for
dramatic effect. Nevertheless, Dukwane's words had enough weight to to
send the men away.

The fugitive, John Muleaux Stevenson, was the superintendent of
Juanasburg, one of the nearby military villages. He was panic-stricken. It
became apparent that he had been visiting Woburn, which had been attacked and destroyed, and the men of the village all killed. Stevenson,
himself, escaped. His story, as related to Cumming, was recorded in the
diary on the same day:

> He said that on Christmas Eve he had gone to Woburn for the purpose
> of holiday and also arranging with the men about some lands ... the cry
> was made of the [Xhosa]s – he ran out and saw a red army of [Xhosa]s
> about 50 yards distant – about 8 of them [the villagers] were just pre-
> paring to have a game at Criket [sic] – when seeing the [Xhosa]s they all
> ran here and there to [illegible] for their guns – that the first who got
> hit was smoking ... Stevenson got his horse saddled and called on Sta-
> cey superintendent of Woburn & Philps, Superintendent of Ely to fly –
> the first said no ... the other asked him to wait but [illegible]. Stevenson
> set off towards the opposite direction of the [Xhosa]s towards Kat
> River.

Later in the day three refugees from Woburn arrived at the mission
house:

> Two Hottentot women and a little white boy came today. Woburn is
> burnt and nearly all there are killed.
>
> We see the smoke of Woburn rising up – an awful sight.

Woburn was not the only place to suffer. Bands of warriors marauded
through the region, bent on the destruction of anything that symbolised
British authority. Throughout the day refugees arrived at Tyumie. Those
in the immediate neighbourhood, such as the trader, Gunn, who operated
a store nearby, had come immediately to the mission on hearing the first
news of the attacks. A message came up from his house. There was a
white man there. He could not come up to the mission because he was
naked. Cumming sent clothes down to him. He was one Sergeant Snodgrass who had been travelling to Fort Hare. He had been waylaid by a
band of Xhosa who had demanded all his clothes, leaving him wearing
only his socks. He was frantic because he had been travelling with his
young son and he and the boy had become separated while trying to escape. The child was afterwards found dead.

The behaviour of Stevenson during the day did not help the situation[608]. He was, no doubt, in shock and was also concerned to justify his abandonment of his companions at Woburn, who had all been killed. When Renton walked over from Mary Chalmers's house to enquire about the fugitive he was sitting outside Cumming's house. At that point he was still expressing his gratitude for his deliverance. "If it had not been for this mission station, I must to-day have been a dead man," he told Renton. He apparently believed that he had been pursued because some Xhosa men who knew him were intent on killing him personally. As a result he would only go outside when he had borrowed some of Cumming's clothes as some sort of disguise. At the same time he was concerned to present himself in the best possible light. Brown stated that

> He was a very overbearing man, not at all of a disposition to undervalue his commission[609], and far enough from being a favourite with the natives.

During the day, in describing his experiences, Stevenson expressed opinions about the Xhosa people that offended John Cumming, to the extent that Cumming ultimately suggested that it would be desirable for him to leave the mission as soon as practicable[610]. This disagreement may have influenced Stevenson's later attitude and behaviour.

Still the refugees came. In the early afternoon the Cummings saw out of the window a small party of men, women, and children approaching from the east – two white men, one with a small boy on his shoulders, two women, one ailing, three more small boys, two elderly Xhosa men and a young Xhosa couple. As they got closer it became clear that it was Niven and his family with the other refugees from Uniondale.

Cumming and Renton rushed out to meet them and escort them to the mission house. They had a harrowing tale to tell[611]. On horseback they had come as far as the Amatole river. There they encountered the first band of Xhosa belligerents. The two escorts provided by Vika tried to explain the situation but, on being threatened, fled, leaving the party to face the danger on their own. Their horses were seized and they were threatened and mishandled, but in the end allowed to proceed. They still needed to cover more than 15 km to reach Tyumie. Rebecca Niven was in poor health and had to be helped all the way. Their next encounter was even more dangerous. Another band of men appeared and expressed the intention of killing the men in the party. Ball, as a non-missionary and former soldier was the chief target. It was Tause Soga who pleaded on their behalf and eventually they were released. They were then helped on their way by for a while by two cattle herders, who were not part of the fighting, and some women who gave them milk and helped to carry the children for a while. One more terrifying encounter with a band of warriors had to be endured. Again the men were threatened with death and again the pleas of Tause led to their release. At last the Tyumie mission came in sight and their immediate ordeal was over. There were, however, still days of tension to come.

About two o'clock in the afternoon two more fugitives appeared at the mission gate. They were two of the CMR patrol that had brought warning of the attacks early that morning. Steadfastly obeying orders, by keeping their guns unloaded rather than following the advice of the missionaries, they had gone on to warn the military villages. Juanasburg received warning and was evacuated. They called at Auckland and then started the journey to Woburn. They had stopped briefly while the missing man dismounted to adjust his bridle, and had immediately been attacked. The two mounted men had escaped but they had little hope for their comrade. Almost immediately their pessimism was negated when yet another naked man, less concerned for his dignity than Snodgrass, was seen striding along the road. It was the missing soldier who had been stripped of his clothes and allowed to go.

That evening the three CMR men and a few of the male refugees left Tyumie to try to make their way to Fort Hare under cover of darkness. Those who remained, not knowing what the next day would bring, tried to make themselves comfortable and get a night's rest.

The following morning Brown renewed his efforts to find some way of reaching Iqibira to find his wife and son. He had to be almost forcibly restrained from leaving on his own. In the early afternoon, however, a party of troops, 50 men of the 91st Regiment and 10 of the CMR, arrived. They had been sent from Fort Hare by Henry Somerset to escort any who wished to leave Tyumie back to relative safety. They had been harrassed all the way and were anxious for a decision to be made as soon as possible. Cumming, Renton, and Niven refused to leave. Stevenson was handed over to the care of the detachment[612]. Brown, knowing that Fort Hare would get him nearer to Iqibira, was anxious to accompany them, but, when Mary Chalmers refused to leave her home, reluctantly remained behind. The refugees, with their escort of troops, made it back to Fort Hare under constant harrassment.

There had still been no certain news of Auckland, although smoke had been seen rising from that direction since the previous day. There was some hope that, because there was a much larger body of men there, they might have been able to fight off an attack. It was not until later on 26th December that a large group of women and children brought news from the village[613]. Unlike Woburn, they had not all been overwhelmed immediately in a surprise attack. The Superintendent, Mr Munro, had been talking to a group of Xhosa who had apparently come for news, after the CMR men had briefly visited the village to warn them. He and a number of the men of the village were suddenly surprised and killed, but nine men with the women and children, had been able to retreat to a roofless blockhouse where for hours they put up a hopeless defence. The men tried to defend the fortification from loopholes, but were picked off one by one as Xhosa men with assegais hid under the loopholes and stabbed them as they fired.

The story emerged from the traumatized women and children and the horror of the situation that they had left behind became apparent. When the number of men defending the flimsy fortress had been reduced to two, the Xhosa had called to them to let the women and children out and they would not be harmed. The men said their farewells; the women and children were sent off towards Tyumie; the last two defenders were then overwhelmed and killed. Many years later an account of their last moments was put together from Xhosa sources[614]:

> The men knew well that any help would be too late, but only wished to get their women into a safe place. They were given time to say Good-bye, and the poor women began their weary heartbroken trudge of seven miles. The men fought bravely, but to no purpose as they were hemmed in on every side. The last man was a big man and strong. When he saw that all were gone or killed, he knelt down and prayed. The natives paused in awe, and looked on. Two young [Xhosa]s, more bloodthirsty than the others, fell on him, one with Assegai, one with Kerrie, and smashed him dead as he knelt there.

That evening the Auckland and Woburn refugees set off for Fort Hare, accompanied only by a few Xhosa women from the mission. There was no reason to suppose that they would be threatened by the Xhosa forces, who were chivalrous to women and children. They reached their destination unmolested.

At last Brown was able to leave Tyumie for Iqibira. The next day a man called Totane had arrived with a message from Maqoma. The import of this was that Maqoma did not want to see the mission abandoned as Chalmers had done in previous wars. He promised that, if the missionaries remained, they would not be harmed. Brown took this as an opportunity. He persuaded Totane to escort him to Iqibira. This time he could not be dissuaded and the pair set off on the following morning, the 28th December.

It was a further two days before a weary George Brown returned to Tyumie[615], bringing some news of Janet and his son. He would certainly not have survived the journey without Totane as escort. On several occasions he was threatened by bands of men. On his journey to Iqibira he and Totane had stopped with a large force of men who turned out to be commanded by Maqoma himself. Maqoma had wanted him to write a letter to Harry Smith on his behalf, but he was reluctant to do so in case he was seen as involving himself in the war, and Maqoma did not insist. Maqoma instructed Totane to take him to Iqibira, and if Janet should not be there to return with him to Tyumie. When they arrived at Iqibira it was to find it destroyed and Stokwe and his men in possession. Brown found out from one of the mission women that Janet and the baby had set out for Fort White that morning with a safe conduct from Stokwe. Hoping that she had reached it safely, Brown and Totane returned to Tyumie.

Another pair of refugees turned up at this point. Tiyo Soga and an elder named Busak[616] had been left in charge of Uniondale when the Nivens left. The next day they had received warning of an imminent attack and had retreated to Vika's place. Shortly afterwards Anta and his men arrived at Uniondale and destroyed it. Almost nothing was left.

Mortification   [Dec. 1850 – Jan. 1851]

The first despatches from Mackinnon, describing the debacle in the Boma Pass, reached Harry Smith at Fort Cox late in the night on Christmas Eve. They came as a bolt from the blue. His self image as a father to the Xhosa, who knew how to handle them, received a blow from which he was not to recover. He could not fail to see the consequences of his folly. The military force on the frontier was far too small to conduct a war; it was thinly stretched, manning the forts that formed the defensive line of the Colony. There were not enough troops in Cape Town to fill the gap. Communications with Britain, with the advent of steam ships, were now faster, but it would be months rather than weeks before any significant support could be received from there. All he could do that night was to send his hasty warning to the mission stations and military villages in the neighbourhood and send despatches to the commanders of the numerous military posts, large and small, along the frontier.

The next morning the extent of his problem became apparent. Xhosa messengers carried the news back and forth. Fort Cox was under siege. Of his senior commanders, Mackinnon was trying to extricate himself from the consequences of the Battle of the Boma Pass, Somerset was himself under siege in Fort Hare, and only Maclean, far away in King William's Town, had any freedom of action. Penned up in Fort Cox, Smith raged and swore. He was forced to send a despatch appointing Henry Somerset as Commander-in-Chief until he could be released. Somerset was his only hope of such release.

Mackinnon and his demoralized men descended from the Amatolas on the eastern side and made their way round along a wagon trail across the plains through Debe Nek to Fort White. They were harried all the way and on one occasion nearly fell into the same kind of trap as on the Boma Pass. The British soldiers were near to panic and it was only the actions of the CMR, bringing up the rear, that were able to hold off the steady attacks by the Xhosa.

On the route they encountered the site of the ambush of a patrol of the 43rd regiment from Fort White. The patrol had been annihilated and the corpses of thirteen British soldiers lay in the sun. When they reached the fort they found that the small garrison remaining there had barely held off the attackers and could not have lasted much longer.

After hesitating for three days, on 29th December, Henry Somerset made an attempt to rescue Smith from Fort Cox. With a force of one hundred and fifty men of the Argylls and seventy of the CMR he set off on a blistering Sunday morning. They had one artillery piece with them, a three-pounder cannon. They had not gone far before massive numbers of Xhosa appeared over the brows of the hills surrounding them. Somerset had no stomach for facing such an overwhelming force and ordered a retreat to Fort Hare. In the confusion the carriage of the cannon was broken and the attempt to save it delayed the retreat. The result was the second major battle of the war and the second defeat for the British. The force was surrounded and the fighting was hand to hand. It was only because the sound of firing brought out reinforcements from Fort Hare that they were not completely overwhelmed. With this aid they fought their way back to the fort. The casualty list was two officers and twenty soldiers dead, one officer and seventeen men severely wounded.

The situation deteriorated rapidly. That evening news came of a major rebellion. A large number of the men of the Kat river region were joined by numerous deserters from the CMR and the new Xhosa police force and had gone to join the Xhosa forces. Their leader was Herman Matroos. They were well armed, and many of them were well-trained in the nature of British military operations. The rebellion was at the time referred to as the Kat River rebellion, although by no means all the Kat River residents supported it and many took part it who were not from Kat River. For want of a better name, it is still called that in modern texts.

That night Somerset managed to get a messenger through to Smith informing him of the defeat and the resulting failure to mount a rescue. A man with Smith's impatient nature could wait no longer. With a troop of the CMR to accompany him, and disguised as one of them, he rode out into the night. They successfully made their way to Fort White and, after leaving orders there, continued to Headquarters in King William's Town. There Smith could contemplate his position.

The one thing in his favour was that, so far, Mhala's amaNdlambe and Phatho's amaGqunukwhebe had remained neutral. Among the amaNdlambe only Siyolo, son of Mdushane, joined the cause of Sandile and Maqoma. Still more importantly, Phatho was still prepared to protect the road between the new port of East London, at the mouth of the Buffalo River. This meant that supplies and communications to King William's Town, only 50 km away, were assured. The old route from Port Elizabeth was very much further over a difficult road, and under constant attack. It was now that Smith underwent a change of heart. Until now, his policy had been to destroy the power of the chiefs over their people. He had a misguided belief that the Xhosa people would welcome their release from "oppression" and happily embrace the ideals of Western culture. In this he was as deluded as in all other aspects of his self belief that he understood the Xhosa. He now performed a U-turn and, for the brief remaining period of his Governorship, he was to propound the belief that government of the Xhosa could only be achieved through the authority of the chiefs. Meanwhile he contemplated the fact that he was at war with them.

There were fears that the Gcaleka would join forces with the amaNgqika. It was also feared that the abaThembu would become involved. Of them only Maphasa, of the amaTshatshu, actually joined the war. He was the son of Bawana, the chief whom John Thackwray had found so disagreeable twenty five years earlier. Maphasa became one of the fiercest antagonists of the British.

The Xhosa strategy was first to attack the key defensive posts, Fort Beaufort, Fort White and Fort Hare. Sandile, Maqoma, and Herman Matroos set up a centre of operations in Kat River Valley where they began to implement this plan.

Royal Visit   [Jan. 1851]

At Tyumie the refugees had left. Those who remained were the Cumming family, Henry Renton and his wife, Robert Niven and his family, and George Brown and his mother-in-law Mary Chalmers. Anxiously they awaited news. Janet Brown and her baby son were believed to have reached Fort White but the country was in uproar and they still had great fears for their safety.

While they waited the fighting raged on. Fort White was known to be besieged. On 7th January it was the turn of Fort Beaufort, which was attacked by Herman Matroos and a large band of rebels. The army held the Fort, while the inhabitants of the surrounding village defended their homes. An early casualty was Matroos himself, who was shot and killed. The fighting continued through the day, until eventually, the attacking forces, demoralized by the loss of their leader, were beaten off. Matroos's body was dragged into the public square and exhibited there.

At last, on the 10th January 1851, Janet was able to make her way to Tyumie. She reached there the following day and was reunited with her husband. Escorted by a Xhosa convert she had not been seriously threatened although she had twice been stopped. She had been accommodated the previous night by one of Sandile's councillors. She brought the news that Fort White had been heavily attacked on the 3rd January. A worrying symptom of the war was that, as soon as the attack was mounted, several soldiers of the Cape Mounted Rifles had deserted to the Xhosa. In previous wars the lion's share of the defence of the Colony had been borne by coloured soldiers. Now everywhere they were deserting and fighting on the other side. The attack on Fort White had been led by Sandile himself. The circumstances of the encounter, however, unlike the Boma Pass battle and the near disaster outside Fort Hare, now favoured the British defenders. They had been able to construct rudimentary fortifications, they were not in an extended line out in open country, and they were in a concentrated force with a single point of command. Disciplined fire from the ordered ranks of men won the day, and the attack was beaten off.

Tyumie was now on its own. Cumming was the incumbent. Renton was the senior man on the spot. He was, however, new in the country; his visit to report on the activities of the missionaries of the United Free Presbyterian Church had been completely overwhelmed by events. Niven and his family were refugees, his wife ailing, and the presence of the children of great concern. The Browns were reunited, but it was only a few months since their enforced marriage, and the domestic situation in Mary Chalmers's house was strained.

They were not without news. While the British Army was immobilized in the scattered frontier forts, awaiting reinforcements, individual Xhosa moved freely through the country. Visitors to Tyumie brought news and messages. The missionaries appear to have occupied themselves by continuing with the business of the mission including the matter of Brown's behaviour[617]. On the 16th January, James Read Jr arrived. He had ridden through the dangerous war zone to find out whether they were safe, and to invite them to take refuge at Philipton.

The most significant visitor arrived with a large retinue on Friday 17th January. A message was brought to Cumming at the mission house announcing the imminent arrival of the Ngqika King[618]:

> 17 Jan 1851: Sandilla comes in the evening asks Sepho down from [illegible] to say that he is coming to see me – invite him to come to Mission house where he would see all the three teachers Mr Renton, Mr Niven & myself as I did not wish to compromise myself by meeting him alone. While met there on important business of mission Sandilla with a number of followers came. Mr Renton addressed him thanking him for his support to the mission and requesting him to continue it. Sandilla in a long harrangue spoke on the efforts of teachers coming to his country & taking his people from him to fight for the Governors & threatened to take the School people of Chumie away us from [sic].
>
> Mr Renton replied requesting that he would allow the people to be neutral. At first he said no – but offered corn [illegible scrawl perhaps meaning that, as a result of the appeal, he agreed to neutrality].
>
> We now see that we are in the hands of Sandilla ...

Sandile was now a figure of authority. He was no longer the immature lad with a crippled leg who had so nearly been overthrown by Maqoma. Maqoma was now the General who provided brains and experience to the war effort, but Sandile was the king and had led his people in battle. Having completed his tirade, he now relaxed. He told the missionaries that he would provide an escort for those who wished to leave Tyumie to reach a place of safety. His condition was that they should not go to a military establishment. Cumming, Renton, and Niven decided that they would go with Read to Philipton. Brown found an obstacle to his doing the same. His mother-in-law was a stubborn woman. Mary Chalmers had lived for many years at Tyumie; much of her married life had been spent there. She had no intention of leaving. Perforce, the Browns decided to remain with her.

That night Cumming provided hospitality for Sandile:

> Sandilla having asked from me a place to sleep in – get Smith's house in old garden for his use – I give him a sheep – bread coffee & sugar – a double blanket.

It was clearly time to move. John Cumming decided to approach Sandile[619]:

> I then applied to Sandille to give us some protection to enable us to reach the Colony. He sent two of his headmen to take us as far as Kat River. We were rather a large party: Mr. Renton, his wife and retinue; Mr. Niven, his wife and family; myself, wife and family, my sister[620]; and others connected with the mission.

The next day the missionaries began packing up for departure. Their first intention was to make for Glenthorn, but they received news that the homestead had been burnt out and the Pringles had taken refuge with John Pringle's brother at the farm Eildon in the Baviaanskloof. They then, on the 20th, made the journey to Philipton which was still very much within the region of hostility.

Turning Point   [Jan. 1851]

Sandile's visit to Tyumie preceded what was to become a defining battle of the war. He was planning an attack on Fort Hare and his forces were gathering in the neighbourhood of the mission.

At 9 a.m. on the 21st January, without warning, the attack began. The garrison in the fort was severely depleted because a detachment had been sent out to escort a wagon train of supplies that had been sent from Graham's Town. There were about 800 Mfengu troops available on the ground. A few British troops manned the artillery in the fort. An estimated 5000 amaXhosa took part in the attack.

The Xhosa commanders had learnt a great deal about British modes of warfare over the years. They now had fire power and disciplined musketry, although it was much inferior to the British artillery. They worked in organized units, following orders and showing the influence of the deserters from the colonial coloured forces. In the nearby village the residents climbed to the roofs of their houses to defend them. The battle lasted five hours with the British army manning the fortress and the Mfengu in the front line of the defence. Eventually Xhosa and rebels were driven off.

After being in a position where they might well have taken the fort, the Xhosa retreated, probably demoralized when the magic sticks of Mlanjeni failed to turn the British bullets to water. Had the Xhosa attack succeeded, the way to the Colony would have been opened, and who knows what the consequences might have been? This was a turning point in the war; the Xhosa, supported by the rebels, once again resumed guerilla tactics, avoiding pitched battles. The war became one of attrition with the Xhosa melting away in the bush and the Colonial forces pursuing them in small engagements and ambushes with the forces of the British struggling to manage the conditions and gain the upper hand.

The Ordeal of Benjamin Booth Jr   [Dec 1850 – Mar 1851]

At the start of the war Benjamin Booth Jr and his wife Matilda were farming at Hammonds, a property owned by Matilda's father Robert

Godlonton near Fort Beaufort, not far from the border of British Kaffraria. During the War of the Axe the couple had remained on their farm and defended it against the threat of attack. In December 1850, however, they did not have this option and, with their children ranging from 1 to 8 years old, they joined the retreat to Fort Beaufort, leaving the farm in the care of their servants.

The death of Herman Matroos did not interrupt the spread of the Kat River rebellion. Matroos's place was taken by his second in command Willem Uithaalder. To the bewilderment of the Booths, the spread of the insurrection resulted in the sacking of their farm. Matilda's letter to her parents in Graham's Town[621] testifies to her complete lack of understanding of the feelings and tensions of the time:

> Who would have thought of our own people joining the [Xhosa]s! – old Jan, the wagon driver, who we have known for so many years, and Piet, who we have brought up from a child. When I left he had a child of his own, and while I was at home I attended upon his wife and child as often as I could, and when I went away provided them with every comfort. The other two men we have also had from children, but they tell me that one of them went away much against his will. The other was old Plaatje. All we have saved is our wagon, three chairs and our bedding and clothes. What we shall do I cannot tell.

Such uncomprehending lamentation was to be repeated over and over again up to the present time by vaguely benevolent white employers when what they perceived as enlightened practices not only failed to win the loyalty of their employees but also provoked active resistance.

The Booths were forced to move to Graham's Town where they had the support of family and friends. Benjamin Sr, widowed since 1847, now lived in Bathurst Street near his daughter Margaret and her husband, Joseph Walker. Matilda's father, Robert Godlonton, could support them, and their experiences were ammunition for his press campaign.

Not long after their move to the town, on Saturday 22nd March 1851, Benjamin Jr found it necessary to travel to Cradock, presumably for some business reason[622]. By this time, although the Xhosa were largely confined beyond the Fish River, the Kat River rebellion was in full swing, and bands of rebels made the road hazardous. It was safer to travel with companions. Benjamin accompanied Charles Trollip, one of the extensive Trollip clan, and a builder called Castings, who was employed by the Trollips[623]. They were mounted and Trollip and Booth each had a second horse on a leading rein attached to his wrist.

The road from Graham's Town to Cradock started off in a north-westerly direction until it reached the line of the Great Fish River, which at that point ran roughly west to east. It then followed the line of the river on the high ground on the southern side. About twenty kilometres from Graham's Town they reached the first point of great danger – de Bruin's Poort. This narrow cleft led down from the high ground to a ford on the river and provided ample cover for an ambush. They had been saving their horses for a rapid gallop through the Poort. This was to no avail. Just before they reached the Poort a band of rebels, waiting in ambush in some thick bush, attacked them with a volley of shots from close range. It was too quick for Benjamin to know what had happened. The horse that he had been leading bolted and dragged him away by the rein tied to his wrist. When it broke loose he was left lying in fortuitous concealment, covered in blood and in great pain. He could hear the sounds of pursuit, a volley of shots and cries of *"Keer hom voor."* He did not know that Castings had died instantly, shot in the heart, while Trollip was careering away on his bolting horse, hampered by the other animal on its leading rein, and pursued by the attackers[624].

When he took stock he was in bad shape. He had been shot in both arms, and one of the wounds in particular was bleeding profusely. He was not sure whether he had been dragged off his mount by the horse he had been leading or whether he had fallen as a result of the shots. He realised that it was vital to stop the bleeding. Both arms were severely injured but he managed in desperation, with the aid of his teeth, to loosen the lace that secured his hat and wind it round his upper arm as a makeshift tourniquet. Once he had gathered himself he began to crawl through the bush away from the scene of action and, when he felt safe enough he doggedly began to plod towards help. Night was approaching.

About ten kilometres away, at the farm Burnt Kraal, Jeremiah Goldswain had had a long day. The band of rebels had been very active in the district and, during the morning, he and his two sons had been following their movements along the Cradock road. They found that the house of a neighbour, Mr Hyde, at Niemand's Kraal had been looted so they followed the tracks of the robbers towards de Bruin's Poort. At noon they gave up and returned home to spend the afternoon checking on their own stock – cattle, sheep, and goats. They rounded them up, confined them in the kraals, and faced a night of remaining on high alert. Jeremiah lay down on his bed, fully clothed, and fell asleep.

At 2 a.m. he was woken by a goat bleating an alarm, but, after looking out of the window and seeing nothing amiss, he again fell asleep. At 5 a.m., his usual rising time, he looked out again and again saw nothing.

> I sad to my wife: "All seames to be quiet: I shall lie down for one hour longer for I feele all most nocked up so I shall lay untill the clock strikes six."

His rest did not last long. Almost immediately he was again woken by the dogs barking at the kraal. He grabbed his gun and went to the window. The dogs were threatening a man who had retreated into a corner of the fence. The intruder saw him appear and called up to him, "Come down, Mr Goldswain." There did not appear to be a threat so he called off the dogs, ran downstairs, and met the man who was now making his way towards the house.

> I hopned the gate and looking at him I said: "Why you are badly wounded." He said: "Yes I ham." "Pray what is your name?" He smiled [and] said: "Booth." Bless me I did not know you: com in." He asked for a glass of water: I gave it him and went and informed Mrs. Goldswain and in a few minets she came down stars. The cause why I did not know him was he was coverd with blood from the cround of his heat down to his feet.

Goldswain removed Booth's shirt, which was stiff with blood, and cut away his vest. He gave a graphic description of his wounds:

> When I had striped him and had washed his bodey and harms I saw that he had been shot with two shots: one had enterd the wright harm jist above the helbo and came out in the thick part of the harm or the muscles of the harm. But I think that it could not be a leaden ball as the wound was jist two inches long and a smal bit of flesh haning like a bell at the uper end of the wound: I think that it must be a piece of the leg of an Iron pot[625]. Above this wound he had with sume dificuty torn off his hat string with his teeth as he was not able to use his harms and to use it as a ligature and this I did not remove as I was afraid that if I loosend it it mite again start bleeding and as Mr. Booth had lost all readey so much blood. It a peared to me that the ball that passed thrue the left harm: it first passed thrue the left waistcote pocket taking one button off of the waistcote and one off of the waistband of the trowsers leveing a black bruse on the bodey a bout three inches long: then striking the Pistole stock – smashing it to peaces – and then entren the left harm cloce by the bend of the harm and out behind the harm and in both caces the bone is not broken.

When the treatment was over Booth drank some coffee and fell into an exhausted sleep. It lasted less than an hour when he was woken by night-mares of being attacked again. Post-traumatic stress had not been recognized as a special condition or given a fancy name at the time, but bad dreams were understood. Jeremiah found him sitting up on the sofa, wide awake, and with blood dripping again from his wound. He was brought into breakfast. He was unable to feed himself because of his wounds so Jeremiah fed him while he told the story on which this account is based. It seems likely that he had finally managed to reach the farm at 2 a.m. – he remembered the goat bleating in alarm – and then waited fearing the dogs, and the possibility of being shot by an alarmed householder. The ability to walk ten kilometres through the night while in serious pain and having lost copious quantities of blood says much for the physical hardihood of the men of the time.

While Benjamin had been asleep, Jeremiah had sent a letter to his son-in-law, a Mr Erskine, asking him to bring his "spring wagon"[626] to transport the victim back to Graham's Town, and another letter to Benjamin Booth Sr, telling him what had happened. Later in the morning Erskine arrived with a posse of seven or eight companions.

The wagon set off for Graham's Town, and the posse to examine the site of the attack at de Bruin's Poort. There they found the grim remains of the previous day's ambush. Castings's body had been partly stripped, his wallet gone but some money still in a pocket. They dragged the body aside and placed it as decently as they could beneath a bush where it would be out of view of scavengers. The horse that had inadverdently saved Booth's life grazed quietly near the scene. The sandy ground was covered with tracks. Several sets of hoofprints led through the Poort down to the river. They followed these, finding Trollip's hat on the ground. From the tracks they deduced that Castings's horse had been captured by the rebels. Eventually on the other side of the river there were only the trails of two galloping horses which disappeared a few kilometres up the Cradock road. They concluded that Trollip must have escaped.

They rode slowly back through the Poort and stopped for a minute's silence where Castings lay, then rode on intending to bring the news to his family and assist in getting a suitable conveyance to bring the body home. A little way down the road they were overtaken by a body of fourteen mounted men.

The previous day Thomas Stubbs, in command of a party of his mounted rangers[627], and his brother William had been patrolling along the Cradock Road. Some time after they had passed through de Bruin's Poort they were overtaken by a cantering horseman, leading another horse. It was Charles Trollip. In distress, he told them of his escape from the ambush and his fears for his companions. Thomas ordered William to take a detail of fourteen men and go back to investigate the scene. It was the next day that they met Goldswain's group, who pointed out Castings's body and brought them up to date on Benjamin Booth's escape.

William's troop pursued the rebels and when they caught up with them, after getting reinforcements from Graham's Town, killed three and captured a further three. Later two others were arrested far to the west at George. They were not regarded as prisoners of war but as rebel criminals. In due course they were tried and executed.

Benjamin recovered from his wounds and, after the war, he and his family returned to their farm.

Scapegoats in the Wilderness   [Jan – Apr 1851]

The refugee missionaries found a very divided community in the Kat River settlement[628]. Their grievances were universally felt but their reactions varied substantially. The years of loyalty, bearing the brunt of the Colonial frontline fighting during Hintsa's war and the war of the axe, could not be discarded by most of the older generation: the call of Mlanjeni led many of the younger generation to follow Herman Matroos into outright rebellion against British rule.

The settlement was sprawled over the Kat River valley, which extended over an area of about eight hundred square kilometres. There were a number of villages and groupings. From the Katberg the Kat river followed a course through the broad valley, first flowing westward, and then, after making a great loop to the north, meandering roughly southwards. A number of tributaries ran into it. The Philipton Mission and its associated village were in the north, on the Readsdale River, which flowed into the Fairbairn, a tributary of the Kat. Seven or eight kilometres downstream on the Kat there was a juncture of the Buxton and Balfour Rivers which then joined the main river from the right, with the Balfour mission and village a few kilometres up the Balfour River. Close to the junction was a large oxbow on the Kat. The land rose sharply within this loop and, at the summit, Fort Armstrong had been constructed, using a similar topography to that of Fort Cox to dominate the surrounding region. Much further south the Mankazana River joined the Kat from the left. This was not the same Mankazana river as that on which John Pringle's farm Glenthorn lay, That was well to the west, a tributary of the Koonap. It was tantalizingly close to Philipton, but the way was blocked by hostile forces. Yet further downstream the Blinkwater stream flowed past Calderwood's old mission site and joined the Kat. Along its banks Herman Matroos's followers had settled.

The refugee missionaries were unable to move further. Immobilized, they set out to make themselves useful to their host. James Read Sr was old and ill. The responsibility for Philipton now rested on the shoulders of his eldest son, James Jr. For both Reads the work of a lifetime was crumbling.

James Read Jr condemned the rebellion itself unequivocally but he was very conscious of the grievances that had led to it. He listed them in a formal letter to William Ritchie Thomson, now the agent for the LMS in Cape Town. In the letter his concern was to try to put the record straight. The grievances of the people of the settlement were real and serious. Nevertheless, not all the Kat River residents were rebels: many were loyal citizens. The actions of the British forces, supposedly against the rebels, were brutal and often against innocent people.

There is little doubt that units of the British army had acted against people in the settlement who were not rebels, although it is true that few families would not have rebels as members. In these actions their houses were burnt, their means of subsistence destroyed, and they were driven into further antagonism. While Henry Somerset was not directly implicated, his command did little to prevent such actions.

In this environment, as elsewhere on the frontier alarming rumours and exaggerations took the place of reliable information. Cumming, Niven, and Renton did their best to help the community in which they found themselves. Many of the residents had been deeply injured by what was happening. Some brought information about what was going on in the environment. Where crimes appeared to have been committed, it was necessary to get the information on record. The missionaries assisted in this by helping with the taking of statements of people who had something to record and were often illiterate or semiliterate. Wounded rebels were certainly brought back to the settlement and were treated by the missionaries, who were the only source of medical help.

In Graham's Town the rumour mill was just as active, fuelled by the fulminations of Godlonton's *Journal*. The columns of the newspaper spewed out a torrent of abuse against the Xhosa and the rebels. The fury of the paper against the rebellion was exercised particularly strongly against the people of the Kat River Settlement, whether or not they were participants in the rebellion. The missionaries who advised them had been a target for abuse since the early days of the settlement. The news was not, of course, provided by professional journalists. It was an uncritical publication of every rumour arriving from people, who had been terrorised. After all, Godlonton himself had seen the effects of the rebellion on his daughter and son-in-law, the Booths.

The situation was exacerbated by Stevenson who had arrived in Graham's Town and found himself the target of accusations of cowardice for having fled from Woburn, leaving his companions to their fate. His defence was to expand his story of having tried heroically to get back to his responsibilities at Juanasburg and to deflect criticism by presenting himself as the hero of Tyumie, providing leadership to missionaries who were paralysed by fear. John Cumming, who had taken Stevenson to task over his attitude to the Xhosa, was a major target of the slander. The

Journal reported what he had to say as undoubted truth. As early as January 11th it was reporting[629]:

> The conduct of the missionaries [Niven and Cumming] is a matter of much talk. Cumming not only refused to accompany the party sent for him [the military escort that had escorted Stevenson from the mission], but would not let them approach within half a mile of his house. He also refused Mr Stevenson a refuge, and told him he must go off, but which he would not do that night. They have since written to Mr. Calderwood in defence of the [Xhosa]s, though Niven escaped from his place in his shirt only.

The ordinary people accepted the false syllogism that was repeated regularly by the paper:

- Missionaries of the LMS and GMS teach the people of Kat river;

- Rebels come from the Kat River;

- Therefore the missionaries teach rebellion.

Even many years later Thomas Stubbs, a man who was intelligent and by no means naïve, could describe the finding of the camp site of the attackers of Benjamin Booth thus[630]

> On going to their fire place he found some pots and kettles and a Bible and Prayerbook open showing they had held their Sunday morning service with the blood of Castings on their hands. This again proves how the Hottentots were misled by those would be philanthropists, the London Missionary Society.

After a few months the war had changed from all-out attack by the Xhosa and rebels to one where the Colonial forces harried the enemy in their retreats in the bush. It became possible to move more safely and Cumming, the Rentons, the Nivens, and Tiyo Soga were able to leave their refuge at Philipton.

Shortly before they left John Cumming received the news that Glenthorn had been destroyed. He was reunited with his family at Glen Avon. The Nivens and Tiyo Soga also moved there, invited by Charles Stretch who was living in a second house on the farm called The Retreat. Renton went to Graham's Town.

Mr A. J. McKenzie, a recent arrival from Fort Beaufort, had in January taken over Pinnock's Hotel in Bathurst Street and was conducting it under the new name of McKenzie's Hotel[631]. Renton engaged a room there on Friday 4th April. McKenzie did not realise what he was in for.

The news that one of the missionaries, who had been the subject of so much vituperation, was in the town spread rapidly. On Saturday, as Renton moved round paying his respects to various acquaintances, he was subjected to insults and harrassment by jeering groups in the streets. By evening the situation had become ugly. McKenzie's Hotel was surrounded by a mob, many of them drunk, calling for action against Renton. At this time Thomas Stubbs was the Field Commandant of Graham's Town. This was the nearest thing the town had to a chief of police; he was responsible for maintaining public order. On this occasion the crowd was persuaded to disperse. Next day the unrest continued. Renton was harrassed going to Church and calling on friends. It was on Monday evening that matters got completely out of hand. Once again the hotel was besieged. This time the crowd had much of the appearance of a lynch mob. They forced their way through the doors and took possession of the ground floor, demanding to see Renton. Stubbs's small force had little chance of preventing them from turning an ugly situation into a full-scale riot.

Thomas Stubbs had no sympathy for any philanthropic opinions and believed as much as anyone in the allegations against the missionaries. He was, however, a responsible citizen who knew his duty. Leaving a few men to hold the stairs, he went upstairs to speak to Renton. He warned him that he could not guarantee his safety unless some means of calming the crowd could be found and suggested that, if Renton were to agree to provide a statement for the crowd in which he agreed to attend a properly organised public meeting and answer questions, Stubbs would read it to the crowd and persuade them to disperse. The tactics worked and there was no further disturbance that night.

A committee of some prominent citizens of the town was duly formed to organize the public meeting. It was chaired by Dr John Atherstone, now a Justice of the Peace. It included Godlonton, William Cock, and Stubbs. There was a certain amount of jockeying for position with Renton being concerned to ensure that his safety was guaranteed and that it was understood that he had been coerced into attending a public meeting, while the committee first appeared to believe that it had been called at his request. The meeting eventually took place in the Court House on the evening of Thursday 10th April, with Renton and the committee members seated on the platform, and what was reported to be the largest attendance ever seen in the town[632].

Atherstone introduced Renton and set out the terms on which the meeting had been called. Before Renton could speak Godlonton leapt up and asked to have the opportunity of clarifying his position. He was allowed to make a somewhat confused self-justifying statement, expressing his good faith and full of inconsistencies. His arguments reported the accusations and then dissociated the speaker from them:

These were some of the grievances on the public mind in connection with Mr Renton, and which had led to an ebullition of public feeling which none more sincerely deplored than himself [Godlonton]. At the same time he was not going to stigmatize it, as some had done, as an unparalleled atrocity. If men, by imprudent meddling, would render themselves obnoxious to public indignation, they must submit to the consequences. ... had the people of this frontier made sterner resistance to the misrepresentations which had been made respecting them by men of Mr Renton's cloth, the calamities which have since overtaken them, and in which they were then involved, would have been entirely avoided. ... He appealed to them [the audience] as generous, independent Englishmen and had no fear for the result.

Eventually Renton was called on to speak. He was a preacher of vigour and experience. In the orotund, oratorical style of the day he set out to demolish the allegation that had been made against Cumming, Niven, and himself.

On Godlonton he did not hold back:

As a private gentleman I can have no feeling against Mr. Godlonton – he is a stranger to me – I have never come in contact with him. But as the conductor of a public journal, I deem his conduct very reprehensible. I have heard many references to his paper as the authority for the allegations and imputations I was called to meet, and I desiderated the articles and extracts in which these are contained, that if I must notice them I might know definitely what it was I had to answer or expose, while some numbers which I saw satisfied me that a system of gross misrepresentation and slander are going on.

He went on to read out the report on the conduct of Cumming and Niven quoted above and followed

"What shall be given unto thee, or what shall be done unto thee, thou false tongue?" – for seldom has so much falsehood and calumny been comprised in so small a space. Here two missionaries are blamed, and the conduct of one of them – especially Mr. Cumming, the resident missionary at the Chumie, and son-in-law of Mr. John Pringle – is represented in a manner to excite reprobation. What are the facts?

He then embarked on an extended eye-witness account of what had happened at Tyumie and thereafter at Philipton. In its course he also demolished Stevenson's boasting. The *Frontier Times* even reported that there were cheers at some points in his speech.

At the end Godlonton again rose in self-justification

... as a public journalist he would fearlessly give currency to whatever he in his judgment might consider it important for the public to know. At the same time, it would be obvious to all, that it was impossible for the editor of a newspaper to guard against inaccuracies in statements transmitted from distant points; they could not examine into the facts, and could only, therefore, rely on the credibility of those who reported them.

This was not quite as outrageous as it seems now. Journalistic ethics were considerably less well-developed than now, and newspapers did not have the resources to cover events on their own behalf; they were forced to rely on letters from correspondents.

The meeting ended inconclusively with a resolution from William Cock who regretted that all questions had not been answered, suggested that a list should be provided for Renton, and called on the people to preserve good order. The immediate danger fizzled out, but the whole affair was the subject of considerable criticism throughout the Colony. The *Cape of Good Hope Observer* editorialized that:

> They [the Graham's Town public] might have corrected the multitudinous reports that naturally arose in consequence of the peculiar position in which the gentlemen assailed were placed by their knowledge of human nature and of what honorable men, under such circumstances, might be supposed to do, to say, or to think. Instead of which they believed, or pretended to believe, all that they heard against these men, and ultimately they placed Mr. Renton upon his defence for crimes, whose imputation would have drawn from him or themselves, at any other period, a simple smile of ridicule.

Stevenson and the *Graham's Town Journal* persisted in the campaign. In an open letter to Renton, written on 25th Dec 1851 and published in the *Journal* on 3rd February 1852, Stevenson made a vituperative attack on Renton[633]:

> I ... acquaintd you of some of the particulars of the dreadful attack by the [Xhosa]s on Woburn village, of which you took notes, without evincing the slightest sympathy or even apprehension for your own safety.

> This divine serenity, coupled with the apparent security and protection which you received from the enemy, while my life was demanded by your ferocious logic sons of light impressed upon my mind the strongest belief that you and some of our brethren were, a few days previous to the [Xhosa] outbreak, in full possession of the intentions and plans of the enemy, ...

This libel seems to have had little effect. Stevenson by this time was an outcast.

> For many years afterwards Stevenson had a most miserable time of it. His fellow colonists treated him with thorough contempt as a cold blooded coward, and no one would have anything to do with him[634]

The disturbance settled down and was for the time being forgotten, but some of the allegations would resurface again and again, even more than forty years later.

War in the Bush   [1851]

When the news of the war reached Britain early in 1851 it provoked widespread indignation. Earl Grey, the Secretary of State, found himself under increasing pressure, and his career was threatened. The reason for the outrage was more the cost of the war than its morality. Colonies were expected to be sources of income, not a drain on the exchequer. This pressure was transferred to Smith in the Colony and did not make his position any easier.

The amaXhosa, having failed to take Fort Hare in a pitched battle, retreated into the bush. There were three main foci of activity – the Waterkloof, the Amatolas, and the Fish River Bush. Sandile found refuge in the Amatolas, Maqoma and Uithaalder in the Waterkloof, and Stokwe and Tola in the Fish River bush, where they were soon joined by Siyolo. Each of these locations was well chosen to cause the maximum difficulty for the British commanders. The mountainous area of the Amatolas were well wooded, providing ample concealment and opportunity for ambush and raids on the farms of the Colony. The Waterkloof was a deep gorge carved out by the apparently insignificant Waterkloof River, a tributary of the Koonap, which, itself, flowed into the Fish. It was located about twenty five kilometres northwest of Fort Beaufort. The Great Fish River was the location of numerous encounters in the previous wars.

The pattern of the war now had army units pursuing the Xhosa and the rebels into their bush strongholds and trying to evict them. Unsurprisingly, the British command had learned nothing from the previous wars or the early encounters of this one. The troops, dressed in inappropriate uniforms, with an emphasis on formal drills and pitched battles, were ill equipped to cope with guerrilla tactics. They were ineffective in providing any defence against the Xhosa forces, who were able to make incursions into the Colony at will. By August, farming in Albany had become impossible and famine was threatened. The army was far too thinly spread to provide any protection to the farmers, and they simply had to abandon their farms and retreat to safety.

After a few months there was little progress. The Xhosa raiders were free to attack isolated farms and pursuit was inevitably unsuccessful when the enemy refused to engage with the pursuers. Complaints by farmers who were suffering from the constant loss of stock grew more strident, and Smith was forced to escalate the war. Reinforcements began arriving in East London, and making the often dangerous journey to King William's Town. Although the road was generally under the protection of Phatho, Siyolo made frequent assaults from his concealment in the Fish River bush. The importance of communications was well understood by the rebels and the Xhosa, and post riders were a regular and vulnerable target.

Almost simultaneously, in two of the theatres of war, the extent of the Xhosa threat was forced home. In the Waterkloof Somerset's forces began a concerted effort to drive Maqoma out, and in the Fish river bush Mackinnon began an onslaught on Siyolo.

On 7th September Lieut.-Col. Thomas Fordyce, who had been left in command of the forces in the Waterkloof region while Somerset was in Graham's Town, led a patrol of 600 men of the 74th Highland regiment up onto the Kroomie heights to attempt an attack on Maqoma. With them was a small Mfengu force and a CMR escort. New in the country, Fordyce was not prepared to accept advice on the conditions from the CMR commander. He set off on his own initiative to clear the Xhosa from the Waterkloof region. His intention was to rest the troops until sunset and then attack the Xhosa who were hiding in the well-wooded regions in the Waterkloof and Fuller's Hoek. The Xhosa had other ideas. While the troops were eating and resting they assembled in large numbers and attacked. The initial onslaught was beaten off. Maqoma, himself then appeared, directing his forces and it became apparent that he was hoping to cut the British off from the pass by which they had ascended and isolate them in an exposed position of the heights. Again the Xhosa were repelled and Fordyce's men began a retreat. Now, however, their supply of ammunition was low. While they had been at the top, the Xhosa had blocked the return path by felling trees. The front of the column was brought to a halt and the Mfengu at the rear, under severe pressure, panicked. The retreat turned into a rout, and, by the time the troops had fought their way to the open plain at the foot of the Kroomie mountains, they had lost fourteen dead and as many wounded. Once the British had reached the plain the Xhosa withdrew, knowing that on the open ground the British held the advantage.

Almost simultaneously, on the Fish River, a similar course of events was playing out. Mackinnon's command had been built up to about 1200 men, the majority from the the 2nd (the Queen's Royal) and the 6th (Royal 1st Warwickshire) Regiments of Foot, and smaller numbers from the 73rd (Highland) Regiment, the Cape Mounted Rifles, and the Mfengu units. His first objective was to clear the Fish River Bush and remove the threat to the communication lines between East London and King William's Town.

Mackinnon had moved his force to Fort Willshire in early September. On the 8th, reports of a large Xhosa force in the neighbourhood caused him to decide to pursue them into the bush[635]. Before first light the force set off. The river flowed at the bottom of a deep gorge. On either side there was dense bush providing ideal cover for an ambush. A small detachment of the Queen's Regiment, under a Captain Oldham, made its way towards the bottom of the gorge to flush out the quarry. On one side of the river Lieutenant Colonel Michel led one detachment along the heights: on the other side Mackinnon led another.

Mackinnon had by now had ample time to apply his mind the nature of the bush war and to gain an understanding of it. He, too, had learnt nothing. Sending Michel and his 150 men into the bush was irresponsible. The Queen's Regiment had only recently arrived in the country and had no experience of the conditions. The men were inappropriately clad and inappropriately trained. In their red jackets they were sitting ducks for Siyolo's men. Once again, with inadequate communications and no clear sight of the enemy, the troops were cut out and slaughtered. The fighting was bloody and no mercy was shown. An attempt at retreat quickly became a rout. There was danger that Oldham's force would be entirely wiped out. On the heights above Mackinnon's troops could hear the noise of fighting. Mackinnon did nothing. Only when troops of the 6th Regiment entered the scene of battle did Siyolo forces retreat, once again disappearing into the bush as if by magic. Of the 150 men, twenty seven, including Oldham himself, were dead, twenty eight were wounded, and eight were missing, never to be seen again.

A few days later the army withdrew from the bush, their objectives unmet.

As was common at the time, there was a rather efficient cover-up. Although there were mutterings that Mackinnon's failure to go to the rescue was due to cowardice, nothing came of them. The reports of the action praised those in command and apparently little was learnt from the experience. Nevertheless, this was the beginning of the eclipse of Mackinnon.

The dissatisfaction with the conduct of the war grew. In Britain and the Colony criticism of Smith and Somerset grew, although Smith's reputation meant that many were prepared to give him some latitude. The British command seemed incapable of learning from experience. The officers, steeped in the methods of the wars against Napoleon, were unable to bring new thinking to their strategy and tactics.

One senior officer was an exception. Colonel Eyre was a career soldier. Initially he, too, placed his faith in traditional methods, but he was nevertheless able to see the inadequacy of Mackinnon's tactics and to begin to consider alternatives. Instead of regarding the officers of the Colonial levies as obviously inferior to the officers of the regular army, he was prepared to listen to them. He also saw that the colonists with the army

Colonel Eyre in the Bush

Detail from a contemporary drawing. Eyre is to the left of the picture. The squatting figure in the lower centre is a civilian guide.

(Historical collection of Museum Africa, Johannesburg, with permission.)

had a wealth of experience in bushcraft. One of these colonists, with whom he discussed things, was his guide, Edward Driver.

Driver was now fifty six years old. He was vastly experienced in bush lore and military operations on the frontier. It is no surprise that, even at this relatively advanced age, he was to be found in the front line. A well-known contemporary drawing[636], depicts Colonel Eyre's camp in the Fish

River bush. Eyre is a tall scholarly figure, bespectacled, immaculately uniformed, wearing a pith helmet with a preposterously high crown. He is surrounded by a large crowd of officers, soldiers, and camp servants. He is gazing shortsightedly into the middle distance at nothing in particular. At a second focal point of the picture, a man squats on his haunches. He is bearded, at ease in loose clothing, and wearing a disreputable slouch hat. He is unidentified, but a figure of consequence in the composition. Driver would have looked and dressed like that, but there is nothing to say that he was actually the model for the artist.

A short while after the debacle in the Fish river gorge that had led to so many casualties, Eyre's detachment was ordered to make another attempt in the same region. Stokwe was now fully engaged against the British with a refuge in a well-wooded kloof that was named after his ally Tola. An attack was planned to drive his forces out of their refuge.

Eyre decided that he needed the support of a force of experienced men. He asked Thomas Stubbs to bring reinforcements from the Albany Sharpshooters and additional supplies of ammunition to Committees Post, where he was now encamped[637]. He also summoned a Mfengu detachment commanded by George Cyrus, who was the government interpreter and Supervisor of Locations in Graham's Town.

When Stubbs arrived with sixteen Albany sharpshooters and Cyrus's force of one hundred and fifty Mfengu, Driver would have been pleased by the addition of a bush-wise frontiersman to the company. He and Stubbs went back a long way and had strong mutual trust. Eyre still had little knowledge of the conditions. He was, however, blessed with intelligence and willingness to profit from experience. Stubbs and Cyrus had travelled through the night and arrived before dawn. Without delay, immediately after breakfast Driver, Stubbs and Cyrus set off to reconnoitre. Eyre, meanwhile, was resting his troops, awaiting the arrival of another force under Colonel Michel which was to provide support on the other side of the river.

The three frontiersmen moved up river. After about six kilometres they saw something white in the bush ahead of them. It was a blanket intended as a signal. They retreated into the bush and moved carefully forward. There was a small herd of cattle ahead of them and they immediately perceived it as a trap intended to entice the army into a narrow kloof where they could be attacked. It was the same tactic that had been used with success against Oldham's force a short while before. Retreat seemed advisable but when they looked back they saw another signal blanket.

"They are in front and behind," said Stubbs. "We seem to be in a bit of a fix."

Driver was beginning to feel his age and did not fancy his chances of escaping from the trap. He suggested: "Yes. I think as you and Cyrus are more active than me, you two had better try and return to the camp. I will manage to hide away along the river until you can bring a party out to attack them and take that lot of cattle. But I am afraid you will have some difficulty in reaching the camp." Stubbs laconically reports: "We did reach it."

Eyre refused to supply any troops to extract Driver as he was planning an early start the next morning and they needed rest so Stubbs took some of his own men and "fetched Driver".

At 3 o'clock the following morning the party set out, intent on attacking the kraal of the chief Stokwe. Cyrus's Mfengu formed the advance guard, and Stubbs's men, to his disgust, were ordered to bring up the rear. One or two kilometres further up river than the point reached by Driver and Stubbs the previous day the Mfengu came on a hut occupied by some wounded rebels. They fired on them but they escaped. The noise of the shots rapidly brought Eyre and Driver to the scene and they were soon joined by Stubbs's rangers who could not keep away from the action.

The Fish River bush is a dense and nearly impenetrable mixture of *euphorbia triangularis*, a small fleshy spiny tree, and other thorny shrubs such as acacias. Eyre, still in Eurocentric military mode, told Stubbs: "I wish you would charge through there and I will march my men round the hill and take them on the flank."

Stubbs told him it was impossible. To a British officer "impossible" was unacceptable. He asked Driver what he thought. Driver replied: "At one time when there were plenty of elephants in the country to make paths through it would have been easily done, but I think it is hardly possible to get through with a horse."

This is an interesting comment. To what extent was Driver aware that it was largely due to the depredations of himself and his fellow ivory hunters that the Eastern Cape elephants had almost disappeared?[638] He probably realised it but did not think it particularly important as there were plenty further north. Only through dedicated conservation efforts in more recent years has the elephant population in what is now the Addo National Park and its environs now been brought up to a viable size. They are worth as much as a tourist asset as their ancestors were as a source of ivory.

Eyre was not one to accept a verdict that what he desired could not be achieved. He lost his temper and told Driver, Stubbs, his aide-de-camp Inglis, and a party of a hundred grenadiers to follow him, and set off into the bush. Within a hundred metres he and his horse were completely trapped and unable to move. Eyre was apoplectic with rage and Inglis nearly paralysed with suppressed mirth. Eyre shouted to a passing soldier to prod the horse with his bayonet and at that point Stubbs took pity on him and cut him loose. It took an hour to work their way through the kilometre of bush and a further four hours to extract the parched and exhausted soldiers from the dense thorns.

The whole expedition ended in a retreat to Committees Post and an abortive attempt to ambush the Xhosa, who wisely never turned up.

Unlike his fellow officers, Eyre was prepared to admit a mistake. He was prepared to learn from his contacts with experienced frontiersmen such as Driver and Stubbs. From the former he began to absorb the techniques of surviving in the bush, from the latter the nature of this kind of warfare. Stubbs was a natural commander who had earned the loyalty of the men of the levy. His concerns were to put them in a winning position without placing them in unnecessary danger. During the campaign Eyre changed from a blinkered British officer to one of the strongest exponents of the stalk and ambush techniques of warfare.

This was not the case with the other members of the British command. In early October Smith, in the face of the reverses suffered by Fordyce and Mackinnon, decided to concentrate all his resources on the Waterkloof.

The Waterkloof gorge ran roughly east to west. To the south was a plateau, the Kroomie heights at the top of a south facing escarpment. To the north was another plateau, a large area of open grassland. At the eastern edge of the gorge a narrow ridge of land separated the Waterkloof gorge from the Fuller's Hoek gorge to the east. The ridge connected the Kroomie heights on the south side with the high ground on the north.

Somerset, following Smith's orders sent Fordyce with the 74th Highlanders to approach from the south up the Kroomie, and Michel with the Queens Regiment to follow the upper Blinkwater and approach from the north. They were then to take the high ground and the ridge and from there to evict Maqoma and his allies from the Waterkloof and Fuller's Hoek. The move took place on 12th October. There was heavy mist on the summit. The only communication between the two divisions was by bugle call and the calls used by the Highland regiments were different from those used by the English. The great push was indecisive. Skirmishing continued until the 6th November, when Fordyce was killed by a coloured sniper while trying to direct his forces from an unprotected position. The troops eventually withdrew, having failed in their objective.

The criticism of the conduct of the war continued. Smith decided on another strategy. Just as in 1834 he and D'Urban had taken the war to Hintsa, blaming the Xhosa king for matters outside his control, now he determined to attack Hintsa's son, Sarhili. The situation was a close parallel to what had happened in 1835. Sarhili was the Xhosa king, recognized as such by the descendants of the House of Phalo – his own Gcaleka, the Rharhabe, and the Mbalu. This did not mean that he had any political control over them. He himself was not a combatant and the arguments that he was harbouring the enemy and their cattle was no better an excuse for an invasion than it had been in Hintsa's time. Smith's decision was a cynical one. The Gcaleka, located beyond the Kei, were vulnerable to invasion, without the natural defences that the combatants had in the Waterkloof, the Amatolas, and the Fish River. They were an easy source of booty. Smith spent six weeks harassing them and returned with the spoils of war – thirty thousand cattle, and other livestock.

Smith wrote a triumphant report to Earl Grey on the success of his mission: back in England Grey was penning a dispatch to Smith with a very different message.

Smith now turned all his attention to Maqoma and his allies. He set out to enforce a scorched earth policy where crops were destroyed and the land was made unliveable. The Xhosa still refused to submit, living off the bush as best they could and refusing to engage with Smith's forces. By March, while the region had been devastated, Smith was no nearer to his goal of defeating Maqoma.

The full story of the war in the bush is impossibly complex, skirmishes and battles throughout the region. News reached the towns in all sorts of ways. Joseph Walker wrote to Godlonton, who was in Cape Town at the time, a letter dated 2nd March 1852[639]

My son Joseph has this moment received a letter from Edward Driver who is in the field [working?] with Col. Eyre & Major Mitchell and he says that the [Xhosa]s fell upon Col. Eyre and took him prisoner and his men rushed forwards and in a desperate fight retook the Col all safe and unhurt so we have spared to us the brave Col Eyre for which I am very thankful to the God of Providence. I believe that the 73 had a dreadful fight on this occasion in which 18 of the brave men of the brave Colonel were killed.

On 1st March 1852, Earl Grey's bombshell arrived in King William's Town. His dispatch informed Smith that he was dismissed from his post as Governor, that his successor was Sir George Cathcart and that Cathcart's arrival in the Cape was imminent. Devastated by the blow, Smith still continued with his campaign, hoping to be able to crown his period of office with a victory, but with no success. At the beginning of April Cathcart arrived and immediately proceeded to the frontier. Smith left to a hero's farewell from the colonists, both on the frontier and in Cape Town. His career was, however, over. In England he was promoted to Lieutenant General and served the home based forces as General Officer Commanding first the Western Districts and then the Northern Districts, but he played no further notable part in affairs of state. He died in 1860.

Cathcart imposed an even stronger policy of seek and destroy. The Xhosa and rebel forces were worn away by attrition. The coloured forces who were regarded as rebels received no mercy, often being shot out of hand or summarily hanged. One of the most successful commanders in the Amatola region was Colonel Eyre, who successfully applied the techniques of stalk and ambush that he had learned in the Fish River Bush in the company of Stubbs, Driver, and other colonists.

By March 1853 it was all over. Sarhili had sued for peace and a peace treaty had been agreed. Siyolo had surrendered and, expecting to be treated as defeated commander, was instead arrested, tried, sentenced to life imprisonment, and sent into exile. Sandile and Maqoma negotiated peace for the Ngqika and were allowed to settle in a region between the eastern edge of the Amatolas and the Kei River. The coloured rebels were granted an amnesty except for their leaders. Uithaalder and Andries Botha were both sentenced to death but their sentences were commuted to life imprisonment.

Postscript [1896]

Many years after the events at Tyumie at the start of the war John and Catherine Cumming, after more than fifty years of marriage, were living in quiet retirement at Glen Avon. Their son, John Pringle Cumming had married Sarah Hart, the daughter of Robert Hart Jr. The Cummings occupied a second house on the farm which had been named The Retreat.

It was forty-five years since the Woburn and Auckland massacres, and there was no memorial to those who had been killed. A journalist, Charles Cowen, had become interested in the affair two years before. He had begun a correspondence to find out more, and had received information from Captain G. Armytage, Stacey's predecessor as Superintendant of Woburn, and W. Dewey, the editor of the *Alice Times*, whom he had known previously when he had worked in the Eastern Cape. Dewey had published an article by Armytage in 1895 about the military graves at

Fort Hare. A further source of information was a set of reminiscences by Stevenson that had been published in 1875[640].

John Stevenson was now an old man living near East London. He was still concerned to justify his behaviour at the time of the massacres, and his flight from Woburn. Shortly after his escape, when he reached Graham's Town, accusations of cowardice led him to construct a view of events which made him the hero of Tyumie, providing leadership to the panic-stricken missionaries. At the time his story had been demolished by Renton's speech, but his article in 1875 had revived his version of the events. At the time his version had been fiercely rebutted in a letter by John Aitken Chalmers, the son of William and Mary Chalmers.

Cowen saw an opportunity to write a book on the dramatic events. He and Dewey interested Mr A. C. Baker, the Civil Commissioner for what was now the region of Victoria West, and, early in 1896, they began a campaign to erect a monument to those military settlers who had been killed in the attacks. Cowen visited Alice and began asking the oldest inhabitants about their memories.

Janet Brown was living in Auckland near Alice. She agreed to give him an account of her knowledge of the affair. Cowan also made contact with Mr A. C. Baker, who also agreed to provide him with information and got in touch with Janet's younger brother, William B. Chalmers in East London, on the same subject[641]. Janet, herself, had of course been alone with her child at Iqibira on the day of the massacres but she wrote him an account of what had happened at Auckland, obtained from talking to Xhosa people who had memories of the events. She was, however, alarmed at the influence that Stevenson's account had had with Cowen. Her brother John, who had taken up the cudgels against Stevenson in 1875, was now dead. She wrote to William telling him of Cowen's questions.

William Chalmers was immediately suspicious of Cowen. He believed that his motive was to write a controversial book with Stevenson's version of events dominating it. He advised Baker to approach John Cumming to obtain his version of the events at Tyumie. Cumming responded with his account of the Christmas Day massacres[642]. Baker appears to have been impressed by this and sent the memoir on to Cowen at the end of May. Chalmers now took up the campaign in earnest. He got further information from Cumming, in particular the pamphlet that had been published in 1851 about Renton's reception in Graham's Town. Reading this incensed him further and he wrote to Cumming[643]:

[It] revived feelings of anger and disgust at Stevenson's black, base, and disgraceful cowardice, and ingratitude towards you. ... [Stevenson] is just the man that would try and take advantage from Mr Baker and make use of him ...

The letter goes on to state that he would publish his brother's letter of rebuttal if Stevenson did not desist.

Baker became convinced. He wrote to Cowen a short time afterwards, stating that Stevenson was unreliable. At about the same time Chalmers received a communication from Cowen which alarmed him even more. It was a pamphlet, ostensibly for private circulation only, printed by the Lovedale Press. It contained an extended introduction by Cowen to a self-justifying account by Stevenson in which he repeated all the claims of his heroism at the time. It does seem that Cowen was inviting comment.

> One aim in this publication is to obtain, from whoever can assist, whatever reliable information they may be able to give me of the events of that time.

The pamphlet is printed with wide margins to allow for comments and Chalmers made full use of these. On 8th July he returned a fully annotated copy of the pamphlet to Cowen. Three days later he sent a copy of his comments to Cumming and commented in the covering letter that Baker was now quite disillusioned with Stevenson and would have nothing to do with him. Dewey too was becoming suspicious. He wrote to Cowen about the pamphlet, stating that it should include the views of Cumming, Chalmers, and Niven. On the same day Chalmers also wrote unequivocally to Cowen demanding that he withdraw Stevenson's account, since it contained lies. He followed it up with a second letter within a few days. He found Cowen's response unsatisfactory: Cowen maintained that he had published the pamphlet privately to establish copyright and prevent uncritical newspaper publication. Cowen, himself, insisted that he was only concerned to get at the truth.

Chalmers then turned to Stevenson, telling Cumming that

> I reminded him that his life was saved by you, and how very kind and hospitable you were to him. I reminded him of the manner in which he was afterwards treated by his fellow colonists for his cowardice in deserting his comrades. I reminded [him] how ungrateful he afterwards proved himself, and how completely demolished he was by Mr Renton in his speech of 1851, and by my brother in his letter of 1874 and what a contemptible figure he cut in the eyes of [the] public. I told him that that speech and that letter were still in existence.

At last his campaign began to take effect. Cowen was finally convinced. He told Chalmers "... I begin to perceive that the mischief and misrepresentation was alive." On 8th November Chalmers wrote to Cumming that

> You will perceive that I have at last got him [Cowen] into the right frame of mind, and that his eyes have been opened about Stevenson.

Cowen, perhaps reluctantly, gave up his ideas and on 18th Feb 1898, Cumming was able to write to Chalmers:

> I suppose that we must bid farewell to Mr Cowen and all his glowing prospects of a sensational book upon the massacre of the Military Settlers near to the Chumie. I have no doubt he was scared by your pen from the attempt.

Chapter 20. Advance and Retreat

Civilisation is hooped together, brought
Under a rule, under the semblance of peace
By manifold illusion

W. B. Yeats, Supernatural songs

Sir George Grey   [1854 – 1861]

Sir George Cathcart's brief tenure as Governor was nevertheless something of a watershed for the Xhosa. It was his responsibility to bring the war to an end. It was he who imposed the consequences of the war upon them. For the Kat River rebels the outcome was equally bleak. The lands of those who had fought against the Colony were forfeit and offered to colonists as farmland. Soon, however, he was to be relieved.

The term of office of the Secretary of State for the Colonies, Earl Grey, came to an end with the replacement of the Whig Government by a short lived Conservative minority government and the subsequent formation of a Whig-Peelite coalition in 1852. The new Secretary of State recalled Cathcart and replaced him with Sir George Grey[644] a former Governor of New Zealand. He took office on 5th December 1854 and served until 1861.

Grey was completely different from the long line of military governors that had served until that point. Intellectually and politically he was at a different level. His instincts were liberal; he saw this as being achieved by extending "civilization", in other words the domination of the Empire, by bringing schools, hospitals, and roads to the Xhosa. At the same time he was Machiavellian in achieving his aims and ensuring that his achievements were recognized by his masters in Britain and by the public[645].

It was under his rule that the ideas were introduced which eventually led to the colonization of the whole region between the Cape Colony and Natal. He saw it as crucial to remove the power of the chiefs. At the same time, where convenient, he made use of Xhosa law and custom to maintain rule. It was done by negotiation and careful use of the carrot and the stick. His intention was always to bring the Xhosa under the rule of western law and custom. He sought to christianize them and bring them into the work force. He regarded this as to their ultimate advantage.

357

The Legislative Council and House of Assembly   [1834 – 1854]

From 1834 the mouthpiece of the colonists in Government was the Legislative Assembly. This was an appointed body headed by the Governor. It included five officials ex officio and between five and seven leading residents of the Colony appointed by the Governor. There was freedom of speech and the Council could introduce legislation. The Governor, however, had both a deliberative and a casting vote, as well as the right of veto. It was never satisfactory. Officials often outnumbered appointed members and could manipulate its procedures. The pressure for a more representative form of government had built up over the years. The pressure was complicated by the rivalry between the eastern and western parts of the colony. There was a strong body of opinion, led by men such as Robert Godlonton, that separate government should be set up for the eastern part of the colony[646].

The trigger that released the pressure for change was the arrival in Cape Town in 1848 of *Neptune*, a convict ship. Earl Grey had determined that, like Australia, the Cape should become a destination for transported convicts. The outrage was immediate. Although Harry Smith sympathised with the colonists in their determination to resist this, he could not go against Grey's orders. He did, however, delay the landing of the convicts while he sent representations back to Britain. Cape Town remained in a state of turmoil. All bar one of the appointed members of the Legislative Council resigned. Those appointed to succeed them were also forced by public opinion to resign. Eventually after several months Grey relented and *Neptune* sailed on to deposit its cargo in Tasmania.

Smith came up with an ingenious plan to heal the situation temporarily. He set up the election of a slate of candidates, from which he would appoint the Councillors according to his prerogative. Those appointed included Stockenstrom, Godlonton, and Fairbairn. This, too, failed when the appointed members resigned because of lack of progress towards representative government. At last, in 1853, a new constitution came into effect, providing for representative government.

Under this constitution two houses were established. The upper house was the Legislative Council, now consisting of fifteen elected members. The four principal officials of the Colony were in attendance with the right to speak, but not to vote. The lower house was the House of Assembly, consisting of forty six members elected on a constituency basis. The franchise was granted on a property qualification. While not set very high, it was enough to exclude most coloured people. The first election in 1854 set Southern Africa off on a long and difficult road to real democracy, which was only reached 140 years later in 1994.

The Great Hunger   [1854 – 1858]

After 1853, as the war wound down, the power of the western Xhosa was broken. Whether they had been combatants, neutral, or allies with the Colony, under Grey's policies their chiefs found themselves salaried officials of the Cape Government, responsible to white magistrates. Those who had been exiled found the loss of their territory hard to stomach. Matters deteriorated with the arrival of another infliction. Lung sickness[647], a disease of cattle, arrived in the country through an imported consignment of beasts. By 1854 it had crossed into the region between Fish and Kei, and it reached Sarhili's people in Gcalekaland across the Kei in early 1855. In spite of strong efforts by the chiefs to control the movement of cattle it devastated the herds of the Xhosa. In some places herds were almost wiped out.

As had been the case a few years earlier, when Mlanjeni had promised invincibility in battle, an unhappy people were ready for a prophet. In 1819 Nxele had brought the Xhosa to war by preaching his version of the Trinity: in 1856 new prophets promised their version of the Resurrection[648].

Mhlakaza was a Xhosa who had been baptised as a Wesleyan and went under the name Wilhelm Goliath in the Colony. When Archdeacon Nathaniel J. Merriman arrived in Graham's Town in 1849 with the responsibility of overseeing the affairs of the Anglican Church in the region, he hired Mhlakaza as a servant. For the next few years the two men travelled the length and breadth of the region on foot as Merriman carried out his duties. They built up a strong relationship. Mhlakaza was of a metaphysical turn of mind, revelled in long religious discussions with his employer, and was soon confirmed in the Anglican Church whose ritual appealed to him far more than the evangelical enthusiasm of the Wesleyans. His ambition was to preach. However, he fell out with his employer and was dismissed in 1853. He moved to Gcalekaland near the Great Place of Sarhili where, like Nxele, he began to preach his own form of religion, a version of Christianity mixed strongly with Xhosa traditions.

Before he left the Colony Mhlakaza had adopted an orphan child, whose parents had both been killed during Colonel Eyre's bloody campaign in the Waterkloof. Peires has made the beguiling suggestion that this child might be the niece that was later living in his household in Gcalekaland[649]. Her name was Nongqawuse.

One day in April the thirteen-year-old Nongqawuse and a younger companion, eight-year-old Nombanda, returned from scaring birds off the crops with a story that two men had appeared to them with a strange prophecy of resurrection. Not much attention was paid to them until they again reported the message on a subsequent day. At this point Mhlakaza decided that they were describing his dead brother, Nongqawuse's father. He accompanied the girls to the place on the Gxara River where Nongqawuse acted as a medium to relay the message of the men. It was a prophecy that the Xhosa must slaughter all their cattle and not plant grain, purifying themselves and getting rid of the bewitched cattle. When this had been done their ancestors would rise from the dead, bringing with them new cattle. There would be a new era of abundance. Initially the message was one of hope for all mankind.

This was not the only prophecy or rumour floating round at the time. One of the more insidious arose from the news that former Governor Cathcart had been killed in the Crimea by Russian forces. Among the Xhosa this news spread rapidly, portrayed as a victory for strange people called Russians. The Russians rapidly became identified with their ancestors and people spoke of the Russians coming out of the sea to drive out the white man.

For Mhlakaza the experience on the Gxara was an epiphany. The prophecy was precisely shaped to fit his mystical temperament. He hastened to Sarhili to tell him of it. The Xhosa were ripe for conversion to a belief in what he said. While Nongqawuse had been the medium, Mhlakaza provided the message. The news spread rapidly. Other chiefs came to see and visit Mhlakaza; some left as converts, others unconvinced. Soon the people were divided into the believers, *amathamba*, and the sceptics, *amagogotya*. Sarhili, after spending time with Mhlakaza had his own mystical experience and became a strong believer. He issued a proclamation that the people should begin slaughtering their cattle and prepare for the new millenium. The stage was set and inexorably the tragedy unfolded.

The division between believers and sceptics cut across all the Xhosa groupings. Sarhili, the Xhosa king and chief of the Gcaleka was a strong believer. Of the Ngqika, Maqoma was a strong believer, Sandile vacillated between belief and scepticism, and their brother, Anta, was an outspoken sceptic. Phatho of the Gqunukwhebe and Ndlambe's successor, Mhala, were also convinced believers. Naturally the Christians, Dyani Tshatshu and Kama of the Ntinde and Gqunukwhebe respectively, were outspoken sceptics, but so was the strongly traditional Anta.

The cattle killing began. For Maclean and Brownlee it was an alarming time. Brownlee, particularly, tried desperately to persuade people to ignore the prophecy but to no avail. Both had a failure of imagination and an inability to understand the mindset of the Xhosa at the time; they ascribed the movement to the chiefs, who were using it as an excuse to invade the Colony. Grey was only too happy to accept their advice on this; he saw it as an opportunity finally to break the power of the chiefs. Brownlee later realised that he had been wrong:

> Talking with me about the Umhlakaza cattle killing delusion he [Charles Brownlee] told me that at one time he had regarded the movement as one initiated by the chiefs to invade the Colony, but that in later years he had rather leant to the view that both chiefs and people, led away by superstitious beliefs, had been equally deluded.[650]

The 18th February 1857 was the day on which the resurrection was to take place. Prophets who supply deadlines for their prophecies are unwise. When the ancestors failed to materialize, starvation was already widespread. Soon desperate people sought food wherever and by whatever means they could. Theft of stock rose substantially.

Sir George Grey arrived at the frontier early in 1857 in order to deal with the crisis. For him the threat was an opportunity to finally break the power of the chiefs. On 3rd March he issued a proclamation threatening death or transportation for any Xhosa who entered the Colony for purposes of theft. Most death sentences were commuted to transportation but this was a dreaded fate. Those convicted were sent to Cape Town or Robben Island and served long terms there. The trials were conducted under procedures set up for the purpose; men were convicted on flimsy evidence without proper defence. The official attitude to relief was that there were many opportunities for obtaining work as labourers and that should be the mechanism for preventing starvation. A Relief Committee was set up in King William's Town under the chairmanship of the Bishop of Graham's Town. It eventually was discontinued given the lack of encouragement from Grey.

The sceptics were blamed by the believers for the failure of the ancestors to return and usher in the new age. Their refusal to kill their cattle had meant that the conditions for fulfilment of the prophecy had not been met. Many of those who remained starved to death. One of the victims was Mhlakaza himself. Thousands flocked to the Colony seeking work. By the end of the great hunger the population of British Kaffraria had fallen from over 100 000 to about 25 000. The effect on Gcalekaland across the Kei was as great. Estimates of the numbers vary widely but the total number of deaths was probably about 40 000. The number who migrated, abandoning their traditional life, was about 150 000.[651]

Land became available in British Kaffraria. Formerly Xhosa land was auctioned off to farmers and speculators. Grey was anxious to increase the white population and had introduced a large party of German immigrants – many of them from the German Legion, a group of mercenaries who had been recruited by Britain for the Crimean war but had been too late to take part in it. White villages and towns began to grow in the region. the existing settlements of East London, King William's Town and Peddie grew rapidly. The new town of Queenstown grew where John Cumming's mission to the Gcina had begun. The German settlers established new villages whose names reflected their origins – Berlin, Hamburg, Stutterheim. Further, the influx of Xhosa west of the Fish River meant that the labour forces in those regions was no longer dominated by the coloured people. Kaffraria was no longer the home of the Xhosa alone. Its demography became much closer to that of the Colony.

The End of Independence   [1854 – 1861]

It was Maqoma, ever the *bête noire* of colonial governors, who first fell foul of the new regulations. In some ways he seems to have gone out of his way to be provocative. An informer called Fusani had been responsible for giving information to the authorities about various cattle thieves, som of whom had as a result been killed. A group of Maqoma's men made an attack on Fusani and killed him. There was some suspicion that Maqoma himself had been involved but there was little evidence. Maqoma at the time was once again drinking heavily. One of his wives fled from him, entering Crown Land. Maqoma applied for a pass to go in pursuit of her but Lucas, the local magistrate, refused it, and was as a result assaulted by the enraged chief. Maqoma then went in pursuit of his wife and as a result was arrested. At this stage Grey took the opportunity to throw the book at him. The case of the murder of Fusani was revived and in one of the dubious trials of the time Maqoma was sentenced to twenty years on Robben Island. He was released in 1869 but after two years again fell foul of authority and was returned to the island without further trial. He died there, embittered and alone.

Grey's next target was Mhala. He was sentenced to five years on Robben island for conspiracy to cause war – this followed from Grey's conviction that the cattle killing had been a plot by the chiefs. Others followed. Soon many others were sent to the island, including Xhoxho, Tola, and Stokwe.

Sandile threw himself on the mercy of the Colonial Government and accepted their authority and a salary, becoming responsible to a magistrate. Bhothomane was old and infirm. Sarhili offered submission but it was refused and a military force was sent against the remaining Gcaleka. They were driven to the other side of the Mbashe River to be settled there.

When Grey left the Colony in 1861 he left two legacies. One was a greatly improved network of schools hospitals and roads. The other was a broken people; the old way of life of the western Xhosa had changed for ever.

Chapter 21. The Next Generation

Our children will not know it's a different country
All we can hope to leave them now is money.

Philip Larkin, High Windows

The Golden Jubilee [1870]

The fiftieth anniversary of the British settlement, like the twenty-fifth, did not go unmarked in Grahamstown[652]. The ceremonies had a different flavour. Where the silver jubilee was a celebration by a group of people in the prime of their lives, pompously and ceremoniously marking their achievements, the golden jubilee was valedictory. Few of those who had landed with such high hopes in Algoa Bay in 1820 still survived: few of those who had survived were in sufficiently good health to take an active part in the proceedings. The celebrants were largely the sons and daughters of the settlers. Those who had survived made great efforts to attend the celebrations.

One of those was John Montgomery, who travelled all the way from the Transvaal to be there. He had been a trader in the early days but had left at the time of the Great Trek. His opinions of his fellow traders had a wry twist[653]:

> These were the men who first opened the roads into the wilderness among the wild tribes where life and property were not safe for one night, and started the trade which others now enjoy, without knowing or caring who were the pioneers: Donald McDonald and [William] McLuckie, who came out in 1819 with Mr Moodie; [James] Weeks and Walker[654] who were the first that penetrated as far as Cradock; [Edward] Driver of Driver's Hill; [William] Thackwray and his sons; John[655] Weakley, [James] Temlett, [David] Hume, Tennant, [Edward] Hanger, the Nordens (John, Ben and Mark), J. Philips, Fossey, Murphy, Anderson, Webber Senior (who still survives), Gleeson, Collins, J[ames] Howse, G[eorge] Wood, Adam Gilfillan[656] and many others whom I forget, who after one or two trips settled down to a more easy way of living. Some of these men took up their abode in Graham's Town and carried on a lucrative trade with the smouses[657]; and others became so stuck up that they would not take their hands out of their breeches pockets without they had gloves on.

A major event on the programme was a lecture on the history of the settlement given by the Rev. Mr H. H. Dugmore[658]. Dugmore was one of those who had been a child in 1820 and was therefore not counted as a "proper settler". He had become one of the many Wesleyan ministers originating from the settler community, and was now a leading citizen of

Grahamstown. His address defined the self-image of the community at the time.

Time, for the people of that era, was a commodity in plentiful supply. Dugmore's address lasted for four hours. It was a eulogy to the achievements of the settlers and there was, perhaps understandably, no great attempt at introspection or self-criticism. He catalogued the achievements of many who had become prominent:

> The elder Cawood, William Hartley, and especially the old veteran Edward Driver, should be induced to write the story of their early adventures, or one of the most exciting chapters of Frontier history will be lost.

He lamented the loss of old friends:

> The Jubilee year had proved the last to several who were hoping to see its completion. My old friend Joseph Walker among the number. Identified with the fortunes of the Settler's city for the best portion of his life, energetic and active in many a work conducive to the highest interest of his fellow townsmen, he has left to us a goodly array of young representatives a name respected and honoured by men of all classes.

He was careful to give credit to the importance of all the Christian denominations that had dominated the religious life of the region, but the Wesleyans got special mention:

> The names of [John] Ayliff, [William] Shepstone, [Richard] Walker,..., [Benjamin] Booth, and others ... are all associated with services that began fifty years ago, and have never ceased. They fed and fanned the flame of piety where it would have died out but for them; and they kindled it in many places where otherwise its light might never have appeared.

While the emphasis was on the English settlers of Albany, the names of Robert Hart and the Scottish settlers were not forgotten, and the listeners were referred to the writings of Thomas Pringle for their story.

A point that Dugmore made was the remarkable longevity of the settlers. To some extent this is a specious statement: the ones who made the largest impression were those who survived the longest. Nevertheless, if we consider our major characters, excluding William Thackwray who died of violence, the average age at death of Joseph and Richard Walker, Benjamin Booth, Edward Driver, Robert Hart, Charles Stretch, John Forbes Cumming, and John Pringle was eighty two. That of their wives was only seventy three, but this was still remarkable in the context of the time.

A Goodly Array of Young Representatives   [1853 – 1870]

By the end of Mlanjeni's war in 1853, Joseph and Margaret Walker were living comfortably in their Bathurst St home. Their family was growing up. Margaret, the oldest, was twenty five. Annie Jane, the baby of the family was five. Joseph Jr, the oldest son, was twenty one. Margaret's father, Benjamin Booth, widowed in 1848, was now retired and living with them[659]. The year 1854 was one of new beginnings for the family. Margaret married William Shaw Copeland on Wednesday 26th July. Exactly two weeks later, Joseph Jr married Dorothy, Edward Driver's, daughter. Their courtship had been quite long. As early as the beginning of 1852, Joseph Jr had been corresponding with his future father-in-law while he was with Eyre in the Fish River Bush[660].

A goodly array of young representatives – Joseph Walker and some of his family. l to r: Benjamin, William, Joseph Walker Sr, Joseph Benjamin (son of Joseph Jr). Rev. W. G. Holford (husband of Ellen), Joseph Jr. (from a photograph lent to the author by the late Miss Gyneth Walker shortly after her 100th birthday)

Two weddings in one year might have been enough for any family, but, on Christmas Eve of the same year, old Benjamin Booth, now sixty eight, married for the second time. His new wife was a widow, Grace Brent (born Elliott). The wedding was celebrated in the Bathurst Methodist Church, of which Benjamin had been a prominent member and lay preacher for much of his life. Benjamin did not live much longer. When he died in 1862 he was once again being cared for by Joseph and Margaret Walker, his daughter and son-in-law.

Joseph Walker was now in a position to let some of the responsibilities for his business fall on his sons. He seems to have been fired with a wish to serve his community. Apart from his service as a municipal commissioner, his name appears on a variety of small committees, usually connected with the Wesleyan Church, running the charitable and social activities of a small town. Some of the committees on which he served give insight into the preoccupations of the time and suggest how much was dependent on the activities of the various religious denominations. Apart from being a trustee of the Wesleyan Chapel, he was on the committee of the Wesleyan School of Industry and Infant School, and the Graham's Town Auxiliary Bible Society. He was superintendent of the Dutch School. These activities were considered important enough at the time to be published in various editions of The Cape Almanac, a directory published regularly in Cape Town.

Thus Joseph and Margaret grew respectably old together. Joseph is remembered by a plaque in the Commemoration Church in Grahamstown. Margaret lived another twenty three years after his death, dying in 1893.

Politicians   [1854 – 1898]

Before the establishment of representative government in the Cape in 1854 the opportunity for participation in public affairs was limited for most of the colonists to local government. It went without saying that it was also limited to men. A few of the prominent – Godlonton, Cock, Fairbairn – served by appointment on the Legislative Council, but otherwise the local municipal councils and various church bodies were the only places to gain experience of participatory government. The new dispensation meant that any citizen who qualified as a voter might be elected to the House of Assembly.

The franchise was certainly not universal. In the first place the thought that women might have the vote was an idea that was yet to come anywhere in the world. It was simply not an issue. Qualification for the voter's roll required the ownership of fixed property worth £25. This effectively excluded most black and coloured people. Registration as a voter

Election campaign in Port Elizabeth Constituency, 1898

On the left is the Progressive Party, dominated by the figure of Rhodes. Joseph Walker Jr is fifth from the left in the bottom row. On the right are the supporters of the Bond. J H Hofmeyr is on the right peering over the wall, Sprigg performs a balancing act and John X. Merriman waves a "Cure for wobbles". The bearded figure in top hat and crown may be intended as a representation of Paul Kruger.

Unknown press source from cutting in author's collection

was also sufficient to qualify one to stand for election to the House of Assembly. To be elected to the Legislative Council, however, required a much stronger qualification – the ownership of fixed property worth £2000. Further, there was no secret ballot. The voter came to the poll and stated his preference to the recorder[661]. In the first elections in 1854 both Robert Godlonton and Andries Stockenstrom were elected to the Legislative Council, representing the Eastern Divisions. The first members of the House of Assembly included several who have featured in our story: Charles Lennox Stretch for the constituency of Fort Beaufort, James Thackwray for Graham's Town, William Gilfillan for Cradock, John Fairbairn for Swellendam, Robert Mitford Bowker for Somerset East, and his brother, Thomas Holden Bowker, for Albany.

To stand for election required a level of public spirit. The sessions were held in Cape Town, except for one in Graham's Town in 1864. They required members to travel large distances and to be away from their businesses and towns for an extended period of time without compensation. This led to several premature resignations. One was Joseph Walker, who was elected in 1866, but resigned before assuming his seat. Which of the three possible Joseph Walkers this was is uncertain. Some sources assume it was Joseph Walker Sr but this seems unlikely for two reasons. Firstly, he was elected for the constituency of King Williams Town: Joseph Walker Sr lived all his life in Graham's Town, although there was some degree of carpet-bagging among the candidates. Secondly, and more convincingly, he was by then almost seventy years old and seems unlikely to have been prepared to undertake the commitments of office, although if he did undertake the commitment his age might have provided a reason for resignation. His nephew Joseph, Richard Walker's son, is another possibility, but he had never shown any particular commitment to public service and lived in Bathurst. If he was so elected the reason for his resignation might have been the failing health of his father, who died the following year. The most likely candidate was Joseph Walker Jr, son of the settler. He was 32 at the time and had political ambitions. At the time he was partner in a firm of merchants, Maynard, Walker & Co., who were trading in East London and King Williams Town. He was in fact later elected to the House of Assembly. If it was him, why did he resign before taking his seat? It is probable that the reasons were financial. During his life he underwent several financial vicissitudes and at about this time he was involved in a great deal of litigation. At the end of 1866 he and his partners were embarking on a major case in the Supreme Court, suing Richard Southey in his capacity as Colonial Secretary, for unpaid debts by the Colonial Government[662]. They alleged that a cargo of hoop iron, carried by a Government vessel, had been negligently destroyed. The sum involved was about £80 which does not sound serious but, compared with average earnings at the time it was equivalent to almost £50 000, a not insignificant sum[663]. The case was to drag on for a considerable time with no resolution.

Joseph Walker Jr again took up an interest in politics in 1879 when he succeeded in being elected to the House. Each constituency had two representatives. Wodehouse, the district containing the town of Dordrecht, had been served for a number of years by John Linden Bradfield and John X. Merriman – the son of the Bishop of Grahamstown. At the election in 1878 Merriman stood for, and was elected to the Namaqualand constituency. His seat for Wodehouse was won by Joseph Walker, who served as as its MHA for nine years. During that period his business problems multiplied. In 1883 Joseph suffered a financial disaster, allegedly brought about by his eldest son Joseph Benjamin[664]. Whatever the reason this led to the necessity for his second son, Arthur, to leave school at the of age sixteen[665].

Joseph lost his seat in 1887. His interest in politics now became that of an ordinary citizen. By the 1898 election he he had settled in Port Elizabeth. At this time Cape politics had moved on. The development of the Afrikaner Bond[666], driven by men like J. H. Hofmeyr, had provided a new thrust for the advancement of the interests of the Dutch speaking people in the Colony and in the new republics. The Jameson raid[667] had broken up the alliance between Rhodes and the Bond.

The election in 1898 was the first at which a secret ballot was introduced. It was also the first in which two distinct parties could be identified The jingoistic Progressive Party was nominally led by Sir John Gordon Sprigg[668], the outgoing Prime Minister, but was dominated by the looming presence and purse of Cecil Rhodes. The liberal members of the Cape Parliament had been split by the scandal of the Jameson raid. Some remained aligned with the Progressives but influential ones like W. P. Schreiner, John X. Merriman, and J. W. Sauer supported the Bond.

The election was hard fought and very close. Joseph Walker was prominent as a supporter of the Progressives. This was the first election in which party lines began to be clearly drawn and the Port Elizabeth Constituency was one where the Progressives were well organized. There was a large committee of several dozen prominent citizens for supporting the campaign and a smaller Executive Committee for organization. Joseph was an active member of the latter. The Committee published flowery invitations in the press to its two desired candidates, asking them to stand. Joseph Walker's name was near the head of the list of signatories in each case. The replies of the candidates, E. H. Walton and James Wynne, are equally flowery.

The press comment by the English language newspapers of the Eastern Cape was overwhelmingly in favour of the Progressives. The *Eastern Province Herald,* the *Graham's Town Journal*, and the *Daily Dispatch* were unashamedly one-sided. Some cartoons[669] show the nature of the coverage. They are crudely drawn, the likenesses for the most part achieved by pasting a photographed head onto the drawing. In one, on the left hand side, a fatherly Rhodes holding a sceptre labelled "British Supremacy" and a small trident labelled "Progress Prosperity Expansion" dominates. Directly below him are the two candidates with a banner "Unity is Strength". Below that is a sober group of their election committee including Joseph Walker. The supporters of the Bond are depicted as a motley rabble on the right. Over a high brick wall peer two prominent supporters of the Bond, the only figures whose faces are drawn rather than represented by photographs. One is J. H Hofmeyr, an eminence grise, not standing for election. The other has a clean-shaven upper lip, a beard, and wears a top hat and crown. It may be meant to represent Paul Kruger, although the cartoonist must then have been ill-informed about his girth – the face is gaunt. Below this are unflattering representations of the Port Elizabeth supporters of the Bond. The cartoon is titled Under which King, Bayonians? This refers to the colloquial name for the inhabitants of Port Elizabeth, which came from the name of Algoa Bay.

The Campaign in Port Elizabeth was a great success for the Committee. Walton and Wynne were elected with 2793 and 2686 votes respectively. The Bond candidate, Jones, got 1110 and a fourth candidate 148. Nationally, however, the result went narrowly the other way.

The Old Veteran   [1830 – 1870]

The old veteran, Edward Driver, was never likely to have written his reminiscences as Dugmore had pleaded. Quite apart from the fact that there were a number of episodes in his life that he probably felt were best forgotten, his lifestyle would not have encouraged practiced fluency with the pen. In 1870, when Dugmore made his speech, the Kelham Ned of 1820 had become a patriarch. He was seventy one years old and never did record his memories.

After the war of the axe, Driver had seen an opportunity for expanding his activities. Opportunities to acquire land became available in the new region of Victoria East – the former ceded territory. Many colonists took advantage of this and acquired tracts of farm land as an investment, often leaving it uncultivated for many years. On 8th March 1848 the southern part of Victoria East was established as the magisterial district of Peddie, centred on Fort Peddie which became the administrative centre. It was in this developing village that Edward and Ann Driver now established themselves.

The Driver family had grown. Their last child, a son, was born in October 1848. They now had eleven surviving children, six daughters and five sons. One daughter had died in infancy. The urge to respectability continued. The Drivers had never before shown much interest in religion but, on 2nd October 1850, the whole family assembled before the Peddie Methodist Minister. All the children were present ranging from twenty-four year old Ann to two year old Arthur. That day all were baptised[670].

These descendants of Edward Driver and Ann Thackwray grew up. Apart from Dorothy's marriage to Joseph Walker Jr, Drivers married and raised families until the number of descendants of the Drivers rivalled that of the Harts.

Edward had no immediate family of his own generation in the Cape. All his connections were with Ann's family. The other members of the Thackwray clan had put their tragic family history behind them and got on with their lives.

Ann's elder sister, Dorothy, and her husband, James Allison, had been married at the beginning of 1827 in St George's, the Graham's Town Anglican church. In 1831 the Wesleyans ran a very successful revival campaign. It was less than a year since the trial and execution of Flora Kiewiet for the murder of Dorothy's brother, William. This had been the culmination of a true *annus horribilis* for the family and the Allisons were ripe for conversion. They joined the Methodist community. The next year the Rev. John Edwards had no difficulty in persuading James Allison to join him as a catechist on a mission to the Griquas in Bechuanaland. James was later ordained and the Allisons spent the rest of their lives in the mission field. They spent ten years near Thabanchu then moved to Swaziland and thereafter to Pietermaritzburg. Dorothy died there in 1864[671].

In 1834 Joseph Thackwray had married Mary, the daughter of Joseph Weakley, a trader who had become a prominent Graham's Town businessman. Joseph set up as a shopkeeper in Cradock and the Thackwrays raised a family who farmed and flourished in the Cradock district. Joseph was the one who gave a home to his widowed mother when her sight failed and her small business ventures came to nothing. She lived until 1850 and the last we hear of the woman who followed her husband from near penury in England to a dangerous and tragic life in the Colony, is the following:

> DIED, at the residence of her son [Joseph] in Cradock in the eightieth year of her age, Mrs. THACKWRAY, Sen., Widow of the late William THACKWRAY. Deceased was one of the original Settlers, and after sustaining with Christian fortitude and meekness the dispensations of the Divine Providence, departed this life on the 19th January 1850, in the full hope of a glorious resurrection at the "last great day."[672]

James Thackwray's wife, Jane, was the daughter of old Benjamin Booth. He had married into the Graham's Town Wesleyan establishment. One sister-in-law was Matilda Booth, the daughter of Robert Godlonton. Another was Margaret, the wife of Joseph Walker. James, too became a Wesleyan. He and Jane had decided that their future also lay in the mission field. They had gone to join James and Dorothy Allison in

Bechuanaland. It was a fateful decision. James became ill with fever – the generic term applied to a number of ill-understood diseases, but most often to malaria. It ruined his health and the Thackwrays were compelled to return to Graham's Town. While James's health never fully recovered, he played his part in the affairs of the town, serving as a Municipal Commissioner after the war of the axe and being elected to represent Graham's Town in the House of Assembly in the first election held in 1853. The first meeting of the House was in 1854. James did not survive long to serve as MHA. His health problems became worse and he died in November of that year at the age of 39.

In the early years of the settlement, Edward Driver had lamented to Cowper Rose that he had been driven to his way of life by financial necessity. His real ambition was to settle down with his family and become respectable. He had now reached a stage where he could realize that ambition. He had established himself as a leading citizen of Peddie.

Apart from the interruptions of Mlanjeni's war in the early eighteen fifties, the Drivers now remained in the village. Edward ran a trading business in the town and in 1854 acquired two farms, Gwanga and Willow Park, a few kilometres to the north-east of the town. The children grew up, married and moved away.

The Peddie district attained the status of a Division in 1858, with a Divisional Council. Edward served as a Divisional Councillor representing the Keiskamma Ward from 1858 to 1861 and representing Peddie village from 1864 to 1871.

Ann had died in 1859, Edward lived on, the patriarch of a growing number of descendants, until he died. The local newspaper reported:

> Died, – At Victoria Saw Mills, Perie Bush, on Saturday, 12th August 1882, Edward Driver, aged 88 years
>
> Deceased was one of the British Settlers of 1820 ...

Rebuilding   [1851 – 1885]

Aa a result of Mlanjeni's war in 1851 the Mission Board of the United Free Church found its activities on the frontier in a parlous state. Of the three Xhosa missions that they controlled, Uniondale and Iqibira had been razed and Tyumie abandoned as a mission, occupied only by Mary Chalmers and her family. The small satellites Kirkwood and Bonkolo were not viable because of the displacement of the people at the time. The new colonial town of Queenstown and its environs enveloped Kirkwood and the site of Bonkolo is now immersed under the town's water supply. The missionary activities of the Board to the Xhosa people had been destroyed. The authorities in Scotland had a serious crisis of confidence about the future of their mission in the Cape. Should their endeavours in the region be halted altogether?[673]

The strain of their experiences weighed heavily on the missionaries who had been at Tyumie on Christmas day 1850. Recognizing this, while considering the future of their missionary activities, the Board summoned Cumming and Niven back to Scotland for a period of furlough.

The whole Niven family sailed for home. John Cumming felt somewhat differently. His family had grown. William Gordon – Willie – had been born in May 1848 and Sarah in January 1850. Perhaps it was not surprising that, with three children under seven, he decided to go alone to Scotland, leaving Catherine and the children with John and Susan Pringle at Glenthorn. Catherine had been born in the Cape and had no personal reason for wanting to go to Scotland. John's mother had died a few years earlier and he had family matters to settle. He was now torn. It was possible that the UPC Mission Board would close down their operations and he might have to consider his future. His earlier wish ultimately to return to Scotland had disappeared. He probably realised that this was a last opportunity to see the country of his birth but his home was now in the Cape.

The Board eventually made its decision. An attempt would be made to resuscitate their mission to the Xhosa. Niven and Cumming were to return to Africa. Niven's brief was to assess the situation. He was to collect information about the situation on the ground and make recommendations about the prospect of success. It does not appear as if he was committed to remain in the long term; his family was to remain in Scotland, and he did indeed return to Scotland nine months later. His wife had been traumatised by her experiences and it is likely that this played a significant part in the decision. Cumming was, however, regarded differently. He was given a one year appointment

> ... with the understanding, that if a favourable opening for the resumption of the mission, or such a field of labour that they consider he may occupy, do not by that period present itself, his connection with the Mission Board will then terminate.

The two missionaries arrived back in Cape Town on October 10th 1853. Niven, following his instructions, had two interviews with Cathcart, the Governor. He was informed of the relocation of the Ngqika and Gqunukwhebe and told that reoccupation of Tyumie, Iqibira and Uniondale would not be permitted. It would have been futile to do so: the congregations had fled and the most committed had settled near Peelton. Both men continued to the frontier, Niven to continue his commission and Cumming to be reunited with his family.

John Cumming rode back to what was now home:

> [22 October 1853] Rode over the hills & by Doorn Kloof ... for Glenthorn. Rode up my dearest ... Found all joyful and well.

Niven's commission was a failure. He visited Sandile, who was smarting over his defeat, depressed by the forced removal of his people from their former territory, and uninterested in accepting any missionaries. He refused permission for the establishment of a mission. Niven returned to Scotland in the middle of 1854 and never returned.

John Cumming set himself the task of building up the congregation in John Pringle's church at Glenthorn. Apart from the Pringle family and their neighbours, there were a number of coloured and Mfengu farm workers. The congregation was small – about twenty five, mainly white – but his efforts were successful enough for his congregation to petition the Mission Board to continue his services, undertaking to provide as much as possible of his salary from their own resources. His real desire, however, was to re-establish the mission to the Xhosa. To this end, in 1855, he paid a visit to Sandile.

By now the Ngqika king had had time to become adjusted to his new situation. Still deeply angry at the loss of the ancestral lands of his people, he was nevertheless prepared to give Cumming a hearing. Cumming wrote afterwards[674]

> The great chief was seated on a skin near to the kraal, with his dirty blanket around him. He had been informed of our arrival, and seemed highly gratified by the object of our visit. He said, that though he had withheld his official word from others, it was only for the purposes of giving it to me personally. ... The school was, in his estimation, a blessing to his people. His counsellors had long ago given their consent, and it was not necessary to call them again. He cheerfully gave his consent to his old teacher, and to his own people of the school but he would not do so to strangers. The country was before us; we might choose what spot we pleased, with one condition only, viz., that we should not bring cattle from the infected districts, as the lung-sickness had not entered his country.

John Cumming lost no time in selecting a site on the Mgwali River, about 25 km north east of the present site of Stutterheim. He then applied for permission from the Government. This was longer in coming. It was not until 5th October 1856 that a letter was received from Sir George Grey's office granting permission. There were many caveats. All missionary activity was undertaken at the missionary's own risk. All arrangements with the chiefs were the applicant's responsibility, and no help could be expected from Government. The agreement, however, had to be re-gistered with the government.

It was not the intention that Cumming, himself, would undertake the mission. His place was now at Glenthorn, from where he could oversee the affairs of the United Presbyterian Church. With a young family, now increased by the birth of Robert in January 1856, the travails of a life in previously unsettled regions would have been severe. In 1857 the Mission Board sent out two missionaries to occupy Mgwali. One was a Rev. Robert Johnston who, after two years helping to establish the mission, was happy to accept a call to a more comfortable congregation in Gra-ham's Town. The other was a far more significant appointment.

When Niven and Cumming had been recalled to Scotland in 1853, Tiyo Soga had accompanied Niven. Charles Stretch had provided hospit-ality for the Nivens and for Soga at Glen Avon after they had eventually been able to leave Philipton. Stretch now provided support for Soga to travel with the Nivens.[675]

In Scotland Soga had attended the Theological College in Edinburgh and had been ordained. He had also met a young Scotswoman, Janet Burnside, and married her. He now returned with Johnston to begin the mission at Mgwali. Soga probably knew what to expect when he arrived. Janet would have had little idea. The idea of a marriage between a Xhosa man and a Scottish woman raised both outrage and interest in the com-munity. The Sogas seem to have risen above it.

By the time Mgwali was opened in 1857 the consequences of the cattle killing were causing devastation. Cumming, Soga, and Johnston loaded a wagon with all the supplies and impedimenta needed to begin operations and set off from Glenthorn, leaving Catherine and the children in the care of the Pringles. They arrived at the site of the mission on 11th September 1857 and found it desolate. They set about building a shelter and establishing themselves at the site.

The starving people ranged over the land searching for sources of food. For the missionaries this was a great problem as they were reliant on what they had brought with them for the future of the mission. On 14th September Cumming wrote a letter to his wife from Mgwali, pre-sumably sending it by messenger to the nearest military post or settlement for onward transmission:

> ... While standing by the waggon we saw Sandilli and a large party com-ing down the hill. Willingly we would have hid ourselves as we thought of the ravages which he and his party would [make] in our provisions. But resolving to face the dreaded visitation we were truly grateful to see the whole party sweep down the road towards Peelton, without

even sending a stray messenger to enquire whose waggons were encamped.

When the two new missionaries were settled Cumming was able to return to his family at Glenthorn where he was to spend the next eleven
years while his family grew up.

 Schooling in the Eastern Cape at this time was a hit or miss affair.
This was a problem for a Scot who wanted his children to have the best
education. John and Catherine made the momentous decision to send
their two older boys to school in Scotland.

Consider the logistics. They were parting with their two older sons for
the several years needed for an education. All arrangements had to be
made by post. Mail from Glenthorn had to be carried by messenger to the
nearest Post Office – probably Adelaide – and then by postcart or rider to
Algoa Bay. From there it went by ship to Scotland. There lodgings had to
be arranged for the boys, and places found at an appropriate school. John
Cumming still had relatives in Scotland, and presumably one of them, or
a colleague from the Church could have acted as agent. Two small boys
then had to be despatched, unaccompanied, half across the world. They
could be placed safely on a ship, but must be met at the other end and
conveyed to their final destination. The ship ran to no schedule and its
time of arrival in Scotland was unknown. Great trust was placed in
agents along the way. All over the Empire similar arrangements were
made for the children of those who served the Government or engaged in
other business in the far-flung colonies.

The despatch of the boys was a major operation:

[21st March 1859] Left with waggon for [Algoa] Bay with John [age 13]
& William [age 11] in order to ship for Scotland. [John] Pringle - Mrs
Cumming Sarah [age 9] and Robert [age 3] accompany.

The journey to the Bay took a week. They arrived the following
Sunday 27th April. But departure of the vessel was more than two weeks
later.

[14th April 1859] Boys embark in the Harrington Capt Haddock. Mrs C
& S and self return in boat - High seas.

It was several years before John Jr and Willam saw their parents again.

The education of girls did not have the same priority. They would not
have careers. Their future was in marriage and, provided that they had
the basics of literacy and numeracy, their remaining education was
largely in social and domestic skills.

[19th Jan 1860] Left in waggon with Mrs C to take Sarah and put her to
school at Mrs Dorringtons Fort Beaufort.

Sarah, living her younger life in very isolated circumstances, never married; she lived with her parents all her life, assuming the management of their household when they retired and seeing to the needs of her father until his death.

John Cumming served the congregation of Glenthorn until his two older sons had finished their education and were off his hands. Under Soga the mission at Mgwali made steady progress. John Aitken Chalmers, son of old William, joined him there at the end of 1860. After some time Soga and Chalmers had built the station up to the point where Chalmers formed a new mission to the people of Oba and Feni, the sons of Tyhali. It was named Henderson Mission[676] and was located on the Thomas River, a tributary of the Kei, about forty km west of Mgwali. Then, in 1868, responding to a request from Sarhili, Soga made another move to establish a new mission at Tutura far across the Kei.

This was the start of a new phase of life for John and Catherine Cumming. Things had changed at Glenthorn. John Pringle, crippled for a number of years by arthritis, had died in 1864, and the farm had been taken over by Catherine's brother. Their eldest son, John, after briefly serving in the Magistrate's office in Tsolo, had married the previous year. His bride was Sarah Jane Hart, one of the many children of Robert Hart Jr and his second wife, Harriet Marillier. Their second son, Willie was just beginning a career in the Colonial Service. The Cummings accepted a call and moved to Mgwali to take over the mission there. Once again John Cumming found himself serving Sandile's Ngqika people. With them was Sarah. Robert was twelve – an age to be away at school, although it is not clear whether he, too, went away to Scotland.

The Cumming family's life at Mgwali lasted for eighteen years. John Cumming's diaries for those years are filled with the minutiae of running a mission – baptisms, marriages, deaths, and drafts of sermons to be preached. They both remained vigorous throughout those years, travelling regularly round the region. Cumming carried out a long correspondence with Charles Lennox Stretch. Catherine was more concerned with family. On 22nd May 1878 she wrote to her grand daughter, Katie, the handwriting carefully formed for a six-year old child to read:

> ... We would like to see Papa and Mama and all our Duckies again
>
> Aunt Sarah says that she wishes she was a bird and she would fly over the hills to see you. Would she not be a funny bird to come walking into the house some day. Aunt Sarah says she is going to write a letter to you so I will not write any more now.
>
> Love to Pa and Ma and You and Harry and Aleyn and Lionel and Ethel for Grandpa and Old Aunt and Aunt Sarah and Grandma. ...[677]

This letter was written against the background of yet another tragedy for the Xhosa. Late the previous year, in far off Gcalekaland, a fight between Mfengu and Gcaleka had broken out at a wedding. It had led to the death of a minor Gcaleka chief. Sarhili was powerless to prevent rapid escalation towards a full-blown war. Since the Mfengu were subjects of the Queen, the new Governor, Sir Henry Bartle Frere, was bound to provide protection. Troops were sent in, Sarhili deposed, and the situation rapidly escalated into war. Soon Sandile's Ngqika were drawn into the fighting.

There was only one outcome possible. The Xhosa were heavily defeated. Sarhili fled and was to remain in hiding until his death in 1893. Sandile retreated into the old haunts of the Ngqika, the Amatolas, to fight a guerilla war. It did not last very long. Just two weeks after Catherine Cumming had written that letter to her granddaughter Katie, news arrived that Sandile's body had been found. He had died of wounds received in an encounter on 29th May.

The Ngqika were expelled beyond the Kei. Tyala, Sandile's councillor and advisor, refused to go. He had advised against the war and had been a strong sceptic of the cattle killing. He was old and defeated. He said he would stay and die in his own place. When an old man loses the will to live death can come fast. He died the next day. John Cumming was present at his death.

Mostert[678] describes Stretch and Cumming in that same year as "two fading old men, both of them ill, weary, too weak to travel to one another ...". Nothing could have been further from the truth. Stretch, a much older man, was indeed near the end of his life – he died four years later – but at that time both John and Catherine were vigorously pursuing their missionary work at Mgwali. Even 7 years later John Cumming was still at work, writing in his diary:

> Sun 6 Dec [1885] Calm peaceful day rose before 5 as usual at this season. Brushed my whole skin with a stiff hairbrush which [had had] a good wash with a towel wet & soap – dried. I rubbed both hands skin to skin.

Magistrates   [1857 – 1929]

When they first grew up, John Forbes Cumming's sons sought a career. Well educated, but sons of a missionary who had small financial resources, they had no capital or land to set themselves up as businessmen or farmers. None felt called to the Church. The obvious career was in government service.

Over the second half of the nineteenth century the advance of the Colony continued. The frontier moved away from Grahamstown, Somerset and Graaff Reinet to the other side of the Kei until the British controlled everywhere from Cape Town to Port Natal. This included what had once been known as No Man's Land, afterwards East Griqualand, which had initially been occupied by Adam Kok's migrant Griquas. The government was administered by a small number of agents and magistrates spread thinly through the new territories. Power was exercised through the authority of the chiefs and using their laws and customs. Where this failed there was always military force to be called upon.

Both of the older Cumming sons entered the Colonial service in magistrates' offices. It was there that they first encountered a new star in the Department.

Walter Stanford was a remarkable young man[679]. He was orphaned in 1857 at the age of 7 when his father, a policeman, was killed in a riding accident. He was quite sickly and his mother decided that the climate near Peddie where they lived did not suit him so she decided to send him to the healthier climate of Glen Grey where her brother, none other than Joseph Warner, was now living. There he was given a basic education by a maiden aunt.

Joseph Warner was at Glen Grey as a result of Mlanjeni's war. He had had to leave his mission, Mvane, and in 1852 was placed at Glen Grey, about 25 km north of his old location. His station was on the other side of the White Kei River and in Thembu territory. In common with many missionaries he accepted a Government position, that of so-called Tambookie Agent, that is diplomatic representative to the Thembu. After a few years Stanford's mother moved to Alice and he rejoined her there in 1860. He was sent to school at the Missionary Institute at Lovedale, which had both black and white pupils. Just two years later, in 1863 before he had turned thirteen, he returned to Glen Grey. His uncle required a clerk in his magistrate's office. Within two years he was being left in charge of the office, taking statements in criminal cases and becoming thoroughly familiar with Xhosa language, law, and custom.

His exploits are only peripheral to our main story but it is worth recording that he was a magistrate by the age of 26, served with distinction in the war of 1877 – 1878, and became Chief Magistrate of East Griqualand in 1885, based in Kokstad. He was awarded the Companionship of the order of St Michael and St George in 1891. Later he served in the Anglo-Boer War and emerged as a Colonel and a Companion of the Order of the Bath. He was briefly a member of the House of Assembly, representing Thembuland, and became a delegate to the National Convention that led to the formation of the Union of South Africa in 1910.

There he tried and failed to get the more liberal Cape franchise system adopted:

> Durban, Tuesday, 20th October 1908. ...
>
> 9. Col. Stanford moved: All subjects of His Majesty resident in South Africa shall be entitled to franchise rights irrespective of race or colour upon such qualifications as may be determined by this convention[680]

This did not imply the kind of universal franchise existing today – in the Cape the property qualifications ensured that only about 8% of the electorate was not white, nor did women count as subjects of Her Majesty for this purpose – but for the times it was a step too far. The motion only had the support of a few liberals such as J. W. Sauer and was rejected by the Convention, but the Cape was allowed to keep their voting system. He served as a Senator of the Union from 1910 to 1929, being knighted in 1919 after service in World War 1.

His impact on this story, however, is that, in 1888, he courted and married Sarah Alice Walker, daughter of Joseph Walker Jr, and that for much of his life he was a close friend and colleague of Willie, John Forbes Cumming's second son.

Glen Avon   [1847 – 1899]

In Somerset, after the war of the axe, the Hart family began to put their troubles behind them. The wool trade was very profitable. Robert Hart Sr was a canny Scot. As time went on he built up a large estate, buying adjacent farms and allocating them to members of his family. Robert's own frugal way of life allowed him to build up a considerable fortune, and he was not above pointing this out. Writing to his friend R. J. Eaton in Graham's Town, he states with Presbyterian smugness:

> My manner of life is very different to many of our country men who reside in Albany I do not keep a dashing carriage nor live beyond my income therefore cannot keep company with them not act the great man I must pay every man and live within my means therefore I believe I am not Esteemed among them as I cannot afford to sport Champaign [like them?] tho when they are thrown on their beam ends they would be good friends with me ...[681]

He turned 70 in 1847 but was as vigorous as ever. His wife, Hannah was not so well. On 1st January 1848 an advertisement appeared in the Eastern Province Herald

> WANTED
> By an aged man and his wife, the latter confined to her bedroom, an elderly female to manage the domestic concerns of their house. A respectable woman with either a son or daughter of 8 or 10 years of age,

and who might be useful in the house, would find this an eligible situation, as liberal wages will be given to a suitable person. Application may be made to R. HART Sen, Glen Avon, near Somerset.

Child labour was not a crime and children were expected to contribute their share of the chores of everyday life.

Hannah's health deteriorated and she died a few years later on 3rd September 1853. Robert Jr now took up more and more of the responsibility for running the home farm. James was out of the picture. After he was released from gaol he did not come back to Glen Avon but returned to farm Roodewal[682].

By 1848 Robert Jr and Harriet had three children; Harriet was ultimately to have a further eight. Other members of the clan had their own young families. Many of them lived close by. The patriarch had made sure that this was the case as he makes clear in his letter to Eaton:

My family whom you have seen in infancy are all comfortably around me and have their own Farmes [owned by Robert in fact] and [estates?] tho Mr Stretch married to my eldest daughter Ann is about 90 miles from me ...

The Stretches, also, were soon to return to Glen Avon and lived for some time in the second homestead, The Retreat.

The educational needs of Robert Jr's family could not be solved by sending the children away to school as had been done for the small Cumming family. Clearly he had a problem. On Saturday 11th March, 1848 he advertised in the *Graham's Town Journal*

The undersigned is desirous of engaging a gentleman and his wife, competent to undertake the education of children of both sexes of different ages from five to fifteen years, on his residence Glen Avon, near Somerset (East). The number of children to be placed under their charge by the advertiser not to exceed ten.

Salary £100 per annum. Use of a small cottage of 3 rooms, a piece of good garden ground which can be irrigated, two milch cows, during summer, and permission to take five more children as boarders on their own account, in which case an additional room will be provided. Meat, meal and butter at the lowest market prices.

Testimonials of character and qualifications for teaching will be expected.

Robert HART Jr.

By 1867 the third generation was growing up and marrying. John Forbes Cumming over the years had always been a welcome visitor to Glen
Avon. He had preached in the chapel that Robert Hart had built and the
two men had much in common. Now John Pringle Cumming, his eldest
son was to marry Sarah Jane, the daughter of Robert Hart Jr. The marriage took place on 7th March at Glen Avon.

But things were about to change at Glen Avon. Robert Hart Sr was
now ninety years old. He was a careful man and his will had been carefully planned, sharing out his large estate among his family[683]. The home
farm was, of course, left to his eld-
est son Robert Jr. What he did not
foresee, however, was that Robert
Jr would predecease him. Robert
Jr died on 18th July 1867, his father less than two months later on
14th September.

Inevitably the estate was complicated: at his death Robert Sr
had more than two hundred descendants. His will started with a
small puzzle. He left a legacy of
£100 to Marian Hart, identified in
the will as his niece. It is not
known how any niece came to be
in the Cape. Robert and Hannah
had come to South Africa without
any family. Robert was estranged
from his father and is not known
to have been in contact with his
siblings. Marian Hart had, in fact,
been married to Richard Walker's
eldest son Joseph[684] since the

John & Sarah Cumming

*Inscribed on back: "John and self in the
greenhouse at Glen Avon"*

middle eighteen forties. The rest of the will was more predictable. The
main Glen Avon farm was left to Robert Jr. The Retreat was divided into
a number of allotments. James was left the farm Roodewal as well as one
allotment of the Retreat. The rest of the estate was divided among his
daughters. Ann and her husband Charles Lennox Stretch were left the
farm Hartfell and a portion of The Retreat. Sara Elizabeth and her husband, Robert Mitford Bowker, got the farm Craigie Burn and a portion of
The Retreat. Margaret, married to the missionary Richard Birt was never
going to be a farmer's wife; she got a portion of The Retreat and £10000.
Ellen had died in 1846 but her husband, William Dods Pringle got part of

The Retreat and £2000. There were common grazing rights provided for all the contiguous farms. The needs of the Presbyterian church at Glen Avon were continued by a legacy of £1300 in trust. There was also an amount set aside for a bursary for a pupil of Gill College, the new tertiary educational institution in Somerset East, founded by Robert's friend Dr William Gill, who left his estate for the purpose[685].

The problems arose with the bequest to Robert Jr, who was dead without the will providing for this contingency. It is difficult to deduce exactly how the situation was resolved. The final distribution account of the estate[686] shows that Glen Avon was, indeed, transferred to Robert Jr, dead or not. His wife, Harriet lived a further 31 years, only dying in 1898. Robert Jr and Harriet had a joint will. Its terms were simple in principle but its consequences were complicated. Whichever spouse died first, the whole estate was divided between their children with the proviso that the survivor would retain all the benefits of the estate until his or her death. As a result the estate of Robert Hart Jr was only finally wound up thirty-three years later in 1900, after Harriet's death[687]. The children of Robert Jr's first wife, Johanna Meintjies, were all adult and making their own way. Harriet's oldest children were a different case. The eldest, Harriet Elizabeth, was already married to a Graaff Reinet farmer, Alexander Stewart. Eldest son Richard was soon to marry and was able to make his own way. Sarah had, of course, just married John Pringle Cumming. The remainder were all dependent in one way or another. The younger daughters ranged from Frances who was 19 to Emily, who was 12. In addition there were two dependent sons, Frederick and Charles, aged 7 and 5 respectively. Harriet therefore became the effective owner of Glen Avon. Her younger children grew up on the farm until the boys could look after themselves and the daughters either married, or continued to live with the family, as was the custom of the time.

Her daughter, Sarah, and her new husband, John Pringle Cumming, settled down to raise a family. He, at that time had a fairly junior position in the Colonial service. His postings were in the new territories to the east of the Kei. These were generally fairly inhospitable places[688]. When he had been a child his mother and her young family had often spent long periods at Glenthorn with her parents. It seems likely that this pattern was followed by the next generation with Sarah remaining at Glen Avon with her young family while her husband was away[689]. By 1884 Sarah Cumming had given birth to eight children. One had died in infancy. The others grew up in what Katie, their first daughter, remembered as an ideal environment. Throughout her life she kept photographs of The Retreat and the Glen Avon homestead hanging in a prominent position in her house. She had two older brothers, two younger brothers and two younger sisters. There were other children on the farm and the surroundings were idyllic.

It was several years after her father's death before Hannah Louisa, Sarah's younger sister, married. Her husband was John Ebenezer Brown, a Scot, who had come out to the Cape from East Lothian. He was a natural farmer and set out to work the home farm with great success. It was in all probability something of a strain when, in the middle eighteen eighties, John Pringle Cumming returned to Glen Avon for good with the intention of working on the farm. In any event a *modus vivendi* was worked out with Browns occupying the old homestead and Cummings The Retreat.

By 1886 John Forbes Cumming was beginning to slow down. The work at Mgwali became more and more burdensome and he diary often shows some concern with his health. It was time to retire. He was seventy eight years old when the Mission Board of the United Free Church agreed that he should retire on a pension of £200 a year. They might have thought twice if they had realised that it was to be paid out for the next twenty-one years. John and Catherine moved to Glen Avon, to join their son John and his wife Sarah at The Retreat.

Tragedy struck the family in 1896 when Bonnie, the baby of the family, died at the age of 12. The remainder grew up. The oldest, Harry, left home as soon as he was old enough to follow an adventurous life, first at the diamond diggings in Kimberley and later in the newly established Rhodesia. Alan married the daughter of the local dominee of the Dutch Reformed Church, J. H. Hofmeyer[690], and went farming in Steynsburg[691]. Katie grew up into an attractive young woman.

When Harriet died in 1898 the complications of the Hart estate were finally worked out. It was agreed that the Browns would purchase the farm from the estate. The price was £13 800. The estate was then liquidated and the proceeds divided among the sixteen heirs. After sundry expenses each received £760 18s 0¾d[692]. An earlier distribution had given each a further £23 7s 9¾d. The Browns took over Glen Avon and it is still in the hands of their direct descendants. The Cummings prepared to leave their home and retire in Somerset East.

The final move away from Glen Avon came in about 1898, and was a wrench for the whole family. John Pringle Cumming acquired a house in Somerset East and called it Altyre, named for the seat of the clan chief of the Cummings in Scotland. There John Forbes Cumming and Catherine lived out their last years. Catherine died in January 1902. It was a sad blow for John. A few months after her death he wrote on black-edged notepaper to his son Willie[693]:

I received the inscription for the stone but act according to your own mind which is agreeable to mine

... the Lord gave and the Lord hath taken away. Blessed be the name of the Lord.

Sarah and I find the situation very lonely.

John Forbes Cumming lived on for five more years after Catherine's death and died on 17th August 1907 in his hundredth year.

New Beginnings   [1883 – 1891]

Being forced to leave school at age sixteen because of financial difficulty is not a good start for a legal career. In the nineteenth century, however, learning on the job was a more viable prospect than it is now. The professions such as law used the system serving articles as a common alternative to first obtaining a degree before entering the profession. An articled clerk using this route was simply an apprentice, with a title chosen to distinguish him from a working class artisan apprentice. He was bound to a lawyer by contract, paid a pittance that was just enough to survive on, and worked hard for his living while studying at night for examinations of the professional body.

Arthur Walker was articled to a firm of lawyers, Innes and Elliott[694], in the growing city of Port Elizabeth. Unlike his elder brother, Benjamin, he was hard working and conscientious and in his twenties qualified as an attorney. He then set out to make his mark by practising as an attorney in several small towns in the Eastern Cape.

In 1891 he was a member of the firm Zietsman and le Roux in Kokstad. He was lodging with his sister and brother-in-law, Alice and Walter Stanford.

Walter Stanford was now Chief Magistrate of East Griqualand. His friend, William Cumming, had moved from Qumbu and was now the district magistrate for Kokstad. At about that time Cumming had a visit from his niece, Katie.

Katie Cumming was now nineteen years old. She and Arthur Walker met. Soon they were engaged to be married and plans began to be made for the wedding that opened our story.

Epilogue

A people without history
Is not redeemed from time, for history is a pattern
Of timeless moments

T. S. Eliot, Little Gidding. Four quartets

The press account of the wedding of Arthur and Katie is written in the breathless prose of a country newspaper's social correspondent, who was also probably editor, chief reporter, and advertising manager:

A very pretty wedding took place at Glenavon, Somerset East, on Wednesday, 28th ult, when Miss Katie Cumming was married to Mr Arthur Walker of Kokstad.

The ceremony was performed by the Rev Mr Leich of Somerset East assisted by the Rev Mr J. F. Cumming, grandfather to the bride, and took place in the family chapel which presented a very pretty appearance. Wreaths of yellow wood and asparagus adorned the windows and clung in artistic groups to the lamp brackets and walls. The pulpit was decorated with ivy and white flowers and backed by a display of Spanish cane which produced a fine effect.

The press report is entirely concentrated on the bridal party. The bridegroom is an unimportant appendage only mentioned when joining the bride at the altar and in the description of his gift to her. The best man is mentioned but not by name. There is no reference to the bridegroom's parents or family who were presumably represented at the wedding.

At the end of the day came the departure:

The bride's going away dress was of myrtle green amazon cloth, handsomely trimmed with deep green corded silk insertion, embroidered in black silk, and a dark green felt hat to match, was trimmed with various shades of light and dark green and natural ostrich plumes. In this stylish costume the bride looked, if possible, more charming than ever, and it is difficult to say which one preferred. The ladies had not arrived at a decision when the happy couple entered their cart and drove off amidst resounding cheers and showers of confetti, blissfully indifferent to the extra luggage attached to their conveyance in the shape of a venerable shoe.

There are no end points in history. Every end is a beginning. The end of our story of the Walkers, Booths, Cummings, Drivers, Harts, and Thackwrays, who came out to the Cape with their dreams of a better future, is the beginning of the story of their two young descendants and their children.

Arthur and Katie drove away from their wedding party to start their married life. Ahead of them and their descendants was the twentieth century – the Anglo-Boer civil war, two world wars, births and deaths, the growth and decay of apartheid, and at last the emergence of a new democracy.

But that is another story.

The End

Appendix 1. Cast

Chief Characters

Cumming, John Forbes: *b.* 14 Jul 1808, *m.* Catherine Pringle 29 Apr 1844, *d.* Somerset East 17 Aug 1907, *ch.* John Pringle, William Gordon, Sarah Cairns, Robert Forbes. *Arr.* 1840 aboard Mary Nixon. Presbyterian missionary associated with Tyumie, Mgwali, and other Cape missions for more than 60 years.

Driver, Edward: *b.* Kelham, Nottinghamshire 1795, *m.* Ann Thackwray 6 Oct 1825, *d.* Pirie Bush King William's Town 12 Aug 1882, *ch.* twelve including Dorothy (wife of Joseph Walker Jr). *Arr.* 1 May 1820 in Calton's party, aboard *Albury*. Trader, elephant hunter, army scout, co-founder of the village of Peddie.

Hart, Robert Sr.: *b.* 5 Jan 1777, *m.* Hannah Tamplin 10 Apr 1804, *d.* Glen Avon 14 Sep 1867, *ch.* 10, incl. Robert Jr., James. *Arr.* 1795 with 98th Argyllshire Highland Regiment and again as ensign in Cape Regiment 1807. Lieutenant, Cape Regiment, Assisted in laying out Graham's Town. Manager Somerset Farm. Granted farm Glen Avon, Somerset East, where he farmed until his death.

Pringle, John: *b.* nr Kelso, Scotland, 21 Apr 1787, *m.* Susan Stretch 26 Mar 1822, *d.* 7 Apr 1764, *ch.* Six, including Catherine (wife of John Forbes Cumming). *Arr.* 15 May 1820 in Pringle's party aboard *Brilliant*. Brother of Thomas Pringle. Prominent farmer.

Thackwray, John: *b.* 8 Sep 1802, *d.* 27 Feb 1828. Son of William Thackwray and Dorothy Pownall. Pioneer and noted elephant hunter.

Thackwray, William Sr.: *b.* 1780, *m.* Dorothy Pownall abt 1800, *d.* Pondoland 8 Oct 1829. *Arr.* 30 Apr 1820 in William Smith's party, aboard *Northampton*, *ch.* John, Dorothy, Ann, William, Joseph. James. Wheelwright, trader, pioneer.

Walker, Joseph: *b.* 26 Jul 1797, *m.* Margaret Booth, 10 May 1827, *d.* Graham's Town, 28 Jan 1870, *ch.* Eleven including Joseph Jr. (husband of Dorothy Driver) *Arr.* 1820 in Geo. Smith's party, aboard *Stentor* and *Weymouth*. Grahamstown merchant and businessman.

Kinsfolk of Chief Characters

Allison, James: *b.* abt 1802, *m.* (i) Dorothy Thackwray 4th Jan 1827 (ii) Mary McC Dunn abt 1867, *d.* 1876. s. of James Allison. *Arr.* 1820 in Scanlen's party, aboard *East Indian*. Prominent missionary in Cape and Natal. Biographical material: Mears [1967].

Booth, Benjamin: *b.* Richmond, Surrey 11 Feb 1786, *m.* (i) Margaret Mortimer abt 1808, (ii) Mrs Grace Brent, 31 Dec 1851, *d.* Grahamstown 28 Apr 1862, *ch.* Margaret, Sarah, Jane, Benjamin Jr, Elizabeth, Mary, Emma. *Arr.* 1820 in Sephton's party, aboard *Aurora*. Father-in-law of Joseph Walker Sr who married Margaret and of James Thackwray who married Jane.

Booth, Benjamin Jr: *b.* 28 Sep. 1820 at Salem, *sn.* of Benjamin and Margaret Booth, *m.* Matilda Barton Godlonton 13 Apr 1841, *d.* 1 Feb 1906.

Booth, Margaret: *b.* 1809 Lambeth England, *dr.* of Benjamin and Margaret Booth, *m.* Joseph Walker 10 May 1827, *d.* 5 Aug 1893, *ch.* Eleven including Joseph Jr. *Arr.* 1820 with parents Benjamin and Margaret Booth in Sephton's party, aboard *Aurora*.

Cumming, John Pringle: *b.* 3 Jan 1846, *sn* of John Forbes Cumming and Catherine Pringle, *m.* Sarah Jane Hart, 7 Mar 1867, *d.* 1911, ch. 8 incl. Kate.

Cumming, Kate: *b.* 28 May 1972, *dr* of John Pringle Cumming and Sarah Jane Hart, *m.* Arthur Walker 28 Jun 1899, *d.* 3rd Sep 1947.

Cumming, William Gordon: *b.* 7 May 1848, *sn* of John Forbes Cumming.

Devenish, John Mears: Ensign, Cape Regiment. *m.* Ellen Stretch 1806. Assistant to Robert Hart on Somerset farm. Brother-in-law of Susan Pringle (*b.* Stretch) and Charles Lennox Stretch.

Driver, Dorothy: *b.* 5 Jun 1833, *dr.* of Edward Driver and Ann Thackwray, *m.* Joseph Walker Jr. 16 Aug 1854, *d.* 5 May 1922, *ch.* Eleven incl. Sarah Alice and Arthur.

Ford, James Edward: *b.* 1769, *m.* Frances, *ch.* Five incl Frances Jane Clarissa. *Arr.* 10th Apr 1820 in Bailie;s party aboard *Chapman.*

Hart, Robert Jr: *b.* 11th Jul 1810, *sn* of Robert and Hannah Hart, *m.* (i) Johanna Meintjies, 14th Sep. 1831, *ch.* six (ii) Harriet Marillier 11th Feb. 1842, *ch.* eleven incl. Sarah Jane, *d.* 18th Jul 1867.

Marillier, Philip Richard: *b.* 18th Feb 1793, *m.* Frances Jane Clarissa Ford, April 1820, *d.* 16th Jun 1880. *Arr.* 10th Apr 1820 in Bailie's party aboard *Chapman. ch.* Nine incl. Harriet Elizabeth and Frances.

Marillier, Harriet: *b.* 6th Jan 1824, *dr* of Phillip and Frances Marillier, *m.* Robert Hart Jr,11th Feb. 1842, *ch.* eleven incl. Sarah Jane, *d.* 1898.

Pownall, Dorothy: *b.* abt 1771, *m.* William Thackwray abt 1800, *ch.* John, Dorothy, Ann, William, Joseph. James, *d.* 18th Feb 1850.

Pringle, Catherine: *b.* 14th Jul 1823, *m.* John Forbes Cumming 29th Apr 1843, *d.* 13th Jan. 1903, *dr.* of John Pringle and Susan Stretch, *ch.* John Pringle, William Gordon, Sarah Cairns, Robert Forbes.

Pringle, Thomas: *b.* 5th Jan 1779, *m.* Margaret Brown 19th Jul 1817, *d.* 5th Dec 1834, *br.* of John Pringle. *Arr.* 15 May 1820 in Pringle's party aboard *Brilliant.* Poet and writer. Fighter for Press freedom in the Cape. Secretary of anti-slavery Society in England after his return from the Cape.

Pringle, William Dods: *b.* 4th May 1809, *m.* Ellen Evelyn Hart 1st Feb 1838, *d.* 2nd Nov 1876, *sn* of Robert Pringle and Beatrix Scott.

Stanford, Col. Sir Walter Ernest Mortimer: *b.* 2nd Aug 1850, *m.* Sarah Alice Walker 7th Jun 1888, *d.* 9th Sep 1933. CMG, CB, KBE. Nephew of Joseph Warner. Colonial Service. Chief Magistrate East Griqualand. MHA. Delegate National Convention 1908 – 1910. Senator, Union of South Africa 1910 – 1929.

Stretch, Charles Lennox, *b.* 6th May 1897, *m.* Anna Hart Apr 1820, *d.* 9th Mar 1889, *br.* of Susan Hart (b. Stretch). Soldier, surveyor, Ngqika Agent, MHA.

Stretch, Susan: *b.* 1796, *m.* (i) Edward Parr, 18th Nov 1812 (no issue) (ii) John Pringle 26th Mar 1822, *d.* 11th Jan 1879, *ch.* six, including Catherine (wife of John Forbes Cumming).

Tamplin, Hannah: *b.* 13th Jul 1777, *m.* Robert Hart Sr 10th Apr 1804, *d.* 3rd Sep 1853, *ch.* ten incl. Robert Hart Jr.

Thackwray, Ann: *b.* 28th Jan 1806, *m.* Edward Driver 6th Oct 1825, *d.* 15th Apr 1859, *ch.* twelve including Dorothy (wife of Joseph Walker Jr), *dr* of William Thackwray Sr. and Dorothy Pownall.

Thackwray, Dorothy, *b.* 7th May 1804, *m.* James Allison 4th Jan 1827, *d.* 23rd Jun 1864, *dr* of William Thackwray Sr. and Dorothy Pownall.

Thackwray, James: *b.* 8th Jan 1815, *m.* Jane Booth 24th Jan 1838, *d.* 1st Nov 1854, *sn* of William Thackwray Sr. and Dorothy Pownall. MHA.

Thackwray, Joseph: *b.* 1st May 1812, *m.* Mary Weakley, 29th Jul 1834, *d.* 5th Jun 1867, *sn* of William Thackwray Sr. and Dorothy Pownall.

Thackwray, William Jr., *b.* 8th May 1808, *d.* abt 27th Oct 1829, *sn* of William Thackwray Sr. and Dorothy Pownall, Farmer.

Walker, Joseph Jr: *b.* 2nd Jun 1832, *m.* Dorothy Driver 16th Aug 1854, *d.* 24th March 1908, *ch.* Eleven incl. Sarah Alice and Arthur, *sn* of Joseph Walker Sr. MHA.

Walker, Arthur Edward Mortimer: *b.* 11th Oct 1867, *m.* Kate Cumming 28th June 1899, *d.* 6th May 1927, *sn* of Joseph Walker Jr.

Walker, Richard: *b.* 8th April 1872, *m.* Martha Littlewood abt 1817, *d.* 6th February 1867, *br* of Joseph Walker Sr., Wesleyan lay preacher, mission storeman, trader.

Walker, Sarah Alice: *b.* 15th Jan 1859, *m.* Walter Stanford 7th Jun 1888, *d.* 11th Dec 1937, *dr* of Joseph Walker Jr.

Other Characters

Ayliff, Rev. John: 1797 – 1862. *Arr.* on La Belle Alliance in Willson's party. Became prominent Wesleyan missionary. Biographical material: Ayliff [1821 – 1851, 1863, 1971]

Bird, Col. Christopher: Colonial Secretary, Cape Colony until 1824.

Bisset, John: 1817 – 1894. *Arr.* 1820 as infant on *La Belle Alliance.* Corps of Guides 1834 – 1835. Thereafter regular officer in C.M.R. Acting Governor of Natal 1875. Published reminiscences [Bisset, 1875].

Boesak, Klaas: Active abt 1820. Leader of a Khoikhoi band of hunters based at Theopolis. Played significant part in battle of Graham's Town. Associate of Landdrost Harry Rivers.

Brown, George: 1813 – 1889. *m.* Janet Chalmers (*dr* of William Chalmers). Missionary of the United Presbyterian Church at Iqibira 1850.

Brownlee, Charles: 1821 – 1890. *sn* of Wesleyan missionary, John Brownlee (1791 – 1871). Himself a Wesleyan missionary later was Ngqika commissioner, followed by a number of positions in the colonial service. Ultimately served as Secretary (i.e. Minister) for Native Affairs in the Cape Government.

Calderwood, Henry: 1808 – 1865. *Arr.* on *True Briton* 1839. Missionary to Maqoma. Later Ngqika Agent, Commissioner and Magistrate for Victoria East.

Campbell, Ambrose: 1799 – 1884: *Arr.* 1820 aboard *Dowson.* Doctor, provocative writer.

Campbell, Duncan: 1782 – 1856. *Arr.* 1820 party leader on *Weymouth.* Assistant Landdrost Graham's Town 1820. Appointed Civil Commissioner for Albany 1828.

Campbell, Thomas: *d.* 1845. *Arr.* 1841 as artisan missionary of GMS. Associated with John Forbes Cumming at Kirkwood and Bonkolo

Chalmers, John Aitken: 1837 – 1888. *sn* of William Chalmers. Missionary. Served at Mgwali and Henderson missions.

Chalmers, William Sr: 1802 – 1847. Missionary of the Glasgow Missionary Society serving at Tyumie. *m.* Mary Munsie, *ch.* Janet Ewing, John Aitken, William Buchanan, Ebenezer.

Chalmers, William Buchanan: 1833 – 1910. *sn* of William Chalmers. Civil Commissioner and resident magistrate of King Williams Town.

Cock, William: 1793 – 1876. Leading Albany businessman. Leader of a party that had arrived on *Weymouth.* Prominent in the attempts to establish a port at the mouth of the Kowie River. Member of the Legislative Council.

Cuyler, Jacob: 1773 – 1854. American born. Son of Abraham Cuyler, the last British appointed mayor of Albany NY. Loyalist in the American war of independence. Family exiled to Canada. Captain in 59th regiment when sent to Cape. Major then Colonel in Cape Regiment. Landdrost of Uitenhage from 1806. Resigned 1823.

Dundas, Maj. William Bolden: Landdrost of Albany, 1825 – 1827. Civil Commissioner of Albany and Somerset, 1828.

Fairbairn, John: 1794 – 1864. Editor. Son-in-law of Dr John Philip. Prominent critic of government and proponent of philanthropic cause. Key figure in campaign for press freedom.

Farewell, Francis: 1784 – 1829. Pioneer and adventurer. Associated with early development of Port Natal.

Fynn, Henry Francis:1803 – 1861. Active in early history of Natal. Associate of Francis Farewell. Became Government Agent with abaThembu and later amaMpondo.

Godlonton, Robert: 1794 – 1884. *Arr.* Bailie's party on board *Chapman*. Graham's Town businessman. owner-editor of The *Graham's Town Journal*, MLA, etc. Father-in-law of Benjamin Booth Jr. who married his daughter Matilda.

Graham, Col. John: 1778 – 1821. British soldier. After service in 90th and 93rd Regiments of Foot was appointed commander of Cape Regiment in 1806. Responsible for expulsion of Xhosa from Zuurveld. Founder of Graham's Town (afterwards Grahamstown).

Halse, Henry: 1817 – 1880. Grew up on frontier having arrived with settlers as infant. Author of an important manuscript of reminiscences [Halse, 1880].

Lochenberg, Jan Nicholaas (Klaas): *d.* 1829. Renegade Boer from Graaff Reinet who lived outside the Colony near Butterworth.

Niven, Rev. Robert: Missionary of the United Presbyterian Church at Uniondale at the start of Mlanjeni's War in 1850.

Philip, Dr John: 1775 – 1851. *Arr.* 1819 as Inspector of Missions for LMS. Cape Town Congregational minister. Strong critic of Colonial government policy

Renton, Rev. Henry: 1804 – 1877. Commissioner of the United Presbyterian Church, sent from Scotland in 1850 to carry out an investigation of its missionary operations in the Cape.

Rivers, Henry (Harry): Landdrost of Albany 1821 – 1825 and Swellendam 1825 – 1842. Treasurer General of the Colony 1842 – 1861.

Shaw, Rev. William: 1798 – 1872. Methodist minister with Sephton's party in *Aurora*. Key to the development of Wesleyan church and missions in the Cape. Biographical material: Boyce [1875], Shaw [1860, 1972].

Shaw, William: Cousin of the Southey brothers. Brother-in-law to Thomas Stubbs. Suspected of being involved in the mutilation of Hintsa's body.

Somerset, Lieut.-Gen. Henry, KCB: 1794 – 1862. Eldest son of Lord Charles Somerset. Served in Cape Regiment 1818 – 1853. Various positions of command on the frontier in the wars of 1834/5, 1846, and 1850 – 53.

Southey, George: 1810 – 1867. Son of 1820 settler George Southey. Served in Corps of Guides 1834/5. Responsible for firing the shot that killed the Xhosa king, Hintsa.

Southey, Sir Richard: 1808 – 1901. Son of 1820 settler George Southey. Led Corps of Guides in 1834/5 war. Later Colonial Secretary, Lieutenant Governor of Griqualand West, MHA.

Southey, William: Son of 1820 settler George Southey. Served in Corps of Guides 1834/5.

Stockenstrom, Anders: 1757 – 1811. Swedish immigrant. Landdrost of Graaff Reinet under Batavian Republic and under British rule. Killed by group of imiDange and Khoikhoi during an apparently peaceful meeting at the beginning of the 1812 campaign to clear the Zuurveld.

Stockenstrom, Sir Andries: 1792 – 1864. *sn* of Anders Stockenstrom. Severe critic of Somerset's and D'Urban's policies. Lieutenant-Governor of Eastern Province. M.L.C.

Stubbs, John: 1779 – 1821. *Arr.* 1820 aboard *Northampton*. Neighbour of William Thackwray.

Stubbs, Thomas: 1809 – 1877. *sn* of John Stubbs. Apprentice of William Thackwray Sr. Led militia forces in the wars of 1834, 1846, and 1850. Author of reminiscences [Stubbs, 1978].

Trappes, Capt: Participated in defence of Graham's Town 1819. Acting District Landdrost 1820 – 21.

Warner, Joseph: 1808 – 1871. *sn* of Henry Warner of George Smith's party in *Stentor.* After service at Clarkebury and Haslop Hills, became a Wesleyan missionary, first at Mvane and thereafter at Lesseyton. Was later "Tambookie agent", i.e. Colonial agent in Thembuland.

Willshire, Lt-Col. Thomas: Commander of British forces at Battle of Graham's Town. Fort Willshire was named after him.

Wood, George: 1801 – 1844. Sephton's party, *Aurora*. Apprentice to William Thackwray. Great friend of John Thackwray. Afterwards a Grahamstown businessman and entrepreneur and reputed to be the richest man in Albany.

Kings and Chiefs

Chungwa (Congo): 1740 – 1812. Chief of the Gqunukwhebe 1793 – 1812. Heir of Tshaka. *sns.* Phatho, Kama, Kobe.

Dyani Tshatshu: Chief of amaNtinde. Converted to Christianity by van der Kemp. Gave evidence to Select Committee on Aborigines in London in1835.

Faku: *abt* 1780 – 1867. King of the Mpondo nation from 1844 – 1867.

Gcaleka: Xhosa king. Great Son of Phalo. Ruled the eastern branch of the divided Xhosa, who took his name. Occupied a region to the east of the Kei centred on the present town of Butterworth

Hintsa: 1789 – 1835, Xhosa King, Chief of the Royal Gcaleka House. Son of Khuwala and descendant in the paramount line of Phalo. *s.* Sarhili.

Jalamba: *d* 1781, Great Son and Heir of Mahote, chief of the imiDange. Treacherously murdered by the commando of Adriaan van Jaarsveld during a meeting on the Zeekoei River.

Kobe: Minor Gqunukwhebe chief. Son of Chungwa. Sometimes called Congo or Kobus Congo by colonists.

Langa: Son of Phalo. Placed in House of Tiso. Founding chief of the amaMbalu.

Maqoma: 1798 – 1873. Right-hand son of Ngqika. Acted as regent of the amaNgqika until coming of age of Sandile. His clansmen were called the amaJingqi after the bull that was presented to him after his circumcision [Stapleton 1991].

Ndlambe (Slambi) *d.* 1828: Son of Rharhabe. Uncle of Ngqika. Regent of the amaRharhabe while Ngqika was a minor. Fell out with Ngqika and the amaNdlambe became a separate chiefdom after the war with the amaNgqika

Ngqika (Gaika) 1778 – 1829: Grandson of Rharhabe in the line of the great house. Became chief of the amaRharhabe as a small child. After the rift with Ndlambe led his own chiefdom, the amaNgqika.

Ngubencuka Vusani *abt* 1790 – 1830: King of the abaThembu 1800 – 1830. His great wife was Nonesi, daughter of King Faku.

Nqeno *d*. 1846: Mbalu chief. Son of Langa.

Nqeto: *d*. 1830: Zulu chief. Leader of the amaQwabe. Lieutenant of Shaka. Fled with his people into Pondoland when Shaka was assassinated and succeeded by Dingane.

Phalo: Xhosa king. The House of Phalo was split by the hostilities between his Great Son, Gcaleka and his brother Rharhabe.

Rharhabe: Son of Phalo. Chief of the western branch of the divided Xhosa.

Sarhili (Kreli): Xhosa King, Chief of the Royal Gcaleka House. Son of Hintsa and descendant in the royal line of Phalo.

Sandile 1820 – 1879: Great son of Ngqika. Chief of the amaNgqika and titular head of the amaRharhabe.

Stokwe: Mbalu chief. Son of Nqeno.

Tyopo: fl. 1827 – 1850. Chief of the amaGcina. His Great Place was in the neighbourhood of the current location of Queenstown. Soga [1930, facing p. 120] gives a genealogy of the amaNgcina which identifies Tyopo as the son of Ngcina. There were actually several generations between the two. Stanford's contemporary account makes it clear that his father was Phato (not the same as the Gqunukwhebe chief). The amaNgcina suffered many vicissitudes and the succession is not clear. At the time of this narrative they offered allegiance to the Thembu king.

Officialdom

Secretaries of State for Colonies

Bathurst, Henry, 3rd Earl Bathurst: 1762 – 1834. Distinguished English politician. Secretary of State (i.e. Minister) for the Colonies 1812 – 1827.

Dundas, Henry, 1st Viscount Melville: 1742 – 1811. Scottish politician. Secretary of State for War and the Colonies 1794 – 1801.

Grant, Charles, 1st Baron Glenelg: 1778 – 1866. Secretary of State for War and the Colonies 1835 – 1839.

Grey, Henry, 3rd Earl Grey: 1802 – 1894. Secretary at War 1835 – 1839. Secretary of State for War and the Colonies 1846 – 1852.

Governors

1797 – 1798	Macartney, 1st Earl (1737 – 1806): Irish Earldom. Governor of Madras 1781 – 1785. First British Ambassador to China 1792 – 1794.
1798 – 1799 1801 – 1803	Dundas, Gen. Francis (acting): 1759 – 1824. British military commander at the Cape during the first occupation. Nephew of Sec. of State, Henry Dundas.
1799 – 1801	Yonge, Sir George (1781 – 1812): 5th Baronet.
1806 – 1807	Baird, Sir David, GCB (1757 – 1829): Army career. Later served in Pen-

insula Wars, created first baronet, was Commander-in-chief for Ireland.

1807 – 1811   Caledon, 2nd Earl (1777 – 1839): Irish peer. Du Pré Alexander, Viscount Alexander, succeeded to his father's title as Lord Caledon in 1802.

1811 – 1814   Cradock, General Sir John Francis (1759 – 1839): Previously Acting Governor of Gibraltar. Later 1st Baron Howden.

1814 – 1826   Somerset, Lord Charles (1767 – 1831): Second son of the 5th Duke of Beaufort. M.P. for Scarborough. Privy Councillor. Father of Henry Somerset.

1820 – 1821   Donkin, Sir Rufane Shaw, GCH, KCB (1773 – 1841) (acting for Somerset): Peninsula war veteran. After his Governorship was M.P. for Berwick on Tweed and later for Sandwich. Commited suicide in Southampton.

1826 – 1828   Bourke Sir Richard, KCB (1777 – 1855): Peninsula war veteran. Later Governor of New South Wales.

1828 – 1833   Cole, Sir Galbraith Lowry, GCB (1772 – 1842): Irish M.P. Peninsula war veteran. Governor of Mauritius.

1834 – 1838   D'Urban, Sir Benjamin GCB, KCTH, KCTS (1777 – 1849): Governor of Antigua, Lieutenant Governor of Demerara Esequibo, Governor British Columbia. Later British Commander in North America.

1838 – 1844   Napier, Sir George Thomas, KCB (1784 – 1855): Peninsula war veteran.

1844 – 1847   Maitland, Sir Peregrine, KCB, GCB (1777 – 1854): Veteran of Waterloo. Lieutenant Governor of Upper Canada and then of Nova Scotia.

1847   Pottinger, Sir Henry, Bart, GCB, PC (1789 – 1856): Governor of Hong Kong. Later Governor of Madras.

1847 – 1852   Smith, Sir Henry (Harry) George Wakelyn of Aliwal, Bart, GCB (1787 – 1860): Peninsula war veteran. Served in USA. Present at burning of the White House and the Capitol in Washington DC. Fought at Waterloo. Military Service in Cape 1828 – 1836. Distinguished military sevice in India.

1852 – 1854   Cathcart, Sir George, GCB (1794 – 1854). Served with Wellington in Napoleonic wars. Later Deputy Lieutenant of Tower of London. After Cape governorship was Deputy to Raglan in the Crimea and was killed at the battle of Inkerman.

1854   Darling, Sir Charles Henry KCB (acting for Grey) (1809 – 1870): Lieutenant Governor of St Lucia and the Cape Colony. Later Governor of Newfoundland, and of Victoria, Australia.

1854 – 1861   Grey, Sir George, KCB (1812 – 1898) : Governor of Australia, and of New Zealand. After service in South Africa served second term as Governor of New Zealand. Later Premier of New Zealand.

Appendix 2. Xhosa Kingdoms and Chiefdoms

Nguni Houses and Clans

The prefixes ama, aba, imi, simply denote a plural and hence also the people constituting the kingdom, house, or clan. The order of the list is alphabetical in the stem.

amaBhaca: One of the displaced peoples during the time of the *mfecane*. Led by Madikane, they were eventually defeated by Thembu, Mpondomise and Xhosa forces

imiDange: Formerly a powerful chiefdom, descended from Mdange, distantly connected to the Royal Xhosa House. By the time of this narrative they were weakened and fragmented. Their most prominent chiefs at the time of this narrative were Habana in first two decades of the nineteenth century, and later Bhothomane.

amaGcina: Thembu chiefdom. Led by Tyopo in the second quarter of the nineteenth century. Although very distantly connected to the Xhosa, after the ravages of the Mfecane they offered allegiance to the Thembu Royal House. Located near current position of Queenstown

amaGqaleka: The Royal Xhosa house. Their kings were in the royal line of succession from Phalo.

amaGqunukwhebe: Independent Xhosa house. They had absorbed many Khoikhoi.

amaHala: Royal House of the Thembu

amaJingqi: Maqoma's people, named after the bull presented to him at the time of his circumcision.

amaMbalu: The house founded by Langa, brother of Gcaleka and Rharhabe.

amaMpondo: Kingdom located in the region of the Umzimvubu River. Their king, Faku, reigned from about 1818 to 1867.

amaMpondomise: Kingdom neighbouring the Mpondo.

amaNdlambe: Rharhabe subgroup with allegiance to Ndlambe.

amaNgqika: Rharhabe subgroup with allegiance to Ngqika.

amaNtinde: Independent chiefdom. For most of this narrative headed by Christian chief, Dyani Tshatshu.

amaRharhabe: Right Hand House of Phalo. A rift between Ndlambe and Ngqika split this house.

abaThembu: Known to colonists as Tambookie. Large kingdom. Royal House the amaHala. Occupying region stretching from Queenstown to Mthatha river and beyond.

amaTshatshu: Associated with the abaThembu. In the eighteen twenties they were ruled by Bawana. By the eighteen forties he had been replaced by his son Maphasa.

amaXhosa: The aggregate of all the descendant houses of a mythical king Xhosa. More straightforwardly those acknowledging the chief of the Gcaleka House as king. Refers mainly to the amaGcaleka, the amaRharhabe, and the amaMbalu, the descendants of the king Phalo, although the amaGqunukwhebe, imiDange, amaGwali, and amaNtinde were descended from Tshawe, an ancestor of Phalo and might be included under the Xhosa umbrella. In modern times the name Xhosa is often inaccurately applied to all who speak the Xhosa language i.e. those who historically originate from a region roughly coincident with the modern Eastern Cape Province. This includes all those listed above and many others.

Relationships among the Xhosa

The genealogy of the Western Nguni kings and chiefs is inherently complicated because it is based on a system of polygamous marriage and the consequently complicated inheritance rules. The lines of descent are of great importance culturally and have been passed down through oral tradition. Inevitably there are inaccuracies and inconsistencies in the information available, particularly for the early generations. The charts below are intended to show the relationships between those rulers who play a significant part in our story.[695]

To understand the line of succession it is necessary to understand the hierarchy of the wives of the chief. When a boy had gone through the circumcision ceremony he became a man, able to marry. An intrinsic part of the marriage ritual was the payment by the bridegroom of the bride price, lobola, to the parents of the bride. This took the form of a number of cattle appropriate to the wealth and status of the betrothed[696]. A young chief might take several wives and have a number of children by them. Eventually, when he was mature, a dynastic marriage would be undertaken. This was usually to the daughter of another, often distant, chief, and an important feature of this marriage was that the lobola was paid, not by the chief himself, but by his people. This wife became the Great Wife; her eldest son was the heir apparent and her house was the Great House. The next most senior wife, often the first wife, was the wife of the Right Hand House. The sons of the Right Hand House had a role as councillors, giving advice to the chief. Because the Great Wife was generally married relatively late in the life of a chief, the Great Son often succeeded his father when he was still a minor. In such cases it was usually the son of the Right Hand House who acted as Regent. Thus Ndlambe acted for Ngqika, and Maqoma for Sandile.

The chiefs did not have absolute power. Their advisors played a vital part and no chief could ignore them without losing adherents. Nor was the succession of the heir a foregone conclusion. Concerns about the capacity of the heir or other political considerations could play a part, as was the case of Ngqika, whose brother was heir apparent and favoured by the elders, but was appointed through the influence of Ndlambe.

The Xhosa kings and chiefs appearing in our story have a common ancestor, Togu, who was active in the middle to late seventeenth century.

The genealogical tables below show the relationship between many of the the various chiefs who play a significant part in our story. The polygamous system means that they are complex. In particular, it is seldom that the name of a wife is known. Only some of the Great Wives of the major figures are recorded. For this reason children have been identified as originating in the Great House or the Right Hand House or a minor House, rather than by the name of their mother. The lines of descent are exclusively patrilineal; the names of the women, who in their time often played a powerful role, have not been recorded in the oral tradition except in a few cases.

Descendants of TOGU

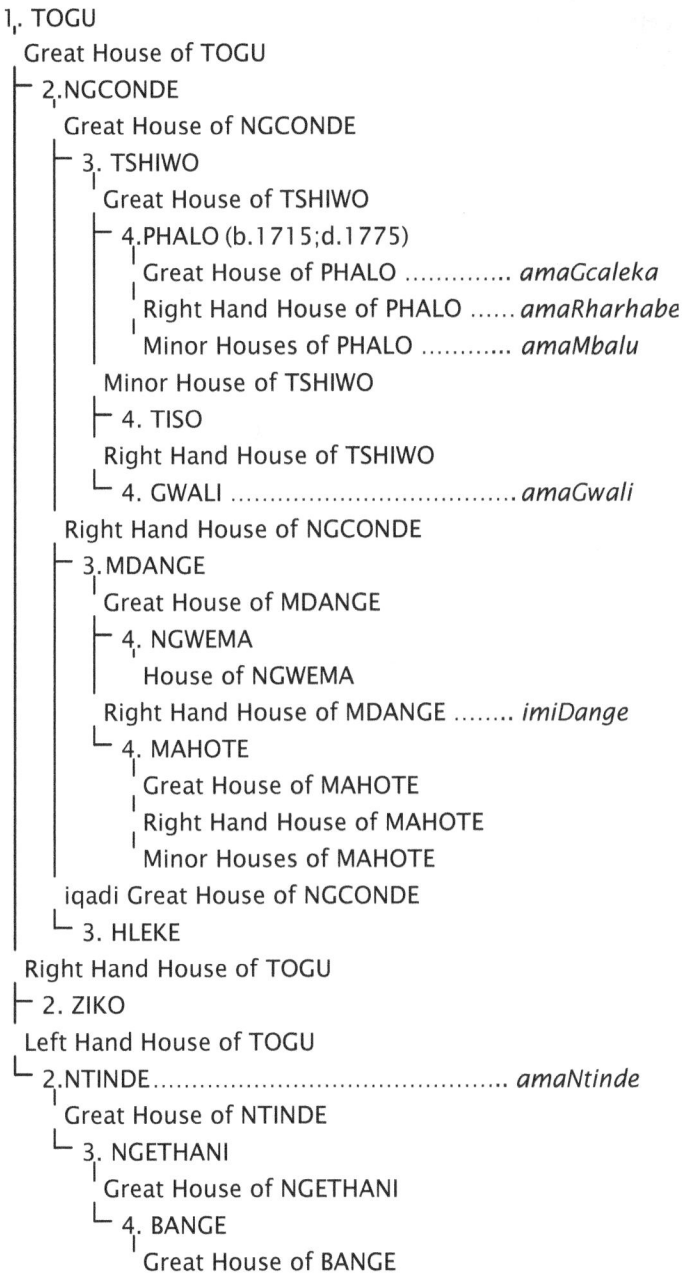

1. TOGU
  Great House of TOGU
  ├ 2. NGCONDE
    Great House of NGCONDE
    ├ 3. TSHIWO
      Great House of TSHIWO
      ├ 4. PHALO (b.1715;d.1775)
        Great House of PHALO .... *amaGcaleka*
        Right Hand House of PHALO ...... *amaRharhabe*
        Minor Houses of PHALO .... *amaMbalu*
      Minor House of TSHIWO
      ├ 4. TISO
      Right Hand House of TSHIWO
      └ 4. GWALI .... *amaGwali*
    Right Hand House of NGCONDE
    ├ 3. MDANGE
      Great House of MDANGE
      ├ 4. NGWEMA
        House of NGWEMA
      Right Hand House of MDANGE .... *imiDange*
      └ 4. MAHOTE
        Great House of MAHOTE
        Right Hand House of MAHOTE
        Minor Houses of MAHOTE
    iqadi Great House of NGCONDE
    └ 3. HLEKE
  Right Hand House of TOGU
  ├ 2. ZIKO
  Left Hand House of TOGU
  └ 2. NTINDE... *amaNtinde*
    Great House of NTINDE
    └ 3. NGETHANI
      Great House of NGETHANI
      └ 4. BANGE
        Great House of BANGE

Origins of the Xhosa Nation

Descendants of Gcaleka

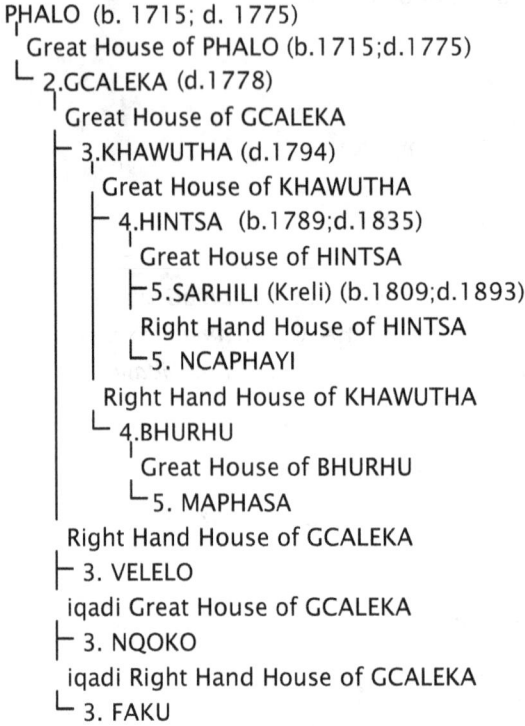

```
PHALO (b. 1715; d. 1775)
 │ Great House of PHALO (b.1715;d.1775)
 └ 2.GCALEKA (d.1778)
    │ Great House of GCALEKA
    ├ 3.KHAWUTHA (d.1794)
    │  │ Great House of KHAWUTHA
    │  ├ 4.HINTSA  (b.1789;d.1835)
    │  │  │ Great House of HINTSA
    │  │  ├5.SARHILI (Kreli) (b.1809;d.1893)
    │  │  │ Right Hand House of HINTSA
    │  │  └5. NCAPHAYI
    │  │ Right Hand House of KHAWUTHA
    │  └ 4.BHURHU
    │     │ Great House of BHURHU
    │     └5. MAPHASA
    │ Right Hand House of GCALEKA
    ├ 3. VELELO
    │ iqadi Great House of GCALEKA
    ├ 3. NQOKO
    │ iqadi Right Hand House of GCALEKA
    └ 3. FAKU
```

(a)

Descendants of Langa

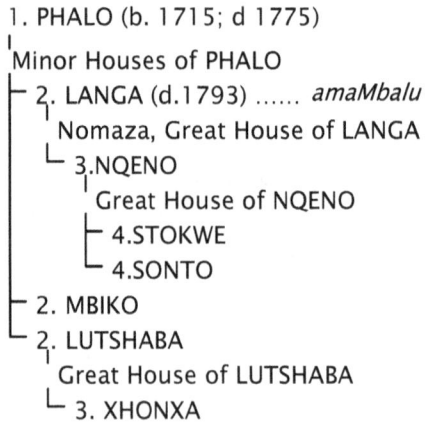

```
1. PHALO (b. 1715; d 1775)
 │
 │ Minor Houses of PHALO
 ├ 2. LANGA (d.1793) ...... amaMbalu
 │  │ Nomaza, Great House of LANGA
 │  └ 3.NQENO
 │     │ Great House of NQENO
 │     ├ 4.STOKWE
 │     └ 4.SONTO
 ├ 2. MBIKO
 └ 2. LUTSHABA
    │ Great House of LUTSHABA
    └ 3. XHONXA
```

(b)

(a) The amaGcaleka, Royal House of the Xhosa; (b) The amaMbalu and other Xhosa houses

Descendants of Rharhabe

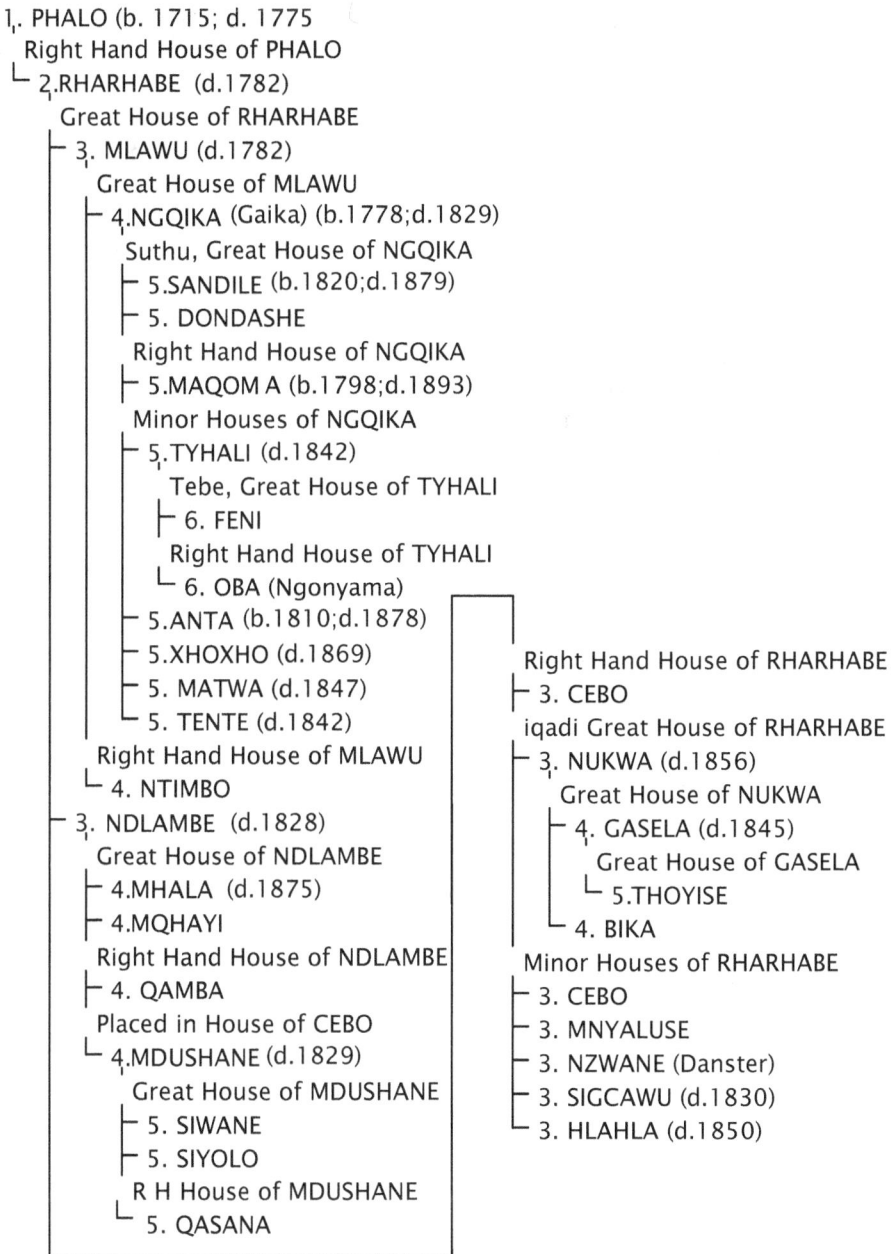

1. PHALO (b. 1715; d. 1775
   Right Hand House of PHALO
   └ 2.RHARHABE (d.1782)
      Great House of RHARHABE
      ├ 3. MLAWU (d.1782)
      │ Great House of MLAWU
      │ ├ 4.NGQIKA (Gaika) (b.1778;d.1829)
      │ │ Suthu, Great House of NGQIKA
      │ │ ├ 5.SANDILE (b.1820;d.1879)
      │ │ ├ 5. DONDASHE
      │ │ Right Hand House of NGQIKA
      │ │ ├ 5.MAQOM A (b.1798;d.1893)
      │ │ Minor Houses of NGQIKA
      │ │ ├ 5.TYHALI (d.1842)
      │ │ │ Tebe, Great House of TYHALI
      │ │ │ ├ 6. FENI
      │ │ │ Right Hand House of TYHALI
      │ │ │ └ 6. OBA (Ngonyama)
      │ │ ├ 5.ANTA (b.1810;d.1878)
      │ │ ├ 5.XHOXHO (d.1869)
      │ │ ├ 5. MATWA (d.1847)
      │ │ └ 5. TENTE (d.1842)
      │ Right Hand House of MLAWU
      │ └ 4. NTIMBO
      ├ 3. NDLAMBE (d.1828)
      │ Great House of NDLAMBE
      │ ├ 4.MHALA (d.1875)
      │ ├ 4.MQHAYI
      │ Right Hand House of NDLAMBE
      │ ├ 4. QAMBA
      │ Placed in House of CEBO
      │ └ 4.MDUSHANE (d.1829)
      │   Great House of MDUSHANE
      │   ├ 5. SIWANE
      │   ├ 5. SIYOLO
      │   R H House of MDUSHANE
      │   └ 5. QASANA

   Right Hand House of RHARHABE
   ├ 3. CEBO
   iqadi Great House of RHARHABE
   ├ 3. NUKWA (d.1856)
   │ Great House of NUKWA
   │ ├ 4. GASELA (d.1845)
   │ │ Great House of GASELA
   │ │ └ 5.THOYISE
   │ └ 4. BIKA
   Minor Houses of RHARHABE
   ├ 3. CEBO
   ├ 3. MNYALUSE
   ├ 3. NZWANE (Danster)
   ├ 3. SIGCAWU (d.1830)
   └ 3. HLAHLA (d.1850)

The amaRharhabe

Descendants of MDANGE

1. NGCONDE
   Great House of NGCONDE
   └ 2. MDANGE
      Great House of MDANGE
      ├ 3. NGWEMA
      │ House of NGWEMA
      │ └ 4. MARULA
      │   House of MARULA
      │   └ 5. YEKWA
      │   House of YEKWA
      │   └ 6. KUSE
      │ Right Hand House of MDANGE
      └ 3. MAHOTE
         Great House of MAHOTE
         ├ 4. JALAMBA(d.1781)
         │ Right Hand House of MAHOTE
         ├ 4. FUNO
         │ House of FUNO
         │ ├ 5. GCEYA
         │ │ House of GCEYA
         │ │ └ 6. MADOLO
         │ └ 5. TOLA
         │ Minor Houses of MAHOTE
         ├ 4. GUDISA
         ├ 4. NJOMOSE
         │ House of NJOMOSE
         │ └ 5. XHASA
         ├ 4. QOBA
         │ House of QOBA
         │ ├ 5. HABANA
         │ └ 5. CHALATA
         ├ 4. NGINZA
         └ 4. MANTLA
            House of MANTLA
            └ 5. BHOTHOMANE

(a)

Descendants of NTINDE

1. TOGU
   Left Hand House of TOGU
   └ 2. NTINDE
      Great House of NTINDE
      └ 3. NGETHANI
         Great House of NGETHANI
         └ 4. BANGE
            Great House of BANGE
            └ 5. CIKA
               Great House of CIKA
               └ 6. TSHATSHU
                  Great House of TSHATSHU
                  └ 7. Dyani TSHATSHU

(b)

Descendants of TSHAKA

(The Gqunukwhebe)

1. TSHAKA (d.1793)
   └ 2. CHUNGWA (d.1812)

      ├ 3. PHATHO
      ├ 3. KHAMA
      └ 3. KOBE

(c)

(a) The imiDange; (b) The amaNtinde; (c) The amaGqunukwhebe

Appendix 3. Maps

The maps have been prepared by the author using the *PlanetGIS Cartographer* software suite. The topographical data originates from the Chief Surveyor General of South Africa. Modern features such as dams, roads and buildings have been removed. It should be recognized, however, that physical features may have changed in the nearly two centuries since the events illustrated by the maps. Erosion and flooding changes the course of rivers, for example. When locations of events and routes are shown, they are best estimates based on contemporary descriptions.

Map 1: The frontier region

The frontier region as it is today. The rectangles show the extent of the maps that follow.

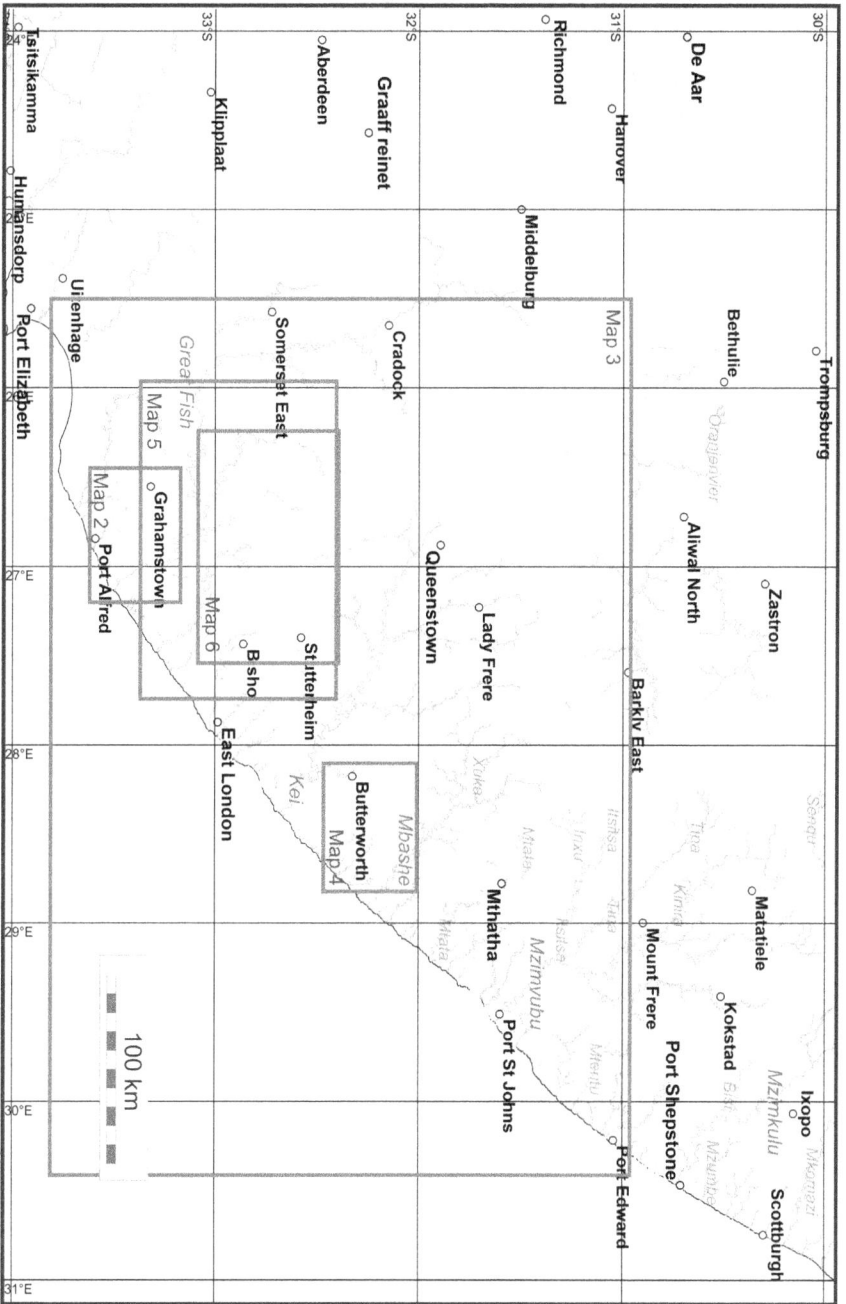

Map 1

Map 2: Early Albany

The settlement in the eighteen twenties, showing various locations that occur in the text.

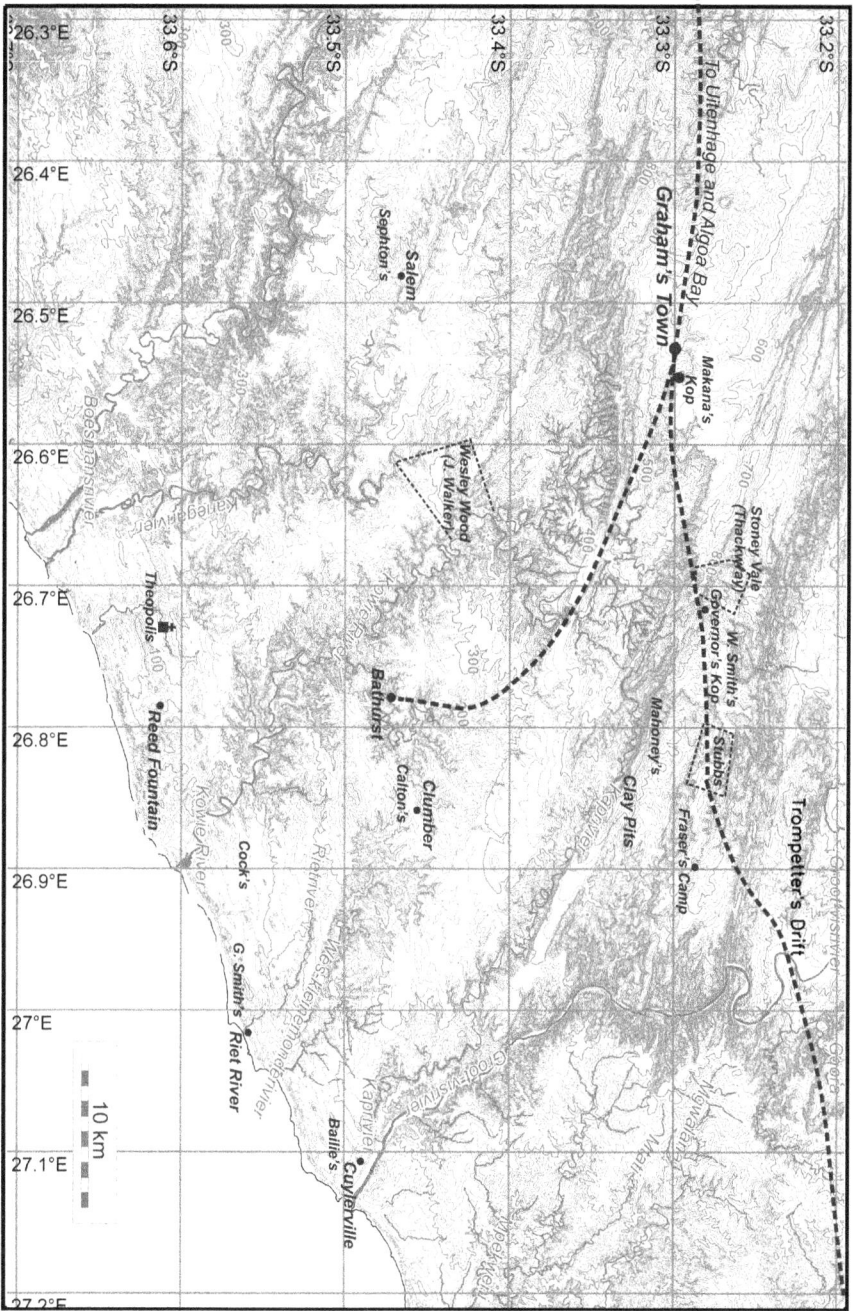

Map 2

Map 3: Nguni Kingdoms

This shows the approximate positions of the various Nguni peoples during the later eighteen twenties. The time of the *mfecane* had caused a number of changes. This represents the approximate situation during the pioneering expeditions of William and John Thackwray, and at the beginning of the war of 1834 – 1835.

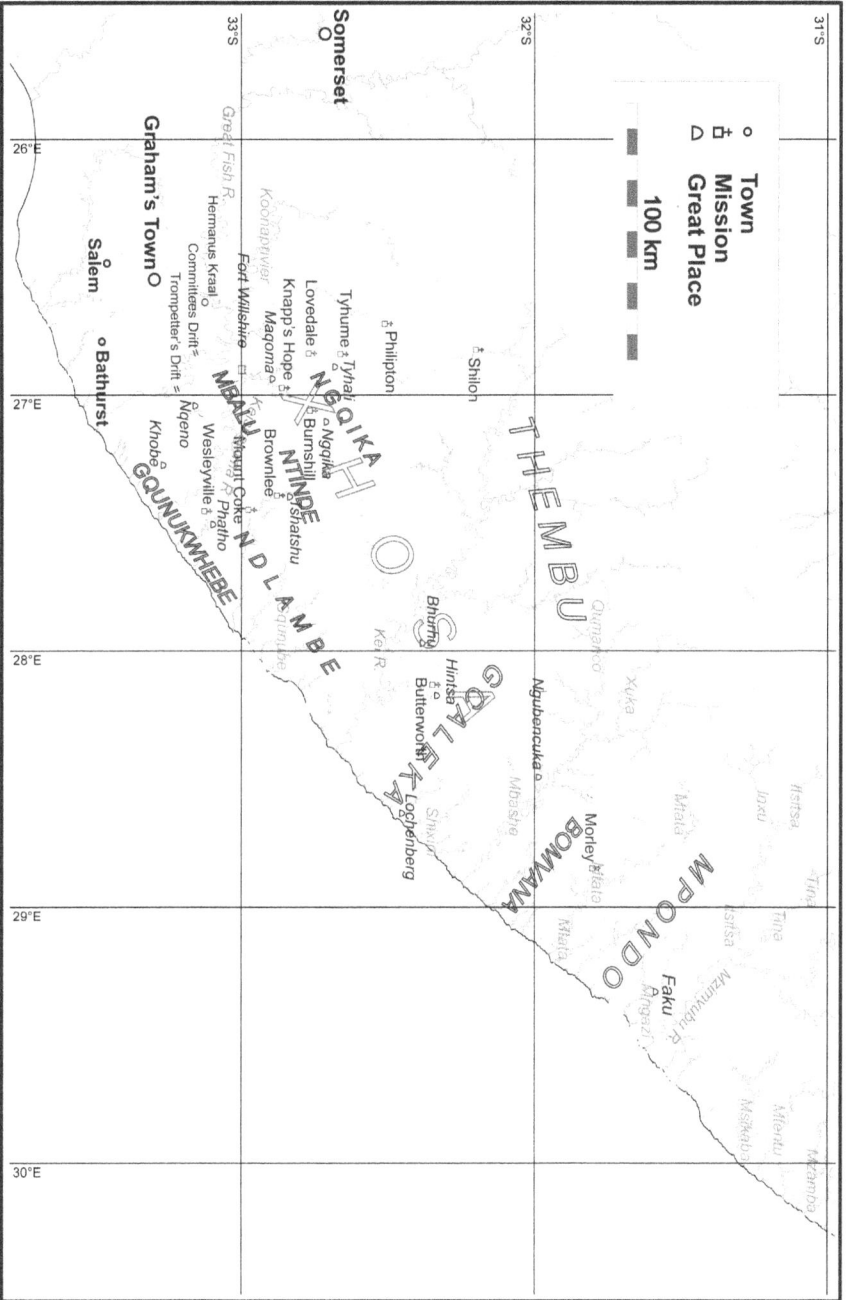

Map 3

Map 4: The pursuit and death of Hintsa.

It is impossible to reconcile the precise topography of the present day site with the map drawn by the army surveyor, C Michel[697], at the time. The map drawn by Pretorius[698] is based on Michel's map. He has added sketched contours. These, however, are not based on any survey. Neither of these maps gives any coordinates. The clue to the site is the fact that the route of the army in Michel's map crossed the Gwadu stream before proceeding to the Nqabara crossing. This is the only site consistent with that. In 180 years, with frequent floods it is quite likely that the perennial line of the river would have changed by erosion within the bounds of the low lying region (the modern contours shown are at 5 m intervals). The oxbows would have become exaggerated. A possible line for the river at the time is indicated, which would bring it closer to Michel's depiction. Michel's sketch shows a relatively straight course for the army from the Gwadu to the Nqabara crossing. The topography makes this unlikely. The dotted line shows a more plausible course.

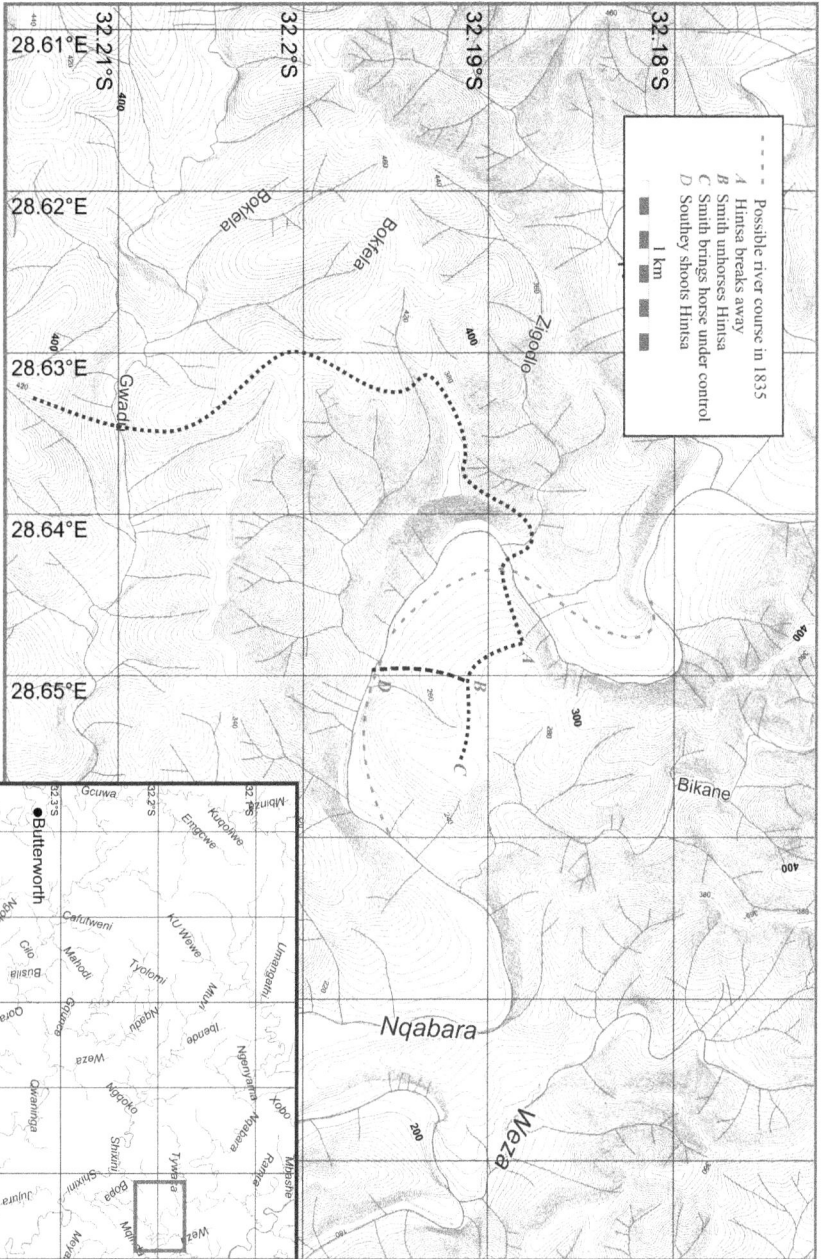

Map 4

Map 5: Events during the War of the Axe

1. 17th April 1846: Somerset's troops defeated at Burnshill and 65 wagons captured by Xhosa.

2. 22nd May 1846: Capture and destruction of 43 wagons by Xhosa forces in Fish River Gorge to east of Trompetter's Drift.

3. Siege of Fort Peddie. Threat extended from end of April to 28th May 1846, when a major attack by united Xhosa forces was beaten off.

4. 7th June 1846: Somerset's forces defeat Ndlambe forces under Mhala and Siyolo in a battle in the Mgwangqa valley.

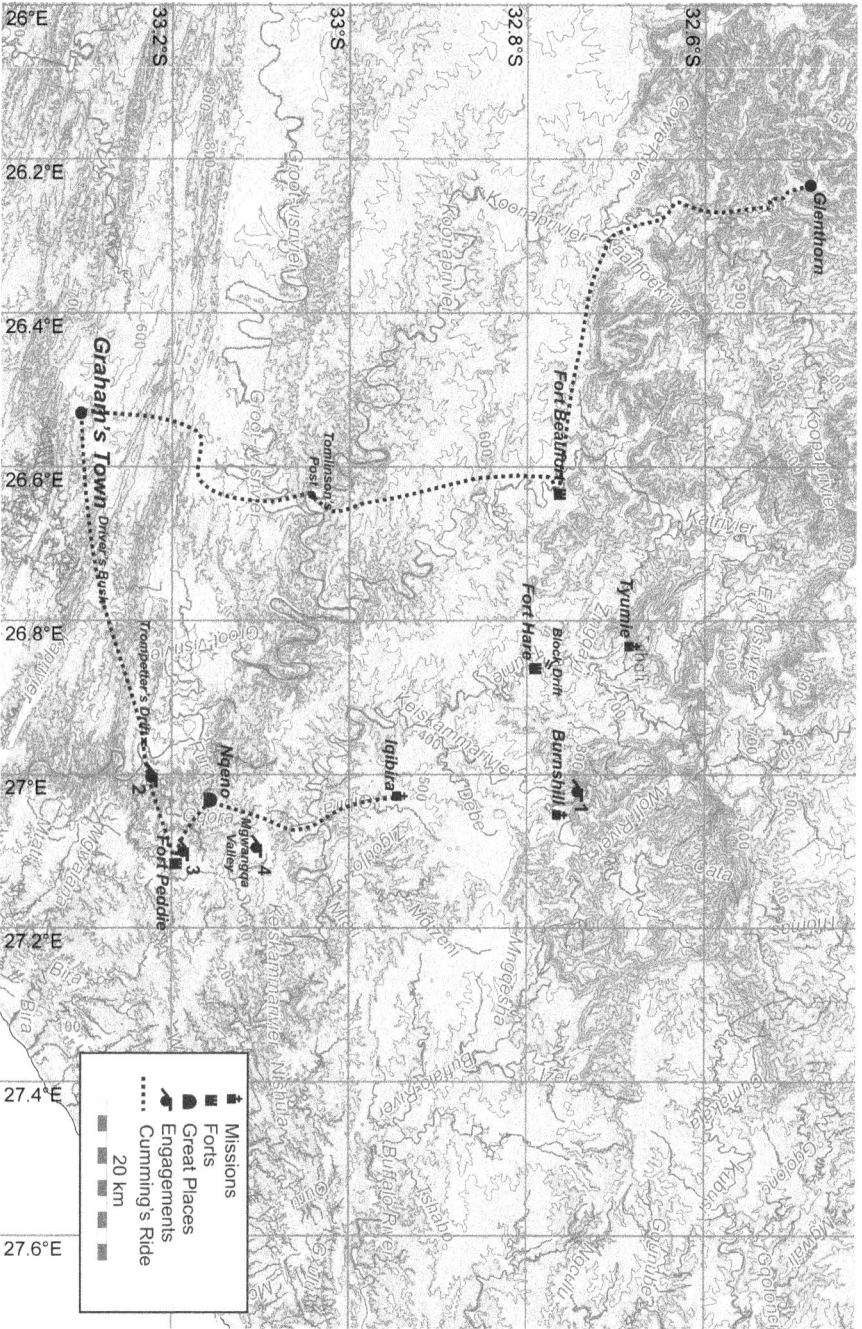

Map 5

26°E
33.2°S
33°S
32.8°S
32.6°S

26.2°E

26.4°E

26.6°E

26.8°E

27°E

27.2°E

27.4°E

27.6°E

Glenthorn

Fort Beaufort

Graham's Town

Tomlinson's Post

Driver's Bush

Trompetter's Drift

Block Drift

Fort Hare

Tyumie

Burnshill

Igibira

Ngeno

Mgwangqa Valley

Fort Peddie

Grootvisrivier

Groot-Vis

Koonaprivier

Koonaprivier

Kwaihoekrivier

Koonaprivier

Katrivier

Zinguiba

Zingcuka

Nohorivier

Keiskammarivier

20 km

Missions
Forts
Great Places
Engagements
Cumming's Ride

Map 6: Mlanjeni's War

Events

1. 24th December 1850: Battle of the Boma Pass.

2. 25th December 1850: Running battle with Xhosa as McKinnon retreated.

3. 25th December 1850: Massacre of villagers at Auckland and Woburn.

4. 29th Dcember 1850: Somerset attempts to break out of Fort Hare to relieve Smith at Fort Cox. Attempt defeated.

5. 7th January 1851: Attack on Fort Beaufort by Herman Matroos driven off. Matroos killed.

6. 21st January 1851: Battle of Fort Hare. Xhosa driven off.

7. 22nd March 1851: Attack on Benjamin Booth Jr at de Bruin's Kloof.

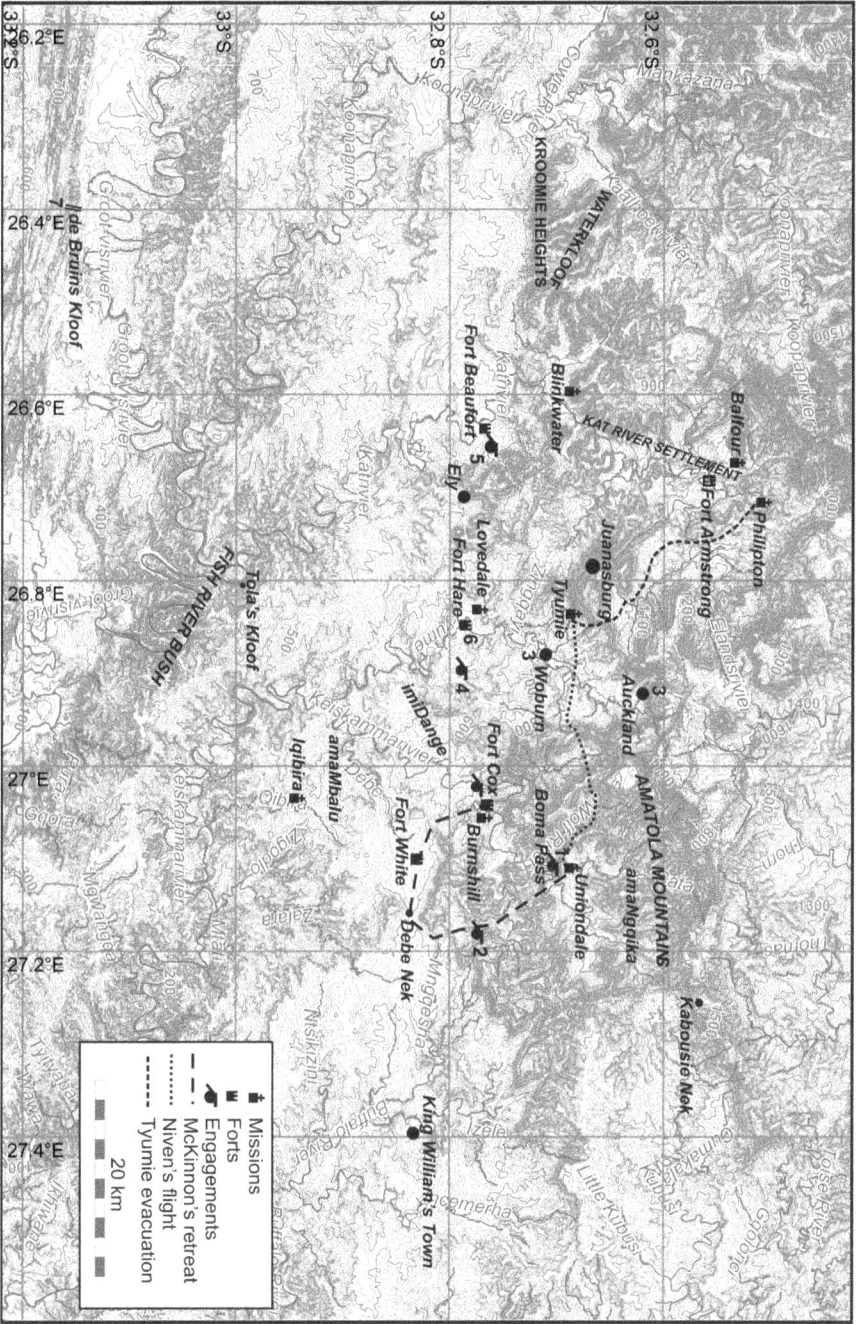

Map 6

Missions
Forts
Engagements
McKinnon's retreat
Niven's flight
Tyumie evacuation

20 km

33.2°S
33°S
32.8°S
32.6°S

26.2°E
26.4°E
26.6°E
26.8°E
27°E
27.2°E
27.4°E

de Bruins Kloof
KROOMIE HEIGHTS
WATERKLOOF
Wankazana
FISH RIVER BUSH
Tola's Kloof
Fort Beaufort
Blinkwater
Balfour
KAT RIVER SETTLEMENT
Fort Armstrong
Philipton
Ely
Lovedale
Fort Hare
Juanasburg
Tyumie
Woburn
Auckland
AMATOLA MOUNTAINS
amaNgqika
imiDange
amaMbalu
Iqibira
Qib
Fort Cox
Fort White
Burnshill
Boma Pass
Uniondale
Debe Nek
Kabousie Nek
King William's Town

End Notes

All citations of sources are made in these end notes using the Harvard system. The sources are arranged alphabetically by author in the list of references that follows. Citations take the form Author [date of publication], or [Author, date of publication]. For unpublished documents the date is the date of writing. Unattributed works such as newspaper articles are cited by the first significant word in the title.

1.   Usages such as "amaXhosa" or "abaThembu" are becoming more common in English. The prefixes "ama" and "aba" simply denote plural forms of the noun in the Xhosa language.

2.   This was the predecessor of the University of South Africa. It was an examining body only, the teaching being done at several independent institutions spread through the colony.

3.   The press cutting has no identification of source other than date. The paper is likely to have been the *Somerset Budget* founded in 1870 and still in existence.

4.   Based on his symptoms, Macalpine and Hunter [1966] suggested that King George suffered from repeated episodes of acute porphyria. Since that time historians have argued whether the king was "mad" or the victim of a hereditary disease. Cox et al. [2005] found extremely high levels of arsenic in his hair. They suggested that this was a contaminant in an antimony based medication which was used routinely and frequently to treat some of his symptoms. Arsenic could have triggered the porphyria. The argument over whether he was mad or not is a matter of semantics – whatever the cause, during periods of illness he was mentally disturbed.

5.   Later 1st Viscount Melville.

6.   A brief biography of Robert Hart is given by ffoliot [1972]. A more romantic account is provided by Bond [1956].

7.   Pronounced "Str'aven".

8.   O.P.R. Births 621/0010 0159 Page 156 1776/1777 carries the birth notice: "HART, Robert son of James HART, Weaver, Strathaven born 5 January 1777."

9.   Some sources, for example ffoliot [1972], incorrectly name his mother as Mary Fleming. His father, James Hart, long after his first wife's death, married Mary Fleming in 1807. By this time Robert was already in South Africa and estranged from his father.

10.   Several references give the name of the regiment as the 91st Argyll and Sutherland Highlanders. This is the regiment that succeeded it. Its first battallion is the 91st of the line, the Argyllshire, and its second battallion the 93rd or Sutherland Highlanders. When Hart joined the regiment it was the 98th Argyllshire which was gazetted on 9th July 1794. It was only in 1798 that it was renumbered as the 91st and much later in 1881 that it was combined with the 93rd. After its formation it was unable to recruit sufficient numbers from Argyllshire and, while its officers were from there (the regiment was commanded by Lt Col. Duncan Campbell of Lochnell and in all 14 of the 30 officers were Campbells), there was extensive recruiting of the rank and file from Glasgow and Edinburgh, and their neighbourhood. See McElwee & Rolfe [1988]

11.   The early history of the Colony is well covered by Mostert [1992]

12.   The growth and development of the white population during this period is discussed in detail by Guelke [1979].

13.   The name "hottentot" has in later times been applied more broadly in a derogatory sense to the general coloured community who are descended from Khoikhoi, former slaves, and people of mixed European and African descent. The word is now regarded as insulting. The usage adopted here is the word "coloured" when it is necessary to describe people falling into what is currently known as the coloured community. Specific descriptors such as Khoikhoi, Cape Malay, or Griqua are used where appropriate. Of course when quoting contemporary sources the use of the word "hottentot" has no pejorative sense.

14.   The changes in Khoikhoi and San ways of life as a result of the pressures exerted by the development of the settlement are discussed, for example, by Elphick [1979].

15.   Armstrong [1979] gives an account of their origins, numbers, and history.

16.   The linguistic division into Xhosa and Zulu is an arbitrary one, not justified by the

languages then spoken. At this time the Zulu and Xhosa languages had not been formalized: even today they are mutually comprehensible and differ less than broad Scots and Home Counties English. The language spoken in the region stretching from the Eastern Cape to Natal was a continuum of mutually comprehensible dialects of the Nguni group of languages. Zulu and Xhosa orthography and grammar were separately formalized in Natal and the Cape, largely by missionaries. A different history might have resulted in a single received standard Nguni language [Branford, 1992]. Only 80 years ago J. H. Soga, son of J. F. Cumming's Xhosa protege Tiyo and his Scottish wife Janet, [Soga, 1931, p vi], with a strong bias towards Xhosa, predicts incorrectly: "It would appear as if, ere long, the so-called Zulu language (which I believe to be really the original Aba-Mbo dialect) will be obliged to justify its existence or, as it is with the Aba-Mbo and Ama-Lala dialects south of the Natal border, give place to the isiXosa." The current politically 'correct' usages "isiXhosa", "isiZulu" in English to describe the languages are no more linguistically correct than would be the use of the word "Deutsch" in English to describe the German language – they are the correct words in Xhosa and Zulu to describe these languages. Hypersensitive writers use them in English but they are not justified by current usage. English usage does, however, seem to embrace "Siswati" for the language of the Swazi people.

17. The complexities are well described by Mostert [1992, Chapter 6, esp. pp 206–210].

18. The prefixes *ama, aba, imi* are simply forms of the plural in Xhosa. Thus amaXhosa implies the Xhosa people, abaThembu the Thembu people, and imiDange the Mdange people. English usage would commonly drop the prefix. Since clans and tribes are commonly named for their chiefs, it is, however, useful to retain the Xhosa prefix for the name of the people. Thus, when the schism between Ngqika and Ndlambe occurred the amaRharhabe people were split into amaNgqika and amaNdlambe.

19. The derivation is from *Thembu* plus *-qua*, a Khoikhoi suffix denoting the plural in the same way as the Nquni prefixes *ama* and *aba* [Dr J. B. Peires, private communication]. Thus *Tambookie* was a version of the Khoikhoi name for the Thembu.

20. The history of the House of Phalo is described by Peires [1981].

21. Not to be confused with Shaka, the great founder of the Zulu nation.

22. New insights into the causes of the first frontier war and the role of the San and imiDange have recently been provided by Peires [2008].

23. I am grateful to Dr J B Peires for clarifying the Xhosa rules of succession. For a discussion see,for example, Soga [1931, p. 49].

24. Throughout the nineteenth and most of the twentieth century Ngqika's name was written in English as 'Gaika'. Presumably this was initially an attempt to represent the 'Ngq' vocalised click sound by 'Ga' followed by 'ika' pronounced 'eeka'. This spelling eventually led to a universal English mispronunciation 'Gy-ka'.

25. Walker [1968, p122].

26. The courteous correspondence in diplomatic language between Sluysken and the British force [Theal, 1897, vol I] suggests the Governor's internal conflict between royalist sympathies and the local political imperative.

27. For an account of the ensuing events see James [1837, vol. 1, pp 300 – 302]

28. Bond [1956, Chapter II]

29. See McElwee & Rolfe [1988, p7]

30. From www.armynavyairforce.co.uk/argyll_&_sutherland_highlanders.htm: "Its first service was at the capture of Cape Town by Sir Alured Clarke, in 1795, when it does not appear to have worn either kilt or tartan, but the national costume was partly resumed on its return to England in 1803."

31. See Bond [1956, p 212]. See also Dunn-Pattison's [1910] account of the campaigns

in his History of the 91st Argyllshire Highlanders. For the capture of the Cape see Theal [1964, Vol. 5, chap. 28].

32. See ffoliot [1972].

33. The British force at the battle consisted of a detachment of 350 marines, 450 men of the 78th Highlanders, and a force of sailors. The 98th Argylls only arrived at the beginning of September.

34. See Barnard [1973, 1994, 1999].

35. See Potgieter, [2003] for an account of the capture of Admiral Lucas's fleet.

36. According to Bond on the basis of his discussions with descendants of Hart, but there is no independent confirmation of this.

37. Lady Anne Barnard's journals and letters [Barnard, 1973, 1997, 1999] show great insight and give a unique picture of Cape Society at the time. Barrow [1806, 1847] describes the first expedition that provided detailed accounts of the people, fauna, and flora of the whole Cape up to and beyond the Great Fish River.

38. See http://www.aboutscotland.com/argylls/91cape.html.

39. Barrow's account of this expedition was published a few years later [Barrow, 1801]. It is still a good read. The interest comes not only from his descriptions of the geography and people of the region (which served as an important source of information for future government officials and travellers), but also for his extensive account of observations of the flora and fauna.

40. See Barrow [1847, p141].

41. The poor man had severe headaches (gout of the head), coeliagra (gout of the stomach), piles, a fistula, and kidney stones.

42. Not to be confused with General John Ormsby Vandeleur and several other military Vandeleurs.

43. See Barrow [1847, p222] and de Villiers [1975].

44. The frontier conflicts that followed these events involved a major rebellion by Khoikhoi workers on the Boer farms, organization of these Khoi under several capable "captains", an alliance with the Gqunukwhebe. The complexities of this 3rd Frontier War are discussed in detail, for example, by Newton-King & Malherbe [1981] and by Mostert [1992, Chaps 9, 10].

45. Thomas Pringle [1826, p9] tells us that: "Mr Hart was a subaltern officer in the military party which accompanied Mr Barrow to the frontier in 1799 ...". This indicates that Hart may possibly have been in the party accompanying Barrow to the frontier rather than with Vandeleur's main force, but this is unlikely. On balance it seems more likely that, as we have assumed, Hart would have been with the main force of his regiment that was transported to Algoa Bay by sea. Pringle's information was presumably obtained through conversations with Robert Hart – Pringle had many of these. Bond [1956], citing family tradition, places Hart in the regimental company of grenadiers, marching with Vandeleur towards Graaff Reinet after disembarking at Algoa Bay. Pringle might have been confused with Barrow's [1801] account of an earlier expedition. The later expedition in 1799 is not part of this work and was only described in the second volume [Barrow, 1804] and consolidated in the first volume in the second edition [Barrow, 1806, vol I]. There is also a description in his autobigraphical notes published much later.

46. See Newton-King and Malherbe [1981, pp 14, 75]

47. Shipp [1890, p 64]. The "tigers" were, of course, leopards, while "hyenas" and "wolves" were synonymous. We can hazard a guess that "Rovee" was a corruption of "Rooi" or "Roode" and Roodewal was intended – "wal being Dutch for "bank." Roodewal, the modern site of Cookhouse, became a military post and also the site of the farm of James, Hart's younger son.

48. It is difficult to follow the chronology of Barrow's [1804, 1806, 1847] accounts of

these events. We use the interpretation of Newton-King and Malherbe [1981].

49. Barrow [1847, pp 229, 230].
50. *Ibid.*
51. According to Ffoliot [1972].
52. See Barrow [1847, pp 232, 233]
53. This comment forms part of a report written during the early part of the second British occupation [Collins, 1809, p. 13], by the Military and Civil Commissioner to the Eastern Cape.
54. An account of the engagement with the *Preneuse* is given by James [1837, vol. 2, pp 346 – 348].
55. Dunn-Pattison [1910, pp 14, 15].
56. This is from unconfirmed information from rootsweb that cites Surrey poor laws http://archiver.rootsweb.ancestry.com/th/read/SOUTH-AFRICA-EASTERN-CAPE/2007-08/1186999443. Hannah's grave at Glen Avon records that she came from Chorlwood but this is presumably a misspelling. Bexhill is about 80 km from Charlwood and in the same county. It is more plausible that Hannah would have met Robert while he was stationed at Bexhill, than in the Channel Islands where they were married, as is often assumed.
57. Equivalent to a modern second lieutenant, the lowest commissioned rank.
58. This regiment, the Sutherland Highlanders, was afterwards merged with Hart's 91st Argyllshire Regiment to form the Argyll and Sutherland Highlanders.
59. The history of these predecessors of the Cape Regiment and Cape Corps is summarised in two papers by de Villiers [1975, 1976].
60. The history of the Cape Regiment from the start of the second occupation to 1870 is described by Malherbe [2002a, b]. There is also the official military record of the time [Cannon, 1842], a near contemporary history covering the period of Robert Hart's service.
61. The story of Graham's service in the Cape is related by Maclennan [1986].
62. See de Villiers [1989, p. 231]
63. See de Villiers [1989, p. 117]
64. Susannah was baptised on 5 July 1809.
65. Accounts of this period are given by Maclennan [1986] and Mostert [1992].
66. Sir Henry George Grey (1767 – 1828) was the brother of the 2nd Earl Grey (later British Prime Minister, and after whom the blend of tea was named.) He is not to be confused with Henry George Grey, the 3rd Earl, or with Sir George Grey, later successively Governor of South Australia, New Zealand, the Cape Colony, and New Zealand for a second term.
67. See de Villiers [1989, p. 235].
68. See Maclennan [1986, p. 85]
69. There are several Riet Rivers in South Africa. This one is not the same as that which flows into the Indian Ocean a short distance west of the Fish River mouth.
70. A more detailed account of events is provided by Maclennan [1986, chaps 14, 15]
71. The author has had access to manuscript notes written by his aunt, Eirene Moberley (b. Walker), who was a grand-daughter of Sarah Hart, the grand-daughter of Robert Sr. In it she states that Hannah Brown (b. Hart), Sarah's sister, was engaged in writing a memoir of her grandfather. In 1931 she took all the Hart papers that she had assembled from various relatives on a visit to her daughter in Cape Town. There she died and one of her sons then destroyed all the papers. This is presumably the fate of the Hart journal.
72. Pringle [1840, p. 95]
73. Pringle [1840] and also quoted by Campbell [1837]
74. The remaining quotations from Hart's journal are from Campbell [1837]

75. The hill, then named Rand Kop was later named Governor's Kop [Cory, 1910, vol. I, p248].
76. In modern Grahamstown, St George's Cathedral dominates Church Square. The square is poorly named: it is an elongated right-angled triangle with the intersection of High St and Hill St forming the right angle. This shape arises from the original layout of the officers' houses. The cathedral is located over the site of the original farmhouse. Hart's lot was near the present intersection of High Street and Bathurst Street. The streams have long since been diverted from their original courses.
77. See Campbell [1837]
78. See Cory [1965, vol. I]
79. Campbell [1972, p. 115]
80. See de Villiers [1989, pp 125, 126].
81. As a younger son of a Duke, Charles Somerset was entitled to be addressed as "Lord Charles" or as "My Lord" but he was not an heir to the estates of the Duke (unless his elder brother had died before succeeding to the title), nor was his title passed on to his sons. Younger sons of noblemen generally had to make their own way in the world (with a little help from their friends and family). The army was the usual route to riches. The Church was an alternative.
82. Mostert [1992, pp 403 – 406] gives a harrowing account of the proceedings. He states that there were three hundred soldiers in attendance and does not mention Fraser. The official military history [Cannon 1842, p. 18] gives the number one hundred and confirms Fraser's presence.
83. See Müller [1987] .
84. Quoted by le Cordeur [1988]
85. See Peires [1981, pp 61 – 63] for an account of these events.
86. Makana ka Nxele – Makana the left-handed – was usually referred to by the colonists as Makana. Nxele means "left-handed". As a consequence the Dutch often called him "Links" meaning "left". Many English speakers misunderstood this and called him "Lynx". The early life and rise to prominence of Nxele is described in a manuscript transcribed from notes by Rev. J. Bennie [1869].
87. The teachings and beliefs of Nxele are described in a nineteenth century manuscript by a Xhosa interpreter, William Kekale Kaye [1869].
88. See Peires [1981, pp 62, 63]
89. See Sheffield [1884, p 97]. This is not a contemporary source but was written to celebrate the opening of the Settlers Memorial Tower in Grahamstown in 1882. Nevertheless it probably represents a typical Colonial view.
90. Rivett-Carnac [1966, p21], without giving a source, states that Mrs Brereton had died on the journey to Graham's Town. Brereton was later in command of the troops responsible for the Bristol massacre of demonstrators during the Reform Bill riots of 1832. He was court martialled and committed suicide during the proceedings.
91. Our account is largely based on that of Stretch [1876]. Mostert [1992, pp 469 – 479] provides details of this campaign and its effects on the attitudes of the amaXhosa towards the British.
92. Maclennan [1986, Chap 23] provides an extended account of the engagement based heavily on a description by Willshire himself in *The Graham's Town Journal*. He also uses oral sources quoted by Kay [1833] and Shrewsbury [1869] to give a Xhosa point of view. As with any battle, the accounts of witnesses often differ. Charles Lennox Stretch was present at the battle and wrote a reasoned account of it [Stretch, 1876]. This paper was written nearly sixty years after the battle when Stretch was an old man, and the fallibility of human memory must be taken into account. Thomas Pringle [1840, pp 97 – 98] gives an account based on conversations with participants,

particularly with Captain Harding who was one of the party that rode out with Will-shire to reconnoitre; these accounts are of course second hand. Cory's [1960, vol. I, pp 385 – 394] history, written in 1910 gives only two explicit primary sources. The first is an interview by Cory of Mrs Mader, the widow of Captain Huntly who died in the battle; the second is a letter from Maj. Fraser to Col. Graham, stated to be in the possession of Sir John Graham of Newlands. Cory quotes parts of the letter at length. However, Fraser was not present at the battle, having been away on a tour of inspection and only having returned the day after the battle.

93. This is according to Stretch [1876]. Mostert [1992, p. 477] has Boesak arriving at the height of the subsequent battle and in the nick of time to save the situation. Pringle writes of the "old Hottentot Captain Boezak" and states that he knew most of the amaXhosa chiefs by sight, suggesting that this could be the same Boesak who was leader of one of the wandering clans that featured in the rebellion of 1799, and that these hunters were the members of his band. Maclennan [1986, p. 195] states that Boesak had some years before been converted to Christianity and was based with his clan at Theopolis.

94. This is Stretch's [1876] version. Cory [1960, vol. I, pp 385, 386] makes no mention of Boesak and states that Willshire had ridden off to "... inspect some horses at a place some twelve miles distant in the direction of Botha's Hill." Pringle [1840, p. 97] states that "... he was taking a morning ride with some of his officers."

95. Cory enumerates 301 troops and 32 armed civilians.

96. In Nxele's own version of theology Tayi was the son of Dalidupu, the supreme Being in a Xhosa Trinity, superior to the Christian Trinity of the missionaries [Peires, 1981, p.70].

97. Cory [1960, vol. I, p. 390, note 2]

98. See MacKenzie & Dalziel [2007, chap. 4]. While merino sheep had been in the country since the time of the Dutch, the suitability of the Karoo regions for their production was established at this time.

99. Assuming, as is probable given Hart's character, that she was conceived and born in wedlock. The Harts were married on 10th April 1804. What family records exist state that Anna was born in 1805.

100. This was a form of tax on freehold property that dated back to feudal law. In feudal times it was a payment made in lieu of services expected from the landowner by his feudal lord. In post-feudal times they were attached to land grants such as those received by the settlers.

101. Makin [1971, p 19] makes the distinction clear.

102. Details of the ship and ships of its type are given by Parkinson [1937].

103. The embarkation list for Smith's party [Theal, 1897 – 1905, vol. XII, p. 448] identi-fies both Walkers as shopkeepers. Smith, himself, is also listed as such and one can speculate whether they had some previous association.

104. According to Sheffield's [1884] list

105. Sheffield [1884] gives her age as 43, Jones [1971] as 48. Walker [1987b] gives her date of birth as 1777 but this is probably based on Sheffield's list. Her death notice in the *Graham's Town Journal* 16 Feb 1850 states that she was in her eightieth year, supporting Morse Jones's date.

106. This is asserted by Walker [1987b]. It is also stated by Nash [1987, p121].

107. The *Northampton* voyage was quite well documented although no copy of the log exists. In the party led by Major George Pigot was his 15 year old daughter Sophia who was the author of a diary [Pigot, 1974]. In Clarke's party was the Stubbs family including Thomas, aged 10. More than 50 years later Thomas, by then a hero of the frontier wars, wrote his Reminiscences [Stubbs, 1978]. These include a lively account of many incidents on the voyage. Sophia Pigot's observations are those of a

naïve upper-class fifteen year old (George Pigot was the illegitimate but acknow-ledged son of George, Lord Pigot, the former governor of Madras) but they have the advantage of immediacy and it is possible to piece together and put in context many details of the voyage. Stubbs's account is delightful and gives marvelous insight into conditions on the voyage. They describe the experiences of a lively, observant ten year old who was into everything on the ship, squabbling with his peers and the ships boys in the crew, and observing the foibles of the adults. His descriptions of some of the rougher passengers show a fine ear for dialogue. They are, however, filtered through the memory of an old man and there is probably a degree of romanticism or even fictionalization. This account of the voyage is largely derived from incidents described by Sophia Pigot and Thomas Stubbs.

108. See Stubbs [1978, p211]
109. Sheffield's lists [Sheffield, 1884] make it clear that William Smith's party sailed in *Northampton*. Morse Jones [1971, p13] erroneously states that William Smith's party sailed in *Weymouth*. However, he correctly places William Smith in *Northampton* on p59 and p156.
110. See Pigot [1974]
111. See Stubbs [1978]
112. On Thursday 13th January 1820 Sophia notes [Pigot, 1974, pp 38, 39] "Some of Papa's people caught the small pox," on the 18th she writes "... the people better of the Small Pox," and on the 25th she contradicts herself with, "Poor Mrs Quince one of our women died of the Small Pox."
113. From a "List of Seventy one grants made in freehold by Sir Rufane Donkin ..." quoted by Theal [1897 – 1905, Vol 14, p 440]
114. Stubbs [1978, p60]
115. In the foreword to the book by E. Morse Jones [Jones, 1971 p vi]
116. See Sheffield [1884, Appendix A, p11] and Jones, [1971 pp 22 – 66]
117. Comparison of the lists of Sheffield and Morse Jones show that approximately 25% of those who actually travelled in Mahoney's party were not on Sheffield's list which was compiled from embarkation lists while about the same number from the latter list never sailed.
118. Sophia Pigot could scarcely have missed a disturbance as serious as that described by Thomas Stubbs and the event that she tersely mentions on 3rd March is the only one that seems to match it. However, Stubbs goes on to end his description of the affair with "...and all was quiet until we reached the line [equator]." The crossing of the equator took place on 16th February and the dates do not accord with this. Stubbs was writing from memory 50 years after the event so he may well have been mistaken in his chronology. If what he describes corresponded to one of the earlier of Sophia's events such as those in late January or early February then one wonders why he said nothing about the later events.
119. Edward's grandson W. I. S. Driver wrote [Driver, 1943] "I remember him well as a well-educated gentleman but we know nothing authentic of his antecedents. He used to say that he came from a place called "Kelham", somewhere in the North of England. That he always went by the name of "Kelham Ned"; that he fought his way up amongst the other boys until, when he left for South Africa in 1820 as a young man, he was "Cock of the Walk". This is easy to credit for, even in later life when I remember him, he was a most domineering and independent old gentleman. And that was his reputation in the family."
120. The background and events leading up to the formation of the Nottinghamshire party are well described by Burton [1971]. This is the major source for our account.
121. See Burton [1971, pp 8, 9]
122. See Driver [1943]

123. See Burton [1971, pp 6 – 7]
124. This information comes from Wikipedia
http://en.wikipedia.org/wiki/Rainhill (Version 31 March 2008).
125. The youngest child Jessie was born in 1795. It is plausible that Catherine died in childbirth.
126. In Sheffield's [1884] list the 10 year old son of Robert is identified as Robt. Dods. This is presumably William as listed by Jones [1971], identified as William Dods by Pringle et al. [1957].
127. In Sheffield's [1884] list John's age on embarkation is given as 29 and his brother, Thomas's, as 30. Jones [1971] has John as the elder at 32 and Thomas the younger at 31. There are a number of other significant differences between the contemporary lists of Sheffield and later work of Jones. Jones had access to far more information than Sheffield; while his information is not without error, in this case his data accord with Thomas Pringle's reminiscences and the Pringle family record [Pringle, 1971].
128. There are two cities called Wilmington, one in Delaware and one in North Carolina. It is not known which.
129. In a letter to his father quoted by Pringle et al. [1957, pp 44 – 47].
130. The trials and adventures of Sephton's party are entertainingly described by Makin [1971]
131. Jones's [1971] list gives his profession as artist. Nash [1987], on the other hand, lists him as a woolstapler. He certainly later practised as an artist in the Cape. Not much of his work has survived. There are miniatures of himself and his wife in the Albany Museum in Grahamstown. Jones [1971] credits him with having painted a picture of Table Mountain but this is probably confusion with a work by another James Ford who taught art in Cape Town at the end of the nineteenth and beginning of the twentieth century and painted *Holiday Time in Cape Town,* a fantasy picture with Table Mountain in the background.
132. Nash [1982, p. 26] refers to his losses which were severe enough for her to describe him and another member of the party as "formerly respectable merchants".
133. Cory Library MS6226.
134. The organization and experiences of Bailie's party are described in detail by Nash [1982]
135. Jones [1971, pp 7 – 15]
136. Pringle [1840, Chapter I]
137. Sheffield [1884, pp 146, 147]
138. Maxwell and McGeogh [1978, p 75]
139. See Jones [1971, p 8]
140. The *disselboom* was shaped from a long straight tree (*boom*) with an adze-like tool called a *dissel.*
141. See Dugmore [1871, p 20]
142. Maxwell & McGeogh [1978, p 7]
143. "Drift" is a corruption of a Dutch word "drif" meaning "ford". It is a common South Africanism. Committees Drift and Trompetter's Drift were major crossing points on the Fish River and, as such, were guarded by military posts.
144. Maxwell and McGeogh [1978, p 75].
145. Dugmore, [1871, p 17]
146. Not to be confused with present-day Cuylerville near Queenstown.
147. Pringle [1840, Chapter II]
148. The village on this site is now known by the less romantic name of Cookhouse, probably named after a small stone kitchen that supplied the troops during the Frontier wars.

149. See Cory [1965, vol. 2, p. 242].
150. Stockenstrom [1887, vol I, p. 129] held a grudge against Henry Somerset that comes through strongly in his autobiography, even though it was first published 67 years later. His opinions of his character should be treated with caution. There are, however, similar opinions expressed by a number of others [Harington, 1980, p. 21].
151. Stockenstrom [1887, vol. I, p.133].
152. Cory [1965, vol. 2, pp 242 – 243] quotes unpublished papers by Bird as evidence of this.
153. See Donkin [1970].
154. The main source for this is Stockenstrom's [1887, vol. 1, 135 – 137] autobiography which is full of dark hints and innuendo. The main facts are probably correct; some of the motives attributed to individuals may be prejudiced.
155. He refers to Knox at this point only as "the enemy" but later refers to the chief primary tool in the whole affair .. getting himself publicly horsewhipped ..." Cory [1965, p. 136] identifies the man horsewhipped as Knox, although he quotes no source; he may have deduced it from the proceedings of the later inquiry which has not been traced.
156. An interesting postscript is that Knox returned to Edinburgh where he became an eminent Professor of Anatomy. That career ended in ignominy when he was associated with the infamous body snatchers, Burke and Hare. Burke was hanged for murdering some of those whose bodies were supplied to Knox, Hare was imprisoned for removing bodies from graves, and Knox, having been found to have purchased the bodies of the victims for his dissections unknowingly, suffered no legal sanction. He was, however, driven from Edinburgh by public opinion, expressed in satire such as
> Doon the close and up the stair,
> Butt and ben wi' Burke and Hare,
> Burke's the butcher, Hare's the thief,
> And Knox the boy that buys the beef!
157. Donkin [1970, pp 93, 94].
158. Donkin [1970].
159. Cory [1965, vol. 2, p. 124].
160. Philipps [1960, p. 88] in a letter to his sister. Both Trappes and Bird were Roman Catholics which may be the root of Philipps's description of Trappes as a "scoffer of religion". Bird afterwards lost his post as a result of his religion.
161. Cory [1965, vol. 2, p. 105].
162. This is according to Cory [1965, vol. 2 pp 105 – 106]. Philipps's account in a letter to his sister [Philipps, 1960, p. 90] claims that he gave an account of the meeting to Trappes under protest and resigned his post voluntarily.
163. In a letter dated Nov 11th 1820, [Philipps, 1960, pp 82 – 84].
164. Donkin [1970]. The mention of Monckton refers only to a discussion which never came to anything.
165. Cory [1965, vol. 2, p. 107].
166. Philipps, [1960, p. 113].
167. Bishop was his given name, not a title.
168. Equivalent to the Public Prosecutor or Attorney General.
169. The sale of commissions in the British Army only ended in 1871. It was regarded as normal practice. A majority in an elite regiment was worth several thousand pounds. In the Cape regiment it would have been worth a small fraction of that.
170. Afterwards created 1st Baron Raglan who brought the military genius of the Somersets to the command of the British troops in the Crimean war.
171. See Pringle [1840, chap. 15], Botha [1984].
172. Established by Lord Charles from the proceeds of a tax on wine and spirits and first opened in January 1822.

173. Pringle [1840, p. 63].
174. Pringle [1824].
175. Pringle [1840, p. 64].
176. Contrary to popular belief, *fraternité* was a later addition.
177. Pringle [1840, p. 67]. It is interesting that Somerset may have regarded the land grant as a personal favour, particularly in the light of his campaign against Donkin for irregularities in the allocation of land.
178. Theal [1964, vol. 5, p. 267].
179. Caused by the fungal species *Puccinia graminis.*
180. Pringle [1840, p. 26]
181. "Neighbour" is a relative term. Somerset farm was about 45 km from Glen Lynden and the last stage of the journey consisted of the broken track described earlier. Nevertheless Pringles and Harts remained in communication.
182. When John Ayliff died he left a manuscript among his papers entitled *The Journal of Harry Hastings* [Ayliff, 1963]. It is the journal of a fictitious character, Harry Hastings, who is undoubtedly Ayliff himself. It is written in a light-hearted style, quite unlike the ponderous formal style of the author's missionary *persona*. The characters are often but not always disguised by pseudonyms and some of the events are embroidered while others may be fictitious. The report of Hart's visit to the settler camp [Ayliff, 1963, pp 79, 80], which would have been the location of Willson's party on the Bush River, is straighforwardly descriptive and there is little reason to doubt that it is an account of a real event.
183. The legend is epitomized by Ritter's [1955] "biography", more properly described as a novel, based on tales the author heard from old Zulu men as a child.
184. Both Henry Francis Fynn [1969] and Nathaniel Isaacs [1836] provided contemporary accounts, but these are regarded with scepticism by many historians.
185. See Hamilton [1998], Wylie [2006].
186. Wylie [2006, p. 437] suggests that there is little doubt that *mfecane* is derived from the Xhosa root *-feca* meaning to crack or bruise. This implies that the word was first applied by the Xhosa to the marauders – those who attacked them – and was distorted by English speakers to *Fitcani* and its variations. Later the meaning was shifted to apply to the events associated with the attacks. Cobbing [1988] maintains that the word was an invention by Walker [1928]: "Walker's neologism, meaning 'the crushing', has no root in any African language ..."
187. See Walker [1928], Omer-Cooper [1960].
188. This point of view was championed by Cobbing [1988]
189. Those interested in following it further can consult the papers in the work edited by Hamilton [2001]. This is a revised collection of papers arising from a colloquium held at the University of the Witwatersrand in 1991.
190. See Wright [2001].
191. Some of the more prominent missions started between 1820 and 1830 were the Wesleyan stations, Wesleyville, 1823; Mount Coke (Ndlambe) 1825; Brownlee's mission (Dyanie Tshatshu) 1826; Butterworth (Hintsa) 1827; Buntingville, 1830; Morley, 1830; the Presbyterian stations, Tyumie, 1820; Lovedale, 1824; Pirie, 1830; Burnshill, 1830; and the Moravian station Shiloh (1828).
192. See Pringle [1840, p. 16]. Clifton was the name they gave to the location of their first temporary accommodation, on a division of Robert Pringle's allotment. They named the whole farm Glen Lynden.
193. See Pringle [1840, p. 23]. Coetzer's mill was a small mill driven by a horizontal water wheel, attached to the upper millstone, which then turned against the lower stone, which was fixed in place. The mill is described by Pringle [1840, p. 21]. The description does not make it clear how the water was made to drive a horizontal

wheel, but the water probably emerged from a chute to exert a force on one side of the wheel.

194. Written in a memorial to Lord Charles Somerset, applying for a grant of land, on April 5ᵗʰ 1823 (quoted by Pringle *et al.*, [1957, p.16])

195. See Pringle [1840].

196. Remarks made by George Thompson [1827, p.32] after a visit to Somerset Farm at the beginning of 1821.

197. See Pringle *et al.* [1957, p.16]

198. See Plaskett [1825]

199. See Stirk [1971, p. 75], Jones [1968, vol. 2, p. 9]. Stirk states that he called the farm Wesley Wood but afterwards refers to it as Wesleywood. A map of the settlement shown by Hockly [1948] shows the farm as split in two with one half belonging to "Wood". This is clearly adapted from Cory's [1965] map which shows the farm as "W. Wood – Jos. Walker" and the date of acquisition. Hockly has taken this as the names of two owners rather than "W.Wood" being an abbreviation for the name of the farm!

200. Goldswain [1949, vol. 2, p. 31] mentions that a manager "had ingaged with Mr J Walker of Grahams Town to cultivate for him and to look after his farm." Goldswain [1949, p. 28] identifies the farm as being at "Cockes partey thirty eight Miles [from Graham's Town] neer the Kowie Mouth." Jones [1968, vol. 3] notes that he had nine cattle stolen from this farm in 1842.

201. See Shaw [1860, p.28].

202. For an authoritative account of the history and economic impact of the frontier trade see Beck [1987].

203. Stubbs [1978, p. 82].

204. *Kraal* is a Dutch word meaning a fenced enclosure to keep cattle or other livestock at night. Because of the central place of cattle in Xhosa life and culture the word was often used by extension to mean the multiple dwellings of a family grouping, surrounded by a fence. The word came from the Portuguese *curral*, which has the same root as the Spanish *corral*.

205. This was long before the construction of the signal tower, the ruins of which are presently on the site. Governor's Kop was the hillock or "kop" on what was to become known as Driver's Farm.

206. See Driver [1943].

207. Honey, a member of Clarke's party, would have been originally located in this neighbourhood.

208. This account is based on the court record of Sykes's trial [Justice Commission, 1821].

209. The court judgement [Justice Commission, 1821] is written in High Dutch with quotes of direct speech in English. The handwriting is poor and the document is fading. The contemporary English translation accompanying it differs. The translator apparently also had difficulty with the handwriting and interpreted "I have closed your gob" as "I have done your job." This does not make sense, and examination of the original supports the reading given here.

210. The weight of the shot is described in the proceedings as 1 grain – in modern parlance about number 8 shot. This would have had a diameter of about 2.2 mm, large enough to cause considerable damage.

211. The primary source for this account is the report by Landdrost Harry Rivers to Lt Col Bird, the Colonial Secretary, of the interrogation of John Stubbs Jr and Thomas Hood [Rivers, 1823]. This is the only evidence from witnesses who took part in the affair and answered direct questions the day after Stubbs's murder. Our account is also reliant on Thomas Stubbs's description [1978, pp 83–87] and Edward Driver's

story told to Cowper Rose[1829]. Thomas Stubbs's account was based on what his brother and cousin told him at the time and filtered through his memory 50 years later when he wrote his reminiscences. Driver was telling the story to Rose while on a hunting expedition and Rose repeated his recollection of it when he wrote his book. Other accounts at the time were also second hand.

212. Covering statement by Landdrost Harry Rivers [1823]

213. 1 lb = 452 g. This suggests that the price of a tusk was about twice that of an ox. Thomas Stubbs [1978, p. 82] remembers that at the beginning of the trade in 1821 they were both worth about the same – about 60 buttons. Maxwell & McGeogh [1978, note 63] express doubts about his memory, basing this on a value in 1825 that suggested that a tusk was worth 16 times as much as an ox. John Stubbs Jr's statement was made within a few days of the trade and supports a much closer equivalence. This simply shows that prices fluctuated according to supply and demand. It is more logical to deduce that by 1825 ivory had become much more valuable than in 1821.

214. The account by Thomas Stubbs [1978, pp 83 – 87] states that John Stubbs Jr and Thomas Hood had been captured by "a lot of mounted Hottentots." Maxwell and McGeogh [1978, p. 11, and note 71, p. 252] take this to mean "a patrol of the Cape Corps", but Rivers's report makes it clear that Boesak was the leader of a group of hunters and that he had previously asked him to keep his eye open for illegal traders. Other parts of the letter make it clear that the practice was for the apprehenders of such traders to receive one third of the goods confiscated. Thus Boesak's motivation was probably that of a bounty hunter.

215. See Rose [1829, pp 212 – 213]. Cowper Rose was a wealthy traveller who visited the Cape in the eighteen twenties and explored widely, afterwards writing a book on his travels [Rose, 1829]. He gave an extended account of an elephant hunt in 1826 for which a settler "Mr D—" was engaged as his guide. He described long conversations round the camp fire with Mr D—who described his life since coming to the Cape. From this description and from Stubbs's account of some of Edward Driver's activities, Maxwell and McGeogh [1978, note 20* p231] identified Mr D— as Edward Driver. Other evidence such as his description of his family are entirely consistent with this identification.

216. Either David Hobson who had been a member of William Smith's party on *Northampton* or his younger brother, William Carey Hobson. They had been settled about this distance to the west of the Stubbs farm. They were later successful merino sheep breeders with a farm that was whimsically called Hobson's Choice. Carey Hobson was also engaged in the illegal trade. A loose sheet in National Archives of S. A., [CO 2662, no page number] gives an account of the interrogation of Carey Hobson for a similar crime by Mr Dyason, the same who had interrogated John Stubbs Jr and Thomas Hood. The interrogation includes questions about whether soldiers at the Drift had been involved in the crime. Hobson refused to answer.

217. In a letter from George Pigot to Robert Wilmot [Theal, 1897 – 1905, vol. 16, pp 72 – 73] and perpetuated by Cory [1965, vol. 2, p. 176].

218. See Prisoners [1823].

219. Quoted by Theal, [1897 – 1905, Vol 15, pp 59, 60]

220. See Theal, [1897 – 1905, Vol 15, pp 108 - 110]

221. Commandos were volunteer militia that had been a feature of colonial life for many years under the Dutch.

222. See Theal [1897 – 1905, Vol 15, pp 365 – 366].

223. Stubbs [1978, p. 211]. The misspelling of the surname is deliberate. This was a satirical description written many years later and the names of those pilloried were lightly disguised.

224. See Rose [1829, p 211]
225. Bell [1963, p66].
226. Halse [1880, p. 8]
227. Beck [1987] has extracted a comprehensive list of those granted licences from the relevant records
228. Beck [1987].
229. See Proclamations [1827, pp. 663-664.]
230. W. I. S. Driver [1943] wrote a memoir of his grandfather for his family. I am grateful to Julie A. Driver for permission to quote from it.
231. Stretch [1988] kept a journal of his exploits. The incident was vouched for by Theopholis Shepstone and Henry Francis Fynn, which is a bit rich since Fynn had been an active trader based in Natal, and was reputed to be a gun-runner and mercenary for Shaka.
232. See Bell [1963]
233. Fynn [1950, p 116]. The spelling of Xhosa names in the early nineteenth century was phonetic (depending on the writer's accent) and often bizarre. The pronunciation and meaning of *Calamaish* has not been deciphered.
234. The evidence for Thackwray's presence at Faku's Great Place in 1825 comes from Fynn [1950, p. 116]. Fynn's "journal" is not a true contemporary journal but an editing of his papers, some of which might have been written well after the events described. The internal consistency of the description of Fynn's 1825 visit to Faku places Thackwray in the neighbourhood at the time. The history of Faku and the Mpondo is given by Stapleton [2001]
235. Bain [1949]
236. Bourke came out as Lieutenant-Governor of the Eastern Frontier but simultaneously Somerset was recalled to meet a number of the allegations made against him during the course of the inquiry. Bourke was then appointed as Acting-Governor and, in line with the recommendations of the commission, the post of Lieutenant Governor was abolished and the affairs of the frontier placed under a Commissioner-General. Somerset refused to resign until the inquiry was complete. Eventually he was formally exonerated and resigned, whereupon Sir Lowry Cole was appointed to the Governorship.
237. See Theal [1897 – 1905, vol. 28, pp 134 – 140].
238. The reasons for Dundas's vacillation relate to the different needs of the northern and eastern borders of the Colony for trade and also to opposite advice that he was getting from the local officials. Stockenstrom was very much opposed to cross-border trade: Dundas was in favour of it. Trade relationships on the northern border were with the Griquas who did not pose a military threat: on the eastern border they were with the Xhosa who did. These matters are discussed in detail by Beck [1987].
239. See Thackwray [1826].
240. The information is contained in a return to the Colonial Secretary made by Dundas [1827], the Albany Landdrost. See also Beck [1987].
241. An extensive study of the missionary trade is included in Beck's [1987] work.
242. See Beck [1987].
243. See Shaw [1972, p. 82].
244. See Complaints [1829].
245. See Beck [1987] for a detailed account of the affair.
246. See Pringle [1840, chap. 11].
247. See Alberti [1968, p 76]
248. John Thackwray is reported to have shot 400 elephants in a single year and Henry Hartley to hold the record of 1200 elephants [Hockley. 1948, p. 142, note 5]. Rose [1829, p. 243] states that Edward Driver told him that he himself had shot 400 and

his Khoikhoi employees another 400.

249. See Hockley [1948, pp 141 – 142].

250. See Meiring [1959, ch. 13]

251. See Whitehouse [2002]. In 1931 the founding herd consisted of only 11: there were 8 female and 3 males, of which only one tusked male bred with the females. Half the females had no tusks. The current herd of several hundred bred from that population.

252. The Convention on International Trade in Endangered Species of Wild Fauna and Flora (CITES), negotiated in 1973 and implemented in 1975.

253. The results of his exploration are described in his monumental book [Burchell, 1822, 1824]

254. The bore (English) or gauge (American) of such a gun is equal to the number of lead spheres, having the same diameter as the barrel, as would total one pound (454 grams) in mass. A four bore gun thus takes a lead ball of a quarter of a pound (113 grams). The diameter of the barrel is just over an inch (26.72mm).

255. See Stubbs [1978, p 87]

256. This description is by Storey [2004].

257. See Selous [1893, p10]

258. See Hockley [1948, pp 141 – 142]. J. Stubbs is probably Thomas's brother, not his father who did not have time to build up a reputation before his death. William Carey Hobson appears as William in the settler lists.

259. Steedman [1835 pp 59 – 69]

260. See Stubbs [1978, p 88]

261. A phrase used by Dick Francis in the novel *Hot Money* to describe a hero who voluntarily went into situations of extreme danger while carefully planning for every eventuality.

262. Dugmore [1871] gave this description during a lecture celebrating the 50th anniversary of the settlement. Contemporary accounts of Thackwray's death are not consistent with this unlikely story. We must assume some oratorical licence but allow that it represents the contemporary view of Thackwray's temperament.

263. Steedman [1835], Rose [1829]

264. See Maxwell and McGeogh [1978, note 20*, p. 231]

265. See Rose [1829, pp 215, 216]

266. Steedman [1835, p 65]. It is, of course, possible that there is some exaggeration in such a hunter's tale.

267. A near vertical rock face.

268. Rose [1829, p243]

269. See Thackwray [1827]. In the April 3 1828 issue of *The Colonist* a letter in the form of an obituary of John Thackwray, signed "A Traveller" appears. The contents of this letter describe an elephant hunt on which the author was guided by Thackwray. Comparison of this with Steedman's [1835] account of an elephant hunt leave no doubt of the identity of "A Traveller." The writer mentions the existence of the letter from Thackwray and suggests that its contents would be of interest to the readers of the journal. In a later issue (April 29th 1828) the correspondent publishes the letter. This, dated October 11th 1827, gives an extended report of the Tembuland expedition on which our account is based. Thackwray writes, "I feel convinced you will be gratified by some account of the journey which I shall proceed to give you as briefly as possible." His confidence is presumably the result of his acquaintance with Steedman on the hunt which must have been at an earlier date than his Thembuland expedition which was in 1827. This can be deduced since the obituary mentions that Steedman obtained permission from Lord Charles Somerset for the hunt. Somerset left the Cape early in 1826. Relevant cuttings from *The Colonist* are preserved in the

Cory Library [MS16488].

270. Barrow [1801, pp 312 – 319]

271. See Rennie [1825].

272. Dr J. B. Peires has been of great help in interpreting Thackwray's spelling to get the correct names and their significance. He has also provided invaluable advice on the relationships between the Thembu leaders that Thackwray encountered.

273. Great-grandfather of Nelson Rohlihlahla Mandela, President of the Republic of South Africa 1994 – 1999.

274. I am very grateful to Dr J. B. Peires [private communication] for identifying Galeyka. He unearthed notes he had made from the unpublished part of the journal of John Ayliff [1821 – 1851]. The September 1832 journal entry refers to Galeka, in Faku's words, the leader of some "little things", being killed in a battle with the alliance of the Mpondo and Mpondomise. He also linked this with the reference in Kay [1833, p. 344] identifying "Galaka" as the son of Gamboshe of the Bomvana. There are thus two references independent of Thackwray's account that place a Galeka/Galaka in the right region at approximately the same time. One of these identifies him as one of the Bomvana. The genealogy of the Bomvana given by Cook [1931] has no Galeka listed as a son of Gamboshe. His son Ntchunga does, however, have a son of the right hand house called Magadule. The identification with Galeyka of the Machadula is significant and it appears that Galeka and Magadule are the same person making Peires's identification probable. Soga's [1930, chap. 20] genealogy calls him Mrazuli.

275. See genealogical table of the Bomvana by Soga [1930, chap. 20].

276. See Peires [1981, p. 89].

277. The Xhosa name for the Kei is Ncibe. "N'Eber" is an attempt by Thackwray to represent the click [J. B. Peires, private communication].

278. Stanford [1958, vol. 1, p. 48] describes Tyopo's parentage and notes that the region in which he was located had originally been totally occupied by the San. Cumming [1834 – 1899, item 430] writes that "As the Bushman dialect is largely composed of clicks, and as Tyopo had been brought up from a boy in their neighbourhood, he could speak like a native".

279. "Mampondo" refers to the amaMpondo people of whom Faku was King. Henry Fynn visited Faku on several occasions.

280. Fynn [1969, p 116]. Fynn's "journal" is a heavily edited compilation from his notes. It is recorded that Fynn returned from this excursion in October 1825.

281. "Entuli" is possibly "Nduli" which means "hill." Near Mthatha (Umtata) there is a hill simply known as Nduli. It is now the location of a small nature reserve, the Nduli nature reserve. There are, however, many other possible locations.

282. This is part of the information provided by Peires [private communication] from Ayliff's [1821 – 1851] journal.

283. Ayliff's [1971] journal is not clear about where he was writing. He states that he was at "the Mission House". At the time he had just been appointed to Salem but could not have been there as this is on the other side of Grahamstown and some dis-tance away. Hermans Kraal was the site where Fort Brown was built.

284. See Ayliff [1971] for that part of the journal dealing with his time within the Colony. A transcription of the complete journal [Ayliff, 1821 – 1851] is in the Cory Library.

285. See Ayliff, [1971, pp 74, 75]

286. The visit to the Woods is according to Bell [1963, p. 95]. Her account is unsubstanti-ated but is likely to have come from her knowledge of the Wood family tradition.

287. See Stubbs [1978, pp 87, 88]. Ayliff's contemporary record and Stubbs's personal recollection agree closely, and are probably near to the truth. Steedman's second-

hand account is very similar.

288. This is Ayliff's description – he is likely to have been trampled as well.

289. See Steedman [1835, p. 75]

290. *South African Commercial Advertiser*, Vol. 5, No. 251, Nov 7th 1829, p 2, col. 4.

291. See Crampton [2004, chapter 7]

292. Mdepa was chief of the Tshomane, a Mpondo clan. He was the son of Tshomane and his great wife Bessie, who was an English castaway who had survived shipwreck as a child and become one of the abeLungu – white survivors of eighteenth century shipwrecks who were absorbed into the culture of the Xhosa speaking peoples. The story of Bessie and her descendants is the subject of Hazel Crampton's book *The Sunburnt Queen* [Crampton, 2004].

293. The use of the word "place" to mean the home or estate of an individual is a common South Africanism. It might have originated from the Dutch "plaas" meaning "farm." No other word seems to adequately describe an establishment like Lochenberg's – an agglomeration of buildings, shacks, and enclosures in both the colonial and Xhosa styles. "Estate" is the nearest equivalent but conveys quite the wrong impression.

294. See Shrewsbury [1994, p 101]

295. See Fast [1994, p. 41]. The two notes 178 and 179 are inconsistent with each other.

296. South African Commercial Advertiser, Vol. 5, No. 251, Nov 7th 1829, p 2, col. 4.

297. Andrew Geddes Bain, later to be the engineer of many roads and passes such as Bain's Kloof, Michell's Pass and the Katberg Pass, kept journals of his travels and records this meeting [Bain, 1949]

298. See Hattersley [1968] and Spencer [1992] for biographical information

299. Since the region was the native land of the Zulus and unoccupied by the British or any other European nation, this seems a little presumptuous of Somerset. There were, however, laws in the Cape restricting the access of British subjects to the region outside the Colony.

300. The account of these events was related by Lochenberg's son to a missionary, Stephen Kay [Kay, 1833, pp 384, 385]

301. See Sinclair [2004]

302. This passage is part of the unpublished document written by Edward Driver's grandson [Driver, 1943].

303. The Civil Commissioner was essentially the Chief Magistrate. These reports dated 17th, 18th, and 25th September are quoted by Leverton [1984, pp 139 – 142].

304. See Leverton [1984, pp 156, 157].

305. No connection of the settlers of that name, Walker was an English traveller.

306. In a letter addressed to W Shepstone at Morley Mission, dated Oct 12th 1829, reporting the murder of the Farewell party. The letter is quoted by several sources, for example Leverton [1984, pp 142, 143].

307. See Steedman [1835, vol I, p 278].

308. See Bain [1949, pp 79 – 125].

309. The word "drift" is a South Africanism meaning a ford

310. See Kay [1833, pp 386, 387].

311. See Walker [1987b].

312. Cane's letter describing the events [Leverton, 1984, pp 142, 143] is dated 12th October. He states that he returned to his pillaged wagon in the evening, presumably within the previous two or three days. His account implies that they were attacked earlier that day, and if we assume that the murders occurred on the previous night we determine a date between the 8th and 10th October.

313. See Soga [1930, p313]. The source of Soga's account is not given. Much of his work is based on oral tradition.

314. All sources depend at various removes on Lynx's account. The most immediate is Cane's letter to the missionary J. W. Shepstone [Leverton, 1984, pp 142, 143]. This is reproduced in several sources. Andrew Steedman [1835, Vol I, pp 272 – 280] gives a more extended account which he states is based on Lynx's story. It includes incidents not reported by Cane – the warning after the traders had retired and details of Lynx's escape. We do not know whether Steedman was able to talk to Lynx or whether his account is an embroidered version of Cane's. There is one direct inconsistency. Cane is unequivocal that "three natives escaped" while Steedman implies that Lynx was the only survivor.

315. Full moon was at 15h16m UT on 12th October 1829 (U.S. Naval Observatory Astronomical Applications Department)

316. See Murder [1829]

317. Letter from Thomas Philipps dated 14 Nov 1829 [Philipps, 1960]

318. See Mrs Thackwray [1830].

319. G. N. Walker [1987b] may have used Philipps as his source.

320. See Jones [1971, p 161].

321. Spencer [1992] records that James Allison was a hatmaker trained by a Boer farmer. Jones [1968, vol. 2, p. 55], without giving a source, records that Allison sold his hatter's business to one J. Boardman on June 15th 1832. This was when he embarked on his mission.

322. See Circuit Court [1830a].

323. See Circuit Court [1830b].

324. John Atherstone was a settler who had received his training at Guy's Hospital, London. He had been District Surgeon of Albany since 1822. He was the father of the better known William Guybon Atherstone who was later to perform the first operation under anaesthetic in South Africa and to identify the first diamond found in South Africa.

325. The most extensive evidence reported in the *Advertiser* was that of John Atherstone and of Elsje Kiewiet, Flora's sister. The correspondent was probably not expert in legal niceties. What is reported as having been said by William on his death bed comes from Atherstone's evidence. Atherstone established that he several times told William that there was no hope of recovery, presumably to establish the admissability of hearsay as a deathbed statement. At the beginning of his description of what Flora told him he stated that, when visiting Flora in custody after William died, he had asked her if she had done it. This was was immediately disallowed by the judge. Nevertheless Atherstone was permitted to describe in great detail what Flora had told him. She, herself, remained silent at the trial.

326. As reported by Atherstone.

327. See Leverton [1984, Vol. 2, p308]

328. See Leverton [1984, pp 156, 157].

329. See Driver [1830].

330. See Brown [1830].

331. In a much later memorial [Driver, 1866] he states that he had never been granted any land, but that all he owned adjacent to Governor's Kop was acquired by purchase.

332. Based on the ratio between average incomes in Britain then and now, this would have been worth about £9000 in today's values [Officer, 2008].

333. *S A Commercial Advertiser*, Vol. 5, No 276, Feb 3rd, 1830, p1, col 15

334. See Leverton [1984, Vol. 2, p. 308].

335. See Godlonton [1844, p. 67]

336. Letter from correspondent dated Oct 30 1829 in *S A Commercial Advertiser*, Vol. 56, Nov 7th, 1829, p2, col. 4.

337. Milton [1983, chaps 10 – 12] gives a succinct overview of the progression of events between 1819 and 1834, culminating in the sixth frontier war. Mostert's [1992] account gives more detail. Developments among the Xhosa are covered in depth by Peires [1981, chap. 6].

338. Peires [2008] clarifies the affiliation of Habana as being of the imiDange. He points out that his father, Qoba was misidentified by Theal as Koba the son of Titi of the amaGwali, and Habana has consequently been misidentified as being of the ama-Gwali by many authors. He points out that "Koba" was correctly identified as descended from Mahota by Collins [1809].

339. See Peires [1981, p. 84] for details.

340. See Rivett-Carnac [1966, p. 75], who is usually at great pains to absolve her subject from any hint of blame for his actions, and is generally laudatory of both him and his father. Harington [1980, p. 21], on the other hand, in his biography of Smith, is of the opinion that Somerset lacked "nerve, ability, judgement, character, energy and intelligence" and that he was "insubordinate, dishonest and corrupt, a war profiteer and racketeer, whose courage was suspect." He quotes letters from Smith to his wife which suggest that his opinion of Somerset was similar – very much at variance with the picture painted in his autobiography [Smith, 1901], or in official reports.

341. Major William Dundas, another member of the Dundas clan.

342. Philipps [1960, pp 303 – 304].

343. See Peires [1981, p. 89].

344. The Moravian account is given by Bonatz [1868, p. 211]. van Kalker's account [Keegan, 2004, p. 21] is essentially the same. The name of the Gcina chief is given as Mtyelela. Both 'Mty' and the 'G' in Galela represent the same soft 'J' [Peires, private comunication].

345. For a biography see Hunt [1974].

346. A sanitised biography of Read is given by Williams [1968]. The account by Mostert [1992, 439 – 441] is less coy.

347. See Stockenstrom [1887, vol. 1, p. 416]

348. The relationship between Hintsa and his neighbours is discussed by Peires [1981, pp 84 – 89].

349. Known to the colonists as Fingos. The name Mfengu comes from the word *ukumfenguza* – to seek work.

350. See Ransford [1972]

351. Like all the missionaries he was a well-meaning man, intent on doing what he perceived as good. His rôle in the events leading up to the invasion of Gcalekaland was unfortunate in that his opinions were strongly coloured by his emotions and he did not seem capable of critical thought. The vituperative attack on him by Majeke [1952] is unfair. Polemics such as this, while containing some truth about the ill effects of some missionary activities, are steeped in presentism and uncomprehending of the motives of the missionary movement.

352. See Peires [1981, p. 88].

353. To be fair to Ayliff, while the Mfengu were not slaves, they were also not of the same status as the Xhosa. They were more in the nature of indentured labour. During the later peace negotiations with Maqoma the acceptance by the Colony of large numbers of Mfengu refugees provoked the cry: "Then why have you detained our Fingoes, who are our Hottentots ..." and Maqoma and Tyhali are quoted as asking "what were they to think of seeing them [the Mfengu with the Kat river Legion] as hitherto they [the Colonial Government] had only to do with English and Hottentots?" [Stretch, 1988, pp 121, 126]. These statements imply that they were regarded as bound to the Xhosa chiefs.

354. See Ayliff [1835]

355. See Jones [1968, vol. 2, p.61]
356. This is Pretorius's [1988, p. 242] account, taken from the record of Driver's evidence at the enquiry into Hintsa's death.
357. Based on the statement by Rowles [1834].
358. This was Driver's own assessment made many years later when trying to get very belated compensation for their loss [Driver, 1866]. While he would have been motivated to represent the size of his herd as being as large as plausible, by 1834 he was undoubtedly already a prosperous farmer.
359. See Halse [1880].
360. This is as claimed by Driver [1866] himself. He was certainly prominent in the later fighting.
361. For a short account of Smith's career see Harington [1974]. There are longer biographies by Lehman [1977] and Harington [1980]. Smith's own interpretation of his career is related in his autobiography [Smith, 1901].
362. The history of the formation and dissolution of the various volunteer groups is confused. Tylden [1954] identifies many of them but is not clear on the relationships between them. Driver's position is from his own statement [Driver, 1866]. The position and ranks of Walker and Wood comes also from their own statements [Walker & Wood, 1835]. In each case these were petitions to the Governor requesting compensation or remuneration and it would have been in the interests of the authors to state their case accurately.
363. See Stretch [1988, pp 23, 24].
364. Richard Southey is the subject of a biography by Wilmot [1904].
365. No connection of the prominent Wesleyan clergyman, William Shaw. In the later inquiry into Hintsa's death he is described as a brother-in-law of the Southeys, but the William Shaw associated with these events had married Eleanor (also called Ellen) Stubbs, sister of Thomas Stubbs. He was, in fact, a cousin of the Southeys.
366. See Campbell [1897, p. 212]. The killing of John Shaw, by a party led by Mqhayi, the son of Ndlambe, is described by Stubbs [1978, pp 102 – 103].
367. See Halse [1880, p. 24]. It is not clear that the Sharpshooters were actually disbanded. A citizen force remained in Graham's Town for the defence of the town.
368. Pretorius [1988, p. 242] states that Driver was not actually a member of the Corps but attached to Smith as a personal guide. This does not seem consistent with the statements of members of the corps such as Bertram Bowker [Mitford-Barberton, 1952, p. 229; Bisset, 1875, chap. 4]. Driver did serve as Smith's personal guide but, given that he was an officer in the Albany Sharpshooters and was vastly experienced in bushcraft, it is probable that Southey recruited him and Smith made use of his talents.
369. See Lehmann [1977, p.159]
370. This is according to Stubbs [1978, p. 106] who is unambiguous in identifying Campbell with initials A.G. There were two Dr Campbell's in Graham's Town at the time. Dr Ambrose George Campbell was a Graham's Town character. Hugely opiniated, and unscrupulous in making unsupported claims to support his political views, he was at this time operating the first hospital in the frontier region. The polemic written under the pseudonym "Justus" [Campbell, 1837] was a condemnation of the Colonial aggression against the Xhosa, but its intemperate tone and unsubstantiated allegations (many well justified) meant that, while it aroused outrage amongst the settlers, it was not as influential as it might have been. Later (1840) Campbell ran a fortnightly journal *Echo* that took a violently opposite view to that of Godlonton's *Graham's Town Journal*.
371. See Stubbs [1978, pp 106, 214].
372. Halse [1880, p. 20]

373. See Andrews [1877, p. 8] who by identifying him as a "major in the Hottentot battalion" makes it clear that this was Wood. Stubbs [1978, p. 106] makes it clear that the contractor was Wood also identifying him as having the rank of major in the Khoikhoi Battalion. Moleskin was a strong finely woven cotton fabric.
374. Andrews uses an abbreviation of "Hottentot" which is more offensive.
375. Stretch [1988, pp 141 & 196]. To put this in perspective, at the present time this would be worth over £600 000 in purchasing power (as calculated using the retail price index), or a staggering £5 800 000 when calculated according to the average earnings in Britain then and now [Officer, 2008], which is probably how contemporaries would have seen it.
376. Maxwell and McGeogh, [1978, p 207], Stubbs's editors, assert that "... Stubbs goes out of his way to exaggerate the foibles of young Wood at points which would have hurt most had Stubbs published in his lifetime." Stubbs's manifestly biased and clearly false allegations regarding Wood's stupidity cast doubt on other allegations that might be more solidly based.
377. Stubbs [1978, pp 111 – 112].
378. Lee is only identified by his surname but this is likely to have been George Lee, a member of Calton's party. Boyce [1875] identifies a Robert Lee as one of the influential Graham's Town group of Wesleyan businessmen, that included Cock, Wood, Godlonton and Walker. The trustees listed on the foundation stone of the Wesleyan Commemoration Church in Graham's Town include, however, a George Lee, together with the same group, so Boyce may have been in error about Lee's first name. No Robert Lee appears on any settler lists. Another candidate is William Lee, a member of Sephton's party.
379. Stubbs [1978, p. 138]
380. See Driver [1866].
381. See Halse [1880, p.6], Le Cordeur [1960, p. 2].
382. A contemporary account of the establishment of the *Commercial Advertiser* and *The Graham's Town Journal* is provided by Meurant [1885]. See also Bell [1963, p. 102], Harington [1973], Gordon-Brown [1979], and Linder [1997, pp 207, 208]. Louis Henry Meurant was the son of a Swiss-born businessman, Louis Balthazar Meurant, who had probably come to the Cape in 1805 as the bandmaster of a British regiment. Louis Balthazar bought a printing press for one George Greig on condition that his son could be apprenticed in the printing trade. Greig was the printer of *The Commercial Advertiser*, edited by Thomas Pringle and John Fairbairn. A few months later Lord Charles Somerset had suppressed it setting off the struggle for the freedom of the press.
383. See Godlonton [1965] and Campbell [1837]. Campbell's polemic was written under the nom-de-plume "Justus." It has been attributed to other authors, including Robert Mackenzie Beverley, a well-known controversialist in England, but the consensus is that Campbell was the author.
384. This was written by Sir Harry Smith [1901, vol. 2, p. 343] in a letter to his wife dated 20 Mar 1835. Another nickname for the town, still used today is "City of the Saints." Usually assumed to be because of the large number of churches, this name is also said to have arisen from a requisition for woodworking tools sent from one of the outlying forts. One item could not be supplied and the order came back with a message, "No vice in Graham's Town," giving rise to a name that stuck.
385. An extract of a letter by Harry Smith to his wife on 27th Feb 1835 [Smith, 1901, vol.2, p. 339]
386. Pretorius [1988] concludes that there was little unambiguous evidence that Hintsa was in any way involved other than that he was aware of the war and some of his subordinate chiefs had joined the attack on the Colony. He is critical of D'Urban for

proceeding with the invasion. He bases this on information coming from James Read and Dr Philip as well as on reports such as that provided by Uys [Graham's Town Journal 20ᵗʰ Mar 1835] that there was no evidence of Colonial cattle in Hintsa's territory. There was, however, a quantity of intelligence to the contrary, predating Uys's report, such as the letter by Walker [1835]. Pretorius's criticism of D'Urban for proceeding to invasion on non-existent evidence neglects the difference between proof acceptable to a court and incomplete military intelligence on the basis of which decisions must be made. There is plenty of cause to criticise the invasion but it is not the case that it was based on hearsay and rumour. Hintsa was certainly not responsible for the attack on the Colony but he was likely to have approved it and he certainly permitted the retreating Xhosa to take refuge with him. On balance it is quite likely that he was waiting to see which way the cat would jump before taking a position.

387. See Walker [1835]. This communication and many others are attachments to a long self-justifying despatch from D'Urban [1836] to Lord Glenelg, the Secretary for the Colonies.
388. See Smith [1901, p. 383].
389. Gilfillan [1970, p.22]
390. Smith [1901, chap. 34].
391. Bisset's [1875, chap. 4] account describes the terrain and the engagement. The description does not make the positions of the Xhosa entirely clear. It was his first time under fire as a 17 yr old and the account was written thirty years later; there may be some exaggeration. He claims 22 000 cattle were retrieved where Smith, who would not have underestimated the number, claims "upwards of 4 000". Smith's [1901, chap. 34] own account does not contain as much detail. The best description of the terrain is that of Halse [1880, p.30]. Most accounts do not clarify the composition of the Xhosa defending force. Andrews [1877, p. 19] is the exception and identifies them as some of Nqeno's amaMbala and amaNdlambe of the clan of one of Mdushane's sons "Ishushane" (who may have been either Siwani or Qasana, probably the latter). In addition they were supported by a group of Khoikhoi rebels led by Louis Arnoldus, a deserter from the Cape Corps.
392. Halse [1880, p.30]
393. These are the words of Bertram Bowker, quoted from his journal by Mitford-Barberton [1952, p. 229]. Driver was 39 years old at the time, 15 years older than Bowker to whom he must have seemed "old". It is not certain that this event happened at Murray's Krantz, but the description of the environment and the people makes it likely.
394. See Driver [1943].
395. Primary contemporary sources for the events in the campaign include Andrews [1835], Gilfillan [1970], and Thomas Holden Bowker [Mitford- Barberton, 1970, pp 131 – 132] each being the diary of a participant in the events written at the time. Many other accounts by contemporaries, which were writen much later [Andrews, 1877; Bisset, 1875; Edgar, 1874; Halse, 1880; Smith, 1901], must be read with scepticism when dealing with events leading to the death of Hintsa, but, allowing for the inaccuracy of memory, can probably be regarded as reasonably accurate for the uncontroversial parts of the campaign.
396. Stretch [1988, p. 61 – 62].
397. Stretch [1988, p. 58].
398. From William Gilfillan's journal [Gilfillan, 1970, p. 36].
399. Entry for April 30ᵗʰ in William Gilfillan's diary [Gilfillan, 1970, p. 36].
400. See Gilfillan [1970, pp 36 – 37].
401. The official position was that Hintsa had suggested this. As Harrington [1980, p. 42]

points out, the initiative more probably came from Smith.

402. Mqhayi was a younger son of the Great House of Ndlambe.

403. Stubbs [1978, p. 108].

404. Thomas Holden Bowker's war diary [Mitford-Barberton, 1970, pp 131 – 132].

405. There were a number of eye-witnesses to the events surrounding Hintsa's death who provided written accounts. In giving weight to these accounts it is necessary to note that there was a significant cover-up largely orchestrated by Smith. As a result many of the accounts written after the events present an official version which in some cases is manifestly untrue. Caesar Andrew's [1835] field diary was written on the spot and differs in significant ways from his reminiscences [Andrews, 1877] which give the official story. William Gilfillan was not a participant in the final action but was a witness from a slight distance. His field diary [Gilfillan, 1970] was written on the spot and remained in private hands until well after his death, when it was included in a publication by a descendant. There is no reason to doubt that his account was a true reflection of what he observed and perceived on the day. Henry Halse was one of those in close pursuit of Hintsa. He managed to avoid giving evidence at the enquiry. Forty five years later he wrote a manuscript of his reminiscences for his family [Halse, 1880]. He was clearly sympathetic to the official version – he writes of the witnesses at the enquiry being "well-primed" – but he does include matters that were firmly suppressed at the enquiry. He was not expecting publication: "I have not written for publication, or even that they should be read until after my death, and then only by my children or near relatives". Subject to the possibility that he may have used official accounts to jog his memory, there is no reason to doubt that the statements he makes are given to the best of his recall. John Bisset came upon Southey and Hintsa immediately after the shooting. As a result of his exploits in the campaign he was accepted as an officer in the army and had a long and distinguished military career. An anonymous contemporary account describing the events in detail is ascribed by Pretorius [1988, p. 239] to Bisset. It contradicts the story in his reminiscences [Bisset, 1875], which present a strict official view and should be regarded with great scepticism. George Southey's supposed journal [Wilmot, 1904, Appendix L] is entirely unconvincing as a contemporary account. It was clearly put together in the form of a journal well after the event and states the official account in words markedly similar to those in other accounts. Richard Southey [Wilmot, 1904, Appendix A] also wrote a brief account that can be discounted. He was not present and is clearly presenting the official picture in a way intended to shield his brother. Early twentieth century historians [Cory, 1965; Walker, 1968] uncritically accept the official version propounded at the time. The analysis of Pretorius [1988] is probably as close as we can get to the truth behind the death of Hintsa. He did not have access to Halse's memoir, Stretch's diary, or Gilfillan's journal but these tend to strengthen his interpretation. Jay Naidoo [1989, chap. 4] comes to a not dissimilar conclusion, although his thrust makes much of the possibility of a planned conspiracy rather than the militarily more likely snafu. He was unaware of Pretorius's work, writing "But astonishingly and to this day [1989], no specific and detailed study has been made (apart from Uys's newspaper articles) of the Hintsa killing". The Pretorius thesis was available in 1970, although it was only published in 1988.

406. See Wilmot [1904, Appendix L].

407. See Andrews [1877, p. 33]. The account shows many signs of having been carefully constructed to accord with the official view. In general this part of it agrees with other eye-witnesses. The statement about the bundle of assegais may have been inserted to support the picture of an armed Hintsa.

408. Bisset [1875, p. 25]

409. Written on the day by Andrews [1835].
410. Andrews [1877] more than forty years after the event.
411. Edgar [1874] describes this athletic feat. How he managed to extract his assegai from the bundle in the circumstances is difficult to understand. On the other hand, if he carried only one assegai, he was unarmed thereafter.
412. Bisset [1875, pp 24, 25]. Naidoo [1989] maintains that chiefs only carried a single ceremonial assegai, but the witnesses all describe a bundle.
413. Halse [1880, p.43]
414. According to the anonymous account ascribed by Pretorius [1988] to Bisset. Smith himself, in his autobiography, surprisingly agrees that he gave a less lurid order that entitled Southey to fire: '... and I desired Mr Southey "Fire, fire at him!" ' [Smith, 1901, vol. 2, p. 47].
415. Edgar [1874].
416. Accounts agree that George Southey fired and hit Hintsa. Caesar Andrews [1877] in his *Reminiscences* is most careful to say that Southey called out a warning in Xhosa: "Southey in the [Xhosa] language cried out to Hintsa that if he would give himself up his life would be saved, but he still continued his course when Southey fired his first shot and hit him in the fleshy part of the left leg." The field diary [Andrews, 1835], on the other hand, makes no mention of any warning, only stating "Mr G. Southey at this moment came near enough to fire and inflicted a flesh wound [in] the leg." Significantly, a pencilled editorial note in a different hand from Andrews's has been added to the diary. It reads: "called to give himself up." No other witness suggest that any warning was given.
417. Halse [1880, p. 43]
418. Andrews [1877, p.34].
419. The evidence surrounding the immediate circumstances of Hintsa's death is heavily contaminated. The contemporary witnesses who wrote down what happened immediately afterwards were outside the main theatre of events. The witnesses who gave evidence at the subsequent inquiry were, in the words of Halse [1880, p. 45], "well primed" and their evidence was often either false or far from complete. Our account is based on the reported statements and conversations of Driver, Julie, and Africa. These are second-hand and cannot be regarded as providing proof beyond any reasonable doubt. They do, however, go a long way to providing a convincing picture on the balance of probability. Driver made comments to a number of officers afterwards. These gave rise to widespread comment. They were reported at second hand by Charles Lennox Stretch [Stretch, 1988, pp 95, 96], serving with D'Urban. Driver is said to have told several people that Hintsa had cried for mercy before he was shot [Stretch, 1988, p. 96]. He also confirmed Hintsa's mutilation. Julie and Africa also made a long statement to Smith's interpreter, a man called Klaas. Klaas gave this these to Ambrose Campbell who relayed it to Dr Phillip. This is the basis of the account of their actions given here. At the inquiry they did not confirm the account, but they were serving soldiers and under pressure from Smith.
420. Driver is reported as stating that he "called lustily for mercy," [Stretch, 1988, pp 95, 96]. If Edward Driver heard this call then Southey must have heard it too.
421. This is from Caesar Andrews's reminiscences [Andrews, 1877, p. 34]. While these are full of misstatements about the actual shooting they can probably be accepted when presenting what he actually witnessed himself.
422. Bisset [1875, p. 26]. Bisset's account is riddled with falsehood and others do not place him on the scene.
423. According to his evidence to the court of inquiry [Report, 1837].
424. See Halse [1880, p. 44]. The role of Ford is not quite so clear cut. There was some suggestion at the enquiry that he was actually medically examining the body rather

than mutilating it.

425. Gilfillan's journal entry for the same day [Gilfillan, 1970, p. 41].

426. See Philip [1828].

427. See le Cordeur [1981, pp 44 – 50].

428. See Stretch [1988, p. 96] in reminiscences appended to his journal.

429. See Halse [1880, p. 44]

430. See Stretch [1988, pp 95, 96]. The thought that it "might be made a personal subject" suggests the possibility of a duel. [This from entry for 17th June]

431. See Stretch [1998]. Simmons and Nourse were officers in the 72nd and the "certain doctor" was Ford. The possibility expressed here that Hintsa's genitals might also have been removed is probably an exaggeration. Other accounts do not suggest this and do not agree as to those responsible.

432. See D'Urban [1835]. The report is addressed to Lord Aberdeen. It was received by his successor, Lord Glenelg.

433. This requires Hintsa to have retained an assegai throughout his headlong flight, during which he was twice shot, the second time seriously.

434. See Andrews [1835]

435. See Andrews [1877]

436. See Sheffield [1884, pp 168 – 169].

437. Halse [1880, p. 44]

438. His presence is according the family tradition of his descendants [Cosser, 1992, p.94]. Thes story was unearthed by Cosser [1992, pp. 94 – 95] as part of an M.A. Thesis in Fine Art. The picture is reproduced in the thesis on page 93. Lalu [2009] is less certain that the picture actually represents the death of Hintsa.

439. Cory Library [MS9456]

440. The guerilla methods used by the Xhosa are discussed in detail by Peires [1981, chap. 9].

441. See Stretch [1988, pp 119 – 121].

442. See Stretch [1988, p. 138].

443. A review of the effects of Glenelg's despatch is provided by Vigne [1988].

444. Halse [1880, pp 44, 45]

445. The proceedings of the Court have been extensively analysed by Pretorius [1988, chap. 6].

446. Pretorius[1988, p. 223]

447. From a document in the Public Records Office in London, quoted by Pretorius [1988, p. 239]

448. Pretorius [1988, p. 242] found that "his attitude before the court is difficult to explain." On the contrary, if we assume that he was determined not to lie, but also not to answer questions that would incriminate his comrades, his attitude is perfectly consistent. The questions that he refused to answer were precisely those that would have incriminated the Southeys and Shaw.

449. See Keegan [1996], le Cordeur [1981] for discussions of this period.

450. See Mostert [1992, pp 796, 797].

451. See Chase [1843].

452. See le Cordeur [1981, p.88]

453. Ransford [1972, chap. 3]

454. This was in a biographical work by Shaw's friend [Boyce, 1875] written about his friend the Rev. William Shaw.

455. This was not Dr Ambrose Campbell, given his standing among the leading citizens of Graham's Town. Dr Peter Campbell, an Irish member of Bailie's party had sailed separately on the *Aurora*, meeting the Wesleyans who settled at Salem. He was a Catholic, but was persuaded by Shaw [1972, p. 42] to join the Salem community. He

later practised in Graham's Town. According to Jones [1971, p. 98] he died in 1837 at the age of 47, implying that the adjective "old" meant affection rather than age. Sheffield [1884, p. x], however, states that in 1850 he was still alive and, at the age of 60, when he was a property holder of note owning a large stretch of real estate in Bathurst St, he married a twenty-year old Miss Cumming – no relation of the family of John Forbes Cumming.

456. This was Dr John Atherstone, District Surgeon and father of the better known William Guybon Atherstone.

457. See Wood & Walker [1835].

458. See Walker [1842].

459. See Faure [1842].

460. This small bank was the ancestor of the National Bank of South Africa, which was later incorporated with Barclays Bank DCO, the predecessor of First National Bank, now one of the "big four" South African commercial banks.

461. See Green [1957].

462. Now Beaufort West.

463. Now Somerset East.

464. The others were William Shepherd, W. R. Thompson, Philip W. Lucas, George Jarvis, George Gilbert, and John Cecil Wright.

465. The troubled history of the attempts to make a commercial port out of the Kowie mouth is described by Turpin [1964].

466. Bennet was a member of Isaac Dyason's party. Dyason's son, Isaac Jr, a marine surveyor, had conducted the first surveys of the estuary in 1820, and had later been the Port Frances harbour master.

467. See Jones [1968, vol. 3, p. 16].

468. See, for example, Nash [1982, chap. 2].

469. The fortunes of Philip Marillier and James Ford can be followed in the account of the history of Bailie's party by Nash [1982].

470. Thomas Philipps [1960, p.159], in a letter to his aunts, the Misses Harries, dated 10th Jan. 1823 describes Ford's troubles and his visit to Ngqika.

471. Sarah Jane Hart, daughter of Robert Hart Jr and his second wife, Harriet Marillier in a letter, see http://marillierfamily.dnsalias.com:1980/ .

472. See de Klerk [1982].

473. Ffolliott [1972].

474. Pringle [1967].

475. See Glen Thorn [1974].

476. See Hart [1844].

477. The charge, the jurors, and the verdict appear in the Court records [Circuit Court, 1845]. These do not include any record of the proceedings. Robert Hart [1847] made an appeal to the Governor, Sir Henry Pottinger for a remission of sentence. Attached to this is a full record of the trial with witness statements and records of cross examination. This was supplied to the Governor by the Attorney-General. The evidence of the three eye-witnesses is entirely consistent. Our account is essentially a paraphrase of the evidence of Jacobus Smit. That of Jan Platje and of Henry Mould is consistent with his but is less complete. The direct speech occurs in the records of the evidence, although it seems that most of the conversation was in Dutch and had been translated.

478. The events surrounding Hart's arrest do not appear in the Court records. The source for this account is a contemporary newspaper cutting from an unidentified journal, supplied to the author by Tombi Peck.

479. See Hart [1845].

480. See Hart [1847]. The Governor, Henry Pottinger, requested advice from Judge Men-

zies. He in turn consulted the Attorney General, William Porter, who, in his advice, disclosed that there had at the time been a further accusation against James of participating in "an unnatural act with a Hottentot." In the circumstances he had felt that justice had been served by the sentence of ten years hard labour, but he could see no justification for a commutation of sentence.

481. This is on the basis of the family tree provided by Oliver Hart [Hart, 2005], a descendant of Wilfred.

482. To the numerate reader the latter is of course correct, since this is the date on which 2000 years had been completed since the starting date. The 1st January 2000 is the date on which the two thousandth year began.

483. John Centlivres Chase in the *Graham's Town Journal* of 25th Jan 1844, reprinted by Godlonton [1844, pp xvii, xviii].

484. The title page of Godlonton's [1844] account gives 10th May as the date. In the text it is stated that it was planned for Tuesday 7th May.

485. The "official" account of the proceedings in Graham's Town is given by Godlonton [1844]; an unexpurgated and personal version comes from Stubbs [1978, pp 137, 138].

486. Equivalent to about £36 in 2009, using comparative retail price indices, but an enormous £350 when using comparative average earnings [Officer, 2008].

487. The direct speech is Stubbs's [1978, p. 138] own reporting.

488. For Maxwell & McGeogh [1978, p. 270, note 226] Wood's behaviour was incomprehensible. Smith, too, was associated with the organization of the banquet; he was scheduled to propose one of the toasts. It is conceivable that their action, in giving Stubbs his say, was intended to cool what was becoming a nasty situation. Stubbs does not suggest that the broken chairs were actually used, and it seems that, once he was speaking, those round him refrained from mayhem and listened.

489. These events in Bathurst are described by Ayliff [1845].

490. See Nottinghamshire City Court [1833].

491. Of course voters were only male. The reform acts of 1832, 1867, and 1884 improved matters but universal male franchise was only achieved in 1918; women got the unrestricted vote in 1928.

492. From *All Things Bright and Beautiful*, the popular Anglican hymn by C. F. Alexander, published in 1848.

493. A small village about 5 miles north of Arbroath. A suitable destination for an early morning walk on a cold December day.

494. The collection [Cumming 1834–1899] was deposited in the South African Library (now the South African National Library, Cape Town Campus) by a descendant, Miss J. C. D. Cumming in 1945. It consists of 457 numbered items – 16 volumes of diaries beginning in December 1835 and ending in 1890, 6 notebooks, numerous letters, copies of addresses and speeches, a variety of ephemera, various printed items, and an incomplete autobiographical narrative (57 pages) of Cumming's life. Unless otherwise stated, all quotations in this chapter are from the first two volumes of the diaries [Cumming 1834–1899, items 1, 2]. The "Narrative" (item 430 in the collection) is a typescript dated 16th July 1896 containing a number of errors in the transcription of names and ending incompletely with a partly charred sheet. Starting on 14th Nov. 1961 the Queenstown *Daily Representative* published an edited version of the narrative in a series of articles, from a version supplied by Cumming's great-grandson John Forbes Cumming. It covers the missing material at the end which amounts to less than a page of the manuscript. Some of the material in the earlier document has been re-ordered and some omitted so as to make the narrative easier to follow. The other editing changes divide the narrative into sections with headings, split paragraphs to reduce the length and insert punctuation.

495. A manuscript family tree in the possession of the author suggests that he had one brother and three sisters but they are unnamed. This was prepared by Eirene Moberley (b. Walker), Cumming's great granddaughter but her sources are unknown. Some would have been conversations with older members of the family. Among the Cumming [1834–1899, item 43] papers is a degree certificate of the Edinburgh Royal College of Surgeons issued to Gulielmus (i.e. William) Cumming in 1826. According to the family tree William, his father, died in 1826 so that the medical Cumming was more likely to have been a brother. There is some evidence in the papers that John Cumming attended lectures in medicine, but he did not qualify as a doctor. There is evidence of correspondence with a sister in the Cumming papers.

496. By this was probably meant the Church of Scotland rather than the Episcopal Church that was associated with the Anglican Church in England. In Scotland there was never an officially established church, although the Church of Scotland was and is the one used by the monarch when in in Scotland. Cumming's church was one of several sects in the fractious Presbyterian community of Scotland.

497. In November 1839, John Williams and James Harris, missionaries of the London Missionary Society, were killed and eaten by cannibals on the New Hebridean island of Erromango in the South Seas.

498. The diary makes it clear that this was the date of arrival. In his reminiscences, *A Narrative,* [Cumming, 1834 – 1899, item 430], written in 1896, he compresses his time in Cape Town to only a fortnight, stating that his arrival was on the 30th September.

499. The peak to the right of Table Mountain as viewed from Table Bay

500. In *A Narrative* [Cumming, 1834 – 1899, item 430] his memory again fails him and he states that he continued the journey in the same ship as he had taken from England. He gives its name as *Norfolk,* which does not agree with his diary.

501. Other examples of five-gaited horses are American harness trotters, and Icelandic horses.

502. Once again in *A Narrative* Cumming's memory fails him. He remembers the ride as lasting an impressive four days [Cumming, 1834 – 1899, item 430, pp 2,3]. The daily diary entries show a different picture, with departure from Algoa Bay on 5th November and arrival at on the 14th. The actual riding time was similar but several days were spent in Graham's Town.

503. [Cumming, 1834 – 1899, item 430, p. 3]

504. [Cumming, 1834 – 1899, item 430, p. 4]

505. In the fashion of the day Cumming refers throughout to "Mr Campbell" without providing a first name. At one point in his narrative [Cumming, 1834 – 1899, item 430, p. 35] he refers to Campbell's marriage to Miss Davanish [*sic*]. John Mears Devenish had been a colleague of John Pringle at Somerset farm and he and his wife Ellen were well known at Glenthorn. Their daughter Elizabeth is known to have married Thomas Campbell in about 1845, which is consistent with the date given by Cumming and allows us to identify Mr Campbell as most probably Thomas. See http://1820settlers.com/ consulted on 17th March 2010.

506. This would have been his Mission or Christian name, given on his conversion and baptism. Many Mfengu refugees found refuge in Missions and became converts.

507. In the typescript of Cumming's reminiscences the name is given as Madosi more than once but in its first appearance is altered by hand to Madori. Stanford [1958, vol. 1, p. 48] notes that the San name of the chief was Madoor, and his Xhosa name Madolo. Bushman's School was taken over after the eighth Frontier war by the Wesleyans, and renamed Mount Arthur.

508. This is not the town of Qumbu in the Transkei region, but a much smaller village.

509. Mthirara was the eldest son of the right hand house. Nonesi, Vusani's Great Wife

had no children.

510. Cumming [1834 – 1899, item 430, p. 9].
511. Abalungu, i.e. white men.
512. "Niven said we would report their conduct to the great chief", assumed to be Sandile since they were near Pirie mission which was in Rharhabe territory.
513. Cumming's spelling, possibly Ngunane.
514. This account is based on Cumming's [1834 – 1899, item 430] reminiscences. Except where otherwise stated all quotations in this chapter are from that source.
515. See Boyce [1834].
516. *Upundlo* was the custom of sexual requisition by the chief [Soga, 1931, Peires, 1981].
517. Both Cumming and Thackwray describe the man as rich and influential and as being associated with Tyopo. The encounters are seventeen years apart.
518. Of course this is a third-hand dramatised account by Cumming [1834 – 1899, item 430]. The actual events may be much as he described; details are indubitably consciously or unconsciously embroidered. The quotation is included to indicate the missionary point of view more than to present an impartial reporter's description of what happened.
519. A *riem* is a leather thong. The word is Dutch. Such thongs were widely used as a substitute for cordage. A *kierie* is a stick fashioned as a weapon. A knob kierie is made from a branch or a sapling in which the portion of the branch joining the tree trunk, or the root is fashioned into a massive knob providing weapon not unlike a wooden mace.
520. Son of the missionary, John Shepstone, Theophilus became a distinguished administrator in both the Cape and Natal, played a prominent part in the history of Natal and the Transvaal, and was eventually knighted for his services.
521. See Stretch [1844].
522. The nature and meaning of the rite of circumcision among the Xhosa is discussed, for example, by Soga [1931, pp 248 – 259] and Ngxamngxa [1971].
523. Stapleton [1991, 1994] describes a man who, when under stress, would get drunk in a tavern, but did not use alcohol in his home.
524. His brother, Tyhali, in a deathbed statement [Tyhali, 1842], complained that he was often too drunk to understand messengers sent to him. The statement was recorded by Stretch, who is otherwise silent on this. Tyhali was by this time completely opposed to Maqoma and may have been prejudiced.
525. See Soga [1931, pp 43 – 45].
526. See Tyhali [1842].
527. For the sequence of events we are dependent on Cory [1965, vol. 4, chap. 7]. While his opinions are always strongly coloured by the prejudices of the time at which he wrote and his language reflects this, there is no reason to doubt his description of the events.
528. For his cricketing career see the Lords Taverners Cricket Archive: http://www.cricketarchive.com/Archive/Players/37/37253/37253.html. While this would be a derisory average for a professed batsman in modern day cricket, to be fair, the batsmen played without pads and the quality of the pitches at that time meant that a side scoring more than 100 in an innings could be well satisfied. On the other hand, neither roundarm nor overarm bowling had yet been legalized; the ball had to be delivered underarm.
529. Elizabeth remarried a few years later and lived to a good age.
530. The Cape of Good Hope Mutual Life Assurance Company had recently been established. It was founded by John Fairbairn on 17th May 1845 and was the predecessor of the giant multinational company The Old Mutual [Benfield, 2004, chap. 1].

531. Nqeno died on April 1st 1846 as noted by Cory [1965, vol. 4, p. 424] who also states that he had a semi-military funeral. Cumming [1834 – 1899, item 430, p. 48] notes that Nqeno was chief when the family arrived at Iqibira at the end of January but that Stokwe had become chief by the time he left the station in May.

532. See Cumming [1834 – 1899, item 430, p. 48]

533. See Cumming [1834 – 1899, item 430, p. 49]

534. See Cumming [1834 – 1899, item 430, p. 48]

535. For fuller accounts see for example Mostert [1992, pp 875 – 877], Milton [1983, pp 156 – 160].

536. See Cumming [1834 – 1899, item 430, p. 49]

537. This is Cumming's rendering of the name. The first name sounds neither like a Xhosa name nor like a baptismal name. Cumming states that he had been baptised by Niven. He was probably Mfengu.

538. This was Ndlambe's brother. He was the same man who had led the group that had killed John Shaw at the beginning of the frontier war in 1834.

539. Probably Sonto.

540. A more complete account of the progress of the war is given by Milton [1983, chap. 18]. It has been helpful in preparing this brief outline.

541. It is ironic that Fort Hare, named after an enemy of the Xhosa, became the site for a university which, before and during the apartheid era, was reserved for black people. Many leaders of the black resistance movements in South Africa and politicians from other African countries were educated there. Now a fully liberated university Fort Hare boasts among its alumni Nelson Mandela, Oliver Tambo, Govan Mbeki, Julius Nyerere, Robert Mugabe, Kenneth Kaunda, Desmond Tutu, and many others.

542. This was Henry, the third Earl Grey. He became Secretary of State for War and the Colonies in June 1846 in the new Whig government of Lord John Russell. He had succeeded to the title the previous year on the death of his father, the second Earl, reformist Prime Minister between 1830 and 1834, and proponent of the eponymous blend of tea. Not to be confused with Sir George Grey, Governor of the Cape 1854 – 1861.

543. According to Cumming [1834 – 1839, item 430] there were 8 children. They included a daughter Janet, and sons John and William Jr. who were afterwards to play a part in Cumming's life.

544. Diary entry for 20th February 1847 [Cumming, 1834 – 1839].

545. See Chapter 6.

546. See Cory [1965, vol. 4, p. 465].

547. See Stubbs [1978, p. 115].

548. See Stubbs [1978, p. 117].

549. Considerable insight into Pottinger's role in the war is provided by the letters and documentation edited by le Cordeur & Saunders [1981].

550. Hulme [1968] lists no fewer than 55 units of levies varying in size from fewer than a dozen to the 400 Mfengu stationed at Fort Peddie. The list is not claimed to be exhaustive.

551. See Stubbs [1978, p. 132]

552. See Cory [1965, vol. 5, pp 13, 14].

553. Quoted by le Cordeur [1988, intro.].

554. At the time several Presbyterian Scots were called to serve the Dutch Reformed Church, the most notable being Andrew Murray in Graaff-Reinet.

555. See Stretch [1849, p. 1, no. 1].

556. See Mostert [1992, pp 834 – 836] for a description.

557. See Cory [1965, vol. 5, p. 17].

558. See Cory [1965, vol. 5, p. 20].
559. Quoted by le Cordeur & Saunders [1981, p. 95] from the collection of Grey's papers held at the University of Durham.
560. Letter in the Brenthurst Collection from Pottinger to Berkeley, quoted by le Cordeur & Saunders [1981, p. 97].
561. Order 154 is quoted in full by Hulme [1968].
562. Quoted by le Cordeur & Saunders [1981, p. 106].
563. See Stockenstrom *et al.* [1854].
564. See Cory [1965, vol. 5, p. 19].
565. Macaulay in his *History of England.*
566. See Le Cordeur & Saunders [1981, pp 151 – 154].
567. In a memorandum written on September 3rd 1847 [le Cordeur & Saunders, 1981, p. 159]. The development of matters to this point and, in particular, the evidence of Calderwood's role is illustrated by many letters and memoranda [le Cordeur & Saunders, 1981, chap. 5]
568. The controversy is described by le Cordeur and Saunders [1981, chap. 7]. Bisset was adamant that he surrendered, but his formal statements differed from his private conversation. Bisset's record in giving evidence at the inquiry into Hintsa's death does not inspire confidence in his veracity.
569. Contemporary accounts of this incident are hard to find. Harriet Ward [Ward, 1848, vol. I, p. 175; 1851, p. 275], writing at the time, describes it with approval, but was not herself a witness. It is described by Cory [1965, vol V, p. 100]. Sheffield [1884, p. 185] – not to be relied on – deplores the action and states that he has failed to find any record of the story and attributes it to "[Xhosa] sympathisers in England." Peires [1981, p. 166] relates it and quotes Mqhayi [1931] as source. Other than Harriet Ward's report, all these accounts were written long after the event. The behaviour attributed to Smith is, however, entirely consistent with his well-documented performance at the great meeting of chiefs a few days later on 17th Dec. 1847 and the story passes the test of plausibility.
570. See Parliament [1968 – 1971, vol. 22, p. 194]
571. I am grateful to Dr J. B. Peires [private communication] for this information.
572. See Parliament, [1968 – 1971, vol. 22, p. 218]
573. Memorial by Stretch [1848, no. 151] to the Governor dated 18th February 1848, later published [Stretch, 1849, pp 9, 10].
574. This is according to Stretch's [1855, pp 8 – 10] own account. Stretch was making the case for his right to the property so allowance should be made for bias. The non-centrality Fort Cox of is arguable since it was close to Sandile's Great Place. More importantly the neighbourhood was in a region of ill-defined boundaries. Lord Charles Somerset's proclamation in 1819, defining the Ceded Territory, was obscure as to the boundary at this point. Henry Somerset had allowed Maqoma to settle to the west of the Keiskamma in the Amatola region where Block Drift was situated. Hare's later determination of the boundary placed Fort Cox outside and Block Drift inside the ceded territory.
575. From Maqoma's point of view, it was his land. From the Colonial Government's point of view he was there on sufferance. Whether he had any right to grant land to Stretch depended on the point of view. There was no formal title. Ngqika'a original cession of the ceded territory was under duress and not within his power.
576. The Lovedale Institute grew into a major educational establishment including a primary and secondary school, a technical institute, a teachers training college, a theological college, and a hospital. In the nineteenth century it took both black and white pupils. It played a pivotal role in black education until it was closed down by Verwoerd's Nationalist government in the nineteen fifties under the provisions of the

Bantu Education Act.

577. Stretch [1848, no. 152] in a letter dated at Mankazana on 16th June 1848.

578. Letter to the Secretary of State written from Mankazana on 29th May 1849 [Stretch, 1849, no. 12].

579. Cape Parliament [1854, pp 613 - 615]

580. A more detailed account of the Brown affair is given by Mostert [1992]. He concentrates on Brown's sexual peccadilloes. Cumming's diary, however, suggests that, while these weighed heavily on their relationship, there were also disputes relating to more professional matters, involving interference by Brown in Cumming's congregation. Cumming's elliptical style, however, makes it difficult to decipher the details of the disagreements.

581. See Cumming [1834 – 1899, item 2].

582. Tiyo Soga was the seventh child of Nosutho, the great wife of Soga, an influential counsellor of Sandile. He was born in the Tyumie valley. His mother was converted to Christianity and Tiyo became a protégé of William Chalmers. He was first educated at Lovedale and when the school was closed at the time of the War of the Axe, it was agreed that he should accompany a teacher, Mr. Govan who had resigned from Lovedale, back to Scotland where he would go to School. He returned in 1848 to become a catechist at the mission.

583. Quoted by Renton in his evidence to the Select Committee on the [Xhosa] Tribes [Parliament, 1968 – 1971, Vol IV, para. 3014]. Mostert [1992, p. 1010] attributes the sentiment to Suthu but Renton's evidence states that this was stated by the regent of the Tyhali clan after his death – an office served by his widow Tebe.

584. Peires [198, chap.1] gives a more detailed account of the character and teachings of Mlangeni.

585. See Smith [1850].

586. See Ross [2003] for an account of the development of the situation.

587. See Read [1852, pp 22, 23].

588. Probably Louis Gustav Tregardt, a younger son of Louis Tregardt (Trichard) the voortrekker. Louis Gustav had been only ten years old at the time of the Great Trek. After the death of his father, his older brothers had made their way to Natal where they were now established. Louis Gustav may well have returned to take over the old farm in the Somerset area when he grew up.

589. See Parliament [1968 – 1971, Vol XXIII, p. 69]

590. This account is largely based on Cumming's [1834 – 1899, item 5] diary entry for 19th Dec. 1850.

591. William Ritchie Thomson, although from Glasgow, now was with the Dutch Reformed Church at Kat River. Many Presbyterians served the sister church at the time. See Williams [1967].

592. See Parliament [1968 – 1971, Vol XXIII, p. 67]

593. See Parliament [1968 – 1971, Vol IV, para. 3048]

594. Smith in a report to Earl Grey dated the following day, 20th Dec. 1850, [Parliament, 1968 – 1971, Vol XXIII].

595. See Brown [1855]. Cumming was present at the meeting and his account is that of an eye-witness. He left a blank in his diary on the day itself (19th Dec. 1850) and wrote his description in that place a few days later (on 24th Dec.). It is not clear from Brown's report whether he was also present or was describing what he heard from the other missionaries. Brown's account was written a few years later (published 1855).

596. Parliament [1968 – 1971, vol23].

597. See Peires [1989, p. 9], Mostert [1962, p. 1003].

598. See A Narrative [Cumming, 1834 – 1899, item 430]. Cumming had previously made

arrangements to take all the occupants of the mission to a safe place in the Colony in the event of hostilities.

599. The old Cape Corps had been renamed the Cape Mounted Rifles in 1827. They were properly referred to as the CMR but the older name was still often used.

600. The route described is that assumed by Bergh & Visagie [1985]. Their map places Fort Cox to the west of the oxbow in the river, on the same bank as Burnshill. It was, as described by Cumming [1834 – 1899, item 430] on the high land of the peninsula formed by the long narrow oxbow. The rest of the route they have mapped is consistent with the demands of the terrain.

601. A primary source for the events at Tyumie on that day are Cumming's diary entry which is clearly written under pressure. Parts are scrawled and sometimes illegible. It is often difficult to follow. He provides a much more coherent account in his manuscript recollections sent to Charles Cowen [1851 – 1896, item B9] but this was written from memory many years later. These recollections, apart from some minor editorial changes, form part of the typescript A Narrative [Cumming, 1834 – 1899, item 430]. Other consistent primary sources are Brown [1855, chaps IV – VI] and Niven [1860].

602. Mary Chalmers's sons, John, William, and Ebenezer were also at Tyumie at the time. William states [Cowen, 1851 – 1896, item B7]: "I may mention my mother and family were on the Gwalie Mission station at the time." [Cowen, 1851 – 1896, item B7]. Gwali was an alternative name for the Tyumie mission. A small tributary of the Tyumie River, the Gwali stream, ran past the mission station. William in extensive marginal notes to a pamphlet by J. M. Stevenson, [Cumming, 1834 – 1899, item 496] gives eye-witness descriptions.

603. Understandably, the writing in Cumming's diary on 25th December 1850 is hard to decipher. The name of the church elder is almost illegible, but appears at first sight to be "Fest –" or "Fast–". Careful examination suggests that the name is Festiri, the brother of Tiyo Soga, who had been at Uniondale but did not accompany the Nivens during their flight. Festiri lived about three kilometres from the mission and it is plausible that the message had come from Tiyo.

604. There are conflicting reports of the response to this. Mostert [1992, p. 1028] states that Cumming refused arms, because the station had always been safe since Ngqika declared it a sanctuary. I have not found the source of this. Brown's [1855, p.55] account is the source used here.

605. The description of Stevenson's arrival and behaviour, including the direct speech quoted, comes from W. B. Chalmers's handwritten marginal notes [Cumming, 1834 – 1899, item 496] in a copy of Stevenson's [1896] own account, which differs radically. Cumming's diary entry, written at the time, is less dramatic: "Called to the door hurriedly on going to the gate found Mr Stevenson superintendent of the Johannesberg [village ?] sitting on his horse who said that he had just escaped from Woburn with his life. I called him down to the house."

606. Ntsikane was one of Ngqika's councillors. He had been influenced by missionaries such as Joseph Williams and had founded a Christian movement in about 1815 or 1816 as a result of a mystical experience [Ntsikane, 1902]. He had preached against the teaching of Nxele in 1819. His son Dukwane was part of the Tyumie community.

607. Chalmers in the private notes sent to Charles Cowen [1851 – 1896, item B7] states: "The writer was nearly eighteen years old at the time, and was present at Gwali when Stevenson arrived there."

608. Stevenson's state of mind on that day is pieced together from remarks made by Renton [Account, 1851], Brown [1855, p. 53], and W. B. Chalmers [Cumming, 1834 – 1899, item 496, manuscript marginal notes; Cowen 1851 – 1896, item B7]. It is rel-

evant to his later behaviour. Chalmers states that throughout the day Stevenson was so incapacitated by terror and shock that he was unable to give any reliable account of the occurrences on the day.

609. As Superintendant of Juanasburg, he was field-cornet.
610. Cumming does not mention the disagreement. Renton, however, reported that Stevenson "was very obnoxious, I understand, to the red [Xhosa]s, and Mr Cumming had represented to him that it would be desirable for him to embrace the first opportunity of going off." Renton used the adjective "red" to describe Xhosa who lived according to tribal custom as opposed to those who had been converted to Christianity. The term comes from the red ochre clay that was used on their faces and bodies. As late as the middle of the twentieth century the term was still used by white people in the Transkei, although by that time it had achieved a pejorative meaning. Renton's use of it was neutrally descriptive, simply distinguishing between converted and unconverted Xhosa people.
611. Niven [1860] describes their experiences in more detail. Mostert [1992, pp 1030 – 1034] gives a more accessible account based on this.
612. Of those present no-one states that anyone other than Stevenson accompanied the soldiers. Mostert states that Ball and two other survivors joined them. Brown, on the other hand, states that the troops left in a hurry under threatened attack. Chalmers suggests that Ball and the other two survivors travelled by night without escort, which seems unlikely.
613. Cumming's [1834 – 1899, item 430, pp 41 – 43] and Brown's [1855, pp 58 – 65] accounts of what was reported from Auckland agree in the significant facts, although they differ in some of the details. Stevenson's [1896] story is confused by the self-serving accounts of his escape from Woburn and has not been given much credence.
614. Summarised by Jessie Brown, a daughter of Janet and George Brown, in 1896 and quoted in a letter from Jessie Brown to Charles Cowen [1851 – 1896, item A7]. The account is in her own words and overlaid by her own feelings.
615. His own account of his adventures [Brown, 1855, pp 70 – 95] is the major source for Mostert's [1992, pp 1050 – 1056] extended description, which is more accessible.
616. Probably "Boesak". This is according to Chalmers [1877, p. 61].
617. Cumming states that they were " met there on important business of mission." (see quotation following). The important business that they had been involved in when the war broke out three and a half weeks earlier had been the Brown affair and Renton's general investigation of the affairs of the mission.
618. See Cumming [1834 – 1899, item 5]. Interestingly, Cumming does not mention Brown's presence at the meeting. Brown's own account agrees quite closely with Cumming's.
619. This does not appear in Cumming's diary or in his reminiscences. Cumming's words are reported by William Ainslie, Catherine's brother-in-law. See Pringle [1957, p. 166].
620. This is the only clear reference to Cumming's having a sister in the Colony. There is a letter in the Cumming [1834 – 1899, item 329] papers to Margaret Cumming in Scotland, presumably a sister, responding to a letter about the death of their mother at the end of 1847. It is possible that Margaret came out to join her brother for a while after her mother's death. In a letter by Catherine to her grand-daughter Kate (copy in the possession of the author) she refers to "Old Aunt" living with them as distinct from her daughter "Aunt Sarah."
621. Quoted by Makin [1971].
622. Contemporary accounts include a newspaper article quoted by Makin [1971], a report of the events by Stubbs [1978, pp 163 – 165], and a lively description,

unhampered by orthography or syntax, by the inimitable Jeremiah Goldswain [1949, pp 143 – 148].

623. The Trollips were a numerous clan. A contemporary newspaper account quoted by Makin [1971] identifies this one as Mr Chas. Trollip. Goldswain [1949] identifies him as Mr J. Trollip. Stubbs [1978] writes only of "one of the Trollips." Maxwell and McGeogh [1978, notes 292, 293] state that William Trollip, Joseph's eldest son was established at the time at Dagga Boer's Nek which was "Trollip country" with farms, a store, and an hotel and imply that this Trollip was one of William's sons, Henry, who with his brother Edward was later killed in the war. This is a red herring. In fact Booth's companion is identified by Gordon [1971, p. 172] as Charles Benjamin Trollip, son of Benjamin and Mary Ann Trollip. Benjamin was the fifth son of the patriarch of the family, the settler Joseph Trollip. Charles was 24 years old at the time.

624. The details of the attack and Booth's escape were reported by Goldswain from Booth's own account. In Goldswain's remarkable spelling the shout was "Keerom voor." Omkeer is to turn. Voor means in front. Keer can mean to stop something. "Keer hom voor!" meaning "Stop him in front", referring to the escaping Trollip, is a more likely phrase.

625. The Xhosa and Khoikhoi used what ammunition they could. Any bits of lead or iron that fitted down the barrel served as shot and behaved like shrapnel.

626. Presumably a sprung horse-drawn vehicle rather than an ox-wagon.

627. The Stubbs Albany Mounted Rangers was formed from the members of Stubbs's sporting club. Stubbs had the rank of field cornet, which meant that he reported to the landdrost but had military duties. Although later, in the Boer republics, a field cornet was a military rank equivalent to second lieutenant, within the rangers Thomas was called captain, and his younger brother William was lieutenant.

628. See Ross [2003].

629. Extract quoted by Renton [Account, 1855; Cumming, 1834 – 1899, item 447].

630. See Stubbs [1978, p. 165].

631. The *Graham's Town Journal* of January 25th 1851 carries an advertisement for the hotel, announcing the change of ownership.

632. The description of the meeting is based on the account published in the *Cape Frontier Times* of April 15th 1851, and reprinted in a pamphlet a few years later [Account, 1855; Cumming, 1834 – 1899, item 447].

633. A copy of the letter is included in the Cowen [1851 – 1896, Item D7] collection.

634. Notes by William B Chalmers [Cowen, 1851 – 1896, item B7].

635. Saks [1993] gives a description of the battle which goes well beyond what is found in other accounts.

636. See Graham & Robinson [1854].

637. This account is based on Stubbs's [1978, pp 157 – 161] description. In particular the direct speech is quoted or reconstructed from his narrative.

638. Destruction of their habitat played as important a part as the direct slaughter by the hunters [Whitehouse, 2002].

639. Godlonton [1830 – 1884, item 117]

640. These were published in the *Sun and King William's Town Gazette* in January 1875 [Cowen, 1851 – 1896, item D1]

641. This section is based on correspondence among the papers of John Forbes Cumming [1834 – 1899, items 257 – 273] and on the papers of Charles Cowen [1851 – 1896].

642. The typescript of John Cumming's [1834 – 1899, item 430] *Narrative* is dated 1896. It starts with his departure for the Cape and end with his return to Glenthorn after his adventurous ride during the 1846 War of the Axe. Within the manuscript, seem-

ingly placed at random, is the self-consistent account of the events at Tyumie which was supplied to Baker. It is also in this form that *A Narrative* was published in the Queenstown *Daily Representative* in 1961. It seems probable that Cumming was engaged in writing his reminiscences when he received Baker's request, and that he jumped ahead in his narrative to supply his version of events. Alternatively the request may have inspired him to begin the task of preparing his reminiscences.

643. Letter dated 17th June 1896 [Cumming1834 – 1899, item 258].

644. Not connected to Earl Grey.

645. See Peires [1989, chap. 2] for a discussion of Grey's influence on the affairs of the eastern Cape Province and the Xhosa.

646. The long and complex history of the eastern Cape Separatist movement is discussed by le Cordeur [1981].

647. Contagious bovine pleuropneumonia caused by a subspecies of the Mycoplasma Mycoides micro-organism.

648. The horrifying story of the cattle killing and the destruction of the Xhosa is narrated and discussed by Peires [1989].

649. Peires [1989, pp 36, 44] provides some suggestive evidence but is firm that there can be no definite conclusion.

650. See Stanford [1958, vol. 1, p.70].

651. See Peires [1989, pp 319 – 322].

652. By 1870 the modern spelling "Grahamstown" was beginning to replace "Graham's Town".

653. See Montgomery [1981, p. 111].

654. This was probably Richard, although the reference raises the possibility that Joseph might have raised early capital for his store by trade. Richard's trade was mostly across the eastern border. There is no other indication that he was ever in Cradock.

655. Actually Joseph Weakley. His daughter married Joseph Thackwray.

656. Tennant, Fossey, Murphy, Gleeson do not appear on the settler lists. There were a number of Andersons and several called Collins. There were several named Phillips but none Philips. This was possibly John Phillips.

657. Peddlars

658. See Dugmore [1871].

659. This is inferred indirectly. In 1845, when his wife Margaret was still alive, the couple were listed in the Cape Almanac as living in Campbell St., a short distance from the Walkers. Her death notice (Graham's Town Journal, 26th June 1847) states that she died at the home of Joseph Walker. The Almanacs for 1850 and 1852 no longer show a place of residence for Benjamin Booth. He was still in Graham's Town; in the announcement of his second marriage he is styled "widower, gentleman, Grahamstown" (Methodist Parish Records, Bathurst Marriages: 1843-1893, transcribed by Ellen Stanton, see http://tree.pagemaker.co.nz/transcriptions/Data/Bathurst/marriages/methodist2. htm). The place of his death, in 1862, was again recorded as the residence of Joseph Walker.

660. Godlonton [1830 – 1884, item 117].

661. This was the usual practice. Massachusetts, the first of the United States to introduce a secret ballot soon repealed it again, and only reintroduced it for the election of Governor in 1889. The West Virginia constitution still permits an open ballot. Britain introduced a secret ballot in 1872.

662. See Maynard [1867].

663. See Officer [2008].

664. Lynette Boreham, one of Arthur's granddaughters, told the author that Joseph Benjamin, known as Uncle Ben, was the black sheep of the family and had been

responsible for the loss of the family fortune. There is little evidence of this at the time in question. Certainly, later around the turn of the century there were a number of cases brought against him either for debt or for failing in his fiduciary duties.

665. Arthur's son Frank writes [Walker, 1987a]: "I believe, owing to unfortunate business associates, grandfather Walker [Joseph Jr] had a bad time financially and Dad left school at an early age ..."

666. See Davenport [1966] for an account of the Bond and the political developments around the 1898 election.

667. A force of Rhodesian and Bechanaland police under Leander Starr Jameson made a botched raid on the Transvaal Republic at the beginning of 1896, hoping to cause the British expatriates in the gold-rich republic to rise in revolt. It failed. Jameson and his associates took the blame.

668. Sprigg's wife, Ellen Eliza Fleischer, was Robert Hart's granddaughter. Her mother, Margaret Hart, had first married her father, James Fleischer, and, after his death, had married Richard Birt, John Cumming's missionary colleague.

669. Cuttings in the possesion of the author. They are by two different artists. The same photograph of Joseph Walker is used in each of them. A clearly identified print of the same original photograph is in the possession of the author, making the identification certain. The source has not been identified. It is not the main Port Elizabeth newspaper, *The Eastern Province Herald,* which did not use cartoons. These may have been part of pamphlets, supporting the candidates.

670. See Donald [1960, p.40].

671. Mears [1967] has written a short biography of James Allison.

672. *Graham's Town Journal,* Saturday 16 February 1850

673. See M'Kerrow [1867, chap. 6] for a contemporary account. The United Free Church existed as one of several Presbyterian churches from 1847 to 1900, when further unification took place. The other major denominations were the Church of Scotland (the established church) and the Free Church of Scotland. Niven and Cumming were its only representatives of the United Free Church in the Cape when it was formed in 1847. Brown came to join them when Niven moved from Iqibira to form Uniondale in 1849. Brown is omitted entirely from M'Kerrow's record. Other Presbyterians among the missionaries belonged to other denominations.

674. As reported by M'Kerrow [1867, pp 441 – 442].

675. See Chalmers [1877, pp 66 – 68].

676. After John Henderson, one of Soga's mentors.

677. A copy of the letter is in the author's possession. The reference to "Old Aunt" is intriguing. There is one earlier reference to Cumming's sister having been with the family at Tyumie in 1850. She might have made her home with her brother and his wife after the death of their mother.

678. See Mostert [1992, p. 1251].

679. The story of his public life is recounted in his own words in his extensive reminis-cences [Stanford, 1958]. A complete biography is yet to be written.

680. See National Convention [1911, p.23].

681. See Hart [1844].

682. He died in Umtata in 1876. His last years were further clouded when he was tried for rape of a minor, a young girl who was in his service. He was found not guilty in the criminal case, but a civil case brought against him by the girl's family awarded damages, which forced him to sell two farms, including Roodewal, which by then had been left to him by his father.

683. See Hart [1860].

684. See Hart [2005]. Marian is assumed to have been born about 1820. There is no record of any family members joining the Harts. Her exact relationship to Robert

Hart is a mystery.

685. Gill College became a High School in 1903 when legislation made it impossible to continue with tertiary education. Gill's bequest was thereafter applied to provide university bursaries for pupils of the school.

686. See Hart [1869].

687. See Hart [1900a,b].

688. J. P. Cumming did not serve as long as his brother Willie and was not so prominent in the service. His career between 1867 and 1881 has not been traced. Stanford [1958, vol. 1, p. 197] notes "Three of us, W. T Brownlee, then magistrate of Qumbu, J.P Cumming, afterwards magistrate of Tsolo, and I climbed to the top of a high peak ... " This was in 1881. By 1885 Cumming seems to have left the service and was permanently at Glen Avon.

689. Their eldest daughter, Kate, the author's grandmother, remembered Glen Avon as her childhood home.

690. This Jan Hendrik Hofmeyer was prominent in the early history of Somerset East, but should not be confused with his famous namesake Onze Jan, or with the latter's equally famous nephew.

691. In a sad postscript, his grandson, Graham Forbes Cumming was stabbed to death in 2003, while transporting workers home from the farm.

692. For those unfamiliar with the currency of the time, this is read as seven hundred and sixty two pounds, eighteen shillings, and three farthings (£1=20s; 1s=12d; 1d=4 farthings).

693. See Cumming [1834 – 1899, #338], dated Somerset East 18th Aug 1902.

694. The firm was established in 1853 and still exists under the name of McWilliams & Elliot.

695. The major sources are Soga [1930], Jackson [1975], and Peires [1981]. Both the latter authors make substantial use of Soga's much earlier work, which, in turn, is based heavily on oral tradition. Jackson provides extensive genealogical charts. His purpose, however, was to clarify the descent of those chiefs who held office (by tradition, or by Government appointment) at the time. Some lines which died out get scant attention. Peires's work remedies this in some cases. The descent of the imi-Dange is a special case. Recent work by Peires [2008] has amplified and clarified this and corrected significant errors.

696. This is still a vital part of the marriage custom among all the African people, whether the marriage is traditional or Christian, although, except in the remote rural regions, the payment is usually in the form of cash rather than cattle.

697. Lalu [2009, p. 83] is one source that reproduces this map.

698. See Pretorius [1988, p. 359].

References

Account, 1855, *An Account of the Reception Given at Graham's Town, to the Rev H, Renton, Special Commissioner of the United Presbyterian Church 1851*, G. J. Pike, Cape Town.

Alberti, L., 1968, *Ludwig Alberti's Account of the Tribal Life and Customs of the Xhosa in 1807, transl. from original German manuscript by W. Fehr*, A. A. Balkema, Cape Town.

Andrews, C., 1835, *Field Diary*, MSB16, 1 (2,3), National Library of South Africa, Cape Town.

Andrews, C., 1877, *Reminiscences of the Kaffir War 1834 – 1835*, Port Elizabeth.

Armstrong, J. C., 1979, The Slaves, 1652 – 1795, in *The Shaping of South African Society, 1652 – 1820*, (R Elphick and H. Giliomee, eds), pp 75–115, Longman, Cape Town.

Ayliff J., 1821 – 1851, *The Journal of John Ayliff*, 3 vols, MS15544, Cory Library, Rhodes University, Grahamstown.

Ayliff, J., 1835, Communication of the Circumstances that Occurred between the Traders and Hintza's Tribe, previous to the rupture, in *British Parliamentary Papers: Colonies Africa*, vol. 21, p. 232, (1971), Irish University Press, Shannon.

Ayliff, J., 1845, *Memorials of the British settlers of South Africa : an address delivered at Bathurst, on 14th May, 1845, in commemoration of the foundation of the settlement in the year 1820, Godlonton*, Grahamstown. Facsimile reprint, 1954, University of Cape Town Library.

Ayliff, J., 1963, *The Journal of Harry Hastings, Albany Settler*, (L. A. Hewson, F. G. van der Riet, eds), Grocott & Sherry, Grahamstown.

Ayliff, J., 1971, *The Journal of John Ayliff 1821 – 1830*, (Hinchliff, P., ed.) A A Balkema, Cape Town.

Bain, A. G., 1949, *Journals of Andrew Geddes Bain – Trader, Explorer, Soldier, Road Engineer and Geologist*, (Lister, M. H. ed.), van Riebeeck Soc., Cape Town.

Barnard, Lady Anne, 1973, *The Letters of Lady Anne Barnard to Henry Dundas, from the Cape and Elsewhere: 1793-1803. Together with Her Journal of a Tour into the Interior and Certain Other Letters* (A.M. Lewin-Robinson, ed), A. A. Balkema, Cape Town.

Barnard, Lady Anne, 1994, *The Cape Journals of Lady Anne Barnard 1797 – 1798,* (Lewin-Robinson, A. M., Lenta, M., & Driver, D., eds), van Riebeeck Society, Cape Town.

Barnard, Lady Anne, 1999, *The Cape Diaries of Lady Anne Barnard 1799 – 1800,* (Lenta, M., & le Cordeur, B., eds), van Riebeeck Society, Cape Town.

Barrow, J, 1801, *An Account of Travels into the Interior of Southern Africa in the Years 1797 and 1798*, Cadell & Davis, London.

Barrow, J, 1804, *Travels into the Interior of Southern Africa in which are Described the Character and the Condition of the Dutch Colonists of the Cape of Good Hope, and of the Several Tribes of Natives beyond its Limits – Vol II*, Cadell & Davis, London.

Barrow, J, 1806, *Travels into the Interior of Southern Africa in which are Described the Character and the Condition of the Dutch Colonists of the Cape of Good Hope, and of the Several Tribes of Natives beyond its Limits – Vols I and II,* (2nd edition with significant additions), Cadell & Davis, London.

Barrow, J., 1847, *Autobiographical Memoir of Sir John Barrow, Bart., late of the Admiralty: including Reflections, Observations and Reminiscences at Home and Abroad from Early Life to Advanced Age*, John Murray, London.

Beck, R. B., 1987, *The Legalization and Development of Trade on the Cape Frontier 1817 – 1832,*

PhD thesis, Indiana University.

Bell, M, 1963, *They Came from a Far Land*, Grahamstown

Benfield, B., 2004, *Life Insurance Company Management: A Universal Primer*, Intrepid Printers, Pietermaritzburg.

Bennie, J., 1869, *Kaffir Legends and History*, Grey Collection , G10b10 (2), National Library of South Africa, Cape Town.

Bergh, J. C. and Visagie, 1985, *The Eastern Cape Frontier Zone 1660 – 1980: A Cartographic Guide for Historical Research*, Butterworths, Durban.

Bisset, Sir J. J., 1875, *Sport and war, or, Recollections of fighting and hunting in South Africa from the years 1834 to 1867: with a narrative of H.R.H. the Duke of Edinburgh's visit to the Cape*, Murray, London.

Bonatz, J. B., (ed.), 1868, Memoir of Sr. Wilhelmina Stompjes, a Kaffir Native-Assistant who departed this life at Shiloh, July 9th, 1863, in *Periodical accounts relating to the Missions of the Church of the United Brethren Established among the Heathen*, vol. 27, pp. 153 – 163 and 209 – 222, Brethren's Society for the Furtherance of the Gospel among the Heathen, London.

Bond, J., 1956, *They Were South Africans*, Oxford University Press.

Botha, H. C., 1984, *John Fairbairn in South Africa*, Historical Publications Society, Cape Town.

Boyce, W. B., 1834, *A Grammar of the Kafir Language*,Wesleyan Mission Press, Grahamstown.

Boyce, W. B., 1875, *Memoir of the Rev. William Shaw, Late General Superintendant of the Wesleyan Missions in South-Eastern Africa*, William Nichols, London.

Branford, W., 1992, South African languages, in *The Oxford Companion to the English Language*, (T. McArthur, ed.), pp 955–956, Oxford University Press.

Brown, G., 1855, *Personal Adventures in South Africa*, Blackwood, London.

Brown, J., 1830, *Memorials Received. John Brown. Withdrawal of Memorial of Edward Driver.* CO 3946 (125), National Archives of S. A., Cape Town.

Burchell, 1822, *Travels in the Interior of Southern Africa, Vol I*, Longman, Hurst, Rees, Orme, Brown and Green, London (reprinted 1967, C Struik, Cape Town)

Burchell, 1824, *Travels in the Interior of Southern Africa, Vol II*, Longman, Hurst, Rees, Orme, Brown and Green, London (reprinted 1967, C Struik, Cape Town)

Burton, C, 1971, *Settlers to the Cape of Good Hope: Organisation of the Nottinghamshire Party*, Historical Society of Port Elizabeth.

Campbell, A. G., 1837, *The Wrongs of the Caffre Nation: a Narrative*, James Duncan, London. (published under the pseudonym "Justus" also ascribed to R M Beverley).

Campbell, C. T., 1897, *British South Africa: A History of the Colony of the Cape of Good Hope from its Conquest 1795 to the Settlement of Albany by the British Emigration of 1819*, John Haddon & Co. London.

Campbell, J., 1974, *Travels in South Africa*, Facsimile reprint, Struik, Cape Town.

Cannon, R, 1842, *History of the Cape Mounted Riflemen; with a Brief Account of the Colony of the Cape of Good Hope*, John W. Parker, London.

Cape Parliament, 1854, *Report of the Select Committee appointed by Resolution of the Legislative Council dated 25 August 1854 to take into Consideration the Allegations contained in the Petition of Mr. Charles Lennox Stretch*, CCP1/2/1/1, National Archives of S. A., Cape Town.

Chalmers, J. A., 1877, *Tiyo Soga: A Page of South African Mission Work*, A. Elliot, Edinburgh.

Chase, J. C., 1843, *The Natal Papers: A Re-print of all Notices and Public Documents Connected with that Territory, including a description of the Country and a History of Events from its Discovery in 1498*, Godlonton, Grahamstown (simultaneously published by Robertson and Collard, Cape Town). Facsimile edition Struik, Cape Town, 1968.

Circuit Court Graham's Town, 1830a, *S A Commercial Advertiser*, Vol. 5, No. 303, May 8th p. 2, col. 4.

Circuit Court Graham's Town, 1830b, *S A Commercial Advertiser*, Vol. 5, No. 306, May 19th p. 2, col. 5.

Circuit Court, 1845, *Record of Proceedings of Criminal Case. Circuit Court, Albany. The Queen versus James Hart. Murder*, CSC 1/2/1/35 (15), National Archives of S. A., Cape Town.

Cobbing, J., 1988, *The Mfecane as Alibi*, J. Afr. History, v. 29, pp 487 – 519.

Collins, R., 1809, Journal of a Tour of the North Eastern Boundary, the Orange River and the Storm Mountains, in *The Record: or a series of Official papers relative to the Conditions and treatment of the Native Tribes of South Africa, Part V*, (D. Moodie, ed.), 1840, facsimile edition 1960, Balkema Cape Town.

Complaints, 1829, *Complaints of Fort Willshire Traders*, CO 3942 (174), National Archives of S. A., Cape Town.

Cook, P. A. W., 1931, *Social Organization and Ceremonial Institutions of the Bomvana*, Juta, Cape Town.

Cory, G. E., 1965, *The Rise of South Africa* (6 vols), Facsimile edition, Struik, Cape Town. Original editions: Vols 1- 5, 1910 – 1930, Longman Green, CapeTown; Vol. 6, 1940, Cape Times, Cape Town.

Cosser, M., 1992, *Images of a changing frontier: World View in Eastern Cape Art from Bushman Rock Art to 1875*, M.A. Thesis, Rhodes University Grahamstown.

Cowen, C., 1851 – 1896, *Papers on the Tyumie Valley massacre*, Collection number A182, William Cullen Library, University of the Witwatersrand, Johannesburg.

Cox, T.M., Jack, N., Lofthouse, S., Watling, J, Haines, J. and Warren, M., 2005, King George III and Porphyria: An Elemental Hypothesis and Investigation, *Lancet*, vol. 366, pp 332 – 335.

Crampton, H, 2004, *The Sunburnt Queen*, Jacana, Johannesburg.

Cumming, J. F. 1834–1899, *The J F Cumming Collection*, MSB139, National Library of South Africa, Cape Town.

Davenport, T. R. H., 1966, *The Afrikaner Bond (1880 – 1911)*, Oxford University Press, Cape Town.

de Klerk, J. C., 1982, The Golden Age of the Golden Fleece, *Merino Breeders' Journal*, vol. 45, no. 2, pp 47 – 51.

de Villiers, J., 1975, Hottentot Regiments at the Cape during the First British Occupation, 1795 – 1803, *Military History J. - S A Military History Society*, vol. 3, no. 5.

de Villiers, J., 1976, The Pandour Corps at the Cape during the Rule of the Dutch East India Company, *Military History J. - S A Military History Society*, vol 3, no. 3.

de Villiers, J., 1989, Die Cape Regiment 1806 – 1817: 'n Koloniale Regiment in Britse Diens, in *Archives Yearbook for South African History*, vol. 52, part 1, Government Printer, Pretoria.

Donald, J. M., 1960, The Founders of Peddie, in *Peddie, Settlers' Outpost*, (Bullock, J. B., ed.), Grocott & Sherry, Grahamstown.

Donaldson, M, 1978, *The Council of Advice*, PhD Thesis, Rhodes University, Grahamstown.

Donkin, Sir R. S., 1970, *Letter Book of Sir Rufane Donkin*, Historical Society of Port Elizabeth and Walmer.

Driver, E., 1830, *Memorials Received. Edward Driver. Government Interference to Obtain Restitution of Articles stolen by Tambookies*, CO 3947 (26), National Archives of S. A., Cape Town.

Driver, E., 1866, *Memorial to His Excellency Sir Phillip Wodehouse*, CO 4142 (40), National Archives of S. A., Cape Town,

Driver, W. I. S., 1943, *Memories of Edward Driver*, Unpublished document in possession of Julie A. Driver.

Dugmore, H H, 1871 *Reminiscences of an Albany settler*, Grahamstown. New edition (van der Riet, F.G., and Hewson L. A. eds) reprinted 1958, Grocott and Sherry, Grahamstown (page references to the latter edition).

Dundas, W., 1827, *Letter from Dundas to Plaskett*, CO 2692 (74), National Archives of S. A., Cape Town.

Dunn-Pattison, R. P., 1910, *The History of the 91st Argyllshire Highlanders: Now the 1st Battalion Princess Louise's (Argyll and Sutherland Highlanders)*, Blackwood, London.

D'Urban, Sir B., 1835, Despatch from Governor Sir Benjamin D'Urban to the Earl of Aberdeen, in *British Parliamentary Papers: Colonies Africa*, vol. 20, pp 695 – 739, (1970), Irish University Press, Shannon.

D'Urban, Sir B., 1836, Despatch from Governor Sir B. D'Urban K.C.B. To Lord Glenelg, in *British Parliamentary Papers: Colonies Africa*, vol. 21, pp 66 – 266, (1971), Irish University Press, Shannon.

Edgar, A., 1874, Reminiscences of the Kaffir War, 1834 – 1835, in *The Friend of the Free State and Bloemfontein Gazette*, nos 1205 – 1214, Bloemfontein.

Elphick, R., 1979, The Khoisan to c. 1770, in *The Shaping of South African Society, 1652 – 1820*, (R Elphick and H. Giliomee, eds), pp 3–40, Longman, Cape Town.

Fast, H. H., 1994, Editorial notes ,in *The Journal and Selected Letters of Rev. William J. Shrewsbury*, by W. J. Shrewsbury, Rhodes University, The Graham's Town Series, Witwatersrand University Press, Johannesburg.

Faure, A., 1842, *Affidavit of Abraham Faure in re Joseph Walker and Christopher Wedderburn versus Marcus Norden*, CSC 2/6/1/21 (228), National Archives of S. A., Cape Town.

ffoliot, P. M., 1972, Robert Hart, in *Dictionary of South African Biography – Vol II*, (D.W. Kruger, ed.), pp 290–291 Tafelberg, Cape Town.

Fynn, H. F., 1950, *The Diary of Henry Francis Fynn*, (Stuart, J. and Malcolm, D., eds), Shuter and Shooter, Pietermaritzburg.

Gilfillan, M., 1970, *The Story of One Branch of the Gilfillan Family in South Africa*, M. Gilfillan, Johannesburg.

Glen Thorn, 1974, 1974: *The 150th Anniversary of the Glen Thorn - Thorn Dale Merino Flock*, CED P SA-MISCELLANEOUS 33, Library of Cedara Agricultural Development Institute, Pietermaritzburg.

Godlonton, R., 1844, *Memorials of the British Settlers of South Africa being the Records of Public Services held at Graham's Town and Port Elizabeth on the 10th April, and at Bathurst on the 10th May, 1844 in Commemoration of their landing in Algoa Bay*, R Godlonton, Grahamstown; reprinted by the South African Library, Cape Town 1971.

Godlonton, R., 1965, *A Narrative of the Irruption of the Kaffir Hordes into the Eastern Province of the Cape of Good Hope, 1834-1835, including Parts I, II and III of the Introductory Remarks*, Struik, Cape Town.

Godlonton, R, 1830 - 1884, *Robert Godlonton Correspondence*, Collection number A43, William Cullen Library, University of the Witwatersrand Johannesburg.

Goldswain, J.,1949, *The Chronicle of Jeremiah Goldswain, Vol II*, (Long, U., ed.) van Riebeeck Society, Cape Town.

Gordon, D. T., 1971, *The Trollops of South Africa*, Shuter and Shooter, Pietermaritzburg.

Gordon-Brown, A., 1979, *The Settlers' Press: Seventy Years of Printing in Grahamstown Covering the Publication of Books, Pamphlets, Directories, Almanacs, Newspapers, with Historical Notes and Anecdotes and Contemporary Illustrations*, Balkema, Cape Town.

Graham, L. and Robinson, H., 1854, *Scenes in Kaffirland and Incidents in the Kaffir War of 1851-2-3 from sketches by two officers of the 43rd Light Infantry*, Dickinson Bros, London.

Green, L. P., 1957, *History of Local Government in South Africa: An Introduction*, Juta, Cape Town.

Guelke, L., 1979, The White Settlers, 1652 – 1780, in *The Shaping of South African Society, 1652 – 1820*, (R. Elphick and H. Giliomee, eds), pp 41–74, Longman, Cape Town.

Halse, H. J., 1880, *An Autobiographical Manuscript of Henry James Halse (1817 – 1880)*, MS 3563, Cory Library, Rhodes University Grahamstown.

Hamilton, C., 1998, *Terrific Majesty: the Powers of Shaka Zulu and the Limits of Historical Invention*, Cambridge MA: Harvard University Press, pp. 5–34.

Hamilton, C. (ed.), 2001, *The Mfecane Aftermath – Reconstructive Debates in South African History*, joint publication of Witwatersrand University Press, Johannesburg, and University of Natal Press, Pietermaritzburg.

Harington, A. L., 1973, The Graham's Town Journal and the Great Trek, 1834 – 1843, in *Archives Yearbook 1969, part 2*, Government Printer, Pretoria.

Harington, A. L., 1974, Sir Harry Smith, *Military History J. - S A Military History Society*, vol. 3, no. 1.

Harington, A. L., 1980, *Sir Harry Smith: Bungling Hero*, Tafelberg, Cape Town.

Hart, R., 1844, *Letter to R. J. Eaton dated 28th Dec 1844*, MS 457, Cory Library, Rhodes University Grahamstown.

Hart, R., 1845, *Memorials Received. R. Hart (Snr) Requesting that his Son J Hart (convict) be allowed to remain in Gaol of Somerset or Grahamstown*, CO 4025 (232), National Archives of S. A., Cape Town.

Hart, R., 1847, *Petition for the Remission of Sentence*, CO 4033 (79), National Archives of S. A., Cape Town.

Hart, R., 1865, *Will*, MOOC 7/1/293 (59), National Archives of S. A., Cape Town.

Hart, R., 1869, *Hart, Robert, Liquidation and Distribution Account*, MOOC 13/1/245 (93), National Archives of S. A., Cape Town.

Hart, R. Jr., 1900a, *Hart, Robert, Liquidation and Distribution Account Second and Final Account*, MOOC 13/1/957 (25), National Archives of S. A., Cape Town.

Hart, H., 1900b, *Hart, Harriet Elizabeth, born Marillier, Liquidation and Distribution Account*, MOOC 13/1/929 (1), National Archives of S. A., Cape Town.

Hart. O., 2005. *Hart Families*, Genealogiese Navorsingsgroep Port Elizabeth, P. O. Box 5836, Walmer. 6065.

Hattersley, A. F., 1968, Francis George Farewell, in *Dictionary of South African Biography –*

Vol I, (W. J. de Kock, ed.), pp 286–287 Tafelberg, Cape Town.

Hockly, H. E. H., 1948, *The Story of the British Settlers of 1820 in South Africa*, Juta & Co., Cape Town.

Hulme, J. J., 1968, Irregular units of the 7th Kaffir War 1846-7, *Military History J. - S A Military History Society*, vol. 1, no. 3.

Hunt, K. S., 1974, *Sir Lowry Cole : Governor of Mauritius, 1823-1828, Governor of the Cape of Good Hope, 1828-1833 : A Study in Colonial Administration*, Butterworth, Durban.

Isaacs, N., 1836, *Travels and Adventures in Eastern Africa*, Edward Churton, London.

Jackson, 1975, *The Ethnic Composition of the Ciskei and Transkei*, Government Printer, Pretoria.

James, W., 1837, *The Naval History of Great Britain from the Declaration of War by France in 1793, to the accession of George IV – 6 vols*, Richard Bentley London.

Jones, E. M., 1968, *The Lower Albany Chronicle* (5 vols), Port Elizabeth.

Jones, E. M., 1971, *Roll of the British Settlers in South Africa*, A A Balkema, Cape Town.

Justice Commission, 1821, *Sykes, William, Vonnis*, CJ 815 (57), National Archives of S. A., Cape Town.

Kay, S., 1833, *Travels and Researches in Caffraria Describing the Character, Customs, and Moral Condition of the Tribes Inhabiting that Portion of Southern Africa*, John Mason, London. American edition with different pagination: 1834, Harper, New York.

Kaye, W. K., 1869, *Kafir Legends and History*, G10b10 (8,9), National Library of South Africa, Cape Town.

Keegan, T. J., 1996, *Colonial South Africa and the Origins of the Racial Order*, David Philip, Cape Town.

Keegan, T. (ed.), 2004, *Moravians in the Eastern Cape, 1828-1928 : Four Accounts of Moravian Mission Work on the Eastern Cape Frontier*, (transl. Baudert, F. R.), van Riebeeck Society, Cape Town.

Lalu, P., 2009. *The Deaths of Hintsa – Post-apartheid South Africa and the Shape of Recurring Pasts*, HSRC Press, Cape Town.

Le Cordeur, B. A., 1960, Robert Godlonton as Architect of Frontier Opinion, 1850 – 1857, in *Archives Year Book for South African History*, vol. 22, part 2, Government Printer, Pretoria.

Le Cordeur, B. A., 1981, *The Politics of Eastern Cape Separatism 1820 – 1854*, Oxford University Press.

Le Cordeur, B. A., 1988, Introduction and editorial notes, in *The Journal of Charles Lennox Stretch*, Rhodes University, The Graham's Town Series, Maskew Miller Longman, Cape Town.

Le Cordeur, B. A., and Saunders, C., 1981, *The War of the Axe 1847*, Brenthurst Press, Johannesburg.

Leverton, B. J. T., 1984, *Records of Natal*, Government Printer, Pretoria.

Lehmann, J. H., 1977, *Remember you are an Englishman – A Biography of Sir Harry Smith 1787 – 1860*, Jonathan Cape, London.

Linder, A., 1997, *The Swiss at the Cape of Good Hope*, Basler Afrika Bibliographen, Basle, Switzerland.

Long, U., 1947, *An Index to Authors of Unofficial, Privately-Owned Manuscripts Relating to the History of South Africa, 1812-1920*, Privately published limited edition, U. Long, Cape Town.

Macalpine I, and Hunter R, 1966, The "insanity" of King George 3d: a classic case of porphyria, *Br Med J.*, 1 (5479): 65–71.

McElwee, W., and Rolfe, M., 1988, *Argyll and Sutherland Highlanders*, Osprey Publishing, Oxford.

MacKenzie, J. M., and Dalziel, N. R., 2007, *The Scots in South Africa - Ethnicity, Identity, Gender and Race 1772-1914*, Witwatersrand University Press, Johannesburg.

M'Kerrow, J., 1867, *History of the Foreign Missions of the Secession and United Presbyterian Church*, Andrew Elliot, Edinburgh.

Maclennan, B., 1986, *A Proper Degree of Terror*, Ravan Press, Johannesburg.

MacQuarrie, J W (ed), 1958, *The Reminiscences of Sir Walter Stanford*, 2 vols, van Riebeeck Society, Cape Town.

Majeke, Nosipho (Dora Taylor), 1952, *The Rôle of the Missionaries in Conquest*, APDUSA, Cumberwood

Makin, A. E., 1971, *The 1820 Settlers of Salem (Hezekiah Sephton's Party)*, Juta & Co, Cape Town

Malherbe, V. C., 2002a, The Khoekhoe soldier at the Cape of Good Hope – How the Khoekhoen were drawn into the Dutch and British defensive systems, to c 1809, *Military History J. - S A Military History Society,* vol. 12, no. 3.

Malherbe, V. C., 2002b, The Khoekhoe soldier at the Cape of Good Hope – Life and Times in the Cape Regiment, *Military History J. - S A Military History Society*, vol. 12, no. 4.

Maxwell, W. A., and McGeogh, R. T., 1978, Editorial notes, in *The Reminiscences of Thomas Stubbs*, Rhodes University, The Graham's Town Series, A A Balkema, Cape Town.

Maynard, H., 1867, *Maynard Walker & Company vs The Honorable Col. Secretary,* CSC 2/1/1/126 (70), National Archives of S.A., Cape Town.

Mears, W. J. G., 1967, *The Revd James Allison Missionary:* A Biographical Outline, Methodist Church of South Africa, Mission and Extension Department, Durban.

Meiring, J., 1959, *The Sundays River Valley: Its History and Settlement*, A. A. Balkema, Cape Town.

Meurant, L. H., 1885, *Sixty Years Ago; Or Reminiscences of the Struggle for the Freedom of the Press in South Africa and the Establishment of the First Newspaper in the Eastern Province*, Saul Solomon, Cape Town.

Milton, J., 1983, *The Edges of War: A History of Frontier Wars*, Juta & Co., Cape Town.

Minutes, 1911, *Minutes of Proceedings of the South African National Convention held at Durban, Cape Town and Bloemfontein, 12th October 1908 to 11th May 1909*, Cape Times Limited, Government Printers, Cape Town.

Mitford-Barberton, I. and R., 1952, *The Bowkers of Tharfield*, Oxford.

Mitford-Barberton, I., 1970, *Comdt. Holden Bowker,* Human & Rousseau, Cape Town.

Montgomery, J., 1981, *The Reminiscences of John Montgomery*, (A Giffard, ed.), Balkema, Cape Town.

Mostert, N., 1992, *Frontiers – The Epic of South Africa's Creation and the Tragedy of the Xhosa People*, Jonathan Cape, London.

Mqhayi, S. K., 1931, *Ityala lamaWele*, Lovedale Press, Lovedale.

Mrs Thackwray's Case, 1830, *S A Commercial Advertiser,* Vol. 5, No.276, Feb 3rd, p1, col. 15.

Müller, A. L., 1987, *The Economic Awakening of the Eastern Cape*, 1795–1820, S A J Economics, vol. 55, pp 26 – 33.

Murder of Lieutenant Farewell and his Party at Natal, 1829, *S A Commercial Advertiser,* Vol.5, No. 251, Nov 7th, p2 col. 4.

Naidoo, J., 1989, *Tracking down Historical Myths : Eight South African Cases,* A. Donker, Johannesburg.

Nash, M. D., 1982, *Baillie's Party of 1820 Settlers: A collective experience in emigration*, A. A. Balkema, Cape Town.

Nash, M. D., 1987, *The Settler Handbook*, Chameleon Press, Diep River.

National Convention, 1911, *Minutes of proceedings with Annexures (Selected) of the South African National Convention held at Durban, Cape Town, and Bloemfontein, 12th Oct. 1908 to 11th May 1909,* Government Printer, Cape Town.

Newton-King, S. and Malherbe, V. C., 1981, *The Khoikhoi Rebellion in the Eastern Cape (1799 – 1803),* Communication No. 5, centre for African Studies, University of Cape Town.

Ngxamngxa, A. N. N., 1971, The Function of Circumcision among the Xhosa-speaking Tribes in Historical Perspective, in *Man: Anthropological Essays Presented to O. F. Raum,* pp 183 – 204, (de Jager, E. J., ed.), Struik, Cape Town.

Niven, R., 1860, *Perils of a Missionary Family in the Caffre Wars of 1850 – 52*, Bell and Bain, Glasgow.

Nottinghamshire City Court, 1833, *City Court Record Books 8th April 1833,* Nottinghamshire Archives and Southwell & Nottingham Diocesan Record Office.

Ntsikana, B., 1902, *The Life of Ntsikana*, Lovedale Press, Lovedale.

Officer, L. H., 2008, *Five Ways to Compute the Relative Value of a UK Pound Amount, 1830 to Present*, http://www.measuringworth.com/ukcompare/.

Omer-Cooper, 1960, *The Zulu Aftermath*, Longmans, Harlow Essex.

Parkinson, C. N., 1937, *Trade in the Eastern Seas, 1793-1813*, Cambridge University Press, Cambridge.

Parliament, Houses of, 1968 – 1971, *British Parliamentary Papers: Colonies Africa, 70 vols*, (Facsimile reprint of originals printed for the British Houses of Parliament), Irish University Press, Shannon. [In references to pagination that of the editors is used rather than that of the original documents.]

Peires, J. B., 1981, *The House of Phalo : a History of the Xhosa People in the Days of their Independence* , Ravan Press, Johannesburg.

Peires, J. B., 1989, *The Dead will Arise: Nongqawuse and the Great Xhosa Cattle-Killing Movement of 1856 - 1857*, Ravan Press, Johannesburg; James Currey, London; Indiana University Press, Bloomington.

Peires, J. B., 2008, The Other side of the Black Silk Handkerchief: The van Plettenberg Agreement of 1778, *Quart. Bull. Nat. Lib. S. A.* , v. 62, pp 9 – 35.

Philip, J., 1828, *Researches in South Africa, Illustrating the Civil, Moral, and Religious Condition of the Native Tribes*, 2 vols, James Duncan, London.

Philipps, T., 1960, *Philipps, 1820 Settler: His Letters,* (Keppel-Jones, A., ed.), Shuter and Shooter, Pietermaritzburg.

Pigot, S., 1974, *The Journals of Sophia Pigot,* (Rainier, M., ed), A A Balkema, Cape Town.

Plaskett, R., 1825, *Decision of His Excellency the Governor, Land Claims 1825*, CO48-69 pp. 87 – 108, National Archives, London.

Potgieter, H., 2003, Maritime Defence of the Cape of Good Hope, 1779 – 1803, *Historia,* v. 48, pp 283 – 308.

Pretorius, J. G., 1988, The British Humanitarians and the Cape Eastern Frontier, 1834 – 1836, in *Archives Yearbook for South African History,* vol. 51, part 1, Government Printer, Pretoria.

Pringle, E., 1967, *These are my People,* E. Pringle, Adelaide, Cape Province.

Pringle, E., Pringle, M., and Pringle, J., 1957, *Pringles of the Valleys: Their History and Genealogy,* E. Pringle, Adelaide, Cape Province.

Pringle, T., 1824, *Some Account of the Present State of the English Settlers in Albany South Africa,* T & G Underwood, London.

Pringle, T., 1840, *Narrative of a Residence in South Africa,* Edward Moxon, London, reprinted 1966, Struik, Cape Town.

Prisoners, 1823, *Report of Prisoners for the Graham's Town District, 31st May – 30 June 1823,* CO 2653 (69), National Archives of S. A., Cape Town.

Proclamations, 1827, *Proclamations, Advertisements, and other Official Notices, published by The Government of the Cape of Good Hope, from the 10th January, 1806 to the 2nd May, 1825,* Cape of Good Hope (at the Government Press).

Ransford, O., 1972, *The Great Trek,* Murray, London.

Read J., 1852, *The Kat River Settlement in 1851: Described in a Series of Letters Published in the South African Commercial Advertiser,* Robertson, Cape Town.

Rennie, G., 1825, *Letter to Major Forbes, Commandant on the Frontier, Baviaans River, July 24th,,* CO 233 (121) National Archives of S. A., Cape Town.

Report, 1837, *Report of the Court of Inquiry into the Death of Hintza.* CO48/185, National Archives, London.

Ritter, E. A., 1955, *Shaka Zulu: The Rise of the Zulu Empire,* Allen Lane, London.

Rivers, H., 1823, *Report to the Colonial Secretary,* CO 2653 (64), National Archives of S. A., Cape Town.

Rivett-Carnac, D. E., 1966, *Hawk's Eye,* Howard Timmins, Cape Town.

Rose, C, 1829, *Four Years in Southern Africa,* Colburn and Bentley, London.

Robinson, A. M. L., Lenta, M., and Driver, D. (eds), 1994, *The Cape Journals of Lady Anne Barnard 1797 – 1798,* van Riebeeck Society, Cape Town.

Ross, R., 2003, Ambiguities of Resistance and Collaboration on the Eastern Cape Frontier. The Kat River Settlement 1829 – 1856, in *Rethinking Resistance: Revolt and Violence in African History,* (Abbinck, J., de Bruijn, M., van Walraven, K., eds), pp 117 – 140, Brill, Leiden Netherlands.

Rowles, J., 1834, Deposition setting forth the Persecution and Robberies by the Caffres, in *British Parliamentary Papers: Colonies Africa,* vol. 21, p. 212, (1971), Irish University Press, Shannon.

Saks, D. Y., 1993, A forgotten Battle of the Frontier Wars, *Military History J. - S A Military History Society,* vol. 9, no. 4.

Selous, F. C., 1893, A *Hunter's Wanderings in Africa: being a narrative of nine years spent amongst the game of the far interior of South Africa : containing accounts of explorations beyond the Zambesi, on the River Chobe, and in the Matabele and Mashuna countries, with full notes upon the natural history and present distribution of all the large mammalia* , Richard Bentley, London. (Reprinted 1981 as A Hunter's Wanderings in Africa, Books of Zimbabwe).

Shaw, 1860, *The Story of my Mission in South Eastern Africa: Comprising some Account of the*

European Colonists; with Extended Notices of the Kaffir and other Native tribes, Hamilton, Adams &Co., London.

Shaw, W., 1972, *The Journal of William Shaw,* (Hammond-Tooke, W. D., ed.), Balkema, Cape Town.

Sheffield, T., 1884, *The Story of the Settlement,* 2nd ed, T & H Sheffield, Grahamstown.

Shipp, J., 1890, *Memoirs of the Extraordinary Military Career of John Shipp, late a Lieut. in His Majesty's 87th Regiment,* 2nd ed., Fisher Unwin, London.

Shrewsbury, J. V. B., 1869, *Memorials of the Rev. William J. Shrewsbury,* Hamilton Adams, London.

Shrewsbury, W., 1994, *The Journal and Selected Letters of Rev. William J. Shrewsbury,* (Fast, H. H., ed.), Rhodes University, The Graham's Town Series, Witwatersrand University Press, Johannesburg.

Sinclair, D., 2004, *The Land That Never Was: Sir Gregor MacGregor and the Most Audacious Fraud in History,* Perseus Books Group, New York.

Smith, Sir Harry, 1850, Proclamation, Encl. 5 in Dispatch to Earl Grey, October 31 1850, in *British Parliamentary Papers: Colonies Africa*, vol. 23, p. 60, (1970), Irish University Press, Shannon.

Smith, Sir Harry, 1901, *The Autobiography of Lieutenant-General Sir Harry Smith, Baronet of Aliwal on the Sutle, G.C.B* – 2 vols, Murray, London.

Soga, J. H., 1930, *The South Eastern Bantu: abe-Nguni, aba-Mbo, ama-Lala,* Witwatersrand University Press, Johannesburg.

Soga, J. H., 1931, *The Ama-Xosa: Life and Customs,* Lovedale Press, Lovedale, Cape.

Soga, T., 1983, *The Journal and Selected Writing of the Reverend Tiyo Soga,* (Williams, D. ed), Rhodes University, The Graham's Town Series, A A Balkema, Cape Town.

Spencer, S. O'B., 1992, *British Settlers in Natal 1824 – 1857: A biographical register,* University of Natal Press, Pietermaritzburg.

Stanford, W. E. M., 1958, *The Reminiscences of Sir Walter Stanford, 2 vols,* (MacQuarrie, J. W., ed.), van Riebeeck Society, Cape Town.

Stapleton, T. J., 1991, The Memory of Maqoma: an Assessment of Jingqi Oral Tradition in Ciskei and Transkei, *History in Africa*, Vol 20, pp 321 – 335.

Stapleton, T. J., 1994, *Maqoma, Xhosa resistance to colonial advance 1798 – 1873,* Jonathan Ball, Johannesburg.

Stapleton, T. J., 2001, *Faku – Rulership and colonialism in the Mpondo kingdom,* Wilfred Laurier University Press, Waterloo, Ontario.

Steedman, A, 1835, *Wanderings and adventures in the interior of South Africa, (2 vols),* Longman, London, (Facsimile edition Struik, 1966.)

Stevenson, J. M., 1896, *The Tyumie Valley Massacres,* Lovedale Press, Lovedale.

Stirk, D., 1972, *Southwell Settlers,* 2nd Edition, (J. M. Berning ed.), D. Stirk, Southwell.

Stockenstrom, A., 1887, *The Autobiography of Sir Andries Stockenstrom, Bart., (2 vols),* (Hutton C. W., ed.), Juta, Cape Town.

Stockenstrom, A., Reitz, F. W., Mettlerkamp, W. S. G., and Ebden, J. B., 1854, *Report of the Select Committee appointed by Resolution of the Legislative Council Dated 25th August 1854 to take into Consideration the Allegations Contained in the Petition of Mr. Charles Lennox Stretch, Ampt. Pub.* CCP1/2/1/1, pp 613 – 615, National Archives of South Africa, Cape Town.

Storey, W. K., 2004, Guns, Race, and Skill in Nineteenth-Century Southern Africa, *Technology and Culture,* Vol.45, pp 687-711.

Stretch, C. L., 1844, Prefatory Note, in *Papers Received from C. L. Stretch, Diplomatic Agent, Relating to Stock Losses on the Frontier 1837 – 1844*, LG600, p.4, National Archives of South Africa, Cape Town.

Stretch, C. L., 1848, *Memorials and Letters of Charles Lennox Stretch*, CO4041, National Archives of South Africa, Cape Town.

Stretch, C. L., 1849, *Correspondence Between C.L. Stretch (late Diplomatic Agent to the Gaika Tribe of Kafirs), the Secretary of State for the Colonies, and the Colonial Government of the Cape of Good Hope*, G J. Pike, Cape Town.

Stretch, C. L., 1855, *Block Drift*, G. J. Pike, Cape Town.

Stretch, C. L., 1876, Makana and the attack on Graham's Town, in 1819, *Cape Monthly Magazine, New Series*, vol. 12, pp 297 – 303.

Stretch, C. L., 1988, *The Journal of Charles Lennox Stretch*, (le Cordeur, B A, ed), Rhodes University, The Graham's Town Series, Maskew Miller Longman, Cape Town.

Stubbs, T., 1978, *The Reminiscences of Thomas Stubbs*, (Maxwell, W. A., and McGeogh, R. T., eds), Rhodes University, The Graham's Town Series, A A Balkema, Cape Town.

Thackwray, J., 1827, *Letter to Andrew Steedman*, MS16488, Cory Library, Rhodes University, Grahamstown,.

Thackwray, W., 1826, *Memorial to the Lieutenant Governor*, CO3932, (630), National Archives of South Africa, Cape Town.

Theal, G. McC., 1897 – 1905, 36 volumes, *Records of the Cape Colony*: Copied for the Cape Government from the Manuscript Documents in the Public Records Office, London, Government of the Cape Colony.

Theal, G. McC., 1964, 11 volumes, *History of South Africa since September 1795*, Struik, Cape Town. Consolidated edition of *Ethnography and Condition of South Africa before A. D. 1505* (vol. 1); *History of Africa South of the Zambezi* (vols 2 – 4); *History of South Africa from 1795 to 1872* (vols 5 – 9); *History of South Africa from 1873 to 1884* (vols 10 – 11).

Thompson, G., 1827, *Travels and Adventures in Southern Africa*, Colburn London. Facsimile edition 1957, Africana Connoisseurs Press, Cape Town.

Turpin, E. W., 1964, *Basket Work Harbour*, Howard Timmins, Cape Town.

Tyhali, 1842, *Statement of Tyali, 14th April 1842*, LG 400 (109), National Archives of South Africa, Cape Town.

Tylden, G., 1954, *The Armed Forces of South Africa: with an Appendix on the Commandos*, Africana Museum, Johannesburg.

Vigne R., 1998, 'Die man wat die Groot Trek veroorsaak het': Glenelg's personal contribution to the cancellation of D'Urban's dispossession of the Rarabe in 1835, *African Historical Review*, v. 30, pp 28 – 44.

Walker, E. A., 1968, *A History of Southern Africa*, 3rd ed. (new impression with corrections), Longman, London.

Walker, F. A. M., 1987a, *Random Memories*, Pietermaritzburg, unpublished (in possession of the author).

Walker, G. N., 1987b, *Genealogical Record of the Forbears and Descendants of Joseph Walker and Dorothy Driver*, Pietermaritzburg, unpublished (in possession of the author).

Walker, J., 1842, *Memorial to the Governor*, CO 4015 (636), National Archives of South Africa, Cape Town.

Walker, R., 1835, Communication from Butterworth, stating the influx of Colonial Cattle into Hintza's territory and their Retention there, in *British Parliamentary Papers: Colonies*

Africa, vol. 21, p. 220, (1971), Irish University Press, Shannon.

Ward, H., 1848, *Five years in Kaffirland: With Sketches of the Late War in that Country to the Conclusion of Peace*, Colburn, London.

Ward, H., 1851, *The Cape and the Kaffirs: A Diary of Five Years' Residence in Kaffirland*, Henry G. Bohn, London.

Whitehouse, A. M., 2002, Tusklessness in the elephant population of the Addo Elephant National Park, South Africa, *Journal of Zoology*, v. 257 pp 249 – 254.

Williams, D., 1967, *When Races Meet: The Life and Times of William Ritchie Thomson, Glasgow Society Missionary, Government Agent and Dutch Reformed Church Minister*, 1794-1891, APB, Johannesburg.

Williams, D., 1968, James Read Sr, in *Dictionary of South African Biography – Vol I*, (W. J. de Kock, ed.), Tafelberg, Cape Town.

Wilmot, A., 1904, *The Life and Times of Sir Richard Southey*, Samson Low, Marston, London.

Wood, G. and Walker, J., 1835, *Memorial addressed to the Governor, Sir Benjamin D'Urban*, CO 3983 (170), National Archives of South Africa, Cape Town.

Wright, J., 2001, Beyond the concept of the 'Zulu explosion' - Comments on the current debate, in *The Mfecene Aftermath – Reconstructive Debates in Southern African History*, (C. Hamilton, ed.), pp 107 – 121, joint publication of Witwatersrand University Press, Johannesburg, and University of Natal Press, Pietermaritzburg.

Wylie, D., 2006, *Myth of Iron: Shaka in History,* University of KwaZulu-Natal Press, Pietermaritzburg.

Index

www.ingramcontent.com/pod-product-compliance
Lightning Source LLC
Chambersburg PA
CBHW050448270326
41927CB00009B/1648